SOCCER IN THE 1930s

Simple or Sublime?

Jack Rollin

A *SoccerData* Publication

Published in Great Britain by Tony Brown
4 Adrian Close, Toton, Nottingham NG9 6FL
Telephone 0115 973 6086
E-mail soccer@innotts.co.uk
www.soccerdata.com

First published 2015

Cover design by Bob Budd.

The Author's Acknowledgements:
Tony Brown for his expertise – and patience – Ashley Hyne for a couple of snippets, Glenda Rollin for sorting software problems and Lorraine Jerram for suggesting the second line of the title.

Printed and bound by 4Edge, Hockley, Essex
www.4edge.co.uk

ISBN: 978-1-905891-92-4

FOREWORD

Nostalgia might be looked upon as a yearning for the past with the unpleasant episodes ignored. Nonetheless it is not essential to have experienced a bygone age to possess feelings for it. The 1930s was such a decade despite the depression, a high rate of unemployment, industrial unrest and events in Europe gathering momentum towards the disaster of the Second World War. Even so, it was looked upon as a halcyon era for football. The sport offered the comforting refuge of escapism.

England considered itself as the *only* country as far as football was concerned. Coaches had spread their message across the globe, properly teaching foreigners how to play the game. Domestically the Football League celebrated its Jubilee and the FA Cup sixty glorious years. Both competitions had been copied far and wide.

The World Cup was instituted, but the four home countries, in dispute with FIFA over broken time payments at the Olympic Games, did not participate. However, an invitation was sent for England to compete in the World Cup! In 1936 a Great Britain team had been entered in the Olympics. From a "results count if nothing else" viewpoint, no country outside the UK defeated England on its own territory, though several did on the continent of Europe. Oddly enough we did not lose to Italy the World Champions, winning once at home and drawing twice away. Yet England fared poorly in the Home International Championship. This despite the disadvantage for Scotland, Wales and Ireland needing to obtain permission for Football League based players released for international duty.

No comparisons have been drawn with later events. It is as it were completed in 1939. Was it a golden era for football or simply a naive one? It will be a matter of opinion.

CONTENTS

Stamford Bridge 1933. Huddersfield's Hugh Turner clears the ball from Chelsea's Hughie Gallacher.

KICK OFF

CHANGES AFTER THE GREAT WAR

During the decade preceding the 1930s, two important measures were taken that affected the game, one concerning its structure, the other the fundamental laws. In the aftermath of the First World War, the Football League effectively doubled its membership with the formation of two regional sections of a Third Division. It was followed by an important change in the off-side law.

This was designed to encourage more goals to be scored. It was to have an immediate and positive effect. The number of goals had reached a ridiculously low level as figures for 4 April 1925 revealed. The full Football League programme of 44 fixtures on that Saturday produced just 71. On 13 December 1924 the Everton v West Ham United match revealed 41 off-side decisions and one goal for the home team!

At a meeting of the International Board in Paris on 13 June 1925, it was decided on a proposal by the Scottish Football Association that a player shall not be off-side if two instead of three opponents are nearer their own goal. The 2-3-5 formation universally in operation and known as "the W formation", had lent itself to fall easily into an off-side trap sprung by defenders, the five forwards leaving themselves vulnerable to such tactics.

However, on 29 August 1925, the first day under the new system, 160 goals were recorded in the 44 Football League matches. Home teams accounted for 105 of them. Aston Villa defeated Burnley 10-0 and there were just two goalless draws! Divisionally, there were fluctuations: First Division 39 goals, Second Division 29, Third Division (South) 42 and Third Division (North) 50.

Huddersfield Town had won the First Division Championship for the previous two seasons. In the first of these they had achieved it on goal average from Cardiff City and just two points separated them from West Bromwich Albion in 1924-25. Not only did Huddersfield establish a record third successive title in 1925-26, but they finished with a five point advantage over Arsenal.

As a further indication of the increase in goals scored and conceded, over these three seasons, Huddersfield registered fifty percent more themselves, while the sixty let in during 1925-26 would have been a sufficient total in the goals-for column to have carried off the first of their championships two seasons earlier! Huddersfield continued to be a force and finished runners-up in the next two seasons adding the FA Cup to their trophy room in the last of these. The Football League presented them with a commemoration shield on 4 June 1928.

The system for separating two teams with the same number of points continued as goal average with the goals conceded divided into the number scored. It was oddly enough in favour of defence rather than attack!

The FA Cup final moved into what was hoped to be a permanent home in 1923 when Wembley Stadium opened. Any accurate assessment of the total number of spectators who attended the inaugural final on 28 April for the Bolton Wanderers v West Ham United tie was impossible as a large proportion of the crowd forced its way in. But the official return from the British Empire Exhibition authorities listed 90,520 through the turnstiles and 35,527 ticket holders for an overall total of 126,047. This has always been considered the recorded attendance though it is likely that some 150,000 were actually present. The start of the match was delayed 40 minutes while the pitch was cleared of many hundreds who had spilled onto the playing area. The FA had to refund money to ticket holders who were unable to reach their seats. In subsequent finals admission was by ticket only.

The 1920s also saw Corinthians, the most famous of staunchly amateur teams, deciding to enter the FA Cup for the first time in their distinguished history. Among tinkering items, players were no longer off-side from a throw-in, a goal could be scored direct from a corner kick and a goalkeeper was compelled to stand still on his goal-line when penalties were taken. In international matches the goalkeeper had to wear a jersey of deep yellow.

At international level, the four British associations resigned membership of FIFA in February 1928 over the issue of payment for broken time. Previously they had left after objecting to the Axis powers Germany and Austria being allowed to continue as members. There had been no UK representation in the 1924 Olympic Games tournament and naturally none in the 1928 series.

Domestically, England had fared poorly in the annual Home International Championship. Indeed, a shared honour with Scotland in 1926-27 was their best performance. In 1928 the Scots – forever known as the "Wembley Wizards" – inflicted a milestone defeat on England at Wembley, winning 5-2. There were some legitimate excuses in the England camp, but the old enemy thoroughly deserved its victory. In 1923-24, Wales came out on top in the four sided tournament having remained unbeaten. The Principality also recorded a unique success when Cardiff City became the first team to take the FA Cup out of England, beating Arsenal 1-0 in 1927. This was the first final to be broadcast on the radio or wireless as it was popularly known. Earlier there had been coverage of a League game between Sheffield United and Arsenal.

Bill 'Dixie' Dean

International matches involving countries outside the United Kingdom had been sparse, but in 1929, England suffered its first defeat against continental opposition losing 4-3 to Spain in Madrid, a slender but ground-breaking reverse. It was a hot, sultry, energy-sapping afternoon which clearly did not suit the visitors. The conditions did not prevent hundreds of perspiring Spanish fans invading the pitch in celebration. There were no correspondents from England present. This was only the 18th match since the war against a team from abroad. England was without George Camsell the Middlesbrough centre-forward, who in the previous two internationals had scored a total of six goals. Unfortunately for England he had been injured against Belgium. In the two games following the defeat in question, he added another five goals!

In 1926-27, Camsell had scored 59 of his club's 122 goals from 37 League games to help them win the Second Division. Both individual and club totals were records for the division. This euphoria was short-lived because the following season his achievement was eclipsed by Bill "Dixie" Dean at Everton who scored 60 in 39 League outings as the team won the First Division title. To pile further misery on Camsell and his team, Middlesbrough was relegated!

Goal scoring records continued to be broken everywhere. Millwall set a Third Division (South) record with 127 goals in 1927-28, while Bradford City managed one more goal the next season in the Northern Section. Quite naturally teams suffered defensively. In 1927-28 Nelson conceded 136 goals in the Third Division (North).

Football was the working man's pastime. But there were many problems affecting it. Not the least of these was the post-war raising of the minimum admission charge from sixpence (2½p) to one shilling (five pence). The downturn in the economy understandably hit clubs hard, too. The undercurrent of industrial unrest following the First World War, which had come close to bankrupting the nation, was of considerable concern. Unemployment was rising. Relations between Government and the triple alliance of railwaymen, transport workers and miners broke down completely late in April 1926 and precipitated the General Strike. The football programme for the season had been largely completed and the actual shut down lasted only nine days. But the miners maintained their stance until it collapsed in six weeks when the men were starved back to the pits.

Then came the Wall Street crash of 1929 that reverberated around the world into the Great Depression and had a devastatingly knock-on effect on life up and down the country. With such a background of uncertainty, the 1930s dawned.

ESTABLISHING THE THIRTIES BASICS

Professional footballers were as a whole better paid than the average worker who was fortunate if he was receiving £2 to £3 a week, though there was no minimum wage for players. The maximum was £8 a week for 37 weeks and £7 for the 15-week off-season. There were bonuses for winning and drawing. Of course there was no obligation on the part of clubs to pay the maximum but players argued that any differential should not apply in the summer when there were no matches!

However, job security was as precarious as for anyone else. If not retained at the end of a season he was either placed on the open-to-transfer list or given a free transfer. While on offer until a change to another Football League club, his registration was retained. The availability of being taken on especially by a Southern League club or other non-league professional competition while transfer-listed by his Football League club was a useful avenue for only a few. Being out of work for the general public forced a stringent means test before any prospect of being paid dole money.

From 1921 referees received three guineas (three pounds three shillings – £3.15p) for officiating at First and Second Division matches, £2.10p for Division Three. Linesmen were paid exactly half the amounts listed. On 30 May 1938 a uniform scale was introduced with referees being paid £3.15p for all Football League matches linesmen £1.50p. A set rate of expenses covering travel and subsistence was also in operation during the 1930s. There was a guinea for hotel accommodation and half that for a meal. As for kit, there was no specific uniform but blazers with an open-necked white shirt and shorts were favoured. Certain individuals had their own preferences.

Experiments were carried out in 1935 with two referees including an England v The Rest trial match and a Football League XI v West Bromwich Albion. But at the League's AGM the motion prompted by Everton's chairman Will Cuff was defeated by 31 votes to 18. At the AGM of the Football Association in 1937 it again failed.

As the economy shrank, miners and those involved in the textile industry were suffering one- third unemployment almost half of steelworkers were laid off and close to two-thirds in shipbuilding were in similar straits. It contributed to a million workers on the dole. At least when attached to a club professional footballers were luckier.

Often frequented spare time amusements included the cinema, music halls, ballroom dancing, greyhound racing and speedway. Again the cheapest admission prices were within a sensible range. Darts and billiards were also favourite pastimes plus betting on the Pools and horse racing. Motor racing was a more expensive hobby. Boxing, golf and cricket headed the other popular sports. There was competition from the two Rugby codes Union and League, ice hockey, tennis, hockey and athletics with excellent national newspaper coverage over several pages and column inches. Baseball and roller derby from America was also introduced. Then the wireless gradually became a captive audience for families at home.

Minimum admission to football matches was one shilling (five pence) and considering the prevailing economic climate the games were well attended. Only in its Jubilee season 1937-38 did the Football League issue official attendance figures. The aggregate was 28,132,933 for 1848 matches in four divisions totalling 88 clubs for an average of 15,225 per game. However, it was not a typical reflection of the times as adverse weather conditions of early season rain and later snow kept crowds down at crucial stages. International matches usually had a minimum entrance fee of two shillings (ten pence) with a varying scale for better accommodation.

While promising youngsters were taken on the ground staff of clubs the majority of players had had either undergone apprenticeships in industry or recruited from full-time employment. Though the school-leaving age was 14 there was compulsory part-time education up to the age of 18. Youngsters had the opportunity of learning a trade at least three years before they could become a professional footballer if so disposed. Previous expertise and exposure to work often led to employment in the same areas once settled in football.

Among the ground staff boys were Stanley Matthews and Freddie Steele at Stoke as well as Jimmy Hogan at Liverpool taken on at Anfield when he was 15. They were certainly in the minority a year or so from being out of school. Matthews later went into business with his father-in-law's sports outfitters.

There were many miners. In any half a dozen various trades represented there would be at least one from the pits. While most had left the mines, Sid Tremain at Hartlepools combined pit work with part-time football. Ex-Army personnel formed another source of recruitment. These were among the best sources. Frequently stated that by merely shouting down a pit a player would emerge was a jest wide of the target as almost all collieries had a football team. Scouts could see potential talent in action. As to the soldiers, their representative games were well publicised in the national press.

Miners and servicemen had something in common: they were physically fit and strong. If they were up to the expected standard on the football field, they were ready made for the requirements of the professional game existing at the time. Contrasting industries also provided those with the necessary aptitude. Alex James who found his greatest fame with Arsenal had worked as a checking clerk in a Scottish steel foundry, oddly enough alongside Tom Adamson, a full-back of Bury and Brentford connections, who was actually born in Lancashire. Though never classed as a part-time player, James had an arrangement to appear a couple of hours a week in the afternoons at Selfridges sports department. One summer when he was in dispute over re-signing for the Highbury club, he attempted to obtain dole money!

Stoke's Stanley Matthews and Freddie Steele

Other players had more than helpful deals with their clubs. When full-back Mike Keeping left Southampton for Fulham in 1932 he continued with his motor trade business in Hampshire. He was allowed to front up at Craven Cottage and elsewhere on weekends plus for the occasional midweek match. "Bunny" Bell of nine goals Tranmere fame and later at Everton was a shipping clerk but also kept a general store in Wallasey! He was allowed to train in the evenings. The professions, too, were involved, schoolmasters among them. Harry Swaby a Grimsby half-back worked on the local fish docks and also trained after work.

As to the variety of backgrounds, Arsenal's Jackie Milne had been a barman at a Glasgow pub, Pat Glover at Grimsby had swapped breaking up machinery for being a railway porter as was his colleague Harry Betmead at one time and also Jim Milne. He was no relation to the Preston player and was employed at Dundee's Lochee West End station. John Jennings at Middlesbrough was formerly a locomotive fireman. Harry Smith at Notts County had been a porter at Harrow while playing for Wealdstone. Jack Smith was at Whitehall Printeries a Leeds printing works when Huddersfield signed him. Alan Fowler later with Swindon was also at Whitehall. In a similar industry, Chelsea forward George Mills had been an estimating clerk in a Bromley printing outfit and Grimsby's Charlie Craven was also involved in a printing capacity. Walter Crook at Blackburn worked in a grocer's shop and Jack Palethorpe of Villa etc., ran errands on a bike for another grocer.

Fred Pincott at Bournemouth had been a bus conductor and when on his father's farm in Scotland Pompey's Bob Salmond had been handy with the plough. Dai Jones at Leicester was originally a fisherman, Neil Dewar a gamekeeper in the Highlands before his Scottish international career, Norwich goalkeeper Harry Duke a salesman, Vince Blore the Palace goalie a baker as well as Villa's Eric Houghton, Ernest Whittam at Chester and Bill Tremelling at Preston. Then again Spurs Bill Whatley actually delivered bread. "Pongo" Waring even sold chocolates and programmes at Tranmere. Harry Duggan of Leeds was a monumental stone mason in Dublin, Fred Howe at Liverpool a plumber and West Ham's Jimmy Collins had worked in his father's butcher shop. Frank Boulton the Arsenal goalkeeper was once a butcher's boy himself. Manchester City's Eric Brook was even a mascot for Mexborough FC in 1919-20!

Arsenal goalkeeper Frank Moss had worked for Leyland Motors, Newcastle full-backs Dave Fairhurst in shipyards and Jimmy Nelson as an apprentice plater in the Belfast shipyards before kicking a ball in Scotland for the first time as an international! Joe Richardson another Newcastle full-back was formerly a blacksmith as was Tom Pickard at Barrow. As a youngster Dennis Westcott picked up some pocket money as a golf caddie at Lytham along with his brother Ronnie who later went to Arsenal. Portsmouth goalkeeper Harry Walker was a motor mechanic but studying psychology.

John Wassall when signing for Manchester United did so in the bacon curing shed where he was employed. Jack Screen of West Bromwich and Norman Wharton originally with Barrow had been electricians. Reading half-back Billy Owen unusually exchanged being a farmer's boy to working in the pits! George Robson who went from Brentford to Hearts had been a truck driver. Others on the road had been Tom Evans at Spurs with a builder's lorry and Jimmy Barrett at West Ham with a tradesman vehicle. Bill Morris with Wolverhampton was a qualified draughtsman. Albert Geldard combined his football with work as an insurance agent during his career. Grimsby wing-half Alex Hall as a builder's joiner took his tools with him on a bicycle. New Brighton's Jasper Kerr favoured four wheels as a confectionery traveller.

Scottish players were more likely to have a separate occupation. Dr James Marshall carried on in his practice with Rangers, Arsenal and West Ham. His Ibrox colleague Jimmy Smith also graduated from university and studied medical gymnastics. The Rangers and Scottish international wing-half George Brown MA graduated from Glasgow University, became a schoolmaster and continued as a part-timer at Ibrox throughout his career. Left-winger Sandy Nicholson was a chartered accountant, Alan Morton an insurance agent complete with bowler and briefcase. Tom Souter of Queen's Park and Rangers was a Glasgow solicitor.

One-time London University graduate Bernard Joy was another in the scholastic profession and at one time at Springgrove Secondary School. He achieved the notable feat of becoming a regular choice at centre-half for Arsenal while retaining his amateur status, having previously played for both Corinthians and Casuals. Not only did he maintain a place in the club's First Division, but he did so training in evenings only! At the end of 1935-36 he went with the Corinthians on a tour of Germany. Howard Fabian a well known amateur was games master at Highgate School. Joe Loughran was another teacher in Birmingham. In 1932-33 Bristol Rovers had two: centre-forward Viv Gibbins at a London School, centre-half Bert Blake at a local one. The scribes were not ignored. Percy Newton who joined Tranmere from Manchester United was a reporter and Hugh McLenahan at Old Trafford worked in a newspaper office.

Centre-forward Wilf Kirkham who had successful scoring achievements for Port Vale – where he hit a club record 153 League goals – and Stoke City, did his teacher training in Sheffield and was another who always dovetailed his twin careers. Upon retirement from football he held two posts as headmaster. However in June 1933 the Stoke Education Committee forbade him to play professional football while he held such a scholastic appointment. Jackie Martin was also content to combine playing with teaching and Aston Villa equally happy about the arrangement. This inside-forward was signed from Hednesford Town and once on Villa's books trained after school hours.

Huddersfield goalkeeper Bob Hesford studied for his BA at Leeds University and also aimed for a Diploma of Education. Part-time football for Fred Lester at Gillingham meant an incredibly early start to the day from four o'clock as a milkman and he did his training twice a week in the evenings. The bigger clubs were not keen on players having other jobs. This did not mean they were against those finishing further education. Cliff Bastin at Arsenal completed his apprenticeship as an electrical engineer.

Some trades required more physical effort and combining such work with playing often presented a full day's toil especially when home was not close by. Charlie Wilson Jones finally settled to play in Wrexham's reserve team after unsuccessful trials with Blackburn and Bolton. He was working as a cobbler in Brymbo and used to cycle five miles there and back to train at Wrexham, before resuming the repair of boots in his workshop. But Birmingham signed the centre-forward and the pedalling stopped.

Bud Maxwell at Preston had been in the boot trade himself as had his North End colleague Harry Lowe at Skelmersdale. Fred Fitton, too in a Burnley shoe store, but Bury's George Matthewson had worked and played for Pelaw Co-op once out of the Army. Albert McInroy of Leeds was formerly a packer at the Preston Co-op! Stan Wood of West Bromwich was a salt packer! At one time Jock Dodds drove a petrol lorry, Ray Westwood his father's dairy van. West Ham's long-server Jimmy Ruffell was once with Ilford Electricity. Dudley Milligan had been a qualified engineer when in South Africa.

The amateur game was another ready-made hunting ground. There was also ample opportunity for the encouragement of part-time players for purely monetary reasons. Clubs also had "nursery" teams playing in amateur football and with semi-professional teams where players could develop in a competitive environment. Amateurs needed to put in the hours if their ambition was to succeed in the professional game. Eric Stephenson was playing for Harrogate and trained in the evenings at Leeds United's Elland Road ground. There was not much spare time for this inside-forward because he was also a Lieutenant in the 30th Battalion Boys' Brigade. He met his wife at church and taught at its Sunday School. Leeds did sign him. He then spent his afternoons as a dry cleaning salesman.

Stepping on the gas was a distinct attribute for a centre-forward. Both Joe Bambrick and Ted Drake had the correct background to it. Bambrick had been a gas worker in Ireland while Drake was an apprentice at the Southampton Gas Company.

Welsh international forward Dai Astley worked in the mines before being taken on by Merthyr at 17. His international colleague Taffy O'Callaghan actually worked in the pits until he was 16! Spurs farmed him out to nursery duty at Barnet and Northfleet. Willie Evans another Spurs favourite was similarly sent to Haywards Sports, another such White Hart Lane "kindergarten." Long serving Leicester City winger and England international Hugh Adcock was another pit boy who developed with Coalville Town. Centre-half for England in eleven matches – ten consecutively – Jack Barker was a Denaby Main miner before joining Derby County from first Denaby Rovers, then Denaby United. Ben Ellis born in Wales worked in the pits and was discovered playing with Bangor in Northern Ireland. Became established in Scottish League football and was capped by Wales. When George Brown later at Aston Villa signed for Huddersfield he was actually on strike at Mickley Colliery as was George Camsell when a pit-boy. Middlesbrough snapped him up! Teenager Herbert Cartwright at Mansfield was even a pit pony handler. Wilf Copping at Leeds had wanted to become a jockey but was too heavy and also became a miner. His subsequent Arsenal colleague Bob John was finished an apprenticeship with a blacksmith as had been goalkeeper Bill Harper his two spells with Arsenal sandwiching a stint in the USA. Another Highbury favourite George Male was once a Lloyd's messenger.

Forest full-back Bill Thompson worked and played for Rolls Royce at one time. Middlesbrough full-back Bob Stuart was employed in a garage when with South Bank. Dundee United's Neil Paterson played as an amateur while employed as a journalist for the locally based D C Thomson group.

At Derby in addition to Barker, Jack Kirby, Tommy Cooper, Errington Keen, Arthur Groves and Jimmy Randall also had mining backgrounds. But George Collin had been a blacksmith, Sammy Crooks had driven a coal truck, Fred Jessop worked as a Cobbler and Jack Bowers at different times had been a baker's roundsman and ironworker. Only Jack Nicholas on the Swansea Town groundstaff before going to the Baseball Ground had an initial association with a football club.

At a similar time Manchester United had two who had been mechanics: Jack Cape and Jack Mellor, Johnny Hall electrician, Walter McMillen engineer, George Vose glass blower and Herbert Heywood moulder. Hugh McLenahan as previously mentioned had worked in a newspaper office, Tommy Manley as an office clerk and Ernie Hine who had gone from being a miner to becoming a publican. Jock Ainsworth was combining his football working in a bedding factory and Hubert Redwood had come from a glass foundry. Arthur Wedgewood was surprisingly perhaps a manual worker, Jack Ball had once delivered fish when playing at Southport but Bill Robertson was a bookmaker.

Sam Weaver of the 35-yard throw-in worked at a Derbyshire pit head before launching his football career that encompassed England honours. Two-goal Jack Allen of Newcastle's Cup win in controversial circumstances also began his working life in the mines. Scottish international defender Bobby Baxter joined Middlesbrough at 20 after a similar background. Sheffield Wednesday full-back Ernie Blenkinsop who won his 26 England caps in succession was the same age when he left the mining industry. Third Lanark full-back Jimmy Carabine a regular choice for Scotland also worked as a miner.

Rapid advancement from toiling underground to being given the opportunity to play professional football was often illustrated and in no better fashion than the experience of George Richardson who was working in the mine at Manton Colliery on the morning of Saturday 8 April 1933. In the afternoon he played for the Colliery team at inside-forward and immediately afterwards was transferred to Huddersfield Town playing in their Central League side on the Monday prior to first team football on the Wednesday. Oddly enough that was his only senior game for Huddersfield but he later played for Sheffield United and Hull City.

The soldier-boys featured everywhere. In November 1930 Aston Villa put seven goals past the Army goalkeeper Lance-Corporal Harry Morton of the Royal Welch Fusiliers in a friendly match, but so impressed they invited him back for a trial with their Colts team when on leave. Though a little under 5ft 10in, he was a commanding presence between the sticks and signed professional forms in March 1931. Perhaps the intimidating name of his original club Middleton Road Primitives proved an asset to his approach. But later on he was hit for another seven – by Ted Drake!

Bill Rawlings had joined the 2nd/3rd Field Ambulance on the outbreak of the Great War and was awarded the 1914 Star. On demobilization he signed for Southampton, Manchester United and Port Vale scored 175 League goals and was twice capped for England. Wee Tommy Magee all 5ft 3in of him was another who won international honours from a military background. He made 394 League appearances for West Bromwich Albion as a midfield player at either inside-forward or wing-half. He actually signed while serving in the trenches in France; the necessary forms being despatched to The Hawthorns. Fred Keenor of Cardiff City and Wales fame had served in the Footballers' Battalion of the Middlesex Regiment.

Of course there were many others who interrupted their careers to serve their country. Bob Kelly was in the Royal Field Artillery during the Great War after establishing himself in first-class football before the conflict. Subsequent to these commitments, his career lasted well into his early 40s and he collected some 14 England caps as a constructive inside-forward. Amby Buckley signed by Fulham as a full-back had played in three Army Cup finals for the Sherwood Foresters and one season played 14 times for the Army. Jimmy Hamilton had served in the Coldstream Guards and at Hartlepools he ran a sub-post office and tobacconists.

For a varied life before professional football Frank Newton who scored 41 goals for Fulham in 1931-32 had been in the Army, Royal Navy, on a Merchant Navy cargo boat, served as a Sergeant in the Calcutta Police and an engineer on the East India Railway. He was born in Quebec – near Durham. In his second spell at Craven Cottage returning from Reading, he had the misfortune to break his leg in a friendly with FK Austria in December 1934. Complications set in, he had to retire and Fulham chairman gave "Bonzo" a job in his company as a brass-moulder.

Movement from the Services to football continued in the 30s but at a slower rate. Several owed their football initiation to when wearing uniform. Centre-forwards were often sharpshooters in both senses. Arthur Frost had seven years in the Army before playing for New Brighton and Newcastle United, From a boy entrant at 14 he had been used to playing every evening when off duty. Tommy Cheetham six years in the Royal Artillery in India before Queens Park Rangers ushered his talent towards an England trial. Billy Hartill had been a Bombardier in the Royal Horse Artillery and played for the Army in Kentish Cup matches against France and Belgium before linking up with Wolves. Dave "Boy" Martin went from drummer boy in the Royal Ulster Rifles bought out for £5 to professional football and Irish international honours. Harry Mordey had learned his football in the Army while stationed in Malta. Born in Malaya he subsequently played for Charlton in 1936.

Charlton Athletic defender Bert Turner was an all-round sportsman in the Welch Regiment serving in the Far East before civilian life. Another who later went to Charlton was Don Welsh who joined the Navy at 15 and was about to set sail for China when Torquay United signed him.

Ex-Soldiers had to wait twelve months before being taken on as professionals. Grimsby had secured goalkeeper George Moulson but had to have him on amateur forms for a year and worked with his brother on Grimsby Docks before signing professionally.

By the quayside was a favourite venue for employment. Both Charlie Rattray at Blackpool and Billy Porter, Oldham full-back had worked at Fleetwood's fish docks, the latter playing for the local club at the same time. Billy Simpson the Nottingham Forest winger started in the shipbuilding trade. Rangers Sam English worked in a shipyard on the Clyde. Goal ace Ted Harper was once a shipwright. Manchester City's Frank Swift with his goalkeeping brother Fred helped with their father's pleasure boat venture. Further off-shore England amateur international Jimmy Coates served on the King's yacht and was always known from his rank as "Rigger."

Motor mechanics included William McGonagle (Celtic), Harold Hobbis of Charlton a machinist, Tom Griffiths of Aston Villa a cabinet maker as were George Stevenson (Motherwell) and Jimmy Gorman (Blackburn), while Leo Stevens at New Brighton had been a conductor on Wallasey Trams. Plumbers included Harold Pearson at West Bromwich and Alf Hanson with Liverpool. Mill workers were various, too. Portsmouth's Billy Smith and John O'Hare at Chelsea employed at Paper mills while wingers Freddie Worrall (Portsmouth) as well as Arthur Cunlifffe (Everton) worked at Lancashire Cotton mills as did Jack Walsh (Millwall), Arnold Whiteside (Blackburn) and Billy Spencer (Stoke). Fulham goalkeeper Alf "bird catcher" Tootill had been a pattern weaver. Jimmy Easson at Pompey began as an engineering fitter. Tom Fenoughty at York and Vince Farrell with Orient were plasterers.

All eyes on the ball. St Andrew's April 1938. Don Dearson scores for Birmingham.

Also plentiful were electricians. Lew Stoker, Birmingham and England wing-half was one. He had played no school football. Don Dearson also at Birmingham was allowed to finish his electrical engineering apprenticeship. Charlie Napier, Celtic and Derby and Raich Carter with Sunderland were two other "sparks." Eddie Perry had worked on an overhead crane.

Maurice Webster the Middlesbrough and England centre-half began as a plumber, Bury's Wally Amos had an apprenticeship as a marine engineer. Bob Adams one-time Cardiff goalkeeper had training as a sanitary engineer. Berry "Nivvy" Nieuwenhuys of Liverpool had been a mining engineer in South Africa and could speak Dutch. Even Bill "Dixie" Dean worked in an engineering plant as did another prolific scorer Dave Halliday. Davie Meiklejohn described as the best post-war player in Scotland had been an engineer, too. Vic Woodley the Chelsea goalkeeper had also had some engineering training as had Laurie Fishlock of Millwall and Walter Robbins at West Bromwich motor engineering. Len Dunderdale of Walsall and Watford had been an engineering fitter. Tommy Johnson of Manchester City, Everton and Liverpool had also had such training, similarly Jimmy Richardson (Newcastle), Jock McDougall (Sunderland) and Jimmy Deacon with Wolves. Bob Pryde at Blackburn was previously a car mechanic. Ken Willingham of Huddersfield had been a metal turner.

The unrelated Bill Richardsons at West Bromwich came from different backgrounds. Centre-half Bill one-time butcher's boy and Tipton Ironworker compared with centre-forward W G Billy who had played for United Bus Co. and became an inspector there.

Almost unique was Tom Burnett a Darlington full-back who played originally for a village team in North Yorkshire and worked as a gardener on the estate of Lord Bolton near Richmond where his father was a woodman. Not exactly having to live hand to mouth was Bill Pendergast who was apprentice to a dentist before drilling in the goals for Chester.

Plenty of well-known names who were butcher's boys at one time: Harold Barton (Sheffield United), Jesse Carver (Newcastle), Peter O'Dowd (Chelsea) and Harold Pearson (West Bromwich). Contrast to those in the building trade: Alf Chalkley (West Ham) – was a scaffolding expert – Harry McMenemy (Newcastle), George Bond (Millwall), George Fitton (Preston),Tom Cochrane (Leeds) and Joe Nicholls ex-Army (Spurs) all bricklayers. George Vose (Manchester United) had been an expert glass-blower, Horace Burrows (Sheffield Wednesday) a maker of coffins and Arthur Riley (Liverpool) who could top them all having been a gold miner! That other South African Gordon Hodgson had been a boiler maker. Johnny Mapson the Sunderland goalkeeper a baker's boy.

James Nichol at Portsmouth had been a pattern maker, Andy Beattie of Preston a quarryman in Scotland. Tommy Nolan sometimes known as "Will" at Port Vale and Bradford was employed as a clerk in Manchester commuting to his football. Goalkeeper Bill Gormlie as a page boy had been playing for Blackpool's Hotel Imperial when he was discovered. Later with Blackburn and became a cinema manager! Celtic centre-forward Jimmy McGrory also became well known in the cinema industry and was a picturehouse proprietor. Irish international goalkeeper Elisha Scott had been a linen cutter.

George Goddard was playing as an amateur with Redhill while working in a local bus garage. He then scored a record 37 League goals for Queens Park Rangers in 1929-30. Alf Lythgoe was in the smelting forge on the LMS railway at Crewe when he was told he had to choose his job or football. He signed for Crewe Alexandra aged 20, but told he was too small for centre-forward. He drifted to Whitchurch, Sandbach Ramblers, Congleton Town and Ashton National until Stockport County recruited him in May 1931. In 1933-34 he scored 46 League goals for them.

He was once handy with a steam hammer, had opened a confectionary and tobacco shop in Stockport in 1939 well placed near the cricket ground. But when he was put on the transfer list with County it immediately raised concerns. However he was fixed up with Ashton National.

Tailoring was the forte of Jack Hallows at Bradford City and he made clothes for any of his colleagues who were interested. Sheffield United full-back Harry Hooper was a tailor's cutter. Shop keeping was another favourite source of income and sometimes other members of the family could be involved. Bolton's Harry Goslin ex-Boys Brigade, opened a cycle shop and often sold caps and leggings to Wanderers fans. His background had been working in the chemical industry playing for Boots Athletic. Sheffield Wednesday's Horace Burrows had a sports outfitters business.

Enterprising Herman Conway who had always been active in the decorating field found when Dave Mangnall arrived at West Ham with transport it helped expanding the business. Others in the painting and decorating game were Fred Barnett at Southend and Syd Roberts with Liverpool. Len Newcomb at Southport started a lending library in his newsagent outlet. Syd Dickinson after his Lincoln time entered the family grocery and provisions business. Scottish international Sandy McNab at Sunderland was another familiar with the grocery retail. At less than 5ft 4in, Bert Davis at Sunderland had a sports outfitters business – with a stool behind the counter. That other pint-sized forward Alex James opened a confectionary and tobacco shop. Of other Highbury favourites Eddie Hapgood was once a milkman, Ray Bowden an auctioneer's clerk and Herbie Roberts an Oswestry gunsmith.

Trevor Smith at Crystal Palace had been a telephone operator. Johnny Spuhler at Sunderland left school and was trained as a joiner as was Jimmy Connor a Roker Park colleague. Johnny Cochrane the Roker Park manager advised him to continue his apprenticeship as he was 20. He did so and was given two afternoons off a week for football training.

Tommy Russell a full-back had played for Cowdenbeath and Rangers before joining Newcastle United. Placed on the transfer list he decided to resume as an electrician at Horden Colliery and started playing three times a week for them!

Plenty of enterprise existed. Bert Sproston who could do his share of plastering, bought up twelve plots of land with his brother who was in the house building trade and played for Sandbach Ramblers. Stoke's Arthur Turner had learned upholstery and this came in use domestically, too. Must be something in the centre-half position for Spurs pivot Arthur Rowe had also worked in the same trade.

In contrast Arsenal's Cup Final goalkeeper Alec Wilson also qualified as a masseur and in the summer looked after Kent County cricketers. He specialized in medical gymnastics and therapy. Newcastle left-winger Tommy Pearson was a laboratory assistant at Edinburgh University when signed from Murrayfield Amateurs. For a time he was assistant curator at the Edinburgh Museum.

Jack Pickering at Sheffield United was articled to a chartered accountant in 1935 and was allowed to train in the evenings. Centre-forward Harry Johnson who left the Bramall Lane club after scoring over 200 goals joined Mansfield and added a further century there. He was always a part-time player, employed as a metallurgist at Hadfields steel company.

Lincoln's Johnny Campbell was initially a chemist's apprentice, studied at a college in Leicester, qualified then started studying to be an optician. Joe James at Brentford had worked in a chemical factory as a fitter's mate. Jimmy Wood of West Ham used to be a chauffeur, Birmingham's England amateur goalkeeper Ken Teweksbury was a jeweller and Jock Thomson Dundee and Everton at one time a wagon builder. Bill Murray turned down an engineering career with a shipyard firm in China for Sunderland football.

Albert Dawes left his father's butcher shop to sign for Northampton. He had previously played for Aldershot and Guildford City as an amateur, having once hit 156 goals for Frimley Green in one season. Charlie Fletcher at Brentford had been in the furniture trade. George Cummings the powerful Villa full-back an iron moulder. West Bromwich's former errand boy Herbert Trentham lost a finger and a thumb when he was a carpenter! Billy Kingdon at Villa had been more fortunate in the same occupation as had Doug Hunt of Tottenham Hotspur.

Arthur Chandler worked for Handley Page aircraft manufacturers before his days at Leicester Oldham's Matt Gray drove a steam roller and later an ambulance! Wally Johnson was a fireman at Southend. He played later with United and West Ham. Leeds' Arthur Hydes made toffee in London, Manchester United goalkeeper Jack Hacking was in the grocery department at Grimshaw Park's Co-op and weighing up sugar when Blackpool signed him! Another one-time grocer was Duncan Urquhart at Hibs. A trio of draughtsmen: George Ritchie (Leicester), Bill Johnstone (Oldham) and Norman Mackay who before he was at Plymouth helped design Dundee's stand.

Many successful careers started late. Dave Mangnall did not play football until he was 16 when he began modestly enough with Maltby New Church FC in the Rotherham Sunday School League scoring over 50 goals one season. Combined mining with Maltby Colliery FC and 35 goals followed by trials with Huddersfield Town, Rotherham United and Doncaster Rovers as an amateur. Leaving his pit job he turned professional with Leeds United. From then came more success and goal scoring. By 1938-39 he had tallied over 150 League and Cup goals for Leeds, Huddersfield Town, Birmingham, West Ham United and Millwall in ten years.

Alec Roxburgh, Blackpool born goalkeeper of Scottish parents, was spotted on the local Pleasure Beach saving penalties after an unsuccessful trial with Manchester City. Any he let in cost him two pence. Blackpool signed him.

Literally plucked from the iron foundry where he toiled, Bob McPhail at 18 was taken to make his debut for Airdrie in a Scottish Cup tie replay. They won and he helped them win the trophy in the final on the ground of Glasgow Rangers for whom he was to play from 1927 to 1939.

Gateshead had a fairly wide spectrum of varying accomplishments at one stage: Norman Harbottle – moulder, Eddie Miller – garage mechanic, Jimmy Quigley – clerk with a bus company, Stan Hornsby – milkman, Tom Conroy – engineer and Joe McDermott – insurance agent.

Few schoolboy internationals escaped detection if they wanted a career in football. Scouting was widespread and well organized by even the most modest of clubs. Louis Rocca was one of the best known as chief scout at Manchester United. A shrewd character he could pull off some odd deals. He once signed an amateur from a Football League club in exchange for three freezers of ice cream for use as fund raisers.

In 1938 the Old Trafford club formed the Manchester United Junior Athletic Club (MUJACS) to promote the development of youth. They also declared their intention of producing three teams of equal first team strength. That same year Preston North End was running two teams in local junior football. Frank Buckley at Wolves even introduced two 16 year old wingers Alan Steen and Jimmy Mullen in March 1939 against Manchester United. They won 3-0 and Steen was a scorer, too.

The main reserve competitions were the Central League and Football Combination. West Bromwich Albion won the Central League three times in succession from 1932-33. The Combination also ran a condensed Second Division for three seasons from 1930-31 but the experiment was not a success. Several non-league clubs used it as a first team competition to augment Southern League commitments. To underline its strength as a club, Arsenal won seven of the ten Football Combination seasons in the 1930s, finished third twice and were runners-up in the remaining season.

In 1938 Arsenal retained 36 professionals and had one on the open-to-transfer list – Alex James. Chelsea also kept 36 but had five on the list. In contrast Accrington Stanley had ten retained professionals and four on the list. Barrow kept just six professionals.

The Southern League, Midland League, Cheshire County, North-Eastern League and Lancashire Combination were among the strongest non-league competitions that also included some reserve teams of Football League clubs. Midweek competitions flourished, too.

The nationwide competition for schoolboys was the English Schools Shield and produced a variety of winners from up and down the country. From 1930 the respective winners each season were Newcastle, Islington, Manchester/Southampton shared, Sunderland, Manchester (the "Cottonopolis boys") twice, Preston/West Ham shared, Liverpool, Manchester and Swansea. These matches were well scouted by the professional clubs.

England did better than Scotland in their Schoolboy International clashes winning five to three with two drawn. England also won the ten against Wales and the six when Ireland entered from 1934. The 1934 match at Highbury drew a 35,600 attendance as England beat Scotland 4-1.

3rd December 1938, Highbury. Ted Drake in action against Birmingham.

Two English teams scoring more than 250 League goals between them in one season illustrated the impact the early years of the change in the off-side law had made on football. Forwards revelled in the freedom putting defenders on the back foot. But once it appeared obvious that the attacking centre-half was outmoded and the "stopper" was not just a passing fancy, defences began the process of coping with the situation again.

The last season of the old law in 1924-25 had seen a total of only 4,700 goals scored in 1848 Football League matches. In 1925-26 it rose to 6,374. For 1929-30 the figure was 6,583 and in succeeding years 6,816; 6.499 (1806 matches due to Wigan Borough withdrawing); 6,512; 6,321; 6,306; 6,119; 6,133; 5,441 and 5,787 in 1938-39.

While Aston Villa had scored a Football League record equalling 128 goals in 1930-31 when finishing runners-up in the First Division to Arsenal – who themselves were scorers of 127 – there were two occasions in later seasons when one day's programme produced as many as 209 goals.

On 2 January 1932, there was an average of 4.75 goals per game as Wigan's demise had reduced the fixtures to 44 that day. Then on 1 February 1936, a full programme of 46 matches again witnessed 209 goals being registered; the average 4.54.

The 1932 occasion saw nine goals, an eight, a seven and two sixes. But 13 teams failed to score – including Arsenal. There was a 5-5 draw, too. For the 1936 goal feast, there were five sixes, but nothing higher and even a goalless draw between Aldershot and Bristol City. Chesterfield actually won 6-5 at Crewe Alexandra. Fourteen teams were without a goal.

Then on 6 January 1934 Stockport County set a Football League record beating Halifax Town 13-0 in a Third Division (North) encounter. It was the Saturday of Herbert Chapman's death so the following Monday might have had more coverage of this Baker's Dozen.

The circumstances of the match came a week prior to Halifax facing Bolton Wanderers in the FA Cup. Two down in 14 minutes to Stockport with the wind against them, it appeared the Halifax players' minds were focusing seven days ahead. This did not help Town's reserve goalkeeper Stanley Milton making his first team debut. First team goalkeeper Walter Shirlaw was to miss his only game that season.

But according to the *Halifax Town Milestones Book 1911-37* there was a humorous side to events. When the tenth goal was scored, Danny Ferguson turned to Hugh Flack asking "How many's that?" "Sure I don't know," replied the Irish full-back, "but I think we're losing!" As a postscript: Halifax led Bolton at one stage and then denied a second when the referee accidentally baulked a Town player who had an open goal. Bolton finally won 3-1. Milton survived the thirteen-goal ordeal to be chosen again.

Stockport's tactics in the first half of keeping the ball in the air failed to yield further goals, so in the second half with the elements against them, they kept it low and profited. The goal timings were 8, 14, 51 (Joe Hill hat trick), 50, 53, 57, 59, 61, 65, 66, 80, 86 and 88. Percy Downes scored four.

For individual aggregate scores, nothing matched the 1935 affair at Prenton Park, the return Boxing Day fixture between Tranmere Rovers and Oldham Athletic. On Christmas Day, Oldham had won 4-1. The Latics made two changes in defence, Tranmere fielded the same eleven. One of the Oldham newcomers was right-back Tommy Seymour who the previous day had been in the Latics reserve team beaten 8-2 at West Bromwich Albion!

On a pitch ankle deep in mud after two minutes, Tranmere went ahead through Ted Urmson. Oldham then lost centre-half Norman Brunskill for 15 minutes with a broken nose. During his absence Rovers added five more goals. Robert "Bunny" Bell opened his scoring after seven minutes, his second after 16 minutes when Tranmere were four ahead and added his fifth just before the interval. Brunskill had returned with face heavily bandaged and instructions not to head the ball, but he had still headed the first Oldham goal after 38 minutes to make it 7-1 to Tranmere!

Nine – one down at the interval, Oldham recovered a little to make the score 10-2 in 63 minutes before the finale. Shortly after Bell's seventh on 68 minutes, which equalled the individual scoring record, he shot wide from a penalty kick! This prompted Oldham into action with two goals in four minutes including a penalty. With three minutes remaining Bell added two more in the 88th and 89th minutes before the final whistle: Rovers 13 Latics 4.

Bell's record-breaking feat resounded for merely a few months, because on 13 April 1936 when Luton Town defeated Bristol Rovers 12-0, Joe Payne scored ten times. It was his first senior game at centre-forward as hitherto he had played six League games at wing-half. He was the only change on the printed programme, a late replacement for Willie Boyd. Payne had had previous amateur experience with Bolsover Colliery as a centre-forward but was farmed out by Luton to Biggleswade Town as a wing-half before being recalled.

However, Payne's final tally of ten was not revealed until later. He had opened the scoring in the 23rd minute Fred Roberts made it 2-0 nine minutes later. But Payne added two more in the 40th and 43rd minutes as Luton led 4-0 at the break. In the 49th minute Payne hit his fourth and six minutes on he had a header which having hit the bar was partially saved by Rovers goalkeeper Jack Ellis before George Martin following up bundled player and ball into the net.

The remaining Payne goals were timed at 57, 65, 76, 84 and 86 minutes, but with the crowd willing him to beat the record of nine goals, it seemed no tenth was likely for Payne. In fact there was a twelfth goal, but scored by Martin.

After the match the referee T.J. Botham (Walsall) confirmed that Payne's header leading to the fifth goal had crossed the line before goalkeeper Ellis was bundled into the net by Martin. "Bunny" Bell graciously sent Payne a congratulatory telegram! It is interesting to note that Boyd had scored ten goals in three FA Cup ties 3, 3 and 4, earlier in the season for Workington before moving to Luton. Incidentally five of the beaten Rovers side including goalkeeper Ellis turned out the following day in the 3-1 win over Torquay United. Boyd had gone to Workington while on Manchester United's transfer list at "too high a price."

Again this is only part of the lone scoring achievements in 1935-36. On 1 February Chester defeated York City 12-0. The game had been in doubt with melting snow, the overflowing River Dee causing flooding and at best an ankle deep surface of mud. By half-time Chester led 8-0, a Football League record at 45 minutes. Frank Wrightson centre-forward for the first time scored four goals. Yet York missed an easy equalising chance!

On 14 December 1935, Ted Drake had scored all seven times for Arsenal away to Aston Villa in a 7-1 win. It was said an eighth attempt had hit the bar and bounced down, the centre-forward claiming the ball had crossed the line. However, according to a report in the *Daily Express* by its Sports Editor Arthur Simmons, there was no mention of woodwork interference, but after Drake's sixth goal, the Villa goalkeeper had saved a header and a shot from him. Only a few weeks earlier Drake had had a mid-week reserve outing to improve his shooting!

Drake's goals were timed at 15, 28, 34, 46, 50, 58 and 89 minutes. The pick of the septet was the second. Bastin found him with a high ball which Drake collected in his stride. With opponents on both sides he forged on between them and drove immaculately in from 15 yards. It equalled the achievement of Albert Whitehurst who had gone seven up on 6 March 1929 for Bradford City against Tranmere Rovers in an 8-0 win. Whitehurst had continued to score ten goals in the next five games including a hat trick and a four-timer, for a total of 17 in six matches.

Seven goals also came the way of Ted Harston when Mansfield Town were 8-2 winners over Hartlepools United on 23 January 1937. Eighty-one League goals in two seasons and he was off to Liverpool where injury curtailed his Football League career.

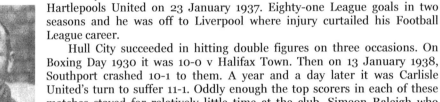

Hull City succeeded in hitting double figures on three occasions. On Boxing Day 1930 it was 10-0 v Halifax Town. Then on 13 January 1938, Southport crashed 10-1 to them. A year and a day later it was Carlisle United's turn to suffer 11-1. Oddly enough the top scorers in each of these matches stayed for relatively little time at the club. Simeon Raleigh who cracked five against Halifax, left during the following season but tragically died after he suffered concussion playing for Gillingham against Brighton & Hove Albion on 1 December 1934. Left-winger Jack Pears who had a hat trick against Southport went to Rochdale after one season and another treble shooter centre-forward against Carlisle, Billy Dickinson retired at the end of his solitary term with Hull.

Ted Harston

Barrow finished their League programme for the season on 5 May 1934 by beating Gateshead 12-1. They took their total of goals in the Third Division (North) to 116 for the season.

There was also an equal sharing of twelve goals between Leicester City and Arsenal on 21 April 1930 when the Gunners rested several players ahead of their FA Cup final. One of the reserves Dave Halliday scored four goals including a hat trick in five minutes. Between 1929-30 and 1938-39 there were twenty examples of matches in which each team scored five times or more.

When Scarborough beat Lincoln City 6-4 in an FA Cup second round tie on 13 December 1930 it was the highest aggregate score for the competition in which a non-league club defeated a League club. In 1934-35 Wigan Athletic became the first non-league club to register a 6-1 FA Cup win on the ground of a Football League club by winning at Carlisle United.

Players scoring at least half of their team's total of League games produced seven such marksmen. In 1930-31 Jimmy Dunne had 41 of Sheffield United's 78 First Division goals. The following season though Leo Stevens managed only 20 in the Third Division (North), it was half of New Brighton's modest 38! In two seasons he managed 33 in 54 League games for them.

Exactly 50 percent of Preston North End's 74 Second Division goals in 1932-33 went to Ted Harper. Jack Bowers scored 34 First Division goals in 1933-34 from Derby County's 68 and in 1935-36 Bert Valentine just made it too, with 30 of the 57 scored by Halifax Town in Division Three (North). There were two such Third Division successes in 1936-37 with identical figures of 55. Joe Payne did so from the 103 scored by Luton Town in the Southern Section, Ted Harston from the 91 produced by Mansfield Town in the North.

Such scoring achievements were not restricted to England. North of the border produced the UK record when Raith Rovers scored 142 League goals in Division Two of the Scottish League in 1937-38. Individually Scotland also had two players registering nine goals in two Scottish Cup ties involving 16 goals. On 17 January 1931, John Simpson the Partick Thistle centre-forward had nine goals in a first round tie against Royal Albert in a 16-0 win and. Rangers leader Jimmy Smith scored the same number when Blairgowrie was beaten 14-2 on 20 January 1934.

The Scots also led on individual goals of eight. On 2 January 1930, Jimmy Dyet scored eight times for King's Park in the 12-2 win over Forfar Athletic. John Calder who had had an unsuccessful trial with Alloa, joined Morton and was another eight goal marksman when Raith Roves were defeated 11-2 on the 18 April 1936. That season he scored 55 goals in all competitions. But King's Park also found themselves on the beaten side with an opponent scoring eight against them. On 13 February 1937 in a second round Scottish Cup tie they crashed 15-0 away to Hearts with Blackpool born Bill Walsh the octet-goal man. He had held the Oldham Athletic scoring record of 32 League goals in 1935-36.

Boyd, too, had achieved something else of note in 1933-34 when he managed to finish top scorer for clubs either side of the border. He had 14 goals for Clyde in 18 League games and another 14 with Sheffield United from 22 such matches. Boyd had played twice on Scotland's 1931 European jaunt against Italy and Switzerland, scoring one against the Swiss. His original claim to fame was scoring more than 200 goals in three seasons for Larkhall Thistle.

Payne was no one-game wonder. As previously mentioned the following 1936-37 season saw him score 55 League goals from 39 matches. Harston equalled the tally from 41 similar games for Mansfield Town that season when leading the Northern Section scorers. Like Harston, Payne also moved higher. Chelsea snapped him up in March 1938 and he was capped for England. Luton, to be fair, had been involved in a game of twelve goals when on 2 September 1933 they defeated Torquay United 10-2. Andy Rennie scored four times.

Nearest in goals scored to Payne's effort in one season was 49 by Tom "Pongo" Waring for Aston Villa in the 1930-31 First Division and the following season in the Third Division (South) by Clarrie Bourton for Coventry City. Of course by the late 1930s such individual totals had disappeared as overall scoring diminished. For example Tommy Lawton with 28 goals for Everton in 1937-38, George Henson 27 for Bradford Park Avenue, Harold Crawshaw (Mansfield Town) 25 and Jack Roberts (Port Vale) 28, were the respective divisional leading scorers. Then 1936-37 had been seen as something of a swansong for the goal-a-game marksmen.

Though perhaps not in the same standard of football, Ray Bowden once scored ten goals for Looe against Tavistock. A Plymouth player was watching and Bowden was promptly signed by Argyle moving on to Arsenal and international recognition. Another ten-goal marksman was Ted Buckley for Tranmere Rovers reserves against Nantwich in 1938 in a 13-0 win. Three of his goals came from penalties and another strike was ruled out through off-side.

Joe Bambrick, of course, hit a half-century of League goals for Linfield in the Irish League in 1929-30 while amassing 94 in all matches that season, including six in internationals, five in Inter-League games and seven in the Irish Cup.

Wingers were often as lethal in front of goal as centre-forwards. Strangely enough all left-wingers! Cliff Bastin at Arsenal scored 33 goals in 1932-33. That same season in Scotland, Tommy McCall had

Jimmy McGrory

one fewer in the Second Division with Queen of the South when they won promotion. Another on the 32 mark was Bob Ferrier for Motherwell in 1929-30, when the Steelmen scored 104 League goals as First Division runners-up. But Ken Dawson helped Falkirk to promotion in 1935-36 when he finished with 39 League goals. Not to be left out of the lethal scoring wide players, in Wales international left-winger Walter Robbins had five against Thames Association for Cardiff City on 6 February 1932. Bert Turner had a nap hand himself for Doncaster Rovers against New Brighton on 16 February 1935. Naturally he was a left-winger.

The Scottish League First Division produced two centre-forwards with 50 or more goals. In 1931-32 Willie McFadyen scored 53 for Motherwell, while Jimmy McGrory of Celtic reached 50 in 1935-36. McGrory's career average was unsurpassed in terms of goals per game at 1.004! McFadyen was also leading scorer in 1932-33 with 45, one more than Barney Battles had registered in 1930-31 with Hearts. Battles father, also Barney had died before seeing his son but had been a Celtic goal scorer, too. The young Barney first played in the USA with Boston and was capped against Canada before Hearts brought him home.

Of players whose careers took them into the period, McGrory registered 408 League goals for Celtic and Clydebank. Hughie Gallacher in an extensive career from 1921 to 1939 for Airdrieonians, Newcastle, Chelsea, Derby, Notts County, Grimsby and Gateshead had 387 and Bill Dean amassed 379 for Tranmere, Everton and Notts County. George Camsell who started with Durham City before Middlesbrough had 345 overall.

Dave Halliday for St Mirren, Dundee, Sunderland, Arsenal, Manchester City and Clapton Orient scored 336, Vic Watson chiefly with West Ham before Southampton reached 313, while Harry Johnson at Sheffield United and Mansfield Town totalled 305.Harry Bedford with Nottingham Forest, Blackpool, Derby, Newcastle, Sunderland, Bradford Park Avenue and Chesterfield scored 308. The only other Scottish player to top a treble century was Bob McPhail with 305 for Airdrieonians and Rangers.

McGrory was one of four players having scored over 300 League goals for one club. He had 397 in Celtic's hoops, Dean finished with Everton on 349, Camsell had 325 by 1939 at Middlesbrough and Vic Watson totalled 298 for West Ham.

While Pat Glover reigned supreme at Grimsby they had Fred Kurz, 17, scoring over 100 goals in two seasons for the reserves having been picked up from Grimsby YMCA in 1935-36. In 1937-38 he had scored 23 goals in half a season in the Central League side.

Lower down the food chain there was no shortage of goals. On 9 February 1933 when Overton Boys beat Laverstock 37-2 a certain Jimmy Holmes scored 26 goals.

Schoolboy marksmen were legendary, too, in the era. Tommy Lawton ploughed in 570 goals in three seasons. Ronnie Rooke playing for Stoke Schools (Guildford) against the Pick of Guildford scored 17 in one match. He later played for Fulham while another Craven Cottager Trevor Smith hit 100 in one season as a schoolboy and 80 in another with Durham Juniors. Stan Foxall at West Ham was credited with 70 goals one season in junior football.

Tom Hopkins as centre-forward for Broad Lanes School scored over a century in one season including nine in one game. But he switched to wing-half when in the Football League with Gillingham.

Monty Wilkinson was another century marksman with Esh Winning Juniors before his Charlton days. At other times he had understudied Hughie Gallacher at Newcastle, Bill Dean at Everton. Straight shooting, too, from the Army. In 1933-34 Corporal Armit from the 4th Battalion Royal Tank Corps scored 105 goals including nine in one match and 20 hat tricks. Little surprise his Battalion won the Army Cup the following season.

Few eclipsed Dennis Kelleher aged 17 of St Joseph's College (Norwood) mid-way through 1935-36 when he had scored 273 goals in three almost seasons. At the half-season he had hit 54 in 19 matches and at Christmas he played for Barnet. He finished that season with 333 and signed amateur forms for Fulham in August 1936.

TACTICS COPING WITH THE THIRD BACK GAME

While forwards found freedom, disorganized defenders dithered. Full-backs pushed to the flanks were required to mark wingers not opposing inside-forwards as wing-halves had previously covered. The centre-half was now detailed to stick rigidly to the other centre-forward, his attacking instincts transferred to the wing-halves. There was never any reference to numbers, systems were always given with letters, W, WM or M.

In fact there remained variations. One wing-half was to be less adventurous than his partner because it would be dangerous for the two in unison to venture too far up field. Already changes were beginning to take shape and the 3-2-2-3 that could be interpreted as such was moving to more of a 4-3-3 pattern. Pushing up an extra forward to confuse the "stopper" centre-half to produce a dual threat also worked at times.

The oft-referred to W formation universally in operation was in fact a squashed representation of the letter, the top three forward points of which were right-winger, centre-forward and left-winger, the lower two being the inside-right and inside-left. Ostensibly there were five forwards without reference to the other six players in the eleven.

As ever players' suitability to one role dictated the choice; either adherence to the play-making role of the attacking centre-half or adoption of the defensive third back. The former had *carte blanche* though the responsibility of keeping an eye on the opposing centre-forward required extra duty cover and co-operation from the full-backs. One could see the disadvantages given the new off-side rule and forwards pressurizing outnumbered defenders.

It also left two small unoccupied, diamond-shaped no-man's land areas in midfield either side of the centre-half who was still obliged to patrol it. Thus the attacking centre-half role was one for an exceptionally gifted and fully-fit specialist able to patrol acres of ground as well as potentially several opponents given the off-side law alteration.

The wing-forwards under the old rule had to pull centres back to keep their inside-forwards on-side. This new off-side altered their role and encouraged them to cut in towards goal with the inside-forwards moving back into midfield to link more directly with their own wingers. In turn the wing-halves deepened into defensive positions. Though the centre-forward role remained largely the same as the focal point of the attack, he no longer had the support of his own centre-half and had the closer attentions of the opposing centre-half. The W formation had become the WM formation with the inside-forward and his wing-half closer to each other with the no-man's land now between the two and their corresponding pair into a spacious six-sided area. The extreme points of the letters were held by the centre-forward and centre-half. Moreover all ten outfield positions were designated in this WM system.

For ease of presentation of course teams continued to be displayed in football programmes in a 2-3-5 formation, though this no longer existed in reality. Occasionally if space on a page necessitated, it was reproduced as 2-3-2-3 with the inside-forwards one row back.

Towards the end of the 30s more teams were using the third back formation and goal scoring was not as free as in the early years. As ever, players comfortable with one system would dictate its implementation; those with other attributes a different agenda. Remarkably the number of goals scored in a season by Arsenal depended on the number of games Alex James played! Yet while Arsenal fashioned the ultimately successful use of the third back, it is another interesting fact that only two of their players figured at centre-half for England during the 1930s, Herbie Roberts and the amateur Bernard Joy. Perhaps the even more surprising statistic is that they contributed just one appearance each and England lost both internationals.

Contrast this with other more adventurous centre-halves like Ernie Hart (Leeds United), Peter O'Dowd (Chelsea) and Tom Graham (Nottingham Forest) who won a dozen caps between them up to 1934 when Jack Barker of Derby County, another pivot with attacking flair won ten England caps in succession. Curious, too, that in O'Dowd's three international exposures the matches were all won and no goals conceded!

The late arrival on the international scene of Stan Cullis (Wolverhampton Wanderers) produced a half-decent compromise between the two options. While his priority was defence he was adventurous and looked to initiate forward movement whenever the opportunity arose. His initial opportunity had come from injury to the more defensive Alf Young.

As to choice of tactics with one or two notable exceptions the club's first team trainer was invariably responsible in addition to his duties involving players' fitness. On match days the trainer would rely on the all-purpose bag, bucket and magic sponge. While Herbert Chapman and Frank Buckley were the two most notable managers as such, many clubs did not even have the figurehead of one making do with a Secretary. Everton, of course, succeeded in gaining promotion, winning the First Division championship twice and the FA Cup without a manager as such until 1939.

Coaching was another grey area. One player was quoted as saying that in the 30s the only coach he saw was a bus. Jimmy Hogan did return from successful stints in Europe notably with Austria to take on Fulham then Aston Villa, but his like was looked upon sceptically by players and generally unappreciated. Anyway he was still listed as Team-Manager. When Chapman died, his successor George Allison was a high profile personality who left football matters in the capable hands of trainer Tom Whittaker. Interestingly enough he was sought by sports people in other fields for his fitness regimes and treatment of injuries.

In Austria the withdrawn centre-forward was introduced which shifted the front formation into an M formation with the two inside-forwards the spearhead, the centre-forward deep with the two wingers. Several English clubs toyed with the plan at odd times, Preston North End for example.

Hogan's influence was based on retention of the ball and often failure to end possession with a definite strike at goal was often too familiar. Whereas the football played by Austria, Hungary and Czechoslovakia was pleasing to the eye, the end result was often in defeat. The Viennese club FK Austria of Hogan fame made several visits to the UK to play club sides. They were admired for their cultural, carpet demonstrations but invariably finished as losers.

However, domestically in terms of where were English top flight managers featured, as an example in 1931-32 among the 22 First Division clubs even Chapman was listed as Secretary-Manager at Arsenal. There were eight others so designated. Derby County had a manager and secretary as did Grimsby Town, Huddersfield Town, Middlesbrough and Newcastle United. Seven clubs registered just Secretaries. Leicester City's Secretary resigned mid-season and was replaced by a Manager!

By 1938-39 eleven Division clubs had a secretary and a manager four had a secretary-manager another four possessed a secretary and a manager while Everton (the champions), Manchester United and Preston North End listed just a secretary.

READ ALL ABOUT IT

The popularity of football was mirrored by the coverage afforded in the national press. In addition there were weekly publications devoting generous space to it, too. There were also a handful of football annuals on the market.

The *Topical Times* produced lively snippets on players and features by top people involved in the game. It also gave away two photographs a week of leading footballers. Its other leading sports featured were boxing, horse racing and cricket. There were extensive Pools forecasts, short stories, serials and answers to a wide spectrum of subjects including sport.

Three other similar publications were *Answers, Sports Budget* and *Football Weekly*. From time to time the latter two plus the *Topical Times* produced detailed *Who's Who* of players with birthplaces, heights and weights included but no dates of birth. In 1934 another comprehensive version came from W M Johnston who in 1931 had published the first *The Football League* featuring the four divisions in some detail goal scorers for each match but without a list of players' appearances for clubs, though with summaries of allied interesting statistics. It continued throughout the period.

For many years the *Athletic News* had been the brand leader for all sports but chiefly the authoritative organ for football until in 1931 it ceased to be as such and merged with the *Sporting Chronicle*. However, it continued to lend its single name to the pocket-sized *Athletic News Football Annual* which for the 1931-32 volume was the 45th issue. Totals of players' appearances and goals plus international and representative matches were included.

The main rival was the *News Chronicle Football Annual* edited by Charles Buchan the former Sunderland, Arsenal and England international. It was a smaller version but did not include appearances and goals, though it did list retained lists and close season signings for English clubs. *The Topical Times Sporting Annual* also featured generous football content. Pools companies also entered the annual market *Cope's Football Annual* and *Littlewoods Football Annual* being two of the more enterprising efforts.

ENTRIES TAKEN FROM THE DAY BY DAY DIARY OF AN INTERNATIONAL PLAYER

The Topical Times ran several months' issues listing the diary of an international player whose identity was snot disclosed. There was evidence it was Billy Cook the Irish international full-back of Everton. This was a typical two weeks taken from the series.

It was a Wednesday in early spring and a sunny morning for a change to bring out the best in him and the other players. It starts with two laps followed by one walking, one running and the sequence repeated. Then a few sprints once the energy is flowing. Off to the gym for exercises and throwing a few left and rights at the punch ball.

Enter the trainer to oversee practice with some not fully inflated footballs, helping the foot and head control, passing and eating up the time with ease and enjoyment. Bath time and back into outdoor clothes. Depending on how well or badly the team is doing, the banter between the players varies. Then it is back to school time with educational classes, nothing too taxing but enough to keep the mind active.

Then in the afternoon more recreation featured on the billiards and snooker table. Evening comes and a visit to the cinema – the first of many such events! One patron spots the player and soon word is passed around the theatre, which can be embarrassing. Such is the price of fame. Back home and it is time for bed.

On Thursday the morning routine resumes followed by a mixture of billiards and table tennis, a quick shower and a later lunch at home. In the afternoon a trip to the country is organised in the car with some friends to visit the Farmers' Market, the ladies particularly enjoying the occasion. However, much of the business conducted by the locals is achieved in the local hostelry! Home for tea and in the evening a boxing show is taken in.

Friday and the early routine at the ground is stepped up all round. After taking a shower the important part of the professional footballers' week means collecting wages. Some players ask for their bonus payments to be kept until the end of the season. The next move is going into town and putting some of the cash into the bank after a shopping trip for essentials at home. Yet another evening out and this time it is a variety show at a local theatre.

Unusually this Saturday there is no match, the team has already been knocked out of the FA Cup. However, at the ground the trainer is busy and always ready for a chat. With the first team inactive, the reserves playing away, it is a fine opportunity for the third string to have a run out on the pitch. Even so, with a cup tie nearby, some of the first team squad consult the club secretary who arranges for passes to be made available for it.

There is still time to go home for lunch which is always referred to as "dinner" and scribble a few notes to be part of a weekly article for the local newspaper. The seats at the match are not the best which is as it should be since the "free-loaders" are the complete outsiders on the day. There is some spice to the event as the visiting team was the one comfortably beaten by his club the previous week.

It turns out to be not the most inspiring of cup matches, the visiting team winning with the only goal in the second half. The losers are due to play his club next Wednesday. Tea at home and yet another evening out, though this time as it is a Saturday night, the choice of picture houses is limited by the large crowds. One of the smaller theatres provides the answer.

Sunday morning and taking the car for a drive into the country and a stop at a local hotel for refreshments is an ideal relaxation. A darts match is in full flow and soon he is making up a foursome. Dinner at home and off to Blackpool in the car with another friend. The weather is colder and the walk around the seafront is bracing to say the least. Tea time and of course another visit to the picture house is a must.

Monday round again and with a match scheduled for the Wednesday afternoon, the tempo of running and sprinting is stepped up. Wall tennis is next, ball practice. After a bath it is billiards and then dinner. With another player a round of golf is organised in the afternoon and he finishes on 82. At last there is a break from the traditional evening performances, with a visit to the local ice skating rink. No participation here, alas, as players are banned from activity in it for fear of accidents.

Tuesday back to training and the inevitable visit to the billiards room where to add a little extra, a small wager is on for what is billiards golf! The call of the cinema is so strong that it is an afternoon matinee with one film then a gangster movie - as it happens - in the evening after tea! With the team being selected in the evening for the following day's League match, it is earlier than usual to bed.

The next morning the postman arrives with the postcard from the club informing him that he has been selected to play at 3.15 pm that afternoon. A quick glance at the morning newspaper confirms the rest of the team is unchanged. Breakfast eaten and next move is a trip to the ground to look over his boots. It is a dry, cold morning but ideal for football. Back home for a light lunch made up of fried fish, tea and a slice of toast. Then off to the match.

With a crowd of some 33,000 in attendance, his team is soon a goal down, but they manage an equaliser. Even so there is no improvement in the second half and twelve minutes from the end the visitors go ahead and add a third near the final whistle to win 3-1. This is an interesting statistic. Since the team adopted the third back system, three goals has been the maximum they have conceded in any one match.

Relaxing after the game and amazingly – guess what – it is back to the "pictures" again!

Thursday morning and no training but at the ground he discovers that he has been dropped from the first team! It will be a run out in the stiffs on Saturday. It will be only his seventh reserve outing since signing for the club five years previously and around 200 first team outings to his credit.

A game of snooker passes the time, though the disappointment lingers. Contemplating on the golf course would appear to be the antidote and meeting a friend he receives four strokes and succeeds in winning 3 and 2. The bye finishes all square

Afterwards he calls in on another player who is recovering from a cartilage operation and has started light training. He has tea with him and his wife followed by a session of table tennis which he loses, two to one. A run in the country again by car with his colleague's family completes the day.

It is Friday and running and sprinting, a massage and then collecting wages. Snooker with his usual opponent, home for dinner then off to the shops, booking seats for a theatre and home for tea. After the variety show with a mate, an early night beckons.

Saturday morning and it is essential he catches the 11.15 am train to play at the ground of the reserve team of which his first eleven is meeting at home. It is a two and a half hours journey, the players whiling away the time with a card school and a sing-song. Next on the menu is lunch at a hotel with a choice of fried fish or boiled mutton. He has the fish with some toast and tea. The ground is ten minutes away.

His team is ahead in ten minutes, but a decision goes against them when the referee awards a penalty, despite the ball hitting hand, not the other way. More misery follows this equaliser because in an accidental collision, he suffers a thigh injury and has to hobble around being of not much use to the team at all. Worse still the opposition scores two more goals and only a penalty save by the goalkeeper prevents a fourth goal. So it is 3-1 again! However, the penalty was just as harsh, having been given for a shoulder charge.

Back to the hotel for tea, on the train and late home with just time to give the car a run out and nurse the painful leg.

Sunday morning and it is essential for a trip to the ground for attention to the leg that the trainer treats with hot water and a massage which considerably improves it. Home for dinner then off to visit the recovering cartilage operation colleague and the chance to gain table tennis revenge which has a satisfactory outcome. Off to the country again with the friend and his wife, tea and cinema in the evening. Driving a modest Morris Eight, the return journey is spoilt by another car not dipping headlights!

Monday morning and the first team unusually called in because there is no mid-week fixture. He does light training and has hot water treatment. There is a notice in the dressing-room that the first team is due to spend some time away for special training at a well-know spa resort. This will involve staying at a first-class hotel, mineral baths and walks in the countryside, plus the best of food. He misses out on this of course, now consigned to the reserve team!

In the afternoon a farmer friend invites him to a rabbit shoot - just watching as the player has no licence and on his own admission would be a danger to others with a gun in his hand!

After tea it seems the obligatory visit to the cinema.

Tuesday morning and not at the ground until ten o'clock while still easing his leg back to full fitness with some light exercise and the trainer insisting that a gentle lap or two will help. More treatment follows this effort. Missing the training routine and concerned about putting on weight, he reduces his food intake and cuts out starchy food for meals.

After usual billiards experience, the club doctor conducts a thorough examination and passes him fit for Saturday. In the evening he is disappointed that he is unable to get into seeing a particular film that interested him because he refuses to queue for it and has to settle for a lesser-known one.

So, it is another Wednesday, more light training and massage. Though not quite 100 per cent, the leg still has a few days to recover completely and now just waiting to see whether it will be the first team card which comes through the post at the end of the week or just the stiffs!

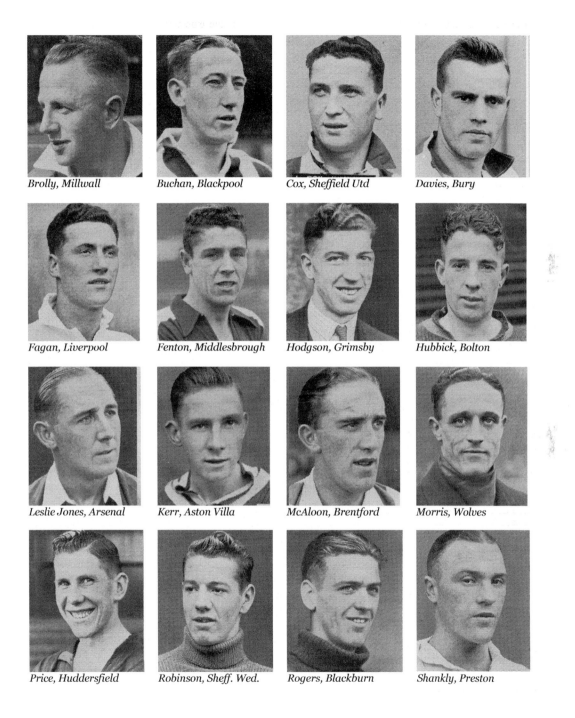

Brolly, Millwall

Buchan, Blackpool

Cox, Sheffield Utd

Davies, Bury

Fagan, Liverpool

Fenton, Middlesbrough

Hodgson, Grimsby

Hubbick, Bolton

Leslie Jones, Arsenal

Kerr, Aston Villa

McAloon, Brentford

Morris, Wolves

Price, Huddersfield

Robinson, Sheff. Wed.

Rogers, Blackburn

Shankly, Preston

FOUR CORNERS

ENGLAND SELECTORS ARE NOT SELECTIVE

The England team that met Scotland at Hampden Park in 1933. Back, players only: Strange, Hart, Hibbs, Cooper, Weaver, Arnold. Front; Hulme, Hunt, Blenkinsop, Starling, Pickering

Team selection by an unwieldy, double-figure committee was the norm as England confidently entered the 1930's international scene on the back of 3-0 and 6-0 respective wins over Ireland and Wales following the surprise, if slender defeat in Spain. There was neither manager nor coach, just one committee man designated to be in charge on a match day. The trainer or team attendant as he was called was left to be responsible for what went on – the pitch. A divergent selection from leading clubs provided a trainer.

For internationals Wembley, which was not owned by the Football Association, was reserved for the visit of Scotland. Wales and Ireland were accommodated around various country venues. Foreign teams were hosted in London either at Stamford Bridge, Highbury or White Hart Lane. There were international trial matches and the Football League played both the Scottish League and Irish League on a regular basis for sources of competitive play to judge the aptitude of suitable material to represent England.

With the argument of whether to stay with the attacking centre-half that most members of the Football Association favoured and ignore the trend to the "policeman" or "stopper," players were often selected from clubs with differing styles.

Four new caps were on parade for what was hoped would be a clean sweep of the championship against Scotland at Wembley on 5 April 1930. Alf Strange came in at right-half, Maurice Webster in the middle of the half-back line Ellis Rimmer on the left-wing and Sammy Crooks on the right. Vic Watson last capped in 1923 was restored to lead the forward line. The effect was remarkable. The "Wembley Wizards" humiliation was avenged. Even three goals in a five minute spell at one stage. Watson and Rimmer each scored twice, David Jack as captain the remaining goal in England's 5-2 victory, though never a one-sided affair. It was England's first outright success in the quadruple tournament since before the First World War and the most convincing victory for 37 years!

However, club before country was painfully evident. Hughie Gallacher was missing for Scotland and was playing for Newcastle United against an Arsenal team which lacked Jack and Alex James both involved at Wembley. The Scots included three Anglos in their side but six from Glasgow Rangers, who incidentally did not have a League game! Gallacher had been pressurised by a struggling Newcastle third from bottom as his deputy Duncan Hutchison, a fellow Scot, was injured; Arsenal equally treading dangerous water seventh from the cellar, none too pleased themselves but achieved a 1-1 draw at St James' Park.

The Football League was unhappy about granting the release of players when internationals were played on a Saturday and while the English players invariably received a better deal, the Scots, Welsh and Irish were usually given short shrift. Moreover at its summer meeting in 1930 the League passed a rule forbidding clubs to release players to associations other than the Football Association. Though then somewhat diluted in its final ferocity, the effect was little different.

Internationals – and by this the Home International Championship – not including England had to be completed by the end of December each year. Three weeks notice had to be given for the release of players without any guarantee of being granted by clubs involved. Players had to be insured and the associations involved required to pay a week's wages for the Saturdays they played for their countries. Wales for example often had to wait until the day of the match to confirm a line-up!

But the same 1930 England eleven against Scotland went to Germany and drew 3-3 in Berlin. It was a brave performance given that Billy Marsden suffered a serious back injury in an accidental collision with Roy Goodall after 14 minutes and though he held out until the interval, did not reappear. In fact his career ended there. Richard Hofmann, a discovery of Jimmy Hogan's, who had all the German goals, was the first foreign player to hit a hat trick against England. Then it was across the border into Austria and a goalless draw with one change at half-back, Sam Cowan replacing Marsden.

For the opening of the 1930-31 Home International Championship, Sheffield United's Bramall Lane was the venue, Ireland the visitors. Five new caps were awarded and the five first half goals should have been six after the break as Strange shot a 75th minute penalty straight at Elisha Scott. With just one change Wales was beaten 4-0 in Wrexham, their first win at the Racecourse Ground since 1912. Jimmy Hampson scored twice to the one on his debut in the previous match. Harry Hibbs saved a 60th minute penalty from Fred Keenor. A month earlier Wales had gone to Scotland with nine newcomers and managed a 1-1 draw. On to March at Hampden Park and a record 129,810 but it ended in a 2-0 defeat for England, a first after seven internationals. With none of his club colleagues on view, this proved to be centre-half Herbie Roberts only cap. The Scots relied completely on locally based talent. It was also the day the "Hampden Roar" was born as Davie Meiklejohn the Rangers centre-half kept Dean quiet. Two second half goals in two minutes from defensive errors and a poor attack said it all.

Roberts was the archetypal third back, a role he fitted after it was manufactured to combat the change in the off side law, He was to be the pillar of Arsenal's answer to free-scoring attacks. One-nil to the Arsenal had its roots there. But few other clubs mastered these negative strategies as successfully and neither did their players. Sadly for his one-cap-wonder's appearance, he was playing a system with which his England colleagues were not too familiar and the Scots exploited the acres of space in midfield.

Off for the early summer tour to familiar territory of France and Belgium. Four new faces were included in the line-up at the Colombes in Paris including "Pongo" Waring at centre-forward. However, the French had not read the script, forgetting that they had lost all six of their previous meetings with England but were deservedly worthy 5-2 winners with victory from forceful wing play. Eventually wasteful after leading with a Crooks goal in ten minutes from a rebound off the woodwork, the visitors were 3-1 down at the interval from goals by Lucien Laurent (15 minutes), Robert Mercier (18) and Marcel Langiller (29), Waring did manage a goal to make it 4-2 after 71 minutes, but prestige had suffered undeniably and Mercier had his second five minutes later. The *Athletic News* was beside itself. Its 18 May issue headlined "Big Blow to British Pride," adding reference to "two shattering blows," the second being the 5-0 defeat suffered by Scotland in Vienna against Austria.

Making just one alteration at inside-forward with the Millwall player Harry Roberts given his only cap, England took it out on the Belgians, winning 4-1 with the new cub from the Lions scoring one of the goals, two others disallowed.

The opening two matches in the domestic competition for 1931-32 witnessed England winning 6-2 in Belfast against Ireland and exactly half that score line over Wales in a well-contested match at rain-soaked Anfield. The latter game introduced Cliff "Boy" Bastin the Arsenal find from Exeter City at outside-left. Against Ireland the six goals were the highest against them since 1912. Jimmy Dunne missed a chance and hit a post before scoring one of the Irish goals. But for the long awaited return fixture with Spain at Highbury in December, Bastin was left out and for once the committee decided not to risk any more newcomers.

Jack Smith of Portsmouth kept his place at inside-right having scored in his first two matches and Dean was plucked back from his lengthy England absence and plunged into the team instead of Waring. The result was something of an anti-climax in that the Spanish Armada was washed up almost before it left port. They were two down in seven minutes and beaten 7-1 with the usually peerless Ricardo Zamora having a nightmare of the jitters in goal. Sammy Crooks, Smith and Tommy Johnson had two goals apiece, Dean the other. Spain's response came when many in the crowd were thinking of an exit to the Underground five minutes from the end.

Five newcomers featured against Scotland at Wembley. It was estimated that 15,000 Scots were in the ground having mostly arrived by special trains to see the All-Tartan mixture. It was their disappointment as the hosts secured a comfortable 3-0 win to top the table once more. A record 92,180 with £19,400 receipts saw Waring restored and linking well with his club colleague Eric Houghton on the left wing. Waring had the first goal plus two late efforts from Bobby Barclay one of five new caps deflected by Allan Craig and Sammy Crooks with two minutes remaining. Sam Weaver another debutant impressed with his long throw-ins, a ploy to be exploited in the future.

For 1932-33, the initial match was at Blackpool's Bloomfield Road, with Ireland as the visitors. Only one uncapped player appeared this time, Arthur Cunliffe on the left wing. A Barclay goal from the little inside-forward settled it. England struggled against a fine Irish defence. But no goals at Wrexham against Wales the better team with three more names unfamiliar to the England line-up. The 25,000 crowd was a record for Wales.

December brought the much-acclaimed Austrians to Stamford Bridge. There was a recall for Jimmy Hampson to lead the attack. He responded with two goals, his fifth in three England games. With the advantage of the elements in their favour, the English team took a 2-0 interval lead but the technically superior Austrians gave a much better performance after the break showing their renowned short-passing capabilities to perfection and had missed a fairly easy chance.

In six minutes they had reduced the deficit. Encouraged, they almost equalized when skipper Walter Nausch hit a post with Hibbs beaten. Houghton's free-kick took a wicked deflection off Schall in the 76th minute. Sindelar reduced the lead within three minutes Crooks restored it. Hibbs was clearly impeded at a corner kick as Austria came within a goal again with five minutes remaining. They were still chasing an equaliser at the finish on the end of a 4-3 defeat. The national press reported the attendance as a disappointing 42,000, but perhaps the super-inflation hitting the continent was responsible for the *Wiener Zeitung* reporting it at 70,000!

George Hunt, one of four new forwards – the trial match at Portsmouth had produced several injuries – was England's marksman at Hampden on All Fools Day 1933, the laugh being on them as Scotland with one Anglo, Dally Duncan on the wing edged it. At left-back Ernie Blenkinsop was making his 26th consecutive appearance, a record for his country. Jack Pickering, one of the new faces, owed his place because Jimmy Easson originally chosen was found to be a Scot!

The Scots mentor James dropped out through injury but managed to be fit enough to play on the day for Arsenal. Joe Hulme was recalled after a five-year absence and missed a sitter, but new boy Johnny Arnold on the other wing fluffed two and like Pickering was never recalled. Jimmy McGrory had the winner in the 80th minute following an opening from Bob McPhail.

The post-mortem on Hampden Park concluded that the game had been decided by the tactics of Ernie Hart operating as an old-style attacking centre-half, Scotland's Davie Meiklejohn as a third back. Oddly enough the players they were marking scored all the goals! Another record 136,259 crowd watched.

Outside of problems caused by injury, individual committee members wanted their own players selected. It was seen again to effect for the tour pairing to Italy and Switzerland who provided the venues. The axe was swung again for the line-up in Rome and amazingly produced six players receiving their first such recognition. Among the sextet was a new centre-half Tommy White in a useful defence, paradoxically a former centre-forward converted at Everton. There was also Eddie Hapgood at left-back and Wilf Copping at left-half. Bastin was back on the wing. He was the England scorer fifteen minutes after Italy's shock fourth minute lead in the 1-1 draw. Arsenal manager Herbert Chapman had travelled officially with the team, an unprecedented departure. In Berne it was more comfortable with three goals in seven second half minutes. Four goals shared by the inside-forwards Jimmy Richardson and Bastin, switched inside to accommodate Eric Brook on the left wing. England players were also in the presence of His Holiness the Pope and Benito Mussolini while in Italy. The impression was that *El Duce* was short stout had a pleasant smile and was charming!

No let up at the start of 1933-34 and a trip to Belfast, the committee finding three new names, two of whom got on the score sheet – Tommy Grosvenor and Jack Bowers in the three goal win over Ireland, who unfortunately had Martin as an early casualty after ten minutes. Unchanged for the visit of Wales to Newcastle's rain-affected St James' Park, there was a disappointment with Wales winning 2-1 to ensure the Championship for the second season. Ten minutes before the interval England lost Allen with an injured knee.

So with France due at White Hart Lane and that 5-2 chastisement in Paris still in the recent memory banks, clearly a different looking team would be selected. As it happened there were relatively few alterations. Hapgood was unavailable, Bastin was omitted and Arthur Rowe came in a centre-half. He was one of three new men, David Fairhurst from Newcastle's Cup-winning team replaced Hapgood, Spurs Willie Hall came in at inside-left and the reliable George Camsell was given his fifth cap.

The crowd was disappointing only 17,097 and those present witnessed a fairly easy passage for England, the rather disjointed French reply to four goals was in the consolation status. Ever ready with his battery charged, Camsell scored twice.

There was some tinkering with the selection for the Scotland match at Wembley on 14 April, but only one newcomer, Raich Carter from Sunderland at inside-right. Bastin in the other inside-forward berth scored on another of his reappearances as did Bowers, back leading the line. A record 92,962 including around 30,000 border invaders paid £20,173 in receipts. Again there had been a background of controversy.

Scotland chanced their tartan arm asking Manchester City for the release of Matt Busby, Jimmy McLuckie and Alec Herd. As a response League President John McKenna ruled against such extravagance. Not one of them played. But Arsenal and Derby each provided three for England. Gallacher was brought back after four years for the Scots who still managed to obtain three other Anglos. In the vogue, too, three goals were knocked in without a reply at the end of it, too, though the intervention of the woodwork three times prevented the visitors from registering. Bastin scored just before the break, Johnny Jackson failing to hold his shot, Eric Brook's free kick was deflected in and Bowers headed the third. Even so it was to the Welsh, thanks chiefly to that flog on the Tyne that the trophy rested.

Middle Europe was the destination on the May agenda. On a hot day, hard and dusty pitch, Hungary was a formidable force and it had been long before the First World War that they had provided opposition for England. Horace Burrows appeared at left-half and another centre-forward Freddie Tilson tried out, otherwise familiar faces of recent times. Tilson scored in six minutes but the Hungarians had two goals. Ahead in 65 minutes through Avar, two five minutes later with Sarosi. On to Prague and Czechoslovakia for a kind of first for England, though in a previous visit the country was still known as Bohemia! This also resulted in the same odd goal in three score line plus another couple of players given a chance in the national team. Tilson opened the scoring after 20 minutes, Nejedly levelling four minutes from the break. The Czechs had the second half and Antonin Puc scored the winner on his 27th birthday. An injury to Tommy Gardner caused a reshuffle.

Ninian Park, Cardiff with a record 36,692 crowd was the starting venue for 1934-35 and it was no surprise in the switch round of players. A new half-back line and three new forwards were on duty including a certain Stanley Matthews on the right wing. Tilson scored twice, Brook once and Mathews on his bow. It was Wales' first defeat since December 1931. Evans suffered a severe facial injury in collision with Hibbs after 70 minutes. Dai Astley refused permission to play for Wales scored a hat trick for Villa! Incredibly Villa's trainer Harry Cooch was designated as England's trainer at Cardiff, his sixth such appointment!

Highbury in November was designated for the arrival of Italy the World Champions. Interestingly enough they had beaten Czechoslovakia in the final but from a neutral aspect, the Italians had been fortunate. With the England match against the Czechs still relatively fresh in the memory, there was additional spice to the fixture. The choice of venue could not have been more appropriate in view of the problems which unfolded over team selection. Originally five Arsenal players were chosen. Then Tom Cooper dropped out with injury and George Male became Gunner No. 6 for his first cap. Tilson cried off injured on the Monday before the game and George Hunt was called up, but he, too, was on the treatment table. That gave Ted Drake a chance as Arsenal's seventh member for his debut at centre-forward. Hapgood, the Highbury captain, was naturally made skipper.

That was not the end of the local connection. Trainer Tom Whittaker was in charge of the team while in the stands, Arsenal manager George Allison was commentating on BBC radio. The Italians were said to be on a £150 a man bonus, plus offers of an Alfa-Romero car and immunity from military National Service.

A sensational start saw England awarded a penalty in only 30 seconds. But the Italian goalkeeper Carlo Ceresoli pulled off a brilliant save from Brook. However the winger made amends in the ninth minute with his first goal heading in a free kick then one from another dead ball kick himself two minutes later.

Alas the seeds of altercation had been sewn already. Italy's centre-half Luisito Monti went off after five minutes with a broken bone in his foot. His version: from a collision with Drake, the alternative one: a stubbed toe. An elbow smashed into Hapgood's face required a broken nose to be patched up and so it went on. Drake made it a comfortable looking score at half-time.

Not that the England players were shrinking violets in the face of a biting December draught. Wilf Copping, who probably invented facial stubble as a deliberate appendage, had the Italians wincing with his no-nonsense tackles and thumping shoulder-charging.

Tom Whittaker attends to Eddie Hapgood's broken nose after the game with Italy

In the second half, ten-man Italy looked more like World Cup winners and caused endless problems without letting up on the physical stuff. Giuseppe Meazza had a couple of goals in as many minutes and only fine goalkeeping by Frank Moss prevented a hat trick.

So England had beaten the World Cup holders but the carted off and walking wounded included Brook with an elbow strapped up, Hapgood sent to hospital, Drake, Bastin and Ray Bowden in the treatment queue. One newspaper report began: "From Our War Correspondent." General opinion seemed to be that continental opposition should not in future be entertained.

February at Goodison Park brought Ireland across the Irish Sea and calmer waters on the field, too. Bastin put England ahead but it was level at 1-1 when Jackie Coulter took a penalty and shot over the bar. The brilliant Bastin secured the winner in the 70th minute. However, there was no luck of the Irish that day. Jackie Bestall made his inside forward debut for England that day at the age of 34 years 226 days.

It was all-the-twos at Hampden, where 30,000 were locked out! There were two untried England starters, Walter Alsford at left-half another centre-forward in Bob Gurney. Indications were apparent that several players on view were not fully fit. One of them Bastin subsequently had a cartilage operation. But two Dally Duncan goals proved enough for the Scots to get the two points and make it a shared twosome for the honours in the final table, England's chance for the title lost by them. But it was a wretched spectacle on a bone hard surface with a light ball and the Scots really had nothing to beat.

Off to Holland and a friendly face in charge of the Dutch in Bob Glendenning, once of Barnsley. Four new forwards and a goal from one of them Fred Worrall provided England's winner in pouring Amsterdam rain, the Dutch amateurs giving a tenacious display. HRH Princess Juliana of the Netherlands was present.

Moreover there was a new look to the start of the calendar for 1935-36 in August with a return to Glasgow for the King George V Jubilee Fund match. No caps awarded for this one-off and another reverse for England losing 4-2 before 56,316. England even used a substitute for the first time, Sep Smith coming on for the injured Jackie Bray.

Ted Sagar the Everton goalkeeper was one of three new caps against Ireland in a fine game even in a gale swept rainy Belfast. Only two of the team chosen had a double figure total in caps. Two Tilson goals and one from Brook after Brown opened for the Irish.

It was the prelude to the German invasion, a prospect which provided endless problems for the authorities. The venue was chosen as White Hart Lane, but the traditional Jewish support for the Spurs club and in the community at large, petitioned against staging it at all. The TUC also sent strong representation to the Government to call it off. There were protesters at the ground a well as at Victoria Station when the German party arrived and a few arrests were made.

Came the match and with some 10,000 visitors inside, there was one large Swastika which blew onto the roof of the main stand just to remind anyone who was unsure of the origin of the opposition. The German national anthem was another giveaway of course, as was the Nazi salute. As an entertainment, the game was pretty mute and with Camsell wheeled out again, the chances of an England victory looked good at least by tradition. He responded with two goals, Bastin a third. Jackie Crayston made his debut at right-half. A fitter looking Hibbs became the first England goalkeeper to record ten clean sheets. Arguments continued over the merits of allowing the game to have gone ahead but merely served to distance the TUC from the Government.

Wales came to the Molineux mud and won, their second goal hoisting their 50th such against England who had six Arsenal players and led. Drake twisted his knee after 42 minutes and suffered a cut eye after a collision with Harry Hanford .The team struggled on to defeat with ten men. Camsell the talisman centre replaced Drake against Scotland, but though he scored after 30 minutes the Scots matched it with a controversial penalty at Wembley on 4 April 1936. Hapgood's heavy tackle on John Crum after 75 minutes was penalised. Tommy Walker either hesitated and replaced the ball or did so because the wind dislodged it from the spot! Anyway Sagar wrongly dived to the left. But at least the standard of football was immensely improved.

In a month it was off to Austria and Belgium where Camsell repeated his single goal effort in each match, but on both occasions there was defeat. It was Camsell's ninth and last appearance and his 18th goal for England! Four uncapped players were given a first choice in the two games including Bernard Joy, Arsenal's amateur international centre-half the last such to play for the full national team. Six Gunners had played against Austria who won 2-1, the Belgians edged theirs 3-2. Perhaps not a surprise to learn Arsenal's Tom Whittaker had been made team attendant for the tour. The club had taken out £65,000 insurance on him and their six players. Austria had expected to lose 4-2, but the England backs were continually drawn out of position by the opposition tactics. Arsenal had had three League games and a Cup Final a week previously.

Given the liberal attitude to firing off invitations to play for England, the committee – which at full strength could number as many as fourteen – came up with six new recipients to be included for the start of the 1936-37 Home International Championship match against Wales at a gusty Cardiff . The new look team succeeded in repeating the score line and defeat of the previous encounter with them. It was England's first defeat in Wales for more than 50 years. The 44,729 was a Welsh record attendance.

Ireland came across to play at Stoke where at times the ball stopped dead on a heavy pitch and with just one newcomer, City left-winger Joe Johnson. England won 3-1 and prepared for a return of foreign visitors of some stature again with Hungary due at Highbury in two weeks. Admission prices ranged from two shillings (10p), half a crown, three and four shillings on the day with bookings at five shillings (25p) seven shillings and sixpence and half a guinea (52½p). Just George Tweedy in goal was unknown internationally. Only the Austrians were rated better than Hungary in Europe. Drake led the goal rush in a six-goal salvo for England with a hat trick, the result being unexpected and the performance well above average. However, despite the score and the heavy, muddy pitch ideal for the home team, the Hungarians control and slick, accurate passing had been widely admired. Their boots at one and a half pounds were half the weight of England's. Sheffield Wednesday manager Billy Walker ordered a set.

The sextet winners became an instant attraction for the Scottish fans who clamoured in their thousands to see them. On 17 April 1937 the attendance of 149,547 was the biggest crowd ever seen in Britain and anywhere in the world for an international match. Incredibly a much altered line-up went to Hampden and lost! The England players wore numbers for the first time. It should not have accounted for them being unable to find each other. Some critics considered that the international trial match preceding the encounter in which the Possibles had beaten the Probables had been a contributory cause of the subsequent performance with Bastin, Brook, Crooks and Drake absent.

George Brown the Rangers left-half proved the Scots' inspiration in the archetypal game of two halves. England gave the Scots a first half lesson in the arts running them ragged from the wings where the Stoke duo of Matthews and Joe Johnson shone. The third City forward Freddie Steele opened the scoring in the 40th minute. But for Carter dallying twice, it might have been three goals. Second half Scotland looked a different outfit. Frank O'Donnell levelled within two minutes, but despite dominating proceedings, it was not until late on that a McPhail double gave them victory at 3-1.

But it was a prelude for England to a Scandinavian tour of Norway, Sweden and Finland. In the three games, eighteen goals were plundered, Freddie Steele getting seven of them. Ten-goal Joe Payne of Luton Town fame and captured by Chelsea, snatched a couple on his debut against Finland, one of seven recruits to the Three Lions on the tour. A record 15 different players had scored goals for England in the season!

Ireland opened the 1937-38 series in Belfast and the tenth successive win over Ireland carried the streak on. A couple made first appearances, Stan Cullis at centre-half and George Mills another Chelsea centre-forward even contrived a treble for himself. In fact it was a proper trio – all in sequence. There was a suspicion of off-side for Mills' first but no doubt of the outcome. Wales, never easy opponents at the time, were sidelined in defeat at Middlesbrough where Stanley Matthews was at his mazy best. Then White Hart Lane was chosen for the December visit of Czechoslovakia.

Joe Payne

Apart from Jackie Morton at outside-left on his initial outing, it was the same team as in the last match. An early injury to Crayston then Mills forced a switch round with Matthews moving to inside-right. He not only scored three times but all with his left foot and achieved the winning goal by racing half the length of the field, his shot clipping Jozef Kostalek on its way. The Czechs, twice level early and late on, were only just bounced out 5-4. Critics voiced opinion that they had topped even Austria's 1932 performance in a fine advertisement for the international game. They had turned out pre-match with training boots and sweat suits and even adopted a third back when the game started.

Inevitably the Scots arrival at Wembley on 9 April would lead to a divergent outcome. Tickets had been sold out in December. Again there were two new boys, Micky Fenton the Middlesbrough centre-forward and Eric Stephenson from Leeds United at inside-left. Scotland included eight Anglos including four of the Preston players destined for FA Cup success and O'Donnell who had just joined Blackpool from North End. Scotland merely required one goal, Tommy Walker as early as the sixth minute. This was not a classic of the genre Fenton missed an easy chance but Scots tactics were better. Critics attempting mitigation blamed a soft ball!

If there had been controversy surrounding Germany's visit to England, it was intensified for the return trip in May 1938. In the interim, the Nazis had taken over Austria and under the Greater Germany banner had acquired several leading Austrian international players. However, it had been agreed that none of these would appear against England. With diplomatic circles in a spin and activity off the field as mesmerising as anything likely to appear on it, the question raised was: "Would the English players give the Nazi salute?" In the end to avoid further international problems, with FA Secretary Stanley Rous ever the peacemaker, it was reluctantly agreed so. The players led by captain Hapgood had merely wanted the players to stand at attention.

The Fuhrer did not attend. However Goering, Goebbels, Hess and Von Ribbentrop were on parade at the Olympic Stadium in Berlin. It was estimated that the crowd numbered around 110,000 on an extremely hot, late afternoon.

Surely the selectors would have been wise to choose tried and trusted players for such an occasion? But the temptation was too much and of course there was Don Welsh at left-half and another new centre-forward in Frank Broome. But it was Bastin who opened the scoring after 12 minutes to settle England down. But the Germans equalised after 20 minutes. Then Jackie Robinson in only his second match restored England's advantage before the half an hour mark and dead on it Broome added England's third. That was not the end of the first half scoring. Matthews added a fourth with five minutes remaining, before Germany again reduced the deficit.

Thus it was 4-2 at the break and any hopes of a German revival were removed when Robinson added his second in the 50th minute. With eleven minutes remaining it was 5-3 only for Len Goulden to make it half a dozen in the 83rd minute.

Sir Neville Henderson the British Ambassador sat next to Goering and infuriated the head of Germany's Luftwaffe by handing him his binoculars every time England scored – to emphasise his missed opportunity of witnessing another hammer blow to the Germans.

The overall opinion of the German press was that England could be considered World Champions, had coped with the weather conditions better and shown stamina, speed and skill far above the performance of their own national team. The following day the few English fans found wandering around Berlin had the courage to wave the Union Jack. It was a brave show of defiance and mercifully there was no trouble.

So with a week to go before the match in Switzerland, there was time to reflect. The same team was chosen against the Swiss and anti-climatically they were beaten 2-1, Bastin scoring from a penalty. Off to France and a few changes, Drake back scoring twice and interestingly enough two centre-halves with Cullis added to the defence. The 4-2 win restored some confidence, though the French had twice levelled.

At the start of what was to prove the last complete season before the start of the Second World War, 1938-39 opened with Wales the hosts at Ninian Park. Once again the Welsh team proved to be incisively formidable opponents. Tommy Lawton, Everton's goal scoring successor to Dean, was the only newcomer in the England side and marked his debut with a penalty. But Wales were worthy 4-2 winners.

This was scarcely any proper preparation for a fixture of this nature on the following Wednesday afternoon for a prestige affair against the Rest of Europe XI at Highbury in recognition of the FA's 75th anniversary. Cullis returned at centre-half with head heavily bandaged before the start and Willie Hall replaced Jackie Robinson at inside-right.

The Duke of Kent is introduced to the England team before the game with the Rest of Europe XI in 1938.

Given the accolades bestowed after the victory over Germany and other successes against Austria, Czechoslovakia, Italy and Hungary albeit on home soil, a representative team selected from chiefly from western European countries with a token Scandinavian thrown in, might present few problems after all.

It comprised five Italians, two Germans and one each from Belgium, France, Hungary and Norway. England managed to find its own referee, too, in Jimmy Jewell! Ex-England international Fred Pagnam long-time coaching in Holland was their trainer. The composite eleven favoured a cut-down WM system which the Germans had tried but given up. So the backs marked the opposing centre-forward the wing halves took the wingers in a straight back four and the centre-half played up behind the five attacking players. Three first half England goals from Hall, Lawton and

Goulden proved sufficient for the effort in front of a crowd of 40,185 receipts of £7,000 from a "two-shilling" gate for a disappointing affair by most reckoning. It was another Royal occasion with HRH The Duke of Kent among the guests.

Doug Wright at left-half and a new left wing pairing of Ronnie Dix and Reg Smith were in the programme for the Newcastle visit of newcomers to England in Norway. Dix was the former teenager prodigy, his partner born Schmidt, not the best surname at the time. But there was satisfaction for the duo, Smith getting two, Dix one after an initial Lawton goal in a foursome-reel.

Only a week elapsed before the venue was Old Trafford and Ireland as the opposition. More changes and the match proved to be a personal triumph for Willie Hall the Spurs inside-forward. He scored five times including a perfect hat trick in 3½ minutes achieved in the 34th, 36th and 38th minutes. Joe Mercer made his debut at left-half, Bill Morris at right-back. Seven goals scored by England.

Months might have gone by, but the attraction of England to Hampden Park and the possibility of another upset brought the Scottish crowds out and another near-150,000 capacity crowd. Though eight visiting players were new to Hampden only one debutant at outside-left in Pat Beasley, but he scored in 70 minutes. Matthews crossed in the 87th minute and Lawton's trademark hanging header was enough to clip the Scots 2-1 for a triple tie with Wales for the home honours. It was England's first win at Hampden in twelve years. Such were the conditions that both teams changed strip at half-time. But England had to borrow a set from the Queen's Park club!

Yugoslavia v England 1939; the Yugoslav goalkeeper Ljubomir Lovric beats England centre-forward Tommy Lawton to the ball.

Despite Prime Minister – waving paper man – Neville Chamberlain's assurances to the contrary, the country was moving into a pre-hostilities mood and the implications for a May tour of Italy, Yugoslavia and Romania presented the Government with a dilemma, whether to call it off or risk one or more international incidents.

With misgivings abounding, the outcome was unexpectedly pleasant. The team was surprisingly greeted with heart-warming affection at all three venues. Italy with just two survivors from the last meeting between the two teams Meazza, now captain, plus Pietro Serantoni, the atmosphere dramatically changed on the field of play!

The 60,000 crowd in Rome paid the equivalent of £17,000, a record for the continent. The Italians on the pitch soon got amongst the England players with the physical stuff. Lawton scored first but Italy hit two, the second a classic of its kind. Silvio Piola punched it in, his follow through blackened George Male's eye! The protests to German referee Dr Peter Bauwens were turned away. Fortunately Hall succeeded in levelling the game.

Afterwards the anti-Fascist Crown Prince Umberto wanted formally to protest over Piola's goal but Rous persuaded him otherwise. Off to the heat of Yugoslavia and with Hapgood suffering an injury early on and Matthews struggling, too, a 2-1 defeat against a determined opponent was not wholly a surprise, though the French referee Georges Capdeville refused Broome a penalty claim. Franco-German co-operation from the men in the middle was hardly in keeping with the times! But the tour ended in victory in Bucharest before a record 40,000 in another muscle matching affair against Romania. Cullis at age 22 was England's captain.

However, escalating events on the continent were about to cause a pause in such international fixtures.

Scotland 1933: Back, players only; Wilson, McPhail, Anderson, Jackson, McGonagle, Brown. Front; Crawford, McGrory, Gillespie, Marshall, Duncan.

Scotland regarded the annual fixture with England as the priority. For these ten matches in the Home International Championship they won five lost four and drew one. In the tournament itself the Scots won the 1935-36 series oddly enough in a season where an extra international was included for the Jubilee Fund; a match they also won 4-2. They shared the title with England twice and there was a three way split with Wales in 1938-39.

All ten competitive games with England were played on a Saturday and while the Football League had a full programme operating on the same day, there was never a similar card in the Scottish League. The nearest to ten fixtures was in 1930 when just Rangers match was not played – and Scotland used several from the Ibrox camp.

Indeed there was no pattern to how Scotland performed during the 30s. Experienced teams were sometimes successful, inexperienced ones often did as well if not better. Home Scots made the majority of appearances with 101 new caps featuring in the ten seasons involved. Of those who appeared regularly even in part of the period, Alan Morton the Rangers winger who was first capped in 1920 took his total number of appearances to 31 by 1932. The next highest was Andy Anderson the Hearts full-back on the winning side against England in 1933 on his debut and making 23 appearances all told. Anderson's club colleague Tommy Walker played in 20 consecutive internationals and scored nine goals. He had studied theology and at one time had ideas of entering the Church.

Understandably Rangers provided many of the more regular selections. Wing-half George Brown played 19 times, inside-forward Bob McPhail 17, centre-half Dave Meiklejohn 15 and Jimmy Simpson who succeeded him 14. Goalkeeper Jimmy Dawson was another from the Ibrox clan with 14 caps.

Top of the Anglo-Scots was centre-forward Hughie Gallacher from a handful of different English clubs. After his debut in 1924 he finished in 1935 with 20 appearances. Wing-half Alec Massie split his Scotland outings with Hearts and later Aston Villa totalling 18. Chelsea right-winger Alec Jackson hat trick hero of the "Wembley Wizards" made his 17th appearance in 1930. Left-winger Dally Duncan achieved his 14 caps while with Derby County.

As to individual matches remember that the "Wizards" included only three Home Scots in 1928. McPhail was on the winning side against England four times but never played at Wembley. Walker was the sole scorer when the Scots won there in 1938. On 9 November 1938 against Wales at Tynecastle it was 1-1 with three minutes left; final score 3-2 to Scotland.

Playing continental opposition was spasmodic. Twelve matches in all over the span. Two matches against France in 1930 and 1932 in Paris. They were won 2-0 and 3-1 with Third Lanark leader Neil Dewar scoring a hat trick. Germany was beaten 2-0 at Ibrox with Celtic's Jimmy Delaney scoring both goals in the 67th and 83rd minutes.

When Austria was at its height in 1931, Scotland played in Vienna and unsurprisingly lost 5-0 when you realize they capped seven new players! Subsequently Scotland drew 2-2 at Hampden in 1933 and 1-1 in Vienna in May 1937 with fewer debutants. Four days after the Viennese visit, Scotland played Italy in Rome with just one more fresh face in Willie Boyd at centre-forward. Italy won 3-0. This was undoubtedly the low point in Scotland's experiences on travel against continental opposition. In fairness four days after the Italian experience, Scotland did win 3-2 in Switzerland.

But the Scots beat Czechoslovakia 3-1 in Prague in 1937 and in the same year 5-0 at Ibrox fielding six new players. Then in 1938 a trip to Amsterdam resulting in a 3-1 win over Holland again with four new players and in December, Hungary was beaten similarly at Ibrox with two more strangers to the international scene.

There was no attempt to take on England merely with familiar names, though naturally calls for English based players being refused might have been a mitigating factor at times. In 1931 when Scotland won 2-0 at Hampden the entire team was chosen from Scottish clubs, similarly in the defeat the following year. The sole Wembley success in 1938 saw four new caps all Anglos, two each from Middlesbrough Dave Cumming the goalkeeper and right-winger Jackie Milne plus the Preston North End pair Bill Shankly at right-half, George Mutch at inside-left. In fact there were eight Anglos including three from Preston on duty that day. When Matt Busby made his debut against Wales in 1933 he was one of eight recruits in the 3-2 defeat. It was his only call-up.

Apart from the lapses against continental opposition and losing to England, the 30s began with three years not losing to Wales and Ireland until 1932 when the Welsh won 5-2 at Tynecastle. Then extraordinarily the pattern changed with Ireland winning twice and Wales once! In between the Scots actually drew with Austria.

However a 3-2 win against Wales in Aberdeen in November 1934 started a seven international unbeaten run until the Welshmen ended it at Dens Park on 2 December 1936. A 1-1 draw against Ireland in Aberdeen in November 1937 launched another septet of undefeated games and was ended in April 1939 when England won 2-1 at Hampden.

Interestingly, in the first ten internationals of the period there were seven different captains for Scotland. Some 15 different players wore the armband in the matches, not because it was handed round, but due to the changes in personnel.

However, James Simpson who followed Davie Meiklejohn at centre-half with Rangers was to skipper the team the most times. Capped on 14 occasions he was captain 13 times consecutively after his debut against Ireland on 20 October 1934.

Overall Scotland won almost twice as many matches as they lost. The figures were 23 wins, seven draws and twelve defeats. There were 102 new players capped though 42 of them appeared just once. No fewer than 15 different centre-forwards were used.

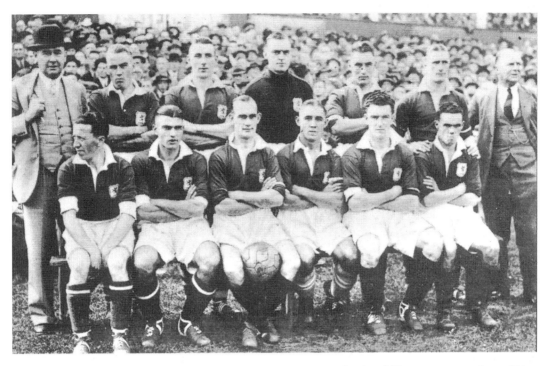

Wales 1935: Players only, back; John (R), Lawrence, John (W), Richards, Phillips. Front; Murphy, Robbins, Griffiths, Jones (L), Glover, Jones (B).

Both Wales and Northern Ireland had to rely heavily on the scraps left to them when trying to prise players from Football League clubs for their international teams. Unlike Scotland who at least had their own domestic competition of more stature, neither the Welsh League nor Irish League was of compatible standard. But passion and spirit made up for material failings.

For Wales the signs in the 1929-30 Home International Championship did not bode well for the decade ahead. Scotland won 4-2 at Ninian Park six goals were conceded to England at Stamford Bridge and incredibly even Northern Ireland hit seven at Belfast's Celtic Park after Wales had ditched most of the previous two teams to include six new caps.

For the next season another wholesale upheaval of players; a mixture of necessity for what was available and trying to improve prospects. For the trip to Ibrox to play Scotland on 25 October 1930 the line-up included nine new caps in a hastily gathered eleven with the bookmakers merely taking bets in excess of a five-goal thrashing. Only veteran centre-half Fred Keenor and goalkeeper Len Evans previously capped against Northern Ireland in 1927 were experienced at this level.

Ted Robbins the ubiquitous FAW secretary since 1909, had always had to beg, manipulate and scheme his way to ensure Wales was represented with as best as could be put onto the field. Off it he was a politician and raconteur supreme. This time the outcome was bordering on the miraculous. The "Unknowns" as they were labelled pulled off a 1-1 draw with Tommy Bamford the debutant marksman.

With so many tasks before him it was not a surprise when one day Robbins left a bag on a platform at Cardiff station with £1,000 in it. He was on his way to Wrexham before realising the mistake, dashed back to find it still there intact! Every player cost the FA of Wales £25 before a ball was kicked.

He would have kept the same team but an injury meant one newcomer against England at Wrexham and a disappointing 4-0 defeat. At the same venue in April there were five newcomers including a goal scorer in Charlie Phillips as the Welsh edged the Irish 3-2. Another first: the kick-off at 6 pm 12,000 attended. Sadly 1931-32 brought three more defeats: unluckily 3-2 to Scotland in

Wrexham with a weakened team, the Scots first success there since 1899, 3-1 to England at Liverpool and 4-0 to the Irish in Belfast where rain cut the crowd to 10,000. Moreover another nine new players were introduced overall. Wales had wanted to play Ireland at Liverpool in 1932!

But what a change of fortune there was in 1932-33 with Wales unbeaten. The Scots were taken out in Edinburgh 5-2 the first win in Scotland since 1906 with Phillips injured in the first few minutes. The crowd of only 3,000 gave Wales an ovation, There was no money in the Wales till. Ted Robbins paid the players and the £150 hotel bill. England was held goalless in Wrexham and Ireland defeated 4-1 at the same venue after a change of tactics. These five points gave Wales its first Home International Championship title since 1927-28. Fred Keenor won his 32nd and last cap against the Scots and over the three matches, four newcomers had appeared. To "cap" it all as it were, an overseas trip was made across the Channel to France and a creditable 1-1 draw in Paris. Moreover the FA of Wales announced a modest profit of £1,000!

Moreover, Wales performed as well in 1933-34. A weakened Scotland was beaten 3-2 at Ninian Park, Ireland held 1-1 in Belfast but due to poor finishing with four new additions then encouragingly England defeated at St James' Park, Newcastle 2-1. So it was the first back-to-back titles for Wales.

But the 1934-35 series began badly with England gaining revenge 4-0 in Cardiff and the Scots having the best of five goals in Aberdeen. Wales did beat the Irish 3-1 at the Racecourse Ground, Wrexham with another three new men on duty. Two of these were a pair of the three Jones boys. They were Wilson Jones the Birmingham centre who scored the first goal and Bryn Jones of Wolves was the other debutant, Les Jones of Coventry City was making his second such appearance. The match was refereed by Dr Peco Bauwens the German official. It was the first time a Home International had been controlled by a foreigner.

Some of the England team off to play Wales at Wolverhampton in 1936. From the left; Rous (FA secretary), Male, Crayston, Drake, Hapgood, and, in the doorway, Bastin and Bowden.

Not unusually Wales had problems fielding a team against England and for once there was sympathy. England agreed to leave travelling reserve Willie Hall of Spurs at home so that Willie Evans also of Tottenham could be made available to play for Wales.

The following season began with a rousing 1-1 draw against Scotland at Ninian Park followed by a welcome if surprising 2-1 success against the English at Wolverhampton in February 1936. Yet a month later with ten of the same team fielded, Wales lost 3-2 in Belfast as well as the chance of the title.

For 1936-37 goals from Pat Glover and debutant left-winger Seymour Morris direct from a corner beat England 2-1. Glover had both goals at Dundee in December and another 2-1 win over Scotland who suffered injuries and hit the woodwork twice. Once again Glover had a brace, Bryn Jones and Freddie Warren also contributed with goals to the 4-1 win at Wrexham against Northern Ireland. It presented Wales with an unbeatable six points and the Championship. In this match centre-half Tommy Griffiths played in his 21st and last international match.

Though there was just the margin of one goal in any of the trio of games in 1937-38, Wales only beat Scotland 2-1 in Cardiff despite injury to Phillips in the first half, losing 2-1 at Middlesbrough to England and by the only goal in Belfast to Ireland where veteran goalkeeper Bert Gray played his 24th international. Ireland missed a penalty.

Robbins had had the usual selection problems for the game with Scotland. Neither Wilson Jones nor Pat Glover were fit, so Eddie Perry of Third Division (North) Doncaster Rovers led the line. Birmingham not only offered three Welsh players but trainer Bill Gibson – a Scot! Billy Hughes, 18, was outstanding on his debut as was his Birmingham colleague Seymour Morris a one-time Cardiff Barracks Bugler Boy.

Then in 1938-39 it was a triple tie for the Championship with England and Scotland, well earned if for nothing else than the 4-2 success over the English at Ninian Park. Scotland won 3-2 in Edinburgh ten minutes from time and the Irish were defeated 3-1 at Wrexham. Against the Scots, Dai Richards made his 21st appearance at left-half. Robbins had recovered from a bout of pleurisy.

Wales had won three domestic titles, as many outright Championships in ten years as England and two more than Scotland. Then in May another trip to Paris but a 2-1 defeat. In this friendly fixture the 57th new cap in 32 internationals was winger Jackie Williams from Wrexham. He proved to be the 17th to make one solitary appearance for his country. The scorer in Paris was Dai Astley his twelfth goal in 13 internationals, easily Wales' most consistent marksman in the period.

PLUCK OF THE IRISH

There was a conflict in Ireland as the football authorities on both sides of the border chose players from the whole of the island and many times players appeared for both Northern Ireland – officially just Ireland – and the Irish Free State; the latter's organization having changed its name from the Football Association of Ireland in 1923.

Ireland's second international in 1929-30 produced a 7-0 victory over Wales at Celtic Park, Belfast with centre-forward Joe Bambrick in his fifth call-up scoring six goals. It was the highest win for 39 years since Wales had been beaten 7-2 in the previous century. But this latest success was squeezed between losing 3-0 to England at Windsor Park and 3-1 to the Scots in Glasgow.

Bambrick, known as "Head, heel or toe" was rampant in domestic football that season scoring 94 in all matches for Linfield. The following season Ireland managed a sub-standard goalless draw with Scotland at Windsor Park but again the filling in the sandwich of losing 5-1 to England at Sheffield and 3-2 to Wales in Wrexham. Against Scotland Fred Roberts the Glentoran centre was tried on his way to outscoring Bambrick with 96 goals overall. It was his only selection. Ex-Army Corporal Jack Jones made his debut as a half-back against Wales in 1930, won seven caps in a row, missed one game then appeared in the next sixteen for a total of 23 appearances.

In 1931-32 defeat by Scotland 3-1 in Glasgow, the Scots missing a penalty by Meiklejohn and Farquharson and Duggan refusing to play as the team had not been nationally selected. After losing 6-2 to England at Windsor Park, there was a welcome 4-0 win against the Welsh at the same venue including three goals in five minutes. Bambrick brought back scored one of the goals Billy Millar another on his debut, while Jimmy Kelly of Derry City on his second appearance had two. Kelly as an example of the double selection in 1936 he played on the left-wing for Ireland against Wales in a 3-2 win and six days later for the Irish Free State in a 1-0 success over Switzerland.

Only one goal in 1932-33 by Sam English, Scotland based with Rangers scoring against Wales in a 4-1 loss after 4-0 and 1-0 defeats respectively home and away against Scotland and England. Against the Scots Billy Cook made his first appearance at right-back. Improved results in the following year's championship after winning 2-1 in Glasgow with four new caps paraded after English clubs refused release of others. One of the newcomers was Dave "Boy" Martin, one time Royal Ulster Rifles drummer boy who scored both goals. Another, the diminutive inside-right Alex Stevenson Dublin born and with Rangers impressed, too. Scott saved brilliantly from a McGonagle penalty.

Two additions to the international ranks against England but three goals conceded at Windsor Park, where Wales were held 1-1 a couple of months later. Martin also scored when the Scots were beaten 2-1 on the same ground in October 1934 with Jackie Coulter of Everton heading the other goal. Injured goalkeeper Elisha Scott did not come out for the second half and centre-half Walter McMillen took over.

The next international was at Goodison Park where England won 2-1 with three new Irish caps selected: Tommy Breen the Belfast Celtic goalkeeper, Jack Brown the right winger who had been part of the £7,750 package when Martin joined Wolverhampton Wanderers and Peter Doherty at inside-right, who had joined Blackpool from Glentoran for £1,500.

Disappointingly Wales won 3-1 at Wrexham with Bambrick back leading the attack and scoring for Ireland. Coulter broke his leg in collision with his Welsh Everton club mate Williams. So on to 1935-36, England winning at Windsor Park 3-1 and the Scots successful in the dying moments in Edinburgh 2-1, but victory over Wales at Celtic Park 3-2, Belfast Celtic's Norman Kernaghan scoring on his bow.

He scored again at Windsor Park before a record crowd of 45,000 when Scotland won 3-1 in October 1936 as did Tom Davis from Oldham Athletic on his first appearance leading the attack in a similar defeat against England at Stoke. This before three defeats in succession came when Wales won 4-1 at Wrexham, when another leader was tried in Cliftonville's Sam Banks. Neither centre was capped again.

England won 5-1 at Windsor Park in October 1937, a game Ireland wanted to be played at Blackpool (!), before Doherty scored to give Ireland a draw with Scotland in Aberdeen and at least three points came from the trio of international games when Bambrick on his eleventh and last international scored the only goal against Wales at Windsor Park, though Brown hit an upright from the penalty spot. Full-back Bertie Fulton made his 20th and last full appearance for Ireland having also won 16 as an amateur international in the same time scale.

Alas 1938-39 yielded no points and just one goal. The Scots won 2-0 at Windsor Park, England crashed seven without replay in Manchester – with another attack leader in Huddersfield Town's Harry Baird – and Wales won in Wrexham 3-1 with debutant Dudley Milligan from Chesterfield scoring in his only such outing, one of four newcomers for an improved Ireland. Of the 58 different players introduced by Ireland in 30 Home International Championship matches, 23 appeared just once.

THE WORLD CUP TAKES STAGE

Before 1930 the nearest competition to a comprehensive international football tournament was as an additional sport in the Olympics. Though there had been an irregularly held South American Championship since 1910, as far as Europe was concerned – even if aware of such an existence at all, completely disregarded it. As far as Britain was concerned, the New World was just another part of the globe outside of the Empire where it had sent coaches to teach the local inhabitants how to play the game.

Since the four home countries were in dispute and thus out of FIFA jurisdiction, there had been no representation in the Olympic football tournament since 1920 over the issue of broken time payments to amateurs. Uruguay winners in 1924 and 1928 were awarded the honour as host nation for the inaugural World Cup in 1930. However, there had been six countries who applied to stage it: Holland, Hungary, Italy, Spain, Switzerland and Uruguay, who was celebrating its centenary and prepared to underwrite the expenses of competing nations as an incentive to make the journey. But the logistics of travelling for European countries to South America produced very few takers.

Thirteen countries accepted. But France agreed because FIFA's President Jules Rimet had given his name to the trophy presented and the French sculptor Abel Lafleur had fashioned the gold cup. The world governing body's representative from Belgium Rudolphe Seeldrayers persuaded his countrymen to agree, too. King Carol of Romania, not noted for his benevolence, actually picked his players and arranged time off from their jobs! Yugoslavia was the other European entry and all four travelled together to Uruguay by ship. However, at a late stage it appears Egypt wanted to attend only to literally miss the boat on its way to Montevideo!

Despite day and night construction on the Centenario Stadium in Montevideo started in February, the project was dogged by heavy rain and was not ready for the finals on 13 July. Early matches were held at two club grounds in the capital. Four groups, three of three teams and one of four at least guaranteed all thirteen two matches. The four Europeans were split up. Apart from the USA and Mexico all other teams were South American.

Uruguay's fiercely rival neighbours Argentina were well supported but arrivals by boat had to be searched for weapons on the quayside. Uruguay military personnel guarded all the visiting players throughout the matches. Belligerent Argentina was involved in several scrapes. Five penalties were awarded in their match with Mexico and Police had to separate fighting players in the game with Chile.

Tough centre-half Luisito Monti though the dominating figure was the chief instigator of the problems.

The bulky-looking USA nicknamed the "shot-putters" by the French included five ex-Scottish professional players and one Englishman. Defeated 6-1 by Argentina in the semi-final, they had the misfortune to lose one player with a broken leg after ten minutes, the goalkeeper injured at half-time and another player in the second half.

Uruguay skippered by full-back Jose Nasazzi with the nucleus of their 1924 and 1928 Olympic squads had a formidable half-back line known as "la costilla metallica" (iron curtain) featuring Jose Andrade, Lorenzo Fernandez and Alvaro Gestido. But they took time to demonstrate their technical edge and territorial supremacy in the final against Argentina. After an argument about which ball to use, the Argies had theirs in the first half and led 2-1, Uruguay's was luckier in the second half and scored three. Belgian referee John Langenus was resplendent in knickerbockers.

Though ahead through Pablo Dorado in twelve minutes, goals from Carlos Peucelle and Guillermo Stabile – claimed off-side – gave Argentina a 2-1 interval lead. Pedro Cea who had scored a semi-final hat trick in the 6-1 semi-final win over Yugoslavia equalized with an opportunist strike and Santos Iriarte made it 3-2 for Uruguay. In the dying moments centre-forward Hector Castro added a fourth with a fine long range effort.

FIFA held eight meetings before deciding to appoint Italy as the 1934 hosts. There were 32 entries and twelve sections in the qualifying competition. With several withdrawals plus protests stronger teams were given every possible advantage to qualify even playing the winners of two inferior teams. In addition Uruguay miffed over the poor European response in 1930 and suffering domestic problems did not compete. Only Brazil and Argentina made the final stages from South America but Egypt became the first from Africa. Sadly whereas there had been groups in Montevideo allowing teams at least two matches, this time the sixteen finalists went into a straight knock-out tournament. Pairings again favoured the strong against the weak. The beaten semi-finalists met in a match for third place. Eight cities provided venues.

Ridiculously Italy had to play a qualifying game with Greece and one wonders what defeat would have meant! There was even another qualifier played in Rome between the USA and Mexico before the main event. The Italians had three Argentine born players of Italian origin including Monti! In the disgracefully over-physical drawn match with Spain seven injured Spaniards and four Italians were subsequently unfit for the replay. Austria thought to be past its best reached the semi-final before narrowly losing to Italy; a scrambled goal in off a post settling it. Czechoslovakia defeated Germany 3-1 in the other semi-final with Oldrich Nejedly scoring twice.

Italy was frustrated in the final by the Czechs close passing game and even went behind in the 70th minute when Antonin Puc scored following a corner. Well supported by fans who travelled by road and rail an upset in front of Mussolini seemed likely. Several chances were missed and one hit a post before the Italians switched their attack. Eight minutes from time Raimondo Orsi's spectacular swerving effort brought the teams level. In extra time Italy's tactics and game plan transformed the match. Angelo Schiavio scored their winning goal. Outstanding in the Italian team was the tireless Giuseppe Meazza. Relief was almost tangible in the capital.

France hosted the 1938 final tournament in deference to Rimet. Nine venues were utilised. Though entries increased to 36, Spain had to withdraw because of the Civil War and after qualifying Austria had to inform FIFA that having been annexed by Germany they had no independent team to participate. England despite being out of FIFA declined an invitation on 6 April. For the first time the hosts (France) and holders (Italy) were exempt from the qualifying competition. This left 15 finalists with Sweden getting a bye. Once again a knock-out system was used.

Charles Sutcliffe the President of the Football League had dismissed the World Cup as a "joke" and his comments on the 1934 tournament that did not include England was akin to a cricket tournament without England, Australia and South Africa. Brazil was the sole survivor from South America, but the Dutch East Indies and Cuba had free passages because their qualifying opponents scratched. Cuba even beat Romania after a replay! In the interim Italy had won the 1936 Olympics. They needed extra time to beat Norway but were fortunate in the semi-final when Brazil bizarrely rested their best two players and paid the penalty.

In a game of eleven goals Brazil edged Poland 6-5 with four-timers on each side: Leonidas da Silva and Ernest Willimowski. Gustav Wetterstrom also scored four for Sweden against Cuba. Brazil had a stormy encounter with the Czechs. Two Brazilians were sent off the field, Czechoslovakia lost one player with a broken leg, their goalkeeper with a broken arm. It finished 1-1 after extra time and there were 15 changes for the replay.

Missing Leonidas, Brazil still managed to push Italy all the way and Vittorio Pozzo was grateful for a Meazza penalty in the 2-1 semi-final victory. The Hungarians kept a hold on Wetterstrom and cantered to a 5-1 win in the other semi-final. Even so, Olle Nyberg had scored for Sweden after only 30 seconds. Brazil doubled Sweden's two goals in the match for third place.

In the final the directness and physical presence of the free-flowing Italians was too much for Hungary's delicacy though it was an enterprising affair, Italy doubling the Magyars two goals. Gino Colaussi opened the scoring for Italy but Gyorgy Sarosi quickly equalized. Meazza laid one on for Silvio Piola and another for Colaussi to give the hosts a 3-1 half-time lead. Sarosi squirmed through for his second goal but Piola had the fourth for the champions who retained their title. Meazza and Giovanni Ferrari were the only survivors from 1934. Pozzo had achieved everything the Fascist regime had wanted.

But FIFA had learned nothing from the initial tournament that only by grouping finalists is there any real incentive to make the World Cup an attractive tournament. The method of qualifying was haphazard and reached farcical levels when countries could reach the final stages without playing at all. The violence shown in some matches was another worrying factor and sanctions needed to be more stringent than hitherto. However, despite the growth of nationalism in sport the World Cup looked likely to continue; the monster FIFA had created becoming too large to put down.

With the International Olympic Committee ignoring the USA for soccer for the 1932 Los Angeles Games worried over the growth of professionalism, the 1936 version in Germany was the only such competition in the 30s. Yet even in the early months of 1936 Austria, Czechoslovakia, France and Italy had all stated their intention of not competing. Austria and Italy did enter in the end and finished as the finalists. Italy won 2-1 after extra time in front of 85,000 in the Olympic Stadium, Berlin. Annibale Frossi scored twice having finished top scorer with seven goals. He had hit three against Japan in an 8-0 win earlier when Carlo Biagi had a four-timer. Frossi wore a headband and spectacles. There was another treble shooter in the match for the Bronze medal Arne Brustad for Norway in their 3-2 victory over Poland.

The tournament was hit by several unpleasant incidents. An Italian player was sent off against the USA but refused to go! Peruvian fans attacked an Austrian player in their team's 4-2 win. Austria protested, a replay was ordered but the Peru team packed its bags and went home.

WORLD CUP WINNERS 1930-1938

Uruguay 1930.

Back; Figoli (trainer, looking away), Gestido, Nasazzi, Ballestrero, Mascheroni, Andrade, Fernandez. Front; Dorado, Scarone, Castro, Cea, Santos Iriarte

Italy 1934.

Back; Combi, Monti, Ferraris IV, Allemandi, Guaita, Ferrari. Front; Schiavio, Meazza, Monzeglio, Bertolini, Orsi

Italy 1938

Pozzo holds the trophy, and players are: Back; Biavati, Piola, Ferarri, Colaussi. Front, kneeling; Locatelli, Meazza, Foni, Olivieri, Rava, Andreolo. Sitting; Serantoni.

Without doubt the 30s "Big Four" on the continent were, in alphabetical order, Austria, Czechoslovakia, Hungary and Italy. In terms of outstanding honours achieved, the Italians as winners of the World Cups in 1934 and 1938 were No.1. However, in technique and application the performance of the so-called "Wunderteam" of Austria prior to Italy's initial success on the world stage certainly eclipsed anything else on the international front at least for a short period.

After beating Czechoslovakia 2-1 on 22 April 1931 they won twelve matches, drew three and had just one defeat – against England – from sixteen games. It ended on 12 February 1933 with a 4-0 win away to France. But after a 2-1 defeat against Czechoslovakia on 9 April 1933 in Vienna a further twelve matches were completed without loss. The fixtures themselves constituted friendly matches and competitive games in the International Cup – the Home Internationals if you prefer to consider them for Middle Europe. Moreover from this record alone is it any wonder that England was regarded as the leading country at the time!

Austria 1934, players only. Back; Platzer, Urbanek, Sesta, Braun, Zischek, Bican, Wagner. Front; Smistik, Cisar, Viertl, Horvath

Unlike the regime or lack of it in England, the Austrians had a two-man setup. Hugo Meisl was the head of operations, Jimmy Hogan his coach. Between them they constructed an entertaining and effective method of play that was a connoisseur's delight to view. They had largely ignored the third back approach. Hogan had always based his methods on the Scottish short-passing game and perfected it with the Austrians. He had some outstanding talent with which to work of course. At best they were semi-professional players but accomplished individuals on the field.

Walter Nausch who could play either wing-half or inside-forward, even full-back if necessary was a cunningly correct calming influence and the player who carried out the ideas of Meisl and Hogan. Not a goal scorer, in fact he managed only one for the Austria in 39 internationals, yet interestingly enough hit a post when Austria lost to England at Stamford Bridge!

Naturally the focus of attention was Matthias Sindelar, definitely a man of central Europe, judging by his background having been born in Koslov on the Austro-Hungarian border in Moravia and living in the Czechoslovakia section of Vienna! His family were Catholic not Jewish as was supposed. As tall and elegant in style as a Viennese waltz, yet lean and wraith-like known as "Der Papierene" – Man of Paper. But to his colleagues he was Motzl. A withdrawn role ostensibly as a centre forward he weaved his artistry leaving others to score. Even so he hit 26 goals in 43 internationals. He had been recovering from a serious illness and had missed seven internationals prior to the run-up against England. Though thought to be one of the best paid players on the continent he worked as a mechanic. On 23 January 1939 he was found dead in his Vienna flat with his girl friend in suspicious circumstances.

Another useful marksman was Anton Schall who could play either inside or outside-left and in 28 internationals scored 27 goals including a couple of four-timers and hat tricks. Right-back Karl Rainer and Josef Smistik a talented influential attacking centre-half both won 39 caps. Defensively Austria was not as formidable but in goalkeeper Rudi Hiden, there was a spectacular and much admired performer who became a professional in France.

Even so a failure of the system with its embedded attacking instincts was in clinically finishing immaculate approach work. Time after time having become pass-masters with the ball, shots were either delayed or off target. Perhaps the fault at least with Hogan might have been through his first experience of coaching in Holland before the Great War. He was taken by the Chairman of the club for whom he had agreed to assist, to a dressing-room where there were eleven left boots. The players all university students were on the field in outdoor clothing shooting at goal with one right boot. That was their notion of the object of the game. At least it was the right attitude, if not Hogan's idea of coaching.

On 24 October 1937 Nausch captained Austria for his last international before the Nazis incorporated the best players into Greater Germany. Franz "Bimbo" Binder was one and added German caps to his Austrian totals. Ironically it was Czechoslovakia who beat Austria that day 2-1 in Prague. In less than a year the same fate awaited the Czechs.

Hungary was regarded as the next best to Austria as far as attractive football was concerned, but they lacked its consistency. They did possess some clever players with two forwards of particular note Dr Gyorgy Sarosi who had a Law Degree as a Doctor of Philosophy and Gyula Zsengeller. Dr Sarosi could play either as an enterprising centre-half or goal scoring centre-forward. From 1931 to 1939 he scored 36 goals in 53 international, his zenith reached when he hit seven goals in the 8-3 win over Czechoslovakia on 19 September 1937, Zsengeller was the other scorer who single-mindedly scored 21 goals in 21 internationals in the same time frame. His best efforts were five of eleven against Greece and a hat trick against Germany on 24 September 1939, weeks into the Second World War. These two were listed in FIFA's team of the 1938 World Cup tournament. Sarosi also represented Hungary at tennis, swimming and fencing.

Hungary at the 1938 World Cup. Sarosi, Szabo, Toldi, Lazar, Turay, Szengeller, Szalay, Sas, Biro, Titkos, Korany

On 10 May 1934 Hungary had surprised England winning 2-1 in Budapest, having previously tried out two teams on international duty on the same day. Bulgaria was defeated 4-1 in a World Cup match, while a 2-2 draw was taking place in an International Cup fixture with the Czechs in Prague. However it was towards the end of the decade that they came more into contention. On 27 September 1936 they defeated a post-"Wunderteam" 5-3 in Budapest. A week later they won 2-1 in Romania. But six weeks before they were due to meet England at Highbury they lost 5-2 to Czechoslovakia in Prague. Then it was the 6-2 chastisement at Arsenal's home. Even so four days later they shrugged off this disappointment to beat the Irish Free State 3-2 in Dublin.

A 5-1 victory in Basle against the Swiss on 11 April 1937 was followed by another setback to Italy in Turin, the Italians scoring twice without reply. Yet there was only two more reverses – strangely enough 4-0 to Portugal among 13 games, ending unlucky for Hungary in the 1938 World Cup final in Paris 4-2 to the Italians again. In the interim they had plundered eight goals off the Czechs, six against Luxembourg and the Dutch East Indies, as many as eleven over Greece and five against Sweden. Lajos Koranyi was right-back in the 1938 World Cup final, his partner Sandor Biro. Goalkeeper Antal Szabo completed this defensive trio having also played in the 1934 World Cup.

The Czechs had been influenced by British coaches from an early date and followed the short-passing Scottish type of football that seemed to be the most favoured by UK coaches to the continent. As to their rating after a 2-2 draw with Austria on 23 March 1930, they had a year's unbeaten run of eight games until losing 2-1 in Vienna to Austria on 12 March 1931. Stung by this defeat they took revenge on first the Swiss with a 7-3 win and then Poland 4-0. A 2-1 success over Italy in an International Cup match on 28 October 1932 was impressive for the Czechs but less so were erratic performances thereafter.

Czechoslovakia 1934: Kalocsay, Boucek, Kopecky, Junek, Puc, Planicka, Burgr, Sobotka, Nejedly, Cambal, Silny, Svoboda, Kostalek, Zenisek, Ctyroky, Vodlicka, Krcil, Patzel

However a 2-1 success against England in Prague on 16 May 1934 was a warm-up boost to the following World Cup where Romania, Switzerland and Germany fell to them. They were considered unfortunate to then lose to the Italians in the final in Rome after extra time. Josef Silny who played against England appeared 50 times for the Czechs and scored 28 goals.

By the time the Czechs came to England in 1937 their results had shown further inconsistency. Even Scotland had won 3-1 against them in Prague seven months earlier. And a week after the England match, the Scots completed a double winning 5-0 at Hampden Park. Not that the standard of passing had deteriorated it was the failure to finish moves with goals.

Among some outstanding performers there was Josef Bican a dual international born in Vienna of Czech parents and capped by Austria notably scoring three against Hungary on 6 October 1935 and two when Hungary beat the Austrians 5-3 on 5 April 1936. On 7 August 1938 "Pepi" Bican scored three for Czechoslovakia against Sweden and four in the 6-2 win over Romania on 4 December which wound down the Czechs international calendar with the Germans now in charge of the country.

Italy get to choose which ball to use during the 1934 World Cup

The 1938 World Cup had seen the end of the careers of goalkeeper Frantisek Planicka and winger Antonin Puc. Both played in the disgraceful 1-1 draw with Brazil and neither appeared in the replay. In fact Puc had been sent off in his 60th international. Oldrich Nejedly had broken his leg and Planicka his arm! Overall Puc had scored 34 goals. Planicka who captained the Czechs had made 73 appearances.

Nejedly who had partnered Puc in many internationals subsequently took his place on the wing and also played in the last international his 43rd having scored 28 goals. Inside-forward Frantisek Svoboda had a ten year international career, also won 43 caps and scored 22 goals.

So, despite those two World Cup trophies, Italy was not looked upon with favour by the purists. This would not have worried Vittorio Pozzo or *IL Duce* who had taken special interest in the exploits of his national football team. They won the games that mattered and most of the others they played, too. Ironically Pozzo had learned the finer points of the game while studying in England! Having been involved in Italy's international organisation previously it was towards the build up of the World Cup finals in 1934 that he assumed total command.

Between 1930 and 1934 of the 35 matches Italy played, they won 23 and drew seven. During this period their sole defeats were at home to Spain, home and away games with Austria and away to Czechoslovakia, plus the Battle of Highbury against England. Thereafter they were just as successful with only two submissions to Czechoslovakia and Switzerland, both on their travels. Thus their impressive record in the 1930s read 65 matches played, 45 ending in victory, 13 draws and just seven losses, a record which far outweighed any other continental country. During this period five of the years saw them undefeated.

By far their most productive sequence came after losing 2-1 in Prague to Czechoslovakia on 10 June 1935 when the Czechs gained revenge for their narrow World Cup defeat. Italy then went 26 games unbeaten before losing to the Swiss in Zurich on 12 November 1939.

Only two players won World Cup medals in both 1934 and 1938, Giovanni Ferrari and Giuseppe

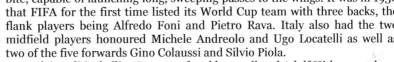

Meazza. Ferrari missed a sitter in his first game, was dropped for a year then became an institution in the team. Meazza was arguably Italy's most talented forward, quick, slick and aware.

There was also Luisito Monti the granite like centre-half Argentine born of Italian parents, played for his birth country in the 1930 and for Italy in 1934. He was just what Pozzo wanted, an attacking style play-maker with bite, capable of launching long, sweeping passes to the wings. It was in 1938 that FIFA for the first time listed its World Cup team with three backs, the flank players being Alfredo Foni and Pietro Rava. Italy also had the two midfield players honoured Michele Andreolo and Ugo Locatelli as well as two of the five forwards Gino Colaussi and Silvio Piola.

Giuseppe Meazza

Italy's political allies Germany fared less well and Adolf Hitler must have envied his neighbour in football terms if probably little else. However, third place in the 1934 World Cup was a worthy effort reinforced by the fact they defeated Austria's "Wunderteam." Yet England had had little difficulty at White Hart Lane when the three goals had flattered the visitors in defeat when they met on 4 December 1935. Even so, they had struck a rich vein prior to this encounter beating Finland, Luxembourg (narrowly), Romania, Estonia, Poland, Latvia and Bulgaria.

Otto Nerz, the German team manager, had fashioned his defence on the third back game, but ditched it in the end. Outstanding was the blond, typical Arian Fritz Szepan who played either as a "stopper" centre-half or constructive inside-forward. He played 34 times for his country and was a clerk in local government. Defensively, too, Reinhold Munzenberg who came back from the international wilderness for the World Cup was an obstacle-like defender either at full-back or as a "stopper." He made 41 appearances. The arrival of Paul Janes at right-back shifted him to the middle. Janes who played 48 times to 1939 was a dead ball specialist, rarely erring in his placements.

Behind them was the tall Hans Jakob. His finest day was when he kept Spain at bay in Barcelona in 1936 in a 2-1 win, one of 38 caps he was awarded. But there was also the Jimmy Hogan discovery of 1927 Richard Hofmann who later became the first foreigner to score a hat trick against England but notoriously sent off in an Olympic Games match that cost him a year's suspension from 1928. Twenty-five appearances yielded 24 international goals. Again when that highly-charged return fixture with the English was looming in 1938 for Berlin, the Germans had put together some at least impressive results on paper, selecting once more some of Europe's weaker nations to demonstrate the prowess of the Fatherland in such sporting events. They did feature two games in one day drawing 1-1 with Hungary in Nuremberg and beating Luxembourg 2-1 at Wuppertal.

Sadly there had been huge disappointments, not the least of them failure in the Olympic Games tournament of 1936 and if the England match two years later was used as a prelude to better things in the World Cup, it flopped disastrously because after a 1-1 draw with Switzerland they lost the replay 4-2 in Paris of all places. By then Austria had been annexed and taken into the Greater Germany complex, the best of the Austrian players became available for selection.

France, though not bracketed with any of the other European nations did arguably record one of the best results against England. In 1931 it was a pretty remarkable 5-2 win. This undoubtedly precipitated the formation of the French professional league. Before this sensational score line they had registered an uninspired own goal win over Germany also in Paris two months previously, suffered defeats to Czechoslovakia and 5-0 to Italy in Bologna. The return fixture in England in 1933 was the French team's first international for six months and the 4-1 defeat of little surprise.

France, as with Hungary, also shared a similar experience during the 1934 World Cup when on the day their first team was losing 3-2 to Austria in the World Cup in Turin, another eleven was beating Holland 5-4 in Amsterdam.

It should be added that from a mixture of stick and carrot they had entered the 1930 World Cup as one of only a handful of European countries so to do. They were rewarded with hosting the 1938 finals and were convincingly beaten by the Italians 3-1.

Oscar Heisserer was the outstanding inside-forward for France and played in the 1938 World Cup. In defence, Etienne Mattler was a fixture at left-back playing in three World Cups. His cap against Wales in 1939 was his 45th. Jean Nicolas had five years in the international area and as forward scored 21 goals in 25 matches. Auguste "Gusti" Jordan was actually born in Austria naturalized in 1937 and was establishing himself in the team in 1938 as a centre-half. He also scored against England in 1938. Another three-time World Cup participant was midfield organizer Edmond Delfour.

Spain, having lowered England's colours for the first time in 1929, also had spasmodic successes, despite playing far fewer international matches than any of their other leading continental countries. In the run-up to that Madrid match they had defeated Portugal 5-0 in Seville and France 8-1 in Zaragoza. They had received genuine and well deserved praise for declining to use any of their obviously paid professional players in the 1928 Olympics.

With the legendary Ricardo Zamora who cost Real Madrid a goalkeeping record fee of £6,000 from Barcelona, having an off-day to say the least at Highbury when the English forwards put seven goals past him, it was a one-off blemish in an otherwise reasonably respectable list of results. However, locals thought he had not played well in the first game against England in 1929. But the unrest that led to the Spanish Civil War interrupted all countrywide football in 1936.

However, Luis Regueiro a scorer against Italy in the 1934 World Cup and who played 25 times for Spain scoring 16 goals, played for the Basque region under the assumed name of Euzadi when the conflict began. Jacinto Quincoces the defender who played twice against England appeared 25 times, too and captained Spain in any absence of Zamora, who conceded only 42 goals in 46 internationals – but ten of them against England!

Interestingly and perhaps not surprisingly, the all-embracing titled but confined to just five countries was the International Cup won by three of the top four countries. Perhaps that was how they viewed their importance. It was played on a home and away group basis. The initial series from 1927-29 was won by Italy, the second from 1931-32 by Austria. Italy took the 1933-35 series and the uncompleted 1936-38 version went to Hungary as Austria was by then part of Greater Germany. Austria, Czechoslovakia, Hungary, Italy and Switzerland were the participants. The outstanding Swiss player was Severino Minelli. First capped in 1930 by 1939 he had played 69 times and was at right back in the 2-1 win over England in 1938.

Yet it was Vienna born Karl Rappan Austrian international a tactical visionary who produced for the Swiss a defensive variation of the Austrian *verrou* (bolt) system that sprung an off-side trap into rapid and effective forward movement from a basis of four defenders in a line, one always acting as cover for the other three. Moreover results improved for the amateurs in 1938. England was beaten 2-1, the Germans held 1-1 in the World Cup and beaten 4-2 in the replay. Interestingly the Italian word for bolt is *catenaccio*.

In Belgium the pressure on them to go to Uruguay in 1930 was also strong. The Braine brothers were famous, Pierre following Raymond, who was once refused a work permit to sign for Clapton Orient! When he wanted to open a bar the Belgian FA threatened his amateur status and instead signed professional forms for Sparta Prague in Czechoslovakia coached by an Englishman, Harry Dick.

A forceful centre-forward Raymond Braine was persuaded by Belgian referee John Langenus to apply to the Belgian FA for reinstatement into the national team. They agreed. He won 54 caps and scored 26 goals. As for Pierre seven years older, he captained the 1930 World Cup team and played on 46 occasions for Belgium. Yet it was Bernard Voorhoof, an inside-forward who played in all three World Cups achieved 59 caps and hit 29 goals by 1939.

Two Swedish players of note were Sven Jonasson and Tore Keller. Jonasson scored twice in the 1934 World Cup finals, once in 1938. He held the record for 252 goals scored in domestic football. Keller a free spirit at times captained Sweden in the 1938 tournament and scored 17 goals in 25 internationals.

The Dutch stayed amateur but had some useful players. They included wing-half Puck Van Heel and Eliza Bakhuys known as "Bep" who had 23 international outings and scored 28 goals. He became a professional in France. Van Heel had 64 caps in his career.

Poland also had a notable goal scorer in Ernest Wilimowski, famous for scoring four goals against Brazil in the 1938 and finishing on the losing side as the South Americans won 6-5. Brazil had several  prominent performers, especially Leonidas da Silva who perfected the bicycle kick and was unaccountably rested against Italy in the World Cup and watched his team lose! Known as the "Black Diamond" or "Rubber Man" he was a fine marksman.

There was also the leading centre-half Domingos da Guia, whose attitude to defending was to cleverly watch where the ball was rather than opponents. Both players were in FiFA's 1938 World Cup players of the tournament.

Apart from meetings in the World Cup and the Olympics, internationals between nations from different continents were rare. The long-running South American Championship was held three times in the 30s. In 1935 held in Peru with Uruguay winners, two years later in Argentina when the host nation beat Brazil 2-0 in the play-off. It was back to Peru in 1939 where again the home team was successful.

Naturally with two Olympic titles in 1924 and 1928 plus the inaugural World Cup in 1930, Uruguay was the leading South American country to the rest of football. They dominated the individual roles in 1930 but especially Jose Nasazzi the right-back and captain and Hector Scarone in

Leonidas da Silva

attack. Their neighbours and final opponents Argentina possessed an equally outstanding player in the fast-moving centre-forward Guillermo Stabile who was top scorer with eight goals in the tournament. His international life virtually finished there as he went to Italy and France to continue his career.

The USA also kept itself in the soccer spotlight though not considered by the IOC to feature the game in the 1932 Olympics they hosted. In the 1930 World Cup, they even had a player chosen for the FIFA team. He was Bert Patenaude decreed to have been the first in the World Cup to score a hat-trick. Thus his four appearances and six goals for his country remained his only international exposure.

Of course the Irish Free State was the only country in the area of the British Isles to enter the World Cup as they were not in dispute with FIFA. They drew 4-4 with Belgium Paddy Moore scoring all four goals and lost 5-2 in Holland for their 1934 contribution. For 1938 they were narrowly beaten 3-2 in Norway and held 3-3 in Dublin for the return match when they made eight changes!

The Irish gave some encouraging displays. In 1936 they drew 3-3 with Hungary and beat the Germans 5-2. In 1938 they drew 2-2 with Czechoslovakia. The following year home and away fixtures with the Hungarians they shared four goals in both matches. They also held Germany 1-1 in Bremen.

Joe O'Reilly a wing-half first capped in 1932 against Holland eventually played in 20 internationals, the last 17 consecutively. Centre-forward Jimmy Dunne who finished his career with Shamrock Rovers after a long stint in the Football League appeared in 15 internationals and scored 13 goals. Moore scored seven goals in nine appearances.

There were other competitions in Europe for national teams. The Balkan Cup finished its first series in 1931 with Romania the winners. Bulgaria won it in 1932 and 1935, Romania again in 1936 and in the unofficial tournament in 1937. Yugoslavia declared winners in the 1934-35 tournament based on a league system. Greece was the only other country involved.

The Baltic states of Estonia, Latvia and Lithuania were involved in a Baltic Cup from 1928 to 1938. Latvia won four times, Estonia three times and Lithuania twice. The 1934 competition was not played and in 1933 the result was annulled.

Two Scandinavian Championships sometimes called the Nordic Cup were completed in the 30s. Norway won the 1929-32 edition and Sweden the 1933-36 competition. Denmark and Finland were also involved and 24 matches were played overall.

The Match of FIFA: Central Europe v West Europe 20th June 1937 Amsterdam

Central Europe, left to right: AJ Jewell (referee), JHA Mooi (linesman), Dr. G Sarosi (Hungary), P Serantoni (Italy), G Meazza (Italy), A Olivieri (Italy), W Schmaus (Austria), S Piola (Italy), F Sas (Hungary), G Lazar (Hungary), K Szesta (Austria), M Andreolo (Italy), O Nejedly (Czechoslovakia), L Cseh (Hungary), W Hahnemann (Austria), P Rava (Italy), B Klenovec (Checkoslovakia)

West Europe, left to right: H Jacob (Germany), EH Bakhuys (Netherlands), BJ Van Caldenhove (Netherlands), L Goldbrunner (Germany), JC Smit (Netherlands), R Paverick (Belgium), E Lehner (Germany), S van den Eynde (Belgium), R Braine (Belgium), E Delfour (France), A Kitzinger (Germany)

PENALTIES

DISCIPLINE – TRAGEDY – INJURIES

Discipline or the lack of it was frequently a topic of newspaper criticism. The unfortunate referee was often accused of failing to deal with rough play. The sliding tackle and obstruction were often singled out as grey areas. Shoulder charging was accepted and there were few instances of the illegal use of the arm, though there were examples of players exchanging blows. Goalkeepers were particularly vulnerable to being charged even when in possession. But it was frequently argued that professional referees would be a step forward in improving overall control.

Frank O'Donnell

While many clubs went years without having a player sent off, dismissal did not always lead to suspension. The other sanction was receiving a caution during a match that often led to a player being fined. Sendings-off invariably meant two weeks suspension and a fine, but there was judgement as to the severity of the incident taken into consideration.

In 1936-37 Frank O'Donnell playing for Preston North End was sent off against Wolves during a 5-0 defeat. He was distraught and upset in the dressing-room. He was the first Preston player sent off in 14 years. The FA subsequently fined him £8 but he was not suspended. However, some players were suspended and handed a £8 fine as well.

Tom "Pongo" Waring of Aston Villa was suspended for 28 days as a result of an incident in the match at Leicester City on 9 February 1933. On 6 January 1934 he was sent off against Tottenham Hotspur, missiles were thrown by the Villa crowd and referee Percy Snape had to be escorted off the field at the final whistle. On 25 February 1939 some spectators threw oranges at Wolves players in the match at Liverpool. The Anfield club was fined 20 guineas.

Frequently in the headlines for a variety of escapades, Waring when at Accrington ran into more trouble. He with two other Stanley players Billy Tyson and Tom Jones were alleged to have been drinking on a train. Waring was fined £10 by the club and all three suspended. Waring stated: "You can find me in Ireland." Eventually apologies all round!

There was the odd case concerning Norwich City v Sheffield Wednesday on 11 September 1937. It was subsequent to the match that it was discovered the Wednesday player Harry Ware had suffered a fractured jaw. No newspaper reports had mentioned it and neither had referee George Gould. However, the Norwich centre-half Peter Burke had been cautioned for the use of an elbow, a rare offence at the time. Even more of a surprise was that Ware joined Norwich on 8 November in a £2,000 deal!

Tom Waring

Tony Leach before a subsequent involvement at Carlisle was ordered off playing for Newcastle United at Tottenham on 20 January 1935. Three weeks later he was suspended for 14 days and fined £10. On 26 October 1935 Duncan McKenzie (Brentford) and Eric Brook (Manchester City) were sent off. McKenzie was subsequently suspended for 14 days while no action was taken over Brook.

Portsmouth's Guy Wharton was sent off against Birmingham on 1 April 1939. He handed a seven days suspension and fined £5 but did not miss playing in the FA Cup final.

Even Jimmy Hogan was fined £5 for entering the referee's room on one occasion when he was unhappy with the official's interpretations. His Villa player Ronnie Starling was also similarly fined over incidents in the match and two other players cautioned.

Arsenal was fined £250 in June 1936 for playing weak teams in the Football League. Twenty-nine different players had appeared in 1935-36 when Arsenal finished sixth. In 1933 Preston had been fined £25 for turning out a weak team in a County Cup fixture at Accrington. Barnsley was fined in 1936-37 for fielding an unregistered player.

On 4 December 1937, Fred Corbett a full-back with Lincoln City was playing at York in a Division Three (North) match when he was injured badly enough to be carried to the dressing-room. After the match he was informed by the referee that he had been sent off! York won the game 3-1. In 1935-36 clubs were given powers to fine players themselves.

On 29 March 1931 the entire Elmsdale Wednesday team and one player from Sutton Wednesday were suspended by the Surrey FA following rough play in the Croydon Midweek Charity Cup semi-final. Five players were ordered off the field, two were taken to hospital. The game was abandoned ten minutes from time. Four players were suspended until the end of the year, eight until the end of the season. In 1932-33 no fewer than 17 Barking players were declared professionals!

Four Bristol City amateurs were declared professional on 3 October 1938 and manager Bob Howison suspended until 6 May 1939. In the interim Clarrie Bourton filled in as player-manager.

Misbehaviour by spectators was usually confined to isolated incidents involving individuals. However, there were several closures of grounds through misconduct by crowds. Early in 1930 Queens Park Rangers' Loftus Road was closed for two weeks. They were not allowed to play within a six-mile radius, but arranged to play Coventry City at Highbury! On 1 March they won 3-1 and were watched by a crowd of 17,903. There were two closures in 1934. Millwall was similarly affected when on 26 April 1934 following incidents a month earlier at the end of the match with Bradford, it was announced that The Den would be closed for the first two weeks of the 1934-35 season. There had been orange peel and paper pellets thrown at officials and players. When orange peel and cushions were thrown at Hull City's match with Preston North End on 21 April 1934, the ground at Anlaby Road was closed for two weeks at the start of 1934-35, but fixture switching did not cause a problem. However, the FA also fined Millwall £100 for crowd misbehaviour on 5 November against Southampton. Again at The Den a spectator threw a missile towards a linesman in another match in 1938-39. More orange throwing when Arsenal entertained Blackpool on Boxing Day 1937 and had several players injured.

On 9 November 1935 incidents in the Carlisle United v Chester game led to Brunton Park being closed for two weeks from 2 December. Referee Ike Caswell having disallowed a Chester goal changed his mind after consulting a linesman. The ball was kicked into the crowd and not returned. Several clubs were instructed to display warning notices as to the conduct of spectators. On 13 September 1937 a missile was thrown in the direction of a linesman in the Preston North End v Charlton Athletic match at Deepdale when a corner was being taken. A policeman was detailed to patrol the area.

On 30 December 1937 it was announced that the Crewe Alexandra ground would be closed for 14 days from 3 January 1938 as a result of incidents on 11 December. But fixtures were reversed! On 6 February 1939 one Southend United player Len Bolan was suspended for 14 days and fined £3. Two others Sid Bell and Alf Smirk were cautioned and similarly fined. The FA also decided to suspend without investigation any players who had been cautioned three times. George Murphy at Bradford City was cautioned twice in games and was fined ten guineas.

However, one of the most serious acts occurred at Brighton on 29 October 1938 during the match with Northampton Town. After referee Reg Rudd had refused the home team a penalty he was struck by a stone thrown from the crowd. Two policemen were despatched to patrol the area. Interestingly enough Rudd had once collided with a player at the same ground, dislocating his shoulder only to resume and finish in charge of the game!

There were also some demonstrations usually aimed at the board of directors of a club where results were not to their liking. Since managers were not as a whole were not high profile figures at the majority of clubs, they often escaped the wrath, but invariably suffered when the board took action against them! On 14 November 1936 it was reported that bad behaviour by spectators had been reported at several venues.

Severe punishment was also imposed in an alleged matter of attempted bribery to fix a series of matches. On 3 January 1939 a Joint Commission of football authorities published a report concerning Stockport County. The Commission found that George Worsley a County Director had offered via Tony Leach a Carlisle United player and former England international, a sum of money to Carlisle players in connection with their two League matches with Lincoln City on 15 and 17 April 1937.

That season Carlisle finished tenth in Division Three (North), Lincoln City runners-up to champions Stockport County, who incidentally beat Lincoln 2-0 on the last day though already crowned. During the season there had been a coincidental series of exchanges between Stockport and Carlisle. Fred Westgarth the County manager resigned. His position was filled by Bob Kelly from Carlisle United. In February, Leach and two other United players joined Stockport, two others made the reverse journey!

As to the April scenario, Carlisle had won the first match and Lincoln the second. Leach had accepted the money and by January 1939 was a Lincoln player! He had distributed the money among the other Carlisle players. The Commission decided that there was no evidence of the truth of the allegations that other officials or players of Stockport County, Carlisle United or of any other club had been cognisant of these actions.

Following these findings Worsley was suspended *sine die* and fined £50. Leach was suspended for 28 days as from 9 January and fined £20. Dave Galloway and Harry O'Grady by then of Tunbridge Wells Rangers were each fined £20, too. John Cliffe, Tommy Kerr, Hugh Mills and Bill Smith of Carlisle United together with Will Adey (Aberdeen), Frank Higgs (Barrow), Jack Johnson (Accrington Stanley) and Norman Roberts (Shrewsbury Town) all at Carlisle at the time of the incident were each fined £15. Stockport paid the costs of the enquiry.

In 1935 the Falkirk manager Robert Orr successfully persuaded Robert Russell an Ayr United player not to play in a crucial relegation match between the two clubs on 9 March. Falkirk won 3-2. Russell admitted the approach had been made to him. Orr was suspended from taking further part in football. The Falkirk club was fined £25 and the match ordered to be replayed. In this Ayr won 3-1 and Falkirk went down to Division Two. Ayr's nickname: The Honest Men.

The 1931 FA Cup semi-final between West Bromwich and Everton at Old Trafford had an attendance of 68,241 but the gates were closed when crowds spilled onto the pitch and there were 333 injuries. One player had to remove a police horse in order to take a corner kick.

There was another scandal involving Arthur Kingscott who had refereed two FA Cup finals in the early part of the century, controversially involved in one incident in which he awarded a goal despite being yards away from the incident. He was the FA's Honorary Treasurer at the time of the 1933 final in April. The usual practice had been for the final official to be presented with some 30 different makes of football for the occasion and they chose one. It was alleged Kingscott, who was in charge of the arrangement, had intimated to the referee Edward Wood that officials in the past had benefited commercially from their choice.

Kingscott, aged 70, was actually in charge of the England international party the following month on its tour to Italy and Switzerland when Herbert Chapman was team manager. In fact Kingscott had been in a similar position for some 20 years during which time England had lost only once! But the subsequent furore over the FA Cup final ball led to Kingscott resigning from his position at the FA on 12 December and he refused to make any apology continually protesting his innocence over the matter. There was no redress either in law or with football's governing body. Kingscott's son Arthur Harold Kingscott had actually been in charge of the 1931 final! As a final irony the 1933 ball was actually selected by the respective team captains from Everton and Manchester City. Kingscott snr died in 1937.

On 13 November 1937 a serious incident occurred at a football match played between British soldiers and native deserters from the Italian Army housed in an internment camp at Isiolo, Kenya. A player from each team came to blows, the referee stopped the match and the Italians in the crowd of around 500 who heavily outnumbered the soldiers attacked players and military personnel with sticks while attempting to gain weapons from the compound. The King's African Rifles were forced to open fire. Nine Italians were killed, ten soldiers and 27 Italians wounded. Order was restored quickly. Matches had been a regular occurrence between the two parties.

There were a few tragic deaths involving domestic players caused by injuries sustained in matches, though with little or no evidence that deliberant violence had led to their subsequent demise. However, as result of rough treatment meted out to him in the match between Sunderland and Chelsea on 1 February 1936, goalkeeper Jimmy Thorpe who was a diabetic and had suffered weight loss for a couple of years, died in a coma four days later. The head and chest injury he sustained had been in a goalmouth melee, though he had indicated to the referee that he was able to continue. As a consequence the FA introduced a ruling that goalkeepers were no longer to be challenged by a foot raised against them once they had control of the ball in their arms. Thorpe had been a Jarrow shipyard engineer before signing for the Roker Park club at 17.

The most widely reported accident led to John Thomson the Celtic goalkeeper who suffered a fractured skull and died after being in collision with the Rangers forward Sam English on 5 September 1931. English was haunted by the incident throughout his subsequent career though no blame was attached to him. But on 1 December 1934 the Gillingham player Simeon Raleigh suffered a fatal injury in a class of heads with the Brighton & Hove Albion player Paul Mooney, who was so affected by the accident that he decided to retire from football. On the same day two amateur players died as a result of injuries sustained. Raleigh had once won a medal for scoring 61 goals for Silverwood Colliery.

On 18 February 1934 Bob Bradley the captain of Carlisle United was found dead in bed. He was 27. Tragedy struck the club again on 31 December 1936 when Jack Round died from a burst appendix. He had played his last game on 29 November. On 6 December 1935 Wolves goalkeeper Jimmy Utterson died of pneumonia. Harry "Popeye" Jones centre-forward of West Bromwich Albion earned a medal from the Royal Humane Society for diving into a canal to save a child from drowning.

When Billy Marsden received an injury playing for England against Germany on 10 May 1930 that ended his career, there was a rush by clubs to demand insurance for players appearing in international matches covering death and total disablement.

Accidents outside the football scene also sadly caused the deaths of several players. Charlton Athletic goalkeeper Alec Wright suffered a spinal injury while diving off a raft into shallow water near the coast at Torquay on 6 September 1934. He died the following day. Only a few days earlier Peter Cunningham who had last played for Crewe Alexander in February 1934, died in a sanatorium. On the last day of 1938 David Ford an Arsenal reserve goalkeeper died from peritonitis.

That same day there were three serious injuries: Edward Dawson the Bristol City goalkeeper fractured his wrist, John Roberts centre-forward for Port Vale dislocated a shoulder and Eddie Perry the Doncaster Rovers centre-forward broke an arm. Preparing to leave the Army and join Liverpool as a professional, Stan Eastham broke his leg in his last service match.

In the summer of 1937 Jimmy Hampson the Blackpool centre-forward who kept a Boarding-House with his wife Betty, went on several fishing trips with the local fishing club in a motor boat. Three miles off Fleetwood the rudder broke and boat struck a buoy and holed the craft on the waterline. It began to ship water, they bailed out and the skipper managed to get them back to shore. On 10 January 1938 having visited his wife who was recovering from illness in a nursing home, Hampson went on another fishing trip in a 40-foot yacht Defender. It collided with a trawler, He was knocked overboard and his body never recovered while another member of the group died similarly.

In 1931 Portsmouth centre-half Bob Kearney was suffering from pneumonia. After a five day illness he died aged 27, leaving a wife and child. A testimonial match when a combined Pompey and Southampton team played a London Representative side raised a substantial amount and in two months the fund reached almost £1,700. Welsh amateur international Sonny Gibbon at Fulham was killed in a motor accident at Deal on 8 April 1935. Celtic inside-forward Peter Scarff contracted pulmonary tuberculosis and died after a long illness on 9 December 1933.

On 31 March 1934 there were three broken legs: Tom Frame (Manchester United), George McLean (Huddersfield Town) and Cyril Pearce (Charlton Athletic). Alex Bell, who had been Manchester City trainer at the FA Cup final and a dietary follower died on 29 November 1934 at the age of 52.

On 8 April 1939 two bad accidents occurred. Sam Russell of Northampton broke his leg at Southend and Sidney Pugh on his debut for Arsenal at Birmingham suffered kidney damage. Five days later Russell had to have his leg amputated.

Grimsby Town goalkeeper George Moulson who was taken to hospital on 25 March 1939 after being injured in the FA Cup semi-final against Wolves was kept in hospital until 4 April.

Joe Ford playing his first game for Newcastle United broke his leg against Grimsby on 16 January 1932 and it proved to be his only Football League appearance. But he recovered from what was a serious injury and played in Scottish League football with Partick Thistle and Leith Athletic.

Aubrey Powell at Leeds suffered a particularly nasty leg injury. His shin bone was protruding from the broken leg. Three operations were necessary before full recovery.

MANAGEMENT

THE TOP TRIO?

HERBERT CHAPMAN

In any field of influence someone said to be "ahead of their time" usually meant the best at that moment. As a football manager Herbert Chapman at Arsenal fitted that latter description. Though his modest enough playing career tended to be readily dismissed, it provided the necessary grounding for what followed in his managerial role.

Born into a large family his father was a coal miner but the young Herbert won a place at Sheffield Technical College and studied mining engineering. In solely Football League terms he played just 38 matches with seven goals mainly at outside or inside-right involving Grimsby Town, Sheffield United and Notts County. Before and after his playing CV embraced Kiveton Park his local club, Ashton North End, Stalybridge Rovers, Swindon Town, Sheppey United, Worksop Town, Northampton Town (three spells) and even Tottenham Hotspur.

His first association with Northampton was in 1901-02 as an inside-forward in their Southern League days. Previously an amateur including his time at Grimsby Town, he turned professional with the Cobblers. Thoughts of an extended career did not exist at the time because he was released to join Sheffield United with the proviso that he could revert to amateur status and continue his mining studies. But in May 1903 he signed as a professional again for Notts County before returning to Northampton for 1904-05. This second sojourn ended in March 1905 when he joined Tottenham Hotspur. In 1905-06 he was their leading Southern League scorer with eleven goals.

Meantime Northampton was suffering the toils bottom for two years. Initially Walter Bull the Spurs player was approached to be player-manager but he declined. He suggested Chapman who consulted his schoolteacher wife then asked Northampton to pay him what they liked! He had to beg the board to buy players as prospects were not good. The policy change helped immeasurably and in 1908-09 Northampton Town won the Southern League championship.

Chapman ended his playing days and in 1912 accepted an offer to manage Leeds City. With the advent of the Great War and regional football, City won the Midland Section of the Football League in 1917 and 1918. But he was certainly caught up in the furore that followed there.

In 1913-14 Chapman had steered Leeds City to fourth in the Second Division, their highest position. However after the war and eight games into 1919-20 the club was expelled from the Football League following financial irregularities including the payment of players during wartime. Failure of the club's directors to co-operate in the inquiry into its affairs, led to the harshness of the decision. Chapman was also unfairly banned. He had spent the war as manager of a munitions factory with little connection with what went on at the club.

Huddersfield Town approached him in 1920 and supported his successful plea for the ban to be removed. Appointed manager he started to turn their fortunes in a spectacular manner. FA Cup winners in 1922 third in the First Division for 1922-23, Champions the next two seasons then prised away by Arsenal's seduction in 1925 on the way to an unique treble.

Chapman the first £2,000 a year football manager, certainly possessed far-seeking views on the game from an early stage in his career. On the playing side his many ideas included strategy when the ball was not in play. He wanted four divisions in the Football League, floodlit football, the use of a white ball, goal-line judges, artificial pitches and European club competitions. He wanted rubber carpet strips along the touchline to cut on the wear and tear on the well trodden surface. His controversial attitude to promotion and relegation was that one half should be promoted the other half relegated to ensure teams would not play the same opposition two seasons in succession. This view seems to have emanated from his playing days when he rarely spent more than one season at a club.

However, when an architect called in to see him at Highbury with plans for the pitch to be raised and water pipes fitted to enable heat to be generated preventing frost from postponing matches, Chapman was unimpressed. The cost £13,000 he thought was a waste as the ground had never suffered from such a calling-off.

As to the theory that Arsenal deliberately used their playing system as a defensive strategy, Chapman was quoted as saying: "Given one point at the kick-off, one goal is sufficient to win a game if my defence is playing correctly and to orders." Make of that whatever you feel appropriate.

There is little doubt that he favoured clubs with a cheque book spending money on improving playing resources. It was nurtured at Northampton and fulfilled at Arsenal. Though he was passionately in favour of coaching for all schoolboys, he was sceptical about signing too many young players because of the risks involved due to the turnover of failure. So much then for the career so tragically cut short in his early 50s at the height of his achievements. What of the man himself? Chunky and chubby, cheerful and a charmer with steely blue eyes, his friendly manner won him many friends inside and outside the game. He even persuaded the London Passenger Transport Board to change the name of the Gillespie Road Underground Station to Arsenal. There had been other interests for Chapman who had studied coal mining and possessed a colliery manager's certificate under Board of Trade guidelines.

Whenever possible he sought to make Highbury available for other matches and encouraged his senior players to coach at Highgate School and other establishments in the vicinity. He thought leading players did not need the Players Union.

He was keen for his players to voice their views and held regular meetings for discussion involving everyone in the club down to the office boy to feel an important part of Arsenal Football Club. Chapman was reported to be suffering from influenza on 4 January. He died two days later.

FRANK BUCKLEY

Frank Buckley was a contrast. Big, broad and brown eyed behind horn-rimmed spectacles, hale and hearty but with an authoritative streak. He was always known as The Major. Unlike Chapman his playing career had been slightly more impressive including one England cap at centre-half. Briefly with Aston Villa and Brighton & Hove Albion he was with both Manchester clubs United and City before two seasons with Birmingham. At Derby County for two years, too, he was playing with Bradford City when the Great War started.

However long before this he had appeared likely to follow his father into the Army. At 18 as an office clerk he signed on for twelve years in the 2nd Battalion of the King's Liverpool Regiment expecting to be sent to the South African War. Instead he was posted to Ireland. Promoted to Corporal then Lance Sergeant he was a Gymnastics Instructor and showed ability at football. Spotted by an Aston Villa scout, Buckley decided to buy himself out in 1903 for £18 and pursued a career in the game. His debut was in a Staffordshire Senior Cup tie against Wolverhampton Wanderers, interesting opponents in view of subsequent events.

At Derby County he collected a Second Division Championship medal as an attacking centre-half. He won an England cap against Ireland in February 1914 but it was not an inspiring debut as the Irish won 3-0 at Middlesbrough. Playing for Bradford City and though in his early 30s he was one of the first volunteers for the Footballers' Battalion of the Middlesex Regiment.

Distinguished wartime service after being commissioned as a Lieutenant, later Captain and then Major as CO of the Battalion, he was seriously wounded in the Somme offensive in July 1916 when shrapnel punctured his lungs seemingly bringing his football career to an end. The metal was removed in Kent and in January 1917 he was back in the front line and mentioned in dispatches during hand-to-hand combat. Poison gas then affected his already damaged lungs.

He was distraught when his batman Thomas Brewer a former Queens Park Rangers player was killed by a sniper's bullet and Buckley offered to pay for the three Brewer children's education.

However in March 1919 he was appointed manager of Norwich City and amazingly turned out for them in a Southern League match! He resigned after a financial crisis at the club and became a commercial traveller for a confectionary manufacturer. But in July 1923 he was back in football as manager of Blackpool. He changed their strip to orange and later tangerine. All his players received conduct instructions.

Blackpool finished fourth in the Second Division, Wolves were Third Division (North) Champions and promoted. In 1927 Buckley was given a three year contract by Wolves and one of his first innovations was a new strip of gold and black. Also the legend of The Major was born.

Affected by the financial problems at Norwich he made it clear at Wolverhampton that football was a business and proceeded to turn deficit into profit even at the expense of results. He inherited a squad of 30 players only five of whom were not local lads. Progress was made after two seasons by finishing ninth then fourth. In 1931-32 Wolves won the Second Division scoring 115 goals.

Almost relegated in 1932-33 two points from safety then 15th, 17th and 15th again in 1935-36 it was not until 1936-37 did Buckley manage to produce better results. Fifth that season and close runners-up a point behind Arsenal in 1937-38, even the League and Cup double seemed within their grasp in 1938-39 only to be runners-up in both competitions.

The Major possessed many ideas and was in favour of floodlighting, numbering players, Sunday football, flying to matches and tip-up seats in stands. He installed many complicated pieces of apparatus at Molineux with the board's approval as well as a rowing machine to improve fitness. But his most controversial innovation was popularly known as the monkey-gland treatment in 1938-39. When Wolves beat Leicester City in the FA Cup, an MP from one of the losers even raised a question in the House of Commons condemning the practice.

Unlike Chapman he was extremely keen on young players and the Buckley Boys were famous. He refereed practice matches coaching the youngsters at the same time. In 1937-38 of 30 professionals, fifteen were under 22, ten under 20 and five under 18. The average age was 23. He also turned Bryn Jones from what appeared to be a journeyman footballer into a record transfer sale when Arsenal paid £14,000 for the Welshman in August 1938. Buckley even named his dog Bryn. Between May 1935 and May 1939 Wolves received £110,658 in transfer fees spending only £42,330 in buying players.

He knew a good player when he saw one. He made his forward-thinking centre-half Stan Cullis captain of the reserves at 18 and the first team at 20. Two years later Cullis skippered England. But The Major was flexible enough to appreciate the advice of those steeped in the game. Following indications – never pleas – from the Wolves trainer, club secretary and even the Molineux groundsman, Buckley relented over a 15 year old youngster named Billy Wright who he had told was not good enough and kept him at Molineux.

A lecture he gave to a referee's society proved a great success. He believed two referees were essential as the game was speeding up, thought linesmen should be given whistles. His players respected him and would stand up when he spoke at club functions.

JIMMY HOGAN

Undoubtedly Jimmy Hogan was the outstanding coach in the 1930s for his work on the continent. From an Irish Catholic family who had landed in Lancashire, his father had wanted him to enter the Priesthood. Jimmy was Head Boy at St Bede's College but was not keen on the church as a career. His football one started as an inside-forward at five shillings a week with his home town team Nelson. Previously he had been with Burnley Belvedere. Following a short time with Rochdale Town he had two seasons in the Football League with Burnley before a return to Nelson. In 1907 he joined Fulham briefly before moving to Swindon Town. At Fulham he had been impressed with the play of several Scots demonstrating their traditional close-passing football. A year later it was back to Lancashire with Bolton Wanderers spending five seasons there. Though he had suffered a serious leg injury this was cured by a bonesetter.

Still only 30 he had already thought about the coaching side of the game. In 1912 he had a short stay as such with Dordrecht in Holland after Bolton had beaten them easily in a friendly while on tour. Injury ended his playing career and Hogan subsequently coached FK Austria which initially proved unsuccessful. He was still in Austria when the Great War began and he was interned but later allowed to coach in Hungary for MTK Budapest. As such he was erroneously labelled as a traitor by some in England.

Football Association Secretary Sir Frederick Wall even contemptuously handed him a pair of Army khaki socks instead of the £200 compensation for being held in a foreign country during the conflict on his first post-war visit to the country. The episode did not feature in Wall's "Fifty Years of Football" in 1934. Wall had lost several family members during the conflict.

In 1918 Hogan coached Young Boys Berne in Switzerland helped the national team coach Teddy Duckworth in preparation for the 1924 Olympics then Lausanne, Dresdner in Germany, Hungaria FC, FK Austria again where he linked up with Hugo Miesl the Austrian national team manager and formed a unique partnership with the "Wunderteam" that caused a stir when they played England. The evening before the Stamford Bridge match Hogan mapped out the tactics on a blackboard and members of the Press were invited.

His basic methods were simple: hours of controlling the ball, keeping it on the ground, creating space running to the right and passing to the left and vice versa. He advocated players getting plenty of use with the ball during the week rather than seeing little of it until Saturday. That was the general idea in England to make players hungry for it on match days.

Hogan had other spells with RC Paris, Lausanne again and briefly back in England with Fulham in 1934. Despite arranging social activities for the players, including a river trip and day out at Newmarket races, the players objected to his training methods and tactics. He was not a devotee of the third back game. He arranged a visit from FK Austria and unfortunately Frank Newton suffered a broken leg!

Hogan fell ill, and had an appendix operation in January. While in hospital the directors sacked him. Then it was abroad again assisting Austria's Olympic squad taking them to the final. Eventually he was persuaded by Fred Rinder the Aston Villa chairman to become team-manager at Villa Park in September 1936. The club had been relegated and suffered a loss of £10,885 largely through transfer dealings.

He also suffered with illness in the family around this time. His youngest son was seriously ill and sent to the Austrian Alps for his health and Hogan had to commute between London and Birmingham when his wife fell ill. But his daughter was a great help to him and the family at the same time, handling the club's merchandising. His older son followed him as a player on the continent.

In 1937-38 Hogan picked a team of 14-18 year olds called the Juniors to play at Perry Barr where the Colts played in the Birmingham Combination. It was another indication of his attention to young players. At Christmas 1938 he gave the players silver matchboxes engraved with the Villa crest. The club sold scarves, ties, badges and cuff links all with the club's logo.

He also took the players away for a week's relaxation at Rhyl. There was plenty of fresh air walking but some sprinting and lapping but no sight of a football during the time. Paradoxically he offered cigarettes and beer at other times putting players in a situation he knew would lead to them questioning their habits!

While many of the senior players were unhappy about Hogan's appointment, he persisted with his ideas and in two years Villa regained their First Division status. Player-power had also been a stumbling block earlier at Fulham, the older professionals objecting to being accused of not knowing how to play the game. This was the curse of the coach c1930s in England. However the Football Association did appoint Hogan as Chief Coach at courses for managers and trainers while he was with Aston Villa. It was while he was collaborating on the FA instructional film that he spotted Reg Lewis a 14 year old who appeared in it. The lad sold cricket scorecards at The Oval while on the ground staff. Hogan recommended him to Arsenal and he played for their Margate nursery!

Hogan never forgot his roots. He returned to his old college had a relaxing day out and most importantly was able subsequently to get the 380 pupils a day off.

Arguably the real reason for the slur of treason rested in the post-Great War refusal of the UK countries to remain in membership of FIFA over any association with Austria, Germany or Hungary. It lingered for much of the period, increasing again as events across the channel developed.

While he was appreciative of the willingness of continental players to listen to his views and follow instructions, he was wary of some of the people in charge of clubs and the politics involved with them. In Hungary there was fierce rivalry with MTK Budapest a Jewish club and bitter rivals with Ferencvaros the Christian one. He was also expected to deliver results wherever he coached – of course! In many places on the continent Hogan was known as "Uncle Jimmy." He was even offered a contract for life by Hugo Miesl to coach the Austrian national team.

GEORGE ARSENAL

Oyster-loving George Allison was no substitute for Herbert Chapman, but as a contrast in styles of a football manager he fitted the requirements for a high profile Arsenal front man to perfection. Twenty-two years working for the William Randolph Hearst organization as the London correspondent of the *New York Herald*, by 1934 he was simply known in Fleet Street as George Arsenal. "By jove, Allison," they would call out to him in that gentle demeanour of the fraternity.

His origin was in the north-east born at Hurworth-on-Tees on 24 October 1883 and at the age of 20 he reported on the same local football matches in which he had played enthusiastically as a full-back. Excited by the prospect of a trial game with Shildon Athletic a semi-professional team he boarded the train at Bishop Auckland and alighted at Shildon leaving his bag and boots on the rack! A pair was given him but two sizes too big and his first kick tore up the turf and damaged his ankle!

After a short spell as assistant to the Middlesbrough FC secretary-manager he packed his bags and moved to London in 1906 and began reporting on Woolwich Arsenal games at Plumstead. He was already becoming an Arsenal fan.

In 1912 he was the European representative for the *International News Service* as well as acting as Arsenal programme editor and club historian. For part of the Great War he served in the Royal Flying Corps. In 1926 he became an Arsenal director.

A year later he had a trial radio broadcast featuring Arsenal's reserves at Highbury and he was readily involved. A few days later on 22 January 1927 the Arsenal v Sheffield United Division One match was broadcast. Seven days later the Corinthians v Newcastle United FA Cup tie at Crystal Palace on 29 January 1927 was also featured.

Of course it was heard by comparatively few listeners on the cat's whisker, crystal set with the *Radio Times* helpfully printing a football pitch divided into eight squares with an assistant helpfully calling out "Square One," to enable the crackle above the commentator's description of the play itself to be followed across the field. Allison possessed a resonant authoritative voice, the broadcast being masterminded by the BBC's Derek McCulloch, "Uncle Mac" beloved of *Children's Hour*.

Allison became a natural and subsequently covered the Derby, Grand National, FA Cup Final and England v Scotland international until the football authorities began to have second thoughts about such broadcasts when other games were being played and spectators were needed at all of them.

On the loss of Chapman, Allison assumed the role and wisely had the correct backup for areas where his expertise was limited. However, he had learned much from always accompanying Chapman to matches. He developed an eye for a good player and with the finances such that he could enter the transfer market without a problem, he was able to keep Arsenal in the forefront of football. Allison did not support the idea of four up and four down for promotion and relegation, in contrast to his mentor.

He was responsible for many successful post-Chapman captures. His first signing was wing-half Wilf Copping from Leeds United and he also persuaded Ted Drake to leave Southampton when the Gunners needed a new centre-forward. Early in the 1937-38 season he went to see Darwen play Great Harwood, the home team's Andrew Davenport having interested him the previous season. Alas the player was injured after ten minutes. Such were the vagaries of scouting even for Arsenal.

Allison also carried on the development of Highbury itself until it was the envy of the football world. But he was always grateful for the legacy left him by Chapman and the staff at Arsenal who made his reign a successful one. On the Monday following Chapman's death, Allison wrote in his *Daily Express* column that he was "sick and sad at heart." Incidentally, the BBC's evening broadcast on that January Saturday in question opened with news of Chapman's passing.

However, early in December 1935 Allison had a breakdown and was sent to the country to recuperate. He returned a few days before Christmas feeling much better and gradually recovered full fitness over the holiday period.

One young amateur player at Highbury taken aside by Allison in 1939 and told professional football was not for him was Len Shackleton.

Portly, passionate and the prime mover for Austrian football in the 30s, Hugo Meisl complete with traditional bowler-hat became focused on fashioning a free-flowing national team that would play attractive close-passing football. If winning became an end product it would be a bonus. He relied on Jimmy Hogan turning the raw material into what was necessary for this to happen.

Meisl, born in 1889 in what was then Bohemia, followed his Jewish family's banking career but was interested in all things football dovetailing into his position in the bank with the same attitude as a choir boy word and pitch perfect would be able to read a comic without being found out.

He had played at inside-forward for FK Austria and first brought Jimmy Hogan to Vienna in 1912 to coach the team. The two stayed close friends. It was in the early 1930s that the pair unveiled what was to become known as the "Wunderteam."

Hugo Meisl

Though Meisl was parental in his attitude to his players, he was strict and expected a correct and obedient approach from them. Fluent in eight languages, he had also refereed the game and became secretary of the Austrian FA having finally quit the bank in 1927.

From 1919 he had been virtually in charge of the national team as well as interests in several Austrian clubs. He was also responsible for instituting the Mitropa Cup for clubs in middle European countries from 1927. The best two clubs were included from Austria, Czechoslovakia, Hungary and Italy who had replaced Yugoslavia by the 1930s while Switzerland was added later. It was played on a home and away knockout system. It was also interesting to note that the winners all came from Austria, Czechoslovakian, Italian and Hungarian clubs.

Friendships were developed with Herbert Chapman in England and Vittorio Pozzo in Italy. He even asked Arsenal's David Jack for his opinion on the third-back system which was not a part of the fluid Austrian carpet game.

The accolade for Austria oddly enough came in the 4-3 defeat when they met England. Shortly before the match at Stamford Bridge on 7 December 1932, the Austrians had played a local team and were whistled off the pitch in a none-too-convincing 2-1 win. Then the chance of a Bohemian rhapsody was ruined by the first half overture until the nerves at playing on English soil were conquered just a little too late in the second act.

Hugo's younger brother Willy was an all-round sportsman and had also played football. His brother picked him in goal against Hungary on 2 May 1920 in Vienna a match ending in a 2-2 draw. Though he also coached the Swedish club Hammarby for two years Willy later worked in Berlin as a journalist for a newspaper until deciding as a Jew it was not the ideal country for him. He immigrated to England in January 1934.

Hugo died of a heart attack on 17 February 1937 and again with Austria part of Greater Germany his future had looked decidedly bleak there, too.

Then again with Vittorio Pozzo lay an affinity for English football but it came from admiring the qualities of Charlie Roberts of Manchester United in the years before the Great War. This attacking centre-half possessed the qualities upon which Pozzo wanted to base his tactics for Italy.

Vittorio Pozzo

Oddly enough 1912 was also a crucial year for him when he was first appointed *Commissario Tecnico* just before the Olympic Games. Born of a well-to-do family in Ponderano in 1886 and studying in Manchester, England in the early 1900s, he settled with no wish to return to home. His family sent a return ticket in an attempt to persuade him otherwise. Furious they cut off his allowance, so he supplemented his living teaching languages in England. Played football in Switzerland for Grasshoppers from 1905 and then Torino a club he helped to form.

He became friends with Hugo Meisl at the Olympics and eventually Herbert Chapman at Arsenal. Pozzo worked for Pirelli until turning long-term to journalism working for *La Stampa*. He dipped in and out of being in charge of AC Milan and the Italian national team until December 1929 when he was given the national reins initially without payment! With the rise of Fascism he wisely decided to toe the party line especially as Mussolini was no dummy when it came to football, before the Dictator later started to show signs of becoming his own caricature. Once when Italy was losing at half-time *Il Duce* threatened the team with military service. They won.

Pozzo knew the Italian mind when it came to dealing with players, aware as individuals they had to be treated as such in order to get the best out of them as a team. He was the main man and left everyone in no doubt of the fact.

While the third back game held no attraction for him, he knew that skill alone with no guarantee of success, he was happy to have physical players like Luisito Monti as the cornerstone of his strategy. Oddly enough the 1938 World Cup success was viewed with wider praise without Monti than the 1934 success with him.

There was neither a Meisl nor a Pozzo for Czechoslovakia, but there was professionalism and foreign players were attracted. However, as far as the national team was concerned there were no fewer than 16 changes of team manager in the 30s. When the Czechs were runners-up to Italy in the 1934 World Cup, they were led by Karel Petru, who had had several other stints at the tiller.

Influenced originally by British coaches and the traditional Scottish passing game, overall results for the national team were reasonable when you understand the varying views that had been passed on to them by the consistent change of individuals in charge.

The Hungarians were also runners-up in the World Cup in the 1938 tournament. MTK Budapest was the leading team after the war and professionalism was introduced by the late 1920's. There were only five different national team managers in Hungary and Karoly Deitz was appointed in 1934 and remained until 1939.

Hogan had also been involved in the post-war development of football in Hungary that was considered second only to Austria in terms of the quality produced on the field of play.

For all Austria's much deserved plaudits they achieved no honours and while the Czechs and Hungarians came close, it was Italy who were twice World Champions.

Interesting to note that of the foreign coaches in Italy during the 30s at one time or another there were 33 Hungarians, eight Austrians, four Czechs, two from Argentina and one each from Brazil, Romania, Yugoslavia and England! The Englishman was William Garbutt with Napoli and Genoa.

ROUS AHEAD OF THE MEMORABLE MEN

The Football Association picked a gem of an administrator in 1934 when they appointed Stanley Ford Rous to succeed the 39-year serving Sir Frederick Wall as Secretary. At the time Rous was a games master at rugby-playing Watford Grammar School and a well respected football referee.

It was a momentous year for this one-time Lowestoft Town goalkeeper. On 28 April he was in charge of the Manchester City v Portsmouth FA Cup Final. The next day he officiated as the man in the middle in Antwerp for the World Cup qualifying match between Belgium and Holland. It was his 34th international having covered matches in all European countries except for Russia, Spain and Portugal.

He had come close to sending off a player in the 1934 FA Cup having to warn Portsmouth full-back John Mackie for threatening remarks aimed at Manchester City winger Eric Brook. Stern words quickly defused the situation.

Suffolk born Rous trained as a teacher and served in the Great War as an NCO in the 272nd Brigade of the Royal Field Artillery in France, Palestine, Egypt and Lebanon. In Egypt he took up refereeing and after the war attended St Luke's College, Exeter where he also qualified as a referee. In 1927 he was appointed to the Football League list. Two years later the headquarters of the FA moved from Holborn Viaduct to 22 Lancaster Gate.

That year he was given his first international assignment and oddly enough it was at the same venue as his last. On 13 March he was in charge of the Belgians game with neighbours Holland in Antwerp. He was also the first to introduce the diagonal system of linesman–referee–linesman in 1933 and used it in the 1934 FA Cup Final. Bolton referee Bert Fogg had previously moved towards similar control a decade earlier. However, it was not until September 1936 that the outline of the system was sent to all referees and linesmen.

In 1938, Rous rewrote the Laws of the Game putting them into a form that was clear cut and easier to follow. He also advocated football club trainers studying psychology, though this idea was never taken up by the clubs. Rous also penned the script for the FA's instructional film "Football and How it is Played" that became a worldwide success.

Shortly after his appointment the FA introduced soccer training for schools with Arthur Grimsdell as coach. The first trials in Essex proved successful and subsequent indications were encouraging until the Elementary Schools announced they preferred schoolmasters to train the boys, not coaches.

Among many active moves, the FA also proposed "probationary professionals" aged 15-17 with £1 a week low and £2 high remuneration with clubs to pay fees for school classes. Those players involved could be reinstated as amateurs if required. There was also worry over an increase in crowd disturbances. A grant was made to the Football League for disabled players. In 1938-39 Bertie Mee the President of the Referees Association asked Rous for clarification on the obstruction law which had been causing many problems. William Pickford wanted the sliding tackle to be banned.

As far as the Football League was concerned Charles Edward Sutcliffe was highly influential. He first became a member of the Management Committee in 1898. From 1927 he was Vice-President then

President from June 1936. For many years he was responsible for producing the Football League fixtures, became most protective of them and battled against the Pools companies who used the fixtures without paying for the privilege of so doing.

The struggle came to a head early in 1936 when at a secret meeting of clubs in Manchester it was decided to withhold the name of the visiting team for clubs playing at home. Reporters overheard proceedings but were persuaded against revealing the details! For three weeks the billboards displayed vague notices akin to: "Everton v ???? 29 February" etc. but though temporarily affected, the Pools companies got wind of what was happening from leakages everywhere and as the Government of the day showed little interest the scheme collapsed.

Sutcliffe was a Rawtenstall solicitor and put his views on every football topic wherever he could find a willing audience. He might well have been advised that the general public could have turned its back on attending football matches where the surprise element of the opposition would have worn thinly and soon. Among many views he was in favour of two referees – but no linesmen – against women playing football –"it's a man's game" – and numbering of players, thought the World Cup was a joke, wanted only English players in the Football League and was not keen on either international matches or foreign club visits. In order for clubs to cut costs he suggested eight-a-side teams, forgetting that three players would be on the dole! One sensible achievement was the 20 percent pool on home matches for the benefit of the majority of clubs struggling. Seemingly well after a serious illness in November, he died on 11 January 1939. He had also believed the home international matches should have been played over three weeks in May.

To encourage better attendances Sutcliffe had advised fans to bring a friend to a game. But he wanted bonuses to players to be scrapped along with managers and trainers! Only local players and amateurs should be signed by clubs. He was vehemently opposed to the Corinthians being given exemption to the early rounds of the FA Cup.

William Pickford was another ubiquitous in football affairs. Lancashire born and into rugby he was converted to soccer on his first viewing. The family moved to the south coast where he divided his time on the *Bournemouth Guardian* as bookkeeper and football reporter. Played for Bournemouth Rovers, became a referee and then enthusiastically influential in the Hampshire FA, graduating to the Football Association's council in 1888 even briefly its President in 1937.

One of his last works was writing the Introduction to *The Story of the Football League* that was published after his death on 5 November 1938. With Alfred Gibson he had compiled the 1905 four volume classic *Association Football and the Men Who Made It*. A year later he penned *How to Referee*.

Ted Robbins was appointed Secretary of the FA of Wales from 1910 and was more than a figurehead involving himself in everything Welsh including acting as team manager, There were also several long-serving people attached to football clubs. George Ramsay came to Aston Villa as a player in 1876, captained the team became a committee member and then secretary until 1935. Nearby West Bromwich Albion had appointed Fred Everiss as Secretary in 1902. Charlie Paynter at West Ham United began with them as a player in 1900, was appointed assistant trainer two years later and trainer in 1912. From 1932 he was team-manager. Sheffield Wednesday's assistant secretary was Eric Taylor who took on the role in August 1929.

Nicholas Lane Jackson known affectionately as "Pa" died on 1 November 1937 in Teignmouth approaching his 88th birthday. Best known as the founder of the Corinthians and a staunch advocate of amateurism, he claimed birth in London altered his age but had started life in Devon. However, he was the man who invented "cap" for international players.

Nine managers or secretary-managers were still in the same place by 1939 though two then had a change. George Jobey had been installed at Derby County since 1915, Charles Webb at Brighton from 1919 as was Charles Foweraker with Bolton Wanderers. Harry Curtis started with Brentford in 1926 while both Major Frank Buckley with Wolves and Jack Tinn at Portsmouth began in 1927. Johnny Cochrane's reign at Sunderland from 1928 ended in 1939 when he briefly took over Reading. Clem Stephenson began his stint at Huddersfield Town in 1929.

Huddersfield Town was the club Leslie Knighton assisted in a managerial capacity and in three years was similarly involved with Manchester City. However, he was surprisingly selected to take over as Arsenal manager in 1919. His tenure ended in 1925 but he landed the position at Bournemouth. Birmingham was his next stop from 1928 until Chelsea secured him in 1933. He left Stamford Bridge at the end of 1938-39.

How much hands-on the training side of football varied with these people. Foweraker at Bolton was more of a desk-jockey concerned with efficient administrative duties, leaving the training of players to George Eccles and then Bob Young. Foweraker previously assistant secretary at Bolton received the Football League's Long Service Medal in 1938.

That chief architect of the off-side trap as a player was Bill McCracken who managed Hull City from 1923 to 1931. After a two year gap he guided Millwall until 1936. His next post was at Aldershot in early 1937.

Then there was "Honest" John McKenna associated with Liverpool for 40 years initially as Secretary then Manager and later Chairman as well as President of the Football League from 1917 until his death on 22 March 1936. Was at the helm when the controversial decision was made to put Woolwich Arsenal up for a place in the expanded First Division in 1919 when they had finished sixth in the Second Division in the last full season of 1914-15.

FROM MODESTY TO MAJORITY

To adequately appreciate the Arsenal success story of the 1930s, it is necessary to examine the politics surrounding their rise from modest beginnings in South London. Formed by workers at Woolwich Arsenal in 1886, who were mostly from the north and midlands employed there on munitions, they shuffled around four different grounds, one of them twice, until settling once again at the Manor Ground in Plumstead .

The need for basics when the team was formed was such that there was no kit, not even a ball. Two of the workers Fred Beardsley and Morris Bates had played for Nottingham Forest and famously contacted their former cub who donated a set of red shirts.

Briefly known as Dial Square FC – after a particular workshop – then as Royal Arsenal, playing successes and growing support prompted the club's committee to decide on turning professional in 1891. Appropriately named, the prime mover behind the idea was John Humble. This was a brave if somewhat foolhardy idea as the deep south of the country was the last outpost of amateurism. The London FA banned them and the club had to rely on friendly opposition, ironically from the midlands and the north. However, they were allowed in the FA Cup which was under the jurisdiction of the Football Association.

In 1893, a limited company was formed and the name changed to Woolwich Arsenal. A successful application was made to the Football League for entry into the Second Division, which was being increased to 16 clubs. The Football League still referred to them as Royal Arsenal until 1896. In 1903-04 there was promotion to the First Division as runners-up. But finances fluctuated until a crisis came in 1910. The club went into voluntary liquidation.

Along came Henry Norris, chairman of Fulham, who had two notions: one to amalgamate with his own club and the other to share Craven Cottage. Neither scheme was welcomed by the Football League. The well-connected Norris, who was Fulham's mayor, a Freemason and personal friend of the Archbishop of Canterbury became Arsenal's majority shareholder. But the team continued to suffer and another blow came with relegation back to the Second Division in 1912-13. Norris, who was chairman by now, had been searching around for alternative accommodation and landed a suitable venue at Highbury in North London, thanks to his Church of England connections. So Woolwich Arsenal upped sticks.

One of Norris' acquaintances was "Honest" John McKenna, Irish born chairman of Liverpool. From 1917, the year Norris was knighted, McKenna became President of the Football League. Whether by inferred influence or other less reputable shenanigans, Arsenal were able to get themselves promoted back to the First Division in 1919 despite finishing only fifth in the 1914-15 Second Division, the last official season until the cessation of hostilities.

Norris appointed Leslie Knighton as manager though the new appointee had only held subsidiary roles at both Huddersfield Town and Manchester City. Norris was very much the iron fist in the iron glove and Knighton had to handle himself carefully in making decisions of his own. But no substantial progress was made in terms of playing success and in 1925 Norris sacked Knighton and persuaded Herbert Chapman to leave Huddersfield Town in the middle of their three-in-a-row championship run. It proved to be a master stroke. That same year the Highbury ground was purchased for £64,000, a sizeable expenditure at the time. Norris also called on his ecclesiastical links to have the ban removed on Good Friday and Christmas Day home matches.

Highbury was then transformed in the 1930s to become the envy of less financially sound clubs. London had not suffered as harshly as industrial centres and naturally there was resentment justified or not towards Arsenal. Between March 1932 and May 1934 Arsenal spent £22,250 on three centre-forwards: Coleman, Dunne and Drake. The team, the ground and even the playing surface was improved.

In the summer of 1932 Chapman arranged for the Highbury pitch to be ploughed up. The top surface was removed by three inches and replaced with one inch of consolidated fibrous turf plus three inches of ordinary turf from the Greystoke Golf Club in Ealing.

In 1931 the banking at the North End was increased and a year later extensive work was started on a new double-decker state of the art West Stand on the existing banking, incidentally opened by the Prince of Wales on 10 December 1932. Seating for 4,000 and standing accommodation for 17,000 it cost £50,000. Electric lifts, ten guineas a season ticket, carpeted lounge, club rooms, cocktail bar, luncheon and tea facilities, tip-up armchair seats for the privileged. A huge clock costing £500 was erected on the top of the North Bank and when this was covered in 1935, it was transferred to the opposite end which became known as the Clock End. Little wonder the turnover was £100,000 a season.

Then in 1936 the pinnacle was reached with a new East Stand at the Avenell Road side of Highbury rivalling the West Stand but with additional installations for players and executive facilities plus an impressive main entrance. There were five floors featuring two tiers each catering for 4,000 seated spectators and a small paddock at the front. The cost was a colossal £130,000. Unsurprisingly Arsenal was known as "The Bank of England" club.

Despite these ground improvements in September 1937 it was said that Arsenal was outgrowing Highbury. While the "bob-a-nob" customers were catered for, there was the ten guinea enclosure and a newspaper reporter noted that the car park paraded "six fur coats and a Rolls Royce owned by the BBC."

Tom Whittaker has the Arsenal men running on the spot

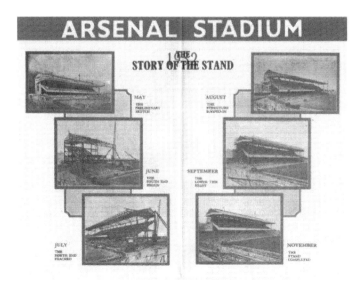

Arsenal's new West Stand at Highbury was opened by the Prince of Wales in 1932

WE WERE THE CHAMPIONS

Arsenal 1930-31, FA Cup winners in 1930. Back; Baker, Lambert, Preedy, Seddon, Hapgood, John.
Centre; Herbert Chapman (manager), Jack, Parker, James, Whittaker (trainer). Front; Hulme, Bastin.

WE ARE THE CHAMPIONS: ARSENAL

Arsenal was undoubtedly the club of the 1930s with five championship successes and two FA Cup wins, yet half-way through the period following their third successive First Division title, not only had they passed their peak, the overall impetus given to goal scoring by the change in the off-side law had already started to fade. Even so, while the Gunners attack became less potent, the defence remained as formidable as ever. In the last six seasons of the decade they conceded less than 50 goals each term.

Many reasons have been put forward to explain the club's overall success. The leadership at the top was fundamental, as were tactics developed under the new off-side law and the financial resources possessed to recruit the best players available. They bristled with internationals, some 28 capped for the four home countries from the end of the Great War. During this same time frame the Arsenal reserve team won the Combination eleven times including five in succession from 1926-27 and on seven occasions in the 1930s alone.

Naturally the untimely death in January 1934 of the club's mentor and manager Herbert Chapman, mid-way through the team's League hat trick, was a crucial factor and though his successor George Allison was a different species of head man, he could not be looked upon as the reason for the subsequent lessening of trophies in the Highbury cabinet. In fact in real terms honours were split evenly between them, each being in charge for two and a half seasons in League championship seasons and one apiece for the FA Cup trophies.

Chapman, secured from Huddersfield Town in 1925 by Sir Henry Norris the controversial Arsenal chairman, when the Yorkshire club was in the midst of its own then unprecedented three-in-a-row titles, was not an instant success if honours were the yardstick. But he gradually fashioned what was to follow. However, in his first season Chapman was able to guide Arsenal to a runners-up position, satisfactorily enough behind Huddersfield, too, following the Londoners' struggles even to stay in the division after the Great War.

Chapman persuaded Norris, who had previously limited transfers to £1,000 and required players to be at least 5ft 8in and eleven stones in weight, to untie his tight purse strings and fixation on the size of new recruits. One of the new manager's first signings was Charlie Buchan from Sunderland, the player who had been a Woolwich Arsenal amateur two decades earlier but had been lost through a dispute over expenses. The gangling Buchan was at 33 a veteran by 1925 and signed for £2,000 plus an incentive clause of a further £100 for each goal scored! This eventually doubled his transfer fee. There were even allegations implicating Norris in an under-the-counter financial transaction.

David Jack (Arsenal) and Tommy Law (Chelsea)

It seems the timing of Chapman's devotion to the "stopper" third back game followed a chastening defeat of seven clear goals at Newcastle on 3 October 1925. Charlie Spencer had been outstanding in the role for United and after discussions with Buchan it was decided to retain the same eleven two days later for the trip to West Ham but with a different system and approach. Arsenal won 4-0 and never regretted the change.

The next season Arsenal reached the FA Cup final for the first time and there was controversy over the goal conceded to Cardiff City, Welsh born goalkeeper Dan Lewis allowing the ball to slip through his arms off his new, unwashed jersey into the net for the only goal. The semi-final was also reached in 1927.

In October 1928, the club paid a record £10,890 to Bolton Wanderers for the tall, elegant David Jack as a replacement for the now retired Buchan. In May 1929 the constructively aware, lethal finishing Exeter City left-wing prodigy Cliff "Boy" Bastin was signed at £2,000 and a month later Scotland's ace Alex James arrived from Preston North End after a £8,750 transfer. However, the pocket-sized schemer was initially unpopular and not fully fit suffering from injuries sustained earlier in his career. Another blow came when following a lost court action, Norris' misdemeanours finally caught up with him and he was banned from football involvement for life. At one time, of course, he had wanted a merger with Fulham!

In 1919, Arsenal who had finished only fifth in the Second Division in 1915 had been elected as one of two additional teams to the First Division receiving ten more votes than relegated Tottenham Hotspur. League President John McKenna, a friend of Norris' had urged clubs to vote for Arsenal because of their longer association with the competition. Yet one of the original twelve Football League clubs Wolverhampton Wanderers had finished higher than Arsenal!

Be that as it may, Arsenal had, it appeared, settled at best as a post-war mid-table team, but the 1929-30 season saw them as low as 14th with eleven drawn matches including a remarkable share of twelve goals with Leicester City on Easter Monday. On 25 September 1929 they had lost 5-2 away to Aston Villa. Only one of the last eleven games ended in victory but that was 8-1 over Sheffield United. Then again the 2-0 FA Cup victory over Huddersfield Town was particularly significant.

Chelsea was beaten in the third round, but Birmingham required a replay before Middlesbrough and West Ham United were defeated. Hull City provided stoic opposition at Elland Road and victory was narrowly achieved at the Villa Park replay. James opened the scoring after 16 minutes, Lambert with two minutes remaining. For part of the match the ominous shape of German airship *Graf Zeppelin* flew over Wembley.

On the field it was all to change dramatically the next season. In 1930-31, Arsenal became the first club based in the south of England to carry off the First Division championship and did so in some style with a record 66 points. The team virtually selected itself. Ten of the eleven who started the season featured in the last match. But centre-forward Jimmy Brain left in September for neighbours Tottenham having scored 139 League and Cup goals in 231 such outings. Alf "Doughy" Baker retired at the season's end after 403 League and Cup appearances. Ostensibly a right-half he had the distinction of having played in every position in the first team including goal.

Bastin was ever present, reliable skipper at right-back Tom Parker missed one, Herbie Roberts, Bob John and the now favourite James were absent just twice each. Of the 22 players used including three goalkeepers, six made only eleven outings between them. Right-half Charlie Jones, once a winger, missed a chunk of games in the early stages, but Bill Seddon proved an able replacement on the 18 occasions required. Of the 127 League goals – one short of the Aston Villa record – Jumping Jack Lambert cracked 38 goals in clusters over 34 games, David Jack 31 in 35 matches. Bastin weighed in with 28. Home and away records were identical. There were 28 wins. Only four League games were lost: at Derby and Villa Park, at home against Newcastle United and Sunderland all spread over the season. At Villa they suffered a 5-1 reverse on 14 March. Three changes were made for the next match including one positional.

Naturally the emphasis was on attack. The threats came from both wings and the double spearhead. Manipulating this strategy was Alex James, lying far deep in his own half, feeding both flanks and cutting long searching passes into the heart of the opposing defence. He was the link between defence and attack in what was virtually a 3-1-2- 4 system; in reality a variation of the WM formation (3-2-2-3) at the time. Ivan Sharpe called him "The little King of no-man's land." Bastin on the left-wing without a close-by inside partner was ideally placed with space to exploit his attacking instincts. Universally of course, teams continued to be listed in 2-3-5 formation.

Individually, Joe Hulme was edgy before a game but fast on the field, crossed and finished well. Bastin was even-tempered able to appreciate his dual role and an accurate marksman. Jack had the knack of allowing the ball to fox his opponents whenever possible. James subjugated his attacking instincts for his deep-lying role and Lambert was a reliable finisher in the air and on the ground.

In 1931-32, Arsenal came close to a League and Cup double but fell in both challenges, just two points adrift of Everton and cruelly defeated at Wembley by Newcastle in the disputed over-the-goal-line affair. Again it was chiefly a settled eleven barring injuries. Eddie Hapgood was absent just once, wingers Hulme and Bastin twice apiece. These two plus Jack and Lambert contributed to all but 14 of the 90 scored in the championship apart from four own goals. Jack scored in nine consecutive matches. In March 1932 Ernest "Tim" Coleman was signed from Grimsby for £8,000.

On 31 October 1931 against Aston Villa, James hit a pass from inside his own half in a straight line. Jack had no more than three touches over 50 yards, feinted and body swerved past five defenders before scoring in the 1-1 draw.

For 1932-33, the racking up of 118 goals helped immeasurably in regaining the First Division crown and Chapman had introduced white sleeves to the red shirts for the first time, after a trial the previous March. On 12 November the new stand was opened at Highbury and Gillespie Road Underground station was now known as "Arsenal." The Gunners beat Newcastle 1-0. Again there was controversy. A classic move involving Hapgood, Bastin and James led on to Coleman's pinpoint pass enabling Hulme casually to walk the ball in. Newcastle claimed off-side. Seven days later Arsenal lost a classic encounter at Aston Villa 5-3. But by Christmas, Arsenal had dropped only six points from a possible 40 having gone to the top in late October. In March and April 1933 Ray Bowden from Plymouth at £4,500 and Ralph Birkett from Torquay were signed in a West Country raid.

Alas, the New Year brought an abrupt stall. In well contested away matches to Sheffield Wednesday and Sunderland, there were 3-2 defeats. The real shock was seven days later when being dismissed by Third Division (South) Walsall 2-0 in the FA Cup, a result that reverberated inside and outside the marble halls of Highbury. For once Chapman had erred. Changes through injury had to be made, but wrong ones and he quickly swung the axe after his own mistakes. Another blip occurred in March when only one point was taken from four games, but the final outcome was positive. On 22 April the 3-1 win at Chelsea secured the title with two matches to spare. Bastin the only ever present scored 33 goals.

The start of 1933-34 saw both flying winger Hulme and James injured in the drawn opener with Birmingham and both, especially the former, missed many matches. Hulme subsequently had a knee operation. Derby were said to be interested in James, who even watched them when off injured! Such was the pull of anything Arsenal on 7 December the *Daily Express* front page story referring to James having been censored by the referee in the Charity Shield match in October and calling him "the world's greatest player," dwarfed the report of Lindburgh's second round the world flight!

Another interesting statistic was on 4 December when Arsenal beat a Vienna XI 4-2 that included eight players who had a week earlier appeared for Austria in the international against Scotland that ended in a 2-2 draw.

The defence conceded only 47 goals, the best such record since the change in the off-side law. But the attack needed strengthening with the reliable Lambert nearing the veteran stage, so the prolific Jimmy Dunne at Sheffield United was recruited, though he proved less lethal in his new surroundings. David Jack was rumoured to be the next Arsenal manager and was also moving closer to the end of his Highbury career. He almost went to Charlton Athletic before leaving for the manager's job at Southend United in the summer, his boyhood town. He had scored 123 League and Cup goals in 206 Arsenal matches. Moreover loss of Chapman's hand on Highbury had been immediately felt, being held by Sheffield Wednesday on 6 January the sad day itself and then three successive League defeats, though in fairness, two FA Cup ties were won.

Even so, interest continued to increase and on 31 January the visit of neighbours Tottenham Hotspur produced a ground record of 68,674 and the highest for any midweek League game with receipts of £5,300. A last minute Bastin goal on 21 February and Arsenal returned to the top 2-1 against Blackburn. FA Cup receipts for the Derby County tie on 17 February yielded £6,154 from a 66,905 attendance and on 3 March Aston Villa attracted 67,366 with £6,366 taken at the gate. While that was the end of the cup run, on 28 April the First Division title was retained. As a postscript both Jack and James played in the last game and George Male was the only ever present.

Late in the campaign George Allison had persuaded one-time gas meter inspector Ted Drake to sign from Southampton in a £6,500 transfer and it proved instantly successful. His seven goals in ten matches helped immeasurably towards the triumph, though the general feeling was that Arsenal had performed well considering the loss of their mentor, but in an overall disappointing season.

In the wake of Chapman's untimely passing, Joe Shaw had been appointed team manager with director Allison given an overall managerial role until his official appointment as secretary-manager on 28 May. However, another constantly stable factor during this changeover period was Tom Whittaker the Arsenal trainer, whose contribution throughout the era was fundamental to the successes achieved on the field. He produced a book on systems for training which was freely available to players.

In 1934-35 there were occasional defeats but never two in sequence. Drake was a revelation scoring a club record 42 League goals and missing just one match. His haul included four four-timers and three hat tricks from the team's 115 goals in total. On 2 February 1935 James of all people scored a hat trick in the 4-1 win over Sheffield Wednesday! Three weeks later on 23 February at Maine Road, the crowd at Manchester City was a colossal Football League record of 79,491. In the crucial game against Everton at Goodison Park on 16 March, goalkeeper Frank Moss dislocated his shoulder, went on the left wing and scored! Drake had the other goal. Easter Monday at Middlesbrough clinched the third consecutive record equalling championship for Arsenal and their fourth in five seasons. Summer invitations came from Africa, South America and even Russia!

James was the deliberately long-shorted short legged genius balanced with a perfect low centre of gravity looking even smaller than his 5ft 6in with sleeves flapping. He subjugated scoring for scheming to suit Arsenal's needs, his fluttering foot a prelude to opening defences. The departed David Jack was a smoker had a sweet tooth, wrote a weekly column for the *Evening Standard* and could have had a Civil Service career, had always appeared taller than a shade off 5ft 11in. He was adroit at allowing the ball to beat opponents by sleight of foot even in front of goal mesmerising defenders with a double-shuffle before the *coup de grace* of a telling shot. It was a priceless pairing.

But 1935-36 saw the previous season's runners-up Sunderland win the championship with Arsenal finishing sixth yet winning the FA Cup against Sheffield United with a Drake goal. Fifteen drawn matches by the Gunners had not helped their championship cause. Still their pull at the box office was irresistible. On 12 October at Chelsea, some 82.905 filled Stamford Bridge for a 1-1 draw; a Football League record standing for all time. Another one, this time personal, befell Drake on 14 December away to Aston Villa. He had nine attempts at goal and scored seven times! Twenty-nine players were used in League games.

Drake was injured playing for England in February and missed most of the rest of the season. But there was FA Cup success and in the semi-final at Huddersfield against Grimsby Town 63,210 attended with receipts of £5,260, both ground records. A heavily-bandaged Drake was back for the Cup Final and scored the only goal.

On the Wembley way, Bristol Rovers and Liverpool were negotiated but old cup foes Newcastle forced a replay before Barnsley and Grimsby Town opened the door to the final. There had been a scare when George Allison collapsed early in December 1935 but he was back at his desk before the holiday period. Thirty-one players were retained, Jimmy Dunne and George Cox listed, the former signed for Southampton, the latter moving to Fulham. In the London Challenge Cup final Alf Kirchen scored three against Brentford.

There was no joy in 1936-37, though 14 internationals were at Highbury, Arsenal in third place with Manchester City top. After a hugely disappointing first dozen games, the Gunners became draw champions with 16 including four in a row during March. Injuries were such that no player was ever present. But the North Londoners stayed as the team everyone wanted to see – and defeat of course. On 17 October away to Charlton Athletic at The Valley, The Gunners won 2-0 in front of 68,160. On 10 April 1937 at Maine Road when Manchester City beat Arsenal 2-0 there were 74,918 present.

Even so, the accumulative statistics were impressive. It had been the sixth time in seven seasons of finishing in the first three, four as champions. In the last eight of the FA Cup, it was the tenth occasion thus far in a dozen seasons including taking two trophies and twice being runners-up. Early in the season Arsenal had approached Wolves for Bryn Jones, with a fee of £10,000 thought to have been offered. It was also rumoured that £12,000 had been mentioned for Hearts Scottish international Tommy Walker.

Still back as winners in 1937-38 the Gunners recorded their fifth League success in eight seasons. Manchester City the previous champions were even relegated despite scoring more goals than any other in the First Division! On 9 October when four goals were shared at Chelsea, the crowd was 75,952. In a see-saw season there were eight changes at the top of the table, goal scoring continued its slump to 1,430 of which Arsenal's contribution of 77 was the lowest by a championship-winning team since Sheffield Wednesday's 86 in 1928-29. But the defence conceded only 44, a figure equalled by Preston North End. Oddly enough in the fifth round of the FA Cup, Preston won 1-0 at Highbury. The receipts were £7,214 from a 72,121 attendance. In January Hulme joined Huddersfield after 372 League and Cup appearances and 124 goals.

On 18 April Brentford beat Arsenal 3-0 at Griffin Park leaving the Gunners, Preston and Wolves level on 46 points, Wolves with a game in hand. In the Brentford match a clearing punch by the home goalkeeper laid out Drake who had to retire to the wing on recovering.

It had not been a vintage championship for Arsenal, but Herbie Roberts was out injured from the end of October, Drake missed fifteen games. Alex James had retired. George Male completed his fifth stint with a championship-winning Arsenal. Eddie Hapgood missed one match with no ever present players among the 29 called upon. One Sunday there were 13 injured players. But reserves proved their worth, the amateur Bernard Joy proving an able deputy for Roberts and the diminutive Eddie Carr brought back from Margate a surprisingly able marksman in the last three crucial wins, the last on the final day with a point to spare over Wolverhampton Wanderers. There was a mere 52 points enough for title number five, only sixteen more points than the bottom club. Bob John retired after 15 years and 467 League and Cup appearances. Roberts with 333 such outings then helped out on the training staff. Again 29 players were used.

Personnel changes had seen some notable replacements for established players no longer at Highbury. Right-winger Alf Kirchen who cost £6,000 after a protracted negotiation from Norwich could also play centre-forward, Reg Crayston £5,250 in instalments from Bradford City and bristle-chinned Wilf Copping ex-Leeds £8,000 as wing-halves all won England caps, as did George Male at right-back. Joy, too, won full international recognition despite his continuing amateur status. Bryn Jones the record £14,000 signing from Wolverhampton Wanderers on 4 August 1938 was a Welsh international inside-forward. The weight of the transfer tag and different environment proved too much of a handicap for him. There was also the need for him and the team to change style as the replacement for James.

Everton won its second title of the decade in 1938-39 with Arsenal in fifth place. This came after Allison had at last managed to convince Wolves over Bryn Jones. With the uncertainty over the situation in Europe, gates suffered all over, Arsenal losing some 5,000 on average over the campaign. Another indifferent start, failing to score in eleven matches, Drake top scorer yet with only 14 goals, even appeared on the right wing with Reg Lewis leading the attack. Again 29 players were paraded on League duty Joy missing just three outings and the Gunners dumped out of the FA Cup at Chelsea in the third round, only the second similar early exit in the decade.

Skipper Eddie Hapgood took his total of League and Cup games to 434. Cliff Bastin who had scored his 150th League goal against Sunderland on 4 February had completed 384 League and Cup appearances as well as scoring 176 goals. The era was at an end.

Arsenal 1935. Back; Bowden, Hill, Compton (L), Moss, Whittaker (trainer), Sidey, Drake, Crayston.
Front; Hulme, Beasley, Bastin, George Allison (manager), Hapgood, Dougall, Copping

Everton 1932. Back: Thomson, Clark, Gee, Sagar, Williams, Cresswell, Bocking. Front: Crichtley, Dunn, Dean, Johnson, Stein, White

Everton, the team the peerless Steve Bloomer labelled the "School of Science," won the First Division title twice in the period and the FA Cup once, but the dawn of 1930 coincided with relegation for the first time in their history. This had come only two seasons after winning the championship in swashbuckling fashion, with Bill "Dixie" Dean plundering 60 League goals, a figure his team scored in home games alone.

That Dean had recovered from horrendous injury from a motor-cycle crash in March 1925 to play again had been amazing. He had suffered a fractured skull, broken jaw, facial lacerations and damage to his right knee spending four months recuperating in a nursing home.

In 1929-30 by early December, Everton though seventh from the bottom remained only two points from it. A mere five wins in the first half of the season they scratched only one point from seven games into April. Amazingly they dropped just one point in the last five games but to no avail. Dean contributed 23 goals in only 25 League outings.

But they regained their status immediately in 1930-31 showing remarkable resilience and scoring 121 goals in the process to finish seven points ahead in the Second Division. League games involving the Goodison Park club averaged over four goals, a feast of scoring indeed. Dean struck 39 in 37 League games, Jimmy Dunn and Tommy Johnson 14 each, Ted Critchley 13, Jimmy Stein and Tommy White ten goals each. There was the statistical quirk of conceding 66 goals, the same figure let in during 1927-28 when they hit 102 themselves. On 7 February 1931 when playing away to Charlton Athletic all five forwards scored in an 18 minute flourish. The final score was 7-0. From 27 December when they defeated Plymouth Argyle 9-1 with Dean scoring four goals they won 14 consecutive League and Cup matches and ended the run beating Reading 3-2 on 7 March 1931.

On 6 December 1930 Dean scored four in the 6-4 win over Oldham. He scored in twelve consecutive League games, a total of 23 in this run. He had another four-timer against Plymouth and two more foursomes in the FA Cup against Southport and Crystal Palace. Everton failed to score only twice in the League at Tottenham and Stoke.

So, despite having Arsenal complete the double over them in 1931-32, Everton still succeeded in carrying off the championship just two points in front of the North London team scoring 116 goals – Dean 45 of them. It was close and at one stage prospects for Everton looked bleak. From December to mid-February they struggled taking only eight points from eleven matches, yet with few changes to personnel throughout. Steady nerves were rewarded.

Perhaps more of a surprise, their challengers suffered, too, so Everton stayed marginally in first place. In full flow with their traditional sweeping passes to the wings and the deadly Dean and others awaiting delivery, they were an attractive, effective combination. They could even afford just three points from the last four outings.

Only three regular players survived these five seasons Warney Cresswell, Critchley and Bill Dean who preferred being called thus. Though there were no ever present players, of the 20 used, eight of them contributed only 34 appearances between them. Goalkeeper Ted Sagar and inside-left Tommy Johnson missed just one game each, Cresswell two.

Wing halves Archie Clark and Jock Thomson missed three games each, centre-half Charlie Gee and Dean were both absent four times, while Critchley and left-winger Stein both made 37 appearances. Right-back Ben Williams, a Welsh international, contributed 33 to the overall total while Scotland cap Dunn at inside-right shared his watch with the versatile White who weighed in with an invaluable 18 goals in 23 outings.

There was no clear cut advantage to any team in the opening weeks until West Bromwich Albion took over for a spell. Everton struck the front in late October and kept ahead while a chasing pack remained theoretically well in touch, albeit lacking consistency.

Naturally there was disappointment in 1932-33 when the team finished eleventh mid-table throughout, too but success at Wembley in the FA Cup provided much cheer. Leicester City, Bury and Leeds United were the early victims and six goals saw off Luton Town. West Ham United was beaten 2-1 at Molineux in the semi-final, then Manchester City in the final with goals from Dean, Dunn and Stein. Left-back Warney Cresswell at 38 years 175 days was the competition's second oldest finalist .A first time novelty in this match was the numbering of players but Everton handed shirts 1 to 11, City 12 to 22!

Then there was a tailing-off to 14th position in the table for Everton in 1933-34. A stuttering start and not one win in the last six matches. Actually there were just two victories in the last 15 and overall 16 drawn affairs. The team was being rebuilt but the foundations were taking time to settle in. Eighth was the finishing slot in 1934-35 with four wins in the last 15 games but there was a cup tie to live long in the memory on 30 January 1935 against Sunderland in the FA Cup fourth round replay at Goodison. On Christmas Day Everton had beaten Sunderland 6-2 in the League.

The teams had drawn 1-1 on 26 January at Roker Park. Four days after there were ten goals on offer for the 59,231 attracted to Goodison. In the first ten minutes referee Ernest Pinckston cautioned three players. There was no more trouble. Leading In 14 minutes through Jackie Coulter he doubled the score on the half-hour. Everton looked settled. But Sunderland cut the margin a minute before the break through Bert Davis.

Everton restored the two-goal advantage on the hour from Alex Stevenson only for Sunderland to reduce it when Connor netted four minutes later and at the death Bob Gurney equalised to send the match into extra time. In 90 seconds Coulter completed his hat-trick yet still the visitors levelled at 4-4 via Connor within two minutes of the extra period. In the 107th minute Gurney missed a sitter. But it was Albert Geldard who turned it for Everton with two memorable goals in the 111th and 119th minutes for a breathtaking 6-4 victory. Wingers had accounted for eight of the ten goals.

Henry Rose in the Daily Express said: "It was the greatest cup-tie I have ever seen." But Bolton ended the run

In the League after that, a further slip to 16th in 1935-36. Everton won just two games in succession – the last pair. Dean missed 13 matches and had a cartilage operation. Everton tried to sign Gallacher during his absence. Jimmy Cunliffe led the scorers with 23 goals. Seventeenth in 1936-37 when there was an unusual statistic: after 3 March a 7-1 win over Leeds was to be the last of the term for the Toffees. A few weeks earlier teenager Tommy Lawton was a scoring debutant in a 7-2 defeat at Wolves.

Fourteenth in 1937-38 with never more than two wins in a row again gave no real hint of better fortune ahead. Moreover they had to step lively in the losing weeks to escape relegation. It should be mentioned that only three points separated the bottom nine clubs! Dean had been injured early that campaign and moved on to Notts County, but his successor was already installed.

Thus teenager Tommy Lawton, plucked from Burnley at the cost of £6,500 in March 1937 took over principal scoring responsibility from the man who had racked up 349 goals in 399 League games. In 1937-38 the youngster scored 28 and reached his 18th birthday on 6 October to become the youngest player to finish a season as the leading scorer in Division One. While Dean and Lawton were roughly the same height and weight, the former seemed heavier, the latter taller. In February 1938 Wally Boyes was signed from West Bromwich for £7,000. On 22 January 1938 Sunderland's FA Cup visit brought 68,158 to Goodison Park.

Everything changed dramatically for Everton in 1938-39. Six straight wins in a flying start, the best since the war, Lawton scoring in each. Though Derby County led at the end of October, Everton had a game in hand. The Rams held them 2-2 at Goodison on Boxing Day, too. It stayed thus until 4 February when Everton won the Merseyside derby at Anfield 3-0 while Derby were losing at Chelsea. The Toffees batteries were recharged by this time, a fine run of 16 games interrupted astonishingly by another 7-0 defeat at Wolverhampton Wanderers on 22 February on a muddy Molineux. Wolves in fact finished four points behind the champions Everton.

Much emphasis had been made on passing and the frequent use of six-a-side practice with rubber boots was thought to have been a contributory factor to the success achieved. For Lawton he always kept up his regime of half an hour's shooting practice each day.

Ten of the squad played mostly all season, only at left-half where ever-reliable Gordon Watson took over from injured skipper Jock Thomson, was there any significant alteration. Norman Greenhalgh at left-back was an ever present player, Stan Bentham at inside-right, Joe Mercer at right-half and Sagar in goal missed only one match, while both right-back Billy Cook and right-winger Tory Gillick were absent only twice. Tommy (TG) Jones at centre-half figured in all but three games, Lawton with 34 goals was absent on four occasions, inside-left Alex Stevenson and his left wing partner Boyes contributed 36 League appearances each. Two of Lawton's non-appearances were due to being on England internationals, Boyes and Mercer were similarly occupied on one occasion. The remaining ten players called upon made only 26 League appearances between them and four of these had just one game. Sagar took his total of League and Cup appearances to 321. Thomson acted as third team coach for their mid-week games.

All this was achieved without a manager as such! Theo Kelly hitherto Secretary, assumed the role in 1939; the last major club to appoint one in this capacity. Previously a loose arrangement between trainers, directors and committee men had been responsible for team selection. Key essentials to this arrangement were Harry Cooke the first team trainer and Chairman Will Cuff.

Everton 1939. Back: Lawton, Jones, Sagar, Cooke (trainer), Mercer, Greenhalgh. Front: Cook, Gillick, Bentham, Thomson, Stevenson, Boyes

WE ARE THE CHAMPIONS: SHEFFIELD WEDNESDAY

With two successive championships in the locker, Sheffield Wednesday appeared favourites to land a Huddersfield Town-equalling three-in-a-row in 1930-31. In 1929-30 early home defeats by Arsenal and leaders Leeds United were swept aside. Second behind Manchester City, the Owls were top in the New Year with a game to spare. Accumulating more in hand on the way, they winged it to the title with 105 goals, ten points clear of the opposition. Between 5 April and 3 May they had played 11 matches.

But there had been controversy in the FA Cup in 1929-30. On 22 March 1930 in the semi-final against Huddersfield the referee blew for time as Jack Allen's shot was crossing the goal line. It was ruled out and Wednesday lost 2-1.

The outcome in 1930-31 proved to be a three-way challenge with Arsenal and Aston Villa. But losing the second game of the season 2-0 at Aston Villa and beaten by Arsenal at Hillsborough in mid-November, their two potential rivals had established a psychological edge.

However, these were the only two reverses suffered by 13 December and on that day a club record 9-1 thrashing of Birmingham put the Owls top on goal average from Arsenal who had a game in hand. Wednesday recaptured the leadership early in the New Year with the Gunners having the benefit of more matches in abeyance.

By February, Arsenal had caught up on its backlog and even Aston Villa had taken second slot thanks to Wednesday suffering three defeats in succession. Yet there had been goals aplenty for the Sheffield club with 102 scored, three fewer than in 1929-30 when there was a gap of ten points ahead of the nearest rivals, contrasting the slender one point advantage in the previous title-winning effort.

In both championship seasons, Wednesday had been able to keep a fairly settled side. In each term they had called upon 22 players. Amazingly only Bob Gregg giving way in 1929-30 to Harry Burgess at inside-left in this usually featured eleven: Jack Brown; Tommy Walker, Ernie Blenkinsop, Alf Strange, Tony Leach, Billy Marsden, Mark Hooper, Jimmy Seed, Jack Allen, Gregg or Burgess and Ellis Rimmer. The additional ten players used filled in when necessary and to advantage it should be added. Brown, Blenkinsop, Strange, Leach, Marsden, Seed and Rimmer were England internationals.

Only Marsden was missing in 1930-31 when again the Owls stuck to most of the successful team of the two previous seasons. Playing for England against Germany in May 1930 he suffered a serious spinal injury which prematurely ended his career. He later coached several clubs in Holland. Chief newcomer was Jack Ball centre-forward from Manchester United, while Charles Wilson a reserve for three seasons took over Marsden's berth. The Owls were third.

After a bright start to 1931-32 from November to February only four matches were won. Ex-Derby players Gavin Malloch at left-half and George Stephenson at inside-left were two of the newer faces. A sustained improvement saw third place reached on Easter Monday. A point behind Arsenal and four below leaders Everton, Wednesday then lost 3-1 at Highbury and their rivals had games in hand, so again it was finishing third.

In 1932-33 there was the same scenario in third though on this occasion the successes were in the middle of the campaign. The championship personnel were still being replaced. Ronnie Starling inside-right and George Beeson right-back were now settling. Starling talented but inclined to beat too many players at a time. Ball scored 33 goals – including eleven penalties – four times more than any other player. Inferior goal average was unhelpful, too. Left-back Ernie Blenkinsop completed 393 League appearances.

Any prospect of a challenge in 1933-34 was damaged when only five games were won to December, though this precipitated an unbeaten League and Cup run of 17 games! Top scorer Ball was transferred by new manager Billy Walker and the final position was 11th. The prize in the following season was winning the FA Cup at Wembley. Wednesday had clear cut wins over Oldham Athletic, Wolverhampton Wanderers, Norwich City and even Arsenal before Burnley in the semi-final at Villa Park.

The final produced a tie of six goals in beating West Bromwich Albion 4-2 with two in the last five minutes from winger Rimmer. He was leading scorer with 26 League and Cup goals and registered in every round. No other Wednesday player reached double figures in the League and the lack of scoring cost them dearly. Third place achieved but five points adrift of runners-up Sunderland and nine behind Arsenal. Walter Millership finally settled to become the first choice centre-half.

That was the last hurrah. Relegation was just avoided in 1935-36 by three points when 20th. The last eleven games produced two wins and seven goals. But the drop became a reality the following term. Again the last dozen matches were the main cause. This time two wins and eleven goals and bottom place. Consistent goalkeeper Jack Brown completed 465 League appearances and had been given a benefit in 1935.

Even 17th in Division Two for 1937-38, bottom early November on goal average, improved until March. They won the last two games home to Burnley away to Spurs to survive by two points. Long serving wingers Mark Hooper and Ellis Rimmer moved on. Hooper had made 384 League appearances and scored 125 goals, Rimmer's respective totals were 382 and 122. Local bragging rights went to neighbours Sheffield United who just edged them out by a point after an exciting 1938-39 won by Blackburn Rovers just a win ahead at the top. Rimmer had previously played for Parkside, Northern Nomads and Whitchurch while had even figured in Everton's third team as an amateur.

An encouraging start was not maintained. By Christmas seventh place was steady until five successive wins in the New Year altered the situation. By mid-February Wednesday had moved to third place on goal average but with two games in hand over United. Unfortunately the old failing in the last third of the season proved costly and third position at the conclusion. Top scorer with 24 goals Doug Hunt had six of seven against Norwich City and the development through difficult seasons of Jackie Robinson as an England inside-forward featured among the few brighter spots.

In the FA Cup, Yeovil took Wednesday to a replay, Chester to two replays as did Chelsea who finally accounted for them.

Sheffield Wednesday 1930. Back:- Hopkins, Francis, Flint (E), Nixon (S), Dickinson (directors). Next to back: Turner, Hodgkiss, Webster, Johnson, Neale, Brown, Dodds, Hargreaves, Mellors, Mills, Feanehough, Rhind (directors). Front standing row: Wardley (director), Jones, Hooper, Harston, Whitehouse, Leach, Blenkinsop, Burgess, Amith, Barton, Trotman, Gunstone, Blanchard (directors). Seated on chairs: Robert Brown (manager), Hooper, Stange, Walker, William Clegg, Charles Clegg, Allen, Rimmer, Gregg, Wilson, Smith, Dean, Stephen. Front of seats: Craig (trainer), Beeson, Seed, Marsden, Hatfield, Goddard, Burridge. Front, with pennants: Wilkinson, Trotter

WE ARE THE CHAMPIONS: SUNDERLAND

Runners-up in 1934-35, Sunderland won the First Division title next time out with just two more points but over a century of goals and eight points clear of Derby County. It was their first such trophy since before the Great War and lifted them to a record joint sixth with Aston Villa.

However, the dawning of the 30s at Roker Park had seen Sunderland ninth in 1929-30 a touch over a point a game along with four other clubs and exit from the FA Cup from a fifth round replay with Nottingham Forest. Thirty-one players used. Dave Halliday moved to Arsenal after 156 goals in 166 League games while Ernie England made his 352nd and last first team appearance. On 19 October 1929 58,519 had seen Sunderland beat Newcastle 1-0. Harry Shaw, left-back was signed from Wolves that season for £7,000.

In 1930-31 two points fewer and two places lower but a semi-final appearance before a 2-0 defeat by Birmingham. Southampton, Bolton after a replay, Sheffield United, Exeter City but only after a replay away, had been the previous victims. Early November Sunderland had been second from bottom in the League table. Bob Gurney scored 31 goals in 38 League games. He had been originally spotted by Charlie Buchan.

No improvement in 1931-32 with just 40 points and out of the cup in a second replay against Stoke City. By the end of January only five wins and the team 20th but only two of the last eleven games ended in defeat and 13th as the final outcome.

They were one place higher in 1932-33 with the same points. Again a falling away and just two wins in the last 13. Still there was considerable interest in the FA Cup sixth round replay with Derby County on 8 March 1933 when Roker Park recorded its highest attendance of 75,118. Though Sunderland lost 1-0 there was cup success later. Ironically the lowest Roker Park gate followed on 29 April when Portsmouth's visit brought only 3,911; the counter-attraction of the live BBC broadcast of the FA Cup final the culprit. During the season attempts had been made to sell Roker Park to the local council.

Seemingly soldiering on as a mid-table team, improvement began in 1933-34, or at least appeared so finishing sixth, though only 44 points gained. A rarity was outside-right Bert Davis as an ever present. Also an even lower gate was recorded on 11 April when a mere 3,841 saw Manchester City draw 0-0.

Then as mentioned a second place behind Arsenal. The strategy of the team was a simple one: all-out attack from every angle. At times they mixed the third back game with five forwards. They were second highest scorers in the First Division in 1934-35 with 90 goals though 25 short of Arsenal's tally. Sunderland was also involved in an FA Cup replay of ten goals with Everton, a classic of the genre. Despite Bob Gurney's 90th minute leveller, they were beaten 6-4 in extra time.

Drawing 16 times proved unhelpful. They took three points off the champions and the seven games lost were twinned with the Gunners. Top after six games and swapping the lead with Arsenal until the New Year, only goal average kept Sunderland second before March when the draw factor was fed in. Just 21 players called upon, six of these making ten appearances in total and only in goal was there much change. Davis and right-half Charlie Thomson were ever present. Another 30 goals came the Gurney way.

Sunderland started August 1935 by losing 3-1 away to the reigning champions. Yet it was Huddersfield Town who made the early impression. That was until 26 October when the Yorkshire side lost 3-0 at Liverpool and Sunderland defeated Sheffield Wednesday 5-1 to lead the table. So tight was it that Sunderland only drawing at Portsmouth allowed Derby to slip in front. But that ended the challenges and Sunderland could even afford to lose 1-0 at Huddersfield on 14 December.

One of the best recalled matches of the season was on 28 December at Roker Park with Arsenal as the opposition. A see-saw goal feast resulted in Sunderland edging it 5-4. It clearly took its toll on the winners; the following week they lost at home for the first time in a year to bottom club Aston Villa 3-1, the Villans first away success!

Of the 109 goals rifled in, Gurney and Raich Carter each picked off 31. Gurney had been the epitome of a consistent scorer, heading their charts for seven years. Carter was a masterly general in midfield as well as an unerring marksman. Gates topped 30,000 on average – 30,378 recorded for League games. Sunderland had an eight-point lead at the end. On 23 November 1935 58,902 watched the north-east derby with Middlesbrough.

There were just two ever present members of the side Thomson and left-winger Jimmy Connor, Carter and Gurney each missed three matches. Inside-left Patsy Gallacher was absent just five times plus helping out with 19 goals. Tom Morrison and Bill Murray, both Scottish born like Thomson shared right-back duties. Well stocked with Scots left-back Alec Hall had been recruited from Dunfermline Athletic and Jimmy Clark from Clydebank Juniors, but right-winger Davis from Bradford. Carter and Gurney were capped for England, left-half Alex Hastings, Connor and Gallacher for Scotland as well as Bob Johnston who took over from Clark at centre-half. Sunderland had offered £13,000 for two Celtic players Jimmy Delaney and John Crum that season.

Murray made his 304th and last appearance and Johnny Mapson made his debut in goal. Sadly there was a tragedy. Goalkeeper Jimmy Thorpe who was diabetic, had suffered injury that accelerated his demise after some rough treatment in the 3-3 draw with Chelsea at Roker on 1 February. He died four days later.

Sunderland won the Charity Shield 2-1 in October 1936, but in the League back to eighth with a leaky defence especially on travel. From a meagre start, top on 21 November before a 1-1 draw with Arsenal in January began a slight decline. Still there was a successful FA Cup run. This included the disposing of Southampton, Luton Town after a replay, Swansea Town and Wolverhampton Wanderers at the third attempt! A 2-1 win in the semi-final was achieved over Third Division Millwall at Huddersfield, then beating Preston North End 3-1 at Wembley in the final with Carter, Gurney and Burbanks on target. In 1937-38, Sunderland tailed off in the League to eighth from a mid-table look all season and then disappointingly doubled the descent to as low as 16th in 1938-39 again without any real impetus all season. Gurney signed off with 228 goals from 390 League and Cup appearances. In March 1939 John Cochrane who had guided Sunderland well during his reign of eleven years resigned and briefly became Reading manager.

Some shrewd business in the transfer market in 1937-38 had seen one-time £10 signing-on fee reserve players Jimmy Clark transferred to Plymouth £3,500, Sandy McNab to West Bromwich £6,500 and Les McDowall £7,000 to Manchester City.

*Sunderland 1936, players only: Back: Carter, Thomson, Hall, Mapson, Hastings, Collin, Clark.
Front: Davis, Gurney, Gallacher, Connor*

WE ARE THE CHAMPIONS: MANCHESTER CITY

Manchester City's best years were wedged in the middle of the 30s as runners-up in the 1933 FA Cup, winners the following year plus taking the First Division title in 1936-37. It represented their peak. While the fall from the summit was swift it was to be gloriously so.

On the way to the 1933 final Gateshead drew with City but then collapsed conceding nine goals in the replay. Walsall, Burnley and Bolton were beaten and Derby, too, by the odd goal in five for the semi-final. In the final, hopes depended on the tactical know-how of inside-left Jimmy McMullan then a 38 year old veteran of Scotland's "Wembley Wizards" fame. But unluckily for him in his last competitive match he wore the No.13 shirt! Everton with correct numbers won 3-0. Fred Tilson City's clever but injury-prone sharp shooter was absent, but made his mark a year later with four of the six goals against Aston Villa in the semi-final and both in the 2-0 Wembley win over Portsmouth.

The 1934 cup-winning team was captained by the veteran Sam Cowan at centre-half. It also included Matt Busby at right-half. At the final whistle young goalkeeper Frank Swift famously fainted! *En route* to the Empire Stadium, City had beaten Blackburn Rovers but needed two attempts at both Hull City and Sheffield Wednesday then accounted for Stoke City before the semi-final. A crowd of 84,569 attended the Stoke tie on 3 March, a record crowd for a match outside London.

Tragically that year saw the untimely death of trainer Alex Bell at 52. Born in South Africa, but a pre-war Scottish international and Manchester United half-back in their famous middle trio, he was a dietary devotee who advertised his regime in the national newspapers.

As to the League, finishing third in 1929-30 after one win in nine from Boxing Day put a brake on any serious hopes of much better fortune allied to inconsistency in the run-in. There was a 10-1 FA Cup replay win over Swindon. England international Tom Johnson completed 354 League and Cup appearances and 166 goals before finding pastures new. City ended eighth in 1930-31 following a stumbling start yet fleetingly fourth in February and down to 14th in 1931-32 with indifferent opening and closing sequences during the season. Half the League games were lost in 1932-33. Another ordinary start, bottom mid-October and still in danger by April before finishing 16th.

In 1933-34 a fifth finish without ever looking capable of anything higher, only once winning three in a row, City then ended a flattering fourth the next season, ten points off the top spot. Cowan was to move on after 407 League and Cup appearances. On 8 December 1934 goalkeeper Frank Swift was carried off injured, Eric Brook went in goal saved a penalty and City won 4-2. In 1935-36 down to ninth where in mid-season seven games produced one point. Busby was transferred to Liverpool for £8,000 in March 1936 but City had signed inside-forward Peter Doherty from Blackpool a month earlier for £10,000. There was little to encourage any thought of honours in the opening weeks of the 1936-37 season, only three wins in the first 13 matches. By Christmas there were a mere 20 points garnered from as many games.

Transformation from Boxing Day produced a stunning unbeaten run of the remaining 22 fixtures. Between 3 October 1936 and 9 October 1937 City scored in 44 consecutive League games. Still plenty of goals were conceded but more scored. By mid-April Arsenal were top, Manchester City second. On 10 April at Maine Road City beat the Gunners 2-0 to establish a lead that remained. At the close City with 107 goals to their credit were top three points ahead of Charlton Athletic with Arsenal third five points behind.

High point was reached on 26 March in a 5-0 win at Liverpool. It caused Ivan Sharpe to describe it as "the most artistic display I ever saw in the Football League." Busby was in the Liverpool side. Overall there were four ever present players, Eric Brook, Jack Percival, Swift and Ernie Toseland. Doherty missed one game, Jackie Bray two and Bobby Marshall four. The other regulars were Sam Barkas, Billy Dale and Alec Herd, while Tilson was only on duty 23 times but scored 15 goals. Nine of the 22 players who turned out contributed only 31 appearances. Doherty was leading scorer with 30, Brook had 20, Herd 15.

When playing Sheffield Wednesday at Maine Road they needed two points to make sure. They were two up then before a memorable third goal. Swift cleared the ball Doherty gained possession and inter-changed passes with Tilson over 40 yards before scoring himself in the 4-1 win. It was their 21st League game undefeated. The last match at Birmingham was drawn 2-2.

Brook possessed a blockbuster of a shot in both feet for a left-winger and had played together with Tilson at Barnsley. On the opposite wing Toseland was very fast. Doherty was simply a class act either fashioning or finishing. Schemer Herd could play centre-forward if necessary and Bobby Marshall who was once an inside-forward succeeded Cowan at centre-half. Left-back ex-miner Sam Barkas was recruited from Bradford City and Percival had assumed the Busby role. City also enjoyed its best average attendance record in 1936-37 at 35,872, the third best in the country with only Aston Villa and Arsenal beating it

Yet with the same squad in 1937-38, City went down, but not without their flair for scoring. In fact the 80 goals were better than any other team in the First Division and they let in three fewer than they scored! It was a Football League record for most goals in a division that still ended in relegation. But their record of scoring in 44 consecutive League games ended. Among the 14 wins there were two at 7-1, a 6-2, 6-1 and 5-3. However, Manchester United passed them having won promotion to the First Division. In February 1938 Jack Milsom was signed from Bolton for £6,000. The following month Sunderland's reserve centre-half Les McDowall arrived in a £7,000 deal.

Barkas, Bray, Tilson and Brook won England caps, Herd for Scotland and Doherty for Northern Ireland. Then after another poor start in the Second Division given these circumstances City did well to finish fifth in 1938-39. Third last in October but games in hand helped at the end. In November 1938 the club paid £10,000 to obtain the signature of England's right-back Bert Sproston from Tottenham Hotspur. He was formerly with Leeds United and had been at Spurs for only four months. Brook completed 494 League and Cup appearances and 177 goals, Toseland 409 while Marshall moved to Stockport County after racking up 355 senior matches. Swift missed his first game in five seasons and had taken his total to 254 League and Cup games.

Manchester City 1937. Back: Chorlton (trainer), Percival, Dale, Swift, Donnelly, Bray, Cassidy.
Front: Herd, Doherty, Marshall, Toseland, Tilson, Brook.

Germany's Der Kicker of 15th February 1938 reports on Aston Villa's cup tie at Charlton. The wording under the picture says "this header from Frank Shell gave Villa the lead". George Robinson later scored Charlton's equaliser.

Aston Villa might be considered the nearly team of the 1930s. They finished second in the First Division championship on two occasions, twice reached the FA Cup semi-final and almost staved off relegation by spending a fortune on players. But support for the Villa Park club stayed consistently high throughout. Significantly no club had a better record against Arsenal.

In 1929-30 they beat the Gunners 5-2, it was 5-1 the following season and the classic 5-3 in 1932-33. However, there was the pay back 7-1 in Villa's relegated term 1935-36.

Disappointment In 1929-30 despite finishing fourth, because Villa had a poor run from mid-December when there was one victory in eight games. Then the memorable 1930-31 campaign when they were runners-up to Arsenal in the title race, Villa managed to score a record 128 League goals, one more than the Gunners. Tom "Pongo" Waring registered 49 of them shooting off the season with two four-timers in the opening three games. He had another foursome later on and a hat trick having registered at least once in 30 matches. He reached his half century with an FA Cup goal in losing out again to Arsenal.

Not that this was a one-man attack. It had a well balanced forward line in many respects with ex-Port Vale right-winger Jack Mandley 5ft 8in, former miner 5ft 5in Joe Beresford sharing the inside-right berth with another pit boy 5ft 10in George Brown of Huddersfield Town fame. The left wing pairing was Billy Walker a shade under 6ft with stalwart service since the Great War and left-winger 5ft 7in Eric Houghton.

Villa scored in every home game and in all but three away. Four players contributed to all but 20 goals, Houghton scoring 30, Walker 15 and Beresford 14 to add to the almost half century from Waring. The team scored four or more goals on 20 occasions, losing 6-4 at home to Derby County, drawing 5-5 at West Ham and only six times at Villa Park did they fail to manage less than four goals. The pinnacle was reached on 14 March 1931 when Villa beat Arsenal 5-1 at Villa Park.

Despite scoring 104 goals the next season Villa finished fifth, Waring scoring 30 this time. Well placed third in the New Year but won just one of the last four. However a more confident start in 1932-33 until Arsenal assumed the leadership in late October. But on 19 November at Villa Park in what has been described as a classic top flight match, Villa defeated Arsenal 5-3 to go top on goal average. There were 17 internationals on view. Arsenal led 1-0 and again 3-2. The first four goals came in 13 minutes and all scoring was finished with less than a quarter of an hour left.

Unfortunately, Villa lost 5-2 at Manchester City a week later! There was a recovery in the second half of the season despite Arsenal's five-goal revenge and just four points in the wake of Arsenal at the end. George Brown hit 33 goals. On 29 April 1933 he scored four in ten minutes in the 5-0 win over Blackburn. Still in the next two seasons Villa could manage only 13th position; an unlucky prelude to relegation in 1935-36 when 110 goals were conceded.

In 1933-34 unbeaten in the last nine but six of these were drawn. That season Villa had 15 internationals on their staff. A similar finale in 1934-35 with only two wins in the last eleven. Dai Astley scored 21 goals and included four hat tricks.

The 1935-36 demotion was not without enormous expenditure in a desperate bid to stave off the drop. Between November and January, some £35,500 was spent on seven players, five of them in a month to early December costing £23,500. They were arrivals with reputable CVs including Alex Massie from Hearts, Gordon Hodgson of Liverpool and George Cummings signed from Partick Thistle who proved the longest surviving at Villa Park of the expensive seven. Some £44,590 was paid out on wages, bonuses, benefits and transfers that season.

It should also be noted that in June 1934 the midland club had secured the signature of Jimmy Allen the Portsmouth centre-half for £10,775. No fewer than 28 Aston Villa players were capped by the home countries while with Villa from the end of the Great War. Of the 30 players used in 1935-36, 17 were either internationals or destined so to become. On 11 January 1936 a crowd of 62,620 saw the Huddersfield FA Cup tie that ended Villa's interest in the competition that season.

There was no swift return. Villa was only ninth in the Second Division in 1936-37 when Frank Broome scored 28 goals, but following a fine spurt Villa lost the last six games. In November 1936 Jimmy Hogan the ace continental coach had been appointed manager. Again there was some resistance against his methods from players out of the 45 professionals there. He was willing to drop so-called stars or switch their positions. He played Allen at centre-forward in the reserves for example. Criticism faded when Villa finished Champions the following season, interestingly letting in only 35 goals and scoring a modest enough 73. Broome scored 20 goals. Top on 1 January back leading in March and won the last four with clear daylight ahead of Manchester United.

In 1938-39 twelfth was the best they achieved in the First Division. Winger Houghton completed his tenth season scoring at least double figures each campaign. Bob Iverson had scored after nine and three-fifths of a second against Charlton on 3 December, the fastest recorded goal confirmed by referee Searle.

As to attendances, Villa's level of support was outstanding. In 1929-30 the average was 27,726 and in successive seasons it was returned as: 30,781; 31,509; 32,249; 30,557; 33,241; 40,864 (when relegated); 37,537; 41,950 (in Division 2 and second best in the Football League) and 39,932 even beating Arsenal's crowd figure. On 30 October 1937 a Division 2 record 67,271 saw the Coventry game.

Villa also had 58 players capped between 1919 and 1939, by far the most of any club. There had been 41 for England, nine for Wales, seven for Scotland and one from Northern Ireland.

The 1932 FA Cup semi-final at Villa Park. Manchester City keeper Len Langford reaches for the ball with Arsenal's David Jack in attendance. Matt Busby (left) and Cliff Bastin (second left) keep their eyes on the ball.

RIGHT AROUND THE PITCH

WEST MIDLANDS

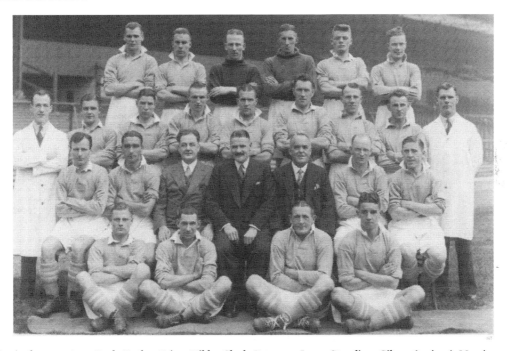

Birmingham 1936-37. Back; Butler, Trigg, Hibbs, Clack, Dearson, Jones. Standing; Gibson (trainer), Morris, Guest, Lea, Sykes, Fillingham, Small, Steel, Tremelling (trainer). Seated; Stoker, Harris, Wiseman (director), George Liddell (manager), Lane (director), Devine, Jennings. Front; Richardson, White, Barkas, Hughes

West Bromwich Albion had a storming finish in 1929-30 winning the last seven games when sixth. It was a prelude to claiming a first when in 1930-31 they pulled off a double with promotion from the Second Division and an FA Cup triumph. Actually it was cup followed by League success because the elevation party celebrated a week after the Wembley affair.

An early home defeat by Everton but in the following pack of the leaders well into the New Year it eventually became a struggle for second place with Spurs. The Throstles had games in hand due to the cup run. Both teams were dropping points, but on the last day Spurs lost at Burnley.

Not that the start on the cup trail was easy. It took three bites at Charlton Athletic, then both Tottenham Hotspur and Portsmouth merely subdued by a single goal. Wolverhampton Wanderers were beaten at the second attempt and Everton in the semi-final at Old Trafford was another by the minimum score.

Neighbours Birmingham provided the Wembley opposition. Billy Richardson – given a second Initial "G" for Ginger to separate him from his unrelated namesake centre-half – scored both Albion goals, the winner under a minute after Birmingham had levelled.

Seven days later it was back to The Hawthorns and of all teams Charlton in opposition for the promotion battle. The cup was paraded to the 52,415 crowd by a non-playing Bert Trentham complete with peaked cap and plus-fours. The Throstles went on to win 3-2, finishing seven points behind Everton. Of the 20 players, three did not miss a League match: goalkeeper Harold Pearson, full-back George Shaw and centre-half Bill Richardson. Wing-half Jimmy Edwards and left-winger Stan Wood were absent just once while Tommy Glidden made 39 League games and all the cup ties becoming the first right-winger to skipper an FA Cup winning side.

Billy "Ginger" Richardson

Sixth the season before the cup glory they were sixth again when back in the First Division for 1931-32. Then in the next few seasons: fourth – using only 18 players in 1932-33 – seventh and then ninth in 1934-35.

Even so, there was another trip to Wembley that season with nine of the class of '31 on view. Jimmy Murphy had replaced long-standing Tommy Magee at right-half and Wally Boyes was Wood's successor at outside-left.

Trailing from the second minute Boyes equalized before the break, though Joe Carter was already limping. In the 70th minute Sheffield Wednesday restored their lead only for Teddy Sandford to level five minutes later. Ginger Richardson squandered an easy chance in extra time and Albion eventually suffered a 4-2 defeat.

Thereafter it was sliding down to 18th in the table despite Richardson scoring 39 goals and only three points from the drop. Incredibly on 20 October 1935 he scored four in a 7-0 rout of Villa at Villa Park! Even 16th in 1936-37 before finally back to the Second Division at the end of 1937-38 after a tight relegation struggle and tenth in 1938-39. In November they signed Joe Johnson from Stoke for £6,000.

Numerous West Bromwich players rendered excellent League service: Carter (414), Glidden (445), Magee (394), Shaw (393) and Ginger Richardson (320 appearances) Richardson scored 328 goals in all matches, Carter (145), Cookson (103) and Glidden (135) in the League. Richardson had been a bus inspector and cost £1,000 when Albion signed him from Hartlepools United in June 1929. He had been recommended to them by Jack Manners a former player.

"WG" scored four goals in five minutes for Albion against West Ham United in November 1931 and three in six minutes on 30 September 1933 out of four goals in a 5-1 win over Derby. He frequently took corner kicks and had an England cap, too, along with Boyes, Pearson, Sandford and Shaw also given international honours in the 1930s, though Ashmore, Carter and Magee had been so honoured in the 1920s. Murphy won 15 full caps for Wales. Sandford moved to Sheffield United after 266 League appearances and 67 goals. He had often played centre-half, too. In a reserve game against Liverpool he scored seven of ten goals. He had been local with a capital "L" having been born in a cottage adjoining the Hawthorns.

Down the road apiece at St Andrew's while there were neither titles nor cups of any significance, at least Birmingham could boast continuous membership of the First Division from 1921, their most consistent chunk of competitive football if at times merely hanging on to their status by the proverbial thread. Exactly half-way in 1929-30 this was only topped once when creeping to ninth place in 1931-32.

The previous season fourth from the bottom but there was a trip to the Cup Final of course and a goal ruled off-side before Albion opened the scoring. Worries that a full Blues side would not be fielded because of injury were dispelled. But "Gentleman" Joe Bradford's volleyed leveller was the only bonus in the 2-1 defeat.

Centre-forward Bradford scored 249 League goals for Birmingham and had the full range of assets, two-footed marksman and an aerial threat. In an era dominated by prolific goal scorers he was capped twelve times by England and hit seven goals. In September 1929 he had scored three hat tricks in eight days: a treble v Newcastle, five goals for the Football League and three against Blackburn.

On the managerial side, Leslie Knighton was poached by Chelsea and former Blues player George Liddell took over in July 1933. They had finished 13th in the table. But 1933-34 came near to relegation just two points away and only three from the drop the following season when 19th. Twelfth in 1935-36 then eleventh in 1936-37 a repeat performance before 1937-38 became another nail-biter with two points to spare in 18th position. Inevitably it had to happen and in last but one place, Birmingham finally succumbed in 1938-39. There had been a huge turnover of players in an effort to find the correct combination, the only consistent figures being the number used in League games: 29, 29, 27, 29, 25 and 32 in the season of relegation. Only on two occasions in these six seasons was there an ever-present on League duty.

Of course there were long-serving stalwarts. None more so than the small but safe-handling goalkeeper Harry Hibbs who had a 16-year career at St Andrew's after signing from Tamworth in 1924, making 358 League appearances up to the end of 1938-39 season. He was capped 25 times by England, too.

As for Wolverhampton Wanderers, with such a high profile manager as Major Frank Buckley, falling in the double aim of League and Cup at the end of the 30s, was all that could be dug out of a disappointing period in the club's history. Yet there were positives obscured by this overall failure.

"The Major," as he was always known, had arrived in 1927 with Wolves in the Second Division. In 1929-30 they improved to ninth, then fourth and in 1931-32 outscored the opposition with 115 goals to edge Leeds United by two points and win promotion. Billy Hartill scored 30 goals. True two points were involved the next season but only to avoid relegation! Hartill the sole ever present hit 33 goals, Wolves were 15th in 1933-34, 17th in 1934-35 with Hartill bagging 27. He left for Everton after scoring 162 League goals in seven seasons. With 15 hat tricks including two 5's and a four timer he had been a consistent marksman – nicknamed "Hartillery" from his days in the Royal Horse Artillery.

On 16 February 1935 Stan Cullis was introduced at right-half for his debut. Wolves ended in 15th position again in 1935-36. Some 20 players had been transferred out in a year. Four teams were fielded each week. Nine ex-juniors were in the first team at times, three others from Third Division clubs. However, fifth place was achieved in 1936-37. Full-back Cecil Shaw transferring to West Bromwich in December 1936 had completed 120 consecutive League appearances at one stage. But the crowd was not happy over the constant sale of players and after losing 2-1 at home to Chelsea on 7 November Wolves were second from bottom.

Wolves became runners-up to Arsenal in 1937-38 only a point in it, too, though the Gunners had superior goal average if it had come to such a question. On 22 January in the FA Cup against Arsenal, the directors were reported to have selected the team. Arsenal won 2-1 after a first minute goal. On 15 April Leicester City had been beaten 10-1 with Dennis Westcott and 18 year old Dickie Dorsett each scoring four goals.

Financially, Buckley pulled off some amazing deals and in a four year period made a more than useful profit, if at times his transactions were at the expense of results. From May 1935 to May 1939 he brought in £110,658 having paid out £42,330 for a healthy credit balance of £68,328. Included in these transfers was the sale of Bryn Jones to Arsenal for a record £14,000. There was an enormous turnover of players at Molineux. At the same time the youngsters figured prominently. Against Brentford on 10 February 1937 the team that won 4-0 had an average age of 20, the oldest 24.

A man who could spot a good player Buckley also brought the best out of Jones who had drifted around without finding a suitable environment for his talents.

In 1938-39, Wolves were chasing the double. On the first day held at Derby 2-2 with Arsenal beating Portsmouth at Highbury and Everton defeating Blackpool away, it was not the start Wolves wanted as they drew the first four before a 1-0 win at Brentford. Arsenal won 1-0 at Molineux on 17 September, too and Wolves lost at Portsmouth a week later.

At the end of October they were even fifth from bottom. But by 10 December a 4-0 win at Charlton Athletic shot them into third place, such was the turnaround. Derby led the pack, Everton second, Arsenal out of it. On 22 February, Wolves astonishingly trounced Everton 7-0 on the Molineux mud. Three days later with the Rams dropping a point, Wolves went second two points behind Everton. But at a crucial stage, Wolves drawing habits returned and ironically their nine defeats were fewer than any other club. On 11 March a 3-2 defeat against Birmingham had been the first for twelve League and Cup games with only one draw! Westcott scored 32 League goals.

The FA Cup was expected to be easier and by the final day with home ties against Bradford Park Avenue, Leicester City, Liverpool, Everton and Grimsby Town (at Old Trafford) stacking up 19 goals in the process. But relegation haunted Portsmouth pulled off a 4-1 upset against the favourites.

Pleased as Punch. Walsall players and directors after their FA Cup win over Arsenal in 1932. Back; Ball, Coward, Bennett, Bird, Salt. Centre: Wait (trainer), Reed, Leslie, Alsop, Sheppard, Cunningham, Lee. Front: Bill Slade (manager) and directors Eyre, Fellows, Lake and Roper.

Shuffled between the northern and southern sections of the Third Division, Walsall finished 17th in 1929-30 and again the next season in the south before a move north for 1931-32 at least improved their standing to 16th. But encouragingly the Saddlers were in fifth place in 1932-33 and fourth next time out with 97 goals of which Gilbert Alsop scored 39.

He had been the hero of the greatest giant-killing act in the FA Cup when on 14 January 1933 when opening the score against Arsenal in a 2-0 win. In 1934-35 Alsop reprised his 39 goals but it was almost half Walsall's total of 81 and they were ten places lower. Tenth in 1935-36 but back in the south for 1936-37 and a struggle at the bottom four points from seeking re-election when 17th. On 11 January 1936 a crowd of 19,882 had seen Newcastle United win a fourth road FA Cup tie 2-0.

Those ominous signs proved right in 1937-38. They were bottom in mid-October then vying with Gillingham for the last two places until a slight revival in December. This double situation returned in the New Year and remained, Walsall winning the final match while the Gills lost enabling the Saddlers to finish 21st but still needing to seek re-election. This was achieved with 34 votes. Bill Bradford brother of the Birmingham player completed 342 League and Cup appearances having been player-coach from 1934.

The reprieve for Walsall lasted no length of time in 1938-39. The first win came in mid-November. Alsop who had been with West Bromwich and Ipswich returned in the second half of the season scored freely again there was too much leeway to make up. Though four more points were obtained from drawn games and just one fewer goal scored than conceded, they were back cap-in-hand at the

Gilbert Alsop

League's AGM. Amazingly 36 votes enabled Walsall to carry on. However the last sixteen had been reached in the FA Cup that season. Alsop had taken his record of scoring to 149 League goals in his two spells from only 188 games.

Arguably the most consistently successful club in the area was Coventry City, Alsop's original club. In an era in which goal scoring reached extensive proportions never achieved before or since, they also eventually contrived to offer sound defence. Sixth in 1929-30, then 14th and 12th it was sixth again in 1932-33.

The record in 1931-32 was unusual. City's games produced 205 goals. Their 108 scored was second highest in the table, the 97 conceded the fourth worst. Clarrie Bourton helped himself to 49 of the goals and had 40 in the next campaign. Coventry finished runners-up in 1933-34 on goal average thanks to improvement at the back and only 54 conceded as well as a century of goals put in. Bourton hit four goals in the 9-0 win over Bristol City. Arthur Bacon had a mid-season five game burst of scoring 2-1-2-5-4 goals.

City were third in 1934-35 and on 16 January 1935 at Cardiff, four goals were registered in the first five minutes to leave the score 2-2. Coventry won 4-2. and a term later came promotion to the Second Division as Champions of the Third Division (South) with a double taking in the Southern Section Cup, beating Swindon Town 5-2 on aggregate. There were 102 goals in the League and just 45 let in, so though only a point kept Luton Town at bay, goal average would have been worth virtually another point. The crucial moment was in the final game when Torquay United were beaten 2-1. Five forwards contributed all but 17 goals in the season. On 27 April 1936 the attendance at Highfield Road for the visit of Luton was 42,809, a figure higher than for the Arsenal v Chelsea derby the same day.

Second Division football brought eighth position in 1936-37, but just 66 goals for and 54 against in the League. In 1937-38 following a confident opening unbeaten in the first 15, a remarkable number coincidences began to be noticed when in a creditable fourth place. Again 66 scored and 45 conceded! In 1938-39 placed fourth once more and 45 in the "against" column for the third time in four seasons.

With the emphasis on being tight at the back, there was fluctuating support from the fans that preferred the attacking enterprise of earlier seasons. In 1929-30 the average was 12,985 and by 1936-37 it had risen to 22,744 and even 25,825 before surprisingly slumping to 19,506 in 1938-39. On 12 March 1938 44,930 had attended the Aston Villa game.

The defence was built around centre-half and skipper George Mason, Birmingham born and culled from amateur football. In view of the club's tight defensive record changes in the rearguard were minimal as you might expect.

Coventry City 1938-39. Back; Astley, Smith, Mason, Hill (trainer), Morgan, Metcalf, Crawley, Boileau. Centre; Taylor, Brown, Roberts, Harry Storer (manager), Davidson, McDonald, Ashall. Front; Frith, Lager, Archer.

EAST MIDLANDS

Derby County figured in the top six of the First Division seven times in the ten seasons, on two occasions as runners-up. Under astute manager George Jobey, they were able to add quality players, launching many to international status. He was a wheeler-dealer capable of upsetting the rules to obtain his quarry.

In 1929-30, Derby trailed ten points behind Champions Sheffield Wednesday, the biggest title-winning margin since 1897 and won only three of their last ten fixtures. Not that this absence of staying power in the season was a one-off experience for them. Next time out it was three wins from last eleven when sixth, in 1931-32 four of 13 ending 15th and only three of 15 the following 1932-33 term that secured seventh spot.

It was worse, too, in 1933-34 when even up to fourth with only two wins from 15 and just a slight improvement in 1934-35 to sixth winning four of the last dozen. Then it was four of 13 in 1935-36 as runners-up before a turnaround in 1936-37. Placed fourth, Derby scored 96 goals and conceded 90 for a ratio of more than four goals per game. As for the last two seasons in the 1930s the Rams failed to win any of their last five each time. In 1935 Jobey had said no more youngsters!

Many put the constant late season demise down to the gipsy curse allegedly inflicted on them in 1895 when the travellers were moved on to make way for the Baseball Ground. At times the quality of individual players made it seem impossible to imagine any voodoo on them could have prevented honours heading to Derby. Centre-forward Jack Bowers signed from Scunthorpe & Lindsey United put goals away with ease, hitting 37 in only 33 League games during 1930-31. In the next three seasons he finished with 25, 35 and 34. In 1934-35 a serious knee injury cut his appearances, but Jobey secured none other than Hughie Gallacher from Chelsea for £2,750 and he responded with a debut goal after six minutes and overall 23 goals from 27 matches.

Such was the international flavour to the attack that in 1936-37 Derby could parade five international forwards of the calibre of Sammy Crooks, Ronnie Dix, Dai Astley, Charlie Napier and Dally Duncan. Crooks had come from Durham City in 1927 and went on to win 26 England caps. Dix, an England cap, was still only 20 when signed but had already established himself as a 15 year old wonder boy with Bristol Rovers, later with Blackburn Rovers and Aston Villa.

Astley had also come from Villa in November 1936 at the cost of £7,500 and was a Welsh international able to play inside-forward as well as leading the line. Charlie Napier, a Scottish international, had arrived a year earlier from Celtic. His fellow Scot on the left wing was Dally Duncan, a Jobey capture from Hull City in 1931.

Of course there were England internationals elsewhere in the team. Centre-half Jack Barker had been signed from Denaby United in 1929 and went on to complete 326 League appearances and win eleven caps. Bowers was another England man as was Tommy Cooper at right-back, an early Jobey recruit from Port Vale, had moved on to Liverpool. Wing-half Ike Keen picked up from Newcastle United was another stalwart in the same mode.

George Stephenson had been another Aston Villa favourite signed and then passed to Sheffield Wednesday. Dave McCulloch arrived from Brentford in 1938, a Scottish cap who had made his name with Hearts to complete another front line of caps at Derby as Napier also joined Wednesday. At one stage Derby had five forwards all qualified to represent Scotland at international level.

In 1935-36 they had lost the first two matches yet by mid-October had climbed to second place. A 3-0 win over Manchester City on 2 November gave them top spot, but a draw at Arsenal cost them a week later. Tucked in behind Sunderland most weeks but never seriously within damaging distance and with the usual slump at a time the Roker men had also faltered, there was an eight point gap for runners-up Derby. On 25 January 1936 a crowd of 37,830 saw neighbours Forest beaten 2-0 in the FA Cup. For the record in 1937-38 the Rams were down to 13th. On 15 January 1938 19 year old Tim Ward made his debut at left-half and kept his place. Derby finished sixth again in 1938-39.

Nottingham Forest had too many slightly uncomfortable seasons in the lower positions of the Second Division. In 1929-30 tenth place was one of their best but it was not until the 11th game before a win and none in the last six. A run of ten without a win around December 1930 contributed to 17th in the season and another December blip in 1931-32 was a prelude to an eleventh finish. On 1 March 1930 there had been a crowd of 44,166 for the Sheffield Wednesday FA Cup tie.

Still it was a considerably more promising season in 1932-33, courtesy of an unbeaten 16 game spell into March and fifth place. Forest stayed out of trouble the next season despite just two wins in the last nine games when 17th. More consistency would have improved ninth place in 1934-35.

Another escape followed in 1935-36 in 19th after scraping only four points from a last possible 16. Fifteen games no goals but three 6's and a nine – Tom Peacock getting four in three of them! That season right-half Billy McKinlay had completed 334 League games and ex-Huddersfield centre-forward Johnny Dent 119 goals in 196 such appearances. Forest, now with a manager in Harry Wightman for the first time, was just a slot higher in 1936-37 thanks to winning four of their last seven and Dave "Boy" Martin scoring 29 goals including eight in successive games. But they continued to live dangerously and in 1937-38 missed the drop by 0.002 of goal average. A 2-2 draw with Barnsley saved them but not the opposition. In 1938-39 with no goals in 13 games and just one win in the last five matches, survival came by 0.05 of a goal when again 20th!

Centre-half Tommy Graham had left in 1938 after eleven seasons, 372 League appearances and two England caps.

Short-lived relegation for Notts County in 1929-30 when there were fourteen games without scoring overall and six successive defeats at the tail end that left them two points short. Bouncing back in 1930-31 as Champions of Third Division (South) scoring 97 goals, conceding 46 and Tom Keetley hitting 39 in only 34 games, they had an eight point margin at the end. Eighteen undefeated from the start was a key to success, too.

Sixteenth in 1931-32 scoring as many as they conceded, Notts finished one place above in 1932-33 when having gone 12 without defeat around November they lost the last seven. Marginally better at that stage in 1933-34 with one win in the final seven leading to 18th.

Notts County 1931/32. From the left; Ferguson, Mills, Smith (HR), Dowsey, Coglin, Bisby, Jakeman, Andrews, Lawrence, Maw, Taylor, Keetley, Haden

Not a surprise when relegation returned after 1934-35. Fourteen matches without a goal, one away win – at Forest – and a mere two wins in the last fourteen, they were bottom seven points from safety. Ninth in the Southern Section in 1935-36 before a strong challenge developed in 1936-37 with veteran signing Hughie Gallacher scoring 25 in 32 matches.

Certainly no hint of it at the start and on Boxing Day they were sixth when the run of 17 without loss began. In February and March jockeyed with Brighton for the leadership. Top at Easter but with free-scoring Luton played two fewer. Yet on 17 April Notts held a four point advantage, Luton reduced to one game in hand. A week later Brighton won at Meadow Lane and only goal average separated Notts with Luton with one game left. Alas, despite leading at Walsall, Notts lost 2-1 and Luton defeated Torquay to win the Championship.

It seemed another effort was on in 1937-38 after a firm opening and top for a time. Gallacher started the season and even Dixie Dean arrived later! Second in January before drifting to eleventh, the same situation occurring in 1938-39 when only one win came in the last nine matches. Full-back Percy Mills had retired in 1939 with 407 appearances to his credit in twelve seasons.

Leicester City were residing in the First Division for 1929-30 finishing eighth, the defence having conceded 90 goals. Eight positions lower in 1930-31 with 95 goals let in and a one goal improvement at the rearguard for 1931-32 when 19th. After one point from nine games, three wins and a draw at the end saved them. Ernie Hine went to Huddersfield after scoring 148 goals.

Exactly the same placing in 1932-33, but the avoidance of demotion came from one draw and three wins on this occasion. Into December there had been a run of 17 without a win. Then in 1933-34 City was 17th following the loss of the last four games.

Living dangerously it was no surprise when 1934-35 brought relegation. Fifteen times they failed to score and not one win was produced in the last six matches. Stalwarts like Arthur Chandler four goal debutant plus top scorer for seven seasons as well as 259 goals in 393 appearances and full-back Adam Black a record 528 appearances given free transfers, while winger Hugh Adcock 434 League games was listed. The 106-goal Inside-forward Arthur Lochhead retired. Though not a prolific goal scorer, Black had found the opposing net with a clearance from his own half on 22 April 1933 against Sunderland. Chandler was a hat trick specialist including six goals in one game, three times hitting five, two of which accounted for City's total and a four-timer.

In 1935-36 the first half of the season was more successful than the second when sixth. Consistent wing-half Sep Smith, a miner who had been recruited in 1929 was rewarded with an England cap.

A new look for 1936-37 reaped a reward. In November £7,500 was paid to Derby for centre-forward Jack Bowers. He responded with 33 goals from 27 matches. In the top two in February, Leicester needed to win their last game to catch Blackpool who had finished their programme. In some style Spurs were despatched 4-1 and the Second Division Championship was won.

Restored to First Division football, Leicester had a revival in February and March, though mostly via drawn games and were 16th. City lost 10-1 to Wolves on 15 April. The short-lived sojourn in the top flight ended in 1938-39. Seventeen games with no goals and a mere two victories from February, Leicester was in the bottom two for many weeks before ending 22nd. Smith took his League appearances to 269.

Midland Counties League title achievements and an impressive FA Cup performance against Arsenal helped Mansfield Town into the Football League, but they had to switch application to the Third Division (South) after six years unsuccessfully trying for the Northern Section. Against Arsenal the Stags captain Chris Staniforth had missed a penalty when the score was 0-0. The squad with a £37 wage bill had trained on eggs and milk.

But Mansfield toiled in 1931-32 until three wins and a draw in the last seven secured 20th position. Harry Johnson the ex-Sheffield United double-century striker and part-timer scored 32 goals the defence let in 108. The Stags were never really happy playing away. The League switched them North in 1932-33 though they managed just one win on travel when finishing 16th. Johnson had 30 League goals. Then three wins out of the last four – their best sequence all season – pushed them to 17th in 1933-34.

However, 1934-35 showed Mansfield in finer fettle, fourth in December and eventually eighth. But again only determined efforts late on proved decisive in 1935-36 with five wins and three draws from nine fixtures made them 19th. In October they had paid Bristol City £250 for centre-forward Ted Harston. He scored 26 goals in 29 games including a treble on his debut at Southport. The previous month Johnson had registered his 100th League goal for the Stags.

Harston more than doubled his contribution in 1936-37, with 55 goals over half the 91 registered. His haul included a seven against Hartlepools, two-fives, a four-timer and three hat tricks. In the close season he was transferred to Liverpool for around £3,000 having scored 81 League goals in 70 outings. Mansfield finished ninth.

Shoved back reluctantly to the South in 1937-38 and with a new attack, one of them Harry Crawshaw finished as the section's leading scorer with 25 goals. On 8 January 1938 a crowd of 15,890 saw the Leicester City FA Cup tie. A reasonable 14th placing was achieved that season. Moreover even though they failed to score in exactly half of their 1938-39 matches, Mansfield managed 16th thanks to 15 drawn games.

With a large turnover of playing staff there had been only five occasions when one player had appeared in all Football League matches in a season.

Adversity was something not tolerated at length by Chesterfield who twice responded to being demoted, restoring their Second Division standing. Quietly fourth in 1929-30 having lost their first three games, there was a different atmosphere in 1930-31 and early topping of the table. The New Year had the Spireites second two points behind the leaders. But points were dropped here and there.

However on 18 April leaders Lincoln lost as did Tranmere, leaving Chesterfield's 3-1 win at Hartlepools a second place on goal average above Rovers but still a point from Lincoln who had a game in hand. A week later both rivals were beaten again and Chesterfield won the title in some spectacular way 8-1 over Gateshead. The last six consecutive wins had produced 26 goals. Albert Pynegar scored 26 of the 102 goals in only 29 games. From Christmas Day 1929 till Boxing Day 1930 they had scored in 46 consecutive League matches.

Bedding down in 1931-32, but second bottom until a Christmas revival, another dip in February until 17th achieved at season's end. Only another such December festival improvement took Chesterfield off the last place in 1932-33, but one win derived from nine games from March and not even winning the last two games prevented relegation in 21st spot.

More personnel changes but a club record ten wins in a row brightened everything in 1933-34 when only 18 players were used! Another nine-match unbeaten run followed before Easter was a disappointment. It was the last fixture with Chesterfield and Barnsley on 60 points, Chesterfield due at

Stockport two points behind but with the superior goal average. Barnsley won while Chesterfield drew 0-0 to finish runners-up. Only 43 goals were conceded; the best in four divisions.

Players came and went at Chesterfield in 1934-35 when the team was tenth. The biggest winning margin in the Third Division (North) Cup was secured 8-1 over Mansfield Town. Nothing indicated optimism for 1935-36, but after being unbeaten in the opening nine games by the New Year a brief spell was enjoyed at the top. This was followed by ten unbeaten games and the Spireites could even afford losing a couple at Easter. Only one point was needed from the last two matches and the Championship was secured in the first such 2-0 against Hartlepools United. The 39 goals let in proved the Football League's fewest that season.

Saltergate had Second Division fixtures again for 1936-37 and the November visit of Sheffield United produced a record crowd of 26,519 for the official opening of the new stand. They finished 15th. On 2 January defender Horace Wass played his 413th League game in more than twelve years. Eleventh

Northampton Town players in training

at the end of 1937-38 after a good opening spurt, it was not until 4 December that a change was made in the forward line. The club produced an impressive sixth in 1938-39 to justify the all-round effort. Left-back Billy Kidd who had made his debut on 12 March 1932 was still well in evidence 272 League games to the good. On 12 February 1938 Joe Devine suffered a broken leg playing against Tottenham .in the FA Cup when the attendance was 30,561.

Northampton Town maintained Third Division (South) status and in six of the seasons covered were well in the top half of the table. Their best was certainly in 1929-30 when there was only one home defeat and but for faltering in February and March might have been higher than fourth.

In-and-out for 1930-31 with spells of eight with no loss, three points from seven games and then one win in the last six left them sixth. Only 18 goals in the first half of the season and a twelve-match sequence without one victory led to 14th in 1931-32. Ex-Arsenal centre-forward Ted Bowen was transferred to Bristol City having scored 114 League goals. Colin Russell scored eight goals in the last seven matches. The Cobblers hit nine in the FA Cup against Met Police, Albert Dawes scoring three.

Had the away form matched the undefeated one at home then eighth place would have been improved upon in 1932-33. Dawes scored 32 goals. He had five goals in the FA Cup against Lloyds. Goalkeeper Len Hammond joined Notts County after making 301 League appearances. A good FA Cup run followed in 1933-34 when Northampton reached the fifth round, but they were 13th in the table. December was unkind to them in 1934-35 but eight wins from nine into April left them seventh.

For 1935-36 when 15th a run of eight without a win was balanced when they lost only four of the last 15. Chopping and changing accounted for 32 players being used. A cup shock losing 6-1 to Walthamstow Avenue galvanized the Cobblers to a five-match winning streak and they were seventh in 1936-37. On 7 November 1936 the attendance was 18,885 for the visit of Luton.

In 1937-38 winning three and drawing five of the last eight aided finishing ninth. Three late recruits from Manchester City were Freddie Tilson, Keiller McCullough and Colin Rodger while Maurice Dunkley made the reverse journey. A good start and ending made up for many mid-season failures in 1938-39 when 17th.

Brentford 1936-37. Back; McKenzie, James, Mathieson, Poyser, Dumbrell. Front; Hopkins, Scott, McCulloch, Holliday, Reid, Richards.

With Arsenal dominating the honours from the metropolis there were slim pickings for the other eleven London clubs sifting around for scraps. Even so there were some worthy achievements from the lower echelons of the League with both Brentford and Charlton Athletic making excellent progress through the divisions.

Tottenham Hotspur gained promotion only to suffer relegation again, West Ham United also demoted but Chelsea managed to hold on to their elevation. Millwall lost its Second Division place if only on a temporary basis.

Fulham did come up from the Third Division (South) but Clapton Orient, Crystal Palace and Queens Park Rangers stayed firmly in the third tier. The ill-fated Thames was washed up after two years in the same environment.

There was precious little joy in the FA Cup as far as actually getting to the final. Chelsea reached the 1932 semi-final and lost to Newcastle United 2-1. West Ham was beaten by the same score the following year by Everton and the same odd goal in three curse hit Fulham against Sheffield United in 1936. However, Millwall created a piece of history in 1937 as the first Third Division club to reach as far. Needless to mention 2-1 was their downfall against Sunderland.

So the success stories involved Brentford and Charlton Athletic. Brentford hit the 30s chasing promotion from the Third Division (South) as runners-up, Charlton 13th in the Second Division but hoping for better fortune allied to also aiming ambitiously for elevation. Both finished the decade in the First Division.

Runners-up Brentford had won all 21 home games in 1929-30 when they fielded an unchanged team in 20 successive games from 2 November to 15 March. Of 18 players used, five played in all 42, two missed one while another was absent twice. Billy Lane scored 33 goals, Jack Lane 18. Brentford scored in every home game hit two 6's and four 5's.They followed up in 1930-31 finishing third then fifth as a prelude to success in 1932-33 when they won the championship, gaining promotion to the Second Division.

From the start the intention was clear; twelve wins and two draws identified the purpose. The squad was strengthened by a trio signed from Middlesbrough: Jack Holliday up front, Billy Scott in midfield and Bert Watson in defence. Holliday scored 38 League goals and 62 points were achieved four points clear of the opposition. On 1 February 1933 Brentford found themselves 4-1 down at Luton. They drew 5-5 with Holliday scoring the nap hand.

A creditable fourth place achieved in 1933-34 failing to score in only three games. The same five forwards who between them scored all but three of the goals and overall missed only five games between them, was the forerunner to another outstanding campaign the following term. This witnessed the lifting of the Second Division title and a place in the First Division five points clear of third place. Only one defeat suffered from mid-February when it was of no consequence.

Only 17 players called upon who cost under £5,000 in total, five ever present and unbeaten at home. Arsenal sent the following telegram: "The League Champions congratulate the Division 2 Champions. Stop. Come up and see us sometime. Stop. A warm welcome awaits you."

The postscript to this episode makes interesting reading for Brentford followers. In the eight First Division matches that followed between the two clubs, Brentford lost only once – away in 1938-39!

Even 1935-36 saw the dawn of life in the top flight with a satisfactory final position of fifth. During these amazing four seasons the nucleus of the squad had remained virtually intact with as many as the same nine players making appearances throughout. One of them, the Wales international winger Idris Hopkins won all his dozen caps in the era. Dave McCulloch from Hearts scored 26 in as many games.

Much of the off-field guidance was due to the shrewd efforts of Harry Curtis secretary-manager and a strong character with the correct knowledge of the requirements needed. Sixth in 1936-37 with McCulloch scoring 31 goals, title hopes only faded at Easter. Brentford was sixth again in 1937-38, but in 1938-39 they won only two of their last eleven and finished 18[th.] However, the FA Cup run in 1937-38 had produced a record gate at Griffin Park for the sixth round tie with Preston North End when 39,626 paid receipts of £2,930. Holliday had scored goals in three different divisions having understudied George Camsell while he was at Middlesbrough. Another secret of Brentford's success was the retention of the nucleus of the playing staff during its rise. Les Boulter was signed from Charlton at £7,000 in February 1939.

Not only did Charlton reach the same goal as Brentford, but did so after recovering from relegation. Thirteenth in 1929-30 then placed 15th in 1930-31 after the turn of the year when they were beaten 6-0, 5-0 and 7-0 in five matches. Then tenth in 1931-32 having picked up in the last dozen games, 1932-33 saw Charlton bottom out in last place, thanks to a general lack of goals. In the summer the club appointed Jimmy Seed as manager and the transformation began in earnest.

Fifth in 1933-34 with leading scorer Cyril Pearce, 26 in 32 games including six in successive games, suffering a broken leg with five weeks left. Another cracking effort in 1934-35 with 103 goals and an unassailable eight point lead as Division Three (South) champions. Ralph Allen was plucked from free-scoring Brentford Reserves in October where he was racking up 149 goals in three seasons and responded with 32 goals in 28 outings. From 8 to 25 December Charlton scored 21 goals in 16 days: 6-0, 6-3, 3-1 and 6-0.

Runners-up in 1935-36 with a three point lead over third place Sheffield United it was promotion to the First Division in successive seasons; an incredible achievement for a club relegated to the lowest division only four years earlier. Harold Hobbis contrived 23 goals from the left-wing. Charlton remained unbeaten at home.

Charlton did not rest. In 1936-37 they were merely three points off winning the First Division title, though they had a vastly inferior goal average to champions Manchester City. Average attendances rose to 31,086. Yet on the pitch it had taken time to settle to the new environment and several players were tried at centre-forward. On 17 October the visit of Arsenal attracted a record crowd to The Valley. Officially it was 68,160 but estimates put it at around 77,000.

It was not until the middle of December and a 2-0 win over Everton that Charlton hit top, with Manchester City eighth. Thereafter Arsenal led with Charlton second until 6 February when The Addicks won 2-1 away to cellar dwellers West Bromwich with the Gunners held at home by Manchester United second from bottom!

In fact it was only goal average that changed things around for the leading pair with Arsenal leading with Manchester City five points away on 13 March. By Easter Monday it was still goal average separating the two leaders, though City had cut their lead to three points.

But it changed dramatically on 3 April when Charlton lost at Sunderland, Arsenal defeated West Bromwich and City won 6-2 at Brentford. City subsequently beat Arsenal 2-0 to consolidate an advantage they did not lose.

Once more the benefit of keeping the same bunch of players had paid handsomely. Among the dozen involved in these rewarding seasons were the goalkeeping discovery Sam Bartram, full-backs Bert Turner and Jimmy Oakes, the adaptable Don Welsh and inside-right George Robinson signed from Sunderland in 1931 who missed only two matches in the three seasons covered. Versatile forward Harold Hobbis broke a leg in February 1938 in the replay with Aston Villa. Some 75,031 were at The Valley for the original tie. Afterwards he had a specially made pair of soft leather boots. In 1937-38 Charlton were top early September fell away and dropped points at crucial times with others similarly affected but still claimed fourth. They even finished third in 1938-39 having been 16th in October up to third in November, slipping in the New Year before recovery.

The scribe who dubbed Chelsea as consistently inconsistent probably pitched it perfectly. Only twice in the top half, one point off relegation in 1938-39, twice losing FA Cup ties to Third Division clubs. But having been runners-up in the Second Division in 1929-30 they kept hold of First Division status through some tricky seasons and narrow escapes. Yet clinching promotion was almost an anti-climatic moment as they had to rely on their nearest rivals losing. In 1930-31 when against Sunderland in a 5-0 win they had eight internationals in the side – five Scots, two English and an Irishman – they finished 12th in the table and again the next season. In 1932-33 a Hughie Gallacher hat trick in a 4-1 win at Manchester City with one game remaining saved them with a two-point safety net. Only weeks before they had taken six goals off Leeds United at Stamford Bridge.

In 1933-34 just eight points gathered by mid-December trailing last but with games in hand a draw with Arsenal in the penultimate fixture put them two points clear again after losing only two of the last nine and placed 19th. Twelfth again in 1934-35 with newcomer Joe Bambrick scoring 15 from 21 games in the second half of the season. But eighth in 1935-36 was the highest position achieved in the 30s. This came about even though no wins were managed for eight games in the New Year. At best they were a mid-table team of fluctuating fortune but certainly entertaining with the outcome of matches often in doubt. Thirteenth in 1936-37 Chelsea scraped only three goals in the last seven matches. They even topped the table in late October 1937 but dropped to tenth. .Joe Payne cost £5,000 from Luton, Jack Smith from Swindon for £3,000 on the same day in March. It still required a further frantic finish in 1938-39 to a single point stay from relegation when Payne scored six in consecutive matches, Chelsea's only goals in the last nine games.

Chelsea did not lack talent. They paid to get it. Harnessing it for sustained periods was the problem. Gallacher was signed from Newcastle United for £10,000 in May 1930, Alec Cheyne the corner scoring king from Aberdeen a month later for £6,000 and £8,500 for Alec Jackson from Huddersfield Town in the following September, just three of 21 international players who figured in the era, only three of whom were not purchased. Thirteen were given recognition while at Stamford Bridge. Crazily there were often two capped players vying for the same position in an international forward line.

Jackson had a difference of opinion with the club and was placed on the transfer list at £6,000 in 1932. He never played in the League again, merely non-league and in France. Reg Groves writing in the *Famous Football Clubs* series on Chelsea reported; "The trouble flared up over trivial things, but it showed that all was far from well at Stamford Bridge. Policy disagreements in the boardroom, training weaknesses, clashes of temperament between star players, all contributed." In the ten seasons only two players were ever present goalkeeper Vic Woodley in 1932-33 and centre-half Allan Craig in 1934-35.

In contrast to the high-priced stars who came and went, there was the reliable Tommy Law at left-back who cost a £10 signing-on fee yet managed to win two caps for Scotland despite being an "Anglo-Scot." To emphasise an earlier point, all three trainers were sacked in 1939.

A couple of stops on the District Line and at nearby Craven Cottage, Fulham seventh in 1929-30 then ninth became Champions of the Third Division (South) in 1931-32 with a club record 111 goals and 57 points. Frank Newton with 43 goals and Herbert "Jim" Hammond adding 31 provided the power in attack. On 7 September 1931 Torquay were beaten 10-2 Hammond scoring four. The team was still scoring if not at the same rate when Fulham finished third in the 1932-33 Second Division campaign. But Newton went to Reading early in 1933-34 and the team were 16th.

Poor away form in 1934-35 led to seventh. Jimmy Hogan was appointed manager, though his methods were not to the liking of the players and eventually the board sacked him while he was in hospital. Then a curiosity in 1935-36 down to ninth when in the last eight games only nine goals were scored – seven of them against Port Vale – and an erratic attack kept them from challenging for honours. Eleventh in 1936-37 Bert Barrett who had England amateur and full caps completed 389 League appearances. On 7 November Ronnie Rooke scored three on his debut in a 5-0 win over West Ham. The Cottagers were placed eighth the next season despite being last on 1 January 1938 and top for six weeks in the autumn of 1938 prior to slipping to twelfth. In a six-goal FA Cup romp on 7 January 1939 against Bury Rooke scored a double hat trick. On 8 October 1938 the visit of Millwall attracted a club record 49,335.

Ex-Manchester City Syd Gibbons at centre-half was 5ft 11in but weighed 13st 7lb. Nicknamed "Carnera" after the boxer he missed only three games in four and a half seasons making 299 League appearances to 1937.

Tottenham Hotspur. Back: McCormick, Sproston, Page, Hall (J), Buckingham, Spelman. Front: Whatley, Sargent, Hall (GW), Morrison, Hall (AE), Lyman

Tottenham Hotspur was nearly always in the shadow of Arsenal. Yet apart from the season they were relegated, invariably in contention and only in 1929-30 finished as low as twelfth. They were third in 1930-31 when former shipwright Ted Harper fashioned 36 goals in only 30 games. Eighth the following term before 1932-33 saw Spurs promoted as runners-up five points ahead of Fulham losing only seven times away in the process and including an indifferent start and finish. George Hunt scored 33 goals.

In fact in 1933-34 they took three points off Arsenal when finishing third, though they failed to score in 13 matches. Hunt had 32 goals this time. Sadly the wheels came off the next season with demotion from the First Division facing the ordeal of 5-1 and 6-0 reverses against the Gunners. Thirty-six players were called upon and there was a run of 16 games without a win. Yet for the FA Cup tie with Newcastle on 26 January a crowd of 61,195 packed White Hart Lane.

In 1935-36 thoughts were entertained of a strong bid to regain promotion but it faded in the second half for a fifth place. Subsequently Spurs were tenth using 30 players in 1936-37 when unusually five players scored League and Cup hat tricks: Johnny Morrison five (including a four timer), Miller four goals, Andy Duncan, George Hunt and Jimmy McCormick a treble each. Hunt went to Arsenal after scoring 125 League goals. Spurs were fifth in 1937-38 after a stutter at Easter. On 11 April they had appointed Peter McWilliam as manager again having previously been in charge from 1912 to 1927. He had been scouting for Arsenal! Spurs finished eighth in 1938-39.

While long-serving players like left-winger Jimmy Dimmock whose thirteen seasons 400 appearances and 100 goals ended in 1931 with moves to Thames and Clapton Orient, there were notable captures including inside-forward Willie Hall from Notts County a year later. Home grown centre-forward Morrison scored 101 League and Cup goals in 154 outings.

But Spurs had some exciting cup ties to recall. One in the FA Cup fifth round on 22 February 1937 witnessed a see-saw 4-3 win over Everton. They had been 3-1 up when the turning point came from a linesman's flag for an Everton foul throw-in causing the referee to call back the penalty he had awarded them for an Arthur Rowe foul on Dean!

Millwall's heroics were also cup related of course while they also recaptured their Second Division status at the end of the 30s. Fourteenth for two seasons prior to 1931-32 when they were ninth place was partially explained by scoring and conceding the same number of 61 goals. Only 19 players called upon. Hit by an uninspiring finish in 1932-33 ended in seventh position the highest achieved before the Lions were relegated in 1933-34 scoring only 39 goals and suffering two runs of eleven games without a win.

Censured over crowd disturbances on 24 March, the Den was to be closed for the first two matches of 1934-35 and with this hanging over the club the last game of 1933-34 ended in defeat against Manchester United who survived in the Lions place.

The highlight in 1934-35 was winning the first six before a twelfth place reprised the next season, while eighth position reflected an improved 1936-37 when the FA Cup produced the plaudits. Seven ties, 23 goals and just four conceded including two in the semi-final against eventual cup winners Sunderland at Huddersfield. Aldershot, Gateshead, Fulham, Chelsea, Derby County and Manchester City were swept aside as Millwall became the first Third Division club to reach as far in the competition. For the Derby game on 20 February 1937 a record 47,478 attended. The Lions also shared the held over Third Division (South) Cup with Watford after both matches were drawn 2-2 and 1-1.

Though a mere one point from the first three games, there was a new manager at The Den in Charlie Hewitt and given funds so to do, he pulled the club round with a run of ten without defeat. Then to the extent that promotion was achieved in 1937-38, the run-in to the title confirmed by just one defeat in the last 17 matches. He strengthened the team with Hearts centre-forward Bill Walsh in October, Southampton right-winger Syd Rawlings in December and inside-right Jimmy Richardson from Newcastle United replacing injured Dave Mangnall. The three top League scorers Mangnall (16 goals), Rawlings (14) and Walsh (11) missed a total of 57 matches between them.

But the defence let in only 37 goals and stalwarts including versatile ever present Ted Smith and wing-half Jim Forsyth who completed 350 League and Cup games in ten seasons. Additionally Millwall won the Southern League Mid-Week Championship and the London Challenge Cup. The oddity of 1938-39 was winning, drawing and losing the same number of League games when in 13th place. It should also be noted that the Duke of Norfolk became club President!

West Ham United lost its First Division standing at the end of 1931-32 after a high seventh in 1929-30 before finishing 18th. Only one point was amassed from the last ten games. Further demotion seemed likely in 1932-33 with the distraction of a cup run and saved by four wins from the last five games; the drop being avoided by only one point ending 20th. For the Birmingham FA Cup tie on 4 March 1933 44,232 were at Upton Park.

At least the remaining six seasons had the Hammers in the top half. In 1933-34 they were briefly third three points from the top before ending seventh. But third in 1934-35 with the agony of failing to go up on inferior goal average was a huge disappointment, though the margin was comfortably in favour of Bolton. Another spirited effort came in 1935-36 leading marksman Dave Mangnall with 23 goals missed most of the second half with injury and though top for many weeks, Easter saw the challenge diminish.

West Ham lost just twice after Christmas in 1936 but had too much ground to make up and sixth was the outcome. Thirty players were used. In 1937-38 a wretched away record contributed to ninth in the table, whereas the culprit was at home in 1938-39 resulting in eleventh place. A protracted FA Cup tie with Spurs began 3-3 at Upton Park, continued 1-1 at White Hart Lane before a Hammers win 2-1 at Highbury.

As to personnel, Vic Watson who cost £50 from Wellingborough completed 15 years in 1935 with 462 League appearances and 298 goals. Another with longevity was outside-left Jimmy Ruffell with 18 years service to 1938 from 505 League games and 159 goals. Centre-half Jim Barrett completed 442 League matches. All played variously for England as did Len Goulden inside-left partner to Ruffell for five years. West Ham paid a record £4,000 for Rod Williams a centre-forward from Reading with a good goals-for-game ratio in November 1937.

Nearby Clapton Orient had enjoyed many years in the Second Division before the 30s. However in 1929-30 twelfth position was to be bettered only once by one place in 1933-34. In 1930-31 goalkeeper Arthur Wood had completed 373 League appearances when Orient finished a relatively comfortable 19th. Sixteenth in 1931-32 and though avoiding the need for re-election, there were several close shaves: on goal average in 1932-33 and with two points to spare in 1938-39.

Despite winning just one of the last eleven, the three-cornered 1932-33 cellar-dweller battle was resolved by Orient conceding twelve fewer goals than either of their fellow sufferers while in 1938-39 losing just one of their last six matches proved the decisive saviour when 20th.

Eleventh in 1933-34, then 14th in consecutive seasons they were twelfth in 1936-37 with the club losing £90 a week, but down to 19th in 1937-38. However, on 23 October 1937 at Brisbane Road 19,896 saw the Millwall game. Financially the club often struggled. There were several moves of venue, too. Two League games were played at Wembley in 1930 plus an FA Cup tie at Highbury with the home facilities requiring improvement. That 1930-31 season the Lea Bridge Speedway ground afforded little touchline space. The League ordered a yard of turf to be added and only after prevaricating did the owners agreed. An Army hut was in use there for extra accommodation at one stage. Meantime both Leyton and Walthamstow Avenue had been approached for sub-letting.

In 1933 closure seemed inevitable after a season of financial crisis and even appeals for players from other clubs, but supporters rallied to raise money. Even the Prince of Wales contributed! On 5 May 1937 the League suspended Orient but removed the ban a month later. In 1933-34 veteran Dave Halliday from Manchester City scored 19 goals in half a season including nine successive games. Surprisingly Orient refused an offer of £10,000 for three players at one time.

Orient also turned inside-left Tommy Mills into a Welsh international having snapped him up from Trocadero a London Hotels League team. Left-half Eddie Lawrence had preceded him in his country's colours.

Crystal Palace threatened to launch concentrated challenges for promotion but was never able to deliver one. Ninth in 1929-30 they were runners-up the next season though the position was over-estimated by having matches in hand at a late stage. However they scored 107 goals with Peter Simpson getting 46 of them.

In 1931-32 four wins and two draws belatedly put respectability on fourth place and one slot lower the following season when no long runs of success materialized. The injury-hit 1933-34 campaign also faced a mid-term nine-match sequence without a win in finishing twelfth. Winger Bert Harry completed 410 League appearances before retiring. Once more in 1934-35 there was no sustained onslaught despite being fifth.

But for a suspect defence, 1935-36 with 32 players called upon would have seen improvement on sixth. Simpson, with 165 League and Cup goals, had joined West Ham but Albert Dawes scored 38 of 96 goals and earned an England trial. Dawes left for Luton early in 1936-37 leading scorer Bob Bigg broke his left leg in February and Palace finished 14th.

Dawes returned but the final outcome in 1937-38 was seventh. Runners-up in 1938-39 points were dropped in the final stages but in reality the three points lost to champions Newport were crucial as Palace had a better goal average. On 18 February 1939 Palace scored three goals in the first five minutes against Walsall and won 4-0.

The restlessness at Queens Park Rangers with its history of folding tents and moving on also reflected the attitude towards improving status. Though third in 1929-30 with George Goddard scoring 37 of the 80 goals, they were way off a decent total of points. Rangers were eighth in 1930-31 and even 13th in 1931-32 due to a mid-season stutter of eight without a win.

They were also on the move again this time to White City where gates rose to 13,303 some five thousand more on average. For the FA Cup tie with Leeds United a record crowd of 41,097 was recorded. Defensive issues led to 16th in 1932-33 and gates were almost halved! That season George Gofton played seven League games and scored eight goals! Back to Loftus Road for 1933-34 and in early autumn Rangers led the table before a fourth position loomed. Goddard went to Brentford after scoring 174 League goals.

In 1934-35 three goals in nine matches from October contributed to 13th, but in 1935-36 with Tom Cheetham recruited from the Army scoring 36 goals Rangers were again fourth. Undefeated in nine games into March helped a ninth place in 1936-37 when £4,000 was turned down for Cheetham. That season they were the only team to beat Luton twice. Still top with two matches left in 1937-38, defeat at Aldershot proved costly and just third spot. Six games into April without a goal ended promise of something developing late in 1938-39 when sixth.

To underline the frustration at Queens Park Rangers they averaged 25 players a season and only on three occasions did they have a player being ever present, two of them different goalkeepers. They ended 1938-39 with another between the posts in 19 year old Reg Allen, signed from Corona FC in March 1938.

Thames Association had been in existence since 1927. Two seasons in the Southern League they were third in 1929-30. The West Ham Stadium ground they used at Custom House, Silvertown had a capacity of 80,000 and the arena held well supported speedway meetings. It was hoped there would be a spin-off for football. Thames had applied for Football League membership in 1929 receiving just one vote. But in 1930 it increased to 20 one more than Aldershot and Thames was elected to Division Three (South) with Merthyr losing its position.

Expectations soon faded. In their first season Thames averaged crowds of 2,315 and finished 20th. One gate of 469 was recorded in December 1930. But winger George Stevens was transferred to Chelsea before entry in the League. In 1931-32 they were bottom with only 23 points gates a little better at 2,623. They did not seek re-election.

IN SUBURBIA

The fringe areas around London produced one successful promotion when Luton Town sustained its challenge from the Third Division (South) mid-way through the period averaging more than 80 goals a season.

Thirteenth in 1929-30, an inconsistent seventh and then sixth in 1931-32 when scoring 95 goals they stalled a little in 1932-33 when despite just one home defeat they won on travel only once dropping to 14th. Unsurprisingly their goals record was 78-78. But the sixth round of the FA Cup was reached that term, even Spurs a victim. A better second half of the programme in 1933-34 restored them to sixth. On 2 September 1933 Torquay were beaten 10-2. The FA Cup visit of Arsenal on 13 January 1934 attracted an 18,641 attendance. Another heavy scoring campaign yielded 92 goals in 1934-35. The widely travelled Jack Ball scored 30 goals in 31 games. That season saw Andy Rennie departing after scoring 146 goals in 307 appearances. Unbeaten spells in October and November and a run of six wins in a row around February threatened a higher finish than fourth.

A notch or two improvement in 1935-36 and top for the first time of Boxing Day. This followed an indifferent opening with two points and two goals from five games as well as using as many as 31 players overall. The defence only conceded 45 goals. Unfortunately six of the last nine fixtures were drawn and despite the amazing 12-0 win over Bristol Rovers with hitherto wing-half Joe Payne getting ten from centre-forward, Luton had to be satisfied with runners-up a point adrift of the top.

Still they proved to be top Hatters in 1936-37 with 58 points and two points clear. They had taken two points off both their nearest challengers Notts County and Brighton & Hove Albion. Of the 103 goals, Payne grabbed over half with 55.

Twelfth from Second Division fare in 1937-38, the campaign ended with three wins after nine games searching for one. Their 89 goals – three more than conceded – proved the highest in the four divisions. Payne went to Chelsea but Luton unearthed Hugh Billington in 1938-39 who responded with 28 goals in 27 appearances. He also scored 14 in 15 Combination games. A slightly disappointing ending but Luton ended seventh.

Neighbours Watford also showed excellent credentials in the second part of the 30s with sixth, fifth then three times fourth place as due reward for their efforts. However, the early seasons were more of a struggle. Fifteenth in 1929-30 and three places lower in 1930-31 when they reached the last sixteen in the FA Cup, fine wins in the last six improved the standing to eleventh for 1931-32 plus quarter-finalists in the cup. Similarly one reverse in the last ten games kept Watford eleventh for 1932-33.

Just one win in the initial eleven matches in 1933-34 led to 15th. Billy Lane scored three in three and three-quarter minutes against Orient beaten 6-0 on 20 December 1933. Four goals came in the first five minutes after a goalless first half, Barnett getting No. 4. Still there was a definite advance in 1934-35 even though the first four games were lost. An undefeated sequence of 15 into February signalled a turn of fortune and sixth position.

In 1935-36 injuries disrupted at times but Watford finished fifth. Long-serving inside-forward Tommy Barnett scored his 100th goal in February. Still it was Luton who spoilt the following season when they completed the double, the Vicarage Road local derby fixture on 20 February 1937 attracting 27,632. Watford also lost two of their last three when in fourth place.

However, there was some Southern Section cup joy gaining revenge on the way by beating Bristol Rovers winners of their final meeting in 1934-35, though the 1936-37 semi-final replay and final had to be held over until the next season. Both final games with Millwall were drawn 2-2 and 1-1, so the trophy was shared. In the earlier 8-3 win over Notts, Willie Black headed four goals.

Fourth again in 1937-38 after a tendency to be inconsistent, they were top at Easter and conceded just 43 goals. Only a New Year improvement altered the outcome to a third successive fourth place. Barnett's eleven seasons had produced 398 League appearances and 144 goals while winger "Taffy" Davies was in his ninth season. Barnett had once scored 100 goals in a season for Longsight.

Reading reorganized after relegation from the Second Division, was just once as low as sixth being regularly among the teams for promotion. For a time Elm Park became a fortress, too. Nineteenth in 1929-30 with only goal average keeping them safe with a better defensive record, the rearguard let them down the next season in finishing 21st. Twenty-six goals conceded in the first five matches provided the key. Though beating Stoke City 7-3 on 3 April with Arthur Bacon scoring six, there were no more victories.

Readjustment produced 97 goals in 1931-32, an unbeaten 13 matches into late March and 16 successive home wins at the end were not enough. Neither was taking three points off Champions Fulham who were two points in front.

Jack Palethorpe had scored 29 goals in 27 games before he was transferred to Stoke City, Moreover, Reading's fourth place in 1932-33 was not improved upon as witness two wins in the last twelve games. There had been 19 consecutive home wins until 1 October 1932. In 1933-34, they remained undefeated at home, dropping only four points. They were sandwiched on goal average in third place. Frank Newton scored 25 in 26 matches after arriving from Fulham.

By now the home advantage was having its effect. From 8 April 1933 there had been no defeats at Elm Park. For 1934-35 Reading stayed second in the wake of Charlton but one point from a last possible six was unhelpful and that came from entertaining the Addicks! However on 16 February the diversion for 30,621 was the fifth round FA Cup tie with Arsenal.

Top for three months during 1935-36, a three-game missing injury to Tommy Tait mid-season was significant. Reading's 55-match unbeaten home run ended in the first of them on 15 January. Third place again only three points behind the champions. Reading was placed fifth in 1936-37, one place lower the next season after a mid-season boost and a Third Division (South) Cup Final succcess 6-2 on aggregate against Bristol City. Reading was fifth once more in 1938-39. Tony MacPhee ex-Coventry scored 25 goals.

Aldershot had come close to a Football League place from the Southern League in 1930 only one vote short of Thames election. But in two years it did happen. Though 17th in 1932-33 the newcomers reached FA Cup fifth round before losing 2-0 at Derby. Goalkeeper Willie Robb (37) had to obtain League permission to play; he finally made 176 appearances! Goals were scarce in 1933-34 fifteen games without one averaging just one a game so 14th was a respectable position especially as there was a lone win in 15 games from January. All this despite unbeaten in the first eight matches then only five games won and 17 goals by Boxing Day. Arthur Tutin picked up from Crook Town was sold to Stoke City.

In 1934-35, only one win away and 14 matches without any goals the Shots were 18th. John Oakes from Spennymoor United was later transferred to Charlton. Scoring remained a problem but eleventh in 1935-36 was encouraging. Yet 1936-37 proved a disaster. Seventeen games without a win from 10 October Aldershot was bottom on 2 January. Only 23 points were obtained, nine below their nearest rivals. But they received 34 votes.

Finding goals was a constant concern, only 39 were managed in 1937-38 and 18th in the table having been 21st on Boxing Day. Transformation of a kind came in 1938-39 and they were even top for a week in October. That month on the 22nd neighbours Reading attracted a 15,611 crowd to the Recreation Ground. Then two key players had to be sold, centre-forward Harry Egan to Cardiff City and full-back George Williams to Millwall. Tenth position was unflattering only five points short of third place and losing their last three games. Cecil Ray scored 22 goals.

Three pleas for re-election proved one too many for Gillingham to stay in the competition. In 1929-30, they were continually hovering around the last two places. Even though they produced three clean sheets at the death, five points and a remarkable 6-0 demolition of Merthyr Town with Fred Cheesmuir scoring a double hat trick, goal average condemned them to re-election.

Thirty-three votes enabled them to carry on and 1930-31 looked more promising until there were only four wins in their last twelve leading to 16th position. But there was more grief when 1931-32 opened with one victory in eleven. Nineteen games without a goal and only 40 in total, they went back cap in hand at the AGM and incredibly received 41 votes. Oddly enough Gillingham had been the only club to inflict home and away defeats on Fulham and prevent them from scoring at home!

An indifferent start in 1932-33 but a definite uplift from a more settled appearance and seventh until ten places were dropped in 1933-34 when unusually five players hit double figures accounting for all but eleven goals.

Worryingly again 1934-35 had all the wrong indications but only one defeat in the last ten kept them four points clear in 20th position. In 1935-36 the first win came in the seventh game but ninth in early February before ending 16th. Eighteen wins in 1936-37 ensured a mid-table eleventh. In these two seasons Jim Watson had scored four hat tricks.

But 1937-38 was the end of the road. One win and a draw away, just 36 goals overall and none in 19 games was a pointer to failure. A solitary win secured in the last nine and it was re-election time having been always in the bottom two from January. Twenty-eight votes awarded and Ipswich Town replaced them.

From a large turnover of players full-back Fred Lester ex-Chatham Town completed 201 League appearances in seven years before joining Sheffield Wednesday.

Southend United had two seasons chasing promotion and one having to apply for re-election before stabilizing in mid-table. Eleventh in 1929-30 they shot off to a fine start winning five in succession to head the Third Division (South). Easter finally wiped off any promotion thoughts.

Not so in 1930-31, third at Christmas and second at the end of March was impressive but there were too many points to make up on the leaders and the Shrimpers finished fifth. Jimmy Shankly completed a club record seven hat tricks from 1928 including five goals against Merthyr on 1 March 1930.

Still it was nearer towards success in 1931-32. Undefeated in the opening 15 games and topping the table, a gentle slide followed. But during that time record gates had come on their visits to Orient and Fulham against whom United took three points! Alas not even an unbeaten run in the last 14 could push United higher than third.

Inconsistency in 1932-33 and 13th before three positions lower in 1933-34, the next move for the club was to forsake the open-to-elements Kursaal for the Greyhound Stadium with David Jack appointed as manager for 1934-35. Son of the first manager Bob Jack he had gone to school locally.

Then the anti-climax of having to seek re-election despite winning three and drawing two of the last seven matches. However, Golders Green was beaten 10-1 in the FA Cup! Harry Johnson scored five goals. Southend was four points adrift of safety. Forty-eight votes proved encouraging. Half-back Dickie Donoven had taken his ten-year stint to 318 League appearances.

A slight improvement came at 18th in 1935-36; new personnel including Jimmy Nelson ex-Cardiff City and Wales full-back, Charles Turner the Leeds centre-half and goalkeeper George Mackenzie both later capped by the Irish Free State. Though centre stage came in the FA Cup when Southend drew 4-4 away to Tottenham, losing the replay before a record 23,634 with 2,000 locked out on Wednesday afternoon 15 January 1936.

Sixth for a time in 1936-37, when manager Jack at 37 years 235 days made his only appearance in the FA Cup against Crystal Palace, but finally tenth. Twelfth placed in both 1937-38 and 1938-39 seasons. From the 1 April to 6 May 1939 Southend played 12 games including four in seven days, scored 12 goals achieved 12 points and managed to beat the champions Newport 5-0 in the sequence. Full-back Dave Robinson reached 317 appearances after ten years then joined the ground staff. Southend also ended Corinthians FA Cup career in 1937-38 and 1938-39.

Jack had played and scored for the "A" team against Islington Corinthians and contemplated a return to Football League action, agreeing on a wage cut if so doing, but had left it to the directors to decide his role.

ON THE EAST COAST

Norwich City 1938-39. Back; Robinson, Taylor, Mackrell, Duke, Milburn, Smalley. Front; O'Reilly, Coleman, Acquroff, Jimmy Jewell (manager), Graham, Furness, Reilly

The Southern League continued to prove an excellent entrance examination for the Football League and Ipswich Town, a fledgling professional club upped from amateur status in 1936 became the latest successful candidate. Though too late for early FA Cup exemption they rattled in 39 goals in the preliminaries including a record 11-0 win over neighbours Cromer. Their first tie produced a 7-0 win over Eastern Counties United with Jack Blackwell scoring a hat-trick. At the League's AGM in 1938 they received 36 votes, eight more than Gillingham.

Seventh was satisfactory as one of five on 44 points and only five places short of third place. After two wins there were nine without one until the settling in process was completed. Ambrose Mulraney scored a hat trick in 15 minutes in a 4-0 win over Bristol City. The FA Cup tie with Aston Villa on 11 January 1939 brought 28,194 to Portman Road.

Their recruitment removed the isolation of Norwich City in East Anglia. The Canaries were perched a comfortable eighth in the Third Division (South) for 1929-30. So, 1030-31 was a shock for them. Bottom in the New Year, a mini-recovery stalled and at the foot again in March, thereafter in the bottom two. But 38 votes enabled them to start re-building and they had beaten Coventry 10-2 with Tommy Hunt scoring five times.

Tenth in 1931-32 and a strong bid for promotion in 1932-33 appreciated. Two undefeated runs of 15 and ten signified the intention but three successive defeats in April proved crucial when City were top. Third place was still encouraging and produced the necessary impetus for 1933-34.

With just one defeat in the second half of the season, Norwich maintained its lead at the top and was able to finish seven points ahead of the opposition to gain Second Division status. Right-winger Billy Warnes and centre-forward Jack Vinall shared with bulk of the scoring with 21 goals each. There was also the brief appearance of Alf Kirchen once a centre-half, destined for Arsenal in attack.

Five players had amassed 71 of the 88 goals: Ken Burditt with 14, Tom Scott nine and Rod Williams six from only eight games completing this contribution. Goalkeeper Norman Wharton kept 16 clean sheets.

Norwich was 14th in the first season in Division Two as defender Joe Hannah ended his 14 year stint after 398 League appearances and two benefits. Eleventh in 1935-36 when City flew from The Nest to Carrow Road with 29,779 watching the 4-3 opener against West Ham, the end of 1936-37 produced a final position of 17th and the departure of manager Tom Parker who had masterminded their promotion. Fourteenth again in 1937-38, an FA Cup visit by Aston Villa attracting 32,172 on 8 January 1938. Then an insipid attack and weak defence led to relegation in 1938-39 on inferior goal average. There were signings of note but too late to turn the tide. But right-half Barney Robinson continued to add to his appearances in his eighth season. On 29 October 1938 HM King George VI attended part of the match against Millwall.

Lincoln City tasted Second Division football for two seasons having been devastated in 1929-30 with a stand-destroying fire. All was made good and the team finished fifth. After losing the first game in 1930-31, ten successive victories set them up but on 25 April a 5-3 defeat at Accrington cost them top billing. They scored 102 goals had 57 points and missed out by a point.

There was almost another late slip in 1931-32 after a strong showing in the New Year. With a narrow points advantage leading the division, one point from the last two matches gave them the Championship on goal average, courtesy of 106 goals and a defence conceding a mere 47. Again 57 points achieved! Allan Hall contributed 42 of their scoring efforts including twelve successive League and Cup games. On 16 January Frank Keetley had scored six of the nine against Halifax. The goalless last home affair with Wrexham had an attendance of 14,938 and film of it shown in local cinemas.

Life was harder in the Second Division and survival in 18th rested on the penultimate game with Manchester United won 3-2 even though it was followed by a 6-0 defeat at Bradford Park Avenue. Hall added 23 valuable goals to make his ratio one every 100 minutes. Alas it was more so in 1933-34 with 25 defeats, 18 games without scoring and only 44 overall. Hall had gone to Spurs for £3,250. Lincoln finished seven points below relegated Millwall.

A spirited attempt was made in 1934-35 amid cost cutting exercises, so fourth place was a worthy response. This was repeated in 1935-36 in the same atmosphere. Centre-half Con Moulson was twice capped for the Irish Free State. On 16 September 1935 skipper Alf Horne scored three penalties for the 3-0 win over Stockport County. For 1936-37 eight consecutive wins into March put them top for a week. Another seven without defeat from April raised promotion hopes but losing at Hartlepools placed everything on the last game at Stockport who had a point and superior goal average despite Lincoln's 103 goals. Lincoln lost 2-0. John Campbell scored 35 goals.

The Imps might have improved seventh place in 1937-38 but for just one win in the last five. Campbell completed 66 consecutive appearances. Lincoln fell away in 1938-39 continually hovering in the lower reaches before ending seventeenth. Still Campbell took his goals total to 104, goalkeeper Danny McPhail completed 309 appearances and wing-half George Whyte was one short of his treble century.

Grimsby Town ended the 30s better positioned in the First Division having had to fight back following relegation. They only scraped by with a point in 1929-30 with five wins and a draw in the last seven matches in a mass scramble involving others, but were 13th in 1930-31. The drop came in 1931-32 even though they won the last three games – their only such successive treble. On 30 April they had won 6-5 at West Bromwich with hat tricksters Max Holmes and Jimmy Dyson.

Thirteenth in 1932-33 the uplift came the next season. Fitness of the playing staff was obvious from seven ever-present players among 18 another missing just once. Top mid-November and never headed. The attack produced 103 goals, the over-elaborate Pat Glover scoring 42 in 39 games! There was a Christmas double over struggling Manchester United 3-1 at Old Trafford with a Glover threesome and 7-3 at home.

In 1934-35 a consolidating fifth place, the highest obtained by the Mariners. Four of the 19 players were ever-present two others missed one game and Glover hit his 100th League goal at Spurs on Boxing Day. However, it was a disappointing 17th in 1935-36. The FA Cup took centre stage that season with Hartlepools beaten in a replay, Port Vale, Manchester City and Middlesbrough before just being edged 1-0 by Arsenal in the semi-final at Huddersfield.

A mid-table twelfth in 1936-37 came as a prelude to later concerns. However on 20 February 1937 Wolves FA Cup visit had attracted 31,651. Nine games before a win in 1937-38 then five in the last seven including the last three successes to escape by two points and 20th. Inside-forward Jackie Bestall the "Mighty Midget" ended twelve seasons with 427 League appearances. He had always possessed a good grasp of tactics and became Birmingham coach in 1938.

Averaging a point a game in tenth place for 1938-39 steadied the Mariners ship. There was also another semi-final encounter. Tranmere, Millwall and Sheffield United both after replays before Chelsea and a semi-final with Wolves. With George Tweedy suffering influenza, Grimsby had the misfortune to lose his deputy George Moulson after 23 minutes and lost 5-0 with Pat Glover taking over in goal. He played the whole game between the sticks on 29 March at Charlton in a 3-1 defeat.

Alec Hall (337 appearances), Harry Betmead (262) and Teddy Buck (354) continued to be the backbone of the half-back line. Glover made 226 appearances and scored 180 goals before moving to Plymouth having suffered a knee injury.

Existence was rarely dull for Hull City with a promotion sandwiched between two relegation terms. Second Division status was lost in 1929-30. The crisis came in March with injuries and involvement in the FA Cup. Half the division was in danger of descending. Inferior goal average cost Hull. But the cup had seen Plymouth, Blackpool, Manchester City and Newcastle (replay) beaten and even Arsenal needed a second try before winning 1-0. The Newcastle game attracted 32,930. Half-back Tommy Bleakley signed off after 368 appearances. Yet that season Hull included future internationals in Sam Weaver, Dally Duncan and Ronnie Starling. In the cup-tie at Plymouth, Stan Alexander scored a hat trick in the 4-3 win, the first treble in the competition proper by a Hull player.

Sixth in 1930-31 and two slots lower in 1931-32, it proved third time lucky in 1932-33. Top in January after an unbeaten 13 matches, the Championship was lifted with a 100-45 goal average which was a Football League record. Bill McNaughton scored 41 times. Hull was also undefeated at home, dropping only three points and just once failing to score.

Fifteenth in 1933-34 and two places higher the following season, this time it was third time unlucky in 1935-36. Financial problems, a list of injuries and a defence conceding 111 goals against 47 from the attack including no wins in the last 16 games with just five drawn, the end was long in sight. Overall only five wins – a Division Two low – and twelve points behind the other relegated club.

Fifth in 1936-37 after a nine-match undefeated start, there seemed to be a real opportunity to regain Second Division fare in 1937-38. With five matches remaining Hull was leading a tight race but losing 1-0 at home to Tranmere they finished third. Only eighteen players were called upon. In 1938-39 Billy Bly was introduced in goal following George Maddison's 430 such outings and left-back Cliff Woodhead completed his ninth season having taken over from Matt Bell who had made 393 appearances to 1931. Hull finished seventh and on 14 January beat Carlisle 11-1 following 6-1 and 6-2 defeats!

At least Newcastle United had an FA Cup success to lighten up what was a gloomy era on Tyneside. Not only was there demotion from the First Division, it was a close run thing that they were not in the Third Division (North) when 1934-35 started.

Even initially in 1929-30 just a point separated the Magpies from the drop out of the top flight. Three wins in the last five matches activated the escape. Hughie Gallacher in his last season at St James' Park scored 29 invaluable goals too, out of his 133 for them overall.

Gallacher returned in Chelsea colours on 3 September 1930. As for 1930-31 17th, not one win in the last seven matches and lack of a reliable marksman. Inside-forward Tom McDonald left for York City after ten years service 341 League games and 100 goals. However, a mid-table finish in 1931-32 – despite one win in the last ten – plus the FA Cup run arriving, too, if at times in a not straightforward fashion. A 1-1 draw at Blackpool was followed by a 1-0 replay win only for those others from the north-western sea-side Southport to prove initially even tougher opposition.

They earned a draw at St James' Park and a repeat of the 1-1 at Haig Avenue. Off to Hillsborough for the second replay Southport collapsed conceding nine goals. Thereafter Leicester City was beaten 3-1 and Watford 5-0 in the sixth round with Jack Allen scoring three. At Leeds Road Huddersfield, Chelsea proved more of a challenge but still defeated 2-1. Thus to the Wembley final and the controversy of the "over-the-goal-line" centre that produced one of Allen's brace in the 2-1 win.

A falling away in the last few weeks was responsible for fifth place in 1932-33 but drawing eleven of their overall 14 games at home in 1933-34 and just one win in the last 14 was a sure-fire way of being relegated. When Sam Weaver who divided his time between wing-half and inside-forward emerged as the leading scorer; perhaps the weakness was obvious. However, on 26 December 1933 Newcastle had scored four goals in five minutes against Everton to win 7-3. After losing 2-0 at Portsmouth four days later they beat Liverpool 9-2 with seven goals in the last thirty minutes!

There was no impact in the next three Second Division seasons in which United finished sixth after losing five of the first six, eighth when Jack Smith, 19, from Huddersfield scored 22 League goals in 31 games and fourth in 1936-37 with five wins at the end. Disaster nearly struck in 1937-38; survival resting on one-tenth of a goal average after two wins in the last 13 fixtures. Ninth place in 1938-39 and a financial loss of £17,000 as an addition to this overall disappointment stamped this largely unhappy flog on the Tyne.

Tees-side at least could say that while there was no cup joy, First Division status was retained if again at times accompanied by fortune. Middlesbrough had its best two 30s seasons at the end. Previously there had been some real scares. In 1929-30 16th position when Jackie Carr one of the four brothers to play for Boro retired after a sterling 20 year service and 421 League games, was followed by seventh, sixth having been their highest all season when while scoring freely the team let in just eight goals fewer. On the last game in 1930-31 George Camsell scored all four in a thrilling eight-goal share with Manchester United.

George Camsell

Camsell, who was to be top marksman for ten seasons from 1926, scored his 200th League goal for the club in 1931-32 but the term produced a slump at the tail end when just four goals came in the last six outings. Only a last five match revival in 1932-33 kept them in 17th place, one higher than the previous season. In the New Year they had been second from the bottom.

A spell of twelve matches without a win consigned Boro to 16th for 1933-34. However, on 18 November 1933 Boro beat Sheffield United 10-3, the highest Division One score for seven years. It became more nerve-wracking in 1934-35 after just three wins in the last 16 matches with a point on the last day enough for safety. Fourteenth in 1935-36 and the quarter-finals were reached in the FA Cup, too.

Already the worst was history and seventh in 1936-37 was welcome with the promise of 17 year old Wilf Mannion at inside-forward and even better in 1937-38 in fifth place when Micky Fenton followed Camsell into the scoring limelight and the England team. There was a full-back of quality in George Hardwick – another 17 year old – emerging, too. The teenager recovered well from putting through his own goal in the first minute of his debut against Bolton. Then in

1938-39 a sound start, slipping back, then briefly third in the New Year and again in early April before ending fourth, their best in the ten seasons. Goals were featured at both ends at almost four a game. Fenton scored 34 in the League. On 21 January 1939 the FA Cup visit of neighbours Sunderland brought 51,080 to Ayresome Park.

Camsell finished his illustrious 14 year association with Ayresome Park with 345 League and Cup goals after signing from Durham City and left-half Billy Forrest completed his tenth season with 307 League appearances.

Hartlepools United toiled at times until finally having to seek re-election to the Third Division (North). At least 1929-30 was a reasonable season for them in eighth place, but only goal average saved the situation in the following term. Harry Simmons scored five against Wigan Borough on 1 January thereafter only 19 were scored overall. In 1931-32 13th when 100 goals were conceded and the position far worse save for winning their last five matches.

Fourteenth in 1932-33 with many goals at both ends, eleventh next time out and twelfth in 1934-35 before another much more settled season ended eighth in 1935-36. On 11 January 1936 some 15,064 saw the Grimsby FA Cup tie. More of an improvement showed in 1936-37 winning 19 matches and up to sixth. Sadly the next two seasons were not encouraging.

For 1937-38 it looked decidedly bleak with no away successes and firmly at the bottom until four draws plus three wins enabled them to survive – but only on goal average! Disastrous start in 1938-39 no points or goals in the first five games and into the New Year with seven straight defeats ended in going cap-in-hand to the League. But with 38 votes they were well supported and re-elected.

Local discovery with Hebburn Colliery, Johnny Wigham made his bow as an inside-forward in 1931 and was still with the club when it had to apply for re-election having made 264 League appearances and scored 102 League and Cup goals.

York City's initial Football League venture in 1929-30 ended in a satisfactory sixth using just 20 players throughout and an effective run at the end. One youngster was Reg Stockill aged 15 years 281 days on the left wing. Twelfth then ninth in 1931-32 with Reg Baines scoring 28 goals before a shock when moving to Bootham Crescent when only an incredible 6-1 win over Darlington in the last game – first win in nine – enabled them to prevent re-election on goal average. Early in October York was 21st, Gateshead 22nd. Back in mid-December 1932 City had even been second in the table. Baines had 29 goals.

Twelfth again in 1933-34 and four wins in the last six during 1934-35 put them into a respectable 15th. York dropped a position in 1935-36 through a leaky defence. Two games of twelve goals: a 7-5 success over Mansfield, but 12-0 loss at Chester. Twelfth once again in 1936-37, with Albert Thompson recruited from the Army scoring 28 goals in League and Cup.

The FA Cup proved a distraction in 1937-38 admiringly forcing a sixth round replay against Huddersfield Town before going down 2-1 n front of 28,123. Baines in what was his third spell at the club from Midland League days, too, was the scorer. He contributed 80 League goals in his 110 appearances. York's victims had been Halifax, Clapton Orient, Coventry, West Bromwich and even Middlesbrough. Bearing in mind City lost their last five League matches, they were still eleventh.

History repeated itself in 1938-39 when again Darlington were beaten 2-1 there in the penultimate game helping towards a one point gap for safety. December and January had seen York suffer some heavy defeats.

One of the stalwarts at either full-back or centre-half was Ted Wass who made 244 League and Cup appearances from 1932 and was a part-timer signed from Chesterfield and working in that town as an engineer. Two others: Baines had been a part-timer employed as a foreman in the Rowntrees chocolate factory, schoolboy international full-back Jack Pinder signed in February 1930 a telegrapher on the railway. Baines three full League seasons at York had yielded consistent League and Cup scoring: 28, 29 and 28 goals.

While Darlington had come to York's rescue a couple of times, nobody came to their aid. But 1929-30 was a good season for them outscoring others with 108 goals and a flourish too late at the end to improve on third place. They had two 8's, a 7 and two 6's. Maurice Wellock scored 34 goals. In 1930-31 the disappointing home record led them to eleventh when unbeaten in the last eight and the finishing place was the same in 1931-32.

In 1932-33 a poor start and ending with just one away win, there were problems throughout with 32 different players used but at least 47 votes in support at re-election. Sixteenth in 1933-34 only two wins away but some silverware gained with the Third Division (North) Cup against Gateshead in a replay, York and Wrexham beaten and Stockport County 4-3 in the final at Old Trafford after being 3-2 down in the 68th minute. Full-back or right-half Hugh Dickson ex-Worksop Town completed his 402nd appearance in his 13th season.

Even top in October 1934 but financial problems required players sold on before a fifth spot at the conclusion Jerry Best scoring 31 in 35 games. Similar moves in and out for 1935-36 the poor away record leaving Darlington twelfth and they lost the section Cup to Chester – at home! Alas rock bottom in 1936-37 with seven successive defeats into March and only two points from the last possible ten. Surprisingly again 47 votes cast in their re-election favour.

One wonders what a similar plea would have ended as in 1937-38 only goal average rescued them following another season with one away win. Consistency surfaced in 1938-39 from eighteenth place with one away win; the fourth time in the 30s.

South Shields were seventh in 1929-30 and basically folded. The enterprise was moved *en bloc* to Gateshead who took their place for 1930-31 finishing ninth. Then such an improvement for 1931-32 as runners-up on goal average though champions Lincoln City had scored twelve more goals and conceded one less. Also Gateshead had lost twice to City. Top at the end of October and vied with Lincoln thereafter.

After a useful start came seventh in 1932-33 and losing the last seven games in 1933-34 including 12-1 at Barrow pushed them to 19th. Jack Wesley, once in the Navy, scored an invaluable 25 goals. Gateshead finished thus in the next season when there was just one away win. Players had to be sold in 1935-36 and leading scorer Jack Allen retired half-way through. Gateshead ended 14th.

In 1936-37 the first win came on 31 October! One win from the last eleven and they were second from bottom on goal average. But they were re-elected with 34 votes. At least lessons were learned. In 1937-38 a good start top four times and a run-in left them fifth. On 25 September 1937 the visit of Lincoln attracted 20,792.

Tyneside hero Gallacher hit 18 goals in 1938-39 and unbeaten in the last seven games Gateshead were tenth. One-time Thornley Albion half-back, George Neilson progressed from Durham City and South Shields to rack up 273 Gateshead appearances.

Just where Carlisle United would have been placed in 1929-30 without the twin scoring powers of Jimmy McConnell with 27 goals and Davie Hutchison with 25 from the 90 goals scored is debatable. Otherwise 15th would have been flattering as the defence conceded 101 goals. On 11 January 1930 the FA Cup tie with Everton attracted 16,806.

Things were turned round in 1930-31 placed eighth with the goal ratio in their favour 98-81, McConnell scoring 36 goals. But 18 defeats were suffered the following season when 18th. One slot lower in 1932-33, 22 loses and the goals dried up to 51 with McConnell now at Crewe, his 124 goals a memory and Hutchison at Luton.

Recruited from the Army the previous season when he had 15 goals in 20 games, Bill Slinger rifled in 31 goals in 1933-34 but Carlisle was 13th. Unluckily, 1934-35 had them bottom suffering 27 defeats, their demise in the season long established. Still 46 votes got them back in the Section. In 1935-36 one win away reported and 13th. Six wins in a row was their best next time when tenth. But subsequent events proved a concern in 1936-37. Allegations came to light of Carlisle players accepting money from a Stockport County director in the last stages of the relegation struggle in the division.

After a bright start in 1937-38 a falling-away in the New Year left them twelfth. Carlisle's hero in 1938-39 was Sam Hunt signed from Accrington Stanley in October and contributing exactly half of United's 66 goals. He scored four, four and three goals respectively against Lincoln, Accrington and Rochdale – his former clubs! Regrettably the defence let in 111 goals and Carlisle were two points off re-election again at 19th.

Clutching cap in hand Barrow was faced with re-election after a 1929-30 season in which they failed to score in twenty matches and achieved only 41 goals. But gaining just seven more votes than Mansfield Town they were re-elected. In 1930-31 16th with Irish international Billy Millar scoring 25 goals and improving on it for 1931-32 with 30 as Barrow moved up to fifth drawing only once.

A ninth position in 1932-33 would have been better but for just one win in the last eight and another late spurt in 1933-34 when the goals were 116 to 94 in favour, was enhanced by winning the last four fixtures. Finished eighth and only 19 players called upon. Jimmy Shankly not of the famous clan had 38 goals, Matt Robinson 25. Gateshead trounced 12-1 in the last game, Shankly getting five, Robinson four.

Nineteen players used again but goals dried up in 1934-35. Though 17th there was no pressing danger throughout and second half disappointment accounted for 15th next time when right-back Billy Host completed 235 League appearances. The position could have been a concern in 1936-37 as Barrow was bottom in January but climbed to 16th. Alas, 1937-38 saw them one place from bottom after again scoring only 41 goals, but perhaps surprisingly re-elected with 35 votes considering their earlier plea. Former England international Freddie Pentland had been appointed manager in January 1938. There was an improvement to 13th in 1938-39 with eight players making 38 or more appearances. That season 20 players were signed for nothing.

As to the FA Cup, in 1931-32 Barrow drew 3-3 at home to Doncaster Rovers. Both the replay and second replay were drawn 1-1 before Doncaster won at the third attempt 1-0 at Leeds. But in 1933-34 and 1934-35 Barrow beat Rovers respectively 4-2 at home and 2-0 away in the same competition.

ATLANTIC COAST AND INLAND

Bolton Wanderers 1937-38. Back; Goslin, Milsom, Atkinson, Young (trainer), Swift, Hurst, Grosvenor, Connor. Centre; Howe, Tennant, Carruthers, Hubbick, Taylor (G), Calder. Front; Taylor (GT), Westwood, Anderson

The bracing off shore air at Southport may have aided re-election twice in succession for the Sandgrounders. But it was a gradual slide and there was some cup cheer. Comfortably settled ninth in 1929-30 when goalkeeper Billy "Salty" Halsall bowed out after 334 League appearances. On 21 September 1929 England amateur international left-winger Jackie Rimmer became the first Southport player to score a hat trick in a Football League game in the 4-0 win over York City. Even fifth in 1930-31 with Archie Waterston scoring 31 goals, Irish international inside-forward Paddy McConnell starring and an FA Cup run to the quarter-finals until Everton popped nine past them.

In 1931-32 hampered by just one win in the last five games but placed seventh. However, after holding Newcastle United twice in the FA Cup they conceded nine goals in the second replay. The home tie produced a gate of 20,010 on 26 January. They finished a mid-table twelfth in 1932-33 but then no win until October 1933, a poor defence and 17 draws, Southport foundered at 18th.

With no success until the eighth match and struggling at home, drifting to one from the bottom in 1934-35 with a large turnover of players, but well supported at re-election with 46 votes. Alas, no improvement in 1935-36 with the number 48 reflecting goals scored and almost double that conceded. Another plea and surprisingly one more vote in favour!

Ominously there were no wins between October and January 1937 but a 14th finishing position with Joe Patrick scoring 29 goals and even runners-up to Chester in the Section's Cup. In 1937-38 despite the division's worst rearguard including letting in ten at Hull, there was triumph in the same Cup beating Bradford City 4-1 in the final after disposing of Carlisle United in a replay, Hartlepools United, Oldham Athletic also second time and Tranmere Rovers. They were placed 16th in the League.

Unbeaten in the first seven games and only three defeats from the first 24 matches in 1938-39 proved an unfulfilled promise, but fourth was still their best position. This time Patrick scored 27.

Blackpool endured a roller-coaster ride having won promotion in 1929-30 with 98 goals and 58 points as Champions, both club records. Centre-forward Jimmy Hampson reached his 100th League goal in 97 matches on 4 January the second of his treble against Southampton. For much of the season they vied with Oldham Athletic. Crucially defeating the Latics 3-0 on 18 April they ended two points ahead of Chelsea and five in front of Oldham.

But Blackpool found the First Division tough conceding a record 125 goals and only one point off relegation in 1930-31 saved by a last day equaliser against Manchester City. The defence let in 102 goals in 1931-32 and twelve fixtures without a win early on. Again it was a point from the drop, courtesy of winning the last two games.

So it was third time unlucky in 1932-33 with sporadic wins and 23 defeats sending them back to Division Two. Adjustment followed in mid-table for 1933-34 and more aware in 1934-35 lying second on 20 April, one point from the last three games left them fourth. Only 19 players were used.

There was a new manager for 1935-36 in Joe Smith and tenth place while the new man sorted matters. Albert Watson, point saver in 1931, left after 353 League appearances. Inside-forward Peter Doherty who had cost £1,000 was sold to Manchester City for £10,000. Bobby Finan scored 34 goals.

For 1936-37 nine successive wins were recorded from mid-November. Into the New Year Blackpool led the table, until held 1-1 at Bloomfield Road by Doncaster Rovers on the last day, Leicester City with a game in hand overtook Blackpool who settled for promotion as runners-up.

Twelfth in 1937-38 introducing Harry Johnston (18) at half-back but losing 248 goal Hampson in a tragic boating accident and 15th in 1938-39 having spent £65,000 on new players including five forwards one of them Jock Dodds from Sheffield United. George Eastham from Brentford cost £8,000 and Willie Buchan from Celtic even £10,000.

Only an Easter revival extracted Preston North End from possible demotion to the Third Division (North) in 1929-30 when 16th. Seventh in 1930-31 but they were down to 13th the next season with ex-Spurs Ted Harper scoring 24 from only 23 games. No defeats from January to April 1933 yet only ninth at the conclusion. Harper weighed in with 37 goals. Midway through the season left-half Bobby Crawford left for Blackpool after 392 League appearances.

With a Committee managing, 1933-34 revealed promotion. Powered along in midfield by Bill Shankly and with a more solid defence, Preston were still in the chasing pack well into the New Year. A 2-1 win at Swansea on 24 March placed them second behind Grimsby Town but only on goal average with two others. This order continually changed but Preston won its last three 1-0, at Southampton the last of them and came second with a point to spare.

A sound start to First Division football in 1934-35 settled the team to eleventh. In 1935-36 February and March were good months and only seventeen players used overall. From the end of November only one change was made until April. The arrival of the O'Donnell brothers Frank and Hugh plus the late appointment of a manager in Tommy Muirhead were other features along with seventh position. On 28 December the first goal in the 4-0 win over Huddersfield was their 2,500th in the League while on 13 April 1936 the 1-0 victory over Bolton produced their 1,600th goal in it.

For 1936-37 a high-scoring FA Cup run accounted for Newcastle, Stoke, Exeter, Tottenham and West Bromwich 4-1 in the semi-final. But Sunderland prevailed 3-1 in the final. Preston was 14th in the table having been the last to win in the division.

With the Committee back in charge, history weighed heavily for 1937-38 and that 50 year old League and Cup double, Preston made strong bids in both competitions. West Ham, Leicester City, even Arsenal 1-0 at Highbury, Brentford and Aston Villa 2-1 in the semi-final put them back at

Wembley. The final was settled sixty seconds from the end of extra time when George Mutch converted a penalty for Preston.

As to the championship effort, 17 drawn games were unhelpful for Preston. Late March just two points behind Arsenal but on goal average from Wolves and Middlesbrough, ten clubs were within six points of the top. But losing at Blackpool and home to Arsenal proved crucial in third place. Despite the chase for honours in April 1938 the club graciously allowed Andy Beattie, Bill Shankly, Tom Smith and George Mutch to play for Scotland against England at Wembley. On the same day they still beat Derby County 4-1! The 64 League goals were divided between nine Scots and Dickie Watmough, an Englishman. In 1938-39 a second half improvement left Preston ninth.

Blackburn Rovers were sixth in 1929-30. Then tenth in 1930-31 with manager Bob Crompton, arguably the most famous Rovers player of all time moving on and the Bruton brothers Jack and Les scoring 37 goals between them. Only a spurt of five wins in the last eight matches of 1931-32 put a better gloss on finishing 16th. Four players scored all but 24 between them with Ernie Thompson hitting 21. With just one win in the final eight outings for 1932-33 it was only one place higher and the worst defence in the division conceding 102 goals. Half-back Harry Healless completed 360 League appearances. Eighth position in 1933-34 was entirely due to an unbeaten record at Ewood Park. Bob Pryde came in at centre-half to stay and impress. On 9 September 1933 Rovers hit all four against West Bromwich in eight minutes.

Blackburn ended 15th in 1934-35 Jack Bruton and Thompson sharing 36 goals but finally crashed into relegation for 1935-36 despite winning four of the first five. There followed a wretched February with a run of eight games without a win and remained at the bottom. The Division Two home record was unimpressive in 1936-37 when twelfth. Right-winger Jack Bruton broke his leg but recovered to record 324 League games and 108 goals. Though 16th in 1937-38 it afforded little optimism for 1938-39 yet with Crompton back at the tiller, it proved a rewarding season.

Save for a wobble in October with three straight defeats, they struck the top in mid-December and from late February maintained first place to ensure the Second Division championship. Outside-left Bobby Langton proved an invaluable addition to the forward line and a cup run to the sixth round confirmed the general advance. Five forwards contributed all but nine of the goals: Albert Clarke 21, Billy Rogers 18, Len Butt and Jack Weddle 16 each plus Langton with 14.

Burnley suffered relegation at the beginning of the era. In 1929-30 they lost their place in Division One on goal average even though they won their last game 6-2 against Derby County. They conceded most goals in the division three short of the century. Eighth in the Second Division in 1930-31 and a further slump in 1931-32 when four wins in the last seven games kept them two points away from the Third Division (North). Centre-forward George Beel completed ten years and bowed out with 316 League appearances and 179 goals.

In 1932-33 after twelve matches without a win early on, history repeated itself with just two points saving a similar fate. Needless to say changes were frequent and for the ten seasons involved only four times was there a player ever present. Thirteenth in 1933-34 and one place higher afterwards when an FA Cup run took them to the semi-final and defeat by Sheffield Wednesday. That 1934-35 season Burnley had accounted for Mansfield, Luton, Forest after a replay and Birmingham. Left-back George Waterfield took his total to 371 League appearances.

But 15th in 1935-36 with the prodigy that was Tommy Lawton introduced late on and 13th in 1936-37. Having made his debut previously as an amateur, Lawton celebrated his professional debut four days later with a goal in 20 seconds and a hat trick on 10 October 1936 in the 3-1 win over Tottenham. Had Burnley's away record matched the one at home in 1937-38 then sixth place would have been improved upon. But 1938-39 the placing was down to 14th.

With the long-serving post-war players drifting into retirement and moving elsewhere, it was readjustment time for Bolton Wanderers after their memorable 20s. Finishing 15th in 1929-30, they were one place higher in 1930-31, former mill hand Harold Blackmore scoring 27 goals. Even 17th the next season when the same marksman ended his Wanderers career with 111 League goals. Demotion followed in 1932-33. Nothing of concern until after Boxing Day and a gentle erosion not hitting last place until one game remained. Even a 5-0 success on the last day did not save them. Winger Billy Butler completed 407 League appearances. On 18 February 1933 the FA Cup tie visit of Manchester City attracted a crowd of 69,912.

Second Division fare and five home defeats were a handicap. Only a twelve-match unbeaten run at the end brought Bolton to third. Whether narrowing of the pitch and new oval goal posts had any effect or not promotion came in 1934-35, kick-started with seven straight wins. Again Wanderers relied on the Jack Milsom – Ray Westwood goal scoring duo. This time they accounted for 61 of the 96 goals. On 5 October 1934 five goals came in eight minutes as Burnley lost 8-0. The defence also showed more stability. Three successive defeats from late March threatened a derailment but runners-up position was subsequently secured with a 1-1 draw at Blackpool. Bolton became FA Cup semi-finalists with Northampton, Plymouth, a three-game marathon with Tottenham and Everton beaten, but a loss to West Bromwich after a replay.

Back in the First Division 13th position before ground improvements were made, but a surprise downturn in 1936-37 when from Christmas Day there was no win for 14 matches. It required strenuous effort from then on until two points separated them from the drop. Full-back Alex Finney signed off his fifteen year two benefits Bolton career with his 483rd League appearance, while promising Stan Hanson was introduced in goal. For 1937-38, flirting briefly with top spot in October, Westwood the dual provider and able finisher in attack had to score 23 as Milsom six seasons top marksman was off to Manchester City.

By 1938-39 when placed eighth, skipper Harry Goslin completed 303 League appearances. Westwood despite being prone to injury had scored 127 invaluable League goals.

Two consecutive re-election applications for Accrington Stanley came within a few votes of losing their status. In 1937-38 they had received 41, but with only 29 in 1938-39 they were just seven votes ahead of Shrewsbury Town. In 1937-38 they had scored only 45 goals. Then they leaked 103 themselves the next season when only eight points had been derived from the first 30 matches.

Previously they had been 16th in 1929-30 after a bright opening, 13th in 1930-31- despite letting in 108 goals – 14th thereafter using only 21 players and 13th again in 1932-33 winning only two of the last ten. In 1933-34 there was rather more of a scare. Only three wins from February including 8-0 v New Brighton left them a mere handful of points off relegation in 20th position. The defence conceded 101 goals. Right-back Jimmy Armstrong completed 260 League appearances. Throughout the period finances remained at a parlous level.

A slight playing improvement came when 18th in 1934-35 thanks to being unbeaten in the last four. The average attendance fell to the League's lowest at 2,785. A much improved ninth standing for 1935-36 with goalkeeper Jack Hacking as player-coach, before finishing 13th again in 1936-37. Bob Mortimer scored 33 goals in 37 League games. There was much relief of a fiscal nature when a fourth round FA Cup replay produced a record Peel Park gate of 11,636 and a victory over Blackburn Rovers. Mortimer scored four of the five in the two cup games – and was promptly signed by Blackburn!

Not that wholesale changes were made each season though the in-and-out of players meantime had been considerable. It was only in 1938-39 when 32 were called upon did this pattern alter.

As to Nelson, on the face of having experienced one season in the Second Division and coming close to quickly regaining their position, failure to be re-elected seemed harsh enough in 1930-31. However, this was their second such application to be readmitted and after enduring a wretched campaign.

In 1929-30 they were placed 19th in the Northern Section, four points clear of the second bottom place, but a disastrous season followed. Twenty-nine matches were lost only 19 points obtained and 113 goals conceded. Yet it was a close run affair at the ballot. First time both new applicants Chester and Nelson received 27 votes. On a second vote Chester had 28, Nelson only 20.

Lancashire lost another club in even more dramatic circumstances. Wigan Borough who had been founder members of the Third Division (North) had excellent facilities, had finished 18th in 1929-30 and even tenth in 1930-31 with gates averaging 5,417. Johnny Jepson scored 28 goals. However, there were serious financial problems not helped by paying too much to sign players and by June 1931 the club owed £800 in wages.

A start was made in 1931-32 but two days after losing 5-0 at Wrexham in their twelfth League game they resigned from the Football League. Their record was expunged from the competition. Yet incredibly Wigan made an application for election at the League's AGM in the summer, receiving not one vote.

MERSEYSIDE AREA

Though Everton took most of the Merseyside plaudits, neighbours Liverpool at least remained in the First Division, seventh as their highest berth but with a couple of scares thrown in along the way. Twelfth in 1929-30 even as promising as sixth into the New Year it would have been higher save for one point from the last six matches.

A ninth place finish in 1930-31 though lying seventh with a game in hand in October, one win in eleven mid-term and inconsistency throughout. Gordon Hodgson scored 36 goals in 40 League games for a club record. The Reds were one place lower in 1931-32 again fifth in November but with a defence conceding 93 goals including the club's then heaviest League defeat 8-1 at Bolton in the finale. However, it was accompanied by an FA Cup bragging 2-1 win over Everton.

Liverpool fell to 14th in 1932-33 with the top half of the table unfamiliar territory but still beating soon-to-be cup winners Everton 7-4. Fifth on 11 November Liverpool was fourth from the bottom at the end of 1933-34 including no wins in a string of 13 encounters, but with the three points taken off the Toffees proving a crucial aid. On a general note Liverpool marginally trailed their rivals in the 30s. Sam English cost £8,000 from Rangers. Neighbours Tranmere visited on 27 January 1934 and 61,036 saw Liverpool win this FA Cup tie 3-1 with English scoring twice.

In 1934-35 they were a respectable seventh on goal average with a draw in the last game despite wayward form, even riding high fifth at the end of December and in March. Right-back Tom Cooper arrived from Derby County and Irish international goalkeeper Elisha Scott – his debut against the Rams previously – bade farewell after 430 League appearances. In 1935-36, losing South African born England international Hodgson after 359 League games and 233 goals proved a blow. A £4,000 transfer to Aston Villa midway through he was a significant loss as goals dried up. Up to sixth into the New Year before the slump to 19th, other teams' failures keeping Liverpool three points from relegation. The scoring void was never adequately filled and notwithstanding the late captures of inside-forward Phil Taylor from Bristol Rovers and ex-Manchester City half-back Matt Busby for £8,500, one win in the last nine left Liverpool again scrambling for results third from the bottom only three points from safety.

They ended a notch higher at 18th in 1936-37. A new manager George Kay was in charge at Liverpool, but again a familiar struggle only three points off the drop. The following two seasons had the Anfield crew exactly in mid-table. In 1937-38, six wins on the trot was the one memorable statistic when eleventh, after being second from bottom in January and again in March. In October 1937 they paid £8,000 for inside-forward Willie Fagan from Preston.

Then in 1938-39 winning, drawing and losing the same number of games made them ideal material for eleventh. This came about after being third from the top late September and into December, too, prior to the customary falling away. Overall the defence often suffered. In the calendar year 1934 it revealed a 9-2 defeat against Newcastle United, 8-1 to Arsenal and 8-0 to Huddersfield Town.

Tranmere Rovers rose spectacularly at the end of the 30s and crashed just as conclusively back to the Third Division (North). They were twelfth in 1929-30, from being fourth in October to below half way by January. Rovers were revitalized in 1930-31 scoring 111 goals in the process. From October they were mostly in second place until losing the last four games and finishing fourth. Jack Kennedy scored 36 goals, Ernie Dixon 31 and Farewell Watts 27.

After a poor start in 1931-32 they were fourth in January and an undefeated run for the last seven kept them there with the attack scoring 107 goals. On Christmas Day 1931 Watts scored five of the nine against Rochdale. For 1932-33 six wins in a row from the end of March was the highpoint in finishing eleventh. Despite topping the division early in 1933-34 there was a slow trickle to seventh. "Bunny" Bell scored 34 League goals.

For 1934-35, an unbeaten start of eight matches promised better things. Top around March, to only fade with one win in the last six ending in sixth place. An even better opening in 1935-36 saw Tranmere undefeated in nine outings. They led the table early January and March but eventually lost runners-up position on goal average. Part-timer and shipping clerk Bell of nine goals against Oldham in the 13-4 match took his total to 33 in 28 League games before being snapped up by Everton for £2,000 on 13 March 1936. He had scored 102 goals in 114 matches. Tranmere won only three more games. On 25 January the FA Cup tie against Barnsley was watched by 22,222.

Two poor spells in 1936-37 with 33 players used, second from bottom in November, last in December but up to 15th in February prior to being placed 19th one point from re-election. Though 1937-38 began slowly Rovers were fifth in December top on Boxing Day. After a slip in March they led by one point with four games remaining. A draw with second placed Doncaster on the last day and they won the title by two points. They had been unbeaten after 19 March, no one scored more than two goals against them with only 41 conceded. "Pongo" Waring scored 22 goals.

The nightmare was 1938-39 again 33 players featuring, only 17 points throughout with just one gained away. No goals in 18 games and firmly bottom from early October. Relegation came early. There had been 31 defeats and Rovers were 14 points beneath their nearest rivals.

Twice having to apply for re-election, New Brighton found themselves backed on both occasions but never able to figure in the top half. Thirteenth in 1929-30 when Dick Johnson scored three hat tricks from his 17 goals, yet after winning the opening game in 1930-31 they went a dozen before another one and eventually ended 19th. More misfortune befell in 1931-32 when they waited for the first victory at the end of October after four goals and one point. Only 38 goals scored and Leo Stevens with 20 had over half of them. With Wigan quitting around the same time, there was only one re-election candidate. New Brighton struck safety in 20th position with only 24 points.

The inevitable was merely postponed. In 1932-33 despite beating fellow sufferers Darlington 7-1 on 8 April they had insufficient credit in the goals-for column to prevent York City surviving on goal average. Their finances were also in disarray. But New Brighton received 47 votes.

From mid-October 1933, they had a curious spell of ten games just scoring goals in their two wins.

No, not Blackpool. This is New Brighton's Tower Ground in the 1930s.

But 15th was an improved position. In 1934-35 they were 16th without real problems with wing-half Jimmy Smedley completing 279 League appearances and Tommy Davis scoring 50 goals in his two seasons. But more concerns developed in 1935-36.

Two wins to the beginning of December and only three points from travel fixtures was a recipe for another re-election stance. Dennis Westcott's ten goals in 18 matches encouraged a vain hope but New Brighton ended bottom with 24 points. On this occasion 38 votes put them back again.

In 1936-37 seven different centre-forwards were tried including full-back Norman Greenhalgh who responded with six goals before joining Everton. Fifteenth that season, New Brighton was two above in 1937-38 with Jack Montgomery scoring 24 goals in 40 matches. They did well to force an FA Cup replay against Tottenham Hotspur.

Sixteenth in 1938-39, New Brighton found Jackie Stamps at Mansfield Town and sold him on to Derby County, similarly sending another striker Arthur Frost out of the Army to Newcastle United; welcome transfers for impoverished coffers.

LANCASHIRE

Having fallen dangerously close to not only insolvency but sampling Third Division (North) football, in addition to two demotions, Manchester United ended the decade on a sounder footing in the First Division.

An unremarkable 17th in 1929-30, Second Division fare beckoned after 1930-31 began with a record loss of the first dozen games, just one away win 115 goals conceded and only 22 points gained from a meagre seven wins. The club was also threatened with having its gas turned off.

Trying to find the right combination in 1931-32, 34 different players were used and United were twelfth. Goalkeeper Alf Steward completed 309 League appearances, half-back Clarrie Hilditch finished his 16th season on 301. The financial crisis was alleviated when James Gibson was co-opted to the board and paid off some pressing debts. Scot Duncan was appointed manager £20,000 was available for signings and led to sixth place in 1932-33. Amazingly £11,000 was spent on transfers and a £700 profit made! Winger Joe Spence completed 481 League appearances and 158 goals.

Alas, when only one point was scrambled in a nine-game run from December 1933, alarm bells rang out at Old Trafford. A rally in April still had fortune hanging by a thread. The last game at Millwall was knife-edged. Whoever lost would be relegated to the Third Division. United won 2-0. Full-back John Silcock bowed out after 423 League games. No less than 38 players had appeared in the season. Of 50 United players 28 were professionals.

At least 1934-35 produced fifth place and launched an all-out bid for promotion in 1935-36. The New Year began with a defeat but there were no more. Fourth in the table in March, a 4-0 win over Burnley on Easter Monday gave United a goal average lead over West Ham in a close race.

Drawn matches were proving costly but Charlton with one game to go leading by a point United had a game in hand. They won it 3-2 at Bury. Despite an anti-climax with both Charlton and United drawing their matches, the Championship came to Old Trafford. United had completed 19 games unbeaten. Though the final advantage was just a point, the Reds defence was far superior having let in just 43 goals with goal average assured.

Sadly eleven winless games into December 1936 heralded another downward spiral with no sustained recovery periods. The manager had his contract extended by five years but a Leeds win after United had completed its programme confirmed relegation! Irish utility man Johnny Carey was signed from St James' Gate.

There was another congested situation at the top of the Second Division in 1937-38 but United led briefly on 26 March. Duncan had resigned three months into the season. With a match left Villa had 55 points Sheffield United had finished with 53 while Manchester United and Coventry were level with 51. Again the Reds goal average was worth a point. Coventry only drew but again it was Bury to play. United won 2-0 and promoted as runners-up. During the season youngsters Stan Pearson and Jack Rowley had shown immense promise in attack. Also the club paid £6,000 to sign Jack Smith, the Newcastle centre-forward in February 1938.

Any prospects of another nose-dive did not happen in 1938-39, though there was a ten-match spell late on without a win. Fourteenth position was satisfactory, the club had set in motion its youth plan with the MUJACS.

Tenth place for Rochdale in 1929-30 gave no indication of the drama to follow in a season of 180 goals – two more conceded than scored. Jack Milsom was sold to Bolton Wanderers for £1,500 in December but Tommy Tippett scored 29 in 30 games including six against Hartlepools. Though there were fewer goals overall in 1930-31, 107 were let in. A second half of the term slump and inferior goal average meant an application for re-election. But 40 votes were secured.

Compared with that, 1931-32 was a total calamity finishing 13 points bellow the nearest team. Four wins, 33 defeats (17 in a row and a record 14 at home), a League record low eleven points with just one away – one only in the last 26 – 135 goals against and only 48 in favour plus serious financial problems. A second successive plea for re-election ensued. With Wigan Borough's earlier withdrawal, only one spot was up for re-election and Rochdale received 47 votes!

Ten new players figured at the start of 1932-33. Ten different centre-forwards tried and 16 games without a win into April 1933, only four wins in the last five lifted Rochdale to the dizzy heights of 18th. No improvement in 1933-34, bottom in January and a third requirement to go cap in hand to the League. Because of the deepening depression there were no other candidates and Rochdale was re-elected unopposed.

In just over four seasons over 100 different players had been called upon. No joy in the FA Cup, just nine seasons without a win. There was yet another sweat at the end of 1934-35. It was reprieved by a 2-0 success over York City with a point and safety to 20th. Marginally better in 1935-36 albeit only in terms of two points from re-election again 20th. No goals in seven of the last twelve outings but a 6-4 win mixed in!

Early in 1936-37 bottom of the table again before improvement and three wins from the last four left a three-point margin in 18th position. Jimmy Wynn scored in nine successive games. Seventeenth in 1937-38 was the best since 1929-30 but the club was £10,000 in debt. At least encouraged by the on-the-field showing, 1938-39 saw 92 goals scored with Wynn claiming 28 and Rochdale was 15th. On 14 January 1939 Rochdale won 7-0 against York. According to *The Survivors* a shilling fund netted exactly a shilling in its first week.

Second Division Bury finished fifth in 1929-30. John Reid Smith broke his nose against Nottingham Forest so lost the chance of equalling Norman Bullock's 31 goals by one. Centre-half Tom

Bradshaw was sold to Liverpool for £8,250 in January but the Shakers were down to 13th the next season. Smith had 27 goals to his credit. Back to fifth for 1931-32 but they registered just one win in the last six games. Smith scored his 100th goal. In 1932-33 they were third at Easter, finally fourth. Worryingly bottom after ten games in 1933-34, a November-launched improvement to February placed Bury twelfth. David Robbie took his total of appearances to 420 and goals to 102.

Milestones, too, in 1934-35 as versatile Bullock completed 505 appearances and 123 goals to take over as manager. Left-winger Wally Amos totted up similar figures of 455 and 122 respectively as well as wing-half Jimmy Porter with 396 appearances. Bury was tenth. They slipped to 14th in 1935-36. Prospects seemed encouraging in 1936-37, but after eight without loss a stumbling January was disappointing and third place at the finale. On New Year's Day 1937 34,386 spectators were at Gigg Lane for the Blackpool match.

Eddie Kilshaw was a promising forward discovery in 1937-38, the Shakers were tenth George Davies scored 25 in only 28 matches, and although 16th in 1938-39 it was not a totally secure situation until late on.

The aspirations of Oldham Athletic in 1929-30 foundered when only two points came from the last possible ten and Blackpool achieved the double over them. Ninety goals were scored and only 19 players used. For the FA Cup 46,471 attended the Sheffield Wednesday tie on 25 January. Twelfth in 1930-31 then a wretched spell to Boxing Day 1931 after a nine-game winless run, the Latics finished 18th three points off re-election.

One point from a run of ten matches and a couple of loan players arrived from Manchester City to help out to 16th in 1932-33. Jimmy Naylor was actually an ex-Latic and Harry Rowley stayed to be moved to Manchester United. In October 1932 full-back Teddy Ivill was transferred to Wolves after 276 League appearances – 224 consecutively at one stage. Oldham had to unload more players in 1933-34 but ended ninth.

Second Division status was lost in 1934-35. Spells of one win in 14, eight defeats in succession and no away wins, Oldham struggled finishing one from the bottom with only 26 points. Readjusting to Third Division (North) life in 1935-36 they were seventh and Bill Walsh scored 32 goals. His total was eclipsed the next season when dual Irish international Tommy Davis hit 33 and the Latics were fourth.

In 1937-38 it was fourth again but they lost the last two including their home record. As for 1938-39 a good start and ending was spoiled by dropping too many points in between and fifth place was the outcome.

For the second year running Stockport County finished runners-up in the Third Division (North) in 1929-30 despite scoring 106 goals, conceding only 44 and achieving the double over Champions Port Vale. Frank Newton scored 36 goals in 35 matches, Andy Lincoln the only ever present had 26. They still fell four points short.

In 1930-31 the New Year found them second three points behind the leaders only to fade and finish seventh. Newton with 34 League goals was transferred to Fulham. Playing staff upheavals fewer points and goals left County twelfth in 1931-32. More changes in 1932-33 and the signing of centre-forward Alf Lythgoe from Ashton National. Nothing sensational happened until January when Stockport remained unbeaten until the end of the season over 16 matches, the finale producing a goal feast victory 8-5 over Chester and third place. Lythgoe introduced mid-season scored 19 in 20 outings. Joe Griffiths had 21 himself.

County were well placed in January 1934 four points behind the leaders with a game in hand. Then there was the 13-0 record-breaking win over Halifax. Another 16-game undefeated run appeared to set up a title tilt that went on until the last match. Two points in arrears they needed victory and help from others. A point was insufficient; Stockport finished third. Lythgoe missed three games but scored 46 of the 115. Another disappointment was in losing the Northern Section Cup Final to Darlington.

In October of 1934-35, Lythgoe a five goal first game scorer, was transferred to Huddersfield Town, personnel changes abounded 33 different players used and seventh place was a result. But the fifth round of the FA Cup was reached and County won the Northern Section pot beating Walsall 2-0. Lythgoe still managed to be joint top scorer with Bill McNaughton on 15 League goals.

Fire destroyed the grandstand and damaged adjacent properties in the summer. Goals became less prolific in 1935-36 and fifth place was well short of a challenge. Not so in 1936-37 with a new stand and optimism higher. That mystical 16 game unbeaten run came again in a two-horse race developing with County and Lincoln.

With two games to go both had the same total of points and they met at Edgeley Park on the last day, a crowd of 26,135 saw a tense affair eventually going County's way 2-0 and the return to Division Two. Down to earth in 1937-38, Stockport was last and relegated. Even the return of Lythgoe late on could not save them. Only 43 goals were scored and four defeats in a row at the end, too.

In 1938-39, the revelation of alleged match fixing in the 1936-37 season had implications for Stockport. On the field of play an unremarkable ninth place in the Third Division (North) but a curious dispersal of goal scoring with six players in double figures accounting for all but four of the League total.

YORKSHIRE

Bradford (Park Avenue) 1933-34. Back: Bartlett (assistant trainer), Parris, Ward, McClelland, Crayston, Purdon, Blackmore, Hogan, Hardy (coach). Next to back: Claude Ingram (secretary-manager), Nuttall (trainer), Skaife, Boardman, Kelso, Hawthorn, Bell, Lewis, Godfrey, Berry & Ward (directors). Seated: Newby (director), Turner (chairman), Copley (director), Allcock, Barrett, Lloyd, Danskin, Suggett, Waddilove, Brearley and Ambler (directors). Front: Dickinson, Bowater, Carson, Robertson.

Judged on the merits of their 1920's triple title triumph, Huddersfield Town made a decent fist of punching their weight at both League and FA Cup levels once again. Though 1929-30 faded away to a First Division tenth when there were no wins in the last five matches, the cup took them to Wembley and a final.

Bury after a replay, Sheffield United, Bradford City and Aston Villa were edged out before Sheffield Wednesday were beaten in the semi-final at Old Trafford; the last four opponents all by the odd goal in three. Arsenal produced sterner opposition winning 2-0 with Town's old mentor Herbert Chapman at the Gunners' helm.

For 1930-31, Huddersfield ended a rather distant fifth place. On 13 December 1930 they beat Blackpool 10-1, George McLean scoring four goals. Centre-half Tommy Wilson had completed 448 League appearances, while in the September, Huddersfield had previously transferred Scotland international winger Alec Jackson to Chelsea for a then record £8,750 fee. As to 1931-32 just one win in the last four games and fourth place, added to a sixth round FA Cup meeting with Arsenal with a similar outcome as at Wembley, in front of a Leeds Road ground record crowd of 67,008. Dave Mangnall, once rejected by Town as a teenager, scored 33 League goals including nine games in succession.

Sixth in 1932-33 occasioned by failing to score at home in eight matches and losing half a dozen games in November into December. Alf Young won the first of his nine England caps as a defensive centre-half against Wales in November 1932. More determined in 1933-34 and leading on 10 March on goal average above Arsenal. Unfortunately McLean suffered a broken leg at the end of the month. Moreover beaten 3-1 at Highbury on 7 April proved a decisive blow and Huddersfield had to settle for runners-up, having lost three of the last seven. Long-striding left winger Billy Smith signed off with a goal on 10 February having notched up 521 League appearances and 114 goals.

Such was the wretched opening to 1934-35 they were bottom at the end of September. Better in the New Year and 16th. Overall 32 players used. In February inside-forward Albert Malam had also broken his leg against Leeds. On 10 November he had scored a hat trick including a twice-taken penalty in the 8-0 win over Liverpool. Among the pacesetters in 1935-36 unbeaten in the first nine games but all eventually in the wake of Sunderland as Huddersfield won only twice in the last nine games before ending third. On 14 December 1935 Ken Willingham had scored in ten seconds against Sunderland, the only goal of the match.

No away wins in 1936-37 and a run of 13 without victory into March put Huddersfield 15th. England right-back Roy Goodall retired with 403 League appearances in 15 years, one of a dozen full internationals in the post-Great War period. Then the FA Cup took centre stage for the remaining two terms. Actually between February 1936 and September 1937 there had been no wins on travel in the League. However, in 1937-38 Hull, Notts, Liverpool, York after a replay were beaten before an impressive 3-1 success over Sunderland in the semi-final at Ewood Park. Then there was that extra time defeat at Wembley against Preston North End. In the League a stumble in December contributed to ending 15th. On the eve of the final, Huddersfield had been actually resting on the bottom of the table, but they beat Stoke City 2-0 on 2 May and climbed seven places.

In 1938-39 the cup again affected First Division results winning only twice in the last eleven matches and merely once away overall produced a 19th slot. Portsmouth proved Huddersfield's undoing in the Cup semi-final 3-1 at Highbury of all places. Previously Forest in a replay, Leeds, Walsall and Blackburn also at the second attempt had been defeated.

Sheffield United may not have won either the First Division or the FA Cup as did rivals Wednesday, but having come dangerously close to dropping down in 1929-30, then experienced relegation, there were bragging rights for the Blades at the close of the 30s when they clipped the wings of the Owls by one point to regain First Division status. But March 1930 began their troubles with one win in eleven attempts and only defeating Manchester United in the last match kept them out of harm's way on goal average. Snapped up from New Brighton, Jimmy Dunne scored 36 of the 91 goals – five fewer than let in. Harry Johnson, with 201 League goals joined Mansfield. In 1930-31 December led to their best sequence with four wins and a draw in finishing 15th. The prolific Dunne racked up 41 League goals.

Five early wins was again a high point and seventh placing in 1931-32 when Irish international Billy Gillespie retired after 448 League appearances and 128 goals while England left-winger Fred Tunstall finished with respective figures of 437 and 129. Dunne, himself, hit 33 this time. Ex-Wednesday goalkeeper Ted Davison became manager. The unbeaten five games were once more on the agenda in 1932-33 into December when tenth. England wing-half George Green had made 393 League appearances, too. Dunne's contribution came from 26 goals.

But in 1933-34 came the crash into the Second Division. Away form was poor, the defence conceded 101 goals and there were never more than two wins in succession. Dunne with 143 League goals was transferred to Arsenal in September. Wing-half Tommy Sampy had reached 340 League appearances. Goalkeeper Jack Smith, an ever-present for three seasons, even played on with a fractured wrist that set itself!

Save for a mid-term dip in form, the Blades might have been higher than eleventh in 1934-35. Prospects improved considerably the next season on two fronts. A run of 22 competitive matches without defeat ended with third place in the table and a narrow loss at Wembley to Arsenal, though "Jock" Dodds hit the bar with a header. This free signing from Huddersfield scored 34 League goals in 1935-36. On 15 February 1936 Bramall Lane had 68,287 for the FA Cup tie with Leeds United.

Just two away wins in 1936-37 and inconsistency kept them seventh but the outlook was good at Christmas 1937 and again in March when in pole position. With two fixtures remaining the Blades were two points ahead of both Aston Villa and Manchester United, who respectively had two and one games in hand. It proved academic because the Blades lost their last game at Southampton to finish third on goal average.

Stirred by this near miss, 1938-39 proved satisfying for Sheffield United in their 50th season. Though Dodds who scored his 100th League goal on 12 September was sold to Blackpool for £10,000 in March, in November the club had paid Derby £2,925 for inside-forward Jimmy Hagan. Several stretches without defeat increased confidence and included the last nine games. Though neighbours Wednesday took three points off them, United had a game in hand as their rivals had completed their programme. A win was all that was necessary to become runners-up and it came convincingly 6-1 against Tottenham Hotspur. A ten-second opener from Harry Hampson and then a hat-trick from Hagan sealed victory and a return to the First Division.

Rotherham United shared United's experience in 1929-30 in that they escaped in 20th position, though in the Third Division (North). Despite conceding 113 goals, including 53 in one spell of twelve, they were two points from having to seek re-election.

As low as 19th at one time in 1930-31 the final berth was 14th after just one defeat in eleven. Billy Hick scored 30 goals in 31 games. A recovery with seven wins from the last ten games in 1931-32 secured 19th. No away wins in 1932-33 and just three points on travel, but two places higher yet again two points from possible re-election.

Not as lucky in 1933-34 because the first home win only came in November and even though away form had improved there were no wins in the last eight fixtures and re-election knocked on the Millmoor door. Fortunately, neither were there other applicants nor the League accepting a request from Nelson, so Rotherham was reprieved. On 13 January 1934 Millmoor had a crowd of 20,198 for the FA Cup tie with neighbours Sheffield Wednesday.

Former Middlesbrough defender Reg Freeman had become player-manager in February 1934 and became manager in the summer. A more settled approach followed with only 20 players used in 1934-35 and ninth place achieved. Eleventh place in 1935-36 and though last in January 1937 five wins and a draw in the last nine matches helped to 17th.

Level at the top at Christmas 1937 but a poor New Year performance with sixth spot at the season's completion. Another down turn following in 1938-39 after a 7-1 opening win against Rochdale but eleventh at the finale, so any other outcome would have been surprising with the same wins and losses, goals for and against!

For Barnsley there was scarcely a dull moment. Twice down and twice back up again from the start in 1929-30 anxious times were forecast. Hovering at the bottom that season winning the last two games left them 17th a point clear. Left-half Charlie Baines achieved 322 League appearances. No away wins in 1930-31 but Easter proved kinder and 19th at the end. Third from the cellar in October and again in February during 1931-32, with four games left Barnsley were two points adrift and eventually succumbed to relegation by 0.05 of goal average.

Third Division (North) in 1932-33 saw them stabilizing in eighth place. Full-back Anuerin Richards was capped by Wales. Still 1933-34 was a vintage campaign. Second early on, new boy Abe Blight a miner from Blackhall who had hit 57 in a season there was scoring goals then Richards broke his leg. Fifth before the turn of the year then an unfaltering 21 games without defeat, unbeaten at home throughout.

Neck and neck on the last day Chesterfield only drew at third placed Stockport, but Barnsley won 1-0 at New Brighton to take the title by a point. Four ever-presents among the 20 used another missing just once yet another absence twice. Of the 118 goals, Blight had 31 in 34 League appearances including four in a 9-0 win at Accrington Stanley, an away record in the division. Barnsley failed to score only twice. All five regular forwards hit double figures. Dickie Spence and Tubby Ashton had 19 each, Harold Andrews 18 and Jackie Smith twelve goals. Smith from West Stanley was barely 5ft 3in and known as "Peter Pan" or simply "Tiny" but still managed to score goals with his head.

Inconsistent in 1934-35 and Blight sustained serious injury with the team 16th. By December 1934 the excellent home record of 36 without defeat ended at last. Relegation avoided by a point in 1935-36 thanks to holding Spurs 0-0 in the last game. The Tykes failed to score 17 times. Reached the sixth round of the FA Cup and lost to Arsenal. In the cup-tie with Stoke City on 15 February a crowd of 40,245 packed Oakwell.

Five wins in the last seven for 1936-37 and 14th. Barnsley won only two of eleven games to Easter in 1937-38 and none at all in the last eight. Tense finale for the drop and Nottingham Forest their level opponents had the better goal average. Result: 2-2, Barnsley relegated by 0.002 of a goal.

All change again in 1938-39, superb defence conceding only 34 goals. Top after six games, seven points clear by Christmas, but Southport had three games in hand. Barnsley kept well ahead, others with congested fixture lists wilted and the Tykes had eleven points to spare at the end winning 30 matches achieving 67 points from only five defeats. Six players scored double figures: Beau Asquith 28 goals, Johnny Steele 17, Danny McGarry 12, George Bullock and Johnny Lang ten each. Asquith equalled the club record scoring five in one game. So it was back in the Second Division at the first try.

Leeds United returned smartly to the First Division after just one season and thereafter had two terms of concern with which to deal. But for 1929-30 in fifth position, their best was a spell of nine without loss early on. Centre-forward Tom Jennings joined Chester after a memorable 112 goals in 167 League matches. With Jennings injured Leeds had given third choice Dave Mangnall a chance after scoring ten of 13 in a reserve game. He scored six in nine outings in Jennings' absence.

In contrast to the previous term, nine games without a win into January forecast trouble in 1930-31. Second from bottom in February and unable to string enough wins together, Leeds finished one point from survival.

But the rewarding 1931-32 Second Division assault began seriously from mid-September with 15 undefeated matches. Top until mid-March but with enough points in reserve to hold on to second place two points behind Wolves despite just two wins from the last ten!

For 1932-33 just one victory in twelve into April took the edge off this First Division season and an eighth place. On 27 December the visit of Arsenal to Elland Road attracted 56,776 for a goalless draw. As previously, a solitary win from ten attempts into January led to ninth in 1933-34. Charlie Keetley who scored his 100th mid-way through a hat trick v Wolves on 11 March 1933, was transferred to Reading having rattled up 108 goals in 160 League appearances. Jennings goal-per-game ratio was just 0.01 better than Keetley's!

Still Leeds were unlucky with injuries in 1934-35 but again had sufficient points to be 18th. Even though there were no wins from the first six games of 1935-36, eleventh was the final standing. Old style attacking half-back Ernie Hart, a former miner, completed 16 years with his 447th League appearances.

Yet another worry in 1936-37 when they won only four of their last 15 fixtures, but crucially included the remaining couple to stay two points clear of relegation in 19th. Gordon Hodgson recruited from Villa in March 1937 went on to score 51 goals in 81 League games. Initially encouraged by second place at Christmas in 1937-38, it was not sustained and with only three wins in a row from the last 14, ninth was the outcome. Full-back Jack Milburn went to Norwich City having totalled 391 League appearances in nine years.

Once more as high as third in November 1938, one win from then until March over 15 matches left Leeds 13th. Wing-half and ex-pit lad Willis Edwards a £1,500 signing from Chesterfield in March 1925 and a 16 times capped England international took his Leeds appearances to 417.

Recovering from an application for re-election, Halifax Town subsequently came close to promotion. But 1929-30 was the real low. With unpaid wages and the bailiffs sniffing round, players had to be sold including Ernie Dixon to Huddersfield Town for £900. He had scored 127 goals in two spells. On the playing front 17 non-scoring games, 44 in total and four wins from the first 25 fixtures. But 40 votes headed the poll.

Not ground-breaking but 17th in 1930-31 and again in 1931-32. Ninety goals were conceded in 1932-33 but 15th position represented progress. The fifth round was reached in the FA Cup but Luton won at The Shay 2-0 before a crowd of 29,235. Incredibly though crashing to a record 13-0 walloping to Stockport County, 1933-34 saw Halifax ninth, 80 goals scored and further optimism. Bill Chambers hit 30 goals. On 2 September 1933 Fred Tunstall scored all four goals in 27 minutes in the 4-2 win against Stockport. Improvement came in 1934-35. Chasing the leaders in the first half of the season, a slip in the New Year was then reversed only for another disappointment at Easter and out of the running. Fourth with two matches remaining Halifax beat already Champions Doncaster away and home to finish runners-up! There had been just two home defeats but ten away and two points adrift. Albert Valentine scored 34 goals.

In 1935-36 Valentine's 30 goals was over half the team's total. They lost the last four games to end 17th. Save for indifferent form in October and November seventh might have been improved upon in 1936-37. Valentine moved on after scoring 88 goals in 114 matches. However, the goal scoring dried up in 1937-38 with only 44 being registered, so 18th was a relief especially as finances were again a worry.

Twelfth in 1938-39 when the FA Cup also produced a marathon seven and a half hour tie with Mansfield in four games, mercifully successful.

Skipper Ted Craig had completed a club record 287 League games and received a benefit while full-back Bill Allsop was still a regular choice in his fifth season.

Bradford City was in the news for passing on players to bigger clubs, but lost Second Division status in the process. In 1929-30 they failed to achieve two wins in a row at any time and were 18th. Six wins in succession into March 1931 raised hopes but only two points from drawn matches left them tenth. Let-back Willie Watson completed 330 League appearances. Jack Hallows scored 19 goals in only 27 games.

A stretch of nine undefeated games into February 1932 proved unrewarding and only scattered wins followed when seventh in the table. Five wins at the start of 1932-33 looked promising but eight defeats in a row to March ended speculation and it was eleventh when the term ended.

In 1933-34 sixth reflected a settled season but without a serious challenge. Left-back Sam Barkas was transferred to Manchester City for £5,000 easing the finances. He won England caps. Problems in 1934-35 from a spate of ten games without a win into late April put them under pressure until rescued by two wins and 20th.

Into April 1936 ten unbeaten games assisted a final position of twelfth. In March City had transferred full-back Charlie Bicknell to West Ham. An ever-present four seasons in a row and 224 consecutive appearances, too of 240. His departure was followed by goalkeeper George Swindin going to Arsenal.

As for 1936-37 it brought relegation after a season of struggle followed by a real downturn around Easter and just one win in the last eleven put them 21st. Neighbours Bradford Park Avenue escaped by three points, courtesy of a double over City! In February right-back Laurie Scott had followed Swindin to Arsenal.

Third Division (North) for 1937-38 yielded inconsistency but 14th before much more encouraging form in 1938-39 emerging from the pack of pursuers in the New Year, before all challenges in the division became fruitless because of Barnsley's lead. City was placed third. There was a trophy gained in the Third Division (North) Cup when Accrington was beaten 3-0; satisfaction after losing the previous final to Southport. Versatile Charlie Moore took his total of appearances to 340 in thirteen years.

For Bradford, usually listed as such minus the Park Avenue, they stayed in the Second Division with really only one uncomfortable season. Certainly goals flowed in 1929-30 with 91 scored and a fourth place after no defeats in the last seven. Six more goals registered in 1930-31 and a sixth position. In November 1930 George McLean was transferred to Huddersfield Town after 250 League appearances had returned 136 goals. Trevor Rhodes scored 19 goals in 21 games.

Six was the predominant number in 1931-32, with an unbeaten half a dozen games to kick-off and another such sequence into March finishing sixth again. The Christmas Day 3-0 win over Leeds attracted a crowd of 32,421. Wing-half Harold Taylor completed 335 League appearances. This time Rhodes had eleven goals from 17 outings. In 1932-33 Bradford was two places lower, again without any sustained challenge for promotion. For 1933-34 with the best defence in the division and one run of seven undefeated into March they were fifth. Blackmore ex-Middlesbrough and Bolton scored 27 goals.

However, drawn games affected them in 1934-35. Sixteen all season including one spell of 13 matches where they were nine of them! Fifteenth was the final position. One place lower in 1935-36 and one away win. Six games late on had failed to produce a win.

Then the problem campaign when slipping into eight games without a win into March, retrieved by seven points scraped from a possible ten at the end when 20th. Three points away from the drop and City the unfortunate losers. Full-back Tommy Lloyd's ten years had produced 328 League appearances.

Seventh in 1937-38, the varying highspots being eight without loss from September and nine matches with only one win to the end of March. The high mark was beating Blackburn Rovers 7-1 with George Henson scoring six goals. He had 27 in the League, the much-travelled Tom Lewis 23, including six successive matches. Ten places down in 1938-39 and again six games without a win into April. Goalkeeper Tommy "Chick" Farr had made 162 League appearances.

While Doncaster Rovers spent two seasons in the Second Division, they were twice close to redressing the situation. Money worries were evident in 1929-30 and the team was 14th. Les Lievesley made his debut on the first day but was injured and did not reappear until February. He still finished leading scorer with 12 goals! During 1930-31 Rovers were one place lower, the high range being five League and Cup wins in a row and 21 goals scored.

Fifteenth once more in 1931-32 with seven defeats on the trot at one stage but there was no need to sell players. A four match FA Cup tie with Barrow took seven and a half hours before victory. However, there was improvement in 1932-33 on the back of an unbeaten home record when in sixth place. Between December 1931 and September 1933 Doncaster stayed unbeaten at home in 33 League games, recording 23 wins and ten draws. Even fifth in 1933-34 with a stunning finish to the season saw only one defeat in 15. This surge was repeated in 1934-35 when just one game was lost in the opening eleven. By mid-February Rovers were second in a tight pack chasing leaders Tranmere four points clear. But Doncaster had two games in hand.

On 30 March Tranmere lost at Stockport and Doncaster took over, still with a couple of matches spare. On 21 April remaining challengers Chester lost and with a late kick-off Rovers knew they were Champions before beating Wrexham 2-1. They still had two games to go.

Nineteen players used, five of them making only 13 appearances between them. The other 14 won medals. Four forwards hit double figures. The financial side was healthier and gates soared. Two home attendances of 23,238 and 27,554 came during the run-in.

Second Division saw second place at Christmas but something of a free-fall from only two further wins nine points and placed 18th. The signs were ominous and in 1936-37 spells of no wins in 14 plus just one in another twelve sank Doncaster to the bottom. Only 30 goals were scored. Wing-half Fred Emery with 417 appearances since 1924 was appointed manager. Wing-half or inside-forward Bobby Smith completed 264 League appearances in eight seasons.

Back in the Northern Section for 1937-38 second prior to Christmas, but needing to catch up on games played it was not until the last two fixtures that positions became clear at the top. Leaders Tranmere won at second placed Hull, Oldham beat Southport and Doncaster lying fourth drew at Darlington to be two points off the top. Last match home to Tranmere and Doncaster required an 8-0 win to overtake a team with vastly superior goal average. It ended 1-1.

It was a similar runners-up position in 1938-39 but Barnsley had the championship tied up long before the finishing line. At Belle Vue on 18 February 1939 Barnsley attracted 34,046.and won 3-1. But Doncaster had drawn 14 games. Six players scored double figures: Mick Killourhy and Eddie Perry 14 goals each, Fred Dell twelve, Charlie Leyfield and Albert Malam eleven each plus George Little with ten.

NORTH WALES AND INLAND

Wrexham twice came close to promotion in 1930-31 and 1932-33. However, 1929-30 was to be remembered for the record 8-0 win over Rochdale with Tommy Bamford scoring four goals. The team was 17th but had seen a 22,715 gate for the FA Cup against Bradford City after defeating West Bromwich.

In 1930-31, a late flurry of eight games unbeaten pushed Wrexham within four points of the top in third place, achieved by .01 of a goal. Seven goals against Crewe with Tommy Lewis the four-timer on this occasion and another seven scored in winning the Welsh Cup against Shrewsbury Town. Bamford had 34 League goals including consecutively in nine matches.

Chester's admission to the Third Division (North) produced the first of the derby clashes and Wrexham took three points. But in 1931-32 tenth was the final position. Bamford scored 31 goals. Near Christmas manager Jack Baynes sadly died.

Then 1932-33 proved a near miss for promotion. With twice as many goals scored as let in – 106 to 51 – five forwards reaching double figures and at Easter third behind Chester and Hull with a game in hand. But having to play three games in four days was a difficult task and though Wrexham remained unbeaten in April four of the eight ended as draws. Two wins in May were essential, but defeat at

Stockport left the final outcome in other's hands and Wrexham finished runners-up two points behind Hull. At one stage at the Racecourse Ground a total of 39 goals were scored in seven successive home games.

Another century-plus of goals for 1933-34 notched with Bamford claming 44 and five of the 8-1 against Carlisle. Maximum points from the last five meant sixth place. In a Northern Section Cup game New Brighton was beaten 11-1, Bamford scoring six goals, Bill Bryant a hat trick. Wrexham were 11th in 1934-35 with nearly thirty fewer goals. Bamford with 175 goals from 204 League appearances was on 17 October transfered to Manchester United. He had set two scoring records. Bryant followed him to Old Trafford six days later.

In 1935-36 just three points from eight games in the New Year led to Wrexham being 18th. Full-back Alf Jones completed his 13th season with 503 appearances. Eighth in 1936-37 the Boxing Day derby with Chester attracted 29,261 but the high scoring days now gone Wrexham came tenth the next term. In 1938-39 just 41 points and 14th position ended the decade disappointingly.

Recruited on a second ballot after a tie with Nelson for the 1931-32 season, Chester adapted quickly to Third Division (North) standards and finished third, Tom Jennings signed from Leeds scored 30 goals. Throughout the 30s they were among the leading contenders. A strong showing from October 1931 put them among the front runners but an eventual third place was seven points behind the leading pair.

Another worthy season in 1932-33 with 94 goals scored Joe Mantle getting 34 of them but marred by a mere two points from drawn games in the last five matches and a fourth position finish. On 14 January 1933 Foster Hedley scored four of the five FA Cup goals defeating Fulham and a week later hit a hat trick in the 4-2 League win over Accrington. On 6 May Gerry Kelly switched from the right-wing to centre-forward scored four including a penalty in the see-sawing 8-5 defeat at home to Stockport!

Tenth in 1933-34 and 30 players used but another determined challenge made in 1934-35. Though unbeaten in 18 League games from 27 October to 16 February, overall 14 drawn matches proved costly as only eight matches had been lost. Ninety-one goals overall but only five points taken from the last six games. With four games left they had been second on goal average from Doncaster Rovers. This time it was third.

Undaunted, Chester did even better in 1935-36 if not quite good enough for promotion. No hint by January lying eighth, but thereafter in the top three, hitting 100 goals and ending runners-up five points shy. Five players had double figures in goal scoring; Paddy Wrightson taking over as chief marksman from Welsh international Ron Williams, who had scored three in eight minutes in the 5-1 opener against Southport. Wrightson registered 18 over eight successive games among 27 goals. Arthur Wilson scored the 100th in the last game v Halifax.

On 1 February 1936 York City had been beaten 12-0 with Charlie Sargeant and Wrightson each scoring four goals. The Northern Section Cup was won 2-1 at Darlington but exceptional manager Charlie Hewitt left for Millwall. Even so but for an injury at Walsall on 21 March that was to end the career of Frank Cresswell when he suffered a broken knee cap after three minutes and the 1-0 defeat ended an eleven game undefeated run, the outcome might have been different that season.

Still among the fancied teams in 1936-37, they dropped only one point in the first nine games and another unbeaten nine in a row into March proved their best. Drawing at Hull on 6 March cost top spot on goal average and again it was third place. Wrightson scored 32 goals. Even so, the Northern Section Cup was retained with a 3-1 win at Southport. Ninth in 1937-38, Wrightson completed his tally in four seasons to 73 goals from 89 League games. A respectable sixth was attained in 1938-39. That season Bill Pendergast scored in 12 successive games and finished with 26 goals in 34 matches. On 25 January 1939 the FA Cup tie with Sheffield Wednesday attracted 18,816.

Crewe Alexandra finished exactly mid-table in 1929-30, having won and lost the same number of games and averaged a point in so doing. Jimmy Scullion scored 29 goals. A win and a draw in the last two matches of 1930-31 helped to an 18th place after hovering in the bottom three, but with an attack scoring 95 goals aided by Bert Swindells and Harry Deacon each netting 22, the disappointment came from losing four of their last six in ending sixth in 1931-32. That season man of 16 clubs Ralph Williams scored 16 goals in only 13 League and Cup games before moving on again! Another effort was aborted when Wigan withdrew. There were two 8-1 wins too, against Lincoln and York. Tenth in

1932-33 and used only 19 players. Four slots lower in 1933-34. After winning the first three they lost eight in a row. Two departures were the Wales international centre-half Fred Keenor after 116 League games, Deacon 118 and 47 goals.

Crewe was thirteenth in 1934-35 again only 19 players used, sixth again in 1935-36 with a leaky defence in evidence. But only 17 players called upon! Yet there was success in the Welsh Cup beating Chester 2-0. Then disquiet in 1936-37 when only two wins came before Christmas Day. With the weakest attack in the section points from drawn matches kept them relatively safe until losing at Stockport on 17 April. A point ahead of bottom club Darlington but with inferior goal average to two others – though with a game in hand – and only four points separating the last seven teams. Amazingly Crewe managed only one more point from three games and yet survived at 20th thanks to other failures around them! However, the Welsh Cup was retained beating Rhyl 3-1 in the replay.

In 1937-38 (19 players called on) and 1938-39 there were no alarms finishing eighth both seasons though in contrasting manner. In the former term they lost only one of the last eleven, while in the latter there was one win in the last seven. There had been 16 consecutive home wins, the last ten in 1937-38, the first six the next season. Ex-Stockport Sunday School team's Swindells left for Barrow in 1938 after eleven seasons, 247 League appearances and 127 goals.

Port Vale championed their way into the start of the decade with 30 wins scoring 103 goals and conceding only 37 on the way to the Third Division (North) title, to enjoy six years in the Second Division. A slight stutter at Easter but five wins at the close produced a Football League record 67 points for the Third Division (North). A week's relaxation in Llandudno in January produced a tonic of six wins on the trot. Despite missing 37 games between them Sam Jennings scored 24, Albert Pynegar 21 and Philip Griffiths 14 goals.

The 1930-31 campaign in the Second Division saw them in a creditable fifth place, the club's highest position but it was hard going in 1931-32. Third from the bottom at Christmas, lost six in a row – later on and with two matches remaining Vale were three points adrift. They won both of them to survive, the last at already promoted Leeds. Versatile Bob Connelly completed 323 League appearances.

Vale steadied at Easter in 1932-33 to be 17th. Stewart Littlewood scored six goals in 57 minutes against Chesterfield in a 9-1 win. Teacher and part-timer Wilf Kirkham left after two spells and 153 League goals to become a Headmaster! Top in October 1933 and second in January their hopes of further promotion ended at the end of March. Despite 16 games without scoring they were eighth.

In 1934-35 they were third from the bottom at Christmas but this time an Easter revival helped towards 18th position. But rock bottom on 7 December 1935 they were unable to shake off the drop zone. The defence let in 106 goals. Two draws from five games at the finish left them a point from salvation. Surprisingly they had beaten Sunderland in an FA Cup replay! The Roker Park team was top of the top division at the time. The tie was initially drawn 2-2, Vale winning the replay 2-0 before 16,677 spectators.

Back to Third Division fare in 1936-37, the Valiants were fourth on Boxing Day and went 13 unbeaten into the New Year. It was not sustained and eleventh was the result. As for 1937-38 a seventh place in October translated to 15th after seven games without a win into April. There had been just one win away. But Jack Roberts 28 goals put him top scorer in the section.

Having previously tried to get a transfer to the Southern Section, they were moved there in 1938-39 but struggled. A run of no-wins in seven into January, third from last in February, then four points were achieved in the last three fixtures for an 18th position.

Stoke City had a new stand to display in 1929-30 and eleventh was their final position as it was the following season when long-serving Bob McGrory became player-coach. Centre-forward Charlie Wilson took his total of League goals to 112. Fourteen drawn games probably cost dearly in 1931-32. Ten matches without loss into January, but sprinkled with draws. The best defence with just 48 goals against but stuck third, two points away from runners-up and promotion. The same eleven had been fielded from 19 September to Christmas Day 1931.

However, an early sequence of eleven without loss signalled another determined intention in 1932-33. Again the rearguard was solid. It was the 16th game before ten goals had been let in. On 11 March Spurs overhauled Stoke's lead for one week when City lost at home to Notts County, before the lead was reversed. With just 39 goals against, Stoke had scored exactly twice as many and though one point was the margin of Championship success, their goal average was far superior. At one stage in the season the forward line's average age had been 20.

In 1933-34 December proved a bad month but a better second half of the term left them twelfth. The FA Cup quarter-finals were also reached and a profit of £13,422 announced. Stoke was even top in October 1934 before finishing tenth, the season McGrory aged 40 became manager after 479 League appearances. In an 8-1 win over Leeds, Stanley Matthews scored four. Though City was never out of the top four during the last three months of 1935-36 – the fourth place representing the highest achieved – Sunderland were running away with the title. Nineteen players were used overall. From 14 December 1935 to 14 September 1936 the same goalkeeper, two full-backs and three halves were paraded in 30 consecutive League games.

Tenth was the placing in 1936-37. Freddie Steele scored 33 League goals that season, while he, Matthews and Joe Johnson figured in attack for England. The visit of Arsenal on 29 March attracted 51,480 to the Victoria Ground. Steele had five goals when West Bromwich was beaten 10-3 on 4 February 1937.

Then there was a relegation battle involving half of the First Division in 1937-38. Twelve games with just a solitary win and Stoke were favourites to go down, one match remaining. But they beat Liverpool 2-0 to grab 17th position on goal average from four other sufferers. Stoke had been unsettled off the pitch with the Matthews saga of wanting a transfer while the injured Steele had missed 19 matches but scored 15 goals. At least in 1938-39 it was ten places higher at the final count. Matthews had made 236 League appearances and scored 47 goals.

SOUTH WALES AND WEST COUNTRY

The short spectacular rise of Cardiff City was already in reverse before 1929-30 dawned with the loss of First Division status. Before the close of the 30s they would be in the Third Division (South).

No hint of a further decline in 1929-30 and with a run of seven undefeated games at the end of March they were a comfortable eighth in the Second Division. But many of the 20s stars were about to leave. Full back Jim Nelson joined Newcastle United.

Reality stepped in from the start of 1930-31 the first win did not arrive until the eighth match. Already among the stragglers with only Reading lower, on 31 January positions were exchanged. The gap widened to five points, Cardiff were nine points from safety and relegated. Playing only 16 games, Jimmy McCambridge scored eight goals.

There were 18 games without a goal and only 14 goals from the second half of the season. Thirty-two players were called upon but at least the replayed Welsh Cup final from the previous season was won against Rhyl. Versatile Welsh international forward Len Davies went to Thames after 305 League games and 128 goals. The national skipper centre-back Fred Keenor joined Crewe after 371 Football League appearances and 61 from Southern League days. Nine unbeaten matches into late April put a shine on ninth place in 1931-32 and with four players scoring double figures there was the appearance of more balance. Irish international Jim McCambridge scored 26 and Walter Robbins who hit five against Thames reached 21. Out bowed legendary Billy Hardy, 40, the formidable wing-half after 20 years and some 600 first team appearances.

But that season had been an illusion because 1932-33 exposed problems. Eight winless games into November and in the New Year Cardiff slumped second from the bottom. Only two wins from the last three games pushed City up to 19th.

A draw on Boxing Day 1933 was only the second point in eleven attempts and they were last. Never above 21st from then on at the foot with one win out of the last dozen and again nine points from the safety margin. But the application for re-election gave them 48 votes.

Alas seven fixtures yielding not one win to the end of February and Cardiff were 19th in 1934-35 and four wins in March contributed to a lift to finishing 20th in 1935-36. Dual Irish international goalkeeper Tom Farquharson retired after 13 years service and 445 League appearances.

Thirty-one different players were used in 1936-37. Oddly enough after the opening defeat City went eight games undefeated. It was their best all season. Struggling from then on, they were rescued by three wins from the last four to be 18th. On 17 January 1937 fire destroyed the grandstand at Ninian Park.

In 1937-38 and 1938-39 there was at least less fretting. Tenth in the former season and in the latter just one point from seven matches to April meant finishing 13th. In 1937-38 Jimmy Collins with 23 goals and Bert Turner with 19 had proved useful marksmen.

In contrast to the 20s, the only FA Cup run of note for Cardiff was in 1938-39 and reaching the fourth round, but disappointment, too, losing the Welsh Cup final to South Liverpool.

While Swansea Town kept hold of their Second Division membership there were four seasons causing anxiety. Even the 1929-30 season raised doubts when only two points were derived from the first six games. Worse, after 20 games just ten points and bottom. Two players were transferred to Everton, replacements signed and with six of the last eight games producing wins, Swansea were 15th.

Not so in 1930-31 though mid-table half-way through, there were half a dozen other strugglers in the lower reaches of the division and concern grew. On 11 April with four games left, the Swans were third from bottom with a point off 21st position. But on 25 April they lost its last match and though Bradford hit five against them Swansea were safe in 20th beating Barnsley 1-0.

Securing Cyril Pearce from Newport County increased the scoring potential in 1931-32 as witness his 17 goals in the initial 13 matches and his final total of 35; an invaluable contribution to 15th at the final reckoning. But he was sold to Charlton Athletic.

In 1932-33 fifth place at the half-way mark, but losing five in a row from February and just three wins from the last seven games left them tenth. Fifteen drawn games and no away wins in 1933-34 meant added burdens, though the fifth round of the FA Cup produced a record attendance at The Vetch on 17 February 1934 of 27,910 when Portsmouth played. Enter the unlucky hero Wilf Milne who had played 500 League games without scoring a goal. In his 501st his penalty beat Lincoln City. Come match 42 at home to Plymouth and Milne repeats the spot kick feat and the Swans paddled on in the Second Division at 19th.

Neil Harris became manager for 1934-35 but mid-season the team was third from bottom. Even so matters improved to 17th. In 1935-36 as players continued to be sold on, centre-half Harry Hanford was transferred to Sheffield Wednesday, yet 13th was encouraging.

They were 13th again in October 1936 and ended up thee places lower. Full-Back Milne had to play in goal twice in emergencies! It was his final season after 587 League matches and earned a benefit. Winning two matches in a row had been a problem in 1937-38 but it needed so to be with a couple of games left. They did and were 18th. Then Jack Warner was sold to Manchester United.

Stuck at the bottom in 1938-39 after eleven games then there was only one win in 19 attempts. The trap door was only avoided by three wins and two draws in five of the last six for Swansea to be safe in 19th place, three points clear.

Few clubs experienced such lows and one high as Newport County. With 34 goals from his 29 games in 1929-30, Tudor Martin helped towards finishing 18th. He had five goals against Merthyr in a 10-0 win. A string of thirteen games without a win to November began their problems.

But 1930-31 was disastrous. The defence conceded 111 goals and wins were infrequent. Only Norwich similarly in the doldrums with Newport eventually twinned with them on goal average. At the AGM, County received only 19 votes, six short of Mansfield and lost their place. Martin had gone to Wolves where in addition to first team chances he hit 60 goals in the Central League.

For 1931-32 it was Welsh League fare as runners-up. But at the re-election vote in 1932 Newport put their name forward for one of the three vacancies as Thames withdrew and regained Football League status with 36 votes.

Yet in 1932-33 the defence let in 105 goals. Despite four wins in the last seven Newport were 21st on goal average between two others and it was back at the voting lobby. Twenty-six votes proved enough.

Only 17 drawn matches kept Newport away from serious harm in 1933-34 as a paltry 49 goals were recorded and eight games won. Four teams were level on points at the conclusion but six away from danger with County 18th. Another season of toil in 1934-35 with 112 goals let in and an unlucky 13 sequence looking for a win into March. Newport was bottom ten points from safety but a surprise 43 votes in favour of retention!

No respite in 1935-36, the rearguard letting in just one fewer than the previous term. Twenty-first and a fifth application for reinstatement rewarded amazingly – given the foregoing – with an unprecedented 40 votes. Clearly the Ironsides were fireproof!

Initially in 1936-37 not a win from the opening eleven games and a continual battle to keep away from the drop zone. Mercifully three wins and a draw from the last six resulted in 19th two points clear. There were also optimistic signs in 1937-38 with just 21 players called upon. Despite 17 games without a goal and only 43 scored, 16 games were drawn. There were five draws in the last eight and a 16th position. On 16 October 1937 a crowd of 24,268 saw the local affair with Cardiff.

Transformed in 1938-39 with twelve undefeated games to Christmas then accountably crashing 8-0 at Swindon; a defeat partially retrieved winning the return the next day 6-4. Yet only 45 goals conceded all told, organized around ever present skipper and centre-half Norman Low, 19 clean sheets and able to finish as Champions of Third Division (South) three points ahead and win a place in Division Two. Low had been a £2,000 record signing from Liverpool in November 1936.

Perhaps the seeming benevolence afforded Newport was in part due to the sad departure of Merthyr at the end of 1929-30. Nine points adrift at the end, bottom from September, accumulating only 21 points (six wins, nine draws) overall having let in 135 goals and in a parlous financial position, they received only 14 votes at the AGM and lost their place, in the wake of fellow Welsh club Aberdare Athletic four years previously.

Bristol City began modestly enough in Division Two during 1929-30 lying fourth in September but third last in December and bottom in February, they escaped 20th on goal average at the end of the season following eight points from the last five matches. In 1930-31 the last nine games produced eleven points and 16th.

However, 1931-32 they were already last in mid-September. Long sequences searching for a win, only six all season just 39 goals, 15 games without one and relegated. A sizeable overdraft meant disposing of players, too. Fifteenth in 1932-33 but two poor spells in 1933-34 of 13 without a win one from the start, last in November and nine of ten winless at the close left them 19th. At least one trophy won with the Welsh Cup in the cabinet. The club also received a welcome £3,750 from Manchester City for centre-forward Jimmy Heale.

Fifteenth again in 1934-35 having recovered from another nine match run trying to find an elusive win, the season was enlivened by a lengthy FA Cup run. Gillingham, Rotherham, two replays with Bury and one each against Portsmouth and Preston included record gates of 42,885 then 43,335. In the League City were two places higher in 1935-36 despite the weakest attack in the division. During 1936-37 the rivalry with Rovers finished with the two of them level on goal average, City 16th the lower.

Still a run of seven undefeated into February looked promising in 1937-38. There were five teams chasing the title but City finished runners-up losing out by just a point. A home defeat by Cardiff proved crucial. Eight times they drew goalless. Discovery Alf Rowles scored a Football League record twelve goals in six consecutive matches, 18 overall in 15 appearances. It included a debut hat trick against Exeter on 15 January. For 1938-39 six without loss to Boxing Day kept interest alive and an eighth placing, but an injury to Rowles ended his career. Manager Bob Hewison was suspended for seven months by the football authorities over illegal payments to amateurs.

Bristol Rovers ended the 30s needing to apply for re-election having been just three times in the top of the table in ten seasons. In fact only goal average saved them in 1929-30. Third last in December and 20th by February, a game in hand in the final week gave them a lifeline when they had been second from bottom. On the last day in a 4-1 win and Jack Phillips scored twice against his former club Brentford. Goalkeeper Jesse Whatley retired after 371 League appearances.

Winning the last five games in 1930-31 pushed them to 15th. Arthur Attwood the only ever present scored 24 goals. Warning signs early on with just two draws from seven matches but 18th in 1931-32 followed by three more successful seasons respectively ninth, seventh and eighth. Former teenage prodigy Ronnie Dix had been transferred to Blackburn for £3,000 in 1932. In 1934-35 there had been the victory in the Third Division (South) Cup final beating Watford 3-2.

That 10-0 drubbing at Luton arrived in 1935-36. Rovers were 17th and in the FA Cup even led Arsenal for an hour before losing! That season Ray Warren was introduced in midfield and started to establish himself. Then the rivalry with their neighbours was given an extra edge the following season with the better attack of the two finished 15th one place above City on goal average. On Boxing Day Rovers had been 20th. In the period, Rovers won five and lost three of the derby games and six were drawn.

For 1937-38 an unbeaten last eight games assisted to 15th but 1938-39 provided a shock. Thirteen games without a win to mid-December and their plight masked by other teams having games in hand at the final reckoning left them bottom, two points from safety. Crisis time and the Eastville Ground sold to the local Greyhound Racing Association as Rovers became tenants. But 45 votes showed confidence in the re-election to the Third Division (South).

Swindon Town experienced their best two seasons at the end of the 30s having had to once apply for re-election. But 1929-30 might have turned out better except for a poor spell of eight games seeking a win into February. Fourteenth was the result and long-serving pre-war winger Bertie Denyer completed 324 League appearances. In the FA Cup Swindon beat Manchester United 2-0 then drew 1-1 with their neighbours City only to crash 10-1 in the replay.

Again in 1930-31 twelfth came about after just two wins in the last ten matches. Harry Morris scored 36 League goals. An end-of-season downturn in 1931-32 saw them losing the last five and ending 17th. However, the real slump came in 1932-33 in Morris' last season after 215 goals in 260 League appearances since 1926.

Bottom in mid-February one win in the last nine and only three in the whole of the second half, the defence leaked 105 goals. Even so it was only on goal average that Swindon was 22nd. At least there confidence at the re-election with 45 votes cast in their favour.

A much better second half of the season in 1933-34 and an undefeated eight games into April left them eighth in the table. But eight places lower in 1934-35 and even 19th in 1935-36. Prospects began to look more positive in 1936-37 with only 21 players used and 13th at the conclusion.

In 1937-38 the period from January to Easter was particularly satisfying with just one defeat and eighth place achieved. In October Swindon paid a record fee of £1,000 for Ben Morton from Torquay. Goals were frequent at both ends in 1938-39, 72 scored but five more let in. The two Newport games illustrated it with 18. Swindon finished ninth. Morton was leading scorer in the Southern Section with 28 goals.

SOUTH OF ENGLAND

Consistency to a fault was the phrase associated with Plymouth Argyle once being admitted to the Third Division in 1920 when the Southern League was virtually taken over *en bloc*. The error was failing six times in succession to finish above runners-up position.

It was different in 1929-30 after a seeming collapse to third and fourth place in the two preceding seasons. Eighteen games without defeat including twelve wins was the impressive opening. Thereafter only four defeats sprinkled here and there. Ninety-eight goals, a club record 68 points, 30 wins, unbeaten at Home Park and only 38 goals conceded. Unsurprisingly a seven point cushion for the championship of the Southern Section.

Goalkeeper Fred Craig retired after 361 League appearances and another 78 from pre-war Southern League days. But the effective left-wing partnership of Jack Leslie and winger Sammy Black honed during the previous seasons proved invaluable again.

Conditioned to Third Division football for so long, the Second Division was not an easy changeover. But they did win a third of their matches in 1930-31 plus four wins and a draw of the last six left them a safe 18th. On 6 December 1930 goalkeeper Harry Cann was injured against Spurs and Fred Titmuss went in goal. Goals from Tommy Grozier and Black (his 100th) won the game. Despite losing the starter in 1931-32 they went eight without losing and ended in fourth place after 100 goals.

A parallel opening in 1932-33 defeat then an eight game unbeaten run, perhaps not a shock given their history! In March ex-Looe forward Ray Bowden was sold to Arsenal for a record £5,000 and Plymouth finished 14th. Tenth in 1933-34 and Jimmy Cookson scored 27 goals in only 29 League games.

Even though there was a stutter from the kick-off in 1934-35 with just one win in the first ten, the final position was eighth. Leslie played his last and 383rd League game in December 1934 and scored his 131st goal. Argyle was one place higher in 1935-36. Then losing merely one of fifteen from mid-September until Christmas in 1936 was one reason for fifth place that term. On 10 October the FA Cup visit of Aston Villa had produced a record crowd of 42,870.

Winning the first game in 1937-38 Argyle were unable to find another in the following eleven and went on to finish 13th. Black ended his fourteen year career after 470 League appearances and 176 goals. In 1938-39 another streak without a win into April, sixteen games without scoring overall, 15th in the table and 34 players called upon reflected change of manager with the legendarily successful Bob Jack giving way to Jack Tresadern.

Torquay United mastered the art of the great escape six seasons no higher than third bottom and with little margin for error. Moreover 1929-30 was a case in point; actually one point from the problem. Concern grew when in eight games into March there were no wins and only four goals scored. Six points were scraped from the last five matches, one point safe but with inferior goal average. Joe Pointon (18 goals) and Les Robinson (16) scored more than half the total number of goals. Ralph Birkett was a debutant right-winger on 8 March 1930 and had involvement in all seven goals scored against Bournemouth.

In comparison 1930-31 was a breeze into eleventh place. Jimmy Trotter had 26 goals. Not so 1931-32 as after beating Bristol Rovers 8-1, the last six games produced a mere one draw. The defence conceded 106 goals and Torquay were 19th. The season started with only 15 players due to injuries and produced heavy defeats. For the fifth game only ten reported fit and a former player had to be quickly recruited. Another respite in 1932-33 in tenth place Torquay losing Birkett to Arsenal as the first United player to win England honours. Then 1933-34 renewed anxiety. Three wins and a draw from the remaining seven enabled United to finish 20th but with points to spare.

Torquay were tenth in both 1934-35 and 1935-36. The last time they scored and conceded exactly the same amount of goals, before 1936-37 brought the need for re-election much closer. Similarly struggling neighbours Exeter still achieved an early season double over United. The last five weeks were worrying. Only five points came from the last nine games but City with a slightly inferior defence had to apply with Torquay 20th.

In 1937-38 no goals in 20 games just 38 overall and the last win in February! United still managed to survive in 20th position again a point from having to seek re-election, though 1938-39 proved only marginally less exacting. Seven away wins but only seven at home and only two wins in he last eight but four points off the bottom two clubs and 19th. Torquay did reach the final of the Southern Section Cup but only one leg of the other semi final took place as time ran out in the season.

Arguably Torquay had the most versatile player in the Football League during the 30s in Albert Hutchinson who completed 317 League appearances appearing in four forward positions, all three in the half-back line and also at left-back! He also contributed 80 goals.

Exeter City came within four points of promotion but had to apply for re-election twice. Their best performances were reserved for the FA Cup.

In 1929-30 let down by just one win in the last twelve they were 16th. Averaging a point a game the Grecians were 13th in 1930-31. Percy Varco scored 25 goals, Harold Houghton 23. Yet the FA Cup captured attention. The sixth round was reached after Northfleet United, Coventry (in a replay), Derby, Bury and Leeds were knocked out to provide a trip to Sunderland. Exeter gave an outstanding display and brought their hosts back to St James's Park. A crowd of 20,984 saw Sunderland win 4-2.

Exeter's results picked up in 1931-32 from just two defeats suffered in 18 matches into February and enabled them to be seventh. Prospects for 1932-33 rose after an indifferent start. From mid-December only two points were dropped in drawn games during a top game surge. On 21 January they won 2-0 at the leaders Brentford and a week later exchanged places with the London club. Though only three more defeats were experienced there were six drawn games and the margin between top and second place grew. Only 21 players were used and Fred Whitlow scored 33 of the record 88 League goals while the defence conceded a club low of 48. Exeter proved creditable runners-up.

In 1933-34 one win – the last – from the last nine left City ninth, but cup fortune appeared again. The Section Cup saw Crystal Palace, Watford, Coventry (after another replay) and two replays with Brighton beaten and then Torquay 1-0 in the final at Plymouth. Whitlow had six of the eleven goals against Palace. The 11-6 score line in that cup tie was actually watched by Arsenal's George Allison.

Exeter finished two places lower in mid-table in 1934-35 from an unimpressive opening when only two wins came from twelve matches. On 4 May 1935 when City beat Aldershot 8-1 the nine goals came in the second half. But it was far worse in 1935-36 with only eight wins the first after thirteen without one and there was just another such success in the final twelve. By 21 March they were bottom. However they topped the poll at re-election with 48 votes.

Not that 1936-37 was any more of a comfort. In the first half of the season three wins came from 22 fixtures. Only Aldershot in free-fall was preventing Exeter being last. Yet again 40 votes were enough to retain membership. However, the FA Cup had been a diversion and the fifth round had been reached. Rod Williams scored 29 of the 59 goals in 41 League games and had seven in the FA Cup, before he had to be sold in the financial crisis.

A third successive application looked possible at the beginning of 1937-38 when one win came in the first ten. True just one other such in the last seven but 17th was well clear. With a fairly settled team and only 21 players used, 14th was comfortable in 1938-39.

Bournemouth and Boscombe Athletic had to plea to be re-elected once in the 30s but was able to settle without further discomfort. In 1929-30 a thirteen-game undefeated run to Christmas Day even promised something higher having climbed to fourth. But the last eleven fixtures brought just two wins and tenth position.

It was tenth again in 1930-31 this time without any dramatic shifts of fortune. Ron Eyre scored 24 goals. In 1931-32 a similar pattern developed but ended 15th. In the third match away to QPR at White City, prolific scoring Eyre registered his 200th League and Cup goal.

Eyre completed nine years service early in 1932-33 after 304 League appearances and 202 goals in the competition alone, his absence raised concerns by the end of March before 18th place was secured.

Fears became reality in 1933-34. From January to March Bournemouth fell from 16th to 21st in a ten-game run with no victories and on the way to letting in 102 goals. They stayed thus until losing 6-0 at Brighton confirmed re-election to be a reality with two games remaining. Bournemouth received 48 votes.

In 1934-35 they were in the last three for several months and 18th early in the New Year. However, by March the danger period was over and 17th was the final position. No such headaches in 1935-36 and an eighth placing, Bob Crompton was briefly in charge. Even better in 1936-37 when the connection of new manager Charlie Bell with his friend Major Frank Buckley had promising young Wolves players arriving at Dean Court, including outside-left Jack Rowley. An unbeaten run of eight at the conclusion lifted Bournemouth sixth.

Disappointment in 1937-38 and with only one win in the last nine games they were 13th. Two places lower in 1938-39 but with Ken Bird in goal and right-back Fred Marsden among the best of the Molineux contingent. Sadly manager Bell died in June 1939. No fewer than 25 players had joined in the moves from Wolves to Dean Court. Rowley progressed, Bournemouth receiving £2,000 from Manchester United. Billy Elliott, 18, was signed by West Bromwich in a £3,000 transfer.

They Meet At Wembley This Week
CUP FINAL TEAMS and CAPTAINS

A group of the Wolverhampton Wanderers
Back—MULLEN, GALLEY, SCOTT, MORRIS, TAYLOR, GARDINER
Front—WESTCOTT, BURTON, M'INTOSH, CULLIS, DORSETT, MAGUIRE

STAN CULLIS

JIM GUTHRIE

A group of the Portsmouth F.C. team
Back—J. STEWART (trainer), SMITH, MORGAN, WALKER, ROWE, HALL, ROCHFORD, WHARTON
Front—GUTHRIE, WORRALL, M'ALINDEN, Mr J TINN (manager), ANDERSON, BARLOW, BAGLEY, PARKER

Portsmouth went to Wembley twice, the second time with their League position in jeopardy, returning to a success there. In 1929-30 they were 13th an earlier FA Cup reverse still lingering around Fratton Park.

By November 1930, Pompey had reached second place and though the momentum was carried into the New Year fourth place represented their highest position from 49 points. The most settled team in the club's history with only seventeen players called upon there were five ever-presents and another five missing just two League games. Only the untimely death of centre-half Bob Kearney robbed them of another likely candidate.

There was much the same approach in 1931-32 despite a mere two wins in the first twelve outings. Of the 21 players involved three were ever-present, one missing a game, two were absent twice and another two made 39 appearances. The main change was at outside-right Freddy Forward being displaced by Freddie Worrall. Eighth was the final position. Pompey lost to Arsenal in the fifth round of the FA Cup.

In 1932-33 Pompey stayed unbeaten until the end of September and topped the First Division before eventually sliding to ninth. Astonishingly eleven players made 36 or more League appearances. But for 1933-34 the cup was again the distraction as they finished tenth. The way to Wembley took out Manchester United in a replay, Grimsby, Swansea and Bolton before Leicester in the semi-final 4-1 at St Andrew's. At Wembley, Pompey led but centre-half Jimmy Allen suffered a head injury and Manchester City edged them 2-1.

In the close season Allen, unhappy over benefit payment, joined Aston Villa for a British record £10,775. The money helped ground improvements. He had been recommended to Pompey by a fan watching him at Poole and had cost £50. As for 1934-35 Pompey started with a club record 39,710 for the 3-3 draw with Arsenal. They were 14th and in 1935-36 back to tenth with the rampant reserves attracting even 12,519 on Boxing Day.

Briefly top in September and remaining third at Easter before drifting down to ninth in 1936-37, with the club owing £13,000! That season saw the departure of goalkeeper Jock Gilfillan after 331 League appearances over nine years, the same such service as full-back Billy Smith with 311 such matches. After ten years half-back James Nichol had completed 353 League games.

At the foot of the table early in 1937-38, the first win not until 20 November, then an upsurge of 33 points from 27 matches and beating Leeds 4-0 in the last game pushed Pompey to 19th and two points clear. John Weddle joined Blackburn after scoring 171 League goals in 368 matches.

The traditional month between semi-final and final caused many a club problems. Pompey found themselves two points off the last relegation place when they beat Huddersfield 2-1 at Highbury in the 1939 semi-final. Lincoln, West Bromwich, West Ham and Preston had been defeated all at Fratton and with clean sheets. They maintained 17th position until the finish of the League programme. But the cup final itself was an unqualified triumph 4-1 over favourites Wolverhampton Wanderers. Only two goals conceded throughout and 15 scored. James Easson moved to Fulham after scoring 102 League goals. Worrall the only Pompey player twice at Wembley took his total to 313 League games. Jimmy McAlinden signed from Belfast Celtic at £7,500 was a dual Irish international and the fee was a record for an Irishman.

Across at Southampton The Dell boys plied their trade in the Second Division and just had a couple of narrow squeaks. Seventh was their highest in 1929-30. But after scoring 26 goals in as many League and Cup games, Dick Rowley was bought by Tottenham for £3,750 in January having scored the winning goal against them on Boxing Day in front of a record 25,203.

The Saints paid a record £2,650 for the Portsmouth captain Johnny McIlwane in 1930-31 and for the first dozen games bagged one more point than goals actually scored. But it was part of their best run, unbeaten from mid-September to late October with five wins and three draws. Ninth was the final position. Centre-half Albert Shelley earned his second benefit after twelve years and retired with 392 League games.

Top in September 1931, Arthur Haddleton scored in eight consecutive League games. A hefty turnover of players led to some fretting until four wins and three draws in the last eight put them 14th. Ted Drake was introduced at centre-forward.

There was a more settled look in 1932-33 with only 21 players used and five wins in the last eight games to ensure 12th place. In February left-back Mike Keeping and outside-left Johnny Arnold were sold to Fulham for £5,000.

More movement away from The Dell in 1933-34 saw Arsenal pay a record £6,000 for Drake in March but a comfortable 14th slot. He had scored a second half hat trick against Bradford City on the opening day. Anxiety arrived early in 1934-35 with one win and six draws in the opening eleven matches. Worse fortune arrived in the New Year though thanks to others failing the Saints were 19th.

The Supporters Club had to help with summer wages! Then came the Jubilee season 1935-36 and late September Saints led the table. But one success in a run of 13 and they were in the bottom half. Sufficient wins thereafter secured 17th. Wing-half Stan Woodhouse completed 351 League appearances and full-back or centre-half Arthur Bradford finished on 306 such matches. Yet only one player had cost money!

Misery was not confined to mid-season in 1936-37; from December to January seven games produced just three draws and from the last dozen outings there was just one win but still a safe 19th. On 16 January 1937 the Sunderland FA Cup visit brought a crowd of 30,380 to The Dell.

Another goal famine opening to 1937-38 though money seemed available as witness a record fee of £2,200 for experienced left-half Frank Hill of Blackpool. Another promising newcomer was Ted Bates at inside-right. Save for the usual April slip-ups 15th was the finishing place. Four straight defeats at the start of 1938-39, bleak spells half-way, a solitary win from the last seven and Southampton were 18th.

Throughout the 30s the FA Cup had been disastrous. Only one tie had been won and two replays lost in ten seasons! The last defeat was 4-1 against fledgling Southern League club Chelmsford City.

In 1932-33 Southampton had put forward a proposal that clubs should introduce a 6d (two and a half pence) gate for the unemployed. It received little support and there were murmurings of "antiquated bodies running the game."

Though short of obtaining promotion, Brighton & Hove Albion was within striking distance of the leaders throughout the period and only once as low as twelfth. They also reached the last 16 in the FA Cup on two occasions.

The exceptional quality of both Plymouth and Brentford meant third place was the only option for other contenders in 1929-30, but Brighton grabbed fifth place as the second half of the season was less successful than the first. Still a club record 87 goals, 30 of them from Hugh Vallance and 28 via Dan Kirkwood, a record gate of 19,193 for Brentford's Boxing Day visit topped by 21,563 for the FA Cup against Grimsby, added up to a fine campaign boosting club funds.

Even so the freehold of the Goldstone ground was purchased in 1930 and improvements put in place. In 1930-31 sixteen unbeaten games took them to second in January before the momentum eased and they were fourth. Geordie Nicol scored 19 goals in only 22 matches. Less formidable in 1931-32 but Arthur Attwood's arrival from Bristol Rovers in November lifted the attack and he scored 25 goals in 27 League games. Eighth was the standing.

For 1932-33 a clerical error forced Brighton to start their FA Cup run in the first qualifying round. Eleven matches were played until West Ham beat them 1-0 in a fifth round replay, the drawn affair having been watched by another record gate of 32,310. Brighton had beaten Chelsea 2-1 on the way. Albion could only manage twelfth place in the Third Division (South). In 1933-34 only twice were there three wins in a row and tenth was the final position. Right-half Reg Wilkinson completed 361 League appearances.

No sustained sequence of wins in 1934-35 never more than two in a row. Albion finished ninth. One run of nine unbeaten into March helped towards seventh in 1935-36, before club records were to be broken the following season. Bowing out was perennial left-winger Ernie "Tug" Wilson after 509 League appearances.

In 1936-37 averaging 10,667 for home games, highest number of wins including away and doubles over opponents they were also third. Additionally only 43 goals were conceded. At one stage Albion dropped to below mid-table before stabilizing in second place until eventually slipping badly at Easter. In 1937-38 eight games unbeaten to New Year's Day had the Goldstone fans believing once more. Though there were only two defeats from the last 15 matches, crucially three points were dropped in the last two of them and Brighton were fifth.

In the top for weeks on end with a sound defence but faltering in the latter stages they were six points adrift of the leaders and placed third in 1938-39. Left-half Dave Walker reached 310 League appearances in ten seasons.

Antonio, Stoke   *Chivers, Blackburn*   *Foxall, West Ham*   *Howe, Bolton*

Lythgoe, Huddersfield   *Salmond, Portsmouth*   *Starling, Sheff. Wed.*   *Westwood, Bolton*

POT SHOTS

POT-POURRI OF THE THIRTIES

In 1938 arrangements were made for a Football League Benevolent Fund of £100,000 to be implemented to assist former players in need. It was hoped £44,000 would come from Division One clubs, £1,000 from each Division Two club and £500 from each of the clubs in the two sections of the Third Division. Permission had been granted from the Football Association to institute the scheme.

There were variations, one suggesting the Third Division clubs would be required to find only £300 which would have slightly reduced the overall target.

Local derby matches would be arranged a week before the Football League programme was to open in August 1938. The idea was for return fixtures to be played at a similar time in 1939. However, there seemed to be some confusion over the actual distribution of the receipts from these matches over either a shortfall or surplus accrued.

The Football League also stated it was prepared to accept money from Pools companies, still a source of contention over fixture copyright, towards the Jubilee Fund. As an example of the income from one match, the West Bromwich Albion v Aston Villa game on 20 August 1938 which was drawn 1-1 produced a crowd of 26,640 and receipts of £1,514.

Finance was a continual source of interest. In 1934 the departing secretary of the FA, Sir Frederick Wall had left clutching a cheque for £10,000. In no time he was on the board of Arsenal by 24 August. However, the FA balance sheet in 1933-34 showed a profit of £133,000. Arsenal as the "Bank of England" club had a typical season's expenditure in round figures as follows:

Players wages, benefits etc.	£17,000
Travelling expenses and kit	£5,000
Gatemen and police	£3,000
Rates, etc.	£3,000
Salaries and bonuses	£5,000
Income Tax	£7,000
Interest on loans	£7,000
Trainers and groundsmen	£5,000
Sundries, including Entertainment Tax at £160 per £1,000	£8,000
Total	*£60,000*

It is interesting to note that in 1938-39 Liverpool had made a profit of £12,000 while Wolves had shown a similar credit figure of £11,000 when they were League and FA Cup runners-up.

Changes to the Laws of the Game in the 1930s included a rule in 1931 that goalkeepers being permitted to carry the ball four steps instead of two. Two years earlier they had been compelled to stand still on the goal-line when a penalty kick was being taken. Also in 1931, instead of awarding a free-kick for a foul throw-in, it reverted to the opposing side.

In 1936 defending players were no longer allowed to tap the ball into the goalkeeper's hands when a goal-kick was being taken. The following year it was extended to when a free-kick was taken inside the penalty area. Also in 1937 the weight of the ball was increased from 13-15oz to 14-16oz. In addition an arc of a circle ten yards radius from the penalty spot was drawn outside the penalty area.

LONG SERVICE AND AWARDS

Benefits for long service included Billy Smith receiving four such awards. On 11 November 1933 in the match with Sheffield Wednesday he had completed 20 years with Huddersfield Town. There were examples of players getting similar recognition with three different clubs. Jimmy McLaren did so with Bradford City, Leicester City and Watford where he played for the last time at 41 years 172 days. He was a former Scottish schoolboy international. Ex-England schoolboy cap Tommy Urwin was the north-east exponent favouring Middlesbrough, Newcastle United and Sunderland in his career.

Amounts donated varied according to length of service. For example in 1935 Sunderland gave £650 to Harry Shaw, Jimmy Connor and Bob Gurney, £500 to Bob Johnston and Alec Hall.

Attempts to limit transfer fees failed. The Football League had ruled in 1922 that all fees should be treated as private and confidential. By the dawn of the 30s the accepted record stood at £10,890 for David Jack's move from Bolton Wanderers to Arsenal in 1928. Of course there were widely different schemes of deferred payments and those in instalments.

When Tottenham Hotspur signed Willie Hall from Notts County in 1932 it was agreed they would pay an additional sum of £500 if the player received international recognition by England. This came about in December 1933 when Hall was given his first cap against France

At the beginning of the 30s fees for internationals were £6 per game, but this was increased to £8 in 1937 and two years later to £10. Attendances for these matches had increased and the pressure to show an appreciation to the players had grown with it. One England player claimed expenses of seven pence at one match!

MUSIC MUSIC MUSIC

And the band played on – eventually. Keen to celebrate promotion to the First Division in 1933, Tottenham Hotspur contacted the Grenadier Guards with a request that should its Band be available to play in front of the crowd at White Hart Lane on the Monday evening of the first home fixture on 28 August against Wolverhampton Wanderers, the club would be delighted. The Guards replied that they were unable to undertake evening commitments but suggested an afternoon kick-off. Spurs agreed and though the attendance of 20,953 was understandably much lower than the usual average crowd for home matches, the team also struck the right note winning 4-0.

Tottenham Borough Silver Band which played at White Hart Lane before and at half-time had the *Spurs March* specially composed for them as a club signature tune. Two years after the introduction Spurs had a run of ill luck and it was played out.

Arsenal was also involved in musical arrangements. On 26 September 1932, the Gunners had travelled to Perth in Scotland for a friendly against St Johnstone and drew 0-0 before a crowd of 15,000. The Perth & District Prize Pipe Band played on the occasion and at the conclusion of the match, players from both sides signed autographs on a drum-skin! George Allison then an Arsenal director and before he became manager signed "Good morning, everybody," his BBC radio greeting and the introduction he made to his weekly column in the *Daily Express*.

Gilbert Stacey the radio broadcaster wrote a march called "Up the Gunners" and dedicated it to George Allison, the players, members and supporters of Arsenal FC.

UNEMPLOYED SHOW ENTERPRISE

With a high rate of unemployment it was not long before competitions were organized for those out of work. Not only in the industrial towns where large numbers were on the dole, but even in the comparatively less insecure environment of London, there was a cup competition arranged with the final being played at Wembley. All unemployed spectators were given free admission. Any player who re-entered the workplace was immediately barred from playing with an unemployed team. The composition of all teams was such that players were not chosen until just before the match was to be played.

The first final at Wembley was on 21 March 1934. A crowd of 2,000 saw Walthamstow Fellowship Club beat Greenwich Trafalgar Club 1-0. Walthamstow also had a penalty kick saved. In the 1935 version for what was the London Occupational Shield, Oral House Club Kennington met St Mark's Fellowship, Poplar. The attendance was doubled and the 3-1 winners St Mark's met the Birmingham League winners.

Walthamstow won again in 1936 beating Burne Occupational Club of Marylebone 3-0 and in the last such final, Richmond Social FC defeated the oddly assembled West Ham Unemployed & Workers Association playing as St Alethia's 4-1 after extra time. Teams reaching the final could have played as many as 24 times along the way.

In the Preston Thursday League in 1935-36 the team designated Unemployed won dropping only one point from 14 matches. It was their third title in consecutive seasons and they had also won the allied cup competition three years out of four.

Fixture-interruptions were not commonplace. It would take exceptional weather conditions to prevent play or postpone matches. Extremely heavy pitches in winter were expected and only snowfalls that could not be physically shifted and touchlines rendered impossible beyond sweeping at half-time were considered a hazard serious enough to prevent kicking the ball around. Weighed down with mud the spherical shape took on medicine ball proportions! However, 29 October 1932 was more than an exceptional day.

It began in pouring rain and a driving wind. The worst affected area was the north-west with games at Blackburn and Blackpool suffering the most. At Blackburn, pools of water appearing at various places and a plunging temperature made life difficult for both the Rovers and visiting Sheffield United players. Blackburn led 3-0 at half-time but both sets of players were freezing cold and exhausted.

Despite a change of kit during the interval it was anticipated the referee would call a halt but he failed so to do. However, numerous players left the field of play to be revived and eventually the official called a halt after consultation with a linesman. But it was only a ten minute reprieve! Though neither dressing-room was happy following what proved a twenty-minute delay and play was resumed only for the referee to collapse! The senior linesman took the watch and whistle. At the end of the affair only eight of the Sheffield players were left on the field with the score still 3-0.

Even so at Bloomfield Road, Blackpool where Chelsea provided the opposition, the situation was far worse. A blizzard off the Atlantic coast added to the torrential rain. Blackpool scored three goals in half an hour and just before the interval Chelsea lost Willie Ferguson with injury. In the second half Chelsea faced the elements and began to struggle. The first to leave the pitch was Eric Oakton. At regular intervals Peter O'Dowd, Harry Miller and Len Allum followed to the dressing-room. Another deserter and the match would have been called off. Blackpool only won 4-0 against the six remaining visiting players.

Ferguson, O'Dowd and Miller were ordered to stay at home in bed on the following day. In the next home programme at Chelsea, manager David Calderhead made it clear the "quitters" were all suffering from exhaustion and he abided by the referee's decision to carry on but believed it was the wrong one. Only one match was postponed in the Football League that day: Swindon Town v Brighton & Hove Albion. However, to emphasise the dreadful elements on the Saturday evening a 110 mph gust of wind was recorded at Folkestone.

Attempts were made to put on the FA Cup tie between Ipswich Town and Reading at Portman Road on 28 January 1939. But it was to no avail as the day before it was found possible to actually row a boat across the pitch!

Fog was a different problem but only one Football League match in the 30s had to be postponed because it prevented the visiting team reaching its destination. It happened to Rotherham United at Hartlepools on 22 December 1934. In addition the same kind of mist had an effect on 21 December 1935.

The train taking midlands referee Ames to officiate at the Exeter City v Bristol Rovers match was delayed by fog and a linesman had to take over until Ames turned up 20 minutes after the kick-off. In order to fill the vacancy on the line for the opening minutes City's reserve centre-forward Jimmy McCambridge was deputised. As a former Bristol Rovers player he was probably the most neutral choice available!

As to travelling problems caused by the fixture list, Charles Sutcliffe the Football League President who prided himself on the application he devoted to producing the League's programme, either he had no grasp of the country's geography or paid little heed to the needs of the clubs involved. On Good Friday 10 April 1936 he arranged for Swansea Town to visit Plymouth Argyle and a trip to play Newcastle United twenty-four hours later. Newcastle themselves had been at home on Christmas Day 1933 and were due to Everton on Boxing Day.

Just as arduous had been the occasion beginning on Boxing Day 1930 when Plymouth Argyle beat Cardiff City 5-1 at Home Park. The Argyle players then set off for what turned out to be a delayed ten hour all night train journey to Liverpool where they were due to play Everton who had not had a game the previous day. Plymouth arrived at 6 am in pouring rain, managed four hours sleep. With a gale blowing at Goodison Park by kick-off time and water covering the pitch, even the toss-up had to be made on the touchline. Not surprisingly Everton won 9-1.

Plymouth seemed fated in such matters. On 30 August 1937 for a Monday evening fixture there was a thunderstorm for the visit of Blackburn Rovers. The train carrying Rovers wing-half Charlie Calladine was becalmed. He decided to de-train and run a mile in time to play in the 2-1 win.

Fixture congestion at the end of the season often caused headaches, too. In 1931-32 Swansea Town had to play Wrexham in a Welsh Cup Final replay and chose the day before their final Division Two match against Bury. Nine of the same team appeared in both games which Swansea won by the same 2-0 score.

On 29 February 1936 Gateshead goalkeeper Derwick Goodfellow missed the train to Crewe and his place had to be taken by trainer Tommy Dawson who had been until then a wing-half. Gateshead won 4-2.

FLY BOYS FACE RESTRICTIONS

The first footballer to be specially flown to a match was an amateur with Bristol Rovers; Vivian Gibbins, a London schoolmaster. At the start of the 1932-33 season injuries played havoc with Rovers team selection. In desperate straits their manager and former international referee Captain Prince-Cox organized a flight from Romford aerodrome to Filton. He was informed that one and a half hours would be required for the journey, so a fast aircraft would be more suitable as Gibbins would be unable to leave before the bell sounded at school! Gibbins had to be at Eastville in time for the 6.15 pm kick-off and actually made it with half an hour to spare, suffering no air sickness on the way.

While the Football League was opposed to clubs flying to matches there was no restriction on flights abroad. Arsenal frequently played on a Saturday and zoomed off to Paris by Imperial Airways to its annual fixture with Racing Club on the Sunday. However, strangely enough they were refused permission to play FK Austria in Paris. On another occasion Arsenal wanted to take to the air for a cup-tie at Newcastle. From 1930-31 season Arsenal made nine such Paris trips winning seven times and drawing the other two games.

On 15 October 1932 Plymouth Argyle officials including one player flew to Stoke on the morning of their match. The Football League was not amused and refused permission for Plymouth Argyle to fly again for a domestic fixture.

West Ham United had to take to the air on 31 October 1936 in an emergency. Three players Albert Walker, Herman Conway and Tudor Martin had travelled by Underground to Paddington on the way to a reserve fixture at Swansea but missed their connection. They contacted manager Charlie Paynter at West Ham and he said: "hire a plane." They contacted Gatwick who provided a sports plane for £25!

Some 50 Villa fans organized a flight from Castle Bromwich to Croydon on the occasion of the match at Arsenal on 10 March 1934. Arsenal won 3-2.

THE MEN IN THE MIDDLE

Calls for referees to become professional were frequent. It was thought the cry for two officials in the middle came from too many of them controlling matches from the middle of the pitch. One unnamed referee a miner, said that he did train to become fit, but there was no regime in place for so doing. Required to run seven to eight miles in a match was a matter of fitness. Bert Fogg who refereed the 1935 FA Cup final was monitored in one match and had run four miles 1,260 yards in the first half and four miles 460 yards in the second half.

At the Football League AGM in 1935 the two-referee proposal failed by 31 votes to 18. Everton's Will Cuff had been one in favour of dual control. Two yeas later at the FA's AGM it was again defeated. Expenses for officials were fairly modest at a guinea for hotel accommodation and half that for a meal.

Naturally referees had their own individual style. Harry Nattrass an ex-miner known as "Natty" who was in charge of the 1936 FA Cup final placed himself under the crossbar at corner kicks! He had played no football himself. He used a match-timer rather than a watch when in the middle. The nickname was most appropriate as he favoured a maroon coloured blazer and shorts. As for Percy Snape, he had played rugby at school.

Reggie Rudd who had been the referee for the 1937 FA Cup final had been persuaded by his Sergeant-Major when in the Army to take up the whistle in the first place. Then George Gould as a lad was due to play when he broke his arm – so refereed the game instead and stayed with it. Rudd was one of many invited to referee international matches abroad – Germany 1 Switzerland 1 on 6 February 1938 in Cologne.

Arthur James (Jimmy) Jewell once attended the same kindergarten school at Kilburn with Rudd. At a match between Watford and Coventry City in 1927, Jewell had been a linesman with Rudd referee. Jewell who also broadcast football commentaries later became manager of Norwich City.

Isaac Caswell was a salesman, for a time a Labour Councillor and also involved in advising the Swedish club AIK Stockholm in the summer months! He was once congratulated after an Arsenal game by Ted Drake for his handling of it. Caswell, known as Ike, had a contract for twelve months to officiate in Argentina. He did not speak Spanish and thought this was actually a help!

But he also had to have a police escort to get him out of a sticky situation when things had not gone well for the home team. One of his suggestions was that penalty kicks should be taken from the exact spot the infringement had taken place.

Despite criticism, British referees were much sought after for foreign international matches. Stanley Rous before his appointment at the FA was one of the most used abroad. Bill Harper the FA Council representative for Worcestershire was a Civil Servant and had refereed in the USA.

Certainly the first to be involved in a World Cup match was Thomas Balway, an English born French official who was a teacher in Paris. He was in charge of the Brazil v Bolivia tie in Uruguay in 1930. Wally Lewington was another familiar on the continent. He was handily placed for such travel as he lived 100 yards from Croydon airport. One of his internationals was when Italy beat Austria 2-0 in Vienna.

However, one domestic occasion presented a problem. Off to handle Blackburn Rovers v Norwich City he caught the wrong train at Blackpool. It was a slow one. He asked the guard if he could do something. At the next signal box the train stopped and a message was passed on to Blackburn for a taxi to be waiting for him! Lewington changed into kit in the guard's van and made it in time though the toss-up was about to be made. His first act was to get the Rovers goalkeeper to change his jersey that was clashing with the opposition colours.

Captain Prince-Cox had controlled some 30 matches in his time, was a boxing promoter, into greyhound racing and later a football manager of course. One of his overseas assignments was the Irish Free State Cup Final. However, the first foreigner to referee a Home International Championship match was the German Dr Peco Bauwens who could speak eight languages.

GETTING BACK TO FITNESS

As medical knowledge improved recovery time from injuries was drastically cut. Cartilage operations that at one time took months to heal, were reduced to weeks. Treatments for various injuries increased with the use of violet and electric rays, sun lamps and a plurostat machine with electrical currents for therapeutic, surgical and diagnostic purposes. Its three uses, firstly to bring bruises to the surface, secondly break down adhesions and thirdly to circulate the blood. All kinds of baths – brine, remedial, Turkish plus a foam variety for half an hour's immersion were other methods employed. Of course the wealthier clubs could afford such equipment, the costs prohibiting the less financially placed from taking advantage.

When Jack Thorogood the Millwall winger was considered for a cartilage operation one of the club's directors who was an osteopath took over and no operation was required.

PEACE IN OUR TIME?

On 29 September 1938 before Neville Chamberlain's visit to Herr Hitler and despite the seriousness of the international situation, it was agreed fixtures would go ahead as normal. In the wake of the Munich Agreement, peace ceremonies were held at grounds on 1 October.

TOP TEN APPEARANCES

Outside of the one-team loyalists dealt with in references to club football, there were many players whose careers into the 1930s topped the 500 mark in League appearances both in England and Scotland. Three even cleared the 600 figure.

Way ahead of the field was Scottish goalkeeper Willie Robb whose figures would have been higher but for appearing during the war for Vale of Leven and Armadale, not to mention Southern League games at Aldershot in 1930-31 and 1931-32 as well as similar matches for Guildford City in 1937-38.

In fact when Aldershot entered the Third Division (South) in 1932 Robb was already aged 37 and special permission had to be obtained from the Football League for him to be registered! He actually began with Birmingham making 40 appearances, was then with Third Lanark totalling 43, Glasgow Rangers 227 and Hibernian 128 games. His Scottish League aggregate amounted to 398 while Football League games for Aldershot came to 176 giving a grand total of 614.

England international right-winger and occasional centre-forward Joe Spence while appearing under Manchester United for the majority of his Football League details added Bradford City and Chesterfield to his career producing final figures of 613 appearances and 195 goals to 1938.

The 31 times capped "Wee Blue Devil" of a Scottish winger Alan Morton was pre-war with Queen's Park before moving to Rangers in 1920. With the amateurs he made 219 League appearances mostly in the war period. His association with Rangers added 382 in the competition or a grand total of 601.

The nearest to 600 after these two was Willie Fotheringham the much travelled Scottish League goalkeeper with 580 split between Airdrie, Dundee, Morton, St Mirren and Queen of the South up to 1937.

Warney Cresswell while serving in the Army during the war had a League game for Hearts. His Football League appearances with South Shields, Sunderland and Everton were 571 giving him 572 overall. An England international full-back he ended his playing career in 1936. In fact South Shields was the starting point for England inside-forward Jack Smith followed by Portsmouth, Bournemouth and Clapton Orient and he reached 571 by 1937.

Patsy Gallagher's lengthy career chiefly with Celtic then Falkirk lasting 20 years from 1911-12 embraced 363 Scottish League games and eleven caps for Ireland. Another two decade player was left-winger Bobby Archibald from 1912-13 with Albion Rovers for a couple of spells ditto Aberdeen and Third Lanark. Then he was at Hibs, Rangers, Ayr, Dumbarton and Raith. This was prior to an English career with Stoke and Barnsley until 1933. So he racked up 320 appearances in the Scottish League, 268 in the Football League.

Scottish international inside-forward Tommy Cairns also showed the same longevity and allegiance to either side of the border. Like Willie Robb he began in England with Bristol City returning home for St Johnstone, Rangers, then Hamilton back to Ibrox before going down south to Bradford City. For the Scottish League there were 419, Football League 146 for a total of 565. There was also a matter of 139 goals in Scotland, 33 in England.

Impossible to forget Hughie Gallacher all 5ft 5in of him with 111 games for Airdrie, then 431 from Newcastle, Chelsea, Derby, Notts, Grimsby and Gateshead thus overall 542 by 1939.

THE FA CUP

The FA Cup enjoyed many of its best supported years in the 1930s with just over half of the Football League clubs establishing record attendances as well as gate receipts, despite the economic climate in existence. Overall entries were continually in excess of the 500 mark, too. Oddly enough the five clubs who shared the First Division championship honours, also gained a cup final success with Arsenal again doubling the achievements of the other four with two wins.

Teams won and then lost on a subsequent appearance at Wembley, the established home of the final since 1923, while others lost and returned to be successful. Freed from the stranglehold of the old off-side law, there were more goals at the Empire Stadium, 31 from the ten finals. The previous ten had scraped only 16.

Understandably the final attracted the highest crowds. From the 1930 final onwards the figures were: 92,488; 92,406; 92,298; 92,950; 93,258; 93,201; 93,384; 93,495; 93,357 and 99,370, that figure reflecting the extensions to Wembley's capacity.

Outside of the final itself, several semi-finals held at League grounds recorded attendances in excess of 50,000, Villa Park being one of the favourite venues chosen over the years. On 16 March 1935 the Sheffield Wednesday v Burnley tie was watched there by 56,625. The same day at Elland Road, Leeds the West Bromwich Albion v Bolton Wanderers semi-final was witnessed by 49,605. A year earlier at Birmingham's St Andrew's ground on 17 March 1934 some 66,544 had seen Leicester City v Portsmouth in the corresponding round.

On 26 March 1938 at Bramall Lane, the home of Sheffield United reported a crowd of 65,129 for Preston North End v Aston Villa. United themselves had been involved in a semi-final on 21 March 1936 at Molineux, Wolverhampton with a gathering of 51,568. There was an even better gate at Leeds Road, Huddersfield that same day when 63,210 saw the corresponding Grimsby Town v Arsenal affair. But far and away the highest at the penultimate stage of the FA Cup was at Old Trafford, Manchester on 25 March 1939, again with Grimsby participating this time against Wolverhampton Wanderers when 76.962 paid £8,194.

Earlier rounds also listed numerous instances of crowds in excess of 70,000 at League grounds. There was also the record other than a final itself when on 3 March 1934 at Maine Road some 84,569 squeezed in for the sixth round tie between Manchester City and Stoke City. Receipts for this match were £5,451. On 5 March 1938, Villa Park housed 75,540 when Aston Villa met Manchester City in a sixth round tie that eclipsed the previous best total of 74,626 at the venue against Walsall on 25 January 1930.

The sixth round on 8 March 1933 also witnessed Sunderland's highest attendance at Roker Park when 75,118 spectators paid £4,566 to see Derby County. Moreover it was Sunderland's trip to White Hart Lane as cup holders in the same round on 5 March 1938 that gave Tottenham Hotspur their best crowd of 75,038 (£5,857).

Villa had interestingly enough set the highest figure at The Valley in the previous round when their visit to Charlton Athletic attracted 75,031. Manchester City was concerned in Sheffield Wednesday's biggest gate when in a fifth round tie on 17 February 1934 at Hillsborough a crowd of 72,841 was recorded with receipts of £5,566. City drew 2-2, won the replay 2-0 and went on to win the cup.

Of the 24 different teams who created record attendances at other grounds, Sunderland was responsible for the most on five occasions. They spread themselves not only in their native north-east, but on Merseyside, in the West Country, London and on the south coast. The first was far off in Devon on 4 March 1931 where 20,984 crammed into Exeter City's St James's Park enclosure for a sixth round replay after the Grecians had stunned Roker Park with a 1-1 draw. Sunderland won at the second attempt 4-2.

Next stop 16 January 1937 at The Dell and 30,380 to see Southampton lose 3-2 in the third round. In 1937-38 Sunderland were, of course, defending their title as cup winners. On 22 January 1938, they won a fourth round encounter at Everton 1-0 in front of 68,158 (£5,877). Then came the earlier mentioned March trip to meet Spurs in the sixth round. But back to the north-east and the fourth round to finish the almost round England tour on 21 January 1939 at Ayresome Park, Middlesbrough watched by 51,080.

Sheffield Wednesday had four record-breaking visits in the period, Arsenal, Aston Villa, Manchester City and Newcastle United three each. The other interesting statistic from these figures is that five of the six clubs all won the cup in the 1930s and the sixth, Aston Villa, had previously taken the trophy six times, a total matched only by Blackburn Rovers.

Perhaps surprisingly, it was Arsenal directly involved in only three record gates during the period in question. However, not an eyebrow was raised when one of them concerned the Huddersfield Town sixth round affair at Leeds Road on 27 February 1932. Some 67,008 paid £4,892 to see Herbert Chapman's new team beat his old one 1-0 and go on to reach the final.

Two years later on 13 January 1934, the Gunners visit to Kenilworth Road, Luton produced 18,641 for the Third Division (South) side. The third occasion fell to West Bromwich Albion on 6 March 1937 in a sixth round tie at The Hawthorns when 64,815 set the 'Throstles' ground record. That occasion was among some spectacular aggregate attendances at these later rounds. On 6 March 1937 three of the four sixth round ties produced ground and receipt records. Wolves had 57,751 (£4,278), nearly West

Bromwich 64,815 (£3,913) and Tottenham 71,913 (£5,714). A year later at the same round all four produced records. Tottenham's crowd was 75,038 (£5,857), Aston Villa 75,540 (£5,508), York 28,123 (£2,735) and Brentford 39,626 (£2,824). On 11 February 1939 the aggregate for the eight ties in the fifth round were 447,719. They included ground records at Birmingham 67,341, Portsmouth 47,614 and Wolves again a new one at 61,.305.

As to the Football League, there were similar records created if not on the scale of the FA Cup figures. In fact more clubs attracted their highest gates in the 1920s League encounters. Just a quarter reported better crowds in the 1930s than in the FA Cup matches.

Way ahead of any other attendance was at Stamford Bridge on 12 October 1935 when the visit of Arsenal produced Chelsea's and the Football League record of 82,905 with receipts of £4,698 as League matches invariably yielded less income than that obtained from the FA Cup where the tradition was everybody paid including season ticket holders.

Arsenal was also involved in Manchester City's best at Maine Road when on 23 February 1935 it was registered as 79,491. The Gunners also established other ground records in the 1930s. On 27 December 1932 at Elland Road there were 56,796 for the Leeds United v Arsenal match. Then on 29 March 1937 Stoke City had 51,480 to see the Londoners. Finally Arsenal's fifth such record was recorded at Deepdale where Preston North End had a crowd of 42,684 on 23 April 1938. As to their own Highbury home, Arsenal noted 73,295 (£5,754) on 9 March 1935 when Sunderland called. In 1933-34 on 16 September Tottenham v Arsenal attracted 56,612 while the return on 31 January produced 68,674 at Highbury.

As far as average League attendances, the Football League issued official figures for its Centenary season 1937-38 revealing the aggregate for the four divisions as 28,132,933 with an average of 15,225 per match. The First Division alone accounted for 11,624,004 at 25,160 per game.

Arsenal's figure for that fifth title winning season was 44,045, the highest average achieved in the history of the competition. Amazingly Aston Villa clocked 41,950 in the Second Division! While Arsenal averaged in excess of 30,000 in each of the ten seasons in question, Villa did so in nine – two in the Second Division – with Chelsea next best with eight, despite struggling year in year out after being runners-up in 1929-30. In fact Chelsea had registered 37,900 back in the 1913-14 season and then another record when peacetime football resumed in 1919-20 revealing 42,860 at Stamford Bridge.

Arsenal led the attendances every season except 1938-39 when Aston Villa returned 39,932 compared with the Gunners 39,102. The loyalty of Villa fans was unsurpassed since they had two seasons in the lower division, but they were not alone in support as overall nine clubs who at some stage had topped 30,000 averages, suffered at least one campaign in the Second Division. Only Liverpool and Sunderland apart from Arsenal who fitted into these statistics, remained in the First Division throughout the 1930s.

Naturally in Scotland the vast areas of Hampden Park and Ibrox were able to accommodate crowds in excess of the figures produced south of the border. On 2 January 1939 the Rangers v Celtic old firm affair in the First Division produced an enormous 118,567 with gate receipts of the comparatively low figure of £5,845. Contemporary reports estimated that at least another 30,000 were locked out!

The corresponding fixture at Parkhead a year earlier on 1 January 1938 between Celtic and Rangers was returned as 83,500 but with receipts at £5,900.

As to the Scottish Cup final, the 26 April 1937 the Aberdeen v Celtic tie was also over subscribed as while 147,365 or 146,433 as elsewhere reported, were inside Hampden Park, a further 20,000 could not gain access.

In contrast the Aberdeen v Rangers Scottish Cup tie on 7 March 1936 was witnessed by 42,663 to set Pittodrie's best. Of course the big two Scottish clubs were the pull for many Scottish League clubs. Yet Rangers with six such records had twice as many as Celtic covering both Scottish League and Cup.

Scotland also led on the international front in the Home International Championship fixtures at Hampden Park against the old foe from England. Due to the number of such occasions when spectators were locked out, on 17 April 1937 the first all-ticket match in Scotland saw 149,547 with impressive receipts of £24,000. Wembley's capacity was in the middle 90,000s and immediately after the 1923 FA Cup final when far too many spectators broke in without paying, all matches at the Empire Stadium were designated as all-ticket.

Scotland's visit on 5 April 1930 saw 87,375 in attendance. On 9 April 1932 it was 92,180 and increased again on 14 April 1934 with 92,363. There was a slight decrease on 4 April 1936 with 93,267 and exactly the same figure was released for the Scotland game on 9 April 1938.

England did use other venues. In fact Wembley was reserved for just the FA Cup final and the invasion by the Scots every other year. In 1938 not even the prestigious England v Rest of Europe was fitted in there; the fixture was held at Arsenal's Highbury ground the attendance 40,185, increased admission prices accounted for the lower gate.

Highbury, White Hart Lane and Stamford Bridge were other London venues selected for foreign opposition. The Football Association also flew the flag around the country for both Wales and Northern Ireland. Both Anfield and Goodison Park were featured in Liverpool, Blackpool's Bloomfield Road ground, St James' Park home of Newcastle United, Molineux the venue for Wolverhampton Wanderers, the Victoria Ground of Stoke City and Ayresome Park for Middlesbrough. Manchester United's Old Trafford was also used on 16 November 1938 for the game with Ireland with an attendance of 40,386.

Italy's visit to Highbury on 14 November 1934 had 56,044 and when Germany came to White Hart Lane on 4 December the following year, there were 54,164 on the day. The Spurs ground had 45,879 when Czechoslovakia were the visitors on 1 December 1937. Interestingly enough the best assembly at Wrexham's Racecourse Ground was for the Wales v Ireland match on 15 March 1939, recorded at 24,318.

As expected the Scotland v England fixture at Hampden Park surpassed anything in size seen south of the border. In 1931 it was 129,810; 1933: 134,710; 1935: 129,693; 1937: 149,547 as mentioned previously and in 1939: 149,269.

VERY DIFFERENT FA CUP FINALS

King George V meets the Huddersfield team at the 1930 FA Cup Final.

The FA Cup final was arguably the foremost event in the football calendar. Invariably there was something memorable happening on the day. In 1930 Arsenal finally broke the stranglehold that the north and midlands had held on the trophy. Masterminded by Herbert Chapman, with the deep-lying Alex James a short-legged artist in long shorts dictating play from no-man's land, Bob John at wing-half and Cliff "Boy" Bastin on the left wing, at 18 years one month the youngest to receive a winner's medal. Overhead flew the *Graf Zeppelin* and below Chapman knowingly overcoming his old club Huddersfield Town. They included Austin Campbell who had played against them for Blackburn Rovers in the 1928 final.

In 1931 the all-midland affair ended with West Bromwich Albion beating Birmingham City with a Billy "G" Richardson brace to achieve a double in taking the cup and winning promotion back to the First Division. Their reserves also won the Central League. Birmingham had two former finalists in Ernie Curtis (Cardiff 1927) and Ned Barkas (Huddersfield 1928). For Birmingham Bob Gregg had his sixth minute headed goal ruled off-side from a free kick by Jimmy Cringan.

Then controversy with the "over-the-goal-line" cross that led to Newcastle United beating Arsenal in 1932. Jimmy Richardson's scuffed centre enabled Jack Allen to level the scores register again and put United on the way to victory. Jimmy Nelson their right-back had won a cup medal with Cardiff in 1927. Arsenal was not involved in a replay and became the first team to score first and lose a Wembley final. It was David Jack's fourth final.

Another innovation for 1933 saw the numbering of players but from 1 to 22 as Dixie Dean spearheaded the correctly numbered Everton to a three goal success over Manchester City. Dean's goal was a tap in after Cliff Britton's cross to him was finger-tipped by goalkeeper Len Langford. The Goodison Park team had reached the final without a replay.

City outside-left Eric Brook became the first to wear a No. 12 shirt in a final. Everton full-back Billy Cook had won a Scottish Cup medal with Celtic in 1931. But the losers became winners in 1934 beating Portsmouth. Trailing with 17 minutes remaining Freddie Tilson omitted from the previous final by Manchester City, boasted at half-time of scoring twice and did so. But already in defensive mode, Pompey then lost centre-half Jimmy Allen with a serious head injury in the 70th minute. In the City goal Frank Swift aged 19, fainted at the final whistle.

Six goals highlighted the 1935 final with Sheffield Wednesday doubling West Bromwich Albion's score, courtesy of two in the last five minutes from eight-goal galloping winger Ellis Rimmer who scored in every round the first such since 1901. He had been handed a lucky horseshoe at half-time. Wednesday had not been involved in a replay. Manager Billy Walker had led the Aston Villa attack in the 1920 final and full-back Joe Nibloe had collected a Scottish Cup medal with Kilmarnock in 1929. Albion's only locally born player was centre-half Bill Richardson.

Ted Drake with a heavily bandaged knee was the lone Arsenal scoring hero in 1936 against Second Division Sheffield United with Herbie Roberts "policing" at centre-half, the granite Wilf Copping at wing-half and flying winger Joe Hulme in his fourth final. After 73 minutes James initiated the move to Bastin who beat Hooper and placed the ball in the middle for Drake to drive left-footed into the roof of the net. It spurred life into Sheffield United. Barton broke through on the right crossed for Dodds to head against the bar with Arsenal goalkeeper Wilson out of position.

In 1937 TV cameras for the first time in a final and Sunderland inspired by local lad and captain Raich Carter after conceding a goal ran out 3-1 winners over Preston North End for whom eleven-goal Frank O'Donnell scored in every round. His brother Hugh who won a Scottish Cup medal with Celtic in 1933 was in the attack, too. Carter, receiving the trophy from HM The Queen with one hand, its stand with the other the Monarch attempted to present him with his medal. The situation was rescued when Alec Hall grabbed the stand. Scots outnumbered others 12 to 10: seven for Preston, five for Sunderland. Americans in London were keen to get hold of one guinea tickets for the final.

But again the defeated Preston returned to triumph in 1938. Many thought the trip by Alf Young was outside the area. With closed eyes George Mutch's in-off-the-bar first Wembley penalty 60 seconds from the end of extra time ended Huddersfield's and Hulme's fifth final outing hopes. For Town's Jimmy "Ginger" Isaac it was his first FA Cup tie. For a second season Preston had not been involved in a replay scored twelve goals and conceded just one. Tallest of the five forwards was Bud Maxwell at 5ft. 8in.

Hot favourites Wolves lost the 1939 final heavily to Portsmouth, first team south of London to succeed in a final remembered for Pompey boss Jack Tinn's luckier spats this time, the "Pompey Chimes" and a tale of nervous Wolves players' shaky signatures in the Wembley visitors book. Bert Barlow signed from Wolves two months earlier was a Portsmouth scorer. They had conceded only two goals in six ties compared with Wolves seven.

Everton 1933. Back; Cooke (trainer), Britton, Creswell, Sagar, Cook, White, Thomson. Front; Geldard, Dunn, Dean, Johnson, Stein, Crichtley

Sheffield Wednesday 1935. Back; Nibloe, Brown, Catlin, Millership, Irwin (trainer), Burrows. Front; Sharpe, Hooper, Surtees, Billy Walker (Manager), Palethorpe, Starling, Rimmer

Preston North End 1938. Back; Shankly, Gallimore, Scott (trainer), Holdcroft, Beattie (A), Batey. Front; Maxwell, Beattie (R), Mutch, Smith, Watmough, O'Donnell

Portsmouth 1939. Back; Jimmy Stewart (trainer), Anderson, Morgan, Rowe, Walker, Wharton, Rochford, Jack Tinn (manager). Front; Worrall, McAlinden, Guthrie, Barlow, Parker

PLAYERS HOBBIES

Domestically in the climate operating families tended to stay together, offspring often remaining at home well into their 20s. Once a player was attached to a club its officials were keen to have him settled preferably in the family environment or in suitable digs with other young players. Good wholesome cooking was popular and mum usually knew how to serve it up.

Naturally accommodation varied. When Jimmy McCambridge was briefly with Sheffield Wednesday his landlady made sure he had health salts, eggs and milk. When he had a slight head cold, she provided a tot of rum and a mustard bath. There was few of that species.

When Bert Sproston left Tottenham Hotspur for Manchester City on 4 November 1938 after a few months following his signing from Leeds United, it was as much to do with missing his home comforts as failing to settle in the" big smoke." He also admitted to suffering from nerves at the time. Sproston was also attending night classes studying commercial subjects. Manchester was not such a distance from Leeds. Interestingly enough on his Manchester City debut on 5 November he was actually listed in the Spurs line-up!

Practically all players were involved in other sporting activities with golf being among one of the favourites but all kinds of outdoor and indoor pursuits were to be found in the off-duty hours of the professional footballer. Outside of the purely bat and ball brigades there were other interesting pastimes.

At George Antonio's home in Stoke, two other City players Jack Challinor and Billy Robson were lodgers. The trio also enjoyed country walks. Three other Stoke players were in digs together: Norman Wilkinson, Harry Brigham and David Jones. The trio formed a dance band. All three could play the piano, while Wilkinson doubled on the saxophone, Brigham on the drums and Jones with the xylophone. They even managed to rustle up a crooner when 17 year old Jack Ford was signed from Frickley Colliery! Another in the Bing Crosby style was Ernie Marshall at Sheffield United. Charlton's goalkeeper Sam Bartram had a decent tenor voice and led the Addicks singing on away trips. Bill Tremelling of Preston was a prize-winning vocalist. Crooning was the forte of Jack Bray at Manchester City.

Outdoors was also a favourite of Charlie Calladine the Birmingham and Blackburn half-back. He liked hiking on the Buxton Moors. It was perfect for his rehabilitation when recovering from an operation. Welsh amateur international Fred Smallwood at Southampton played the trumpet in a dance band and that other famous left-winger Eric Brook of Manchester City fame was a ballroom dancing expert – as was his young daughter.

Before he was married, Jackie Robinson shared a house with two other Sheffield Wednesday players Jack Thompson and George Drury. Robinson was useful in the decorating stakes. At Lincoln 16 year-old Tom Callender was living with his cousin Jack Callender. At Gateshead for a time a regular training game was played between the married men and the single ones. Albert McInroy the goalkeeper had to play centre-forward for the married crowd to make up the numbers.

Next to living at home or in suitable accommodation, players often found themselves living in close communities. At one stage the majority of Manchester City players were in residence on a nearby housing estate to the Maine Road ground. Not everyone was that near. Bert Valentine lived in Wigan and had to train at Halifax. He would get up at 6.30 am catch a train at 8 o'clock and arrive at Halifax at 10 am. After training the return journey would get him back for lunch at 2 o'clock. When Jack Boottie was with Grimsby from February 1938 he was living in Wolverhampton and had a 150 mile trip to home games.

Cars were not too plentiful and expensive to run even though petrol at 6d (two and a half pence) a gallon was thought exorbitant. When "Bunny" Bell was transferred to Everton, he arranged to pick up two of the players Harry Morton and Norman Greenhalgh plus masseur Harry Cook from their digs at New Brighton, on the way to training.

For those married men their leisure time outside of other sporting interests with golf high on the agenda, there was time for hobbies and under the eagle eye of "her indoors" the garden was often a priority on the list. Chelsea goalkeeper Vic Woodley was another flower grower, but also indulged in some useful cabinet-making inside.

It was almost outdoors for Alec Scott the Wolves goalkeeper who was a breeder of rabbits. Pets generally were popular. Fred Jessop at Derby County had a cat and a dog. Both got on famously! Several clubs had their own mascots. Manchester City's was a bull terrier called "Peter" and one of the puppies of the Liverpool mascot "Sucks" was looked after by Jim Harley. Anfield also featured "Girlie" the Great Dane at one time. Stockport County's was "Billy" a bulldog.

Huddersfield Town's Reg Mountford also had a rabbit called "Fluffy" and a Dalmatian known as "Wanton!" Ernie Jackson at Sheffield United was a greyhound owner and his "Prince" was successful on the circuit. Carrying them around was no problem – he was also a weight-lifter. Torry Gillick at Everton was into racing greyhounds, too and ran them at Glasgow before coming to England. But for Leeds United's Bob Browne, "Bobby" the Budgie was the household pet. Then for cramming as much into his leisure time Tom Grosvenor with Bolton Wanderers was a keen tomato grower, gardener, kept poultry and pigeons and had a prize bull terrier known as "Pete!" Manchester City's Jack Bray was also enthusiastic about his poultry farm. Another City stalwart Jack Percival kept pigs and bred greyhounds! George Bargh at Preston had three Golden Retrievers and when not out with them also grew tomatoes in a hot house. Port Vale's Sam Jennings "Lucy" was an Alsatian, too.

Villa full-back Danny Blair spent some time early on farming in Ireland. He found gardening at home much easier as a result. Burnley defender Alick Robinson was also keen on his garden as were Dai Hopkins at Brentford and Walter Crook at Blackburn. When in 1935 Alf Lythgoe moved into a house in Huddersfield it needed a deal of TLC but he transformed it with flowers, a lawn and bushes. Reading and woodwork were two other of his hobbies. Burnley's Bob Johnson was an expert shot with a rifle. Card tricks and conjuring became a remunerative hobby, too, for Albert Geldard at Everton and Bolton Wanderers; thus sleight of foot and hand.

Musical instruments offered a wide range for those so interested. Blackburn's Bob Pryde played the violin as did Eddie Perry of Fulham, who also had a pleasing voice. His pride was a Cremona violin that was 200 years old. Another violinist was Joe Richardson the Newcastle full-back. The Villa and Wales centre-half Tom Griffiths was a cellist and Bury winger Arthur Smith played the church organ as did Welsh international Jimmy Murphy at West Bromwich. Liverpool's South African forward Berry Nieuwenhuys was a ballroom dancer to championship standard, too and the club's pivot Fred Rogers a bass singer in a local male voice choir. Winger George Mee at Mansfield coupled singing with being an all-round entertainer.

George Mutch of FA Cup final penalty fame played the banjo as did Bob Done at Liverpool. Sheffield Wednesday winger Ellis Rimmer had been a music hall pianist at one time and kept up his

playing in leisure time. The accordion was Jackie Mandley's choice at Aston Villa. Goalkeeper Ron Dunn ex-Army bandsman played solo cornet in the Crystal Palace Prize Band. Alf Lythgoe was a jazz drummer.

For Ted Catlin the Sheffield Wednesday full-back, holidaying abroad meant staying on the lookout for clocks to add to his collection. Former trades were most helpful when it came to a spot of DIY at home. Peter Doherty at Manchester City had been involved in a family building operation and found his skills in demand domestically. Joe Cockroft at West Ham was a keen motorist and interested, too, in anatomy. Amateur photography was high on Bill Murray's interests at Sunderland.

An offshoot of sporting interests saw Alf Young the Huddersfield Town and England "stopper" centre-half take his role as Vice President of his local cricket club with a positive attitude. He organized whist drives, raffles and sales of work in order to raise funds.

Peter Doherty

While holidays at home were usual there were others who travelled on the continent in the summer. Tom Holley at Leeds United was interested in languages. He became so advanced in French and German that he read books written in both while on holiday abroad. Yet one wonders how Stan Cullis another of the centre-half mould found as much time as he did when his interests ranged from being able to speak the European language Esperanto, was fluent in French could write shorthand and had a certificate for bookkeeping.   Tommy Lawton was an avid reader of Edgar Wallace crime stories and Edward G Robinson films. However, he considered a late night was to be ended at 11 pm.

Other accomplishments included the unusual situation of a trio of caricaturists with Chester – Harold Howarth, Arthur Wilson and Billy Horsman. Another supremely gifted in such sketching was the Chelsea full-back George Barber. He drew all the players at Stamford Bridge and his work was often published in magazines.

The collecting of favourite items had Bradford City manager Dick Ray with countless tobacco pipes. He once gave one to Billy Meredith the Welsh wizard winger and 25 years later he still possessed it.

Many clubs were keen to look after the after-hours education of their players. In 1937-38 Crystal Palace had 26 professionals and two nights a week they sent them on evening classes to study English, commercial subjects, geography and maths. There were two schoolmasters taking them – and no cane! Earlier on, Derby County manager George Jobey had three schoolboy internationals: Jack Halford, Syd Lowe and George Hannah. He arranged night classes for them in bookkeeping, shorthand and typing.

Indoor pursuits had Willie Chalmers while at Bury taking up rug making. West Bromwich Albion's George Shaw was neatness personified. He was a prize rose grower outside and fancy embroidery fanatic inside, much admired by wife and children!   Gordon Reed the Gateshead centre-forward spent the summer season playing his guitar and crooning on Hastings Pier and the winter in a Newcastle dance band.

Len Massarella the Sheffield Wednesday winger gave up steeplechasing, though he kept his interest as the family owned Silver Mint an Olympic winner.

GOING ABROAD TO PLAY

Peter O'Dowd

France's 5-2 win over England in 1931 was the catalyst for the formation of a professional league across the Channel in 1932. It also provided a magnate for English players. One of the highest profile departures was Peter O'Dowd the Chelsea and England centre-half.

While his three caps had been on the winning side with no goals conceded; an interesting anomaly for a cultured, accomplished attacking centre-half in the fast-developing era of the third back game, he was not always appreciated.

A Yorkshireman from Halifax, he attended St Bees Grammar School in Bradford and subsequently played variously for Apperley Bridge and Selby Town, had a trial with Bradford Park Avenue before signing amateur forms for Blackburn Rovers, turning professional there in December 1926.

From March 1930 he was at Burnley who paid £3,000 before Chelsea signed him in November 1931 after a £5,250 transfer deal. He was one of many players at Stamford Bridge not to see eye-to-eye with the management and with the French set-up bedding down after a couple of years, in September 1934 O'Dowd went to play for Valenciennes in France. At the time he had a drapery business in Weybridge. It was said the French club had paid £3,000 for his services.

He was chosen to play for the North of France against visiting Sheffield Wednesday and was the outstanding player on the field in a 3-2 win. However, a scandal erupted when with two other British players he was accused of throwing a game. Beaten 6-1 at home by Lille, O'Dowd had admittedly had a poor afternoon. Initially banned then reinstated. The trio appealed to the French FA and were each awarded £66 in compensation.

In March 1937, O'Dowd came back to England and signed for Torquay United but had the misfortune to break his leg. His last Football League outing was at Millwall on 30 October 1937 when Torquay lost 7-0. However, the report of the match bore no criticism of O'Dowd's performance. Another Chelsea international, Scottish inside-forward Alec Cheyne spent two seasons with Nimes before returning to Stamford Bridge. Andy Wilson the Scottish international also once with Chelsea, went to Nimes in 1931 after leaving Queens Park Rangers. He also had a stint in Holland with Groningen.

While O'Dowd was an exception, many other players were sought after and were told to cross the Channel stating their intention was to work as shop assistants. It back fired a number of times. Bob Pollard of Exeter City, QPR and Cardiff, was one who got caught out and even found himself in jail overnight until his club St Etienne sorted matters out! A colleague there was Tommy Flannigan who had been around the Football League circuit without being able to find a permanent base. He stayed three months. There were five professionals the others were all employed by the club owner.

Yet another player with Blackburn connections in France was Fred Kennedy. Manchester United had signed this Rossendale United product of an inside-forward in the 1920s and his later clubs included Everton, Middlesbrough, Reading and Oldham. Back at Rossendale then Northwich when on the Latics transfer list, he signed for Racing Club Paris until Blackburn Rovers brought him back in 1933 for a season. Then it was back to Paris and in 1934-35 he scored 16 goals when they finished third. He won a championship medal in 1935-36. Kennedy scored 19 League goals that season. There were only three foreign players there, goalkeeper Rudi Hiden and centre-half Gusti Jordan both Austrians. There had been a succession of coaches at Racing Club – all English: Curtis Booth, Peter Farmer, Jimmy Hogan from 1934-35 and Sid Kimpton once of Southampton. Hogan's older son Joe was actually based on the continent and played for both Lausanne and Racing Club in Paris.

Billy Fraser tried his luck with Marseille where Charlie Bell was manager. He only had a couple of friendly games while deciding on the offer of £8 a week during the season, £6 out of it – close to the Football League structure, though other clubs paid more. Having left Fulham he decided to return home and signed for Northampton Town. The ball used in France was slightly smaller and encouraged better control.

George Gibson was also at Valenciennes with O'Dowd for a time. A centre-forward he had been with Leicester City. However, he was only loaned to the French club and while an equally successful player there, he was implicated in the scandal along with O'Dowd. Actually he had had a taste of French football previously when he played under floodlights for Leicester against Racing Club Paris. Much travelled forward Jack Ball had a spell with Excelsior Roubaix in 1935-36 before returning to Luton Town

England schoolboy international left-winger Les Miller from Romford played for Barking Town and after an unsuccessful trial with Northampton Town also decided to try his luck in France with Sochaux. He married a French girl, too. So well did he play across the Channel that Tottenham Hotspur signed him in September 1936, to be the first professional to be transferred from a French club. Sochaux manager in the early 30s was Vic Gibson a Scot who also played in Spain for Espanol before a 25 year coaching stint with various French clubs.

Three Southampton players Peter Dougal, George Harkus and Harold Rivers also went over to France. As with the experience of Miller, Bert Lutterlock had started out as an amateur with Tufnell Park before playing with Lille. He came back to England to play for Wolves, Aldershot and Luton as a full-back.

William Aitken one-time at Newcastle also had spells in France with Cannes, Reims and Antibes, but not before being in Italy with Juventus. But Fred Bartlett actually signed for Queens Park Rangers after being with Club Francais.

At Charlton, George Green the Welshman who had been recruited from Barry Town had a breakdown and the club decided to send him to Spain to recuperate, arranging for him to play for Espanol at Barcelona to help restore his fitness. Harry Lowe the ex-Spurs player was manager there. All went well until the Spanish Civil War. Green quickly returned to The Valley. Charlie Slade did some coaching in Spain, too, chiefly connected with Sevilla.

Irish international Pat O'Connell once of Sheffield Wednesday became Barcelona coach in 1935. When the Spanish Civil War began during 1936-37 while *La Liga* stopped, the Republican area managed to organize a Mediterranean League. A businessman arranged for Barcelona to tour Mexico and the United States. They made enough money to survive the crisis at home, but only four players returned with O'Connell, the remainder deciding to become exiles themselves in Mexico and France.

Among a number of refugees affected by the conflict in Spain was Sabine Barinaga who was housed in an English convent having escaped from the Basque region. A 16 year old he went to Southampton as a centre-forward for 1938-39 and scored 13 goals in a dozen B team games. His mother was in Barcelona, his father in France.

Many Scottish players had immigrated to North America in the 1920s and with soccer booming at the time there it seemed a wise move for many of them. Alas the stock market crash changed all that and most came back. One with a difference was Alec "Sandy" Archer, who followed his family to Canada and played both ice hockey and soccer for Winnipeg Scottish. He had to mark Hughie Gallacher in one match and managed to keep him fairly quiet. Archer returned to his skates and the UK to play hockey for Wembley Lions but also signed soccer forms for Watford.

When Villa's Danny Blair was playing for Providence in the USA he was paid 50 dollars a week. Joe Kennaway also had some five years with Providence. This goalkeeper was capped for Canada against the USA and when he came to Scotland to play for Celtic he added a couple of Scottish caps, too.

Full-back Alec "Sandy" Wood had to play as an amateur for Leicester City in 1932 because though Scottish born he had become an American citizen. He played four times for the USA in the 1930 World Cup and later for Nottingham Forest.

Versatile forward Jimmy Brown had a similar Scottish background to Wood and actually played in the same four World Cup internationals. He appeared for a host of American clubs before coming to Manchester United in 1932 then joining Brentford and Tottenham Hotspur in the following years. It had been said there were six Scots in the USA team for the 1930 World Cup. Actually one was English George Moorhouse formerly of Tranmere Rovers. But the USA coach Bob Millar, was Scottish. Jim McGuire a centre-half went to the States from Scotland played for Brooklyn and returned via Celtic to Northampton prior to returning to Brooklyn.

On this familiar route Barney Battles of 44 goal Hearts fame was capped for the USA against Canada in 1925, later played for Scotland. He also suffered an injury retired took up occupation as a masseur, became fit again and resumed playing with Hearts!

David Imrie also originated in Scotland and had been playing in Chicago when he returned to the UK. He signed for Clapton Orient in 1931 and scored a hat trick against Northampton. But it was to Northampton that Scot Jim McGuire went from Celtic having returned from the USA. Alec Stevenson at Brentford had gone from Airdrie to play for Detroit before the return trip and thence to Griffin Park.

Naturally the first footballers to venture abroad were those with a coaching agenda with their active careers completed. By the 1930s there were still those apart from Jimmy Hogan engaged with high profile clubs on the continent

When England lost to foreign opposition for the first time 4-3 to Spain, Freddie Pentland had assisted in the coaching of the Spanish national team. An England international himself of a pre-war vintage he had been successful there at club level, chiefly with Athletic Bilbao. Introducing a short-passing game there he also signed ten 18 year olds from other clubs and was able to win League and Cup honours. In 1933 he was appointed manager of Atletico Madrid.

Long-serving Bob Glendenning had taken over from a succession of English coaches in charge of Holland in 1924. He had played for Barnsley and Bolton Wanderers in his career. Another familiar with the coaching scene in the Netherlands was one-time Swindon player Bob Jefferson. There was similarly in the land of windmills and dykes Gus Smith from 1919. A wider travelled export with coaching qualifications was Charlie Bell, a Scot who had burst onto the Football League the day after Boxing Day 1913 by scoring twice for Woolwich Arsenal in a 2-1 win over Leicester Fosse his only outing for the Gunners!

He had two spells coaching Sporting Club in Portugal, Wigan Borough, Padova, Marseille, Nice and Mansfield Town before ending the 30s in charge Bournemouth, where he died on 5 June 1939. One-time centre-forward Horace Williams who had played extensively inside and outside both English and Scottish Leagues had a spell coaching Lucerne in Switzerland.

However, by far the most successful national team manager was Cornishman Alfred Crowle with Mexico! Cornish miners had introduced football to the country in the early part of the 20th Century. Crowle was heavily involved in these embryo days until in 1935 he was put in charge of the national team on a brief tour of Central America. In a week they beat El Salvador 8-1, Guatemala 5-1, Cuba 6-1, Honduras 8-2 and Costa Rica 2-0! Five games 100 percent and Crowle then retired!

Kingstonian, Amateur Cup winners 1932-33. Players only. Back; Rassell, Broderick, Urpeth. Centre; Lee, Daley, Keen. Front; McCarthy, Gibson, Whitehead, Macey, Okin

There was something of a slump in amateur football with the discontinuation of the annual Amateurs v Professionals meeting in the Charity Shield and hit by petrol rising to 6d (two and a half pence) a gallon, so that many sought the alternative of using creosote in their car tanks!

However the FA Amateur Cup was still the primary competition after the FA Cup itself. In the 1930s the most successful teams hailing from the south with only Bishop Auckland twice winners disputing the southern-softies stranglehold on it. Dulwich Hamlet won it three times, twice beating Leyton.

The Hamlet ground at Champion Hill which was revamped in 1933 was the largest amateur venue in the country able to hold 40,000 spectators. It was the site for several England international fixtures and an Amateur Cup final.

Of course the most notable amateur club existing was the Corinthians, though until 1922 their rules had forbidden entry into competitive football. Then they became associate members of the Football Association. Bizarrely they plumped for the FA Cup rather than the Amateur Cup. But with their halcyon days long gone, in 1939 they amalgamated with Casuals to form Corinthian-Casuals, though the merger idea was first mooted in March 1937.

Corinthians came in for much criticism over their decision to enter the FA Cup, though it was largely unjustified. What was a scandal was their exemption until the first round proper. They kept up their annual fixtures with Queen's Park. The high point for Corinthians was on 25 March 1935 when they won 7-1 with John Warfield scoring all seven goals, albeit against an opposing team out of true form.

Interestingly enough, Casuals themselves did not hold the same agenda and in fact won the 1936 Amateur Cup beating Ilford 2-0 in a replay at Upton Park a favoured venue for these finals. The two heaviest defeats suffered by teams in the final were in 1930 when Bournemouth Gasworks Athletic lost 5-1 to the holders Ilford at Upton Park and two years later when Marine (Liverpool) was beaten 7-1 by Dulwich Hamlet on the same ground.

Four of the seven goals were scored by Horace Moseley who later played briefly for Millwall and Bristol City. Two other Hamlet goals came from their most illustrious player Edgar Kail who won England amateur and full international honours.

The only all-Northern final was in 1939 when Bishop Auckland defeated Willington 3-0 during extra time at Sunderland's Roker Park home. It was their eleventh final and seventh win. All three goals were scored by Laurie Wensley, 19, who thus followed his father Harry who had won his medal in the corresponding 1921 final. It was the teenager's second treble having had a three-timer against South Bank earlier on. Bishops previous success in 1935 – its first for 13 years – was achieved against Wimbledon after a replay. Initially at Middlesbrough the teams had drawn goalless. A week later at Stamford Bridge, Bishop Auckland won 2-1. The Dons opened the scoring in three minutes but were worn down and Bishops also hit the crossbar twice.

In the 1929-30 competition, Ilford made it clear early on their intention of retaining the cup. In the first round they beat Eastbourne 13-1 and including the final scored 30 goals. They were, however, held to a goalless draw in the semi-final against Northern Nomads before winning the replay 4-2. But the outsiders Gasworks had done well to dispose of Wycombe Wanderers, Welton Rovers, Barnet and Percy Main Amateurs before a fine 2-0 semi-final success over Wimbledon at Portsmouth.

Still Barnet gained savage revenge giving the Gas men the works in the first round in 1930-31 when they won 9-3. In the final Wycombe won with a follow up attempt after a penalty was saved against Hayes. It was Wanderers first Amateur Cup win. Ilford stayed in scoring mood in 1931-32 with a 10-2 success at Worthing in the second round. Dulwich just won its semi-final against Kingstonian 1-0 at Selhurst Park before a crowd of 30,000.

Kingstonian went one better the following year, though their final opponents were unfortunate to have to struggle in the replayed final with ten players for all but ten minutes before losing 4-1. The original tie ended 1-1 at Dulwich Hamlet, the replay staged at Darlington's Feethams Ground. Yet plucky Bournemouth Gasworks had thrown away many chances in their semi-final against Stockton at New Cross before losing 2-1.

In the 1934 final Dulwich included six of their 1932 final side. They had started the cup campaign beating Casuals 2-1 when there were eight amateur internationals on parade in the match. The final against Leyton was a chapter of accidents. Two Hamlet players collided and were absent in the second half while Leyton also suffered more than a few knocks. It was Dulwich's third cup triumph.

For the 1935 final against Bishop Auckland, The Dons featured Leslie Smith, 16, the youngest finalist. He subsequently turned professional with Brentford.

There had been a marathon second round tie in 1934-35 involving HMS Victory and Leytonstone. After two goalless draws they shared six goals. The third replay went into extra time before HMS Victory won 5-3. However Leytonstone protested that one of the Navy team was ineligible and a further replay was ordered. This time HMS Victory won 2-1. The tie had lasted nine and a half hours. Goals, too, in the third round when Bishop Auckland hit Farsley Celtic 11-1, six of the team getting on the score sheet. In 1935-36 the Casuals had seen Bishops off in the third round scoring four without reply. They were held 1-1 in the final at Selhurst Park but won the replay at Upton Park 2-0.

The 1936-37 final was a repeat of the all-London affair in 1933-34. Again Dulwich Hamlet with four of the previous final team was the winner, this time 2-0 though both sides missed penalties. A crowd of 33,516 watched at Upton Park. In earlier rounds HMS Victory sunk almost without trace losing 8-0 to Clapton and Casuals had the misfortune to suffer injury to their goalkeeper in successive rounds, losing to Dulwich 1-0.

The all-Kent final in 1938 saw Bromley beat Erith & Belvedere 1-0 at Millwall's The Den ground for their first cup in 27 years. Erith needed three attempts before disposing of Leytonstone in the third round. Dulwich suffered its first home defeat in the Amateur Cup for ten years when Barnet won 3-1 at Champion Hill. The 1939 affair was spoiled by the wind and the tie was hanging in the balance until a Willington player mistakenly hearing a referee's whistle picked up the ball. Bishop Auckland scored from the resulting play.

Bromley was also involved in an FA Cup tie against Apsley on 26 November 1938 that attracted a crowd of 4,178. A year earlier Dulwich Hamlet entertaining Aldershot in the corresponding round was said to have had 20,000 in attendance and as such the highest gate in the round. Actually it 14,573 but still the highest! Before turning professional with Chelsea, George Mills had scored over 100 goals for Bromley.

The Southern Counties Amateur Championship had been around from before the Great War, its Northern equivalent almost as long. Hertfordshire won four times in the period, Essex three, while Surrey and Sussex had one each. Suffolk was awarded a final when the fixture with Hampshire was not played. In 1926 it was decided to institute a representative fixture between the South and North. In the 1930s the Southern section won seven, lost two and drew once.

As to Amateur International matches Scotland had entered late having not met England until 1926 and neither Ireland nor Wales before 1930. There were no fixtures against continental countries in the era apart from the Great Britain entry in the 1936 Olympics in Berlin. England and Scotland shared five wins each in the 30s, England won all ten against Wales and six against Ireland who had three wins and a draw.

Scotland won five against Ireland and drew once. Scotland met Wales eight times but not after 1937 winning five, losing only once and drawing twice. England favoured Dulwich Hamlet for the Scots games, around the south for Wales and a variety of venues for Ireland. The Scots varied it for Wales but Ireland was always hosted in Glasgow.

It was left to individual clubs to accept invitations to play abroad. However, the Middlesex Wanderers formed soon after the turn of the century provided collective tours for players. Though its original aim restricted it to those with Middlesex County honours, its popularity forced expansion outside its borders. But it did keep its "Old Boys" elitism.

The man at the head in the 30s was Bob Alaway who had good connections throughout the soccer spectrum. One of these trips was in 1931 to Paris and a four-sided tournament involving Racing Club de France, Cercle Athletique de Paris and Hayes, the beaten Amateur Cup finalists. Wanderers met Racing Club in the final, led at the interval but were dumbstruck when the French brought on three substitutes and drew 1-1! Protests were of no avail. The French coach was Peter Farmer, a Scot! Middlesex Wanderers also played under excellent floodlights in Holland and drew 1-1 with FK Austria, once known as the Vienna Cricket and Football Club.

Olympic Games 1936, England v Poland. Polish forward Hubert Gad rises above Bernard Joy.

It was back to Holland the following year and ten games in two weeks – with cricket in between! In 1933 and France even against professional opposition the Wanderers acquitted themselves well including against Racing Club Roubaix coached by Bill Hewitt an ex-Wanderer himself. Then an international tournament in Holland in 1934 with Belgium and France represented. New ground was broken the following year to Norway, sightseeing always a feature of the outings.

There had been no football tournament in the 1932 Olympics in Los Angeles, even though the USA had competed in the 1930 World Cup, but with the same Games uppermost, 1936 represented just a short trip to the Rhineland in Germany. In fact it was an eleventh hour decision to actually compete in the Berlin Games football tournament with all four home countries contributing players. Bernard Joy of Arsenal and England was appointed captain the trainer was Bill Voisey of Millwall fame. Great Britain beat China 2-0 but lost to Poland in the quarter-final round. Despite leading, the UK team was 5-1 down at one stage before recovering three goals with amazingly two from centre-half Joy! As a response to this Charles Wreford Brown the FA's member in charge of the party hoped it would persuade teams to ditch the third back game.

Extended excursions meant time off their own work commitments for these amateurs and in 1937 the Football Association tour to Australia and New Zealand curtailed the numbers available from those with Middlesex Wanderers links. Twenty matches were played including one in Ceylon with 18 won and only two lost in Australia. Meantime the Wanderers went to Switzerland.

Disappointment in 1938 when the planned trip to Norway had to be cancelled because of the Norwegians being involved in the World Cup finals in France. But in 1939 the Wanderers' Jubilee was celebrated in Turkey.

In addition the Islington Corinthians arranged a world tour starting in October 1937 and even a few Wanderers were co-opted. Holland, Switzerland, Egypt, India, Burma, Malaya, Macao, Indo-China, China itself – even Shanghai held by the Japanese, too! The Philippines, Japan, the USA and Canada completed the eight months 95 game round the world trip. The organization of such a venture beggars belief. Only seven matches were lost, including three in a barren spell of four games.

Islington Corinthians World Tour 1937-28. Back; Tarrant, Bradbury, Manning, Wingfield, Dance, Longman, Martin, Pearce, Lowe. Centre: Buchanan, Miller, Clark (captain), Tom Smith (manager), Wright, Sherwood, Avery. Front: Braithwaite, Read. The lion's name is not known.

Almost half of the party gave up their day-to-day jobs, the remainder were either fortunate enough to have the financial resources to take time out or had benevolent employers; truly a tour for the privileged. These specific Corinthians had played their inaugural fixture on 8 September 1932 at Tufnell Park against Barnet the North London Thursday champions. Sir Frederick Wall and the four Islington MPs were in attendance. The match was drawn 1-1. Subsequently the Islington Corinthians competed in this competition.

The Metropolis also had a competition for both professional and amateur clubs. It was the London Challenge Cup and comprised 16 teams, all eleven London professionals and five from the amateur spectrum. Arsenal won it three times, QPR twice and Brentford, Fulham, Millwall, Spurs and West Ham once each.

As to the leading all-amateur competitions in the south, the Athenian and Isthmian Leagues were the strongest. Walthamstow Avenue won the title five times, Barnet and Romford twice each and Barking won once. For the Isthmians, Wimbledon had four championships, Leytonstone and Kingstonian two each then Dulwich Hamlet and Nunhead one each. Easily the most prestigious in the north was the Northern League. Shildon won it four times in a row from 1933-34, Bishop Auckland and Stockton each had two successes, Ferryhill Athletic and Willington one each.

In the 1936-37 FA Cup, Walthamstow Avenue had a splendid win. In the first round proper they beat Northampton Town 6-1 in front of 7,568 spectators. For the second round it was 1-1 with Exeter City when the tie was abandoned in fog after 65 minutes, the attendance a ground record of 11,131. Only 8,000 watched the replay when Avenue lost 3-2.

The Isthmian League played two representative matches in France winning 2-1 in 1937 and losing by the same score the following year. The London League had actually visited Paris on odd occasions from as early as 1905. In the seven meetings in the 1930s they won three and drew three. Club visits to the continent became more frequent, too.

However, by far the most impressive performance by any amateur club in the timescale was produced by Southall in 1935-36. They excelled but overstretched themselves and sadly won nothing. Because of successes in four cup competitions their League commitments suffered to the extent that they were playing two games in one day and even six in a week at the end! Their outstanding performance was beating Third Division (South) club Swindon Town 3-1 in the FA Cup first round proper. It earned them an exemption to the fourth qualifying round. In the next round they took eight goals off Newport (IW) before losing 4-1 at Watford, but tiredness in the last quarter of an hour when 1-1 was a telling factor. In cup games alone they scored over 100 goals. In 1935-36 Leavesden were also involved in some 17 cup ties of varying standards. In addition, they had been concerned in an amazing end to the London League title. They, Finchley and the P.O. Engineers had the same points and almost identical goal average. Champions Leavesden's was 1-50th of a goal better than Finchley's and the Engineers missed second place by just 1-125th of a goal!

The triangular Kentish Cup was won four times each by Belgium and France while the British Army took the other two titles. The long-standing Army Cup itself produced a three-time winner in the 1st Battalion Sherwood Foresters from 1930 onwards. No regiment won more than once in the next seven years. The other three-sided competition for the Inter-Services Championship saw the Navy surprisingly having the better of the exchanges winning five outright and sharing in one triple tie. The Army won twice and the RAF once in 1939.

As to the University Match, Cambridge held the edge over Oxford, the Light Blues winning four times to the Dark Blues three with three drawn games. While the first five were staged at Stamford Bridge from 1933-34 Highbury provided the venue with the 1939 match held at Dulwich Hamlet. On 8 December 1937 in the 60th Battle of the Blues, Cambridge beat Oxford 3-2 at Highbury. Their third goal was Light Blues 100th in the series.

The Amateur Football Alliance's competitions were well served, too, with the Arthur Dunn Cup given generous reportage at times, with the sports coverage spread over many pages in the daily and weekend newspapers. It seemed if there was a ball kicked a report followed somewhere.

Semi-professional football was once the south's response to the Football League concentrating on the north and midlands via the Southern League. But when the Football League wanted to expand it needed to take the south's competition virtually *en bloc*. Despite this wiping out of its components, the Southern League survived by also accommodating reserve teams from the Football League.

By the 1930s there were Eastern and Western sections and from 1933 for three years a Central group, too. By 1936 a single division of 16 clubs was increased to 18 the following season and even 23 in 1938. A mid-week section was added from 1936.

Most non-league clubs had three different types of player: full-time, semi-professional and amateur depending on resources to which category was predominant. They were able to accommodate Football League players transfer-listed by their clubs and awaiting a chance to resume a career in the largely full-time game. There were no summer wages and in many instances it was pay-for-play only.

While the Southern League catered for the bulk of clubs in the southern part, there were other well-established competitions in various other areas of the country. The Midland League was paramount in the central areas, the North-Eastern League in the north-east and the Lancashire Combination in the north-west. Football League clubs had tie-ups with several using them as nursery outlets for younger players. The Birmingham & District League and Cheshire County League were two other prominent competitions.

Reserve teams of Football League clubs appeared in all of these competitions as well as others around the country and were equally successful in winning titles. Both Middlesbrough and Sunderland stiffs were among the honours in the north-east as well as Grimsby Town and Barnsley in the midlands. However, interestingly enough in both 1937-38 and 1938-39 the winners of the Southern League, Midland League and North-Eastern League were non-league outfits. The Lancashire Combination was dominated by non-league clubs with South Liverpool and Lancaster Town winning three titles each, Chorley and Darwen two each.

The FA Cup was the knock-out tournament providing the opportunity for glory. But giant-killing was restricted to the fourth round stage and then only twice reached. In 1933-34 Workington began in the fourth qualifying round with a 3-3 draw at Manchester North End before winning the replay 6-3. They then beat Southport, Newport County and Gateshead before losing 2-1 to Preston North End.

It was not until 1938-39 when Chelmsford City had a decent run in the competition that a semi-professional non-league club as such achieved a similar feat. Only recently formed from the old amateur Chelmsford FC, they were in their first Southern League season. Though excused the Extra Preliminary Round the newcomers had to start in the Preliminary Round and began by beating Barking 2-1 away. From then on it was Ford Sports (Dagenham) 6-2 away, Crittall Athletic 4-3 at home and Romford 3-1 away before Dulwich Hamlet became the first non-Essex opposition and beaten 5-1 at New Writtle Street. In the first round proper, Kidderminster Harriers 4-0, Darlington 3-1 and Southampton 4-1 were all victims at home before Chelmsford went crashing 6-0 at Birmingham.

In 1933-34 Bath City did exceptionally well to hold Charlton to a goalless draw in the FA Cup before losing the replay 3-1. Their team included two groundsmen employed by the club, an insurance agent, ironmonger, mason, carpenter and builder's labourer. The other four were full-time professionals. After the replay centre-forward Ernest Coombs and centre-half Jack Carter were both transferred to Blackburn Rovers, inside-forward Harold Butt to Charlton!

Yeovil & Petters United had to allow Welsh international Wilf Lewis to join Bath City shortly after scoring a hat trick against Dartford in an FA Cup replay on 1 December 1932. It was the club's first hat trick in the competition proper. Yeovil had a succession of player-managers including David Pratt, who later moved to Orient, Hearts and Bangor as a manager. Like many non-league bosses, he had to act as manager, office boy and telephone operator, but still managed to sell five players. Then Dave Halliday arrived and scored goals including a hat trick against Ipswich Town before accepting the position of manager at Aberdeen. He had previously signed Charlie Smith from Exeter and took him to Pittodrie! Travel was never a Halliday problem. When with Clapton Orient he was living in Manchester. In 1937-38 the Yeovil weekly wage bill was £25. The Somerset club reported a 11,800 attendance for their FA Cup tie with Liverpool on 12 January 1935, though it was the smallest of the ties that day. At one time in 1938-39 Yeovil had seven aircraft workers locally employed and before one cup-tie were given a week's holiday with pay to prepare for the occasion.

Even when modest members of the Birmingham Combination in 1933-34 Cheltenham Town beat Carlisle United 2-1 away in the FA Cup and attracted a 10,389 crowd when losing at home to Blackpool 3-1 in the third round. Player-manager George Blackburn at left-half had been an England international. The team included a market gardener and a council clerk. In the third qualifying round replay they had lost to Llanelly but protested over an ineligible player and had the result reversed.

Colchester United sold Reg Smith to Wolves and Cliff Fairchild to Arsenal in 1937-38. As part of the deal a Challenge Match was agreed between the two purchasing clubs to be played at Layer Road and before a crowd of 14,000 Wolves beat Arsenal 1-0.

Loss of League status did not prevent Gillingham from making a strong bid for Southern League honours in 1938-39 finishing third. Harry Rowley formerly with Manchester United scored 38 goals for them. The previous season Kidderminster Harriers had snapped up Johnny Dent from Nottingham Forest and he responded with 93 goals in two seasons.

Macclesfield Town plundered 142 Cheshire League goals in 1933-34 but only finished second. Bert Valentine contributed 84 of the goals including 15 hat tricks. He moved on to Halifax Town. Midland League debutants in 1934-35 were Peterborough United a crowd of 4,035 watching their first 4-0 win over Gainsborough Trinity. Their best score in the competition came on 31 December 1938 when Boston United was beaten 12-0. Charlie MacCartney scored half of the total.

Scunthorpe & Lindsey United beat Lysaghts Sports 11-3 on 29 October 1938 in an FA Cup tie Harry Johnson scoring five goals. He had 15 of the 31 they scored in their cup run that season. Goals flowed freely for Shrewsbury Town, too. In 1933-34 Joe Taylor scored 68 including two 6's, a four timer and three hat tricks. In 1935-36 Bill Hewitson hit 72 in League and Cup with a six, four 4's and six trebles. The following season when Shrewsbury hit 197 goals in all competitions Ernie Breeze the full-back and captain was tried at centre-forward against Bangor and hit six in an 11-1 win.

The Cheshire League famous for its goal scoring also saw Wigan Athletic producing two outstanding forwards. In 1932-33 William Chambers scored 60 goals, 39 of them in the League. Then in 1934-35 Jack "Nipper" Roberts a former England amateur international produced 46 in the League out of his 66.

Shrewsbury had long held hopes of gaining Football League status and once elected were determined to have a railway halt built in close proximity to the ground. On 13 January 1934 Cheltenham Town might have had the lowest FA Cup on the day but the visit of Blackpool attracted 10,389! Two weeks later it was a similar tale in the next round when Preston North End visited Workington when the 15,321 was the smallest but a ground record. That season Workington beat Chopwell Institute 16-1 in a League game, Andy Lincoln scoring five goals.

Margate who had acted as a nursery club for Arsenal wanted a better deal but the connection was ended and instead Arsenal entered a third team in the Southern League for the first time in 1938-39 with home games on Enfield's ground.

However, in 1935-36 in the FA Cup Margate had beaten Crystal Palace 3-1 in an FA Cup second round tie. Scorer of a hat trick including a penalty was wing-half Jim Evans, who signed for Arsenal the following season.

Folkestone had a trio transferred to Wolves: Len Smart, Cyril Tucker and Alex McIntosh the latter who settled down to first team experience to such an extent that the Molineux club sent a further donation. The visit of Yeovil on 10 December 1938 for a second round FA Cup tie, Folkestone hired a number of motor lorries to provide access for more spectators. The gate was 5,000. Two 17 year olds attracting attention were Fred Durrant at centre-forward and Tony James on the right wing. They had transferred Jack Vinall to Sunderland in 1931.

Due to meet Ipswich Town on 26 November 1938 on the occasion of their first tie in the FA Cup proper the wage bill at Street FC for a week at the time was £14. The same season Chorley had not played at this stage since 1900. They drew 1-1 with Horden Colliery Welfare. Goalkeeper McIntosh, a labourer, asked his employers for time off to play in the replay. He was told he would lose his job. He played all the same. Horden won 2-1, but Chorley rallied round McIntosh.

The non-league circuit continued to attract leading players trying their hand at being player-managers. In 1938-39 former Fulham defender Sid Gibbons held the post at Worcester City, The same season Ernie Hart the England international centre-half found a similar niche with Tunbridge Wells Rangers and Allan Sliman from Chesterfield at Chelmsford City.

Dulwich Hamlet players celebrate their 1937 Amateur Cup win. From the left; Murray, Robbins, Morrish, Hugo.

ACROSS THE HALF WAY LINE

SCOTTISH SET-UP AND RANGERS SUPREME

Rangers 1933-34, with the Scottish Cup, Glasgow Charity Cup and the Scottish League Championship trophy. Back; Dawson, Gillick, Craig, Hamilton, McDonald, Fleming, Jenkins. Centre; William Struth (manager), Marshall, Cheyne, Simpson, Kennedy, Smith, Drysdale, McPhail, Dixon (trainer). Front; Main, McAulay, Gray, Venters, Meiklejohn, Hart, Brown, Archibald, Nicholson

Rangers had the edge over Celtic in the 1930s winning seven First Division titles and five Scottish Cups to their opponents two and three honours respectively. While Motherwell was the only other championship winner, the last two seasons produced East Fife and Clyde as Scottish Cup winners. East Fife had finished third in the Second Division and became the first club outside the top flight to win the trophy.

The composition of the Scottish League had two divisions of 20 teams, the experiment of a Third Division having been abandoned in the 1920s after just two seasons. Two up and two down for promotion and relegation purposes was sustained throughout.

In November 1932 the Second Division expelled Bo'ness and Armadale as they were unable to meet £50 match guarantees to visiting clubs. Bo'ness had had a similar problem in 1931 but had been re-elected. Armadale played 17 matches in 1932. From 1933-34 onwards the remaining 18 clubs carried on. Edinburgh City elected to the Second Division in 1931 only twice succeeded in avoiding the wooden spoon when 15th in 1935-36 and 17th in 1937-38. City had replaced Clydebank who disbanded in July 1931 having been hard hit by the downturn in local industry.

Motherwell the surprise club had finished second in Division One in 1929-30 five points behind Rangers but outscoring the championship with 104 goals. Third the next season and champions themselves in 1931-32 reversing the five point margin and again registering one more goal than Rangers this time scoring 119 goals.

Second place in 1932-33 but yet again one more goal than Rangers with 114, runners-up in 1933-34 but finishing seventh, twice fourth then fifth and even as low as twelfth in 1938-39.

Naturally Rangers were the dominating force. Only once out of the top two and that was when third in 1937-38. They overshadowed Celtic who were fourth, runners-up, third, fourth, third, runners-up, Champions (1935-36), third, Champions again (1937-38) and runners-up.

The Ibrox clan's 1929-30 title was their fourth in succession and they also won every competition for which they had entered: League, Scottish Cup, Glasgow Cup and Glasgow Merchants' Charity Cup. In the Scottish Cup Queen's Park, Cowdenbeath after a replay, Motherwell and Montrose brought them to the semi-final where Hearts were beaten 4-1. Partick Thistle held them to a goalless draw in the final before a crowd of 107,475. Rangers won the replay 2-1 with a record midweek attendance of 103,688. Perhaps a little fortuitously the Charity trophy was won by toss of a coin after goals and corners had been shared with Celtic.

However, the 2-1 New Year's Day win over Celtic was their first Ne'er day victory at Parkhead since 1902; a portent of what was to follow. This significant victory came in the midst of an eleven match winning streak into February. With seven games remaining and an eleven points lead, the championship was almost there. The 3-0 win at Ayr sealed it a week later. Five forwards hit double figures in the League and accounted for all but 13 of the 94 goals. Jimmy Fleming scored 27 but goalkeeper Tom Hamilton was the only ever present.

After a 14 match 14 win tour of North America, the League trophy was retained in 1930-31 thanks chiefly to a devastating finish launched from a an 8-0 win over Clyde on 14 February in which Jimmy Smith scored five. With two games remaining Rangers were a point in front of Celtic and four ahead of Motherwell. But it still required a 4-0 last day win at East Fife to ensure a club record fifth title in a row and the 19th overall.

The distribution of the 96 goals saw Smith scoring 21 in the same number of games, inside-forwards "Doc" Marshall and Bob McPhail each scoring 20. Bob McGowan had ten from a dozen outings at centre-forward and contributed the 3,000th Rangers League goal on 20 December. Right-back Dougie Gray was the sole ever present.

For 1931-32 there was another new leader of the attack in Sam English from Coleraine. He responded with 44 League goals and 56 in all competitions. Despite this impressive contribution, Rangers were runners-up. Motherwell 4-2 winners over Rangers at Fir Park in the third game proved worthy champions even though Rangers edged the return at Ibrox 1-0. The season was marred by the accidental but fatal injury to Celtic goalkeeper John Thomson in a collision with English on 5 September in the goalless draw at Ibrox.

Rangers slipped up on 17 October losing at home to Queen's Park and were unable to regain the leadership thereafter. But there was Scottish Cup success. Brechin was beaten 8-2, Raith 5-0 and Hearts 1-0 both away, Motherwell 2-0 before the 5-2 semi-final win over Hamilton. In a replayed final with Kilmarnock, Rangers succeeded 3-0 following a 1-1 draw. Again the attendances were incredible considering the depressed state of the country, respectively 111,982 and 104,695.

In 1932-33 the first game was lost 2-0 away to St Mirren. But it was one of only two such defeats. Rangers took three points off runners-up Motherwell, enough to give them the championship. Yet even in October Motherwell had a one point lead and kept it in the 2-2 draw at Ibrox. Again it was late on before the title was destined for Ibrox. A two point lead with two games to play then Motherwell dropped a point to Third Lanark and it was over. Smith scored 33 goals, McPhail 29 but only George Brown at left-half played in all League games. One-time Queen's Park amateur Alan Morton "The Wee Blue Devil" retired from his impish left-wing role with 382 League games to his credit and went straight onto the Board of Directors!

Another foursome reel was produced at home in 1933-34 with the League, Scottish Cup, Glasgow Cup, Merchants' Cup plus the unofficial British Championship success in beating Arsenal home and away respectively 2-0 and 3-1. Only two defeats were suffered in the League against tenacious Motherwell early on and away to St Johnstone in November. Even so Motherwell still led in December matching Rangers effort week by week. But a 4-2 success over them in January put Rangers top and eventually only two points were required from three remaining fixtures.

In the Scottish Cup Blairgowrie, Third Lanark, Hearts after a replay and Aberdeen brought St Johnstone as the semi-final opposition. Rangers won 1-0. In the final five goals were scored against St Mirren without reply.

Smith was leading scorer with 41 goals in only 32 matches, McPhail 22 from just 25 outings and Fleming 16 from just 13 League games! Fleming had scored nine times in a 14-2 Scottish Cup win over Blairgowrie! But again only versatile defender Whitey McDonald was ever present. Right-winger Sandy Archibald retired after 513 League games since during the Great War.

Rangers had to be content with the League and Cup double in 1934-35. The medical move to London in July 1934 of Dr James (Doc) Marshall to Arsenal was a blow after 200 League appearances and 111 goals. Smith six-hit Dunfermline Athletic in a 7-1 win but a 3-2 defeat at Dundee put Aberdeen and Clyde ahead of them. Still a 1-1 draw at Celtic Park and Rangers were top though having played a game more but led again late September. Trailing leaders St Johnstone with a game in hand in second place but losing 2-1 at Clyde on 20 October caused some concern.

On 3 November Rangers beat leaders St Johnstone 3-1 to reduce their lead to a point. Despite being level on points with Celtic top at the end of the year Rangers had two games in hand. Rangers recovered and even though Scottish Cup commitments interrupted the programme, the indications were promising and Rangers were three points ahead of Celtic at the conclusion. Cowdenbeath, Third Lanark, St Mirren and Motherwell were dismissed in the Scottish Cup and Hearts 2-0 after a semi-final replay. Hamilton Academicals were edged 2-1 in the final.

Smith with 36 goals was leading scorer though he missed six games. There were no ever present players but other personnel changes with younger players like Tory Gillick bedding in at Ibrox and scoring 17 goals himself. Long serving Fleming moved to Ayr United with 176 League goals to his credit from 225 games.

The Scottish Cup was the major honour in 1935-36, third in a row. Gray and McPhail picked up their sixth winner's medals with the club. Not even a grandstand 16 game undefeated run into April prevented Celtic from winning its first Scottish League title in ten years. On 21 September Celtic won 2-1 their first at Ibrox since 1921. In mid-October Aberdeen led, Rangers third behind Celtic. It stayed that way until Ne'er Day when Rangers gained revenge in a memorable 4-3 win. Three days later the order was Aberdeen, Rangers, Celtic with a game in hand. By Cup final day 18 April when Rangers beat Third Lanark 1-0 in 90 seconds, they were six points adrift of leaders Celtic despite that unbeaten sequence. Celtic had led from February with two games in hand. Four days later Celtic had clinched their title and Rangers only finished second on goal average from Aberdeen. Goalkeeper Jerry Dawson and full back Dougie Gray played in all League games, Smith scored 31 from 28 goals. Centre-half Davie Meiklejohn bowed out after 490 League games. Mid-season Gillick was sold to Everton for a record £8,000. For that third in a trio of Scottish Cup wins had seen East Fife, Albion, St Mirren and Aberdeen slip away in Rangers wake before the semi-final disposal of Clyde 3-0.

For 1936-37 Rangers recaptured the title. Again Aberdeen proved early motivators and though Rangers had a run of 17 without defeat they were only third behind Celtic. Even mid-December they were fourth with Hearts above them. Still another 13 game unbeaten run from January improved the situation and with Aberdeen tucked into second, the third and four places were disputed between Celtic and Hearts. Motherwell even stole fourth place from Hearts at the end. Dawson appeared in all 38 League games for Rangers again, Smith led the marksmen with 31 goals. Rangers actually lost twice to Hearts.

Celtic refused to be written off and ended 12 points better off than third placed Rangers in 1937-38. Dundee led initially but late September Rangers in an unbeaten run of 16 that included seven draws were top with Motherwell and Dundee following. The lead changed with Motherwell ahead in October and Hearts in November. It was not until mid-December than Celtic showed in front on goal average from Hearts. Incredibly Rangers were just a point behind with a game in hand! New Year's Day saw Celtic win the Auld Firm derby 3-0 before a record 83,500. It heralded a collapse and only two of the next nine were won. Overall the 13 drawn matches contributed to the downturn.

Normal service was resumed at Ibrox in 1938-39, Rangers having the cushion of an 11 point lead at the finale after an indifferent start. They even crashed 6-2 at Celtic Park on 10 September. By 1 October Celtic, Rangers and Queen of the South were in that order on goal average. Rangers took over and though Celtic had a game in hand, the lead increased and by January Rangers were nine points to the good in the middle of a 17 game undefeated run. On 2 January a record 118,567 packed Ibrox with an estimated 30,000 unable to gain admittance. Rangers won 2-1. At the end only eight points separated second to seventh place. Rangers were unbeaten at home. Alex Venters scored 35 goals from 33 League appearances. Jock Shaw who cost £2,000 from Airdrie slotted comfortably in at left-back and Willie Waddell looked just as promising as a winger at only 17. Willie Thornton continued to establish himself in attack, too. However, stalwarts like Gray (485 League games), Smith (225 League goals) and McPhail (231) were still aboard. McPhail had cost £4,500 from Airdrie in 1927 where he had won his first of seven Scottish Cup medals.

The man at the tiller deserves special mention in view of the foregoing. They were astutely managed by Edinburgh born Willy Struth who had assumed control in 1920 on the passing of his predecessor William Wilton, who died in a boating accident in which Struth was the only other occupant. He was to enjoy a lengthy and rewarding reign at Ibrox. A stone mason by trade and athletically a professional sprinter at one time he held coaching positions at both Clyde and Hearts before becoming assistant manager at Rangers in 1914.

Rangers had at least one representative in every Scotland team against England in the 30s and ever present appearances were not always feasible for such players. From 1919-20, Rangers won 15 of the 20 Scottish League titles. From the 1933-34 season Rangers had the better of the friendly exchanges with Arsenal, winning three times to Arsenal's one victory, the other two games being drawn.

STEELMEN SHOW METAL

Motherwell 1933. Back; Wylie, Crapnell, Wales, Blair, McGlory, Telfer, Johnstone, Ellis.
Front; Dowell, McMennemy, McFayden, Bob Ferrier, Stevenson, Ogalvie, McKenzie

Motherwell enjoyed seven seasons of consistency from 1926-27 during which they were never out of the top three places, From 1929-30 they outscored all opposition for four consecutive seasons and in 1931-32 won the Scottish League Championship amassing 119 goals to finish five points ahead of Rangers with Celtic 13 points further away. While the area suffered industrial depression, the team continued to be well supported.

In 1929-30, the death was announced of the Steelmen's former star Hugh Ferguson at only 33. Losing to Hearts at home and Ayr away in September, Motherwell then tightened up at the back and showed more emphasis on attack. After Celtic was beaten 2-1 came a 6-1 crash at Partick Thistle. Then a 4-2 defeat away to Rangers, who also knocked them out of the Scottish Cup. But on 15 March Motherwell completed a sensational double over Celtic winning 4-0 at Parkhead. Nine goals were taken off Queen's Park, too and the Steelmen finished runners-up at the final analysis. Bob Ferrier scored 32 goals from outside-left.

Negotiations towards signing Ben Ellis a Welsh half-back with Bangor in Ireland were finalized in October 1930. On Christmas Day, Motherwell fielded what proved to be the finest attack in the club's history: Johnny Murdoch, John McMenemy, Willie McFadyen, George Stevenson and Bob Ferrier. They beat Thistle 3-0. All five were capped at least once by Scotland. A League and Cup double was even a possibility. Top of the table in the spring they were also in the semi-final of the Scottish Cup after accounting for Bathgate, Albion, Hibs and Cowdenbeath. But after beating St Mirren in the semi-final, a late own goal cost them a final win over Celtic and they lost the replay. Motherwell had led the original tie 2-0 with eight minutes left. McGrory pulled one back and Alan Craig had the misfortune to head an own goal. Then it was third place in the Championship.

However, for 1931-32 it was a vastly different outcome. By mid-September they were third a point behind leaders Rangers and Kilmarnock on goal average. At the end of October though held 2-2 by Celtic, Motherwell had a two point lead over Rangers but had played one more game. Even losing 1-0 at Ibrox over the holiday they kept top spot. Celtic was beaten 2-0 in the Scottish Cup but Rangers knocked them out in the fourth round.

Even in January they had 40 points and 92 goals. On 12 March Motherwell won 4-2 at Parkhead for another double over the Hoops. Two weeks later Rangers lost 4-3 at Third Lanark and though they had played two games fewer than Motherwell, the Steelmen were seven points to the good. With Rangers involved in the cup final replay they had three games in hand but Motherwell just needed to avoid defeat in their last match to ensure the title. They beat Clyde 3-0 but it had been over weeks before. Motherwell had become only the second team outside the Glasgow pair to win the Scottish League since 1904.

Only Celtic avoided defeat at Fir Park. Just two were lost away, five drawn. McFadyen scored 53 of the 119 League goals. Goalkeeper Alan McClory and Ellis were ever-present among the 19 players used. Allan Craig and Willie Telfer missed one each, Bob Ferrier was absent twice, Stevenson three times and McFadyen played only 34 League games.

There was no let up in 1932-33 and in mid-September Motherwell were breathing down Rangers necks a point adrift but with a game in hand. They drew at Ibrox only to lose three in a row to Hearts, Celtic and Partick dropping to fifth before a revival by December just a point behind Rangers. Then into the New Year with only goal average separating. On 11 February Rangers won 3-1 at Fir Park and shortly after Motherwell slumped 4-2 at Queen's Park. But they recovered and also had cup commitments. Hamilton was beaten, seven goals taken off Montrose and five off Dundee. Shared six goals with Killie then hit them 8-3 in the replay. Motherwell defeated Clyde 2-0 in the semi-final reaching the final again only to lose 1-0 to Celtic. Motherwell finished runners-up three points behind Rangers. In January 1933 Craig was sold to Chelsea for £4,000. McFadyen hit 45 League goals. On 29 October 1932 Motherwell lost at home for the first time since 7 September 1929.

As for 1933-34 a similar scenario and a 2-1 win over Rangers at Fir Park on 2 September put Motherwell top. Six points ahead for some weeks then halved in the New Year. Losing 3-0 at Celtic on 10 March Motherwell were one point ahead of Rangers who had two games in hand. A week later Partick won 3-2 at Fir Park, too. On 21 April Motherwell did lead again in their last fixture, but Rangers winning the Scottish Cup that day, still had three to play and were a point behind. They were four points ahead at the end. This time McFadyen scored 38 goals.

For 1934-35, Motherwell slipped to seventh with McFadyen contributing 33 goals, were fourth next time out 18 points below the winners Celtic. They were fourth again in 1936-37 and beat Celtic 8-0 on a Friday night in April as the Hoops were due to attend the FA Cup final the following day. In fairness Celtic had suffered an injury to their goalkeeper. Alex Stewart signed from St Johnstone for £250 scored six times. Motherwell then finished fifth and down to twelfth in 1938-39. But they sold right-winger Duncan Ogilvie to Huddersfield Town for £2,900 in March 1936 and bought him back in December 1937 in the deal taking 249-goal McFadyen to Leeds Road, Huddersfield. McMenemy went to Partick Thistle for £1,000 in September 1936 and changes continued. Stewart was transferred to Falkirk in November 1938 for £900. Centre-forward Dave Mathie was signed from Wishaw Juniors. In December 1938 defender Willie Kilmarnock was signed at 17. On 27 August 1938 Ellis the penalty expert scored three from the spot against Kilmarnock!

Sheffield born Ferrier became assistant manager in May 1938. He had played 19 seasons for the Steelmen with 626 League appearances and 259 goals. At the end of 1938-39 his left-wing partner Stevenson had completed 510 League appearances in 16 seasons with 169 goals. Ellis took his total to 279 League appearances. In the Scottish Cup final Clyde proved the better team though the four-goal margin did not reflect Motherwell's effort.

Celtic 1933. Back; Thomson (A), Hogg, Kennaway, Napier, McGrory, McGonagle. Front; Thomson (R), Geatons, McStay, Wilson, O'Donnell

There were slim pickings for Celtic in the years between the wars, just two Scottish League titles in the 1920s and two in the 1930s. They did slightly better in the Scottish Cup with three in each decade. For 16 years Celtic had in Jimmy McGrory one of the most consistent goal scorers in first class football anywhere in the world, who averaged a goal a game throughout his career. His 397 League goals in the Hoops came from only 378 games. Yet it did not yield the honours for his club his record might have suggested.

Originally a left-winger and not tall at 5ft 6in, his first Celtic senior game was at inside-right and he was even loaned out to Clydebank in 1923-24 where he was turned into a centre-forward, hinting as such to Celtic officials when he scored the winning goal at Parkhead against them.

Three times finishing third and twice fourth, the 1930s were difficult times for the club but the fewer successes were memorable and well earned. Initially the cup provided the honours. In 1931, Motherwell proved stubborn final opponents after Kilmarnock had been defeated 3-0 in the semi-final. East Fife, Dundee United and Morton had been beaten away, Aberdeen at home in the fourth round. Two down to Motherwell with eight minutes remaining Celtic forced a replay Allan Craig unluckily heading through his own goal. Celtic won the replay 4-2. Two seasons on and again Motherwell stood in the way before McGrory scored the only goal.

In 1929-30, a fourth place eleven points behind champions Rangers with one spell of four successive defeats mid-season. McGrory missed twelve games with injury. Runners-up the following season but again adrift of a late challenge and ten League matches drawn including two of the last three.

Naturally the fatal accident to goalkeeper John Thomson on 5 September 1931 cast a long shadow over the club and its supporters following the collision with Rangers centre-forward Sam English. The brave Thomson had twice suffered concussion in successive matches in a previous season. But Joe Kennaway plucked from football in the USA proved a fine replacement. Again Celtic was in the wake of both leaders and runners-up respectively 18 and 13 points short when third.

Fourth in 1932-33 but drew twice with Rangers who finished 14 points in front as Champions. In the Scottish Cup Celtic beat Dunfermline 7-1 away, Falkirk, Partick and Albion after a replay. Then after edging Hearts 2-1 in the semi-final replay, Motherwell again proved stoic opponents in the final before Celtic won 1-0. McGrory was absent eleven times again in 1933-34 and unusually was not top scorer. Frank O'Donnell had 22 League goals. No serious challenge with Rangers 19 points as Champions and Motherwell 15 ahead with Celtic third. Three stalwarts ended their association: Jimmy McStay, Alec Thomson and Peter Wilson. McStay with 406 League appearances, Thomson with 391 League appearances and topped 100 first team goals plus Wilson after 344 League matches.

A far more concerted effort followed in 1934-35 after an inauspicious beginning that had Celtic languishing 13th after a handful of games. On 15 October manager Willie Maley appointed Jimmy "Napoleon" McMenemy as coach and Celtic won its next nine matches! By 1 December they were third and second from then on as Rangers had two games in hand. They cleared the backlog late to win the title by three points from Celtic.

In 1935-36, the first Scottish League title for ten long years was distinguished, though it began with losing 3-1 at Aberdeen on Willie Lyon's debut, too. But there was no other reverse until 14 December when Celtic lost 1-0 at Dunfermline Athletic, while on 21 September the 2-1 win at Ibrox had put them top. On 19 October, McGrory overhauled Steve Bloomer's world record 352 first class goals. Celtic won its last eleven matches and remained five points ahead of the field.

Though Rangers won a see-saw by the odd goal in seven at Parkhead on 1 January only another 1-0 defeat at Hearts on 1 February blighted the League campaign. It was Celtic all the way from then and only twice held to a draw for extra measure. They scored 115 goals five more than their nearest rivals and conceded only 33, ten fewer than the Ibrox team.

McGrory who was absent six times, scored in 29 League games, a total of 50 goals. Only twice did Celtic fail to find the net. Of the 21 players used Bobby Hogg, Lyon, Willie Buchan and Johnny Crum were ever present, George Paterson missed just two games. Eight players contributed only 21 appearances between them. Early dismissal from the Scottish Cup was for once an asset. Moreover the omens were there when on 21 September the Celts had won at Ibrox for the first time since 1920-21.

Celtic had a steady defence and devastating attack Jimmy Delaney and Buchan on the right wing, McGrory leading the line and Crum and Frank Murphy forming the left flank. Disappointment followed in 1936-37 when finishing third this time nine points behind the Champions Rangers. However, Celtic won the Scottish League title again in 1937-38 appropriately enough in their Golden Jubilee season. It was their 19th such Scottish League championship. Though the winning margin was just three points they had twice beaten runners-up Hearts. The 114 goals scored were just one goal fewer than two seasons earlier. All this achieved without McGrory from mid-October on his way to retirement and the managerial reins at Kilmarnock after 397 League goals alone and 470 overall for the club.

For extra measure the prestigious Empire Exhibition Cup was won. Firstly Sunderland 3-1 in a replay after a goalless draw, Hearts by the minimum then Everton similarly 1-0 in the final with a Crum goal.

Changes up front were needed as Buchan was sold to Blackpool in November and replaced by Malky MacDonald converted from an attacking centre-half to inside-forward. Crum moved to replace McGrory and Johnny Divers slotting in at inside-left. Unusually six players reached double figures scoring: Crum 24, Divers 19 (from only 20 games) Joe Carruth 15 (from 19), Buchan 13 before his move and Murphy ten goals. Only Hogg and Crum were ever-present, Murphy and Paterson missed just one and goalkeeper Kennaway and Lyon two each.

Squeezed between these two seasons was the Scottish Cup success in 1937. Yet Stenhousemuir took them to a replay, before Albion and East Fife proved easier before Motherwell in the fourth round. Clyde were the 2-1 semi-final losers. Though final victory was against Aberdeen 2-1 at Hampden Park, the quarter-final against Motherwell was the tricky tie of the run. Eight goals shared before the replay saw Celtic edge home 2-1.

In 1938-39, McGrory's Killie suffered a 9-1 drubbing at Parkhead to open the season, but Celtic finished eleven points behind champions Rangers. Inconsistency cost dearly, for despite eight goals and three sixes including a 6-2 win over Rangers, the middle of the season saw crucial points dropped with the attack unaccountably miss-firing. On 1 April 1939 Jimmy Delaney sustained a severe fracture of the right arm. The legendary Willie Maley retired after a world record 42 years at the tiller.

CLOSE TO THE TOP THREE

Aberdeen and Hearts were the only Scottish teams apart from Celtic, Motherwell and Rangers to finish as high as runners-up in the Scottish League. They were also the most consistent after these three.

In 1929-30 Aberdeen ended in third place though seven points from the top. They failed to score in only one League game and Benny Yorston scored 38 times in as many games leading the League marksmen. A poor start hindered expectations the following season when sixth before 18 November 1931 proved a fateful day for the club.

Five players including Yorston who had scored 101 League goals were axed and put on the transfer list for an alleged betting scam though no charges were ever brought. Aberdeen was seventh, their lowest position in the 30s. A mid-season slump saw no wins and only three points in eight games.

In 1932-33 the centre-forward position was solved with the signing of Paddy Moore from Shamrock Rovers and he responded with 27 goals in 29 games with the Dons sixth. Ninety goals were scored in 1933-34. Inside-forward Willie Mills scored 28 and Matt Armstrong finally emerged with 14 goals from only 12 games leaving Aberdeen fifth.

Armstrong was in full flow in 1934-35 with 31 goals and missing only two League games. He also registered in eleven successive matches. The Dons reached the Scottish Cup semi-final before losing 2-1 to Hamilton Academicals. Again sixth place was secured in the League.

But 1935-36 saw a vast improvement. The first game produced a 3-1 win over Celtic at Pittodrie and Rangers were to perish there in November. In mid-October Aberdeen moved top though having played a game more than the Auld Firm duo. This false position remained and was underlined as they had played two more fixtures. But in mid-February with Dons in a Scottish Cup commitment, Celtic went top and stayed there. Aberdeen was third but had achieved the double over Rangers. Ninety-six goals were registered, beaten a mere three times and Armstrong averaging a goal a game on 30 strikes.

Prospects seemed even better in 1936-37. Unbeaten and leading in September, not dislodged when edged out 3-2 at Celtic Park, the first reverse in a dozen games. However, on 6 February a 1-0 defeat at Motherwell cost top spot and Rangers led on goal average with two games in hand. Aberdeen had already lost ground. In fact their last eleven games were to yield only 11 points. Second place was seven points behind Rangers. Armstrong and Billy Strauss each scored 24 goals. The Dons were also runners-up in the Scottish Cup after Inverness Thistle, Third Lanark, Hamilton Academicals and Morton had been defeated. Celtic edged Aberdeen 2-1 in the final.

Back to sixth in 1937-38, Mills with 114 League and Cup goals joining Huddersfield Town for £6,500 in March. Then Aberdeen scored 91 goals in 1938-39 when third and another Scottish Cup semi-final defeat 3-1 by Motherwell after a replay. In March 1939 Aberdeen discarded its black and gold stripes for red shirts and white shorts. Long serving right-back Willie Cooper in his 12th season took his League and Cup appearances to 338 having made 163 consecutive League appearances at one stage. Armstrong had scored 155 League and Cup goals.

Hearts, runners-up position came in 1937-38, the season following Aberdeen's second place. The Edinburgh club's worst season in the period had seen them tenth in 1929-30. The following season when ending fifth, Barney Battles bludgeoned 44 of the 90 League goals from 34 games. In November 1930 he scored successive hat tricks against Motherwell, Dundee and St Mirren and his four-game absence was due to an appendicitis operation. In other matches he added a further 22 goals.

After eighth place in 1931-32 plus 53,496 v Rangers in the Scottish Cup on 13 February 1932, improvement followed in 1932-33. A 1-0 success over Dundee on 17 September and Hearts were third on goal average below Motherwell but with a game in hand of leaders Rangers a point in front. With only four points separating the top eight the race was wide open. Introduced at 17 was Tommy Walker a schoolboy international inside-forward.

By February, Rangers were forging ahead, Hearts third three points behind Motherwell but having played one more. These positions remained. Sixth in 1933-34 but another step up in 1934-35 in spite of an indifferent opening phase, tenth after six games. Hearts were third briefly in October but second on 10 November with one point separating the first four teams. Slipping in the New Year, Hearts were gradually falling behind in points from the leaders and were third. Another teenage inside-forward debutant was Andy Black. Ex-Third Lanark centre-forward Dave McCulloch was top Scottish League scorer with 38 goals.

On 21 September 1935 in the derby with Hibs, Hearts were four up at half-time. Thereafter it went 5-0, 6-0, 6-1, 6-2, 6-3, 7-3 and 8-3. Alex Massie was transferred to Aston Villa in December 1935 for £6,000, a month after McCulloch joined Brentford for £3,000. Hearts were fifth again for the next two campaigns before the best effort in 1937-38 produced a sustained performance. Pacesetters Dundee gave way to Rangers but by mid-October Hearts had moved up to third. On 27 November a crushing 3-0 win at Ibrox Park put Hearts top on goal average from Motherwell. But on 25 December Hearts lost 3-0 at Third Lanark and Celtic took over again on goal average. That was how it panned out. Hearts completed the double against Rangers, but Celtic beat them twice. On 27 November 1937 Black became one of few players to score a hat trick against Rangers scoring in the tenth, 15th and 63rd minutes. In 1938-39 Hearts were mostly in the chasing pack behind Rangers when fourth. Right-back Andy Anderson took his League appearances to 313 over ten seasons, Black scored his 105th League goal.

If collectively disappointing, individually Hearts produced several outstanding players who often figured in the Scottish international team, goalkeeper Jack Harkness, Anderson and Massie among them.

THE SURPRISE CLAN

Hamilton Academicals though twice placed as low as 13th finished fourth in 1934-35. In mid-September they were fourth two points off the leaders then improved to third. In December they remained unbeaten at home as well as being level with Rangers and Hearts on goal average having played one more game in a tight race.

Then Falkirk ended their home record and defeat at Celtic left them moving out of the leading pack, though with games in hand through Scottish Cup commitments, the situation was still promising. A 2-1 semi-final cup win over Aberdeen at Celtic Park followed by beating Hearts 2-0 in the League on 6 April left them only three points off second place but with Rangers coasting it at the top. By now the backlog of games had been completed. Rangers edged Hamilton 2-1 in the Cup final and fourth spot in the championship represented Accies best season during the period.

In 1929-30 they had been placed unlucky 19th then twice tenth before up to eighth in 1932-33 before they were eleventh in 1933-34. Outstanding at centre-forward was David Wilson, an Englishman signed from Hebburn Colliery in 1928-29. He went on to score 256 League goals in 329 League games. In 1936-37 he scored 35 goals. Despite his small stature his tenacity and marksmanship made him a dangerous leader.

Hamilton also developed the talent of Alex Herd from a teenage inside-forward who scored on his debut into a rewarding transfer to Manchester City on 3 February 1933 after he had scored 25 goals in 27 League games. On 7 January he had scored three penalties against Partick Thistle. Jim McLuckie accompanied him in the same move to Maine Road. Both won Scottish international recognition. A record crowd of 28,690 had watched Hearts beaten 3-1 on 3 March 1937 in the third round of the Scottish Cup. Sixth in 1935-36 then eighth in the rankings, down to 13th and seventh in 1938-39.

Kilmarnock forced a Scottish Cup final replay against Rangers in 1932 with a 1-1 draw before losing the replay 3-0. East Fife, Albion Rovers, Dundee United in a replay, Dunfermline and Airdrieonians had been previously defeated. Their final scorer was Bud Maxwell a local lad. He became one of three players subsequently transferred to Preston North End where they won FA Cup winners' medals. Maxwell scored 103 goals in four seasons for Killie. Centre-half Tom Smith was the next for Deepdale followed by inside-forward Bobby Beattie.

Though Rangers had beaten them in the 1932 final, Kilmarnock enjoyed some success against the Ibrox club. On 16 February 1933 they beat Rangers 1-0 in a third round tie watched by 32,745. It was the Ibrox club's sole cup reverse between 1931 and 1937. Seventh in 1933-34 was Kilmarnock's highest placing in the 30s. In 1929-30 Rangers had loaned Bobby McGowan to them and he responded with 18 goals in only 15 matches including five against Morton and four against Ayr. Oddly enough he was to be signed by Killie in 1937-38 and scored eight times in a dozen games. That season Killie had a fine run in the Scottish Cup beating Dumbarton, Celtic 2-1 Ayr after a replay and Rangers 4-3. Then East Fife beat them in the replayed final. Another scoring oddity came in a Scottish Cup tie against Paisley Academicals on 18 January 1930 with Jimmy Weir scoring six in the 11-1 win. He thus trebled his total over two seasons.

Killie finished eighth in 1929-30, eleventh in 1930-31, then ninth, 14th and seventh for 1933-34. Ninth in 1934-35 then eighth, eleventh before becoming as low as 18th in 1937-38 only two points from the drop. By 25 September they were bottom after nine games bracketed with four other strugglers. A mini-revival was not maintained and they stayed second from the bottom into the New Year. With Morton appearing doomed already, at least Kilmarnock remained in touch with those clubs above them.

A 6-0 Scottish Cup win over Dumbarton acted as a stimulus in the League and on 12 March Rangers were beaten 2-1 at Rugby Park leaving them twelfth. Exhausted by their cup exploits Killie managed only five more points. Relative calm returned in 1938-39 when tenth.

In 1931, Kilmarnock had seen the departures of Mattha' Smith after 16 years service 415 League games and 109 goals as well as Peerie Cunningham who in six years had scored 100 League goals. A year later Scottish international full-back Joe Nibloe was transferred to Aston Villa.

Partick Thistle had their best three seasons from 1929-30 being placed sixth (actually third time in a row), fourth and sixth again in that order. They also had their best season in the Scottish Cup in the first of these reaching the final and forcing a goalless draw with Rangers before being edged out in the replay 2-1. While 107,475 had seen the original game, the evening kick-off on a Wednesday produced 103,668! Their earlier victims had been Dalbeattie Star, Dundee United, Aberdeen, Falkirk and Hamilton.

In 1930-31 The Jags recorded their highest win 16-0 against Royal Albert from Larkhall. Johnny Simpson scored nine goals. With the club in financial straits, Simpson was later sold to Plymouth Argyle for £2,750. Twelve wins in a row in 1932-33 but middle of the table, then a colour change to red and yellow in 1934.

At the end of the 1938-39 season Partick wing-halves Alex Elliot and Eddie McLeod had respectively made 369 and 394 League appearances; a remarkable pairing of consistency in over a dozen seasons.

Clyde amazingly retained its Division One status and as an added bonus won the Scottish Cup in 1939 in convincing style. Settled as a mid-table team their only worrying season was 1935-36 when 18th. By early November they were bottom but only two points separated the last seven clubs. Results improved in a continuing tight group with the Bully Wee fourth from the last place. A 4-0 home defeat by Celtic pushed them 18th, just a point off relegation. With no wins on travel and losing 5-3 away to Airdrie on 4 April they were in the last two. A welcome 1-0 win over Hearts was followed by beating Queen of the South 3-0 in the penultimate fixture. With Airdrie held at Arbroath and Ayr also having completed their programme, Clyde was safe.

The backcloth to the 30s for Clyde centred on its Shawfield ground where greyhound racing was oddly enough well supported. The Bully Wee's foxy Chairman John McMahon eventually did a deal with the GRA and kept the wolf from the door.

Scottish International full-back Danny Blair joined Aston Villa in 1931 after 179 League appearances. He had previously played in North America. But 1938-39 was unquestionably Clyde's best season. They were ninth in the table with a cup run as a bonus. St Johnstone was beaten 2-0, Dundee 1-0 after a goalless draw brought the daunting prospect of a visit to Ibrox Park to face Rangers. Incredibly Clyde won 4-1 with Willie Martin scoring all four goals. Third Lanark was then beaten 1-0 as were Hibs in the semi-final. A goal in 30 minutes in the final against Motherwell and an early second half strike for 2-0 took the fight out of the Fir Park side and two further goals made it 4-0. Martin the ex-Queen's Park Scottish amateur international scored 20 League goals that season.

In 1933-34 centre-forward Willie Boyd was transferred to Sheffield United and had the distinction of being top scorer for both clubs that season. He registered 91 League goals in four seasons for Clyde.

Coincidentally, Queen's Park's best season also secured ninth place. For the Spiders it was 1932-33. They also outstandingly held Rangers three times to draws. In December at Hampden it was 0-0 and in February 1-1 at Ibrox in the Scottish Cup 1-1 in the replay then losing 3-1 at the third attempt. The amateurs also defeated Motherwell 4-2 on 25 February, won 4-3 at Partick and 3-2 at Falkirk.

In 1933-34 the legendary James (J B) McAlpine, inside or outside left, completed 473 League appearances for the Spiders scoring 164 goals in continuous service from 1919.

Unfortunately 1938-39 ended their sojourn in the top echelon. After five matches they were unbeaten at home but obtained no points from travel. Then Ayr won at Hampden and Queen's Park were 19th. After eleven games they were bottom. Encouraging wins away at Albion Rovers and at home to Hearts then Aberdeen revived hopes plus an amazing 5-4 success at Kirkcaldy against Raith Rovers lifted them to 14th.Then the tailing-off and after losing 8-3 at Tynecastle to Hearts on 4 March they were 19th. Raith looking candidates for the drop was beaten 3-0. But with one match to play the Spiders chances looked good enough. St Mirren had to play Celtic, while Queen's Park was at home to Queen of the South. The Spiders won 2-0 but the Paisley outfit edged Celtic 2-1 and stayed up. Martin before his move to Clyde scored a club record 30 League goals.

Naturally the calls on Queen's for players for Scotland's amateur international team were always a problem with Scottish Division One requirements ever present. It was to the club's credit that they continued to maintain such high standards. They also supplied James Crawford, Robert Gillespie and Willie Wiseman to the full Scottish eleven.

The highest crowd was against Rangers in the Scottish Cup on 18 January 1930 when 95,772 saw Rangers win 1-0.

THE BOUNCING BACKERS

Of the teams bouncing back and forth between the leading divisions, Third Lanark twice won the Division Two championship. Fourth in 1929-30, they proved worthy title winners in 1930-31 eleven points clear of runners-up Dundee United and scoring 107 League goals. But in two seasons they were back down before immediately rallying to regain Division One status.

In 1931-32 a 4-3 win over Rangers on 26 March pushed them to third, though well away from the leaders Motherwell and their victims in second place. But Celtic had games in hand and caught Third Lanark to take third place. Neil Dewar scored a club record 35 League goals.

The Hi-Hi came 13th in 1932-33 when Dewar was transferred mid-season to Manchester United only to fare badly the following season. After seven games they were second bottom. The first home win did not materialize until beating Airdrie 3-1 on 21 October. After 14 April, Third Lanark laid 18th with two matches remaining while Airdrie had a game in hand and were a point behind. Airdrie won, Third Lanark lost and despite a George Hay hat trick against Partick Thistle in the last match, Airdrie took the necessary point against Ayr.

Making a confident start in 1934-35 in Division Two the first defeat was not until 20 October 2-1 at Arbroath and the first home reverse a week later by the same score against King's Park cost them first place. This was recaptured by the middle of December and maintained. With one match remaining, Arbroath with inferior goal average were promoted anyway leaving Third Lanark to cement the title 3-1 against Forfar.

Thereafter the Hi-Hi settled back to Division One fare finishing ninth, sixth, ninth again and 15th during the remaining seasons. In 1935-36 Hay scored 27 League and Cup goals. That season Third Lanark reached the Scottish Cup final losing 1-0 to Rangers having beaten Hearts, Leith Athletic, Dumbarton, Morton and Falkirk.

Stalwarts included right-back Jimmy Carabine capped by Scotland, centre-half Jimmy Denmark transferred in 1937 to Newcastle United and Dewar another Scottish international who returned in 1937-38 via Sheffield Wednesday. He scored 101 League goals for Third Lanark. On 22 January 1938 in the Scottish Cup some 45,335 saw Celtic win 2-1.

Morton experienced two relegations squeezing in one temporary promotion. In 1931-32 Dick Black scored 38 League goals in 37 League games and joined Manchester United before the season's completion. He also scored three goals in each of two top flight games against Celtic! But having hovered in the danger area for three seasons, 1932-33 proved the Greenock club's downfall. By early November they were 18th just a point above the last two. December was kinder before the New Year down turn stuck them firmly 19th throughout. Robert Keyes was Morton's leading scorer with 13 League goals and ex-Falkirk's Tim Morgan scored eight in as many games at the tail end.

Division Two produced several challenging attempts with fifth, sixth and third finishes before 1936-37. Then the only home defeat was suffered on 28 November when Airdrie won 1-0. Morton scored an eight, a seven and four sixes at Cappielow though the away form was not as impressive. The last match at King's Park was lost 2-1 but Ayr had already become Champions leaving Morton as runners-up. Morton also excelled in the Scottish Cup. After sharing six goals with Murrayfield Amateurs they won the replay 6-1 then drew with Partick before another replay win. A fourth round 4-1 success over Queen of the South was followed by a losing semi-final against Aberdeen 2-0 at Easter Road. The previous season they had reached the fourth round.

Alas after ten matches in Division One at the start of 1937-38 Morton was bottom and soon after became a fixture there. Black was back via St Mirren and scored 23 League goals. In 1938-39 they were twelfth in Division Two.

Dundee United had won promotion the season before 1929-30 but was cash-strapped until Newcastle United paid £4,050 for Duncan "Hurricane" Hutchison after three games. He had scored 68 League goals in just over two seasons. Still the fans were unhappy over the transfer. Defence was the real problem 109 goals conceded and five points away from safety.

In 1930-31 a clearout of staff produced better results. Into the New Year prospects improved noticeably. While Third Lanark had been runaway winners, second place was more open. In fact on the last day Dundee United entertained Dunfermline. They had a point advantage and a better goal average and in effect won 2-1 anyway. Only 18 players were called upon. It was their fifth change of status in seven years!

With only four Division One wins in the first half of 1931-32 then beating Celtic 1-0 on Boxing Day there were only four more in the season and United went down again letting in 118 goals scoring only 40 themselves, eight points from safety. Only a spirited finale brought them 13th in Division Two in 1932-33. After 17th in 1933-34 a mid-season revival in 1934-35 helped towards fourth place when only 16 players were used throughout, including two trialists ignored by the Scottish League who maintained United had the League record with 14!

But it was a season of record breaking for the club: 105 goals, most in one game 9-6 v Edinburgh City, 8-0 away at Brechin, 17 games unchanged and Arthur Milne aged 19, scoring 23 in just 18 League games after a debut four-timer including hat trick in nine minutes v Queen's Park.

Subsequently United were seventh, twice 14th and ninth in 1938-39. In six consecutive matches from 7 March to 13 April 1936 they had scored 42 goals: 6-3, 6-1, 6-1, 8-2, 4-3 and 12-1. Milne scored 77 League goals in only 73 League games before joining Hibernian. Hutchison did return in 1935 and completed 199 League appearances in his two spells plus 123 goals to his credit. In 1938-39 Willie Black was signed from Morton and scored 23 goals in 28 League games.

Albion Rovers fared slightly better overall. Following their second stint in Division One they stayed up for a while. Three points off runners-up in 1929-30 and 101 goals to their credit, they slipped down to ninth when "Bunty" Weir completed 84 goals in three years. Rovers were 16th then fifth in 1932-33. John Renwick scored 42 League goals. Then the drama unfolded in 1933-34. Little indication early season but a good home record if poor away, still left them within two points of the top. Late November eight points from the leaders. First away win in December but a 3-2 victory over Dunfermline in January and only three points separating them. Fluctuating form affected the pacesetters and a gap of seven opened above Albion.

On 31 March a 4-2 win against King's Park put Albion second on goal average behind Dunfermline. The Fifers and Arbroath had completed, Albion had one more to play a point behind the pair. A 3-2 win at Dundee United confirmed the title.

In 1934-35 Airdrie loaned John Connor to Albion and his eight goals in six games including both in a 2-2 draw at Rangers staved off the drop. Renwick had scored 86 goals in four seasons. They were 16th in Division One for two seasons but bottom in 1936-37 with only 16 points and 116 goals conceded. Wing-half Murdy Walls completed 375 League appearances in 15 years with the club. On 8 February 1936 some 27,381 had seen the Scottish Cup tie with Rangers.

Even so Albion returned at once as runners-up to runaway Raith Rovers though again it was a nail-biting time. Second place was the only real target and there were plenty of candidates. Rovers were fifth in March still with a precious game in hand. On 20 April this was won comprehensively 7-0 against East Stirling, to leave Albion one point ahead of Airdrie. On the last day Airdrie shared ten goals at Dundee United but Albion drew 1-1 with Montrose and went up.

In 1938-39 they were bottom of Division One early November with six points from 15 games and last in the New Year, too. A 5-0 win over Hamilton on 4 March put them 18th and a point at Clyde on 8 April and they were 17th. Then two successive wins at home 1-0 v Aberdeen and 2-1 v Raith and 16th at the close.

Cowdenbeath also suffered demotion and thereafter needed five seasons before winning the Division Two championship in 1938-39. After 16th in 1929-30, seventh in 1930-31 then twelfth and 17th, relegation descended. In 1933-34 never far from the last place and four points adrift in the New Year it increased to five and doubled at the death. In November they had accepted an offer from Rangers for local boy inside-forward Alec Venters who had shown immense promise and good enough to be capped for Scotland two months earlier.

In the 1930-31 Scottish Cup, Cowdenbeath beat Queen of the South 3-2 away, St Johnstone 4-0 away after a 1-1 draw and St Bernards 3-0 to face Motherwell in the fourth round losing 1-0. Life in Division Two showed a gradual improvement with twelfth in 1934-35, tenth in 1935-36 and sixth in both 1936-37 and 1937-38. It was consolidated in fine fashion during 1938-39. Unbeaten and table-topping the first defeat was in the tenth game. A 5-0 defeat at Dundee on 28 January was only the second reverse. With eight games left the lead was eight points with a game to spare. Remaining unbeaten and a Championship lead of twelve points at the end. No home defeats just two away and of the 120 League goals Rab Walls scored a record 54 after 37 the previous season.

Only once above half way, Airdrieonians continually fought the spectre of relegation from Division One. The Diamonds heydays of the 20s with Gallacher and McPhail were long gone. Twelfth in 1929-30 they were ninth the following season. Fourteenth in 1931-32, the next season was a worry. Just seven points from the first 15 games and bracketed with the bottom team last by December. The dizzy heights of 18th in February and stayed there to avoid the drop. John Connor loaned from Celtic scored an invaluable 22 League goals in 21 matches. Mid season Scottish international full- back Jimmy Crapnell the last jewel in the crown moved to Motherwell after 227 League appearances.

Yet 1933-34 was even more of a concern. Sixteenth mid-November and only two points off the foot. By mid-February one of four in trouble but with Cowdenbeath drifting it was one from three. On 21 April Airdrie beat luckless Cowdenbeath 3-1 one point clear with a game in hand. This was drawn 1-1 away to Queen of the South, leaving Airdrie two points ahead of Third Lanark. Thirds won their last but Airdrie drew with Ayr and finished 18th again.

After the relative calm of 14th in 1934-35, the inevitable came in 1935-36. No hint after ten games until a run of consecutive defeats left them second from the bottom in November. Third from the bottom in the New Year and last in March several other teams were struggling. Even two wins and two draws in the last five games did not save Airdrie. Incredibly Connor who had been signed the previous season was second highest Scottish League Division One scorer with 33 goals!

Division Two life was easier and reflected in fourth, third and fourth again. In 1937-38 Robert Hogg scored 31 League goals in 28 matches and full-back Jock Shaw was transferred to Rangers having missed only eight games in five seasons.

Dundee was twice eighth and retained its Division One status until 1937-38. By a strange twist of fate that opening phase was by far their best in the decade. Six straight wins and table-topping until the wheels came off in October and a 6-0 defeat away to Rangers. Below half-way in the New Year and out of the Scottish Cup, then came the shock. The Ibrox boys were entertained at Dens Park on 5 February and found themselves 4-1 down at the interval. The final score was 6-1 with Arthur Baxter scoring a hat trick and Archie Coats two goals. Then only seven points were accumulated from eleven games. Another run of poor results before another 6-1 win over St Johnstone put them back into the top half of the table. But another slump and early April Dundee was 17th. But playing catch up with outstanding matches along with half a dozen teams on the same points, it was a blow when Celtic won home and away games against Dundee.

With two matches remaining, Morton already relegated six teams including Dundee were on 31 points another had 30. Thanks to its better goal average Dundee were actually 13th – perhaps an unlucky number. Moreover they crashed 5-0 at Falkirk and only had a goalless draw at Ayr, thus finishing 19th a point from safety. One more point and they would have been 14th!

In Division Two sixth place in 1938-39 but Dundee was never in contention. Coats had not missed a League game in his five seasons at Dens Park and scored 122 goals. The record crowd was set on 14 February 1931 when 38,091 watched Aberdeen in a 1-1 Scottish Cup draw.

Among the Scottish Division One clubs who were relegated during the 30s, three of them: St Mirren, Falkirk and Ayr United won back their status the following season. St Mirren had been fifth twice in the first three seasons, 15th in between, seventh in 1933-34 and down to 17th in 1933-34. But in 1934-35 finished second bottom and relegated. Alas for the Love Street team their talisman centre-forward Davie McCrae had signed for the French club Stade Rennes mid-way through the previous season. He had scored 222 League goals in over ten seasons.

St Mirren also reached the Scottish Cup final in 1934. However, in the first round they had found themselves a goal down to Penicuik Athletic before forcing a 2-2 draw. Winning the replay 4-1 they also won 4-0 at Brechin City with a McCrae hat trick. The scalp of Celtic was taken in the fourth round from a goal in each half and Motherwell in the semi-final with a Jimmy Knox treble. But Rangers coasted the final scoring five clear goals.

However, in 1935-36 the Saints were runners-up in the Second Division and promoted scoring 114 League goals. Goal a game Jimmy Knox scored 33 of them. Even so the team found the going tough again 16th, 14th then 18th when close to the drop once more in 1938-39, only to respond sensationally by beating Celtic 2-1 in the last game with goals from Willie McLintock the top scorer with 21 goals and Knox to ensure continuance in the top flight. Knox at inside-forward contributed 246 League games and hit 141 goals by 1939.

Falkirk won the Division Two championship in 1935-36 with a record 132 goals – one of five teams to top a century that term – and accompanied St Mirren back to the Scottish Division One. Kenny Dawson was leading marksman with 39 goals and he and Robert Keyes made an effective striking duo. The team adjusted themselves better and were placed seventh, fourth and fifth in the next three seasons.

The Bairns had lost their prolific marksman Evelyn Morrison when he was transferred to Sunderland midway through 1929-30. He had scored 43 League goals the previous season having been snapped up from neighbouring Stenhousemuir a season earlier. Seventh in 1929-30, then 14th, in 1931-32 long serving defender Tom Ferguson completed a club record 449 League appearances in 13 seasons. In a run of eight seasons he missed only two matches. Jimmy Bartram left for Northampton Town in 1935 after 61 goals in three seasons. Dawson with 102 goals signed for Blackpool in November 1938. On 25 August 1937 there had been a record crowd of 22,618 for the visit of Rangers to Brockville Park.

Ayr United went down in 1935-36 after several narrow squeaks. In 1929-30 they had been ninth, two points from the drop in 1930-31, 17th in 1931-32 and 16th in 1932-33. Up to eighth in 1933-34 they were two points from relegation in 1934-35. Yet after demotion Ayr recovered in confident fashion to win the Division Two title in 1936-37 scoring 122 goals in the process. They won all home games except for drawing with runners-up Morton. Terry McGibbon who had been leading scorer in 1933-34 with 35 goals – the season 23,220 saw Celtic in the Scottish Cup on 3 February 1934. McGibbon improved on his best with 39 in 1935-36. In five seasons he rattled in 119 League goals. That season Andy McCall moved to St Johnstone after 228 League appearances. Ayr were placed 14th in 1938-39.

In two strange ways, 1937-38 was a satisfying one for Ayr. In the Scottish Cup they defeated East Stirling, Queen's Park and Morton both after replays but having held Kilmarnock to a 1-1 draw lost the replay 5-0. In the League they drew 15 matches including the feat of holding both Rangers and Celtic home and away. Such was the close contest to avoid relegation that at the season's end only three points separated teams ranked 9th to 19th. On the last day of the season Ayr drew 0-0 with Dundee to survive by one point having won only one of their last seven fixtures.

Relegation hit St Johnstone in 1929-30, finished fifth in Division Two and then won promotion in 1931-32 as runners-up to East Stirling on goal average. Though St Johnstone scored 102 goals it was nine fewer than their rivals who had conceded three more goals. Jimmy Benson scored 38 of their tally.

Once back in Division One they acquitted themselves well. In 1932-33 they were fifth behind Rangers the Champions, Motherwell, Hearts and Celtic – a formidable foursome. Ninth the next season they also reached the Scottish Cup semi-final before losing to Rangers. Then in 1934-35 they were fifth again when the order above was: Rangers, Celtic, Hearts and Hamilton.

They were never in danger during the rest of the 30s, seventh, twelfth then eighth twice. Among some notable players Scottish international and rarely absent from League duty goalkeeper Sandy McLaren moved to Leicester City mid-way through 1932-33 as the Saints most capped player. Winger Jimmy Caskie arrived in 1933-34 and was transferred to Everton for £3,000 during 1938-39. At the same time Andy McCall who had scored 28 League goals in 1936-37 joined Huddersfield Town.

Highest attendance was 20,658 on 3 March 1934 for the Scottish Cup tie with Queen of the South. St Johnstone won this fourth round tie 2-0.

Hibernian having been two off the relegation spots in 1929-30 went down the following season. The decline in performances on the field and problems off with the depression plus financial problems dating back to expenditure on ground improvements were contributory causes. Relegation came with Ayr winning its last game after Hibs had completed their programme.

After finishing seventh in 1931-32 the next season saw Hibs winning 15 of their first 18 games. But when Bo'ness and Armadale were expelled for not meeting guarantees, four fixtures were lost. However Hibs won the title with five points clear. On 4 March the visit of neighbours Hearts in the Scottish Cup had produced a ground record of 33,759.

But only once in subsequent seasons did Hibs finish even half-way and struggles against relegation continued. In 1933-34 they were 16th then eleventh, 17th (two points clear) 17th again, tenth and finally 13th in 1938-39. For 1935-36 hovering in the danger zone personnel changes disrupted the team. Only two points separated the bottom four. It was imperative for a win at Dunfermline in the last game. Willie Black was the saviour and two seasons later he joined the Fifers. They were 17th again in 1936-37 but without the same anxiety. For the following season they snapped up former Dundee United centre-forward Arthur Milne who had been hurt in a Liverpool trial and then overlooked. He scored 37 League goals in 66 appearances. In 1938-39 Hibs reached the Scottish Cup semi-final before losing 1-0 to Clyde. The colours were changed, too, with bright green shirts and white sleeves introduced.

TEAM CREATING HISTORY

Of the clubs winning promotion, none did so more spectacularly than Raith Rovers in 1937-38. Oddly enough it seemed their best chances had passed them by, finishing fifth, fourth, third, sixth and eighth from 1929-30 onwards. In 1934-35 the Kirkcaldy side had dropped to 13th and 17th for the next season. They did rally to eighth in 1936-37 and it proved a prelude to an outstanding season never previously accomplished in British football history.

Despite six new players in the team they settled down quickly. Top by 4 September the first loss was on 9 October at Cowdenbeath. There was only one other defeat at home to East Fife on Ne'er day with a record 19,500 at Stark's Park. In the return game with Cowdenbeath on 29 January their 100th goal in the League was confirmed.

An 8-3 win at Alloa with four matches left secured the title and the 142 goals scored was a UK record. The winning margin was eleven points. Only 16 players were used, six ever present. Norman Haywood scored 47 League goals, Tommy Gilmour 35, Jock Whitelaw 26 and Francis Joyner 21 before his transfer to Sheffield United for £1,650 on 7 April 1938 after promotion was assured.

As expected from such a mammoth total of goals there were three 8s, one 7, five 6s and three 5s. There was a goal in every League game. Additionally in the Scottish Cup, Edinburgh City was beaten 9-2. Of the 43 first team matches played only once did Raith fail to score and that in a goalless Fife Cup draw with Cowdenbeath. Haywood, Gilmour, Jimmy Morrison and Peter Cabrelli appeared in all matches and Haywood scored 55 goals overall.

Alas, the uplift proved too much for the Kirkcaldy team propping up the table after ten games and hovering in the danger zone thereafter. Yet incredibly on 7 January they beat Celtic 4-0 at Stark's Park. A week later they won 4-2 at Motherwell. A run of success was needed, it did not happen. Odd wins were insufficient and last place became a permanency. Ninety-nine goals were conceded. Out of the Scottish Cup first time 1-0 to Rangers but there was a gate of 21,747 at Stark's Park.

Queen of the South accomplished promotion but barely held on to it. Seventh, sixth and ninth in 1931-32 when though scoring 99 goals, they let in 91. Jimmy Rutherford scored a club record 41 League and Cup goals. But 1932-33 told a different tale. Finally shaking off Dunfermline Athletic for runners-up position, a matter of five fewer drawn games left them behind Champions Hibernian who had lost the same number of times as The Doonhamers. Left-winger Tommy McCall scored 32 goals. Right-back Willie Savage made his debut on 1 October in the 10-0 win over Bo'ness as a trialist and stayed seven seasons making 234 League appearances. The end result was promotion for Queen of the South and in 1933-34 they acquitted themselves more than satisfactorily in fourth place.

Celtic, Hibs and Hearts were beaten twice and Motherwell away! Only Rangers achieved the double over them. There was the old defensive failing and eight goals were conceded at Dundee on 2 September before five wins in succession shortly afterwards. On 23 December they won at Celtic 1-0 and were in the top half. A 4-1 win over Aberdeen on 10 March and Queens were fourth. With two games remaining third but only one point from the last two left them fourth. Unfortunately it was a struggle in 1934-35. Five consecutive defeats by the end of March, then fortunately three points from the last two matches ensured 17th position.

Fifteenth in 1935-36 though again the second half of the season was more troubled. The same situation was not the case in 1936-37; bottom after ten games and well into February five points from relegation. With two fixtures left three points separated them from Dunfermline. They cancelled each other out and Queens were 18th.

After 20 games in 1937-38 only five points separated eight strugglers. This shrunk to two points in the New Year. In March the Dumfries team was only a point from safety and had played one more. Ten teams were level. On 30 April Queens won 3-2 at Rangers to survive at 16th! In 1938-39 came the relief up to sixth.

Arbroath seemed to be plying peacefully as a mid-table Division Two side before a strong challenge developed in 1933-34. On 23 September they were fourth one point from the top. By 4 November level top in second place with hopes rising. On 23 December the tenth home win was secured and briefly top on goal average. Though the home record was lost early in the New Year by the end of January they again led. Five teams were chasing promotion with only three points between them.

Though unbeaten in their last four they finished third on inferior goal average having scored seven fewer than Dunfermline and conceded one more goal just a point off the leaders. Ever present Alex Brand scored 33 League goals.

However, the opening phase of 1934-35 was anything but encouraging. Second from bottom after five games proved misleading and by late October Arbroath was fifth from the top then second in mid-December. A fine run-in produced an unbeaten eleven matches and promotion two points behind Champions Third Lanark plus beaten only twice at home. A mere 42 goals were conceded, fifteen clean sheets but still let in two 5's and a six.

Eleventh in Division One in 1935-36, then 14th, eleventh again before the slide arrived in 1938-39. Seventeenth early October and bottom in November there was no real improvement until winning the last two matches. They were three points from relegation in 17th position. Brand completed 165 League appearances in six seasons and took his goals tally to 112. Right-back Willie Fordyce completed 317 League games having missed only 13 in nine seasons. On 9 September 1936 the visit of Aberdeen attracted 12,800.

Though Dunfermline Athletic failed to gain another point in 1933-34 when their goal average was far superior to Albion Rovers in the Second Division Championship race even though losing both games to them, their equally superior goals for and against enabled the Pars to win promotion after being level with Arbroath. The Fifers had been tenth and third from 1920-30 and repeated the sequence from 1931-32 being only two points short in 1932-33. In 1934 the experienced Scottish amateur and full international inside-forward Willie Chalmers once of Queen's Park was signed.

Division One also brought the much-travelled Bobby McGowan to East End Park. He responded with 56 goals in 74 League games in the next three seasons but could not prevent relegation. After finishing 15th and 14th they were 19th in 1936-37. Back in Division Two Roly Robertson scored 34 League goals as an ever present in 1937-38 while in 1938-39 Willie Black another with a well trodden track record was signed from Watford in October and finished with 32 League goals. Dunfermline had finished ninth and fifth in these two seasons. No Scottish Cup runs as the fourth round was the furthest reached.

Fortunes eventually swung in a positive way for Alloa Athletic following a poor showing in 1929-30 when they were last but one having conceded 104 goals. Twice 13th and then eleventh in 1932-33, the Wasps were then 15th and tenth before improvement in 1935-36 to fourth. Down to ninth and eleventh in 1937-38 the breakthrough came in 1938-39.

They won the first three games and led the table. The Wasps buzzed between third and fourth places into the New Year. On 4 February they won 2-0 at Stenhousemuir and were second two points behind Cowdenbeath. A surprise 3-1 defeat by bottom club Edinburgh City on 18 March and crucially 4-1 at home to strongest challengers East Fife with one match remaining threatened to end promotion aspirations. On 26 February 1939 the Scottish Cup visit of Dunfermline drew 13,000.

Cowdenbeath was already assured of the title and promotion. East Fife had completed its 34 matches with one more point than Alloa. Airdrie had also ended and had an inferior goal average to Alloa. On 29 April, Alloa drew 1-1 with Brechin to take runners-up position thanks to a defence conceding only 46 goals. John Fitzsimmons signed from Celtic was leading scorer with 22 goals. Alloa had also reached the fourth round of the Scottish Cup that season.

Within three seasons Leith Athletic, East Fife and East Stirlingshire were promoted to Division One and within four years all were back in Division Two. Leith and East Fife finished one and two in Division Two during 1929-30 separated by goal average. Leith took the title conceding 16 fewer goals despite scoring 22 less!

In 1930-31, East Fife scraped only 20 points and laid seven points from safety while Leith had settled in 17th position, two points from demotion themselves. East Fife had let in 113 goals one less than they had scored the previous season. Arthur McGachie who had scored 37 League goals in 1929-30 was top scorer with just 14.

Leith's leading marksman in 1930-31 was James Laidlaw with 17 goals from 27 League games, John Crawford made most appearances missing just four games. But the Edinburgh club's Division One career ended in 1931-32 having conceded 137 goals and mustering just 16 points. Crawford again had the most outings being absent just twice. James Nicol scored 19 goals in 29 League games.

East Fife meanwhile came eighth in Division Two and apart from 13th in 1933-34 well in the top half thereafter. In 1934-35 Phil Weir completed 100 League appearances and 215 goals. On 9 September that season Joe Cowan hit seven goals against Dumbarton. However, 1938-39 proved an exciting struggle for promotion as previously recorded; inferior goal average costing runners-up position.

There had been immense success for the Methil team the previous season recording their highest win on 11 December 1937 beating Edinburgh City 13-2 and a marathon Scottish Cup effort. Victims were Airdrie (away), Dundee United 5-0 and Aberdeen (away) after a draw produced a fourth round tie with Raith Rovers. Again East Fife won the replay 3-2 away. In the semi-final at Tynecastle St Bernards also took them to a second game at the same venue with the same score before another 2-1 result there!

The lengthened final proved just as absorbing, the initial meeting with Kilmarnock ending 1-1. The Hampden Park replay looked to be heading the same way 2-2 at full-time before East Fife scored twice in the extra period to win 4-2. Thus East Fife became the first Division Two club to win the trophy. Their revenue for ten matches was £10,000. Danny McKerrall, a Falkirk reserve was transferred in an injury emergency and scored in both games. John Harvey from Hearts had to be signed, too, replacing David Herd in the replay because of injuries! These two won cup medals.

The week of their final success, East Fife played four times: Monday lost to East Stirling with reserves playing, Wednesday the cup replay win, Thursday beat Forfar in the League and Friday hit seven against Dundee United!

During this time Leith Athletic had finished 16th in the 1932-33 Division Two then stuck mid-table before back to 16th in 1938-39. Not much Scottish Cup success either but Neil Paterson the amateur and writer scored a hat trick against his former club Buckie Thistle on 25 January 1936.

East Stirling finished twelfth in 1929-30 with John Renwick scoring 34 goals. He added 25 the following season when the team moved to seventh. He had left when East Stirling won the 1931-32 Division Two championship by 0.057 of a goal better than St Johnstone, who ironically had been the only team to win at Firs Park that season. The aftermath in 1932-33 was savage; relegated shipping 115 goals, four more than they had scored in 1931-32. The goals columns were reversed respectively 55 against and for in these two seasons.

East Stirling were ninth, 14th eighth, seventh and 13th in 1937-38. Mid-way through the season Robert Kemp who had played left-half and left-wing moved to St Bernards having completed 278 League appearances. Then in 1938-39 a disappointment with 130 goals conceded and second last. By an odd fact, ex-Third Lanark's Malcolm Morrison established a club record with 36 League goals from a total of 89.

However, in March 1934 East Stirling was suspended by the Scottish League for failing to meet their match guarantee against Morton. The ban was lifted after four days on club assurances.

ROUNDING UP THE SCOTTISH SCENE

Eleven other Scottish clubs were involved in Division Two though three of them did not complete the ten seasons. Also in 1928-29 Bathgate and Arthurlie had resigned. Bathgate's record did not feature in the final table, yet Arthurlie having failed to complete its last four matches was recorded. So for 1929-30 both Brechin City and Montrose were readmitted. Clydebank resigned in 1931 having finished 18th and 19th in the two previous seasons, while Bo'ness and Armadale were expelled in November 1932 unable to meet match guarantees.

Edinburgh City replaced Clydebank and with the disappearance of the other two clubs, Division Two was reduced to 18. While Bo'ness had finished 13th, last and 14th previously, Armadale had been placed 15th then 18th twice. Bo'ness had also reached the Scottish Cup fourth round in 1930-31, forcing a replay against Kilmarnock. In later seasons they finished as a runner-up in the Scottish Qualifying Cup in 1935, 1936 and 1938. Armadale folded.

Alas Edinburgh City, the capital's amateur equivalent to Queen's Park in Glasgow, appeared out of their depth. Bottom four seasons consecutively, they were 15th in 1935-36 and one off the foot in 1937-38, thus finishing last six times in eight seasons.

However, St Bernards another Edinburgh based club, was the most consistent of the others involved. Never lower than 14th they were third twice, fourth once and fifth on two occasions. They also enjoyed a run in the Scottish Cup in 1937-38 with Motherwell one of their victims on the way to the semi-final and taking East Fife to three games before narrowly losing out to the eventual winners.

In 1938-39 George Brooks in his second stint there scored 17 goals in 21 League games and the much travelled winger George Grant who had been a member of the team during the cup run made it 43 goals in 53 games over two seasons. He went to Clapton Orient. On 18 February 1939 late choice Jimmy Johnstone scored all six in the 6-2 win over Forfar.

Stenhousemuir recovered from being 17th twice in succession to be fourth in three successive seasons with 1933-34 providing the best effort at moving up. A 6-3 win at Alloa on 28 October and they led the division. Dropping to fifth in the New Year and even sixth but they were only three points from the top plus a game in hand. On 24 March the double completed over Alloa with four matches left, three points from leaders Dunfermline and still one fixture fewer. Sadly successive defeats at Brechin and St Bernards derailed the chances. Fifth in 1934-35 it was as a mid-table team that the Larbert team ended the 30s. Twice they scored nine goals. On 2 February 1935 they beat Montrose 9-4 and 16 April 1937 it was 9-2 against Dundee United. In 1936-37 Robert Murray in his second season scored a club record 31 League goals.

The Scottish Cup offered a few memories. In 1932-33 they beat Morton 1-0 Third Lanark 2-0 before losing 3-2 to Clyde. There was even a 1-1 draw with Celtic in 1936-37 before losing the replay 2-0 as well as a 1-1 draw with Motherwell the following season. Scorer against Celtic was right-winger Charlie Howie in two spells sandwiching Nottingham Forest for two seasons he made 231 League appearances.

King's Park was sixth in 1929-30. That was their highest but also twice seventh in consecutive seasons 1933-34 and 1934-35. Centre-forward James Dyet had two seasons with the club initially in 1929-30 when he scored 25 goals in only 16 League games and then in 1933-34 when he recorded 16 in 20 matches. His first outing was record-breaking. On 2 January 1930 against Forfar Athletic he scored eight goals in a 12-2 victory; a record individual score for a debutant. In between these stints he played for Falkirk had a trial with Middlesbrough and then joined Dundee United. Alex Haddow had scored hat tricks in five consecutive matches in 1932: 4-5-3-3 3.

Forfar Athletic scored three more goals than they conceded and won three more than they lost in 1929-30 when eighth. Dave Kilgour with 45 League goals scored almost half the total. Twelfth the following season, 1931-32 when sixth was to be the highest. During the remaining seasons the Loons were just below mid-table.

The club's top score came on 26 December 1936 when Stenhousemuir was beaten 8-1. Willie Black was leading scorer that season with 37 goals. Defensively the worst two seasons were 1937-38 and 1938-39 when respectively 100 and 138 goals were conceded.

Sixth place was also a peak for Dumbarton in the 30s. It was in 1933-34 when only four points were dropped at home, the only winners at Boghead Park being East Fife and Leith Athletic. In 1931 half-back Harry Chatton who had been capped by both Ireland and the Irish Free State retuned to the club after stints in his own country plus the USA.

In 1937-38 Jimmy Smith became player-manager. He had once set an unbeatable Scottish League record of 66 goals for Ayr United in 1927-28. Ever-present Smith scored 29 League goals in 1937-38, the team's best scoring season with 85 goals.

In 1929-30 Montrose had their highest win beating Solway Star 8-0 in the Scottish Cup and reached the last eight to celebrate the return to League football. After the eight goals, both Inver Citadel and Albion Rovers after a replay were beaten before losing 3-0 to Rangers. However, in 1934-35 Montrose conceded 105 League goals .Goalkeeper Wastell Gerrard was signed in 1929-30 from Motherwell and stayed for six seasons. The following term the Gable Endies were eighth.

The best scoring outcome was in 1938-39 with 82 goals to their credit. Hugh Adam scored 30 of them and Joe Rodi 16. Rodi had led the marksmen in 1937-38 with 20. In the same 1938-39 season Montrose had the satisfaction of knocking out Scottish Cup holders East Fife 2-1 on their own ground.

Defensively Brechin City had a tortuous time letting in more than one thousand goals in ten seasons! In 1938-39 though they again had more than a century of goals against them, they finished as high as tenth and the 82 goals in the" for" column was their best in the 30s. Ever present Alex Watson scored 24 League goals.

In fact 1937-38 had been their worst season with three defeats of 10-0 in League games and an overall 139 goals in the "against" column.

Leaks in defence were prevalent in the Scottish Cup, too. But in 1934-35 after Leith had been beaten 3-2, Brechin held Raith then won the replay 4-2 away before defeat against Hamilton. They also did well to win 2-1 at Kilmarnock in 1936-37. Even so 15 ties in ten seasons had seen 54 goals against them. In February Dennis Quigley who was leading scorer with 11 goals joined Grimsby Town but Norman Brand finished with 17 from 20 League games.

Yet Edinburgh City's record was dreadful. In eight seasons and bottom six times they conceded 980 League goals. In 1931-32 the deficit was 146 goals a record for Division Two, though the 78 they scored themselves represented an offensive peak! In 1936-37 the seven points they scrambled in the entire term was also a record low in the division.

But the following season they accomplished the unusual Scottish Cup feat of disposing of Hibs at Easter Road 3-2 in a first round tie, the home team's Arthur Milne failing with a penalty that would have ensured a replay. Peter Carruthers scored twice for City. By 1939 he had made 115 League appearances and scored 42 goals.

However, with their amateur status, several players were chosen for Scottish Amateur international honours including goalkeeper Desmond White who later joined Queen's Park. There had been an unusual event on 28 August 1937 when Forfar Athletic visited. Among the crowd of 500 was the Earl of Strathmore. He saw eight goals equally shared!

In 1938 the leading reserve competition for Scottish League clubs known as the Scottish Alliance was replaced when the Division One clubs formed their own league for reserve teams. This meant Beith and Galston the two non-league clubs still retaining membership and Dundee relegated from Division One were thus ineligible to participate.

Belfast Celtic and Linfield shared the Irish League honours with one interruption from Glentoran in 1931. Celtic won five including the last four championships, while Linfield was successful in 1930, 1932, 1934 and 1935. Irish Cup honours were also divided between these three clubs, though with a different outcome. Glentoran winning three times, Belfast Celtic twice and Linfield on five occasions.

Even though the Welsh League was not as strong a competition as either of its two Irish counterparts, Wales had the benefit of teams playing in the Football League, though again when international considerations had to be met, they also faced the usual restrictions on access to players. There was also the benefit of English based teams in geographical proximity to the Principality being allowed in the Welsh Cup.

Accordingly from 1933 onwards Chester, Bristol City, Tranmere Rovers and Crewe Alexandra in successive years were all cup winners until 1938 when Swansea Town won. Cardiff City in 1930, Wrexham in 1931 and Swansea in 1932 had been the first three winning teams but in 1939 even non-league South Liverpool took the Welsh Cup.

With 14 teams in the Irish League the season was supplemented by several established cup competitions apart from the main Irish Cup. Thus the City Cup, County Antrim Shield and Gold Cup provided ample opportunities for honours. Additionally to the big three clubs, the Gold Cup was also won by twice by Portadown and once each by Distillery, Coleraine and Cliftonville. The City Cup saw Derry City – who entered in 1929-30 – winning in 1935 and 1937, Distillery in 1934 and Portadown in 1939. Derry also shared honours with Linfield in 1938. However the County Antrim Shield remained the preserve of Celtic, Glentoran and Linfield in varying degrees. There were also many other minor competitions. Also in 1934 Ballymena FC was expelled and replaced in the Irish League by Ballymena United.

Players on both sides of the border were an attraction for Football League clubs. The Irish Football League's representative matches against their English equivalent provided the source for talent spotting. A steady stream of high calibre players made the crossing and in fairness there were ample opportunities for those English based to make the reverse journey should they be interested. Three Irish League matches were played against the League of Ireland in 1930, 1938 ad 1939.

Joe Bambrick, Dave "Boy" Martin, Peter Doherty, Jimmy McAlinden, Tommy Breen and Jackie Coulter were among those who made the international grade from sound grounding in the Irish League. Former Corporal Jack Jones of the King's Own Scottish Borderers had eight seasons with Linfield, two with Hibernian and another two with Glenavon as a half-back. Bambrick in ten years of Irish football had scored some 618 goals.

An outstanding youngster was Norman Kernaghan of Belfast Celtic. He was 17 years three months old when he played for Ireland against Wales in 1936 and had been as young as 16 years nine months when he was selected to play for the Irish League against the Football League.

To a lesser extent the same applied to the Irish Free State though with international players being selected for both national teams there was an inevitable overlap. However since the southern part of the country played fewer international matches it was only when joining English clubs did such talent gained honours. Until 1934 there had been only eight fixtures, thereafter 21.

Again the failure to receive the necessary release from English and Scottish clubs for international fixtures was a deterrent to any form of consistent selection. Worse, too, playing on a Sunday, it was often required that English based players were in action on successive days.

Domestically, the FAI Cup was dominated in the early 30s by Shamrock Rovers. Including the 1929 final they won five in a row. Cork won in 1934 and Bohemians a year later before Shamrock were winners again in 1936. Waterford, St James Gate and Shelbourne were the next most successful cup teams.

In terms of League honours, Shamrock did not fare as well, though they won in 1931-32 and had two in succession 1937-38 and 1938-39. Bohemians also had a treble triumph in 1929-30, 1933-34 and 1935-36. Shelbourne in 1930-31, Dundalk in 1932-33, Dolphin 1934-35 and Sligo Rovers 1936-37 shared the remaining titles.

Membership of the League of Ireland had begun modestly enough in 1921-22 with eight clubs. Bohemians and Shelbourne were among the founders still going a decade later with Bohs the only ever present. Due to a dispute Shelbourne missed out competing in 1934-35 and 1935-36.

Both the Welsh League and League of Ireland held representative matches against each other. The latter also met the Irish League and the Scottish League though the fixtures were spasmodic.

On 1 March 1930 the Irish League won 6-1 in Dublin and there was a similar score on 3 May in Swansea when the Welsh League was successful. A year later on 2 May there was a better result for the League of Ireland when Jim Munro the Cork centre-forward scored all three goals in a 3-1 win over the Welsh League.

In Llanelly on 13 February 1932 they again won 4-2. Later that year on 16 October in Dublin again the Irish won 2-0 There was not another fixture until 18 March 1935 in Dublin but a further 2-1 success. On 17 March 1937 an international flavour was introduced when the Yugoslav First Division representative team was beaten 3-2 in Dublin.

A year on to the day, there was more ground breaking when the Irish League visited Dublin and won 3-1. A return fixture in Belfast was held on 11 March 1939 and revenge for the League of Ireland 2-1. Six days later in Dublin and another first as the Scottish League was met and beaten 2-1.

The Irish team that lost 1-3 to England at Stoke, November 1936. Players only, back: Fulton, McCullough, Breen, Jones, Doherty. Front: Brown, Stevenson, Davis, Cook, Mitchell, Kelly

FREE KICKS

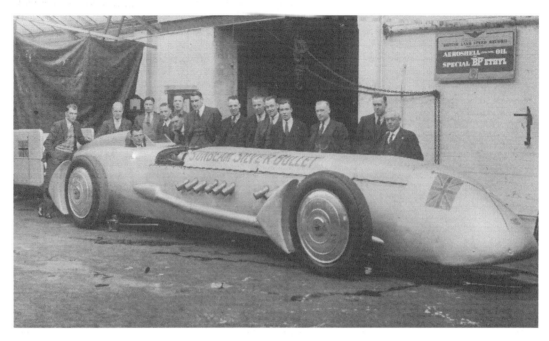

The 1934 FA Cup-winning Manchester City team spent time at Southport before the final, and are pictured with the Sunbeam Silver Bullet. The driver Jack Field, a Southport garage owner and racing driver (second from the right) hoped to break the British land speed record on Ainsdale beach, but was unsuccessful. From left to right; Herd, McLuckie, Cowan (at the wheel), Bray, Cassidy, Busby(top), Bell (trainer, bottom), Swift, Dale, Marshall, Tilson, Toseland, Brook, Jack Field, Wood (director). Photograph by courtesy of Garth Dykes.

AN ODDLY INTERESTING GAME

George Bowater scored one of the goals by which York City beat Burton Town away in the FA Cup first round in November 1934. Transferred, he scored one of the goals by which Burton beat York away in the cup's first round in November 1935.

More frequent cup familiarity hit the "aitches" when Halifax Town and Hartlepools United were drawn against each other on the same ground in 1933-34, 1934-35 and 1935-36. Curiously, too, Halifax had all three ties at home and drew them 1-1. Halifax won the first replay 2-1 at Hartlepools, lost the second there 2-0 until in 1935-36 it was a bit of a marathon. A goalless draw led to a third meeting at St James' Park which Hartlepools won 4-1 but only after extra time.

Cup thrashings can leave indelible marks. Other times the pain can be remedied. In 1934-35 Midland League Scunthorpe United suffered a 7-0 trouncing by Coventry City in an FA Cup first round tie. The following season the two teams were paired again at the same stage. But with George Young performing heroics in goal the "Scunny" boys managed a 1-1 draw. With a home replay the outlook seemed bleak after 30 minutes with City 2-0 ahead. But United responded with three goals before half-time and a fourth ten minutes before the end. That season, too, Coventry won the Third Division (South) Championship.

Tweaking the facts just a trifle Jimmy Oakes a full-back from Hanley, Staffordshire, who played for Port Vale and Charlton Athletic, had the distinction of playing for both clubs in the same Football League game! On Boxing Day 1932, he was left-back for Port Vale in a Division Two game against Charlton at The Valley when the match was abandoned because of bad light. Three weeks later, Oakes was transferred to Charlton and when the rearranged fixture took place on 26 April 1933 he was the Addicks left-back and helped them to beat Port Vale 2-1.

Players moving around were not uncommon. Darlington born Alec Mackay signed for Southport on 12 September 1933 having already been with four League clubs among a handful of others, despite being just 13 days past his 20th birthday. His five previous clubs had been Albert Hill Juniors, Darlington Railway Athletic, Newcastle United (trial), Crook Town, Stanley United, Bolton Wanderers, Bournemouth & Boscombe Athletic and Southport. He made just one Football League appearance for Southport then joined the Somerset Constabulary!

Joe Miller variously played for Largs Thistle, Port Glasgow Thistle, Morton, Arthurlie, Johnstone, Nuneaton Town, Aberdare Athletic, Middlesbrough, Dublin Dolphins, Hibs, Ards, Bournemouth, Ballymena and Ross County. Born in Ireland won three caps but he was thought to have been a Scot!

Players making Football League appearances for three different clubs in one season were not unusual. During 1937-38 there were as many as four. Jimmy Richardson played in all three divisions starting with Huddersfield Town in Division One, scoring twice in ten games. Transferred to Newcastle United in Division Two he scored three goals in 14 appearances and finished in Division Three (South) with Millwall scoring five goals in twelve such outings.

Charlie MacCartney had four games for Carlisle, one for York and two for Darlington. Jack Beattie began with 19 for Birmingham, made three for Huddersfield from 5 January to 9 February and 15 for Grimsby. Clarrie Bourton left Coventry after five games, made eight appearances at Plymouth and finished with 19 at Bristol City. Though he did not play for Tottenham in 1937-38, George Hunt was still with them before moving to Arsenal making 18 appearances and ending the season at Bolton Wanderers with five League outings.

Then there was Ernie Dixon centre-forward who even managed three clubs in six weeks during 1929-30: Halifax, Huddersfield and Nelson. It had been his second stint with Halifax and he later played for Tranmere for three seasons.

Royalty was not a stranger to football. King George V attended the 1930 and 1934 FA Cup finals as guest of honour and was accompanied by his wife Queen Mary for the 1932 match. In 1937 King George VI and Queen Elizabeth were both at Wembley then the King on his own for 1938 and 1939. In 1931 the Guest of Honour was the Duke of Gloucester, in 1933 the Duke of York and in 1935 the Prince of Wales. Only 1936 missed out on a royal occasion, but the monarchy was in some turmoil at the time. On 25 January 1936 a two minutes silence was held at grounds and "Abide With Me" sung in honour of the late King George V.

The insularity of England in particular was painfully obvious on many occasions. The respected Corinthian F N S Creek referred to: "a so-called World Soccer Championship was held in Italy."

In the 1930s a hole large enough to take a horse and cart opened up overnight at Watford's Vicarage Road ground. It took all morning to fill it in and replace the grass in time for the afternoon match.

Before the 1930 FA Cup final at Wembley a group of boys tried to tunnel their way into the Stadium under the turnstiles at the Eastern End. Somebody stepped on to the tunnel roof and it collapsed.

In the summer of 1939 with war clouds gathering, filming continued at Denham Studios on "The Arsenal Stadium Mystery" from the Leonard Gribble book that had been serialised in the *Daily Express* in March. The story concerned the murder of a player from the fictitious Trojans, a kind of Corinthians playing against Arsenal. Film of the Gunners last game of the season against Brentford wearing white shirts was used with Oxford University players filling in for close-up shots where necessary. Arsenal manager George Allison had a leading role and the Arsenal players appeared as themselves. Leslie Banks and Greta Gynt starred in it. Oxford players received four guineas a week, Arsenal double that figure.

The actor Clifford Mollison, Arsenal's Eddie Hapgood, Tom Whittaker and Cliff Bastin, listen to producer Anthony Asquith during the making of The Lucky Number in 1932. The film was shot in and around Highbury Stadium and at Gainsborough's studios in Twickenham.

Since Arsenal had perfected the third back game and Herbie Roberts was the epitome of the "stopper" centre-half, he managed to put through his own goal twice in 90 seconds when the Gunners were held to a 3-3 draw by Derby County on 8 October 1932. Not to be outdone, on 20 January 1934 Henry Kingham who went on to make 250 League appearances for Luton Town was also responsible for two own goals in another match of six, though it was Queens Park Rangers who won 4-2.

In 1937 two amateur teams were playing a minor cup tie. The outside-left of one team was late in arriving at the ground and missed the kick-off. As he stood by the touchline awaiting the referee's permission to join the game his team attacked and forced a corner on the left. The referee acknowledged his arrival and waved him to come on. He did so took the corner and scored direct – all without stepping further onto the field!

Selecting players for England trial games who had already either played for Scotland or were about so to be chosen caused some embarrassment as Jimmy Easson (Portsmouth) and Jock Dodds (Sheffield United) both fell into that category.

The Spanish Civil War ended the national league competition, but in Republican areas for a time at least a Mediterranean League was in operation on the east coast and a Basque competition in the north. Even when Austria had been taken over by Germany and its national team disbanded, on 3 April 1938 a team was assembled to play Germany in Vienna in an attempt to forge a sporting link with the new alliance. It was a difficult day for the Austrians who were far superior, not to humiliate their "masters" though the temptation ended when they scored twice late to win 2-0 thanks to goals from Karl Sesta and Matthias Sindelar. The latter insisted his team wore red and white, the national colours not traditional white shirts and black shorts.

On 12 March 1939 a crowd of 20,000 watched the final of the Jubilee Cup on Gibraltar. The Home Fleet drew 2-2 with the Mediterranean Fleet.

Playing more than one game on the same day was not unusual. Goalkeeper Fred Swift played for Oldham Athletic against Preston North End in a Division Two match at Deepdale on the morning of Easter Monday 2 April 1934 and for their reserves against Preston reserves in a Central League game at Boundary Park in the afternoon. Mention of Oldham and the nine goals plundered by "Bunny" Bell of Tranmere fame, the centre-forward was sold to Everton for £2,000 and in his first game as a Toffee he failed to score for their reserves – against Oldham!

Then unusually Bristol City won two cups on the same day on 1 May 1939. The first team defeated Swindon Town 2-0 in the Bath Coronation Cup, while the reserves took the Berkeley Hunt Cup with a 7-4 win over a Berkeley & District League XI.

Show business personalities did not readily flock to football but film star Anna Neagle supported West Ham United as a girl until Hollywood fame changed her into following Arsenal. Comedian Arthur Askey was an Everton fan and Liverpool could claim to have two comics Billy Bennett and Ted Ray as supporters along with the Bud Flanagan and Chesney Allen duo. Ray had actually played as an amateur in Liverpool's third team before he became a radio star.

Ipswich Town became the latest new club to enter the Football League in 1938 and the team contained former Chelsea forward John "Jock" Hutcheson who had been out of the game injured for two years and had received compensation. He was refused Football League approval to be reinstated, played in the Southern League side but was allowed to play in the FA Cup and even scored against Aston Villa!

Height or the lack of it was illustrated when Fred Le May was given his debut at outside-right for Thames in October 1930. He stood just 5ft and weighed 7st 10lb. He subsequently played for Watford and Clapton Orient. In 1937-38 Rochdale signed an outside-right Thomas McMurray from Glenavon. He was released towards the end of the same season to join Tunbridge Wells Rangers. At 5ft 2in he was one of the shortest and also one of few Irishmen to play county cricket for Surrey. Slightly taller was Sid Tufnell with Blackpool, an inside-forward or wing-half. He was a quarter of an inch under 5ft 3ins.

Anything over 6ft was regarded as exceptionally tall. Few came as near as Joe Nicholls at 6ft 4in and 15 stone. A Grenadier Guardsman and ex-bricklayer he was his Battalion heavyweight boxing champion. He handled goalkeeping chores with Spurs and Bristol Rovers very well, too.

But neighbours Bristol City claimed Jack Neale a centre-half signed from Berkeley in the Gloucester League tipped it at 6ft 5in when signed in 1937. Another 6ft 4in goalkeeper was Jack Doherty signed by Celtic from Derry City in November 1937.

Even at the age of 16, Ernie Gregory on the West Ham United ground staff was 6ft and weighed 13st 7lb. He was allowed to play for Leytonstone and was selected for the London FA team in Brussels for the 2-1 win against the Red Devils in November 1938.

Even younger was Ray Russon, 14, snapped up by Tottenham Hotspur and put on their ground staff after he was spotted playing for Doncaster Schools on Boxing Day. An inside-forward he was already half an inch over 6ft.4in.

Other sports celebrities tried their hand at the soccer game with some success. Doug Finlay was an Olympic hurdler and was a Flying Officer in the RAF. In a friendly against Oxford University he scored the fly boys goal in a 1-1 draw. Welsh rugby international Wilfred Wooller scored seven goals in a Cardiff Docks Cup game and signed for Barry Town. Some tried their hand at refereeing. Dave Mangnall when at Millwall became the man in the middle for the annual Boxers v Jockeys match at The Den in 1937. While many footballers played county cricket, Alf Hanson (Liverpool) and Louis Page (Burnley) played for England at Baseball.

Alex James stature – or what there was of it – was accentuated by his extra long shorts, thought to have been arranged as a stunt by the eminent *Daily Mail* cartoonist Tom Webster, who always featured the pint-sized schemer that way while James was with Preston. He liked the idea and bought a pair of shorts to fit the cartoon.

Breaking down the value of any player who cost a substantial fee in the first place, the case of David Jack at Arsenal made interesting reading. With his transfer from Bolton Wanderers, wages and bonuses, for the 181 League games and 113 goals scored, each came cost £120 and each goal £75. As a 15 year old with Plymouth Argyle youth team he had played in a Devonshire Cup final.

"Pongo" Waring was one of the better paid players. How? When he was at Tranmere Rovers he was given one penny each Saturday by the then manager Bert Cooke.

Unusual scoring habits abounded. Alf Lythgoe scored five goals in each of two Football League matches with different clubs in different divisions in the same season. He scored five for Stockport County against Southport in a Division Three (North) match on 25 August 1934 and five for Huddersfield Town against Blackburn Rovers in Division One on 13 April 1935.

While there were Scottish Cup finalists who made it to the FA Cup last stage, only one succeeded in winning Irish Cup and FA Cup teams in successive seasons. Jimmy McAlinden did it with Belfast Celtic in 1937-38 and Portsmouth in 1938-39.

Match days are the busiest for club secretaries. John Peters the Arsenal Secretary from 1914 saw so little of home games, that when on holiday he actually paid to see a game – in full.

Long service without hitting the limelight did occur. Cyril Webster was an Everton professional inside-forward from May 1929 until the end of 1938-39, but was never selected for first team football. Norman Young at Aston Villa went from 1926-27 until 14 September 1935 before his first team debut. Nearly three months after Young made his debut he started to drive for the fixture at Manchester City. It was a misty morning but thick fog came down and he left his vehicle. He started walking, the fog lifted a little and he got a lift. Visibility worsened. He took to his feet again, this time running almost three miles to the nearest station. He arrived five minutes too late for the train, but it had been held up, too! Eventually he reached Maine Road but the day ended in a 5-0 defeat, the full-back understandably in not too good a shape for 90 minutes play. That was his last first team game for Villa, before joining Barnsley.

Bands of brothers appeared here and there. In 1937-38 West Ham United had three of the same family who all favoured the right-half position by choice. They were the Scottish born trio of David, Jim and Bob Corbett, while a fourth brother was also a right-half for Hearts.

Life with the Lyons was somewhat different. In 1939 Tommy Lyon a Glasgow born Scottish inside-forward was with Chesterfield while his brother Willie born in Birkenhead was a centre-half with Celtic. Previously on 13 February 1937 Tommy had played for Albion Rovers in a Scottish Cup tie in which the Celtic opposition included his brother Willie. Celtic won 5-2.

Multi-packs of the same family existed. The Shankly clan of five from Glenbuck developed Bill at Carlisle and Preston, John at Blackpool after service with Portsmouth and Luton plus Jimmy variously with Sheffield United, Southend, Barrow and Carlisle. Two others remained in Scottish football Bob with Alloa and Falkirk, Alec or Sandy at Ayr and Nithsdale, though the latter's career as the first born was also completed in the previous decade.

The Keetley five from Derby were Charlie, Frank, Harold, Joe and Tom, though Harold and Joe had finished their careers in the 1920s. Marksmen all, they held variously scoring records in middle England. Frank Keetley scored six goals in 21 minutes for Lincoln City against Halifax Town on 16 January 1932. Brother Tom with Notts County scored three goals in each of three consecutive Division Two matches away from home against Plymouth, Manchester United and Chesterfield in October-November 1931. He scored 284 career League goals with Bradford, Doncaster, Notts and Lincoln.

He was listed by Notts County at the end of 1932-33 with a fee of £750 on his head. He thought this would prevent him finding another League club so he went into business in charge of a wayside hotel outside Derby. Then Lincoln came in for him!

Three Curran brothers from Ryton-on-Tyne played in the Football League. Frank was with Southport, Accrington and Bristol Rovers, Andy also at Accrington after Blackpool while Jimmy was at Barnsley and Southend.

Another trio involved at New Brighton the Stevens family. Leo a former tram conductor was leading scorer in 1930-31 and 1931-32 when he managed half the total. From a brood of 13 children, five brothers among them, two others Jack and Bill were also Rakers. Jack like brother Leo scored twice on his debut, Bill played in the reserves.

Naturally the Jones boys from Merthyr figured prominently. Four of the five brothers initially followed their father into the pits. Ivor the oldest was capped ten times by Wales after service in the Great War, William known as Shoni played for Merthyr and Ton Pentre, Emlyn for Merthyr, Everton and Southend and Bert for Southend and Wales. Bryn was variously with Glenavon, Aberaman, Wolves and Arsenal of course. Emlyn even joined Barrow in 1938 having had knee problems and was playing in Birmingham League football.

The Wallbanks family from the north-east moved around various clubs. Fred did manage three years at Bradford City at one time, Jimmy even five years with Millwall. Jack spent four seasons at Barnsley and also scored virtually a goal a game with Chester. In 1938-39 William Wallbanks was at Spurs and Harry known as "Choppy" as he came from Chopwell was on Fulham's books.

Then there was the Milburn clan, chiefly at Leeds United where Stanley, Jack and James were resident while George was at Chesterfield.

The McMenemy family was headed by Jimmy "Napoleon" McMenemy, a former bricklayer. He had six sons three of whom played professional football. John played for Celtic and Motherwell, Harry for Newcastle United and Frank for Northampton. They were all inside-forwards like their father who had been a long-time pre-war Celtic player.

Across the Irish Sea Jack "Soldier" Jones was capped for Ireland at amateur and full level. He played for Linfield, Hibernian and Glenavon. His father and four uncles all gained honours. Brother Sam played for Blackpool, his brother-in-law Billy Mitchell at Chelsea and Distillery. Uncle Joe Burnison was with Distillery and Bolton, Uncle Sam Distillery and Bradford PA, Uncle Harold with Distillery and Uncle Johnny at Glenavon.

Two players with the same name with the same club at the same time were also not rare. In 1932-33 Grimsby Town had two Charlie Wilsons on their books. Both played together in first team matches. Charlie Wilson was a midfield player variously at half-back and inside-forward who had previously played for West Bromwich Albion and Sheffield Wednesday. Charles Henry Wilson a full-back or right-half had been with the club since 1923 and was a Cleethorpes lad.

West Bromwich had also two William Richardsons with no other initials. The club's centre-half Bill Richardson was called thus while centre-forward Billy Richardson was given the extra initial of G for "Ginger." He became known as either Billy or W G. A more novel way of separating came at Newport County when they had two called Billy Owen. They decided to call one of them WE as he was formerly with Exeter City and the other WM as he had been with Manchester City.

Leeds United had two called John Kelly who were either inside or centre-forwards in 1934-35. They decided to call one Jack, the other Mick who formerly served in the Irish Guards. At Burnden Park, the two known as George Taylor were respectively referred to as "half-back" and "winger."

Overkill on the Jones name at Wrexham in 1932-33 with full-back Alf, winger Arthur and two centre-forwards Charlie Wilson and Ozzie all figuring in the first team. Moreover the Chairman was Dr Edward Jones.

Keeping it in the family at Walsall in April 1936 Harold Wait was in goal for Walsall at the age of 43 while his son Harry junior was in goal for the reserves.

George Ansell was the first University player to become a professional footballer and the first to play for two different Football League teams, Brighton in 1931 and Norwich in 1935. A triple Oxford Blue as a forward he also assisted Corinthians. Before the start of 1938-39 a combined Oxford and Cambridge team toured Jamaica.

Herbert Chapman tried to sign Rudi Hiden a pastry cook and the Austrian international goalkeeper. The Arsenal manager deposited £2,000 in an Austrian bank but the British Ministry of Labour insisted on a two-year residential qualification. Hiden was actually turned back at Dover when he attempted to land! Arsenal did get a foreign goalkeeper Piet Keizer a Dutchman, but he was an amateur and wholesale fruiterer.

Premature retirement through injury meant anxious times for future employment. But Frank Moss became the manager of Hearts at the age of 27 in March 1937. An England international goalkeeper, his career had been terminated prematurely with Arsenal after injury. Not such an outcome hit Willie Evans a pit lad from Wales who made the grade with Tottenham Hotspur having been picked for an England amateur trial originally! Fine control and a rapid-shooting left-winger he was the club's penalty taker, too. Won Welsh international honours and in 1932-33 scored 28 League goals including eight spot kicks. Recovered confidence after one injury but suffered knee problems and after one unsuccessful operation was given a free transfer. Signed for Fulham, had another operation but was forced to retire at 25 and was given a job coaching at Craven Cottage.

Southampton celebrated its Jubilee in 1935-36 with a 600lb cake in the shape of a football field displaying two teams and 50 candles. It was the centrepiece at a dinner at which the club's original captain Arthur Fry was one of the guests of honour.

When Tommy Lawton signed professional forms for Burnley he did so on a Friday at the mill owned by Chairman Tom Clegg. The following day he scored after 20 seconds against Tottenham Hotspur and completed his hat trick. Previously he had played as an amateur having been spotted scoring three goals for Rossendale in a Lancashire Combination match when still only 14.

Proof of loyalty to a club when cup final tickets were in the offing, prompted one Sheffield Wednesday fan to send his scrapbook of the Owls matches to substantiate his case. He was looked after and his cuttings returned.

Jimmy Connor was a Belfast Celtic player but he lived at Downpatrick 30 miles away. On Friday nights he would walk to the ground! Arriving Saturday morning he would have a nap, then dine on eggs and sherry and be fully fit for the match!

In 1938-39 Celtic started its Scottish Cup venture by beating Burntisland Shipyard 8-3, but the three goals conceded represented the most they had conceded to a non-league team.

Popular then, as now. Spot the ball, 1931.

Penalty experts were worth a place in most teams. But just as handy to have on the staff were goalkeepers with a decent record for saving spot kicks. In 1929-30 Herbert John Emery saved nine out of ten penalty kicks he faced in Rotherham United first and reserve team matches during 1929-30. When Stranraer beat Bo'ness 5-3 in the final of the Scottish Qualifying Cup in 1937-38 at Somerset Park, Ayr their goalkeeper Andrew Loudon saved three penalties.

When Billy Owen stepped up to take a spot kick for Exeter City against Bournemouth on 27 March 1937 he had not failed from a penalty kick in 53 consecutive attempts. This became a first and the match was drawn 1-1. Then on 14 December 1935 three penalties had been awarded in seven minutes all for handball in the Charlton Athletic v West Ham United match. Charlton converted both of their spot kicks, West Ham their one. The game ended 2-2.

On 27 September 1930, Queen's Park were entertaining Celtic at Hampden Park but losing 3-2 when the referee prematurely ended the game with two minutes remaining. He recalled the teams from the dressing room over the miscalculation and James McAlpine succeeded in equalising from a penalty for a 3-3 draw.

In 1934-35 394 penalty kicks were awarded in the 1,848 Football League matches and 131 were missed. On 5 January 1935 at Liverpool, Arsenal's Eddie Hapgood headed a goal after his penalty kick had been partially saved. Of course it did not count as a penalty kick. Anyway, who needs penalties? In 1931 in the first round of the Glasgow Charity Cup Rangers beat Celtic by two goals and three corners to two goals and one corner.

Praise from an experienced opponent is often the highest accolade for any player. On 18 December 1937 Liverpool's Johnny Shafto scored with an overhead kick to put his team ahead against Arsenal at Anfield after 19 minutes. Opposing centre-forward Ted Drake congratulated him on his worthy strike. Liverpool won 2-0.

Even the man-in-the-middle came in for praise on 7 December 1935 when Everton were well beaten 6-1 at West Bromwich Albion. Referee Teddy Wood was congratulated by none other than "Dixie" Dean for his handling of the afternoon's encounter!

Humour in defeat is not always appreciated. After Aldershot had been beaten 9-2 away to Clapton Orient in a Division Three (South) match on 10 February 1934, the vanquished team took late afternoon tea in a local hotel. The head waiter reported to the directors in charge of the Aldershot party of 20 that he had laid "nine on one side, nine on the other, with the remaining two, one at each end..."

What's in a name? When the British Universities played their German equivalent at Wembley in 1937 the visiting goalkeeper was called Bonk.

The banning of transfers after the deadline in March was sacrosanct. Only in exceptional circumstances did the Football League relaxed this ruling. It happened towards the end of 1935-36 when Blackburn Rovers were granted permission to play Kevin Joseph Hamill, an amateur goalkeeper despite the fact that the club was involved in a relegation struggle in Division One.

On 14 March the regular choice goalkeeper Cliff Binns had broken a fibula in a League game at Everton. He was replaced by Jack Hughes, but on Good Friday 10 April, Hughes suffered a spinal injury against Liverpool. Jimmy Barron was called upon for two games but in the second of these on Easter Monday at Liverpool he broke his wrist.

Two days later, on 15 April Rovers secured the services of Hamill from Seaforth Social Club and he played at home to Portsmouth on 18 April, finishing on the winning side 3-1. However, in the last two games of the season Blackburn fielded John Pratt who had been signed earlier as an amateur from Preston. After all this effort Blackburn who had used five different goalkeepers in these nine games over a period of six weeks, they were still relegated. Hamill went back to his Social club after his one Football League outing.

Hughes like the others all eventually recovered their injuries. He had won Welsh amateur and full international caps in his time. When earlier playing for Aberystwyth he used to take their penalties, running from goal to hit the ball from the spot!

Car ownership was not universal by any means but when Fred Westgarth was manager of Stockport County he banned players using motor cycles and pedal cycles – because the latter developed the wrong muscles for football.

At one time Matt Busby even decided that walking was better training than driving a car to the daily sessions at a club. He also pinpointed the moods of players that could their performances including winning, losing, off form, off colour, confidence and domestic problems.

Confidence or a lack of it affected Freddie Steele at Stoke in 1938-39. He lost his scoring touch concerned over his pregnant wife and worried by an old knee injury. In the opening weeks of the season he scored only five goals. He was rested while medical opinion was divided over the treatment for his cartilage problem. Thinking an inferiority complex might be the problem he was sent to a psychiatrist twice a day for several weeks. On 3 December he was brought back against Huddersfield, scored regained his confidence and goal scoring habits.

Touring and trips abroad became popular for many clubs. On 6 April 1932 Coventry City made their first such venture to Holland playing a Dutch XI at Sparta's ground in Rotterdam. They won 3-0 with goals from Ernie Cull, Jock Lauderdale and Clarrie Bourton.

Queen of the South undertook one on 4 May 1936. Initially in France losing 4-3 to Bethune looking tired two days after their journey they recovered to beat Seti 2-1 and Charleville 5-0. On to Luxembourg then North Africa where in Algiers they beat the Spanish club Racing Santander 1-0. Unfortunately the crowd pelted the Queens players with stones. Jackie Gordon suffered a broken collar bone Joe Tulip was sent off but returned later when the Scottish team managed to have twelve players on the field!

Prestige was at stake on 11 April 1937 when Charlton Athletic was invited to play the French national team in Paris. Italy had originally been designated to play a friendly against France but had had to cry off. The previous day Charlton had beaten Huddersfield Town 4-0 at The Valley. Showing no sign of fatigue, Charlton beat the French 5-2 with two goals each from Don Welsh and George Tadman and one from Harold Hobbis.

Paris was also the setting on 10 May 1933 when Sunderland experienced its first exposure to floodlit football and defeated Racing Club 3-0. George Gibson scored twice, George Ainsley the other goal. Interestingly enough Gibson later in his career played for two French clubs Valenciennes and Racing Club de Roubaix.

West Ham United was among the leaders when venturing abroad and made frequent trips to Europe. Chelsea trainer Tom Whitley reckoned he been abroad some 30 times. Once with Spurs in Budapest they were without a goalkeeper. He filled in and let in 18!

Celebrating its Division One Championship in 1937, Manchester City travelled to Germany to play five matches. Most of the opposition seemed to be connected with the Army and had been sent away for special training. The smaller continental ball was used for one half of the matches. Two games were drawn in Duisburg and Wuppertal but Schweinfurt was beaten 3-2. A Berlin representative team at the Olympic Stadium had Nazi guards standing to attention round the pitch. City lost 3-2 and 3-2 in Stuttgart.

There seemed no obvious reason why the FA banned Wolves from touring Hungary at the end of 1936-37. However, Aston Villa's much publicised visit to Germany in 1938 began by sea in the "Europa" and opened with a 3-2 win over a German Select XI that included nine Austrian internationals! It was played in a heatwave in the Reichssportfield in Berlin. The crowd was numbered at 110,000 and the visitors left to the derision of the German spectators for refusing to give the Nazi salute. Then Villa then won 2-1 in Stuttgart in front of 70,000 but lost 0-1 in Dusseldorf.

At the conclusion of 1935-36 Aston Villa and Blackburn Rovers the only two original members of the Football League who had not suffered demotion at some stage were both relegated.

Though the actual definition of the role of manager in the 1930s was vague, some of those thus designated moved around frequently. Harold Wightman was with four different clubs in separate divisions in a period of 12 months during 1935-36. He was assistant manager to George Jobey at Derby when the previous season ended and during the summer he was appointed secretary-manager of Luton Town. He became manager of Mansfield Town in January 1936 and took the reins at Nottingham Forest in May 1936. The clubs involved were respectively from Division One, Division Two, Division Three (South) and Division Three (North).

As to the first ex-professional receiving the Football League long service medal as a manager, it was David Calderhead who was presented with it in 1932 having taken over the reins at Stamford Bridge with Chelsea in 1907. He had been player-manager with the club during the early part of his reign with the club. When Tranmere Rovers appointed a secretary-manager for 1937-38 he was Jim Knowles a former film extra!

Influence of the gentle sex was in evidence for Duggie Reid at Stockport County. Down from Scotland to Manchester he gained employment as an apprentice plumber through his sister! He was a wing-half converted to centre-forward. Then for Bill Forrest, Middlesbrough centre-half, born in Scotland, he eloped to Gretna Green to be married.

Colleagues' advice often paid dividends. Alf Lythgoe was about to join Winsford but his fellow Stockport player Jack Stevens persuaded him to stay. He shortly after moved to Huddersfield for £3,500. All went well until a torn tendon, two cartilage problems and an ankle injury. He suffered a drop in wages, too before returning to Stockport.

Stephenson rocketed on the promotion train in successive seasons. It was George of that ilk initially with Preston North End when they gained promotion to Division One in 1933-34. The following season he had joined Charlton Athletic when they rose to Division Two and again when they entered the Division One in 1935-36. Jack Palethorpe gained promotion with Stoke City in 1933 for Preston North End in 1934 and was in Sheffield Wednesday's FA Cup winning team in 1935.

Persistency paid off for George Hunt after unsuccessful trials with Barnsley, Sheffield United and Port Vale. He even scored four of five goals in a United trial! It all changed after playing for Regent Street Congregationals. He was picked up by Chesterfield and from then on it was Spurs, Arsenal and Bolton all among the goals as a centre-forward.

Foreign players were pretty thin on the ground unless you wanted to include Scots, Welsh and Irish in the Football League. By far the most arrivals came from South Africa and though several stayed and became settled, just as many returned having failed to make any impression. However, in October 1937 two Argentines, half-back Augustus Corpa and inside-left Casca Rinaldi were signed by Barrow. They were working on a naval contract at the docks.

Celtic had a Swedish goalkeeper called Julius Hjuliana, a Jewish player called Jerry Solis and an Egyptian Abdul Salim who played several Alliance matches for the club with only bandages around his feet.

Born in Argentina as Francisco Enrique Gonzalez and at one stage serving in the South Wales Borderers this forward played for Aston Villa, Bournemouth, Norwich, Newport, Shelbourne and Barrow before changing his name to Frank Peed.

Then there was Jack Acquroff with Spurs then Folkestone followed by League experience with Hull, Bury and Norwich who was born in Chelsea of Scottish parentage, but had Russian ancestry!

Charlie "Spider" Preedy was Arsenal's goalkeeper in the 1930 FA Cup final. Renowned as a bit of a show-boater he had been born in Neemuch, India and was previously with Charlton Athletic and Wigan Borough.

India as part of the Commonwealth was the birthplace of many others including Reg Tricker (Clapton Orient), John Armand (Swansea Town), Paddy Mills (Birmingham), Johnny Price (Fulham), Alf Quantrill (Bradford) and George Bellis (Wolves). Jack Butler of Arsenal hailed from Ceylon but as stated there were many from South Africa.

The brothers Frank and Reg Osborne, respectively Tottenham Hotspur and Leicester City, Arthur Riley and Gordon Hodgson (Liverpool) plus David Murray (Bristol Rovers) and Alex Berll (Manchester City trainer) were just a few emanating from the Cape.

Not exactly "foreign" but for West Bromwich Albion the unusual signing of centre-forward George Dudley who was playing for Vono Sports but had previous Scottish League experience with Albion Rovers and King's Park. He was the first Scot to sign for Throstles for 30 years. Jock Rutherford Gibson at Sheffield United had been born in Philadelphia, USA.

There were few black players in the Football League. Jack Leslie at Plymouth and Eddie Parris who was capped for Wales while with Bradford Park Avenue being the only such home international. Similarly Jewish players, the best known being Les Goldberg of Leeds United and Dave Morris at Swindon Town.

The purely amateur player who made the most appearances into the 30s was England amateur international Jack Burns a versatile midfield player either at inside-forward or wing-half. He played for Queens Park Rangers and Brentford and completed 262 Football League appearances until 1936. He was a schoolmaster. Viv Gibbins another in the teaching profession managed to be capped at England amateur level and twice in the full international team in the 1920s.

Tom Priestley the Chelsea and Ireland international inside-forward wore a skull cap to hide his baldness. A schoolmaster he later became a headmaster of a school in Londonderry. George Weinand Huddersfield's South African forward was deaf but had little difficulty in sport, having also played tennis, rugby and cricket against the Australians.

The first Cup Final to be broadcast was Cardiff City v Arsenal on 23 April 1927 with a commentary given by George Allison, then a director of Arsenal!

Arsenal probably staged the first match in which any parts were shown either live or in recorded form for television. It was a practice game at Highbury on Thursday 16 September 1937. At the time BBC studios and transmitter were located at nearby Alexandra Palace. The first complete televised showing of a football match had been in August 1936 when the BBC screened a film of the Arsenal v Everton game at the start of the season. Arsenal won 3-2. However, the first live transmission came from Germany in November 1936.

On 16 September 1937 BBC TV cameras at Highbury conducted another trial for such broadcasting with John Snagge commentating. However, it was reported that he was "stiff" and clearly lacked the ease in front of the cameras displayed by Arsenal manager George Allison.

With the football authorities not entirely happy with broadcasting matches while others were being played, the BBC provided coverage for listeners around the Empire.

As for cinema newsreels for the 1937 FA Cup final, there were hidden cameras at Wembley and autogyros and aeroplanes in the air filming the event.

Life after football took on an unusual slant for Percy Varco a goal scoring forward whose playing record saw him get goals for Aston Villa, Queens Park Rangers, Norwich City and Exeter City, some 84 in 165 League games. A broken knee cap at Rangers certainly interrupted his career which finished with one first team game for Brighton & Hove Albion on 17 December 1932. He was able to play in local football, became a fish merchant and served two spells as Mayor of Fowey in Cornwall his home town while running the local Aquarium. Dave McLean of Huddersfield fame had a spell as East Fife manager. Also at Forfar he was elected to the Town Council beating eight other candidates for the position.

Jack Seagrave managed to play more than the full complement of 42 League games in 1935-36. Beginning with Southport he played in 29 successive Third Division (North) fixtures, the last against Chesterfield to whom he was transferred! He completed 15 consecutive games for them making 44 League appearances in total.

Another unique performance came in 1934-35 from Harry Adamson at Bradford City. He managed to be top scorer in every competition the club entered. In addition to getting ten of twelve Division Two matches, he led the scorers in the Midland League, Yorkshire League and its Mid-week equivalent.

Schoolboy aspirants often faced fiscal fences. Wally Ardron brought up in Swinton, Lancashire at least had a schoolteacher who was football minded. But he supplied the boys with boots at six shillings (30p) a pair which they had to repay at 6d (2½p) a week. Ardron paid one shilling (5p) but found the outlay outside his pocket. However, the master told him to score three goals and he could keep the boots. Ardron duly obliged. Subsequently he played for Denaby United and was transferred to Rotherham United for £100 making his first team debut in 1938-39.

Eric Westwood played for Manchester Boys against Southampton Boys in the 1933 English Schools Shield Final. The matches were played at Maine Road and The Dell. His first two League games for Manchester City were against Tottenham Hotspur at Maine Road on 5 November 1938 then the following week at The Dell against Southampton.

In September 1933 20 Public Schoolboys were invited to Highbury for soccer training organized by the Corinthians with the blessing of Arsenal

Mark Hooper destined for Sheffield Wednesday left school and shortly afterwards played in four cup finals in a week: Durham Professional, Northern League, Durham Senior and Sunderland Shipyards! He won two, lost two.

Harold Barton who joined Sheffield United as a winger had been an outstanding athlete at school winning the 100, 220, quarter-mile, half mile, mile, high and long jump. But the school rule that three prizes was the maximum!

Another outstanding sprinter at school was Ken Willingham who actually represented England Boys at international level. His dedication to getting fixed up at Huddersfield Town was such that he worked all night to ensure his trial was next day.

Manchester United goalkeeper Len Langford helped out with older students. He acted as manager-trainer for the Manchester University team that had a successful tour of Germany and Austria. Fulham's long-serving Bert Barrett lectured on the game to a boys club in Worthing.

Sam Cowan of Manchester City cup final fame had only played his first game at 17 as a joke. He wore only one football boot, too! Subsequent to his football career he became a qualified masseur.

Not all promising schoolboys continued once starting on the ladder. Gasworks apprentice Norman John Catlin was a centre-forward with Bitterne Boys Club and scored 17 goals in an English Schools Shield match finishing with 62 in 13 matches for Southampton Boys. Capped at schoolboy level, had a season as an Arsenal amateur, signed for Southampton played six first team games then decided to quit and join the Cunard-White Star line as a clerk.

However, in August 1938 Redfern Froggatt the 13 year old son of former Sheffield Wednesday captain Frank Froggatt, won the Sheffield Schools football dribbling and came second in the sprint and had already excelled at cricket for Sheffield Boys.

While some daylight still existed between the cricket and football seasons to a reasonable extent, there were a couple remaining who played both sports at the highest level. James Scot Symon played five times for Scotland at cricket in 1935-38 including a game against Australia. He was the only one to play for Scotland at both sports. In 1938 at Forthill he took 6-33 in the Aussies first innings of 213. John Arnold the Southampton and Fulham outside-left played for England against New Zealand at Lords in 1931 and at football against Scotland in 1933. Others played county cricket including Joe Hulme for Middlesex and Ted Drake for Hampshire.

Jim Hammond at Fulham was a Sussex county cricketer and in addition to 316 League games for them he scored 151 League and Cup goals for them and acted as 12th man for England in a Test Match against Australia. Huddersfield's George Weinand when living in South Africa had a knock against the visiting Australians.

LNER locomotive 2866 "Nottingham Forest"

In 1936-37 The London and North Eastern Railway introduced a batch of 23 locomotives for express passenger work in East Anglia with Football League club names and appropriate club colours on accompanying panels. There were a number of anomalies. No. 2858 had its named changed from *Newcastle United* to *The Essex Regiment*. No. 2859 *Norwich City* had originally been named *Rendelsham Hall* but the nameplates were incorrectly spelled. Then in 1938 the *Norwich City* nameplates were put on it as 2859 had had a name change of its own to *East Anglian* in 1937! As to No. 2870 *Tottenham Hotspur* it was originally named *Manchester City* before later becoming *City of London*. In May 1937 *Tottenham Hotspur* had actually been named in a ceremony at Hoe Street Station, Walthamstow by Spurs chairman Charles Roberts.

When No. 2854 *Sunderland* was needed for working the Cup Final special in 1937 it was under general repair, so on 17 April, No. 2851 *Derby County* was sent to Gorton to acquire 2854's number and nameplates before being the *status quo* a month later. Even so it should be mentioned that an official photograph for Works purposes only, taken at Darlington showed No. 2849 as *Darlington* when it was later *Sheffield United!* Doubly confusing as the engine was originally allotted the name *Derby County*...

As far as the LNER was concerned, Sir Nigel Gresley the company's chief steam locomotive engineer also designed a restaurant car specifically for the Arsenal Football Club's use on the north-east coast line.

On 2 March 1935 Arsenal lost its sixth round FA Cup tie 2-1 at Sheffield Wednesday. After the match a Police motor cycle escort took their coach to the station where the announcer cried out: "London train on Platform 3, Arsenal Football Club party to the right, ordinary passengers to the left."

When Plymouth Argyle hosted Everton in a third round FA Cup tie at Home Park on 10 January 1931, the pitch was rolled by a Corporation steam roller. But it was Argyle who were flattened 2-0.

Travel problems could have delayed repercussions, quite naturally. Reg Osborne of Folkestone missed his train due to fog, so was unable to be signed 14 days before the team's FA Cup tie against Bristol Rovers on 25 November 1933.

Coventry City set off for Exeter City on 11 April 1931 but missed their connection at Gloucester. They changed on the train, arrived four minutes late. A 15 minute start delay and Coventry managed to recover sufficiently to win 3-2.

On Good Friday 1939 Lincoln City had to put Jimmy Connor in goal for his debut. Regular choice Dan McPhail was ill and Jack Thacker missed his train. Connor kept a clean sheet in a 1-0 win and stayed for the rest of the season.

Haverfordwest were away to Troedyrhiw on 4 December 1937 in a Welsh Cup tie. Due to a car breakdown the visitors had to start with ten players. Soon down to six when one went off injured. But by skilful use of off-side tactics they kept the score down to one against and the missing players arrived near half-time. Codd who had started off in goal resumed his normal centre-forward place and scored twice in a 2-1 win!

Occasionally it needed some fast moving to get to a game. Willie Hall the Spurs inside-forward was playing golf when he learned he had been picked for an England trial. He was five miles from White Hart Lane, raced to the ground, had a quick massage, packed his bags and just made the FA party on the way to Liverpool.

Treasured possessions of clubs are invariably displayed in boardrooms. The ball used in Walsall's third round FA Cup success against Arsenal on 14 January 1933 when they won 2-0, was preserved in a glass case in the secretary's office. Receipts from this match had been £1,487 from a 11,149 crowd after the club increased prices of admission.

When the north stand at Brighton & Hove Albion's Goldstone Ground was being built in 1930 the excavation revealed an 18th century cannonball.

The lucky horseshoe that helped bring the FA Cup itself to Barnsley in 1912 was still being displayed at Oakwell 25 years later.

While sports like Rugby numbered their players, the Football League steadfastly refused to introduce them. In 1933 the year when for the first time the Football Association numbered players in the FA Cup Final from 1-22, Tottenham Hotspur's proposal for numbers to be introduced was heavily defeated at the League's AGM. The meeting was in no mood for change it seems as Sheffield United's scheme for unemployed persons to be admitted at a minimum charge of sixpence (2½p) received little support and Derby County's idea for doubling promotion and relegation from two to four clubs failed to reach a three-quarters majority.

Sam Weaver of Newcastle United perfected the art of the long throw-in, but he was not the only player so to do. Frank Bokas famously entered the record books when he actually "scored" from such a throw. Actually there was an own goal involved. The occasion was a fourth round FA Cup tie at Oakwell between Barnsley and Manchester United on 22 January 1938. United were leading through Johnny Carey until the 13th minute. Barnsley left-half Bokas took a throw-in from a point in line with the edge of the penalty area. He floated the ball high into the goalmouth. United's goalkeeper Tom Breen was caught too far forward and though he got a hand to the ball he could not prevent it dropping behind him under the bar for the equaliser! The match finished 2-2, Barnsley lost the replay 1-0.

However, the interesting fact about Bokas was that while working as a miner at Bellshill near Glasgow he lost the little finger of his left hand in an accident. But as a junior playing in Scotland he had managed to achieve other such goals for Kirkintilloch Rob Roy.

In 1930-31 the Dewar Charity Shield was revived for the first time since the split between the FA and the AFA in 1907. Arsenal met the Corinthians at Highbury before a crowd of 12,000 who paid £823, the sum being handed over to the National Playing Fields Association. The amateurs led twice but were beaten 5-3.

The Sheriff of London Shield between the same two clubs was held at Highbury on 26 October 1932. It was the Corinthians Jubilee year. They were 61 down at half-time and were beaten 9-2. Ernest "Tim" Coleman scored five Arsenal goals.

This Shield was also played at White Hart Lane on 2 May 1934 between Tottenham Hotspur and the Corinthians, who after leading 4-3 at half-time lost 7-4. Bernard Joy played for the Corinthians and George Hunt the centre-forward he was marking scored a hat trick.

In 1938-39 when Arsenal had five players released for international duty, their next opponents Preston North End offered to play the fixture as a friendly and arrange the League game later when the Gunners were better represented. Arsenal declined with thanks and minus the famous five still won 1-0.

Despite ominous signs on the continent in 1938-39, there was optimism and expansion in certain areas. Manchester United made it clear they intended to build three first-teams of equal strength and reckoned they were just five players short of the target. Arsenal having moved its nursery connection from Margate entered a team in the Southern League with home matches on Enfield's ground. Everton announced they were to field four teams with the additional one playing in the Bootle JOC League. At Goodison Park the underground heated practice pitch was also receiving interested glances, too. Blackpool decided to enter five teams: Division One, Central League, West Lancashire, Mid-Week and Fylde League.

Appropriately named players turning out for a particular club included Andy Lincoln making his Football League debut for Lincoln City on 31 August 1931 scoring twice in a 6-0 win over Hartlepools United. Yet it was a second such Imps first outing as he had figured in their Midland League days, too.

While FA Cup rules forbade a player appearing for two different clubs in one season, the North and South sections of the Third Division had no such restriction for their cup competitions. You could appear for different clubs as long they were not in the same section. Hence goalkeeper Jack Beby having the unusual distinction of conceding eleven goals while with Crystal Palace, yet picking up a winner's medal with Darlington!

Bryn Jones

Costing a world record fee of £14,000 in 1938 it was a sobering thought that at one time Bryn Jones had experienced heartache years beforehand. Working the late shift at the Pit, he ran home, no time for tea, caught the bus to Swansea for a trial – and failed. He later had a trial with Southend when his brother Emlyn was there but was again turned down.

Hughie Gallacher's last move was from Grimsby to Gateshead at a modest £500 fee. In 1925 it had been £6,500 from Airdrie to Newcastle and subsequently to Chelsea £10,000, Derby £3,000, Notts County £2,000 and Grimsby £1,000.

Welsh international centre-half Tom Griffiths moved from Wrexham to Everton, Bolton, Middlesbrough and Aston Villa for a total of £18,000. This was all before a return to Wrexham.

In March 1936 Southampton transferred Bill Light to West Bromwich Albion for £2,000 the highest fee for a goalkeeper at the time.

Many trials proved inconclusive and failure to realize the potential of promising talent could prove costly. Full-back George Roughton went to Manchester United but they were unsure. Meanwhile he signed for Huddersfield and the Old Trafford club then had to pay a fee for him.

Clem Stephenson when manager of Huddersfield Town had first spotted Jimmy Richardson aged 16 when he was playing in north-east minor football. He had been a schoolboy international inside-forward. Stephenson lost track of him and Richardson was playing for Blyth Spartans when Newcastle United signed him. Eventually Stephenson got his man via there.

Harry Boileau a wing-half had played for Bedworth Town. Then there was an opportunity when he volunteered to fill a gap in a Coventry City third team trial. After 20 minutes he was called off the pitch and signed in August 1931.

Lewis Stoker at Birmingham was given a two-month's trial when he came from West Stanley, but did not actually get a game and signed anyway! Willis Edwards was on his way to Blackburn for a trial when a train companion turned out to be a Chesterfield official who persuaded him to go to Saltergate instead.

Jack Hill, Durham City centre-half, was wanted by Bob Jack, Plymouth manager. They met in a Durham street and Hill could not make up his mind. They tossed a coin, Hill said "heads" and signed for Argyle.

Dave "Boy" Martin was still in the Army when he was recommended to Norwich City. They sent a scout to watch him in a unit match and decided not to sign him! Phil Griffiths was invited for a trial at Stoke City. It did not work out, but he stayed in the area and signed for Port Vale.

Albert Stubbins made a similar close move in the north-east after being turned down by Sunderland. He opted for Newcastle United, scored twice in a trial game and was promoted to twelfth man before his actual debut.

The value of a player could change dramatically season to season. Jimmy Smith of Ayr's record 66 goals in a season cost Liverpool £5,000. He was transfer-listed and played for Tunbridge Wells Rangers, moved to Bristol Rovers. He was later given free transfers to Newport County and Notts County.

Transfer-listed Football League players seeking clubs often advertised themselves in magazines with full details of career and even addresses! But in 1932 Scottish international winger Alex Jackson of "Wembley Wizards" fame was so well known he was quickly approached by Ashton National when Chelsea put a fee of £6,000 on his head. He was offered £15 a week plus share of the gate receipts over a certain figure. Only half fit and tired by the journey from London he could not score the goals expected of him. After a few weeks the contract was cancelled by mutual consent. He admitted he had flopped and handed back the money which would have crippled the club. It was said he was receiving £30 a game. Jackson had attracted a crowd of 6,000 for his debut though this was not a club record attendance. Joined Margate in February 1933 and in the next few seasons he drifted across the Channel to Nice, Le Touquet and Nimes destined never again to play in the Football League.

Players often found professional football by chance when a scout sent to view one prospect found another candidate instead. But when Bury's chief scout Jimmy Porter on a day off was teaching a friend to drive when they came upon a football match at Prescot, stopped to watch. Porter saw Eddie Kilshaw who worked at ICI in Prescot and eventually signed him. At 17 he had three reserve games before his first team debut against Aston Villa.

Joe James was playing for a Battersea Church team on Wandsworth Common when he was spotted by Brentford manager Harry Curtis.

Strange patterns at Christmas included 1936 when not one Division 1 home team won, the nearest was a goalless draw between Charlton and Sunderland. On Boxing Day with reversed fixtures there were eight home wins and three draws! Then on Christmas Day 1937 in the Third Division (North) there were no home wins, four draws and five away wins. One match was abandoned at 0-0 in the fog, another postponed because of it.

Not to be outdone the Northern Section of the Third Division on 14 March 1931 had produced all eleven home winners, the visitors scraping only four goals. On 6 November 1937 from the full programme of 44 Football League fixtures, there were 14 home wins, 13 home defeats and 17 drawn games. On the opening day of the same season there had been only three away winners, two in

Division One and one in the Third Division (North). On 17 November 1934 all the fixtures in Division Two resulted in home wins.

Then on 30 January 1937 of the 16 FA Cup ties and 19 Football League matches there was not one away victory. With a difference, too the Newcastle United v Portsmouth match on 5 December 1931 which ended 0-0 was played throughout without one corner kick being taken.

At various times there were suggestions for an Anglo-Scottish League to run concurrently with the existing competitions; floodlit football in midweek; discussions over studs, half-studs or rubber grips for footwear; Sunday soccer, a tournament for clubs knocked out in the third round of the FA Cup; The midweek competition for England and Scotland was to include four teams from each country. Amazingly one was for an International League – but only for the four UK countries!

Floodlighting could be installed for £3,000 but it was thought few clubs had the financial resources to erect them. The clamour for a manager to be appointed for representative teams was occasionally answered. In 1934 Dick Ray the then Leeds United incumbent was put in charge of the Football League team against the Scottish League. Ray left Leeds the following year and Bradford City two years later.

Though goal scoring began to diminish in the latter part of the 30s, in 1936-37 Derby County scored 96 and conceded 90. In one three-match sequence they lost 5-2 at Preston, beat Arsenal 5-4 and lost 6-2 at Brentford. Hat tricks were also the vogue at Crewe Alexandra in 1938-39. Tom Foster and Fred Chandler had one each, Leo Stevens and Matt Johnson both twice. Stevens and Arthur Rice also scored four-timers.

Arsenal had fans in many parts of the world. One in British Guiana, South America sent a gift of a monkey skin and a little bag of gold dust. Supporters travelling to away matches in the constraints of the time had a varied kind of agenda depending on their means. In 1935-36 one Preston North End fan based in Harrogate managed to travel to all home and away games by car, but another unemployed and more local to Deepdale could make away games by leaving at the latest Thursday on foot.

When the agreement to use Wembley had seven years to run, the owners of White City wanted to put in a bid and were preparing to increase its size by 50 percent at a cost of £250,000. Wembley estimated expansion of the Empire Stadium to 130,000 would cost £60,000. For the 1937 FA Cup final there were 1,540 cars, 26 motor cycles and 513 coaches in five car parks.

Players had superstitions about their footwear. Some kept the same pair until they wore out, others insisted on a new pair every season – providing the club could stand the cost! Willis Edwards at Leeds United had the same pair for eight years until the repairers told him they were fed up trying to mend them. Preston defender Frank Gallimore who clung to his boots, patched re-soled and only discarded when the toe-caps collapsed. There was also widely differing ideas of how to break in new boots. Wearing a couple of sizes too small and immersing feet and boots in water was one theory. Putting on the left boot seems to have been less favourable than beginning with the right one before a game.

When George Drury was transferred to Arsenal from Sheffield Wednesday he suffered a loss of form. He went to manager George Allison and asked him if he could contact his former club and attempt to get his old pair back. He did and Drury's old form returned.

Goalkeepers with a fixation about their sweaters included Jack Brown of Sheffield Wednesday. Though it was becoming frayed and threadbare in parts he insisted on keeping it for matches. Jack Leckie of Cardiff City disliked green. When he played for Raith Rovers and Bray Unknowns in Ireland he wore yellow. At Port Vale he had to wear green and suffered several injuries. It was the same at Stockport County. So at Cardiff he was happy with white.

For general superstitions Freddie Worrall at Portsmouth took some beating. He never went onto the field without at least three mascots: a pocket horseshoe, white heather tucked into each stocking and a small white elephant attached to a tie-up. He was also the player who put manager Jack Tinn's lucky spats in place on Cup Final days.

But Eric Houghton at Aston Villa probably topped that. He averted his gaze at a funeral procession, always took in weddings, was frightened of cross-eyed men but seeing a sailor was lucky. If he left home and realised he had forgotten something, he would return and count five before venturing out again. He would collect small mascot trinkets and keep them until his luck ran out. Would throw them away and again start searching for more. Strangely enough, Alex James believed looking at funerals was lucky!

One day playing in goal for Stoke City at Derby County, a spectator threw a miniature chanticleer towards Norman Lewis. He kept in his pocket. Feeling the ball before a match is not so much of a superstition but a sensible move as he is the only player allowed to handle it.

The order in which players came onto the field affected Arthur Turner at Stoke City, too. Always insisting on being last in line, one day he was left in the dressing-room and the match almost started without him! Sep Smith the Leicester City wing-half and Jack Hacking the Oldham Athletic goalkeeper who had played for England during his career always made sure they came eleventh.

Two players at the same club wanting to be last out was fairly common, too. Johnny Arnold at Fulham had it to himself until Eddie Perry was signed and the scrum followed for last man. There was a ritual at Arsenal for a time, too. James would be first out, drop the ball to Hapgood who would back-heel it to Male. Hapgood would make for the goal post kick the left one, then the right. Chelsea usually came out in twos and threes! Wilf Copping at Arsenal would never shave on match days and his facial bristles became a trade mark.

The same peg in the dressing-room was another must for the serious followers of the routine. There was never a No.13 it seems but Stoke's Victoria Ground had a 12a.

Eric Houghton

When Stoke manager Bob McGrory was a player he always made a point of giving someone a shilling (five pence) before he entered a ground on match days. Charlton manager Jimmy Seed was a collector of lucky objects originally when he was a player. Over the years he had a tiepin, three-penny-piece, horseshoe and even a lump of coal!

Jack Tennant the Bolton full-back was given a two-headed penny by a friend and he had it for many years until he was tempted to try his luck with heads or tails. Someone called "heads" and he never felt the same about the coin afterwards.

Frank Newton at Fulham made sure his wife wished him good luck before leaving home for a game. Then came the FK Austria friendly at Craven Cottage and because it was unusual to play on a Monday evening the routine was not followed. Newton was injured and played his last game.

Sandy McNab at West Bromwich Albion always had sausage and chips on a Friday evening, left for home in the same gear and kissed his daughter three times. Before the kick-off he always insisted Cecil Shaw follow him onto the field. Ted Catlin at Sheffield Wednesday looked after the yellow golf sweater given to him by his colleague England amateur international goalkeeper Haydn Hill and a ring of blue-white enamel made for him by an unemployed man in Sheffield.

Sheffield Wednesday's Ronnie Starling had a kind of non-playing/playing lucky charm when with certain clubs getting to the FA Cup semi-final. It happened when he was at Hull 1930, Newcastle 1932, Wednesday 1935 and Villa 1938. He played in the last two semi-finals.

Alf Young at Huddersfield had already won England international honours but was struggling with his form. The club almost transferred him to Rotherham United. Then someone gave him a model of a black cat with one eye and he was back to his best. Forget to take the cat with him and he was injured in the FA Cup tie with Portsmouth.

Black cats lucky? Try telling Hughie Gallacher who thought they were just the opposite. Even a white sparrow was not to the liking of Barnsley fans after another bad run.

Village school children at Pentre, Broughton were given a holiday to watch Wales play Ireland at Wrexham on 27 March 1935 as two former pupils Tom Griffiths and Wilson Jones were playing. Jones making his debut scored one goal in a 3-1 victory. Also appearing for the first time was the unrelated Bryn Jones. Children sometimes benefited from the generosity of players. Jock Dodds the Scottish International gave a complete rig-out to boys at his former school at Leadgate, County Durham.

Everton goalkeeper Ted Sagar playing against Leicester City on 27 December 1938 dislocated his shoulder and was rushed to hospital, given gas, had the limb put back. He returned to the match playing on the wing! Everton won 3-0. Sagar had once dislocated a finger, put it back in place himself and continued after this DIY.

Charlie Calladine attracted attention from Football League clubs while playing for Scunthorpe. He had his appendix removed just after Birmingham signed him. They gave him three months rest and the recuperation period paid off.

On 29 March 1937 Southend United goalkeeper George MacKenzie cracked his wrist bone playing against Brighton. He had his arm and wrist put in splints and resumed in goal until his captain told him to get out on the right wing. One down at the time, Southend won 2-1.

The unlikelihood of being able to earn more money at one club rather than another usually divided players into two categories, the one-club man or the wanderer. Bobby Crawford with 392 League games for Preston North End left for Southport after missing only one game in his last seven seasons at Deepdale. It also included 187 consecutive appearances.

Fellow wing-half Joe Cockroft arrived at West Ham United in 1933 from Gainsborough Trinity and made his debut on 14 April against Chesterfield. He did not miss a first team game until 2 April 1938 against Tottenham Hotspur, after a run of 217 League and Cup matches.

Something about that position because George Whyte at Lincoln City who made 299 League appearances for them was another chiefly left-halt and made 183 consecutive League appearances from 3 March 1934 until 3 September 1938.

Wanderers included the like of Harry Lovatt who listed Wood Lane United, Red Street St Chad's, Audley, Port Vale and Preston before making his Football League debut with Crewe Alexandra. He subsequently played in the League for Bradford City, Wrexham and Leicester City – after a stint with Scarborough – Notts County and Northampton in 1931. Then back to the non-league circuit with Macclesfield, Stafford and Winsford United.

Inside-forward Les Roberts was in a class of his own. From Cradley Heath St Luke's he went to Aston Villa in 1921, Redditch then Bristol Rovers and made his Football League debut with Chesterfield. No League games at either Sheffield Wednesday or when back for a Rovers return, but more League experience with Merthyr, Bournemouth and Bolton. Swindon, Brentford and Manchester City were added before Exeter, Crystal Palace and Chester brought him to 1933-34. Rotherham was his next stop prior to outside the League again with Scunthorpe. In 1936 he started two seasons with New Brighton before finishing his career with South Liverpool. Three seasons at Swindon had been his longest spell anywhere.

Jack Downing made his debut for Darlington against Carlisle United on 29 April 1933 scored a hat trick in a 5-2 win and after playing in the next and final game of the season left the club!

Not to be confused with the Goodison Park trainer Harry Cooke, Everton's masseur Harry Cook, who celebrated 17 years at Goodison Park in 1937, had marvellous manipulating hands but was blind. He had been injured in the Great War after attempting to shoot a Turkish soldier his enemy had thrown a grenade which exploded in front of Cook and left him sightless. He had a detailed memory of his players, noting that Lawton had a longer tibia than the others, Dean had slightly thicker ankles and Charlie Gee had two cartilage scars by one knee.

The professional Powderhall Sprint Championship was well competed for by players who had to use fictitious names in the races, though most people knew who they were. Liverpool full-back Jim Harley was one of the successes in it and ran under the name of J H Mitchell. All competitors had handicaps over the 130 yard race. When he won in 1936 he had had a nine yard handicap and won in 12 and six-sixteenth seconds.

All-rounder of note was Reg Halton at Bury. He had cups for swimming, Tennis, table tennis, darts and was one of several County Cricketers.

Player with the longest name was christened Arthur Stanley Sackville Redvers Trevor Boscawen Griffith Trevis. His parents named him after Sir Arthur Boscawen the former MP for Dudley whom the Trevis family had admired. The young Trevis played for Leamington Town, Old Hill Amateurs, West Bromwich Albion, Chester and Worcester City as a wing-half. He was known as "Bos."

Tom "Pongo" Waring of much travelled fame inherited his nickname from a cousin who preceded him at school. Willie Miller arrived at Everton from Partick Thistle in 1935 with a reputation as an inside-forward, to such an extent that he had been dubbed "Golden Miller" after the famous Cheltenham Gold Cup horse. But he found he going tough moved on to Burnley, Tranmere before returning to Scotland with Falkirk

Ex-professionals as referees were thin on the ground. In fact there was only one in the 1930s. He was George William Jones a centre-half who had played for Nottingham Forest, Mansfield Town and Grantham in the 1920s. Then George Stephenson the Liverpool referee raised an important point after taking charge of a match involving deaf and dumb players. He was able to control it by using a handkerchief! But he also said there was nothing to stop him from using it in Football League games as there was no reference to a whistle – just signals from the official in the middle.

Former referees becoming managers was not as unusual. Herbert Hopkinson took over as Rochdale manager in 1932 and the renowned Jimmy Jewell became Norwich City secretary-manager in 1939.

While the ball that started at kick-off time invariably finished the 90 minutes, referee Eddie Wood once used his discretion on a particularly unpleasant afternoon. Rain had churned the pitch and the ball become increasingly heavy. After two players were dazed after heading the ball, he called for a clean replacement.

On 14 March 1936 the referee appointed for Bradford City v Doncaster Rovers failed to appear. A linesman replaced him and Doncaster's twelfth man George Flowers ran the line, thus earning more money that day than any of his colleagues – £1.11s.6d (£1.58).

Three Southend United players were found guilty of poaching on 16 September 1934. Police had stopped their lorry containing 62 rabbits and four guns. One player was fined £1, the others ten shillings (50 pence) and their firing equipment confiscated.

Money being tight a young Dennis Westcott trained in the evenings at Everton but found the two shillings (ten pence) fare too much and quit. Having started with Wallasey Grocers then Leasowe Road Brickworks he was turned down by West Ham United before landing a contract with New Brighton and thence on to Wolves.

Clubs did sometimes remember to make a donation when signing players when no transfer fee had to be paid. Centre-half Walter Winterbottom signed for Manchester United in 1936-37 having played for Royton Amateurs near Oldham. He was studying to become a teacher. He went to Old Trafford from Mossley, who received a £50 gift as a result. Sheffield Wednesday made a similar gesture to West Wylam in the case of Jackie Robinson signed at 16. Bolton, too, gave some financial help to Brierley Hill Alliance from whom they had signed Ray Westwood.

When Portsmouth Tram Boys beat Palmer Sports 40-0 on 8 October 1934, nine different players scored goals, but the leading marksman was appropriately named Boss who had ten goals to his credit.

In a Watford and District League game in January 1938, Garston Old Boys beat Watford British Legion 18-1. The Garston goalkeeper scored twice, the two full-backs one each and the half backs contributed another four goals.

In the 1938 Southend Schools Cup Final, Westborough beat West Leigh 5-0. It was their 14th game of the season and their 148th goal having conceded none. Left-winger Ken Evans with 36 goals to his credit was chosen to play for England v Ireland in a schoolboy international.

While players tended to be known in their own specialized positions, the utility player was worth his wages. In 1935-36 Charlie Sillett at Southampton played 23 games at right-back, nine on the left side, eight times at left-half and even twice led the attack. Another position this Army man had was being a boxer and had once fought Jack Petersen. But Torquay United's Albert Hutchinson spread his 317

League appearances to 1939 from left-back, all three half-back positions, two inside-forward places, plus centre-forward and on the left wing!

On 11 April 1936 Fred Sharman whose usual position was centre-half, played centre-forward for Leicester City against Tottenham Hotspur. His immediate opponent was Doug Hunt also playing out of position at centre-half having previously played centre-forward. Sharman scored in a 1-1 draw. The following Saturday, Hunt led the Spurs reserve attack and was marked by Leicester's Sharman playing centre-half!

Pat Glover had to deputise in goal for Grimsby Town in emergencies and in order to keep him up to scratch he often played for the A team in that position.

Long distance goals from defenders were rare. However, full-back Walter Crook playing for Blackburn Rovers against West Bromwich Albion at Ewood Parkin 1939 scored with a wind-assisted effort from 70 yards in a 3-0 win. Well, it was 1 April.

Running on the turf was one familiar activity for a footballer, but treading the boards was rare for one of them. Arthur Gale at West Bromwich Albion was a Manchester schoolmaster but interested in amateur dramatics. However, he landed the role of Tony Chute in "The Quaker Girl" opposite the BBC radio artiste Doris Brookes. John Reid Smith at Bury was another theatre actor. Gale had played in all West Bromwich's FA Cup ties in 1934-35 but was left out of the final team. That, presumably, was Show Business!

On 1 October 1938 in the wake of the Munich Agreement, Charlton Athletic guests for the 4-4 draw with Bolton Wanderers were the Prime Minister Neville Chamberlain and the Rector of Charlton.

West Ham United managed three one-game-one-goal players. Cliff Ette in 1933-34, Dick Bell and Cliff Hubbard both in 1938-39.

A treble of a different kind was achieved by Charlie Davis, centre-half of Mansfield Town when he appeared in their opening League game on 29 August 1931. He had previously achieved first Football League day appearances at Torquay United in 1927 and York City in 1929.

Three in a row Mersey golf titles for Tom Cooper right-back at Liverpool. The runner-up in the 1938 tournament was Eric Brook left-winger at Manchester City.

George Collin was with West Stanley three times, Arsenal and Bournemouth in between. Injured while at Dean Court he regained fitness was signed by Derby and became a regular choice at left-back.

In 1935-36 three Male brothers were chasing various cup medals, George with Arsenal in the FA Cup, Len with Ilford in the Amateur Cup and Charles employed by Scotland Yard in the Civil Service Shield. Ilford lost their game. George Male also acted as trainer-coach to the Southern Amateur League club The Norsemen in 1937-38.

Sheffield Wednesday manager Jimmy McMullan had to decide how to split the £165 talent money for third place in 1939. Twenty-one players had appeared and he divided the number of appearances each made from the total of 462 into the sum available. It worked out at seven shillings and a penny halfpenny a game. Two ever present players received £15 each.

High-scoring matches often resulted from one team suffering the loss of an injured player. When Stoke City defeated West Bromwich Albion 10-3 on 4 February 1937 the Throstles goalkeeper Billy Light was a casualty in the first few minutes. There were two debutants for Stoke that day, goalkeeper Doug Westland and left-back Jimmy Harbot, the latter having his only City first team outing.

In a difficult environment for the Players Union to improve conditions for its members, when the Football League declined the offer from the Pools companies of £5,000 towards publishing its fixtures, they asked if the money could be handed over for ex-players in need. In April 1930 the League refused to meet a deputation from the Union over players on the transfer list receiving no wages. By 1933 some £24,000 had been handed over by the Union for injured players.

In 1936 the Football League agreed with Players Union secretary Jimmy Fay to promote the idea of players becoming referees.

The vexed question about the Pools irritated the Football League and several ex-players were regularly giving their forecasts in the press including Charlie Roberts, Harry Bedford, Jock Rutherford, Harry Hampson and Alec Troup.

Arsenal's Herbert Chapman wrongly suggested that "players would refuse £4 a week to go on the dole for a few shillings." The Union later claimed one Arsenal player joined the organisation after he was transferred to another club.

In 1934 the Union was at odds with the Football League who wanted injured players to be placed on half wages after a month.

When Manchester City were parading with the FA Cup after their 1934 success a silver golf cup was thrown at the players from an upstairs window. It was caught appropriately enough by goalkeeper Frank Swift. Then there was the "Tom Lawton Trophy" presented by the Everton and England centre-forward to his old Bolton school in 1939 for House Shield purposes.

An unnamed Director was examining his club's accounts and questioned the manager over £100 spent on seven trialists as only two had been signed. The manager replied that he knew he could sell the two on for £500. But the Director asked him why he had given the other five trials in the first place. Ah! Well.

Some professions had strict rules about playing football. Dr John Bone had been a professional with Motherwell and St Mirren. When employed at the Royal Hospital in Winchester he was granted permission to play for Portsmouth but without any remuneration.

Peace finally broke out in amateur football in May 1934 when the Amateur Football Association had its differences with the Football Association finally settled. The newly designated Amateur Football Alliance was given representation on international selection committees and the Amateur Cup. However their many long-running competitions carried on as before.

As to what happened to the players of the Manchester United cup winning team of 1909 by 1935, one had died in the war, another in 1934. One was working in the mines, another on the docks. One was living in London. Billy Meredith was one of three working as a hotelier and Charlie Roberts had a couple of stationery and newsagent businesses in Manchester and District. Harold Halse was still looking for a job in football!

Tottenham Hotspur ran seven teams at one time. They included two at Northfleet their nursery and a couple of teenage colts' sides there. The Northfleet coach was James Anderson who had not played professional football but had been on the ground staff at White Hart Lane.

When Jackie Robinson made his debut for Sheffield Wednesday against West Bromwich on 22 April 1935 he wore the boots of Ronnie Starling the player he was replacing. Robinson was a scoring debutant, too, in the 1-1 draw.

Publicity was frequently localized. In 1933 Stockport County announced in a local cinema advert: "Come to Edgeley Park and see what you think of Alf Lythgoe." He was 5ft 8in, 10st 7lb had positioned sense for a centre-forward, two good feet, a ten yard burst of speed and swerve. Despite being rejected at Crewe for being too small at 17 he had made the grade. Four First Division clubs watched him in November 1933. Middlesbrough offered £5,000, Stockport turned down a £4,000 offer. Even went to Wolves for a trial and was told: "Go where you shouldn't be and shoot when you ought not to." He resumed at Stockport and was top scorer with 46 League goals in 1933-34. Another Lythgoe fad was to rub olive oil on his legs every evening to keep his muscles in trim.

When Bournemouth manager Charlie Bell signed Willie Sellars, a goalkeeper from St Anthony's, in 1937, the agreement was completed in a cinema.

Centre-half Tom Lockie had four seasons with Rangers before moving to Leith Athletic in 1931. From then on he changed clubs every year – Barnsley, York City, Accrington Stanley and Mansfield Town. Went back to York in 1936 stayed and became trainer.

Vic Wright, an inside-forward with Rotherham United was twice transferred for four figure sums of money. He went to Sheffield Wednesday soon returned but was later sold to Liverpool.

While Ted Harston was scoring freely for Mansfield Town in 1935-36 and 1936-37 with 26 and 55 League goals respectively, the second and third highest scorers in both seasons were Arthur Atkinson and George Anderson on each occasion scoring ten and eight goals respectively. Harston was once taken ill; rumours spread around that he had died and frantic officials rushed to his home to find him fit and well.

On 21 December Swansea Town's George Lowrie aged 18, was involved in an exchange deal in which Les Vernon and Joe Beresford were transferred to Preston North End.

You could say Everton were bright sparks. What with their electrically heated training ground they also had an all-electric laundry at Goodison Park.

Bradford (Park Avenue) goalkeeper Chick Farr narrowly avoids punching his half-back Bob Danskin in the game with Fulham at Craven Cottage, October 1937

THE CLOSE SEASON

CLOSE SEASON THEN CLOSED SEASON

The 1939 close season proceeded with the usual heartache for those players being either given free transfers or placed on the transfer list. There was the additional concern of militia training by age groups that had been brought in as well as many players already opting to join Territorial units as the situation on the continent worsened.

Austria had been tacked on to Germany, Czechoslovakia gradually dismembered and the Russo-German pact threatened Poland in a sandwich. Meanwhile Spain was licking its wounds after the Civil War in which both Italy and Germany had given men and material support to Franco's winning side against the Republican government.

The Football Association had been against England's May tour to Italy, Yugoslavia and Romania but it had passed off extremely well off the field with no unpleasantness of any kind. The official report said: "Once again an outstanding feature of the tour has been the splendid sportsmanship shown by every member of the team. The captains Hapgood and Cullis set an excellent example." The FA's tour to South Africa was another success as was the Scottish FA's tour of the USA and Canada. There were still many British coaches operating in Europe particularly in Holland. Alex James, who had been refused Football League status because of his link with a Pools company, had friends in Poland and was coaching there. He was quoted £25 for coaching the national team.

However, domestically clubs went about getting prepared for the new season. At the AGM of the Football League the retiring clubs were voted back. In the Southern Section of the Third Division, Bristol Rovers received 45 votes, Walsall 36. The former League club Gillingham had 15, Chelmsford City and Colchester United one each. In the North, Hartlepools United had 38 and Accrington Stanley 29. Missing out were Shrewsbury Town with 22, South Liverpool five and Scunthorpe & Lindsey United four. Neither Burton Town nor Wigan Athletic received a vote.

The watering of pitches was to be allowed with the exception of the months of November, December, January and February. There had been an enormous rough when Everton crashed 7-0 at Wolverhampton's Molineux ground, the visitors claiming the pitch had been heavily watered when unnecessary.

For the first time, too, players in the Football League would have numbered shirts but it was only agreed by the slender margin of 24 to 20. But the four up and four down promotion and relegation issue was lost by 28 to 21.

There would be an increase of six representatives of the League on the FA's Council and due to the passing away of three long-serving administrators, the Rt.Hon. The Earl of Athlone KG was appointed President of the FA and Mark C Frowde its Chairman. Will Cuff of Everton was elected President of the Football League.

The Third Division clubs decided to abandon their sectional cup competitions. One semi-final was still outstanding from 1938-39 and was to be slotted in for the new season. In place of it, the teams finishing second and third in each section would compete for two cups. The winners would meet for gold medals. For the FA Cup 538 entries had been received.

David Jack the Southend United manager proposed that the pooling of home gate receipts be increased from 20 percent to 100 percent to help the majority of clubs striving to pay their way. On 5 June it was revealed that the FA's assets were £138,515!

There were discussions about moving all fourth, fifth and second round matches in the FA Cup to midweek, the inception of a countrywide reserve competition, scrapping bonuses to players, the problem of gland treatment and television.

The Scottish League programme began on 12 August with the Football League starting two weeks later. On September 3 the Prime Minister Neville Chamberlain announced that Great Britain had declared war against Germany. All sport and entertainments were immediately cancelled.

For further reading please refer to *The Men Who Never Were* and *Soccer at War*.

THE HONOURS BOARD

Contents:

In the 1930s, "Ireland" (governed by the Irish Football Association) was commonly used for today's "Northern Ireland". The Republic of Ireland (the Football Association of Ireland) was known either as "Eire" or the "Irish Free State".

HOME INTERNATIONALS

19/10/1929, Ireland 0 England 3, Windsor Park, Belfast. Att: 40,000
Ireland: E.Scott (Liverpool), S.R.Russell (Bradford City), R.Hamilton (Rangers), J.Miller (Middlesbrough), J.H.Elwood (Bradford Park Ave), W.McCleery (Linfield), H.A.Duggan (Leeds United), R.W.Rowley (Southampton), J.Bambrick (Linfield), L.Cumming (Oldham Athletic), P.J.Kavanagh (Celtic)
England: J.H.Brown (Sheffield Wednesday), W.Cresswell (Everton), E.Blenkinsop (Sheffield Wed), W.Edwards (Leeds United), E.Hart (Leeds United), A.F.Barrett (Fulham), H.Adcock (Leicester City), E.W.Hine (Leicester City), G.H.Camsell (Middlesbrough), J.Bradford (Birmingham), E.F.Brook (Manchester City)
Scorers. England; Hine, Camsell 2 (1 pen)
Referee: T. Small (Scotland)

26/10/1929, Wales 2 Scotland 4, Ninian Park, Cardiff. Att. 20,000
Wales: A.Gray (Manchester Central), B.D.Williams (Swansea Town), A.Lumberg (Wrexham), S.R.Bennion (Manchester United, F.C.Keenor (Cardiff City), R.F.John (Arsenal), W.Davies (Notts County), E.O'Callaghan (Tottenham Hotspur), L.S.Davies (Cardiff City), C.Jones (Arsenal), F.C.Cook (Portsmouth)

Scotland: J.D.Harkness (Hearts), D.H.Gray (Rangers), J.Nibloe (Kilmarnock), J.D.Gibson (Aston Villa), J.A.Johnstone (Hearts), T.Craig (Rangers), A.S.Jackson (Huddersfield Town), T.A.Muirhead (Rangers), H.K.Gallacher (Newcastle United), A.W.James (Arsenal), A.L.Morton (Rangers)
Scorers: Wales: L.S.Davies, O'Callaghan.
Scotland; Gallacher 2, Gibson, James
Referee: W McLean (Ireland)

20/11/1929, England 6 Wales 0, Stamford Bridge, London. Att. 32,945
England: H.E.Hibbs (Birmingham), T.Smart (Aston Villa), E.Blenkinsop (Sheffield Wed), W.Edwards (Leeds United), E.Hart (Leeds United), W.Marsden (Sheffield Wednesday), H.Adcock (Leicester City), E.W.Hine (Leicester City), G.H.Camsell (Middlesbrough), T.C.Johnson (Manchester City), J.W.Ruffell (WHU)
Wales: D.Lewis (Arsenal), B.D.Williams (Swansea Town), A.Lumberg (Wrexham), T.P.Griffiths (Everton), F.C.Keenor (Cardiff City), R.F.John (Arsenal), W.Davies (Notts County), L.S.Davies (Cardiff City), W.L.Lewis (Huddersfield Town), C.Jones (Arsenal), F.C.Cook (Portsmouth)
Scorers: England; Camsell 3, Johnson 2, Adcock
Referee: W. McLean (Ireland)

01/02/1930, Ireland 7 Wales 0, Celtic Park, Belfast. Att. 25,000
Ireland: A.Gardiner (Cliftonville), A.McClullage (Burnley), R.P.Fulton (Belfast Celtic), W.McCleery (Linfield), J.Jones (Linfield), T.Sloan (Linfield), J.Chambers (Bury), R.W.Rowley (Southampton), J.Bambrick (Linfield), J.McCambridge (Ballymena), J.Mahood (Belfast Celtic)
Wales: R.J.Finnegan (Wrexham), A.R.Hugh (Newport County), T.Jones (Manchester United), E.Lawrence (Clapton Orient), F.C.Keenor (Cardiff City), J.Pugsley (Charlton Athletic), W.Davies (Notts County), B.Williams (Bristol City), T.J.Martin (Newport), S.Davies (Rotherham United), F.C.Cook (Portsmouth)
Scorers: Ireland; Bambrick 6, McClullage
Referee: T. Crew (England)

22/02/1930, Scotland 3 Ireland 1, Celtic Park, Glasgow. Att: 30,000
Scotland: R.C.Middleton (Cowdenbeath), D.H.Gray (Rangers), W.Wiseman (Queen's Park), J.D.Gibson (Aston Villa), D.D.Meiklejohn (Rangers), T.Craig (Rangers), A.S.Jackson (Huddersfield Town), G.Stevenson (Motherwell), H.K.Gallacher (Newcastle United), A.W.James (Arsenal), A.L.Morton (Rangers)
Ireland: A.Gardiner (Cliftonville), S.R.Russell (Bradford City), R.Hamilton (Rangers), R.McDonald (Rangers), J.Jones (Linfield), T.Sloan (Linfield), J.Chambers (Bury), R.W.Irvine (Portsmouth), J.Bambrick (Linfield), J.McCambridge (Ballymena), J.H.McCaw (Linfield)
Scorers: Scotland; Gallacher 2, Stevenson
Ireland; McCaw
Referee: A. Josephs (England)

05/04/1930, England 5 Scotland 2, Wembley, London. Att: 87,375
England: H.E.Hibbs (Birmingham), F.R.Goodall (Huddersfield Town), E.Blenkinsop (Sheffield Wed), A.H.Strange (Sheffield Wednesday), M.Webster (Middlesbrough), W.Marsden (Sheffield Wednesday), S.D.Crooks (Derby County), D.N.Jack (Arsenal), V.M.Watson (WHU), J.Bradford (Birmingham), E.Rimmer (Sheffield Wednesday)
Scotland: J.D.Harkness (Hearts), D.H.Gray (Rangers), T.Law (Chelsea), J.Buchanan (Rangers), D.D.Meiklejohn (Rangers), T.Craig (Rangers), A.S.Jackson (Huddersfield Town), A.W.James (Arsenal), J.W.Fleming (Rangers), G.Stevenson (Motherwell), A.L.Morton (Rangers)
Scorers: England; Rimmer 2, Watson 2, Jack
Scotland: Fleming 2
Referee: W. McLean (Ireland)

20/10/1930, England 5 Ireland 1, Bramall Lane, Sheffield. Att: 39,064
England: H.E.Hibbs (Birmingham), F.R.Goodall (Huddersfield Town), E.Blenkinsop (Sheffield Wed), A.H.Strange (Sheffield Wednesday), T.Leach (Sheffield Wednesday), A.F.Campbell (Huddersfield Town), S.D.Crooks (Derby County), G.Hodgson (Liverpool), J.Hampson (Blackpool), H.A.Burgess (Sheffield Wednesday), W.E.Houghton (Aston Villa)
Ireland: E.Scott (Liverpool), A.McClullage (Burnley), R.P.Fulton (Belfast Celtic), J.Jones (Linfield), W.Reid (Hearts), W.McCleery (Linfield), H.A.Duggan (Leeds United), R.W.Irvine (Connah's Quay), J.Dunne (Sheffield United), W.Gillespie (Sheffield United), J.H.McCaw (Linfield)
Scorers: England; Burgess 2, Crooks, Hampson, Houghton. Ireland; Dunne
Referee: J. Thomson (Scotland)

25/10/1930, Scotland 1 Wales 1, Ibrox Stadium, Glasgow. Att: 23,106
Scotland: J.Thomson (Celtic), D.H.Gray (Rangers), J.R.Gilmour (Dundee), C.D.McNab (Dundee), R.Gillespie (Queen's Park), F.R.Hill (Aberdeen), D.M.McRorie (Morton), G.C.Brown (Rangers), B.J.Battles (Hearts), G.Stevenson (Motherwell), A.L.Morton (Rangers)
Wales: L.Evans (Cardiff City), F.T.Dewey (Cardiff Corinthians), W.Crompton (Wrexham), W.Rogers (Wrexham), F.C.Keenor (Cardiff City), E.Ellis (Oswestry Town), W.S.Collins (Llanelly), J.E.Neal (Colwyn Bay), T.Bamford (Wrexham), W.W.Robbins (Cardiff City), W.R.Thomas (Newport County)
Scorers: Scotland; Battles. Wales; Bamford
Referee: C.E. Lines (England)

22/11/1930, Wales 0 England 4, The Racecourse, Wrexham. Att: 11,282
Wales: L.Evans (Cardiff City), F.T.Dewey (Cardiff Corinthians), W.Crompton (Wrexham), W.Rogers (Wrexham), F.C.Keenor (Cardiff City), E.Ellis (Oswestry Town), A.L.Williams (Wrexham), J.E.Neal

(Colwyn Bay), T.Bamford (Wrexham), W.W.Robbins (Cardiff City), W.R.Thomas (Newport County)
England: H.E.Hibbs (Birmingham), F.R.Goodall (Huddersfield Town), E.Blenkinsop (Sheffield Wed), A.H.Strange (Sheffield Wednesday), T.Leach (Sheffield Wednesday), A.F.Campbell (Huddersfield Town), S.D.Crooks (Derby County), G.Hodgson (Liverpool), J.Hampson (Blackpool), J.Bradford (Birmingham), W.E.Houghton (Aston Villa)
Scorers: England; Hampson 2, Bradford, Hodgson
Referee: H. Watson (Scotland)

21/02/1931, Ireland 0 Scotland 0, Windsor Park, Belfast. Att: 20,000
Ireland: A.Gardiner (Cliftonville), J.McNich (Ballymena), R.P.Fulton (Belfast Celtic), W.McCleery (Linfield), J.Jones (Linfield), T.Sloan (Linfield), H.Blair (Portadown), E.Falloon (Aberdeen), F.C.Roberts (Glentoran), J.Geary (Glentoran), J.H.McCaw (Linfield)
Scotland: J.Thomson (Celtic), J.S.Crapnell (Aidrieonians), J.Nibloe (Kilmarnock), P.Wilson (Celtic), G.Walker (St Mirren), F.R.Hill (Aberdeen), J.L.Murdoch (Motherwell), P.Scarff (Celtic), B.C.Yorston (Aberdeen), R.L.McPhail (Rangers), A.L.Morton (Rangers)
Referee: H.E. Hull (England)

28/03/1931, Scotland 2 England 0, Hampden Park, Glasgow. Att: 129,810
Scotland: J.Thomson (Celtic), D.Blair (Clyde), J.Nibloe (Kilmarnock), C.D.McNab (Dundee), D.D.Meiklejohn (Rangers), J.Miller (St Mirren), A.Archibald (Rangers), G.Stevenson (Motherwell), J.E.McGrory (Celtic), R.L.McPhail (Rangers), A.L.Morton (Rangers)
England: H.E.Hibbs (Birmingham), F.R.Goodall (Huddersfield Town), E.Blenkinsop (Sheffield Wed), A.H.Strange (Sheffield Wednesday), H.Roberts (Arsenal), A.F.Campbell (Huddersfield Town), S.D.Crooks (Derby County), G.Hodgson (Liverpool), W.R.Dean (Everton), H.A.Burgess (Sheffield Wednesday), J.F.Crawford (Chelsea)
Scorers: Scotland; McGrory, Stevenson
Referee: A.J. Atwood (Wales)

22/04/1931, Wales 3 Ireland 2, The Racecourse, Wrexham. Att: 11,000
Wales: W.R.John (Walsall), B.D.Williams (Everton), W.Crompton (Wrexham), F.C.Keenor (Cardiff City), T.P.Griffiths (Everton), D.Richards (Wolves), C.Phillips (Wolves), D.J.Astley (Charlton Athletic), T.Bamford (Wrexham), W.James (WHU), F.W.Warren (Middlesbrough)
Ireland: W.Diffin (Belfast Celtic), A.McClullage (Burnley), R.P.Fulton (Belfast Celtic), S.J.Irving (Chelsea), J.Jones (Linfield), W.McCleery (Linfield), H.A.Duggan (Leeds United), R.W.Rowley (Tottenham Hotspur), J.Dunne (Sheffield United), J.McCambridge (Cardiff City), J.H.McCaw (Linfield)
Scorers: Wales; Phillips, Warren, Griffiths
Ireland; Dunne, Rowley
Referee: W.P. Harper (England)

19/09/1931, Scotland 3 Ireland 1, Ibrox Stadium, Glasgow. Att: 40,000
Scotland: R.Hepburn (Ayr United), D.Blair (Clyde), R.McAulay (Rangers), A.Massie (Hearts), D.D.Meiklejohn (Rangers), G.C.Brown (Rangers), J.Crawford (Queen's Park), G.Stevenson (Motherwell), J.E.McGrory (Celtic), R.L.McPhail (Rangers), J.Connor (Sunderland)
Ireland: A.Gardiner (Cliftonville), J.McNich (Ballymena), R.Hamilton (Rangers), W.McCleery (Linfield), J.Jones (Linfield), W.A.Gowdy (Hull City), H.Blair (Portadown), R.W.Rowley (Tottenham Hotspur), J.Dunne (Sheffield United), J.Geary (Glentoran), J.Chambers (Nottingham Forest)
Scorers: Scotland; Stevenson, McGrory, McPhail
Ireland; Dunne
Referee: I. Caswell (England)

17/10/1931, Ireland 2 England 6, Windsor Park, Belfast. Att: 40,000
Ireland: A.Gardiner (Cliftonville), S.R.Russell (Derry City), R.P.Fulton (Belfast Celtic), R.McDonald (Rangers), J.Jones (Linfield), W.Mitchell (Distillery), J.Chambers (Nottingham Forest), P.McConnell (Southport), J.Dunne (Sheffield United), J.McCambridge (Cardiff City), J.Kelly (Derry City)
England: H.E.Hibbs (Birmingham), F.R.Goodall (Huddersfield Town), E.Blenkinsop (Sheffield Wed), A.H.Strange (Sheffield Wednesday), T.Graham (Nottingham Forest), A.F.Campbell (Huddersfield Town), S.D.Crooks (Derby County), J.W.Smith (Portsmouth), T.Waring (Aston Villa), E.W.Hine (Leicester City), W.E.Houghton (Aston Villa)
Scorers: Ireland; Dunne.
England; Houghton 2, Waring 2, Hine, Smith
Referee: H. Watson (Scotland)

31/10/1931, Wales 2 Scotland 3, The Racecourse, Wrexham. Att. 10,860
Wales: A.Gray (Tranmere Rovers), A.Richards (Barnsley), A.Lumberg (Wolves), T.Edwards (Linfield), T.P.Griffiths (Everton), E.Lawrence (Notts County), P.H.Griffiths (Everton), E.O'Callaghan (Tottenham Hotspur), E.M.Glover (Grimsby Town), W.W.Robbins (Cardiff City), E.R.Curtis (Birmingham)
Scotland: J.D.Harkness (Hearts), D.Blair (Clyde), R.McAulay (Rangers), A.Massie (Hearts), D.D.Meiklejohn (Rangers), G.C.Brown (Rangers), R.Thomson (Celtic), G.Stevenson (Motherwell), J.E.McGrory (Celtic), R.L.McPhail (Rangers), A.L.Morton (Rangers)
Scorers: Wales; Curtis (pen), O'Callaghan.
Scotland; Thomson, Stevenson, McGrory
Referee: I. Caswell (England)

18/11/1931, England 3 Wales 1, Anfield, Liverpool. Att. 15,000
England: H.E.Hibbs (Birmingham), T.Cooper (Derby County), E.Blenkinsop (Sheffield Wed), A.H.Strange (Sheffield Wednesday), C.W.Gee (Everton), A.F.Campbell (Huddersfield Town), S.D.Crooks (Derby County), J.W.Smith (Portsmouth), T.Waring (Aston Villa), E.W.Hine (Leicester City), C.S.Bastin (Arsenal)
Wales: A.Gray (Tranmere Rovers), B.D.Williams (Everton), B.Ellis (Motherwell), C.Jones (Arsenal), T.P.Griffiths (Everton), R.F.John (Arsenal), C.Phillips (Wolves), E.O'Callaghan (Tottenham Hotspur), D.J.Astley (Aston Villa), W.W.Robbins (Cardiff City), F.C.Cook (Portsmouth)
Scorers: England; Smith, Hine, Crooks.
Wales; Robbins
Referee: W.F. Bunnell (England)

05/12/1931, Ireland 4 Wales 0, Windsor Park, Belfast. Att. 10,000
Ireland: E.Scott (Liverpool), J.McNich (Ballymena), R.P.Fulton (Belfast Celtic), W.McCleery (Linfield), M.Pyper (Linfield), W.Mitchell (Distillery), J.Chambers (Nottingham Forest), R.W.Irvine (Derry City), J.Bambrick (Linfield), W.Millar (Barrow), J.Kelly (Derry City)
Wales: A.Gray (Tranmere Rovers), S.Lawrence (Swansea Town), H.E.Foulkes (WBA), S.R.Bennion (Manchester United), T.P.Griffiths (Everton), E.Ellis (Oswestry Town), T.J.Jones (Sheffield Wednesday), W.James (WHU), T.Bamford (Wrexham), W.W.Robbins (Cardiff City), J.E.Parris (Bradford Park Avenue)
Scorers: Ireland; Kelly 2, Millar, Bambrick
Referee: P. Snape (England)

09/04/1932, England 3 Scotland 0, Wembley, London. Att: 92,180
England: H.F.Pearson (WBA), G.E.Shaw (WBA), E.Blenkinsop (Sheffield Wed), A.H.Strange (Sheffield Wednesday), J.P.O'Dowd (Chelsea), S.Weaver (Newcastle United), S.D.Crooks (Derby County), R.Barclay (Sheffield United), T.Waring (Aston Villa), T.C.Johnson (Everton), W.E.Houghton (Aston Villa)
Scotland: T.Hamilton (Rangers), J.S.Crapnell (Airdrieonians), J.Nibloe (Kilmarnock), C.D.McNab (Dundee), A.Craig (Motherwell), G.C.Brown (Rangers), A.Archibald (Rangers), J.Marshall (Rangers), N.H.Dewar (Third Lanark), C.E.Napier (Celtic), A.L.Morton (Rangers)
Scorers: England; Crooks, Barclay, Waring
Referee: S. Thompson (Ireland)

17/09/1932, Ireland 0 Scotland 4, Windsor Park, Belfast. Att: 40,000 Referee: W.P. Harper (England)
Ireland: E.Scott (Liverpool), W.Cook (Celtic), R.P.Fulton (Belfast Celtic), E.Falloon (Aberdeen), J.Jones (Linfield), W.A.Gowdy (Sheffield Wednesday, E.J.Mitchell (Cliftonville), T.J.Priestley (Coleraine), W.Millar (Barrow), S.English (Rangers), J.Kelly (Derry City)
Scotland: A.McLaren (St Johnstone), D.H.Gray (Rangers), J.S.Crapnell (Airdrieonians), A.Massie (Hearts), J.A.Johnstone (Hearts), W.Telfer (Motherwell), J.Crawford (Queen's Park), G.Stevenson (Motherwell), J.E.McGrory (Celtic), R.L.McPhail (Rangers), J.M.King (Hamilton Academicals)
Scorers: Scotland; McPhail 2, McGrory, King

17/10/1932, England 1 Ireland 0, Bloomfield Road, Blackpool. Att: 23,000
England: H.E.Hibbs (Birmingham), F.R.Goodall (Huddersfield Town), E.Blenkinsop (Sheffield Wed), A.H.Strange (Sheffield Wednesday), J.P.O'Dowd (Chelsea), S.Weaver (Newcastle United), S.D.Crooks (Derby County), R.Barclay (Sheffield United), W.R.Dean (Everton), T.C.Johnson (Everton), A.Cunliffe (Blackburn Rovers)
Ireland: E.Scott (Liverpool), W.Cook (Celtic), R.P.Fulton (Belfast Celtic), W.Mitchell (Distillery), J.Jones (Linfield), W.McCleery (Linfield), H.A.Duggan (Leeds United), P.Moore (Aberdeen), J.Dunne (Sheffield United), J.Doherty (Cliftonville), J.Kelly (Derry City)
Scorer: Barclay
Referee: H. Watson (Scotland)

26/10/1932, Scotland 2 Wales 5, Tynecastle, Edinburgh. Att. 31,000
Scotland: A.McLaren (St Johnstone), D.H.Gray (Rangers), D.Blair (Aston Villa), H.M.Wales (Motherwell), J.A.Johnstone (Hearts), J.R.Thomson (Everton), J.Crawford (Queen's Park), A.Thomson (Celtic), N.H.Dewar (Third Lanark), A.W.James (Arsenal), D.Duncan (Derby County)
Wales: W.R.John (Stoke City), B.D.Williams (Everton), B.Ellis (Motherwell), F.C.Keenor (Crewe Alexandra), T.P.Griffiths (Bolton Wanderers), D.Richards (Wolves), C.Phillips (Wolves), E.O'Callaghan (Tottenham Hotspur), D.J.Astley (Aston Villa), W.W.Robbins (WBA), D.J.Lewis (Swansea Town)
Scorers: Scotland; Dewar, Duncan. Wales; O'Callaghan 2, Griffiths, Astley, J. Thompson (og)
Referee: W.P. Harper (England)

16/11/1932, Wales 0 England 0, The Racecourse, Wrexham. Att. 25,167
Wales: W.R.John (Stoke City), B.D.Williams (Everton), B.Ellis (Motherwell), J.P.Murphy (WBA), T.P.Griffiths (Bolton Wanderers), D.Richards (Wolves), F.W.Warren (Middlesbrough), E.O'Callaghan (Tottenham Hotspur), D.J.Astley (Aston Villa), W.W.Robbins (WBA), D.J.Lewis (Swansea Town)
England: H.E.Hibbs (Birmingham), F.R.Goodall (Huddersfield Town), E.Blenkinsop (Sheffield Wed), J.Stoker (Birmingham), A.Young (Huddersfield Town), J.T.Tate (Aston Villa), S.D.Crooks (Derby County), D.N.Jack (Arsenal), G.Brown (Aston Villa), E.A.Sandford (WBA), A.Cunliffe (Blackburn Rovers)
Referee: S.Thompson (Ireland)

07/12/1932, Wales 4 Ireland 1, The Racecourse, Wrexham. Att. 8,500
Wales: W.R.John (Stoke City), B.D.Williams (Everton), R.F.John (Arsenal), J.P.Murphy (WBA), T.P.Griffiths (Bolton Wanderers), D.Richards (Wolves), W.E.Richards (Fulham), E.O'Callaghan (Tottenham Hotspur), D.J.Astley (Aston Villa), W.W.Robbins (WBA), W.Evans (Tottenham Hotspur)
Ireland: E.Scott (Liverpool), W.Cook (Celtic), T.Willighan (Burnley), W.Mitchell (Distillery), J.Jones (Linfield), W.McCleery (Linfield), W.Houston (Linfield), S.English (Rangers), J.Dunne (Sheffield United), J.Doherty (Cliftonville), J.Kelly (Derry City)
Scorers: Wales; Robbins 2, Astley 2
Ireland; English
Referee: G. Hewitt (England)

01/04/1933, Scotland 2 England 1, Hampden Park, Glasgow. Att: 134,170
Scotland: J.Jackson (Patrick Thistle), A.Anderson (Hearts), P.W.McGonagle (Celtic), P.Wilson (Celtic), R.Gillespie (Queen's Park), G.C.Brown (Rangers), J.Crawford (Queen's Park), J.Marshall (Rangers), J.E.McGrory (Celtic), R.L.McPhail (Rangers), D.Duncan (Derby County)
England: H.E.Hibbs (Birmingham), T.Cooper (Derby County), E.Blenkinsop (Sheffield Wed), A.H.Strange (Sheffield Wednesday), E.Hart (Leeds United), S.Weaver (Newcastle United), J.H.Hulme (Arsenal), R.W.Starling (Sheffield Wednesday), G.S.Hunt (Tottenham Hotspur), J.Pickering (Sheffield United), J.Arnold (Fulham)
Scorera: Scotland; McGrory 2. England; Hunt
Referee: S.Thompson (Ireland)

16/09/1933, Scotland 1 Ireland 2, Celtic Park, Glasgow. Att: 27,131
Scotland: J.D.Harkness (Hearts), A.Anderson (Hearts), P.W.McGonagle (Celtic), A.Massie (Hearts), A.Low (Falkirk), W.Telfer (Motherwell), J.M.Boyd (Newcastle United), A.Venters (Cowdenbeath), J.E.McGrory (Celtic), R.L.McPhail (Rangers), J.M.King (Hamilton Academicals)
Ireland: E.Scott (Liverpool), T.Willighan (Burnley), R.P.Fulton (Belfast Celtic), J.McMahon (Bohemians), J.Jones (Linfield), W.Mitchell (Chelsea), H.Blair (Swansea Town), A.E.Stevenson (Rangers), D.K.Martin (Belfast Celtic), J.Coulter (Belfast Celtic), J.Mahood (Ballymena)
Scorers: Scotland; McPhail. Ireland; Martin 2
Referee: E.J. Wood (England)

04/10/1933, Wales 3 Scotland 2, Ninian Park, Cardiff. Att. 40,000
Wales: W.R.John (Stoke City), S.Lawrence (Swansea Town), B.Ellis (Motherwell), J.P.Murphy (WBA), T.P.Griffiths (Middlesbrough), D.Richards (Wolves), C.Phillips (Wolves), E.O'Callaghan (Tottenham Hotspur), D.J.Astley (Aston Villa), W.W.Robbins (WBA), W.Evans (Tottenham Hotspur)
Scotland: J.Kennaway (Celtic), A.Anderson (Hearts), D.Urquhart (Hibernian), M.W.Busby (Leicester City), J.Blair (Motherwell), J.S.McLuckie (Manchester City), F.R.McGurk (Birmingham), J.McMenemy (Motherwell), W.MacFadyen (Motherwell), J.F.Easson (Portsmouth), D.Duncan (Derby County)
Scorers: Wales; Evans, Robbins, Astley
Scotland; MacFadyen, Duncan
Referee: E.J. Wood (England)

14/10/1933, Ireland 0 England 3, Windsor Park, Belfast. Att: 40,000
Ireland: E.Scott (Liverpool), S.E.Reid (Derby County), R.P.Fulton (Belfast Celtic), W.S.McMillen (Manchester United), J.Jones (Linfield), S.Jones (Distillery), H.A.Duggan (Leeds United), A.E.Stevenson (Rangers), D.K.Martin (Belfast Celtic), J.Coulter (Belfast Celtic), T.J.Priestley (Chelsea)
England: H.E.Hibbs (Birmingham), F.R.Goodall (Huddersfield Town), E.Hapgood (Arsenal), A.H.Strange (Sheffield Wednesday), J.P.Allen (Portsmouth), W.Copping (Leeds United), S.D.Crooks (Derby County), A.T.Grovesnor (Birmingham), J.W.Bowers (Derby County), C.S.Bastin (Arsenal), E.F.Brook (Manchester City)
Scorers: England; Grosvenor, Bowers, Brook
Referee: H. Watson (Scotland)

04/11/1933, Ireland 1 Wales 1, Windsor Park, Belfast. Att. 20,000
Ireland: E.Scott (Liverpool), S.E.Reid (Derby County), R.P.Fulton (Belfast Celtic), W.Mitchell (Chelsea), J.Jones (Linfield), S.Jones (Blackpool), E.J.Mitchell (Glentoran), A.E.Stevenson (Rangers), D.K.Martin (Belfast Celtic), J.Coulter (Belfast Celtic), J.Kelly (Derry City)
Wales: L.Evans (Birmingham), S.Lawrence (Swansea Town), D.O.Jones (Leicester City), A.Day (Tottenham Hotspur), H.Hanford (Swansea Town), D.Richards (Wolves), C.Phillips (Wolves), E.O'Callaghan (Tottenham Hotspur), E.M.Glover (Grimsby Town), T.J.Mills (Clapton Orient), E.R.Curtis (Birmingham)
Scorers: Ireland; Jones. Wales; Glover
Referee: M.C. Hutton (Scotland)

15/11/1933, England 1 Wales 2, St James' Park, Newcastle. Att. 15,000
England: H.E.Hibbs (Birmingham), F.R.Goodall (Huddersfield Town), E.Hapgood (Arsenal), A.H.Strange (Sheffield Wednesday), J.P.Allen (Portsmouth), W.Copping (Leeds United), S.D.Crooks (Derby County), A.T.Grovesnor (Birmingham), J.W.Bowers (Derby County), C.S.Bastin (Arsenal), E.F.Brook (Manchester City)
Wales: W.R.John (Stoke City), S.Lawrence (Swansea Town), D.O.Jones (Leicester City), J.P.Murphy (WBA), T.P.Griffiths (Middlesbrough), D.Richards (Wolves), C.Phillips (Wolves), E.O'Callaghan (Tottenham Hotspur), D.J.Astley (Aston Villa), T.J.Mills (Clapton Orient), W.Evans (Tottenham Hotspur)
Scorersa: England; Brook. Wales; Astley, Mills
Referee: S. Thompson (Ireland)

14/04/1934, England 3 Scotland 0, Wembley, London. Att: 92,363
England: F.Moss (Arsenal), T.Cooper (Derby County), E.Hapgood (Arsenal), J.Stoker (Birmingham), E.Hart (Leeds United), W.Copping (Leeds United), S.D.Crooks (Derby County), H.S.Carter (Sunderland), J.W.Bowers (Derby County), C.S.Bastin (Arsenal), E.F.Brook (Manchester City)

Scotland: J.Jackson (Chelsea), A.Anderson (Hearts), P.W.McGonagle (Celtic), A.Massie (Hearts), T.M.Smith (Kilmarnock), J.Miller (St Mirren), W.L.Cook (Bolton Wanderers), J.Marshall (Rangers), H.K.Gallacher (Chelsea), G.Stevenson (Motherwell), J.Connor (Sunderland)
Scorers: England; Bowers, Bastin, Brook
Referee: S. Thompson (Ireland)

29/09/1934, Wales 0 England 4, Ninian Park, Cardiff. Att: 36,692
Wales: W.R.John (PNE), S.Lawrence (Swansea Town), D.O.Jones (Leicester City), J.P.Murphy (WBA), T.P.Griffiths (Middlesbrough), D.Richards (Wolves), C.Phillips (Wolves), E.O'Callaghan (Tottenham Hotspur), R.Williams (Newcastle United), T.J.Mills (Leicester City), W.Evans (Tottenham Hotspur)
England: H.E.Hibbs (Birmingham), T.Cooper (Derby County), E.Hapgood (Arsenal), C.S.Britton (Everton), J.Barker (Derby County), J.Bray (Manchester City, S.Matthews (Stoke City), E.R.Bowden (Arsenal), S.F.Tilson (Manchester City), R.W.Westwood (Bolton Wanderers), E.F.Brook (Manchester City)
Scorers: England; Tilson 2, Brook, Matthews
Referee: S. Thompson (Ireland)

20/10/1934, Ireland 2 Scotland 1, Windsor Park, Belfast. Att: 39,752
Ireland: E.Scott (Belfast Celtic), J.Mackie (Portsmouth), R.P.Fulton (Belfast Celtic), W.S.McMillen (Manchester United), J.Jones (Linfield), W.Mitchell (Chelsea), H.A.Duggan (Leeds United), W.A.Gowdy (Linfield), D.K.Martin (Belfast Celtic), A.E.Stevenson (Everton), J.Coulter (Everton)
Scotland: J.Dawson (Rangers), A.Anderson (Hearts), P.W.McGonagle (Celtic), A.Massie (Hearts), J.M.Simpson (Rangers), A.C.Herd (Hearts), W.L.Cook (Bolton Wanderers), G.Stevenson (Motherwell), J.Smith (Rangers), P.Gallacher (Sunderland), J.Connor (Sunderland)
Scorers: Ireland; Martin, Coulter
Scotland; Gallacher
Referee: H.N. Mee (England)

21/11/1934, Scotland 3 Wales 2, Pittodrie, Aberdeen. Att. 26,334
Scotland: A.McClory (Motherwell), A.Anderson (Hearts), P.W.McGonagle (Celtic), A.Massie (Hearts), J.M.Simpson (Rangers), G.C.Brown (Rangers), W.L.Cook (Bolton Wanderers), T.Walker (Hearts), D.McCulloch (Hearts), C.E.Napier (Celtic), D.Duncan (Derby County)
Wales: W.R.John (PNE), S.Lawrence (Swansea Town), D.O.Jones (Leicester City), J.P.Murphy (WBA), H.Hanford (Swansea Town), D.Richards (Wolves), I.J.Hopkins (Brentford), R.Williams (Newcastle United), D.J.Astley (Aston Villa), T.J.Mills (Leicester City), C.Phillips (Wolves)
Scorers: Scotland; Napier 2, Duncan
Wales; Astley, Phillips
Referee: S. Thompson (Ireland)

06/02/1935, England 2 Ireland 1, Goodison Park, Liverpool. Att: 32,000
England: H.E.Hibbs (Birmingham), C.G.Male (Arsenal), E.Hapgood (Arsenal), C.S.Britton (Everton), J.Barker (Derby County), W.Copping (Arsenal), S.D.Crooks (Derby County), J.G.Bestall (Grimsby Town), E.J.Drake (Arsenal), C.S.Bastin (Arsenal), E.F.Brook (Manchester City)
Ireland: T.Breen (Belfast Celtic), W.Cook (Everton), R.P.Fulton (Belfast Celtic), W.A.Gowdy (Linfield), J.Jones (Linfield), W.Mitchell (Chelsea), J.Brown (Wolves), P.D.Doherty (Blackpool), D.K.Martin (Wolves), A.E.Stevenson (Everton), J.Coulter (Everton)
Scorers: England; Bastin 2. Ireland; Stevenson
Referee: W.E.Webb (Scotland)

27/03/1935, Wales 3 Ireland 1, The Racecourse, Wrexham. Att. 16,000
Wales: J.I.Hughes (Blackburn Rovers), B.D.Williams (Everton), R.F.John (Arsenal), J.P.Murphy (WBA), T.P.Griffiths (Middlesbrough), D.Richards (Wolves), I.J.Hopkins (Brentford), L.J.Jones (Coventry City), C.W.Jones (Birmingham), B.Jones (Wolves), C.Phillips (Wolves)
Ireland: T.Breen (Belfast Celtic), J.Mackie (Portsmouth), R.P.Fulton (Belfast Celtic), K.McCullough (Belfast Celtic), J.Jones (Linfield), W.A.Gowdy (Linfield), H.A.Duggan (Leeds United), J.Brown (Wolves), J.Bambrick (Chelsea), P.D.Doherty (Blackpool), J.Coulter (Everton)
Scorers: Wales; Hopkins, C.W. Jones, Phillips Ireland; Bambrick
Referee: Dr P. Bauwens (Germany)

06/04/1935, Scotland 2 England 0, Hampden Park, Glasgow. Att: 129,693
Scotland: J.Jackson (Chelsea), A.Anderson (Hearts), G.Cummings (Patrick Thistle), A.Massie (Hearts), J.M.Simpson (Rangers), G.C.Brown (Rangers), C.E.Napier (Celtic), T.Walker (Hearts), H.K.Gallacher (Derby County), R.L.McPhail (Rangers), D.Duncan (Derby County)
England: H.E.Hibbs (Birmingham), C.G.Male (Arsenal), E.Hapgood (Arsenal), C.S.Britton (Everton), J.Barker (Derby County), W.J.Alsford (Tottenham Hotspur), A.Geldard (Everton), C.S.Bastin (Arsenal), R.Gurney (Sunderland), R.W.Westwood (Bolton Wanderers), E.F.Brook (Manchester City)
Scorers: Scotland; Duncan 2
Referee: S.Thompson (Ireland)

05/10/1935, Wales 1 Scotland 1, Ninian Park, Cardiff. Att. 37,568
Wales: W.R.John (Sheffield United), S.Lawrence (Swansea Town), R.F.John (Arsenal), J.P.Murphy (WBA), T.P.Griffiths (Middlesbrough), D.Richards (Wolves), C.Phillips (Wolves), B.Jones (Wolves), E.M.Glover (Grimsby Town), L.J.Jones (Coventry City), W.W.Robbins (WBA)
Scotland: J. Jackson (Chelsea), A.Anderson (Hearts), G.Cummings (Patrick Thistle), A.Massie (Hearts), J.M.Simpson (Rangers), G.C.Brown (Rangers),

J.Delaney (Celtic), T.Walker (Hearts), M.W.Armstrong (Aberdeen), W.Mills (Aberdeen), D.Duncan (Derby County)
Scorers: Wales; Phillips. Scotland; Duncan
Referee: A.J .Caseley (England)

19/10/1935, Ireland 1 England 3, Windsor Park, Belfast. Att: 28,000
Ireland: E.Scott (Belfast Celtic), S.E.Reid (Derby County), C.A.Allen (Cliftonville), W.Mitchell (Chelsea), J.Jones (Linfield), R.J.Browne (Leeds United), J.Brown (Wolves), K.McCullough (Belfast Celtic), J.Bambrick (Chelsea), P.D.Doherty (Blackpool), J.Kelly (Derry City)
England: E.Sagar (Everton), C.G.Male (Arsenal), E.Hapgood (Arsenal), S.C.Smith (Leicester City), J.Barker (Derby County), J.Bray (Manchester City, R.J.Birkett (Middlesbrough), E.R.Bowden (Arsenal), S.F.Tilson (Manchester City), R.W.Westwood (Bolton Wanderers), E.F.Brook (Manchester City)
Scorers: Ireland; Brown. England; Tilson 2, Brook
Referee: W.E. Webb (Scotland)

13/11/1935, Scotland 2 Ireland 1, Tynecastle, Edinburgh. Att: 30,000
Scotland: J.Jackson (Chelsea), A.Anderson (Hearts), G.Cummings (Patrick Thistle), A.Massie (Hearts), J.M.Simpson (Rangers), A.C.Hastings (Sunderland), J.Delaney (Celtic), T.Walker (Hearts), M.W.Armstrong (Aberdeen), W.Mills (Aberdeen), D.Duncan (Derby County)
Ireland: E.Scott (Belfast Celtic), W.Cook (Everton), R.P.Fulton (Belfast Celtic), K.McCullough (Manchester City), J.Jones (Linfield), W.Mitchell (Chelsea), H.A.Duggan (Leeds United), A.E.Stevenson (Everton), J.Bambrick (Chelsea), P.D.Doherty (Blackpool), J.Kelly (Derry City)
Scorers: Scotland; Walker, Duncan. Ireland; Kelly
Referee: H. Nattrass (England)

05/02/1936, England 1 Wales 2, Molineux, Wolverhampton. Att. 27,519
England: H.E.Hibbs (Birmingham), C.G.Male (Arsenal), E.Hapgood (Arsenal), W.J.Crayston (Arsenal), J.Barker (Derby County), J.Bray (Manchester City), S.D.Crooks (Derby County), E.R.Bowden (Arsenal), E.J.Drake (Arsenal), C.S.Bastin (Arsenal), E.F.Brook (Manchester City)
Wales: W.R.John (Sheffield United), D.O.Jones (Leicester City), B.Ellis (Motherwell), J.P.Murphy (WBA), H.Hanford (Swansea Town), D.Richards (Brentford), I.J.Hopkins (Brentford), C.Phillips (Aston Villa), D.J.Astley (Aston Villa), B.Jones (Wolves), W.Evans (Tottenham Hotspur)
Scorers: England; Bowden. Wales; Astley, B.Jones
Referee: W.E.Webb (Scotland)

11/03/1936, Ireland 3 Wales 2, Celtic Park, Belfast. Att: 20,000
Ireland: E.Scott (Belfast Celtic), W.Cook (Everton), R.P.Fulton (Belfast Celtic), W.A.Gowdy (Hibernian), J.Jones (Hibernian), R.J.Browne (Leeds United), N.Kernaghan (Belfast Celtic), T.J.Gibb (Cliftonville),

D.K.Martin (Wolves), A.E.Stevenson (Everton), J.Kelly (Derry City)
Wales: W.R.John (Sheffield United), T.P.Griffiths (Aston Villa), D.O.Jones (Leicester City), J.P.Murphy (WBA), H.Hanford (Sheffield Wednesday), D.Richards (Brentford), I.J.Hopkins (Brentford), C.Phillips (Aston Villa), D.J.Astley (Aston Villa), B.Jones (Wolves), W.Evans (Tottenham Hotspur)
Scorers: Ireland; Kernaghan, Gibb, Stevenson
Wales; Phillips, Astley
Referee: H. Nattrass (England)

04/04/1936, England 1 Scotland 1, Wembley, London. Att: 93,267
England: E.Sagar (Everton), C.G.Male (Arsenal), E.Hapgood (Arsenal), W.J.Crayston (Arsenal), J.Barker (Derby County), J.Bray (Manchester City, S.D.Crooks (Derby County), R.Barclay (Sheffield United), G.H.Camsell (Middlesbrough), C.S.Bastin (Arsenal), E.F.Brook (Manchester City)
Scotland: J.Dawson (Rangers), A.Anderson (Hearts), G.Cummings (Aston Villa), A.Massie (Aston Villa), J.M.Simpson (Rangers), G.C.Brown (Rangers), J.Crum (Celtic), T.Walker (Hearts), D.McCulloch (Brentford), A.Venters (Rangers), D.Duncan (Derby County)
Scorers: England; Camsell. Scotland; Walker (pen)
Referee: W.R. Hamilton (Ireland)

17/10/1936, Wales 2 England 1, Ninian Park, Cardiff. Att: 44,729
Wales: A.Gray (Chester), H.G.Turner (Charlton Athletic), R.F.John (Arsenal), J.Warner (Swansea Town), T.P.Griffiths (Aston Villa), D.Richards (Brentford), I.J.Hopkins (Brentford), B.Jones (Wolves), E.M.Glover (Grimsby Town), L.J.Jones (Coventry City), S.Morris (Birmingham)
England: G.H.Holdcroft (PNE), B.Sproston (Leeds United), A.E.Catlin (Sheffield Wednesday), T.Smalley (Wolves), J.Barker (Derby County), E.R.Keen (Derby County), S.D.Crooks (Derby County), W.R.Scott (Brentford), F.C.Steele (Stoke City), R.W.Westwood (Bolton Wanderers), C.S.Bastin (Arsenal)
Scorers: Wales; Glover, Morris. England; Bastin
Referee: W.McLean (Ireland)

31/10/1936, Ireland 1 Scotland 3, Windsor Park, Belfast. Att: 45,000
Ireland: T.Breen (Belfast Celtic), W.Cook (Everton), R.P.Fulton (Belfast Celtic), W.S.McMillen (Manchester United), J.Jones (Hibernian), W.Mitchell (Chelsea), N.Kernaghan (Belfast Celtic), K.McCullough (Manchester City), D.K.Martin (Nottingham Forest), J.Coulter (Everton), J.Kelly (Derry City)
Scotland: J.Dawson (Rangers), A.Anderson (Hearts), R.F.Ancell (Newcastle United), A.Massie (Aston Villa), J.M.Simpson (Rangers), G.C.Brown (Rangers), A.D.Munro (Hearts), T.Walker (Hearts), D.McCulloch (Brentford), C.E.Napier (Derby County), D.Duncan (Derby County)
Scorers: Ireland; Kernaghan.
Scotland; McCulloch, Munro
Referee: T.J.Thompson (England)

18/11/1936, England 3 Ireland 1, Victoria Ground, Stoke. Att: 47,882
England: G.H.Holdcroft (PNE), C.G.Male (Arsenal), A.E.Catlin (Sheffield Wednesday), C.S.Britton (Everton), C.W.Gee (Everton), E.R.Keen (Derby County), F.Worrall (Portsmouth), H.S.Carter (Sunderland), F.C.Steele (Stoke City), C.S.Bastin (Arsenal), J.A.Johnson (Stoke City)
Ireland: T.Breen (Belfast Celtic), W.Cook (Everton), R.P.Fulton (Belfast Celtic), K.McCullough (Manchester City), J.Jones (Hibernian), W.Mitchell (Chelsea), J.Brown (Coventry City), A.E.Stevenson (Everton), T.L.Davis (Oldham Athletic), P.D.Doherty (Manchester City), J.Kelly (Derry City)
Scorers: England; Worrall, Carter, Bastin
Ireland; Davis
Referee: W.E.Webb (Scotland)

02/12/1936, Scotland 1 Wales 2, Dens Park, Dundee. Att: 23,858
Scotland: J.Dawson (Rangers), A.Anderson (Hearts), R.F.Ancell (Newcastle United), A.Massie (Aston Villa), J.M.Simpson (Rangers), G.C.Brown (Rangers), A.D.Munro (Hearts), T.Walker (Hearts), D.McCulloch (Brentford), W.Mills (Aberdeen), D.Duncan (Derby County)
Wales: A.Gray (Chester), H.G.Turner (Charlton Athletic), B.Ellis (Motherwell), J.P.Murphy (WBA), T.P.Griffiths (Aston Villa), D.Richards (Brentford), I.J.Hopkins (Brentford), B.Jones (Wolves), E.M.Glover (Grimsby Town), L.J.Jones (Coventry City), S.Morris (Birmingham)
Scorers: Scotland; Walker. Wales; Glover 2
Referee: Dr A.W. Barton (England)

17/03/1937, Wales 4 Ireland 1, The Racecourse, Wrexham. Att: 19,000
Wales: A.Gray (Chester), H.G.Turner (Charlton Athletic), D.O.Jones (Leicester City), J.P.Murphy (WBA), T.P.Griffiths (Aston Villa), D.Richards (Birmingham), I.J.Hopkins (Brentford), B.Jones (Wolves), E.M.Glover (Grimsby Town), L.J.Jones (Coventry City), F.W.Warren (Hearts)
Ireland: T.Breen (Manchester United), W.Cook (Everton), R.P.Fulton (Belfast Celtic), T.Brolly (Millwall), J.Jones (Hibernian), W.Mitchell (Chelsea), J.Brown (Coventry City), P.D.Doherty (Manchester City), S.J.Banks (Cliftonville), A.E.Stevenson (Everton), J.Coulter (Everton)
Scorers: Wales; B.Jones. Ireland; Stevenson
Refree: A.J. Jewell (England)

17/04/1937, Scotland 3 England 1, Hampden Park, Glasgow. Att: 149,547
Scotland: J.Dawson (Rangers), A.Anderson (Hearts), A.Beattie (PNE), A.Massie (Aston Villa), J.M.Simpson (Rangers), G.C.Brown (Rangers), J.Delaney (Celtic), T.Walker (Hearts), F.O'Donnell (PNE), R.L.McPhail (Rangers), D.Duncan (Derby County)
England: V.R.Woodley (Chelsea), C.G.Male (Arsenal), S.Barkas (Manchester City), C.S.Britton (Everton), A.Young (Huddersfield Town), J.Bray (Manchester

City), S.Matthews (Stoke City), H.S.Carter (Sunderland), F.C.Steele (Stoke City), R.W.Starling (Aston Villa), J.A.Johnson (Stoke City)
Scorers: Scotland; McPhail 2, O'Donnell
England; Steele
Referee: W.McLean (Ireland)

23/10/1937, Ireland 1 England 5, Windsor Park, Belfast. Att: 36,000
Ireland: T.Breen (Manchester United), W.E.Hayes (Huddersfield Town), W.Cook (Everton), W.Mitchell (Chelsea), J.Jones (Glenavon), R.J.Browne (Leeds United), N.Kernaghan (Belfast Celtic), A.E.Stevenson (Everton), D.K.Martin (Nottingham Forest), P.D.Doherty (Manchester City), O.Madden (Norwich City)
England: V.R.Woodley (Chelsea), B.Sproston (Leeds United), S.Barkas (Manchester City), W.J.Crayston (Arsenal), S.Cullis (Wolves), W.Copping (Arsenal), A.Geldard (Everton), G.W.Hall (Tottenham Hotspur), G.R.Mills (Chelsea), L.A.Goulden (WHU), E.F.Brook (Manchester City)
Scorers: Ireland; Stevenson
England; Mills 3, Hall, Brook
Referee: W.E. Webb (Scotland)

30/10/1937, Wales 2 Scotland 1, Ninian Park, Cardiff. Att: 41,800
Wales: A.Gray (Chester), H.G.Turner (Charlton Athletic), W.M.Hughes (Birmingham), J.P.Murphy (WBA), H.Hanford (Sheffield Wednesday), D.Richards (Birmingham), C.Phillips (Aston Villa), L.J.Jones (Arsenal), E.Perry (Doncaster Rovers), B.Jones (Wolves), S.Morris (Birmingham)
Scotland: J.Dawson (Rangers), A.Anderson (Hearts), G.Cummings (Aston Villa), A.Massie (Aston Villa), J.M.Simpson (Rangers), G.C.Brown (Rangers), R.F.Main (Rangers), T.Walker (Hearts), F.O'Donnell (PNE), R.L.McPhail (Rangers), D.Duncan (Derby County)
Scorers: Wales; B.Jones, Morris. Scotland; Massie
Referee: C.E. Argent (England)

10/11/1937, Scotland 1 Ireland 1, Pittodrie, Aberdeen. Att: 21,878
Scotland: J.Dawson (Rangers), A.Anderson (Hearts), G.Cummings (Aston Villa), D.McKenzie (Brentford), J.M.Simpson (Rangers), A.C.Hastings (Sunderland), J.Delaney (Celtic), T.Walker (Hearts), J.Smith (Rangers), R.L.McPhail (Rangers), R.Reid (Brentford)
Ireland: T.Breen (Manchester United), W.E.Hayes (Huddersfield Town), W.Cook (Everton), M.Doherty (Derry City), W.S.McMillen (Chesterfield), W.Mitchell (Chelsea), J.Brown (Coventry City), J.McAlinden (Belfast Celtic), D.K.Martin (Nottingham Forest), P.D.Doherty (Manchester City), J.Coulter (Grimsby Town)
Scorers: Scotland; Smith. Ireland; Doherty
Referee: A.J. Jewell (England)

17/11/1937, England 2 Wales 1, Ayresome Park, Middlesbrough. Att: 30,608
England: V.R.Woodley (Chelsea), B.Sproston (Leeds United), S.Barkas (Manchester City), W.J.Crayston (Arsenal), S.Cullis (Wolves), W.Copping (Arsenal), S.Matthews (Stoke City), G.W.Hall (Tottenham Hotspur), G.R.Mills (Chelsea), L.A.Goulden (WHU), E.F.Brook (Manchester City)
Wales: A.Gray (Chester), H.G.Turner (Charlton Athletic), W.M.Hughes (Birmingham), J.P.Murphy (WBA), H.Hanford (Sheffield Wednesday), D.Richards (Birmingham), I.J.Hopkins (Brentford), L.J.Jones (Arsenal), E.Perry (Doncaster Rovers), B.Jones (Wolves), S.Morris (Birmingham)
Scorers: England; Matthews, Hall. Wales; Perry
Referee: W.E. Webb (Scotland)

16/03/1938, Ireland 1 Wales 0, Windsor Park, Belfast. Att: 15,000
Ireland: J.F.Twoomey (Leeds United), W.Cook (Everton), R.P.Fulton (Belfast Celtic), T.Brolly (Millwall), W.S.McMillen (Chesterfield), R.J.Browne (Leeds United), J.Brown (Coventry City), P.Farrell (Hibernian), J.Bambrick (Chelsea), A.E.Stevenson (Everton), J.Coulter (Grimsby Town)
Wales: A.Gray (Chester), H.G.Turner (Charlton Athletic), W.M.Hughes (Birmingham), G.H.Green (Charlton Athletic), T.G.Jones (Everton), D.Richards (Birmingham), I.J.Hopkins (Brentford), L.J.Jones (Arsenal), E.Perry (Doncaster Rovers), B.Jones (Wolves), F.W.Warren (Hearts)
Scorer: Ireland; Bambrick
Referee: H.R.A. Mortimer (England)

09/04/1938, England 0 Scotland 1, Wembley, London. Att: 93,267
England: V.R.Woodley (Chelsea), B.Sproston (Leeds United), E.Hapgood (Arsenal), C.K.Willingham (Huddersfield Town), S.Cullis (Wolves), W.Copping (Arsenal), S.Matthews (Stoke City), G.W.Hall (Tottenham Hotspur), M.Fenton (Middlesbrough), J.E.Stephenson (Leeds United), C.S.Bastin (Arsenal)
Scotland: D.S.Cumming (Middlesbrough), A.Anderson (Hearts), A.Beattie (PNE), W.Shankly (PNE), T.M.Smith (PNE), G.C.Brown (Rangers), J.V.Milne (Middlesbrough), T.Walker (Hearts), F.O'Donnell (Blackpool), G.Mutch (PNE), R.Reid (Brentford)
Scorer: Scotland; Walker
Referee: W.R. Hamilton (Ireland)

08/10/1938, Ireland 0 Scotland 2, Windsor Park, Belfast. Att: 40,000
Ireland: T.Breen (Manchester United), W.E.Hayes (Huddersfield Town), W.Cook (Everton), W.S.McMillen (Chesterfield), M.T.O'Mahoney (Bristol Rovers), R.J.Browne (Leeds United), J.Brown (Birmingham), J.McAlinden (Belfast Celtic), D.K.Martin (Nottingham Forest), A.E.Stevenson (Everton), J.Coulter (Chelmsford City)
Scotland: J.Dawson (Rangers), J.Carabine (Third Lanark), A.Beattie (PNE), W.Shankly (PNE), J.Dykes (Hearts), G.D.Paterson (Celtic), J.Delaney (Celtic),

T.Walker (Hearts), J.Crum (Celtic), J.Divers (Celtic), T.Gillick (Everton)
Scorers: Scotland; Walker, Delaney
Referee: H.R.A. Mortimer (England)

22/10/1938, Wales 4 England 2, Ninian Park, Cardiff. Att: 55,000
Wales: W.R.John (Swansea Town), W.J.Whatley (Tottenham Hotspur), W.M.Hughes (Birmingham), G.H.Green (Charlton Athletic), T.G.Jones (Everton), D.Richards (Birmingham), I.J.Hopkins (Brentford), L.J.Jones (Arsenal), D.J.Astley (Derby County), B.Jones (Arsenal), R.H.Cumner (Arsenal)
England: V.R.Woodley (Chelsea), B.Sproston (Tottenham Hotspur), E.Hapgood (Arsenal), C.K.Willingham (Huddersfield Town), A.Young (Huddersfield Town), W.Copping (Arsenal), S.Matthews (Stoke City), J.Robinson (Sheffield Wednesday), T.Lawton (Everton), L.A.Goulden (WHU), W.Boyes (Everton)
Scorers: Wales; Astley 2, B.Jones, Hopkins
England; Matthews, Lawton (pen)
Referee: W.R. Hamilton (Ireland)

09/11/1938, Scotland 3 Wales 2, Tynecastle, Edinburgh. Att: 34,810
Scotland: J.B.Brown (Clyde), A.Anderson (Hearts), A.Beattie (PNE), W.Shankly (PNE), R.D.Baxter (Middlesbrough), A.Miller (Hearts), J.Delaney (Celtic), T.Walker (Hearts), D.McCulloch (Derby County), R.Beattie (PNE), T.Gillick (Everton)
Wales: W.R.John (Swansea Town), W.J.Whatley (Tottenham Hotspur), W.M.Hughes (Birmingham), D.J.Dearson (Birmingham), T.G.Jones (Everton), D.Richards (Birmingham), I.J.Hopkins (Brentford), L.J.Jones (Arsenal), D.J.Astley (Derby County), B.Jones (Arsenal), R.H.Cumner (Arsenal)
Scorers: Scotland; Walker 2, Gillick
Wales; Astley, LJ Jones
Referee: T.J. Thompson (England)

16/11/1938, England 7 Ireland 0, Old Trafford, Manchester. Att: 40,386
Ireland: J.F.Twoomey (Leeds United), W.E.Hayes (Huddersfield Town), W.Cook (Everton), T.Brolly (Millwall), W.S.McMillen (Chesterfield), R.J.Browne (Leeds United), D.Cochrane (Leeds United), A.E.Stevenson (Everton), H.Baird (Huddersfield Town), P.D.Doherty (Manchester City), J.Brown (Birmingham)
England: V.R.Woodley (Chelsea), W.W.Morris (Wolves), E.Hapgood (Arsenal), C.K.Willingham (Huddersfield Town), S.Cullis (Wolves), J.Mercer (Everton), S.Matthews (Stoke City), G.W.Hall (Tottenham Hotspur), T.Lawton (Everton), J.E.Stephenson (Leeds United), J.R.Smith (Millwall)
Scorers: England; Hall 5, Lawton, Matthews
Referee: P. Craigmyle (Scotland)

15/03/1939, Wales 3 Ireland 1, The Racecourse, Wrexham. Att: 22,997
Wales: G.Poland (Wrexham), H.G.Turner (Charlton Athletic), W.M.Hughes (Birmingham), G.H.Green (Charlton Athletic), T.G.Jones (Everton), D.J.Dearson (Birmingham), I.J.Hopkins (Brentford), L.M.Boulter (Brentford), E.M.Glover (Grimsby Town), B.Jones (Arsenal), R.H.Cumner (Arsenal)
Ireland: T.Breen (Manchester United), W.Cook (Everton), M.P.Butler (Blackpool), T.Brolly (Millwall), J.Leatham (Belfast Celtic), E.Weir (Clyde), D.Cochrane (Leeds United), A.E.Stevenson (Everton), D.Milligan (Chesterfield), P.D.Doherty (Manchester City), J.Brown (Birmingham)
Scorers: Wales; Boulter, Glover, Cumner
Ireland; Milligan
Referee: Dr A.W. Barton (England)

15/04/1939, Scotland 1 England 2, Hampden Park, Glasgow. Att: 149,269
Scotland: J.Dawson (Rangers), J.Carabine (Third Lanark), G.Cummings (Aston Villa), W.Shankly (PNE), R.D.Baxter (Middlesbrough), A.McNab (WBA), A.McSpadyen (Patrick Thistle), T.Walker (Hearts), J.Dougall (PNE), A.Venters (Rangers), J.V.Milne (Middlesbrough)
England: V.R.Woodley (Chelsea), W.W.Morris (Wolves), E.Hapgood (Arsenal), C.K.Willingham (Huddersfield Town), S.Cullis (Wolves), J.Mercer (Everton), S.Matthews (Stoke City), G.W.Hall (Tottenham Hotspur), T.Lawton (Everton), L.A.Goulden (WHU), A.Beasley (Huddersfield Town)
Scorers: Scotland; Dougall
England; Lawton, Beasley
Referee: W.R. Hamilton (Ireland)

FIFA MATCH

Central Europe 3 Western Europe 1, 20 June 1937, Amsterdam, 30,000.
Central Europe: Olivieri (Italy); Sesta (Austria), Schmaus (Austria) (sub: Rava (Italy)), Serantoni (Italy), Andreolo (Italy), Lazar (Hungary), Sas (Hungary), Meazza (Italy), Piola (Italy), Dr Sarosi (Hungary), Nejedly (Czechoslovakia).
Western Europe: Jakob (Germany); Paverik (Belgium) (sub: Joakin (Belgium), Caldenhove (Holland), Kitzinger (Germany), Goldbrunner (Germany), Delfour (France), Lehner (Germany), R Braine (Belgium), Bakhuys (Holland), Smit (Holland), Van den Eynde (Belgium).
Scorers: Central Europe: Sas 2, Nejedly. Western Europe: Bakhuys.
Referee: A.J.Jewell (England).

HOME COUNTRIES AND EIRE
v. OTHER COUNTRIES

AUSTRIA

Austria 0 England 0, at Hohe Warte, Vienna,
14 May 1930, 61,000.
Austria: R.Hiden, K.Rainer, J.Tandler, H.Klima,
L.Hoffman, J.Luef, I.Siegl, W.Nausch, F.Gschweidl,
J.Horvath, F.Wessely.
England: H.E.Hibbs (Birmingham), F.R.Goodall
(Huddersfield Town), E.Blenkinsop (Sheffield Wed),
A.H.Strange (Sheffield Wednesday), M.Webster
(Middlesbrough), S.Cowan (Manchester City),
S.D.Crooks (Derby County), D.N.Jack (Arsenal),
V.M.Watson (WHU), J.Bradford (Birmingham),
E.Rimmer (Sheffield Wednesday)
Referee: J.Mutters (Holland).

Austria 5 Scotland 0, at Hohe Warte, Vienna,
16 May 1931, 45,000.
Austria: R.Hiden, R.Schramseis, J.Blum, G.Braun,
J.Smistik, K.Gall, K.Zischek, F.Gschweidl, M.Sindelar,
A.Schall, A.Vogel.
Scotland: J.Jackson (Patrick Thistle), D.Blair (Clyde),
J.Nibloe (Kilmarnock), C.D.McNab (Dundee),
J.McDougall (Liverpool), G.Walker (St Mirren),
A.R.Love (Aberdeen), J.Paterson (Cowdenbeath),
J.F.Easson (Portsmouth), J.Robertson (Dundee),
D.H.Liddell (East Fife)
Scorers: Austria: Zischek 2, Sindelar, Schall, Vogel.
Referee: P.Ruoff (Switzerland).

England 4 Austria 3, at Stamford Bridge, London,
12 December 1932, 42,000.
England: H.E.Hibbs (Birmingham), F.R.Goodall
(Huddersfield Town), E.Blenkinsop (Sheffield Wed),
A.H.Strange (Sheffield Wednesday), E.Hart (Leeds
United), E.R.Keen (Derby County), S.D.Crooks (Derby
County), D.N.Jack (Arsenal), J.Hampson (Blackpool),
W.H.Walker (Aston Villa), W.E.Houghton (Aston Villa)
Austria: R.Hiden, K.Rainer, K.Sesta, K.Gall, J.Smistik,
W.Nausch, K.Zischek, F.Gschweidl, M.Sindelar,
A.Schall, A.Vogel.
Scorers: England: Hampson 2, Houghton, Crooks.
Austria: Zischek 2, Sindelar.
Referee: J.Langenus (Belgium).

Scotland 2 Austria 2, Hampden Park, Glasgow,
29 November 1933, 62,000.
Scotland: J.Kennaway (Celtic), A.Anderson (Hearts),
P.W.McGonagle (Celtic), D.D.Meiklejohn (Rangers),
P.R.Watson (Blackpool), G.C.Brown (Rangers),
D.H.Ogilvie (Motherwell), R.F.Bruce (Middlesbrough),
W.MacFadyen (Motherwell), R.L.McPhail (Rangers),
D.Duncan (Derby County)
Austria: P.Platzer, A.Janda, K.Sesta, F.Wagner,
J.Smistik, W.Nausch, K.Zischek, J.Bican, M.Sindelar,
A.Schall, R.Viertl.
Scorers: Scotland: Meiklejohn, McFadyen. Austria:
Zischek, Schall.   Referee: J.Langenus (Belgium).

Austria 2 England 1, at Praterstadion, Vienna,
6 May 1936, 60,000.
Austria: P.Platzer, K.Sesta, W.Schmaus, J.Urbanek,
H.Mock, W.Nausch, R.Geiter, J.Stroh, M.Sindelar,
J.Bican, R.Viertl.
England: , E.Sagar (Everton), C.G.Male (Arsenal),
E.Hapgood (Arsenal), W.J.Crayston (Arsenal), J.Barker
(Derby County), W.Copping (Arsenal), R.Spence
(Chelsea), E.R.Bowden (Arsenal), G.H.Camsell
(Middlesbrough), C.S.Bastin (Arsenal), H.H.Hobbis
(Charlton Athletic)
Scorers: Austria: Geiter, Viertl. England: Camsell.
Referee: J.Langenus (Belgium).

Austria 1, Scotland 1. Praterstadion, Vienna,
9 May 1937, 63,000.
Austria: P.Platzer, K.Sesta, W.Schmaus, K.Adamek,
J.Pekarek, W.Nausch, R.Geiter, J.Stroh, M.Sindelar,
C.Jerusalem, J.Pesser.
Scotland: J.Dawson (Rangers), A.Anderson (Hearts),
A.Beattie (PNE), A.Massie (Aston Villa), J.M.Simpson
(Rangers), A.McNab (Sunderland), J.Delaney (Celtic),
T.Walker (Hearts), F.O'Donnell (PNE), C.E.Napier
(Derby County), T.Gillick (Everton)
Scorers: Austria: Jerusalem. Scotland: O'Donnell (F).
Referee: J.Langenus (Belgium).

BELGIUM

Belgium 1, Irish Free State 3, Molenbeek, Brussels,
11 May 1930, 18,000.
Belgium: A.Badjou, T.Nouwens, N.Hoydonckx,
P.Braine, A.Hellemans, J.De Clercq, L.Versijp,
F.Adams, M.Vanderbauwhede, J.Moeschal, D.Bastin.
Irish Free State: T.G.Farquharson (Cardiff City),
W.Lacey (Shelbourne), J.McCarthy (Bohemians),
W.Glen (Shamrock Rovers), M.T.O'Brien (Norwich
City), F.McLoughlin (Fordsons), H.A.Duggan (Leeds
United), J.J.Flood (Shamrock Rovers), J.Dunne
(Sheffield United), A.F.Horlacher (Bohemians),
L.Golding (Shamrock Rovers)
Scorers: Belgium: Bastin.
Irish Free State: Dunne J 2, Flood.
Referee: R.Melcon (Spain).

Belgium 1, England 4, Molenbeek, Brussels,
16 May 1931, 30,000.
Belgium: A.Badjou, T.Nouwens, C.Joacim, C.Simons,
A.Hellemans, J.Moeschal, L.Versijp, B.Voorhoof,
J.Capelle, J.Van Beeck, Stan Van den Eynde.
England: H.Turner (Huddersfield Town), F.R.Goodall
(Huddersfield Town), E.Blenkinsop (Sheffield Wed),
A.H.Strange (Sheffield Wednesday), S.Cowan
(Manchester City), J.T.Tate (Aston Villa), S.D.Crooks
(Derby County), H.Roberts (Millwall), T.Waring (Aston
Villa), H.A.Burgess (Sheffield Wednesday),
W.E.Houghton (Aston Villa)
Scorers: Belgium: Capelle. England: Burgess 2,
Houghton (pen), Henry Roberts.
Referee: Dr. P.J. Bauwens (Germany).

Irish Free State 4, Belgium 4, World Cup, Dalymount Park, Dublin, 25 February 1934, 35,000.
Irish Free State: J.Foley (Cork), J.Lynch (Cork Bohemians), T.Burke (Cork), P.Gaskins (Shamrock Rovers), J.O'Reilly (Aberdeen), J.Kendrick (Dolphin), W.Kennedy (St James's Gate), D.Byrne (Coleraine), P.Moore (Aberdeen), T.O'Keefe (Cork), J.Kelly (Derry City)
Belgium: A.Vandewijer, J.Pappaert, P.Smellinckx, J.Van Ingelghem, F.Welkenhuyzen, D.Bourgeios, L.Versijp, J.Brichaut, J.Capelle, A.Saeys, Stan Van den Eynde (Francois Van den Eynde).
Scorers: Irish Free State: Moore 4. Belgium: Capelle, Stan Van den Eynde, Francois Van den Eynde.
Referee: T.Crew (England).

Belgium 3, England 2, Heysel, Brussels, 9 May 1936, 40,000.
Belgium: A.Badjou, R.Paverick, P.Smllinckx, P.Dalem, E.Stijnen, A.De Winter, J.Fievez, R.Lamont, J.Capelle, H.Isemborghs, A.Franckx.
England: E.Sagar (Everton), C.G.Male (Arsenal), E.Hapgood (Arsenal), W.J.Crayston (Arsenal), B.Joy (Corinthians), W.Copping (Arsenal), R.Spence (Chelsea), S.Barkas (Manchester City), G.H.Camsell (Middlesbrough), J.Cunliffe (Everton), H.H.Hobbis (Charlton Athletic)
Scorers: Belgium: Isemborghs 2, Fievez. England: Camsell, Hobbis.
Referee: Dr. F.J.Van Moorsel (Holland).

CZECHOSLOVAKIA

Czechoslovakia 2 England 1, Letna, Prague, 16 May 1934, 35,000.
Czechoslovakia: F.Planicka, L.Zenisek, J.Ctyroky, J.Kostalek, S.Cambai, R.Kreil, F.Junek, J.Silny, J.Sobotka, O.Njedly, A.Puc.
England: F.Moss (Arsenal), T.Cooper (Derby County), E.Hapgood (Arsenal), T.Gardner (Aston Villa), E.Hart (Leeds United), H.Burrows (Sheffield Wednesday), S.D.Crooks (Derby County), J.Beresford (Aston Villa), S.F.Tilson (Manchester City), C.S.Bastin (Arsenal), E.F.Brook (Manchester City)
Scorers: Czechoslovakia: Nejedly, Puc. England: Tilson.
Referee: J.Langenus (Belgium).

Czechoslovakia 1 Scotland 3, Sparta, Prague, 15 May 1937, 35,000.
Czechoslovakia: F.Planicka, J.Burgr, J.Ctyroky, J.Kostalek, J.Boucek, K.Kolsky V.Zlatnik, F.Svoboda, J.Sobotka, V.Kopecky, A.Puc.
Scotland: J.Dawson (Rangers), R.B.Hogg (Celtic), A.Beattie (PNE), C.M.Thomson (Sunderland), J.M.Simpson (Rangers), G.C.Brown (Rangers), J.Delaney (Celtic), T.Walker (Hearts), F.O'Donnell (PNE), R.L.McPhail (Rangers), T.Gillick (Everton), 1
Scorers: Czechoslovakia: Puc. Scotland: Simpson, McPhail, Gillick.
Referee: Dr.P.J.Bauwens (Germany).

England 5 Czechoslovakia 4, White Hart Lane, London, 1 December 1937, 45,879.
England: V.R.Woodley (Chelsea), B.Sproston (Leeds United), S.Barkas (Manchester City), W.J.Crayston (Arsenal), S.Cullis (Wolves), W.Copping (Arsenal), S.Matthews (Stoke City), G.W.Hall (Tottenham Hotspur), G.R.Mills (Chelsea), L.A.Goulden (WHU), J.R.Morton (WHU)
Czechoslovakia: F.Planicka, J.Kostalek, F.Daucik, A.Vodicka, J.Boucek, K.Kolsky, J.Riha, F.Kloz, J.Zeman, O.Nejedly, A.Puc.
Scorers: Matthews 3, Crayston, Morton. Czechoslovakia: Nejedly 2, Puc, Zeman.
Referee: J.Langenus (Belgium)

Scotland 5 Czechoslovakia 0, Hampden Park, Glasgow, 8 December 1937, 41,000
Scotland: W.Waugh (Hearts), A.Anderson (Hearts), G.Cummings (Aston Villa), G.Robertson (Kilmarnock), R.Johnston (Sunderland), G.C.Brown (Rangers), P.S.Buchanan (Chelsea), T.Walker (Hearts), D.McCulloch (Brentford), A.Black (Hearts), D.Kinnear (Rangers), 1
Czechoslovakia: F.Planicka, J.Kostalek, F.Daucik, A.Vodicka, J.Boucek, K.Kolsky, J.Riha, J.Sobotka, J.Zeman, O.Nejedly, A.Puc.
Scorers: Scotland: McCulloch 2, Black, Buchanan, Kinnear.
Referee: T.J. Thompson (England).

Czechoslovakia 2 Ireland 2, Sparta, Prague, 18 May 1938, 17,000.
Czechoslovakia: F.Planicka, J.Burgr, F.Daucik, J.Kostalek, J.Boucek, V.Kopecky, J.Riha, L.Simunek, V.Bradec, J.Ludl, O.Nejedly.
Ireland: G.McKenzie (Southend United), P.Gaskins (St James's Gate), W.C.Gorman (Bury), J.O'Reilly (St James's Gate), M.T.O'Mahoney (Bristol Rovers), C.J.Turner (WHU), K.P.O'Flanagan (Bohemians), J.Dunne (Shamrock Rovers), T.L.Davis (Tranmere Rovers), J.J.Carey (Manchester United), T.O'Keefe (Waterford),
Scorers: Czechoslovakia: Nejedly 2, l pen. Ireland: Davis, Dunne J.
Referee: R.Barlassina (Italy).

FINLAND

Finland 0 England 8, Pallokentta, Helsinki, 20 May 1937, 9, 533.
Finland: P.Salminen, F.Karjagin, A.Pyy, K.Oskanen, E.Lahti, A.Rinne, P.Virtanen, K.Wecksrom, A.Lehtonen, P.Larvo, Y.Kylmala.
England: V.R.Woodley (Chelsea), C.G.Male (Arsenal), E.Hapgood (Arsenal), C.K.Willingham (Huddersfield Town), H.A.Betmead (Grimsby Town), W.Copping (Arsenal), A.J.Kirchen (Arsenal), J.Robinson (Sheffield Wednesday), J.Payne (Luton Town), F.C.Steele (Stoke City), J.A.Johnson (Stoke City)
Scorers: England: Payne 2, Steele 2, Kirchen, Johnson, Willingham, Robinson.
Referee: R.Eklow (Sweden).

FRANCE

France 0 Scotland 2, Colombes, Paris, 18 May 1930, 25,000.
France :A.Thepot, M.Anatol, M.Capelle, J.Larent, M.Banide, A.Chantrel M.Kauffmann, H.Pavillard, M.Pinel, E.Delfour, P.Korb.
Scotland: J.Thomson (Celtic), J.Nelson (Cardiff City), J.S.Crapnell (Airdrieonians), P.Wilson (Celtic), G.Walker (St Mirren), F.R.Hill (Aberdeen), A.S.Jackson (Huddersfield Town), A.G.Cheyne (Aberdeen), H.K.Gallacher (Newcastle United), G.Stevenson (Motherwell), J.Connor (Sunderland)
Scorers: Scotland: Gallacher 2.
Referee: R.L. Van Praag (Belgium).

France 5 England 2, Colombes, Paris, 14 May 1931, 35,000.
France: A.Thepot; E.Mattler, M.Capelle, L.Finot, J.Kaucsar, P.Hornus, E.Liberati, E.Delfour, R.Mercier, L.Laurent, M.Langiller.
England: , H.Turner (Huddersfield Town), T.Cooper (Derby County), E.Blenkinsop (Sheffield Wed), A.H.Strange (Sheffield Wednesday), T.Graham (Nottingham Forest), J.T.Tate (Aston Villa), S.D.Crooks (Derby County), G.T.Stephenson (Sheffield Wed), T.Waring (Aston Villa), H.A.Burgess (Sheffield Wednesday), W.E.Houghton (Aston Villa)
Scorers: Mercier 2, Laurent, Langiller, Delfour.
England: Crooks, Waring.
Referee: J.Langenus (Belgium).

France 1 Scotland 3, Colombes, Paris, 8 May 1932, 8,000
France: A.Thepot; M.Anatol, A.Chardar, E.scharwath, J.Kaucsar, J.Laurent, E.Liberati, J.Alcazar, R.Mercier, R.Gerard, M.Langiller.
Scotland: J.D.Harkness (Hearts), J.S.Crapnell (Airdrieonians), J.Nibloe (Kilmarnock), A.Massie (Hearts), R.Gillespie (Queen's Park), J.Miller (St Mirren), J.Crawford (Queen's Park), A.Thomson (Celtic), N.H.Dewar (Third Lanark), R.L.McPhail (Rangers), A.L.Morton (Rangers)
Scorers: France: Langiller (pen). Scotland: Dewar 3.
Referee: A.Carraro (Italy).

France 1 Wales 1, Colombes, Paris, 25 May 1933, 25,000.
France: R.Defosse; J.Vandooren, E.Mattler, C.Delmer, G.Verriest, E.Delfour, M.Polge, N.Lietaer, J.Nicolas, R.Rio, M.Langiller.
Wales: W.R.John (Stoke City), R.F.John (Arsenal), S.Lawrence (Swansea Town), J.P.Murphy (WBA), T.P.Griffiths (Middlesbrough), C.Jones (Arsenal), T.J.Jones (Sheffield Wednesday), L.J.Jones (Cardiff City), T.Bamford (Wrexham), W.W.Robbins (WBA), F.W.Warren (Middlesbrough)
Scorers: France: Nicolas. Wales: Griffiths.
Referee: R.L. Van Praag (Belgium).

England 4 France 1, White Hart Lane, London, 6 December 1933, 17,097.
England: , H.E.Hibbs (Birmingham), F.R.Goodall (Huddersfield Town), D.Fairhurst (Newcastle United), A.H.Strange (Sheffield Wednesday), A.Rowe (Tottenham Hotspur), W.Copping (Leeds United), S.D.Crooks (Derby County), A.T.Grovesnor (Birmingham), G.H.Camsell (Middlesbrough), G.W.Hall (Tottenham Hotspur), E.F.Brook (Manchester City)
France: R.Defosse; J.Vandooren, E.Mattler, C.Delmer, M.Banide, E.Delfour, R.Courtois, R.Gerard, J.Nicolas, R.Rio, E.Veinante.
Scorers: England: Camsell 2, Brook, Grosvenor. France: Veinante.
Referee: J.Langenus (Belgium).

France 0 Ireland 2, Colombes, Paris, 23 May 1937, 16, 688.
France: L.Di Lorto; A.Ben Bouali, R.Diagne, F.Bourbotte, G.Meuris, E.Delfour, M.Lauri, K.Ignace, R.Courtois, M.Frutuoso, A.Aston.
Ireland: T.Breen (Manchester United), W.O'Neill (Dundalk), J.J.Feenan (Sunderland), J.O'Reilly (St James's Gate), C.J.Turner (Southend United), C.Moulson (Notts County), J.Brown (Coventry City), D.Jordan (Wolves), J.Dunne (Southampton), P.Farrell (Hibernian), W.J.Fallon (Notts County),
Scorers: Ireland: Jordan, Brown.
Referee: A.Krist (Czechoslovakia).

France 2 England 4, Colombes, Paris, 26 May 1938, 46,920.
France: L.Di Lorto; H.Cazenave, E.Mattler, F.Bourbotte, G.Jordan, R.Diagne, R.Courtois, M.Brusseaux, J.Nicolas, O.Heisserer, A.Aston.
England: V.R.Woodley (Chelsea), B.Sproston (Leeds United), E.Hapgood (Arsenal), C.K.Willingham (Huddersfield Town), A.Young (Huddersfield Town), S.Cullis (Wolves), S.Matthews (Stoke City), F.H.Broome (Aston Villa), E.J.Drake (Arsenal), L.A.Goulden (WHU), C.S.Bastin (Arsenal)
Scorers: France: Jordan, Nicolas. England: Drake 2, Broome, Bastin (pen).
Referee: L.Baert (Belgium).

France 2 Wales 1, Colombes, Paris, 21 May 1939, 23,000.
France: J.Darui; J.Vandooren, E.Mattler, F.Bourbotte, G.Jordan, R.Diagne, J.Bigot, O.Heisserer, D.Koranyi, E.Veinante, J.Mathe.
Wales: G.Poland (Wrexham), H.G.Turner (Charlton Athletic), W.M.Hughes (Birmingham), G.H.Green (Charlton Athletic), H.Hanford (Sheffield Wednesday), J.Warner (Manchester United), J.J.Williams (Wrexham), D.J.Astley (Blackpool), C.W.Jones (Birmingham), D.J.Dearson (Birmingham), S.Morris (Birmingham)
Scorers: France: Bigot, Koranyi. Wales: Astley.
Referee: L. Franken (Belgium).

GERMANY

Germany 3 England 3, Grunewald, Berlin,
10 May 1930, 60,000.
Germany: W.Kress; F.Schutz, H.Stubb, C.Heidkamp,
L.Leikngerger, H.Mantel, J.Bergmaier, J.Pottinger,
E.Kuzorra, R.Hofmann, L.Hofmann.
England: , H.E.Hibbs (Birmingham), F.R.Goodall
(Huddersfield Town), E.Blenkinsop (Sheffield Wed),
A.H.Strange (Sheffield Wednesday), M.Webster
(Middlesbrough), W.Marsden (Sheffield Wednesday),
S.D.Crooks (Derby County), D.N.Jack (Arsenal),
V.M.Watson (WHU), J.Bradford (Birmingham),
E.Rimmer (Sheffield Wednesday)
Scorers: Germany: Hofmann R 3. England: Bradford 2,
Jack.
Referee: J.Mutters (Holland).

Germany 3 Irish Free State 1, Kampfbahn Rote Erde,
Dortmund, 8 May 1935, 35,000.
Germany: F.Buchloh; P.Janes, W.Tiefel, P.Zielinski,
L.Goldbrunner, J.Bender, E.Lehner, O.Siffling, A.Lenz,
L.Damminger, J.Fath.
Irish Free State: J.Foley (Celtic), P.Gaskins (Shamrock
Rovers), L.Dunne (Manchester City), P.O'Kane
(Bohemians), C.Lennon (St James's Gate),
F.Hutchinson (Drumcondra), P.Ellis (Bohemians),
P.Moore (Aberdeen), A.Rigby (St James's Gate),
J.Donnelly (Dundalk), P.Monahan (Sligo Rovers)
Scorers: Germany: Damminger 2, Lehner. Irish Free
State: Ellis.
Referee: A.Krist (Czechoslovakia).

England 3 Germany 0, White Hart Lane, London,
4 December 1935, 54,164.
England: H.E.Hibbs (Birmingham), C.G.Male
(Arsenal), E.Hapgood (Arsenal), W.J.Crayston
(Arsenal), J.Barker (Derby County), J.Bray
(Manchester City), S.Matthews (Stoke City), H.S.Carter
(Sunderland), G.H.Camsell (Middlesbrough),
R.W.Westwood (Bolton Wanderers), C.S.Bastin
(Arsenal)
Germany: H.Jakob; S.Haringer, R.Munzenberg,
P.Janes, L.Goldbrunner , R.Gramlich, E.Lehner,
F.Szepan, K.Hohmann, J.Rasselnberg, J.Fath.
Scorers: England: Camsell 2, Bastin.
Referee: O.Olsson (Sweden).

Scotland 2 Germany 0, Ibrox Park, Glasgow,
14 October 1936, 50,000.
Scotland: J.Dawson (Rangers), A.Anderson (Hearts),
G.Cummings (Aston Villa), A.Massie (Aston Villa),
J.M.Simpson (Rangers), G.C.Brown (Rangers),
J.Delaney (Celtic), T.Walker (Hearts), M.W.Armstrong
(Aberdeen), R.L.McPhail (Rangers), D.Duncan (Derby
County)
Germany: H.Jakob; R.Munzenberg, A.Munkert,
P.Janes, L.Goldbrunner, A.Kitzinger, F.Elbern,
R.Gellesch, O.Siffling, F.Szepan, A.Urban.
Scorers: Scotland: Delaney 2
Referee: H.Nattrass (England).

Ireland 5 Germany 2, Dalymount Park, Dublin,
17 October 1936, 30,000.
Ireland: ,J.Foley (Celtic), W.O'Neill (Dundalk),
W.C.Gorman (Bury), J.O'Reilly (St James's Gate),
C.J.Turner (Southend United), N.Connolly (Cork),
P.Ellis (Bohemians), J.Donnelly (Dundalk), T.L.Davis
(Oldham Athletic), P.Moore (Shamrock Rovers),
M.Geoghegan (St James's Gate)
Germany: H.Jakob; R.Munzenberg, A.Kunkert,
J.Rozinski, L.Goldbrunner, A.Kitzinger, E.Lehner,
O.Siffling, K.Hohmann, F.Szepan, S.Kobierski.
Scorers:Ireland: Davis 2 (1 pen), Donnelly 2,
Geoghegan. Germany: Szepan, Kobierski.
Referee: W.E. Webb (Scotland).

Germany 3 England 6, Olympia-Stadion, Berlin,
14 May 1938, 120,000.
Germany: H.Jakob; P.Janes, R.Munzenberg, A.Kupfer,
L.Goldbrunner, A.Kitzinger, E.Lehner, R.Gellesch,
J.Gauchel, F.Szepan, H.Pesser.
England: V.R.Woodley (Chelsea), B.Sproston (Leeds
United), E.Hapgood (Arsenal), C.K.Willingham
(Huddersfield Town), A.Young (Huddersfield Town),
D.Welsh (Charlton Athletic), S.Matthews (Stoke City),
J.Robinson (Sheffield Wednesday), F.H.Broome (Aston
Villa), L.A.Goulden (WHU), C.S.Bastin (Arsenal)
Scorers: Germany: Gellesch, Gauchel, Pesse. England:
Robinson 2, Broome, Matthews, Goulden.
Referee: J. Langenus (Belgium).

Germany 1 Ireland 1, Weserstadion, Bremen,
23 May 1939, 35,000.
Germany: H.Jakob; P.Janes, J.Streitle, A.Kupfer,
H.Rohde, A.Kitzinger, E.Lehner, W.Hahnemann,
J.Gauchel, H.Schon, W.Arlt.
Ireland: G.McKenzie (Southend United), W.O'Neill
(Dundalk), M.Hoy (Dundalk), J.O'Reilly (St James's
Gate), M.T.O'Mahoney (Bristol Rovers), E.Weir
(Clyde), K.P.O'Flanagan (Bohemians), J.Dunne
(Shamrock Rovers), P.Bradshaw (St James's Gate),
J.J.Carey (Manchester United), W.J.Fallon (Sheffield
Wednesday)
Scorers: Germany: Schon. Ireland: Bradshaw.
Referee: Dr O. Remke (Denmark).

HOLLAND (NETHERLANDS)

Holland 0 Irish Free State 2, Olympic Stadion,
Amsterdam, 8 May 1932, 30,000.
Holland: G.Van der Meulen; M.Weber, S. van Run,
B.Paauwe, W.Anderiesen, P. van Heel, F.Wels,
W.Volkers, W.Lagendaal, J.Mol, J.van Nellen.
Irish Free State: M.McCarthy (Shamrock Rovers),
J.Daly (Shamrock Rovers), P.Byrne (Shelbourne),
J.O'Reilly (Brideville), M.T.O'Brien (Watford),
P.Kinsella (Shamrock Rovers), W.Kennedy (St James's
Gate), A.E.Stevenson (Dolphin), P.Moore (Shamrock
Rovers), A.F.Horlacher (Bohemians), J.Kelly (Derry
City)
Scorers: Irish Free State: O'Reilly, Moore.
Referee: J.Langenus (Belgium).

Holland 5 Irish Free State 2, World Cup. Olympic
Stadion, Amsterdam, 8 April 1934, 38,000.
Holland: A.van Male; M.Weber, S.van Run,
H.Pellikaan, W.Anderiesen, P.van Heel, F.Wels,
L.Vente, B.Bakhuys, K.Smit, K.Mijnders.
Irish Free State: J.Foley (Cork), P.Gaskins (Shamrock
Rovers), P.Byrne (Drumcondra), J.O'Reilly (Aberdeen),
H.A.Chatton (Cork), J.Kendrick (Dolphin), W.Kennedy
(St James's Gate), J.Squires (Shelbourne), P.Moore
(Aberdeen), W.Jordan (Bohemians), P.Meehan
(Drumcondra) [A.F. Horlacher (Bohemians)]
Scorers: Holland: Bakhuys 2, Smit 2, Vente. Irish Free
State: Moore, Squires.
Referee: Dr P.J.Bauwens (Germany).

Holland 0 England 1, Olympic Stadion, Amsterdam,
18 May 1935, 33,000.
Holland: L.Halle; B.Caldenhove, S.van Run, B.Paauwe,
W.Anderiesen, P.van Heel, F.Wels, D.Drok, B.Bakhuys,
K.Smit, K.Mijnders.
England: H.E.Hibbs (Birmingham), C.G.Male
(Arsenal), E.Hapgood (Arsenal), T.Gardner (Aston
Villa), J.Barker (Derby County), H.Burrows (Sheffield
Wednesday), F.Worrall (Portsmouth), G.R.Eastham
(Bolton Wanderers), W.G.Richardson (WBA),
R.W.Westwood (Bolton Wanderers), W.Boyes (WBA)
Scorer: Worrall.
Referee: Dr P.J.Bauwens (Germany).

Irish Free State 3 Holland 5, Dalymount Park, Dublin,
8 December 1935, 35,000.
Irish Free State: W.Harrington (Cork), W.O'Neill
(Dundalk), W.McGuire (Bohemians), W.Glen
(Shamrock Rovers), P.Andrews (Bohemians), J.O'Reilly
(Brideville), P.Ellis (Bohemians), J.Donnelly
(Dundalk), P.Moore (Shamrock Rovers), A.F.Horlacher
(Bohemians), J.Kendrick (Dolphin)
Holland: L.Halle; M.Weber, B.Caldenhove, H.Paauwe,
W.Anderiesen, P.van Heel, F.Wels, D.Drok, B.Bakhuys,
K.Smit, J.van Nellen.
Scorers: Irish Free State: Horlecher 2, Ellis. Holland:
van Nellen 2, Drok, Bakhuys, Smit.
Referee: Dr P.J.Bauwens (Germany).

Holland 1 Scotland 3, Olympic Stadion, Amsterdam,
21 May 1938, 50,000.
Holland: A.van Male; M.Weber, B.Caldenhove,
B.Paauwe, W.Anderiesen, P.van Heel, F.Wels, H.van
Spaandonck, L.Vente, F.van der Veen, B.de Harder.
Scotland: J.Dawson (Rangers), A.Anderson (Hearts),
J.Carabine (Third Lanark), T.B.McKillop (Rangers),
J.Dykes (Hearts), G.C.Brown (Rangers), A.D.Munro
(Blackpool), T.Walker (Hearts), F.O'Donnell
(Blackpool), A.Black (Hearts), F.Murphy (Celtic).
Scorers: Holland: Vente. Scotland: Black, Walker,
Murphy.
Referfee: C.E.Argent (England).

HUNGARY

Hungary 2 England 1, Ulloi, Budapest,
10 May 1934, 35,000.
Hungary: J.Hada; J.Vago, L.Sternberg, A.Szalay,
G.Szucs, G.Lazar, A.Rokk, I.Avar, G.Sarosi I, G.Toldi,
T.Kemeny.
England: , F.Moss (Arsenal), T.Cooper (Derby County),
E.Hapgood (Arsenal), J.Stoker (Birmingham), E.Hart
(Leeds United), H.Burrows (Sheffield Wednesday),
S.D.Crooks (Derby County), H.S.Carter (Sunderland),
S.F.Tilson (Manchester City), C.S.Bastin (Arsenal),
E.F.Brook (Manchester City)
Scorers: Hungary: Sarosi I, Avar. England: Tilson.
Referee: R.Barlassina (Italy).

Irish Free State 2 Hungary 4, Dalymount Park, Dublin,
15 December 1934, 27,000.
Irish Free State: J.Foley (Celtic), P.Gaskins (Shamrock
Rovers), P.Bermingham (St James's Gate), P.O'Kane
(Bohemians), C.Lennon (St James's Gate),
A.F.Horlacher (Bohemians), R.Griffiths (Walsall),
J.Donnelly (Dundalk), A.Rigby (St James's Gate),
P.Moore (Aberdeen), W.J.Fallon (Notts County)
Hungary: J.Hada (A.Szabo); J.Vago, L.Sternberg,
G.Seres, G.Szucs, A.Szalay, G.Markos, J.Vincze, I.Avar,
L.Cseh II, P.Titkos.
Scorers: Irish Free State: Donnelly, Bermingham (pen).
Hungary: Avar 2, Markos, Foley (og).
Referee: J.Langenus (Belgium).

Hungary 3 Ireland 3, Hungaria Uti Stadium, Budapest,
3 May 1936, 15,000.
Hungary: A.Szabo (G.Hori); G.Futo, S.Biro, B.Magda,
J.Turay, J.Dudas, F.Sas, J.Vincze, G.Sarosi I, L.Cseh II,
T.Kemeny.
Ireland: W.Harrington (Cork), W.O'Neill (Dundalk),
W.C.Gorman (Bury), W.Glen (Shamrock Rovers),
C.Moulson (Lincoln City), J.O'Reilly (Brideville),
H.A.Duggan (Leeds United), J.Donnelly (Dundalk),
J.Dunne (Arsenal), O.Madden (Cork), W.J.Fallon
(Notts County)
Scorers: Hungary: Sas, Sarosi I 2. Ireland: Dunne J 2,
O'Reilly.
Referee: Dr J.Brull (Czechoslovakia).

England 6 Hungary 2, Highbury, London,
2 December 1936, 36,000.
England: G.J.Tweedy (Grimsby Town), C.G.Male
(Arsenal), A.E.Catlin (Sheffield Wednesday),
C.S.Britton (Everton), A.Young (Huddersfield Town),
E.R.Keen (Derby County), S.D.Crooks (Derby County),
E.R.Bowden (Arsenal), E.J.Drake (Arsenal), H.S.Carter
(Sunderland), E.F.Brook (Manchester City)
Hungary: A.Szabo; J.Vago, S.Biro, G.Lazar, G.Sarosi I,
J.Dudas, L.Sas, J.Vincze, L.Cseh II, G.Zsengeller,
P.Titkos.
Scorers: England: Drake 3, Brook, Britton, Carter.
Hungary: Vincze, Cseh II.
Referee: L. Le Clerq (France).

Ireland 2 Hungary 3, Dalymount Park, Dublin,
6 December 1936, 30,000.
Ireland: J.Foley (Celtic), W.O'Neill (Dundalk),
W.C.Gorman (Bury), J.O'Reilly (St James's Gate),
C.J.Turner (Southend United), C.Moulson (Notts
County), P.Ellis (Bohemians), J.Donnelly (Dundalk),
T.L.Davis (Oldham Athletic), P.Moore (Shamrock
Rovers), W.J.Fallon (Notts County),
Hungary: J.Palinkas (A.Szabo); G.Polgar, J.Vago,
J.Turay, G;Szucs, J.Dudas, L.Cseh II, J.Vincze, G.Sarosi
I, G.Toldi, P.Titkos.
Scorers: Ireland: Fallon, Davis. Hungary: Cseh II,
Toldi, Titkos.
Referee: H.Nattrass (England).

Scotland 3 Hungary 1, Ibrox Park, Glasgow,
7 December 1938, 23,000.
Scotland: J.Dawson (Rangers), A.Anderson (Hearts),
A.Beattie (PNE), W.Shankly (PNE), R.D.Baxter
(Middlesbrough), J.S.Symon (Rangers), A.McSpadyen
(Patrick Thistle), T.Walker (Hearts), D.McCulloch
(Derby County), A.Black (Hearts), T.Gillick (Everton), 1
Hungary: A.Szabo; L.Koranyi I, S.Biro, G.Polgar,
J.Turay, J.Dudas, P.Titkos, L.Cseh II, Dr G.Sarosi,
G.Toldi, L.Gyetvai.
Scorers: Scotland: Black, Walker (pen), Gillick.
Hungary: Dr G Sarosi (pen).
Referee: H.Nattrass (England).

Ireland 2 Hungary 2, The Mardyke, Cork,
19 March 1939, 12,000.
Ireland: G.McKenzie (Southend United), W.C.Gorman
(Brentford), M.Hoy (Dundalk), J.O'Reilly (St James's
Gate), C.J.Turner (WHU), E.Weir (Clyde),
K.P.O'Flanagan (Bohemians), J.Dunne (Shamrock
Rovers), P.Bradshaw (St James's Gate), J.J.Carey
(Manchester United), T.Foy (Shamrock Rovers),
Hungary: A.Szabo; L.Koranyi I, S.Biro, G.Lazar,
B.Sarosi III, I.Balogh I, S.Adam, G.Zsengeller,
F.Kolloth, I.Kiszely, L.Gyetvai.
Scorers: Ireland: Bradshaw, Carey. Hungary:
Zsengeller, Kollath.
Referee: H.Nattrass (England).

Hungary 2 Ireland 2, MTK Stadium, Budapest,
18 May 1939, 15,000.
Hungary: A.Szabo; K.Kis, S.Biro, A.Szalay, G.Szucs,
I.Balogh I, J.Szanto, Dr G.Sarosi, F.Kollath, I.Kiszely,
A.Nagy I.
Ireland: G.McKenzie (Southend United), W.O'Neill
(Dundalk), M.Hoy (Dundalk), J.O'Reilly (St James's
Gate), M.T.O'Mahoney (Bristol Rovers), E.Weir
(Clyde), K.P.O'Flanagan (Bohemians), J.Dunne
(Shamrock Rovers), P.Bradshaw (St James's Gate),
J.J.Carey (Manchester United), W.J.Fallon (Sheffield
Wednesday),
Scorers: Hungary: Kollath, Sarosi.
Ireland: O'Flanagan 2.
Referee: Dr P.J.Bauwens (Germany).

ITALY

Italy 3 Scotland 0, Stadio Partito Nazionale Fascista,
Rome, 20 May 1931, 25,000.
Italy: G.Combi; E.Monzeglio, U.Caligaris, A.Ferraris IV,
F.Bernardini, L.Bertolini, R.Constantino, R.Cesarini,
G.Meazza, Ferrari Giovanni, R.Orsi.
Scotland: J.Jackson (Patrick Thistle), D.Blair (Clyde),
J.Nibloe (Kilmarnock), C.D.McNab (Dundee),
J.McDougall (Liverpool), J.Miller (St Mirren), A.R.Love
(Aberdeen), J.Paterson (Cowdenbeath), W.G.Boyd
(Clyde), J.Robertson (Dundee), D.H.Liddell (East Fife)
Scorers: Constantino, Meazza, Orsi.
Referee: Dr P.J.Bauwens (Germany).

Italy 1 England 1, Stadio Partito Nazionale Fascista,
Rome, 13 May 1933, 50,000.
Italy: Combi; V.Rosetta, U.Caligaris, M.Pizziolo,
L.Monti, L.Bertolini, R.Constantino, G.Meazza,
A.Schiavio, Ferrari Giovanni, R.Orsi.
England: H.E.Hibbs (Birmingham), F.R.Goodall
(Huddersfield Town), E.Hapgood (Arsenal),
A.H.Strange (Sheffield Wednesday), T.A.White
(Everton), W.Copping (Leeds United), A.Geldard
(Everton), J.R.Richardson (Newcastle United),
G.S.Hunt (Tottenham Hotspur), W.I.Furness (Leeds
United), C.S.Bastin (Arsenal)
Scorers: Italy: Ferrari Giovanni. England: Bastin.
Referee: Dr P.J.Bauwens (Germany).

England 3 Italy 2, Highbury, London,
14 November 1934, 56,044.
England: F.Moss (Arsenal), C.G.Male (Arsenal),
E.Hapgood (Arsenal), C.S.Britton (Everton), J.Barker
(Derby County), W.Copping (Arsenal), S.Matthews
(Stoke City), E.R.Bowden (Arsenal), E.J.Drake
(Arsenal), C.S.Bastin (Arsenal), E.F.Brook (Manchester
City)
Italy: C.Ceresoli; E.Monzeglio, L.Allemandi, A.Ferraris
IV, L.Monti, L.Bertolini, E.Guaita, P.Serantoni,
G.Meazza, Ferrari Giovanni, R.Orsi.
Scorers: Italy: Meazza 2. England: Brook 2, Drake.
Referee: O.Olsson (Sweden).

Italy 2 England 2, San Siro, Milan,
13 May 1939, 70,000.
Italy: A.Olivieri; A.Foni, P.Rava, T.Depetrini,
M.Andreolo, U.Locatelli, A.Biavati, P.Serantoni,
S.Piola, G.Meazza, G.Colaussi.
England: V.R.Woodley (Chelsea), C.G.Male (Arsenal),
E.Hapgood (Arsenal), C.K.Willingham (Huddersfield
Town), S.Cullis (Wolves), J.Mercer (Everton),
S.Matthews (Stoke City), G.W.Hall (Tottenham
Hotspur), T.Lawton (Everton), L.A.Goulden (WHU),
F.H.Broome (Aston Villa)
Scorers: Italy: Biavati, Piola. England: Lawton, Hall.
Referee: Dr P.J.Bauwens (Germany).

LUXEMBOURG

Luxembourg 1 Ireland 5, Luxembourg Stadion,
9 May 1936, 8,000.
Luxembourg: JP.Hoscheid, JP.Frisch, V.Majerus,
J.Schmit, Alfred Kieffer, J.Fischer, O.Stamet, A.Schmit,
L.Mart, R.Geib, T.Speicher.
Ireland: W.Harrington (Cork), W.O'Neill (Dundalk),
W.C.Gorman (Bury), W.Glen (Shamrock Rovers),
C.Moulson (Lincoln City), J.O'Reilly (Brideville),
H.A.Duggan (Leeds United), J.Donnelly (Dundalk),
J.Dunne (Arsenal), P.Ellis (Bohemians), J.Kelly (Derry
City)
Scorers: Luxembourg: Mart. Ireland: Dunne J 2, Kelly
2, Donnelly.
Referee: Dr P.J.Bauwens (Germany).

NORWAY

Norway 0 England 6, Ulleval, Oslo,
14 May 1937, 20,000.
Norway: H.Johansen; N.Eriksen, O.Holmsen,
F.Ulleberg, J.Juve, R.Holmberg, O.Frantzen,
R.Kvammen, A.Martinsen, M.Isaksen, A.Brustad.
England: V.R.Woodley (Chelsea), C.G.Male (Arsenal),
A.E.Catlin (Sheffield Wednesday), C.S.Britton
(Everton), A.Young (Huddersfield Town), W.Copping
(Arsenal), A.J.Kirchen (Arsenal), T.Galley (Wolves),
F.C.Steele (Stoke City), L.A.Goulden (WHU),
J.A.Johnson (Stoke City)
Scorers: England: Steele 2, Kirchen, Galley, Goulden,
Holmsen (og).
Referee: E.Ulrich (Denmark).

Norway 3 Ireland 2, World Cup, Ulleval, Oslo,
10 October 1937, 28,000.
Norway: T.Blohm; R.Johannessen, O.Holmsen,
F.Ulleberg, N.Eriksen, R.Holmberg, O.Frantzen,
R.Kvammen, A.Martinsen, M.Isaksen, A.Brustad.
Ireland: G.McKenzie (Southend United), J.Williams
(Shamrock Rovers), M.Hoy (Dundalk), J.O'Reilly (St
James's Gate), C.J.Turner (Southend United),
P.Kinsella (Shamrock Rovers), T.Donnelly
(Drumcondra), J.Donnelly (Dundalk), J.Dunne
(Shamrock Rovers), W.Jordan (Bohemians),
M.Geoghegan (St James's Gate)
Scorers: Norway: Kvammen 2, Martinsen. Ireland:
Dunne J, Geoghegan.
Referee: Dr P.J.Bauwens (Germany).

Ireland 3 Norway 3, World Cup, Dalymount Park,
Dublin, 7 November 1937, 27,000.
Ireland: G.McKenzie (Southend United), W.O'Neill
(Dundalk), W.C.Gorman (Bury), J.O'Reilly (St James's
Gate), C.J.Turner (Southend United), T.Arrigan
(Waterford), K.P.O'Flanagan (Bohemians),
H.A.Duggan (Newport County), J.Dunne (Shamrock
Rovers), J.J.Carey (Manchester United), T.Foy
(Shamrock Rovers),
Norway: S.Nordby; R.Johannessen, O.Holmsen,
K.Henriksen, N.Eriksen, R.Holmberg, K.Eeg,
R.Kvammen, A.Matinsen, O.Frantzen, J.Hval.

Scorers: Ireland: Dunne J. O'Flanagan, Duggan.
Norway: Kvammen 2, Martinsen.
Referee: J.Gibbs (England).

England 4 Norway 0, St James's Park, Newcastle,
9 November 1938, 39, 887.
England: V.R.Woodley (Chelsea), B.Sproston
(Manchester City), E.Hapgood (Arsenal),
C.K.Willingham (Huddersfield Town), S.Cullis
(Wolves), J.D.Wright (Newcastle United), S.Matthews
(Stoke City), F.H.Broome (Aston Villa), T.Lawton
(Everton), R.W.Dix (Derby County), J.R.Smith
(Millwall)
Norway: H.Johansen; L.Martinsen, O.Holmsen,
K.Henriksen, N.Eriksen, R.Holmberg, K.Brynildsen,
R.Kvammen, A.Martinsen, M.Isaksen, A.Brustad.
Scorers: England: Smith 2, Dix, Lawton.
Referee: J.M.Martin (Scotland).

POLAND

Poland 6 Ireland 0, Legia, Warsaw, 22 May 1938,
25,000.
Poland: E.Madejski; W.Szczepaniak, A.Galecki,
W.Gora, J.Wasiewicz, E.Dytko, R.Poiec I, L.Piontek,
F.Scherfke II, E.Willimowski G.Wodarz.
Ireland: G.McKenzie (Southend United) [W.
Harrington (Cork)], P.Gaskins (St James's Gate),
W.C.Gorman (Bury), J.O'Reilly (St James's Gate),
M.T.O'Mahoney (Bristol Rovers), C.J.Turner (WHU),
K.P.O'Flanagan (Bohemians), J.Dunne (Shamrock
Rovers), T.L.Davis (Tranmere Rovers), J.J.Carey
(Manchester United), T.O'Keefe (Waterford).
Scorers: Poland: Wodarz 2, Piontek 2, Wilimowski,
Wasiewicz.
Referee: F.Majorszky (Hungary).

Ireland 3 Poland 2, Dalymount Park, Dublin,
13 November 1938, 34, 295.
Ireland: G.McKenzie (Southend United), W.C.Gorman
(Bury), M.Hoy (Dundalk), J.O'Reilly (St James's Gate),
M.T.O'Mahoney (Bristol Rovers), R.Lunn (Dundalk),
K.P.O'Flanagan (Bohemians), J.Dunne (Shamrock
Rovers), P.Bradshaw (St James's Gate), J.J.Carey
(Manchester United), W.J.Fallon (Notts County)
Poland: E.Madejski (R.Mrugala); W.Szczepaniak,
A.Galecki, W.Gora, E.Nye, E.Dytko, R.Piec I, L.Piontek,
J.Wostal, E.Wilimowski, G.Wodarz.
Scorers: Ireland: Fallon, Carey, Dunne J. Poland:
Wilimowski, Piontek.
Referee: Dr P.J.Bauwens (Germany).

ROMANIA

Romania 0 England 2, Stadionul ANEF, Bucharest,
24 May 1939, 40,000.
Romania: D.Pavlovici, ; R.Burger, L.Sfera, V.Cossini,
A.Juhasz, R.Demetrovici, C.Orza, S.Ploesteanu,
I.Bodola, N.Reuter, S.Dobay.
England: V.R.Woodley (Chelsea), C.G.Male (Arsenal),
W.W.Morris (Wolves), J.Mercer (Everton), S.Cullis
(Wolves), W.Copping (Leeds United), F.H.Broome

(Aston Villa), L.A.Goulden (WHU), T.Lawton (Everton), D.Welsh (Charlton Athletic), L.C.Smith (Brentford)
Scorers: England: Welsh, Goulden
Referee: J.Langenus (Belgium).

SPAIN

Spain 1 Irish Free State 1, Estadi Olimpic de Montjuich, Barcelona, 26 April 1931, 50,000.
Spain: R.Zamora; Ciriaco, J.Quincoces, Marti, Sole, Castillo, Piera, Goiburu, Samitier, Arocha, Gorostiza.
Irish Free State: T.G.Farquharson (Cardiff City), G.Lennox (Dolphin), P.Byrne (Dolphin), J.Robinson (Dolphin), H.A.Chatton (Shelbourne), S.Byrne (Bohemians), J.J.Flood (Shamrock Rovers), C.Dowdall (Cork), P.Moore (Shamrock Rovers), C.Reid (Brideville), P.J.Kavanagh (Celtic)
Scorers: Spain: Arocha.Irish Free State: Moore.
Referee: S.Romanhino (Portugal).

England 7 Spain 1, Highbury, London, 9 December 1931, 55,000.
England: H.E.Hibbs (Birmingham), E.Blenkinsop (Sheffield Wed), A.H.Strange (Sheffield Wednesday), C.W.Gee (Everton), A.F.Campbell (Huddersfield Town), S.D.Crooks (Derby County), J.W.Smith (Portsmouth), W.R.Dean (Everton), T.C.Johnson (Everton), E.Rimmer (Sheffield Wednesday)
Spain: R.Zamora; Zabalo, J.Quincoces, Cilaurren, Gamborena, Roberto, Vantolra, Leon, Samitier, Hilario, Gorostiza.
Scorers: England: Smith 2, Johnson 2, Crooks 2, Dean. Spain: Gorostiza.
Referee: Dr P.J.Bauwens (Germany).

Irish Free State 0 Spain 5, Dalymount Park, Dublin, 13 December 1931, 35,000.
Irish Free State: T.G.Farquharson (Cardiff City), G.Lennox (Dolphin), L.Doyle (Dolphin), W.Glen (Shamrock Rovers), H.A.Chatton (Dumbarton), F.McLoughlin (Cork), J.J.Flood (Shamrock Rovers), P.Gallagher (Falkirk), D.Byrne (Shamrock Rovers), A.F.Horlacher (Bohemians), P.J.Kavanagh (Celtic)
Spain: Blasco; Ciriaco, Zabalo, Leon, Gaborena, Roberto, Vantolra, Luis Regueiro, Samitier, Arocha, Gorostiza.
Scorers: Spain: Luis Regueiro 2, Arocha, Samitier, Vantolra.
Referee: J.Langenus (Belgrium).

SWEDEN

Sweden 0 England 4, Rasunda Solna, Stockholm, 17 May 1937, 34, 119.
Sweden: G.Sjoberg; N.Axelsson, W.Skold, F.Berg, Sven Andersson, Ernst Andersson, G.Josefsson, E.Persson, S.Jonasson, K.E.Grahn, Axel Nilsson.
England: V.R.Woodley (Chelsea), C.G.Male (Arsenal), A.E.Catlin (Sheffield Wednesday), C.S.Britton (Everton), A.Young (Huddersfield Town), W.Copping

(Arsenal), A.J.Kirchen (Arsenal), T.Galley (Wolves), F.C.Steele (Stoke City), L.A.Goulden (WHU), J.A.Johnson (Stoke City)
Scorers: England: Steele 3, Johnson.
Referee: J.Langenus (Belgium).

SWITZERLAND

Switzerland 2 Scotland 3, Charmilles, Geneva, 24 May 1931, 10,000.
Switzerland: C.Pasche; S.Minelli, R.Ramseyer, E.Loichot, O.Imhof, G.Gilardoni, E.Kramer, A.Syrvet, A.Buche, A.Abegglen, M.Fauguel.
Scotland: J.Jackson (Patrick Thistle), J.S.Crapnell (Airdrieonians), J.Nibloe (Kilmarnock), C.D.McNab (Dundee), G.Walker (St Mirren), J.Miller (St Mirren), A.R.Love (Aberdeen), J.Paterson (Cowdenbeath), W.G.Boyd (Clyde), J.F.Easson (Portsmouth), D.H.Liddell (East Fife)
Scorers: Switzerland: Buche, Fauguel. Scotland: Easson, Boyd, Love.
Referee: A.Carraro (Italy).

Switzerland 0 England 4, Neufeld, Berne, 20 May 1933, 26,000.
Switzerland: F.Sechehaye; S.Minelli K.Bieser, G.Gilardoni, O.Imhof, E.Hufschmid, W.von Kanel, A.Abegglen, R.Passello, M.Abegglen, A.Jaeck.
England: , H.E.Hibbs (Birmingham), F.R.Goodall (Huddersfield Town), E.Hapgood (Arsenal), A.H.Strange (Sheffield Wednesday), J.P.O'Dowd (Chelsea), W.Copping (Leeds United), A.Geldard (Everton), J.R.Richardson (Newcastle United), G.S.Hunt (Tottenham Hotspur), C.S.Bastin (Arsenal), E.F.Brook (Manchester City)
Scorers: England: Bastin 2, Richardson 2.
Referee: Dr P.J.Bauwens (Germany).

Switzerland 1 Irish Free State 0, Nordstern, Basle, 5 May 1935, 23,000.
Switzerland: R.Bizzozzero; S.Minelli, L.Gobet, F.Defago, W.Weller, E.Muller, L.Amado, A.Poretti, L.Kielholz, E.Bosch, A.Jaeck.
Irish Free State: J.Foley (Celtic), P.Gaskins (Shamrock Rovers), L.Dunne (Manchester City), P.O'Kane (Bohemians), C.Lennon (St James's Gate), F.Hutchinson (Drumcondra), J.Daly (Shamrock Rovers), P.Ellis (Bohemians), A.Rigby (St James's Gate), J.Donnelly (Dundalk), P.Monahan (Sligo Rovers)
Scorers: Switzerland: Weller (pen).
Referee: A.Beranek (Austria).

Ireland 1 Switzerland 0, Dalymount Park, Dublin, 17 March 1936, 32,000.
Ireland: W.Harrington (Cork), W.O'Neill (Dundalk), W.C.Gorman (Bury), W.Glen (Shamrock Rovers), C.J.Turner (Southend United), J.O'Reilly (Brideville), P.Ellis (Bohemians), J.Donnelly (Dundalk), J.Dunne (Arsenal), A.F.Horlacher (Bohemians), J.Kelly (Derry City)
Switzerland: G.Schlegel; S.Minelli, W.Weiler, F.Defago,

F.Jaccard, E.Muller, E.Diebold, L.Kielholz, A.Frigerio, J.Spagnoli, G.Aeby.
Scorer: Ireland: Dunne J.   Referee: J.Langenus (Bel.)

Switzerland 0 Ireland 1, Wankdorf, Berne,
17 May 1937, 25,000.
Switzerland: R.Bizzozzero; S.Minelli, A.Lehmann, H.Liniger, S.Vernati, E.Lortscher, A.Bickel, P.Aebi, E.Rupf, W.Karcher, G.Aeby.
Ireland: T.Breen (Manchester United), W.O'Neill (Dundalk), J.J.Feenan (Sunderland), J.O'Reilly (St James's Gate), C.J.Turner (Southend United), C.Moulson (Notts County), J.Brown (Coventry City), D.Jordan (Wolves), J.Dunne (Southampton), P.Farrell (Hibernian), W.J.Fallon (Notts County)
Scorers: Ireland: Dunne J.
Referee:W.J.Lewington (England).

Switzerland 2 England 1, Hardturm, Zurich,
21 May 1938, 25,000.
Switzerland: W.Huber; S.Minelli, A.Lehmann, H.Springer, S.Vernati, E.Lortscher, L.Amado, E.Walaschek, A.Bickel, A.Abegglen, G.Aeby.
England: V.R.Woodley (Chelsea), B.Sproston (Leeds United), E.Hapgood (Arsenal), C.K.Willingham (Huddersfield Town), A.Young (Huddersfield Town), D.Welsh (Charlton Athletic), S.Matthews (Stoke City), J.Robinson (Sheffield Wednesday), F.H.Broome (Aston Villa), L.A.Goulden (WHU), C.S.Bastin (Arsenal)
Scorers: Switzerland: Aeby, Abegglen (pen). England: Bastin (pen).
Referee: Dr P.J.Bauwens (Germany).

Ireland 4 Switzerland 0, Dalymount Park, Dublin,
18 September 1938, 31,000.
Ireland: G.McKenzie (Southend United), W.C.Gorman (Bury), M.Hoy (Dundalk), J.O'Reilly (St James's Gate), M.T.O'Mahoney (Bristol Rovers), R.Lunn (Dundalk), T.Donnelly (Shamrock Rovers), J.Dunne (Shamrock Rovers), P.Bradshaw (St James's Gate), J.J.Carey (Manchester United), W.J.Fallon (Notts County)
Switzerland: W.Huber; S.Minelli, A.Lehmann, H.Springer, S.Vernati, E.Lortscher, A.Bickel, A.Abegglen, L.Amado, E.Walaschek, G.Aeby.
Scorers: Ireland: Bradshaw 2, Dunne J, Donnelly.
Referee: H.R.A. Mortimer (England).

YUGOSLAVIA

Yugoslavia 2 England 1, BSK Stadion, Belgrade,
18 May 1939, 40,000.
Yugoslavia: L.Lovric; Z.Pozega, E.Dubac, P.Manola, P.Dragicevic, G.Lehner, S.Glisovic, D.Vujadinovic, A.Petrovic, F.Matosic, N.Perlic.
England: V.R.Woodley (Chelsea), C.G.Male (Arsenal), E.Hapgood (Arsenal), C.K.Willingham (Huddersfield Town), S.Cullis (Wolves), J.Mercer (Everton), S.Matthews (Stoke City), G.W.Hall (Tottenham Hotspur), T.Lawton (Everton), L.A.Goulden (WHU), F.H.Broome (Aston Villa)
Scorers: Yugoslavia: Glisovic, Perlic. England: Broome.
Referee: G.Capdeville (France).

OTHER INTERNATIONALS

8 May 1935, King George V Jubilee Fund, unofficial international, England XI 0 Anglo-Scots 1, Highbury Stadium, London. Att: 8,944
England XI: H.Wright (Charlton Athletic), F.Channell (Tottenham Hotspur), E.Hapgood (Arsenal), J.Crayston (Arsenal), B.Joy (Casuals), H.Miller (Chelsea), J.Morton (West Ham United), Alexander (Millwall), J Holliday (Brentford), W.Hall (Tottenham Hotspur), H.Hobbis (Charlton Athletic)
Anglo-Scots: J.Jackson (Chelsea), J.Nibloe (Sheffield Wednesday), D. Blair (Aston Villa), J.Hutchinson (Chelsea), R. Salmond (Portsmouth), J.Thomson (Everton), F.Hill (Arsenal), J.Beattie (Blackburn Rovers), J.Maxwell (Preston North End), G.Mutch (Manchester United), W.Cook (Bolton Wanderers)
Scorer: Anglo-Scots; Mutch
Referee: L.Brown (London)
The Anglo Scots played in the red shirts of Arsenal

21 August 1935, King George V Jubilee Fund, unofficial international, Scotland 4 England 2, Hampden Park, Glasgow. Att: 56,316
Scotland J.Jackson (Chelsea), A.Anderson (Hearts), G. Cummings (Partick Thistle), A.Massie (Hearts), J.Simpson (Rangers), G.Brown (Rangers), J. Delaney (Celtic), T.Walker (Hearts), M.Armstrong (Aberdeen), W.Mills (Aberdeen), D.Duncan (Derby County)
England: H.Hibbs (Birmingham), G.Male.(Arsenal), E.Hapgood (Arsenal), C.Britton (Everton),W.Millership.(Sheffield Wednesday), J.Bray (Manchester City) (sub. at half-time: Smith (Leicester City)), J.Morton (West Ham United), H.Carter (Sunderland), R.Gurney (Sunderland), R.Westwood (Bolton Wanderers), W.Boyes(West Bromwich Albion)
Scorers: Scotland; Walker 2 (1 pen), Delaney, Armstrong. England; Westwood, Gurney
Referee: Webb (Scotland)
The use of a substitute for an injured player was contrary to the laws of the game at the time.

Germany 4 Republic of Ireland 1, 6 May 1936, Cologne.
Germany: Mombre, Hoenig, Class, Vogel, Hooss, Pleiser, Elbern, Dahmen, Euler, Gauchel, Boergs.
Republic of Ireland: W.Harrington (Cork), W.O'Neill (Dundalk), W.C.Gorman (Bury), W.Glen (Shamrock Rovers), C.Moulson (Lincoln City), J.O'Reilly (Brideville), H.A.Duggan (Leeds United), J.Donnelly (Dundalk), J.Dunne (Arsenal),A. Horlacher (Bohemians), J.Kelly (Derry City)
Scorers: Germany: Boergs, Gauchel, Dahmen, Harrington (own goal). Ireland: Dunne
Although the opposition was listed as "Germany", their team was selected only from clubs in the Rhineland. Consequenlty this game is not included in the official records.

England 3 Rest of Europe 0, 26 October 1938, Highbury, London, 40,185.
England: V.R.Woodley (Chelsea), B.Sproston (Tottenham Hotspur), E.Hapgood (Arsenal), C.K.Willingham (Huddersfield Town), S.Cullis (Wolves), W.Copping (Arsenal), S.Matthews (Stoke City), G.W.Hall (Tottenham Hotspur), T.Lawton (Everton), L.A.Goulden (WHU), W.Boyes (Everton)
Rest of Europe: A.Olivieri (Italy); A.Foni (Italy), P.Rava (Italy), A.Kupfer (Germany), M.Andreolo (Italy), A.Kitzinger (Germany), A.Aston (France), R.Braine (Belgium), S.Piola (Italy), G.Zsengeller (Hungary), A.Brustad (Norway).
Scorers: England: Hall, Lawton, Goulden.
Referee: A.J.Jewell (England).
To celebrate the F.A.'s 75th anniversary. The Rest of Europe team is sometimes labelled as "FIFA".

ENGLAND INTERNATIONAL TRIAL MATCHES.

England 1 The Rest 6, Anfield, Liverpool, 12 March 1930, 12,000.
England: Hibbs (Birmingham), Cooper (Derby County), Blenkinsop (Sheffield Wednesday), Edwards (Leeds United), Wilson (Huddersfield Town), Campbell (Huddersfield Town), Adcock (Leicester City), Hine (Leicester City), Camsell (Middlesbrough), Stephenson (Derby County), Tunstall (Sheffield United).
The Rest : Brown (Sheffield Wednesday), Goodall (Huddersfield Town), Hapgood (Arsenal), Strange (Sheffield Wednesday), Webster (Middlesbrough), Marsden (Sheffield Wednesday), Crooks (Derby County), Jack (Arsenal), Bradford (Birmingham), Johnson T (Everton), Brook (Manchester City).
Scorers: England: Tunstall. The Rest: Jack 3, Strange, Marsden, Johnson.
Referee: W.E.Rycroft (Nelson).

England 3 The Rest 2, Highbury, London, 4 March 1931, 14,282.
England: Turner (Huddersfield Town); Goodall (Huddersfield Town), Blenkinsop (Sheffield Wednesday), Strange (Sheffield Wednesday), Talbot (Aston Villa), Campbell (Huddersfield Town), Crooks (Derby County), Hodgson (Liverpool), Dean (Everton), Johnson T (Everton), Houghton (Aston Villa).
The Rest: Spiers (Tottenham Hotspur); Cooper (Derby County), Roughton (Huddersfield Town), Oliver (Fulham), Cowan (Manchester City), Tate (Aston Villa), Bruton (Blackburn Rovers), Smith J (Portsmouth), Hampson (Blackpool), Burgess (Sheffield Wednesday), Bastin (Arsenal).
Scorers: England: Dean 3. The Rest: Burgess 2.
Referee: G.T. Gould (South Norwood).

England 1 The Rest 4, Leeds Road, Huddersfield, 16 March 1932, 8,444.
England: Hibbs (Birmingham) [Turner (Huddersfield Town]; Goodall (Huddersfield Town), Blenkinsop (Sheffield Wednesday), Strange (Sheffield Wednesday), O'Dowd (Chelsea), Campbell (Huddersfield Town), Crooks (Derby County), Smith J (Portsmouth), Dean (Everton), Johnson T (Everton), Bastin (Arsenal).
The Rest: Pearson (West Bromwich Albion), Shaw (West Bromwich Albion), Hapgood (Arsenal), Stoker (Birmingham), Young (Huddersfield Town), Weaver (Newcastle United), Hulme (Arsenal), Barclay (Sheffield United), Waring (Aston Villa), Tilson (Manchester City), Houghton (Aston Villa).
Scorers: England: Bastin.
The Rest: Waring 2, Hulme, Barclay.
Referee: H.Bateson (Huddersfield).

England 1 The Rest 5, Fratton Park, Portsmouth, 22 March 1933, 15,103.
England: Sagar (Everton); Cooper (Derby County), Blenkinsop (Sheffield Wednesday), Britton (Everton), Barker (Derby County), Keen (Derby County), Crooks (Derby County), Grosvenor (Birmingham), Coleman (Arsenal), Carter H (Sunderland), Bastin (Arsenal).
The Rest: Moss (Arsenal); Male (Arsenal), Hapgood (Arsenal), Strange (Sheffield Wednesday), White (Everton), Copping (Leeds United), Hulme (Arsenal), Starling (Sheffield Wednesday), Hunt (Tottenham Hotspur), Pickering (Sheffield United), Arnold (Fulham).
Scorers: England: Bastin.
The Rest: Hulme 2, Hunt 2, Pickering.
Referee: E.G.Walliker (Wiltshire).
Players were numbered for the first time in an international trial match.

England 1 The Rest 7, 21 March 1934, Roker Park, Sunderland, 13,500.
England: Morton (Aston Villa); Goodall (Huddersfield Town), Roughton (Huddersfield Town), Willingham (Huddersfield Town), Allen (Portsmouth), Copping (Leeds United), Worrall (Portsmouth), Beresford (Aston Villa), Milsom (Bolton Wanderers), Westwood (Bolton Wanderers), Bastin (Arsenal).
The Rest: Nicholls (Tottenham Hotspur); Cooper (Derby County), Hapgood (Arsenal), Stoker (Birmingham), Hart (Leeds United), Weaver (Newcastle United), Matthews (Stoke City), Carter H (Sunderland), Gurney (Sunderland), Furness (Leeds United), Brook (Manchester City).
Scorers: England: Willingham. The Rest: Carter 4, Gurney 2, Brook.
Referee: T.J. Thompson (Northumberland).

England 2 The Rest 2, The Hawthorns, West Bromwich, 27 March 1935, 12,846.
England: Sagar (Everton); Male (Arsenal), Hapgood (Arsenal), Britton (Everton), Barker (Derby County), Bray (Manchester City), Geldard (Everton), Carter H (Sunderland), Drake (Arsenal), Westwood (Bolton Wanderers), Bastin (Arsenal).
The Rest: Swift (Manchester City); Chennell (Tottenham Hotspur), Barkas (Manchester City), Gardner (Aston Villa), Millership (Sheffield

Wednesday), Alsford (Tottenham Hotspur), Crooks (Derby County), Eastham (Bolton Wanderers), Gurney (Sunderland), Sandford (West Bromwich Albion), Brook (Manchester City).
Scorers: England: Drake 2.
The Rest: Gurney, Brook.
Referees: Dr A.W.Barton (Repton College) and E.J. Wood (Sheffield) *as this match was also used as a trial for a two-referee system.*

Probables 3 Possibles 0, Old Trafford, Manchester, 25 March 1936, 10,000.
Probables: Holdcroft (Preston North End); Rochford (Portsmouth), Barkas (Manchester City), Willingham (Huddersfield Town), Young (Huddersfield Town), Cockroft (West Ham United), Matthews (Stoke City), Carter H (Sunderland), Richardson W G (West Bromwich Albion), Dawes (Crystal Palace), Hobbis (Charlton Athletic).
Possibles: Kirby (Derby County); Griffiths (Manchester United), Stuart (Middlesbrough), Stoker (Birmingham), Vose (Manchester United), Smith S (Leicester City), Birkett (Middlesbrough), Eastham (Bolton Wanderers), Cheetham (Queens Park Rangers), Goulden (Wes Ham United), Cunliffe (Middlesbrough).
Scorers: Probables: Richardson 3.
Referee: H.Dedman (Blackpool).

Probables 2 Possibles 0, Turf Moor, Burnley, 17 March 1937, 6,024.
Probables: Woodley (Chelsea); Male (Arsenal), Catlin (Sheffield Wednesday), Britton (Everton), Young (Huddersfield Town), Bray (Manchester City), Kirchen (Arsenal), Bowden (Arsenal), Tilson (Manchester City), Westwood (Bolton Wanderers), Brook (Manchester City).
Possibles: Tweedy (Grimsby Town); Compton L (Arsenal), Barkas (Manchester City), Jobling (Charlton Athletic), Cullis (Wolverhampton Wanderers), Welsh (Charlton Athletic), Matthews (Stoke City), Robinson (Sheffield Wednesday), Clayton (Wolverhampton Wanderers), Goulden (West Ham United), Johnson J (Stoke City).
Scorers: Probables: Tilson, Bowden.
Referee: J.E.Williams (Lancashire).

Probables 1 Possibles 1, Goodison Park, Liverpool, 13 October 1937, 7,000.
Probables: Woodley (Chelsea); Sproston (Leeds United), Barkas (Manchester City), Willingham (Huddersfield Town), Young (Huddersfield Town), Bray (Manchester City), Geldard (Everton), Hall (Tottenham Hotspur), Gurney (Sunderland), Goulden (West Ham United), Brook (Manchester City).
Possibles: Bartram (Charlton Athletic); Compton L (Arsenal), Stuart (Middlesbrough), Crayston (Arsenal), Cullis (Wolverhampton Wanderers), Copping (Arsenal), Kirchen (Arsenal), Scott (Brentford), Richardson W G (West Bromwich Albion), Bowden (Arsenal), Morton (West Ham United).
Scorers: Probables: Gurney. Possibles: Richardson.
Referee: H.T.Wright (Macclesfield).

INTER-LEAGUE MATCHES

The Football League XI that met the Scottish League in 1935. Back; Tilson (Man. City), Britton (Everton), Moss (Arsenal), Hapgood (Arsenal), Bray (Man. City). Front; Matthews (Stoke), Barker (Derby Co.), Cooper (Derby Co.), Hall (Tottenham), Bowden (Arsenal), Brook (Man. City)

Football League 7 Irish League 2, Goodison Park, Liverpool, 25 September 1929, 18,000.
Football League: Davies (Everton); Cresswell (Everton), Jones (Blackburn Rovers), Edwards (Leeds United), Hart (Leeds United), Campbell (Huddersfield Town), Toseland (Manchester City), Hine (Leicester City), Hampson (Blackpool), Bradford (Birmingham), Page (Burnley).
Irish League: McMullan (Ards); Reid H (Glentoran), Frame (Linfield), Pollock (Belfast Celtic), Reid D (Ballymena), McCleary (Linfield), Mackie (Coleraine), McCracken (Linfield), Bambrick (Linfield), Geary (Glentoran), Mahood J (Belfast Celtc).
Scorers: Football League: Bradford 5, Hampson, Hine.
Irish League: Mahood J 2.
Referee: E.J. Wood (Sheffield).

Irish League 1 Scottish League 4, Windsor Park, Belfast, 9 October 1929, 10,000.
Irish League: McMullan (Ards); Reid S (Distillery), R P Fulton (Belfast Celtic), Pollock (Belfast Celtic), Reid D (Ballymena), McCleary (Linfield), Mackie (Coleraine), McCracken (Linfield), Bambrick (Linfield), Geary (Glentoran), Mahood J (Belfast Celtic).
Scottish League: Jackson (Partick Thistle); Crapnell (Airdrieonians), Nibloe (Kilmarnock), McNab (Dundee), Craig (Motherwell), Thomson (Dundee), Love (Aberdeen), Cheyne (Aberdeen), Battles (Hearts), Stevenson (Motherwell), Ferrier (Motherwell).
Scorers: Irish League: Bambrick.
Scottish League: Battles 4.
Referee: H.E.Hull (Barnsley).

Scottish League 2 Football League 1, Ibrox Park, Glasgow, 2 November 1929, 40,000.
Scottish League: Thomson J (Celtic); Gray (Rangers), Nibloe (Kilmarnock), McNab (Dundee), Johnstone (Hearts), Craig (Motherwell), Archibald (Rangers), Muirhead (Rangers), Battles (Hearts), Stevenson (Motherwell), Morton (Rangers).
Football League: Hibbs (Birmingham); Cresswell (Everton), Blenkinsop (Sheffield Wednesday), Edwards (Leeds United), Hart (Leeds United), Marsden (Sheffield Wednesday), Adcock (Leiceser City), Hine (Leicester City), Jack (Arsenal), Johnson (Manchester City), Brook (Manchester City).
Scorers: Scottish League: Muirhead, Stevenson. Football League: Jack.
Referee:W.Bell (Motherwell).

Irish League 2 Football League 2, Windsor Park, Belfast, 24 September 1930, 12,000.
Irish League: McDonald (Ards); McGinnigle (Coleraine), R P Fulton (Belfast Celtic), McCleary (Linfield), J Jones (Linfield), Mitchell (Distillery), Houston (Linfield), Cassidy (Ballymena), Bambrick (Linfield), Frewen (Belfast Celtic), McCaw (Linfield).
Football League: Brown (Sheffield Wednesday); Goodall (Huddersfield Town), Hapgood (Arsenal), Strange (Sheffield Wednesday), Webster (Middlesbrough), Cadwell (West Ham United), Crooks (Derby County), Jack (Arsenal), Hampson (Blackpool), Walker (Aston Villa), Houghton (Aston Villa).
Scorers: Irish League: Bambrick 2. Football League: Hampson 2.
Referee: H Watson (Glasgow).

Football League 7 Scottish League 3, White Hart Lane, London, 5 November 1930, 21,738.
Football League: Spiers (Tottenham Hotspur); Goodall (Huddersfield Town), Blenkinsop (Sheffield Wednesday), Strange (Sheffield Wednesday), Leach (Sheffield Wednesday), Campbell (Huddersfield Town), Crooks (Derby County), Hodgson (Liverpool), Hampson (Blackpool), Carter (West Bromwich Albion), Houghton (Aston Villa).
Scottish League: Thomson J (Celtic); Gray (Rangers), McGonagle (Celtic), Wilson (Celtic), Craig (Motherwell), Hill (Aberdeen), Thomson R (Celtic), Thomson A (Celtic), Battles (Hearts), Stevenson (Motherwell), Ferrier (Motherwell).
Scorers: Football League: Hampson 3, Crooks 2, Hodgson, Campbell. Scottish League: Ferrier 2, Battles.
Referee: H.E.Hull (Barnsley).

Scottish League 5 Irish League 0, Firhill Park, Glasgow, 8 October 1930, 10,170.
Scottish League: Jackson (Partick Thistle); Crapnell (Airdrieonians), Gilmour (Dundee), McNab (Dundee), Watson (Hamilton Academicals), McLeod (Raith Rovers), McRorie (Morton), Stevenson (Motherwell), Battles (Hearts), Ballantyne (Parttick Thistle), Ferrier (Motherwell).
Irish League: McDonald (Ards); McGinnigle (Coleraine), Gibson (Glentoran), McCleary (Linfield), J Jones (Linfield), Mitchell (Distillery), Houston (Linfield), Cassidy (Ballymena), Bambrick (Linfield), Frewen (Belfast Celtic), McCaw (Linfield).
Scorers: Scottish League: Battles 3, Ferrier, Gilmour.
Referee: J. Thomson (Burnbank)

Football League 4 Irish League 0, Bloomfield Road, Blackpool, 23 September 1931, 15,233.
Football League: Turner (Huddersfield Town); Jackson (Liverpool), Keeping (Southampton), Edwards (Leeds United), Graham (Nottingham Forest), Tate (Aston Villa), Hulme (Arsenal), Beresford (Aston Villa), Hampson (Blackpool), Bestall (Grimsby Town), Houghton (Aston Villa).
Irish League: A.Gardiner (Cliftonville); McNinch (Ballymena), Mitchell (Coleraine), Edwards (Linfield), Jones (Linfield), McCleary (Linfield), Chambers (Coleraine), McCracken (Linfield), Bambrick (Linfield), Borland (Belfast Celtic), Tierney (Belfast Celtic).
Scorers: Football League: Hampson 3, Houghton.
Referee: A.E.Fogg (Bolton).

Irish League 3 Scottish League 2, Windsor Park, Belfast, 3 October 1931, 14,584.
Irish League: A.Gardiner (Cliftonville); McNinch (Ballymena), Mitchell (Coleraine), Edwards (Linfield), Jones (Linfield), McCleary (Linfield), Blair (Portadown), McCracken (Linfield), Bambrick (Linfield), Barnard (Glentoran), Kelly (Derry City).
Scottish League: Dawson (Rangers); Brown (Dundee), McAuley (Rangers), Black (Aberdeen), Walker (St Mirren), McLeod (Partick Thistle), J.Crawford (Queen's Park), Moffatt (Hamilton Academicals), Boyd (Clyde), Stevenson (Motherwell), Bertram (Airdrieonians).
Scorers: Irish League: Kelly 2, Bambrick. Scottish League: Crawford, Boyd.

Scottish League 4 Football League 3, Celtic Park, Glasgow, 7 November 1931, 51,000.
Scottish League: Jackson (Partick Thistle); Crapnell (Airdrieonians), McGonagle (Celtic), Meiklejohn (Rangers), McStay (Celtic), Brown (Rangers), Thomson R (Celtic), McMenemy (Motherwell), McGrory (Celtic), McPhail (Rangers), Morton (Rangers).
Football League: Hibbs (Birmingham); Goodall (Huddersfield Town), Blenkinsop (Sheffield Wednesday), Edwards W (Leeds United), Graham (Nottingham Forest), Edwards J (West Bromwich Albion), Crooks (Derby County), Smith J (Portsmouth), Dean (Everton), Bestall (Grimsby Town), Bastin (Arsenal).
Scorers: Scottish League: McGrory 2, McPhail, McGonagle (pen). Football League: Bastin 2, Smith J.
Referee: J.Hudson (Glasgow).

Irish League 2 Football League 5, Windsor Park, Belfast, 1 October 1932, 17,000.
Irish League: Breen (Belfast Celtic); McClure (Portadown), Mitchell S (Coleraine), Mitchell W (Distillery), Jones (Linfield), Harkin (Derry City), McPherson (Ballymena), Irvine (Derry City), Bambrick (Linfield), Devan (Coleraine), Kelly (Derry City).

Football League: Moss (Arsenal); Cooper (Derby County), Blenkinsop (Sheffield Wednesday), Stoker (Birmingham), O'Dowd (Chelsea), Weaver (Newcastle United), Worrall (Portsmouth), Hine (Huddersfield Town), Brown (Aston Villa), Pickering (Sheffield United), Wood (West Bromwich Albion).
Scorers: Irish League: Bambrick, Devan. Football League: Brown 3, Worrall, Wood.
Referee: H.Watson (Glasgow).

Scottish League 4 Irish League 1, Ibrox Park, Glasgow, 19 October 1932, 10,000.
Scottish League: Kennaway (Celtic); Crapnell (Airdrieonians), Hay (St Mirren), Massie (Hearts), Walker (St Mirren), Telfer (Motherwell), J.Crawford (Queen's Park), McMenemy (Motherwell), Boyd (Clyde), Stevenson (Motherwell), King (Hamilton Academicals).
Irish League: Breen (Belfast Celtic); McClure (Portadown), Mitchell S (Coleraine), Mitchell W (Distillery), Jones (Linfield), Walker (Glenavon), Houston (Linfield), Irvine (Derry City), Bambrick (Linfield), Devan (Coleraine), Kelly (Derry City).
Scorers: Scottish League: Boyd 2, Stevenson, Telfer. Irish League: Devan.
Referee: H.Watson (Glasgow).

Football League 0 Scottish League 3, Maine Road, Manchester, 9 November 1932, 29,603.
Football League: Hibbs (Birmingham); Goodall (Huddersfield Town), Blenkinsop (Sheffield Wednesday), Strange (Sheffield Wednesday), Talbot (Aston Villa), Campbell (Huddersfield Town), Hulme (Arsenal), Smith J (Portsmouth), Brown (Aston Villa), Johnson (Everton), Houghton (Aston Villa).
Scottish League: Jackson (Partick Thistle); Crapnell (Airdrieonians), McGonagle (Celtic), Meiklejohn (Rangers), Johnstone (Hearts), Geatons (Celtic), Archibald (Rangers), Marshall (Rangers), Dewar (Third Lanark), McPhail (Rangers), Napier (Celtic).
Scorers: Scottish League: Napier 2, Dewar.
Referee: G.T.Davies (Bury).

Irish League 3 Scottish League 0, Windsor Park, Belfast, 30 September 1933, 25,000.
Irish League: Pinkerton (Derry City); Wright (Belfast Celtic), R P Fulton (Belfast Celtic), McCullogh (Belfast Celtic), J Jones (Linfield), McCleary (Linfield), Houston (Linfield), E D R Shearer (Derry City), Martin (Belfast Celtic), Coulter (Belfast Celtic), Kirby (Distillery).
Scottish League: T G Smith (Queen's Park); Morgan (Dundee), Warden (Third Lanark), Wilson P (Celtic), Watson (Hibernian), Hutchison (Falkirk), Archibald (Rangers), McMenemy J (Motherwell), Maxwell (Kilmarnock), Venters (Cowdenbeath), Mooney (Airdrieonians).
Scorers: Irish League: Martin 2, Kirby.

Football League 4 Irish League 0, Deepdale, Preston, 4 October 1933, 14,400.
Football League: Sagar (Everton); Beeson (Sheffield Wednesday), Trentham (West Bromwich Albion), Britton (Everton), Allen (Portsmouth), Copping (Leeds United), Crooks (Derby County), Grosvenor (Birmingham), Bowers (Derby County), Bastin (Arsenal), Brook (Manchester City).
Irish League: Pinkerton (Derry City); Wright (Belfast Celtic), Charlton (Derry City), McCullogh (Belfast Celtic), J Jones (Linfield), McCleary (Linfield), Houston (Linfield), E D R Shearer (Derry City), Martin (Belfast Celtic), Coulter (Belfast Celtic), Kirby (Distillery).
Scorers: Football League: Bowers 2, Crooks, Bastin.
Referee: P.Robinson (Blackburn).

Scottish League 2 Football League 2, Ibrox Park, Glasgow, 10 February 1934, 60,000.
Scottish League: Kennaway (Celtic); Anderson (Hearts), McGonagle (Celtic), Massie (Hearts), Simpson (Rangers), Brown (Rangers), Main (Rangers), Stevenson (Motherwell), Fleming (Rangers), McPhail (Rangers), Nicholson (Rangers).
Football League: Sagar (Everton); Shaw (West Bromwich Albion), Blenkinsop (Sheffield Wednesday), Willingham (Huddersfield Town), Allen (Portsmouth), Copping (Leeds United), Bruton (Blackburn Rovers), Beresford (Aston Villa), Bowers (Derby County), Weaver (Newcastle United), Bastin (Arsenal).
Scorers: Scottish League: Simpson, McPhail. Football League: Beresford, Bowers.
Referee: T.Dougray (Rutherglen).

Irish League 1 Football League 6, The Oval, Belfast, 19 September 1934, 13,500.
Irish League: Utterson (Glenavon); McNinch (Ballymena United), R P Fulton (Belfast Celtic), Patton (Distillery), Jones (Linfield), Leathon (Glentoran), Brown (Belfast Celtic), Grant (Derry City), Martin (Belfast Celtic), Duffy (Derry City), Kelly (Derry City).
Football League: Sagar (Everton); Cooper (Derby County), Roughton (Huddersfield Town), Britton (Everton), Cowan (Manchester City), Robinson (Burnley), Matthews (Stoke City), Carter (Sunderland), Tilson (Manchester City), Westwood (Bolton Wanderers), Brook (Manchester City).
Scorers: Irish League: Brown. Football League: Tilson 2, Brook 2, Matthews, Westwood.
Referee: S.Thompson (Belfast).

Scottish League 3 Irish League 2, Firhill Park, Glasgow, 3 October 1934, 8,000.
Scottish League: Kennaway (Celtic); Hogg (Celtic), Cummings (Partick Thistle), Massie (Hearts), Blair (Motherwell), McKennon (Motherwell), Ness (Partick Thistle), Davidson (St Johnstone), McFadyen (Motherwell), H Bremner (Queen's Park), Reid (Hamilton Academicals).
Irish League: Utterson (Glenavon); Hair (Linfield), R P Fulton (Belfast Celtic), Gowdy (Linfield), Jones (Linfield), McCleary (Linfield), Brown (Belfast Celtic),

K McCullogh (Belfast Celtic|), Martin (Belfast Celtic), J L Donnelly (Linfield), Kelly (Derry City).
Scorers: Scottish League: McFadyen 2, Ness. Irish League: Martin 2.
Referee: M.C. Hutton (Glasgow).

Football League 2 Scottish League 1, Stamford Bridge, London, 31 October 1934, 20,000.
Football League: Moss (Arsenal); Cooper (Derby County), Hapgood (Arsenal), Britton (Everton), Barker (Derby County), Bray (Manchester City), Matthews (Stoke City), Bowden (Arsenal), Tilson (Manchester City), Hall (Tottenham Hotspur), Brook (Manchester City).
Scottish League: Kennaway (Celtic); Cooper (Aberdeen), McGonagle (Celtic), Massie (Hearts), Simpson (Rangers), Herd (Hearts), Main (Rangers), Miller (Partick Thistle), McCulloch (Hearts), Napier (Celtic), Reid (Hamilton Academicals).
Scorers: Football League: Brook 2. Scottish League: McCulloch.
Referee: W.P.Harper (Stourbridge).

Football League 1 Irish League 2, Bloomfield Road, Blackpool, 25 September 1935, 26,000.
Football League: Swift (Manchester City); Beeson (Sheffield Wednesday), Barkas (Manchester City), Crayston (Arsenal), Barker (Derby County), Robinson (Burnley), Worrall (Portsmouth), Carter (Sunderland), Lythgoe (Huddersfield Town), Westwood (Bolton Wanderers), Boyes (West Bromwich Albion).
Irish League: Scott (Belfast Celtic); Millar (Glentoran), C Allen (Cliftonville), McCullough (Belfast Celtic), Jones (Linfield), Browne (Derry City), Kernaghan (Belfast Celtic), E D R Shearer (Derry City), McNally (Distillery), Conwell (Portadown), Kelly (Derry City).
Scorers: Football League: Boyes. Irish League: McNally, Kelly
Referee: H.Nattrass (England).

Irish League 2 Scottish League 3, Windsor Park, Belfast, 23 October 1935, 5,000.
Irish League: Scott (Belfast Celtic); Millar (Glentoran), C Allen (Cliftonville), McCullough (Belfast Celtic), Jones (Linfield), McCleary (Linfield), Kernaghan (Belfast Celtic), Gowdy (Linfield), E D R Shearer (Derry City), Weldon (Distillery), Kelly (Derry City).
Scottish League: Dawson (Rangers); Anderson (Hearts), Cummings (Partick Thistle), Massie (Hearts), Simpson (Rangers), Paterson (Celtic), J Crawford (Queen's Park), Buchan (Celtic), Armstrong (Aberdeen), Harrrison (Hamilton Academicals), Mooney (Airdrieonians).
Scorers: Irish League: Shearer 2. Scottish League: Harrison 2, Buchan.
Referee: W.McLean (Belfast).

Scottish League 2 Football League 2, Ibrox Park, Glasgow. 30 October 1935, 13,300.
Scottish League: Dawson (Rangers); Cooper (Aberdeen), McGill (Aberdeen), Massie (Hearts), Simpson (Rangers), Brown (Rangers), Main (Rangers),

Walker (Hearts), McGrory (Celtic), Venters (Rangers), Rodger (Ayr United).
Football League: Sagar (Everton); Male (Arsenal), Hapgood (Arsenal), Smith S (Leicester City), Young (Huddersfield Town), Bray (Manchester City), Birkett (Middlesbrough), Bowden (Arsenal), Camsell (Middlesbrough), Tilson (Manchester City), Brook (Manchester City).
Scorers: Scottish League: Massie, Brown. Football League: Bowden, Camsell.
Referee: W.E. Webb (Glasgow).

Scottish League 5 Irish League 2, Ibrox Park, Glasgow, 2 September 1936, 15,000.
Scottish League: Dawson (Rangers); Anderson (Hearts), Cheyne (Rangers), Geatons (Celtic), Blair (Motherwell), Brown (Rangers), Delaney (Celtic), Walker (Hearts), Armstrong (Aberdeen), Harrison (Hamilton Academicals), Murphy (Celtic).
Irish League: Lamb (Portadown); Millar (Glentoran), R P Fulton (Belfast Celtic), McNinch (Glentoran), Carlyle (Derry City), Martin (Derry City), Kenaghan (Belfast Celtic), E D R Shearer (Derry City), Redfern (Newry Town), Baird (Linfield), Kelly (Derry City).
Scorers: Scottish League: Delaney, Walker, Armstrong, Harrison, Murphy. Irish League: Shearer, Baird.
Referee: J.Baillie (Scotland).

Irish League 3 Football League 2, Windsor Park, Belfast, 23 September 1936, 16,000.
Irish League: Lamb (Portadown); Millar (Glentoran), R P Fulton (Belfast Celtic), Edwards (Linfield), Carlyle (Derry City), Walker (Belfast Celtic), Kernaghan (Belfast Celtic), Baird (Linfield), E D R Shearer (Derry City), Duffy (Derry City), Kelly (Derry City).
Football League: Sagar (Everton); Rochford (Portsmouth), Shaw C (Wolverhampton Wanderers), Willingham (Huddersfield Town), Barker (Derby County), Bray (Manchester City), Birkett (Middlesbrough), Bestall (Grimsby Town), Steele (Stoke City), Westwood (Bolton Wanderers), Brook (Manchester City).
Scorers: Irish League: Kelly 3. Football League: Steele, Westwood.
Referee: S.Thompson (Belfast).

Football League 2 Scottish League 0, Goodison Park, Liverpool, 21 October 1936, 34,000.
Football League: Holdcroft (Preston North End); Male (Arsenal), Catlin (Sheffield Wednesday), Britton (Everton), Gee (Everton), Keen (Derby County), Crooks (Derby County), Richardson (Huddersfield Town), Dean (Everton), Westwood (Bolton Wanderers), Bastin (Arsenal).
Scottish League: Dawson (Rangers); Anderson (Hearts), Shaw (Airdrieonians), Geatons (Celtic), Smith (Kilmarnock), Brown (Rangers), Delaney (Celtic), Walker (Hearts), Armstrong (Aberdeen), McPhail (Rangers), Kinnear (Rangers).
Scorers: Football League: Westwood, Bastin.
Referee: H.N.Mee (Mansfield).

Irish League 2 Scottish League 3, The Oval, Belfast, 1 September 1937, 11,000.
Irish League: Twoomey (Newry Town); Lavery (Belfast Celtic), R P Fulton (Belfast Celtic), J Doherty (Derry City), Carlyle (Derry City), Walker J (Belfast Celtic), Kernaghan (Belfast Celtic), McAlinden (Belfast Celtic), Turnbull (Belfast Celtic), Duffy (Derry City), Kelly (Derry City).
Scottish League: Dawson (Rangers); Hogg (Celtic), Carabine (Third Lanark), Geatons (Celtic), Shankly (Falkirk), Smith (Dundee), Delaney (Celtic), Buchan (Celtic), Coats (Dundee), Black (Hearts), McNee (Hamilton Academicals).
Scorers: Irish League: Kernoghan, Turnbull. Scottish League: Buchan 2, Black.
Referee: H.Nattrass (England).

Scottish League 1 Football League 0, Ibrox Park, 22 September 1937, 30,000.
Scottish League: Dawson (Rangers); Hogg (Celtic), Carabine (Third Lanark), Robertson G (Kilmarnock), Dykes (Hearts), McKenzie (Motherwell), Delaney (Celtic), McKinnon (Partick Thistle), Stewart (Motherwell), Venters (Rangers), Caskie (St Johnstone).
Football League: Woodley (Chelsea); Sproston (Leeds United), Barkas (Manchester City), Willingham (Huddersfield Town), Cullis (Wolverhampton Wanderers), Bray (Manchester City), Matthews (Stoke City), Galley (Wolverhampton Wanderers), Steele (Stoke City), Westwood (Bolton Wanderers), Ashall (Wolverhampton Wanderers).
Scorers: Delaney.
Referee: M.C.Hutton (Glasgow).

Football League 3 Irish League 0, Bloomfield Road, Blackpool, 6 October 1937, 14,700.
Football League: Woodley (Chelsea); Sproston (Leeds United), Barkas (Manchester City), Willingham (Manchester City), Young (Huddersfield Town), Bray (Manchester City), Geldard (Bolton Wanderers), Hall (Tottenham Hotspur), Mills (Chelsea), Goulden (West Ham United), Brook (Manchester City).l
Irish League: Twoomey (Newry Town); Lavery (Belfast Celtic), R P Fulton (Belfast Celtic), Doherty (Derry City), Carlyle (Derry City), Martin (Derry City), Kernoghan (Belfast Celtic), McAlinden (Belfast Celtic), E D R Shearer (Derry City), Duffy (Derry City), Kelly (Derry City).
Scorers: Football League: Hall, Mills, Goulden.
Referee: L.E.Gibbs (Reading).

Scottish League 6 Irish League 1, Ibrox Park, Glasgow, 7 September 1938, 20,010.
Scottish League: Dawson (Rangers); Hogg (Celtic), Carabine (Third Lanark), Elliott (Partick Thistle), Lyon (Celtic), Miller (Hearts), McSpadyen (Partick Thistle), McKinnon (Partick Thistle), Martin (Clyde), Black (Hearts), Caskie (St Johnstone)
Irish League: Kelly (Glenavon); Monoghan (Portadown), R P Fulton (Belfast Celtic), McIvor (Newry Town), McKinley (Ards), Rosbotham (Linfield), Todd (Glentoran), McAlinden (Belfast Celtic), Taylor (Glentoran), Donnelly (Linfield), Kelly (Derry City).
Scorers: Scottish League: Martin 2, Black 2, McSpadyen, McAlinden. Irish League: Todd.

Irish League 2 Football League 8, Windsor Park, Belfast, 21 September 1938, 14,000.
Irish League: McCurry (Cliftonville); Adams (Distillery), R P Fulton (Belfast Celtic), McIvor (Newry Town), Carlyle (Derry City), H Walker (Belfast Celtic), Todd (Glentoran), McAlinden (Belfast Celtic), E D R Shearer (Derry City), Duffy (Derry City), McCormick (Linfield).
Football League: Woodley (Chelsea); Sproston (Tottenham Hotspur), Hapgood (Arsenal), Willingham (Huddersfield Town), Cullis (Wolverhampton Wanderers), Welsh (Charlton Athletic), Matthews (Stoke City), Robinson (Sheffield Wednesday), Lawton (Everton), Goulden (Wesr Ham United), Morton (West Ham United).
Scorers: Irish League: McIvor, Shearer. Football League: Lawton 4, Welsh, Robinson, Goulden, Morton.
Referee: P.Craigmyle (Scotland).

Football League 3 Scottish League 1, Molineux, Wolverhampton, 2 November 1938, 28,389.
Football League: Woodley (Chelsea); Sproston (Tottenham Hotspur), Greenhalgh (Everton), Willingham (Huddersfield Town), Cullis (Wolverhampton Wanderers), Gardiner (Wolverhampton Wanderers), Matthews (Stoke City), Hall (Tottenham Hotspur), Lawton (Everton), Dix (Derby County), Boyes (Everton).
Scottish League: Brown (Clyde); Hogg (Celtic), Hickie (Clyde), Geatons (Celtic), Lyon (Celtic), Paterson (Celtic), Delaney (Celtic), Walker (Hearts), Martin (Clyde), Venters (Rangers), Kinnear (Rangers).
Scorers: Football League: Dix 2, Boyes. Scottish League: Walker.
Referee: T.J. Thompson (Leemington-on-Tyne).

AMATEUR INTERNATIONALS

The England amateur team that played Wales in 1937. Back; Sowerby, Tunnington, Lodge, Mitton, Burchell, Shield. Front; Parr, Matthews, Lewis, Thornton, Riley

1929-30
Ireland 0 Scotland 3, Londonderry, 12 October 1929.
Scorers: Scotland: McDonald, Moncrieff, Ross.

England 7 Ireland 2, Crystal Palace, 16 November 1929.
Scorers: England: Ashton 4, Coates 2, Rimmer. Ireland: McMahon, Kelly.

Scotland 1 Wales 0, Hampden Park, 8 February 1930.
Scorer: Scotland: McLelland.

Wales 1 England 2, Aberystwyth, 15 February 1930.
Scorers: Wales: Davies-Owen. England: Smithies 2.

Scotland 1 England 0, Hampden Park, 15 March 1930.
Scorer: Scotland: McDonald.

1930-31
Scotland 1 Ireland 0, Aberdeen, 20 September 1930.
Scorer: McLelland.

Ireland 3 England 1, Cliftonville, 15 November 1930.
Scorers: Ireland: Miller 3. England: Gibbins.

Wales 1 Scotland 2, Swansea, 7 February 1931.
Scorers: Wales: Pugh. Scotland: Anderson, Cordiner.

England 5 Wales 0, Bournemouth, 14 February 1931.
Scorers: England: Gibbins 2, Warnes 2, Hegan.

England 2 Scotland 1, Stamford Bridge, 21 March 1931.
Scorers: England: Gibbins, Hegan. Scotland: Crawford.

1931-32
England 3 Ireland 2, York, 14 November 1931.
Scorers: Whewell, Coates, Smithies. Ireland: Martin 2.

Scotland 1 Wales 5, Tynecastle, 2 January 1932.
Scorers: Cumming. Wales: Davies J 3, Davies G, Davies-Owen.

Wales 1 England 3, Swansea, 27 February 1932.
Scorers: Wales: Evans W. England: Creek 2, Kail.

Ireland 4 Scotland 0, Cliftonville, 2 March 1932.
Scorers: Ireland: McClelland 2, Priestley, McCaw.

Scotland 3 England 1, Hampden Park, 19 March 1932.
Scorers: Anderson, Dodds, Russell (og). England: Ashton (pen).

1932-33
England 1 Wales 0, Torquay, 21 January 1933.
Scorer: England: Cornelius.

Scotland 6 Ireland 0, Celtic Park, 28 January 1933.
Scorers: Scotland: Dodds 3, Crawford 2, Harvie.

Ireland 4 England 3, Cliftonville, 18 February 1933.
Scorers: Ireland: Martin 2, McKnight, McCaw. England: Cornelius 2, Finch.

England 1 Scotland 0, Dulwich, 25 March 1933.
Scorer: Roberts.

Wales 2 Scotland 0, Bangor, 8 April 1933.

1933-34
Wales 3 England 5, Bangor, 27 January 1934.
Scorers: Wales: Vale, Jones S, Robbins (og). England: Fabian 2, Evans F, Lewis, Burns.

England 4 Ireland 0, Ilford, 17 February 1934.
Scorers: England: Lewis 2, Shearer, Finch.

Scotland 4 Wales 0, Greenock, 10 March 1934.
Scorers: Scotland: Anderson 3, Paul.

Scotland 3 England 2, Hampden Park, 24 March 1934.
Scorers: Scotland: Whitehead 2, Bremner. England: Shearer, Finch.

Ireland 4 Scotland 1, Cliftonville, 25 April 1934.
Scorers: Ireland: Billingsley 2, Connell, Hewitt. Scotland: Whitehead.

1934-35
England 6 Wales 1, Wimbledon, 19 January 1935.
England: Simms 3, Burns, Sanders, Finch. Wales:
Williams JH.

Ireland 2 England 4, Cliftonville, 16 February 1935.
Scorers: Ireland: Bruce, Kernaghan. England: Simms 2,
Shearer, Finch.

Wales 2 Scotland 5, Aberystwyth, 16 February 1935.
Scorers: Wales: Mills 2. Scotland: Dodds 3, Crawford,
Bremner.

England 2 Scotland 1, Dulwich, 23 March 1935.
Scorers: Simms, Finch. Scotland: Dodds.

Scotland 2 Ireland 3, Ibrox Park, 17 April 1935.
Scorers: Martin 2. Ireland: McNeill, Tarrant, Gibb.

1935-36
England 5 Ireland 0, Blackpool, 15 February 1936.
Scorers: England: Charlton 3, Finch 2.

Scotland 1 Wales 1, Dumfries, 15 February 1936.
Scorers: Scotland: Martin. Wales: Mudford.

Wales 3 England 7, Portmadoc, 29 February 1936.
Scorers: Wales: Jones G 2, Williams J. England:
Charlton 3, Thornton 3, Shearer.

Scotland 1 England 0, Inverness, 14 March 1936.
Scorer: Scotland: Whitehead.

Ireland 3 Scotland 5, Cliftonville, 22 April 1936.
Scorers: Ireland: Foye 2, McNeill. Scotland: Dodds 2,
Kyle 2, Wright.

1936-37
England 9 Wales 1, Portsmouth, 23 January 1937.
Scorers: England: Sowerby 3, Riley 3, Matthews, Parr,
Thornton. Wales: Leahy.

Ireland 5 England 1, Cliftonville, 13 February 1937.
Scorers: Ireland: Lyness 2, Gibb 2, Banks. England:
Matthews.

England 0 Scotland 1, Dulwich, 13 March 1937.
Scorer: Scotland: Kyle.

Wales 0 Scotland 2, Bangor, 27 March 1937.
Scorers: Scotland: Kyle, Whitehead.

Scotland 3 Ireland 0, Cathkin Park, 21 April 1937.
Scorers: Scotland: Martin, Kingdon, Duffy (og).

1937-38
Wales 2 England 8, Rhyl, 29 January 1938.
Scorers: Wales: Griffiths 2. England: Parr 4, Anderson
3, Finch.

England 1 Ireland 1, Leicester, 19 February 1938.
Scorers: England: Wood. Ireland: Fulton.

Scotland 2 England 5, Hampden Park, 12 March 1938.
Scorers: Scotland: Kyle, Whitehead. England: Gibbons
3, Edelston, Thornton.

Ireland 2 Scotland 1, Cliftonville, 13 April 1938.
Scorers: Ireland: Moore W, Kelleher. Scotland:
Kingdon.

1938-39
England 5 Wales 2, Cheltenham, 28 January 1939.
Scorers: England: Gibbons 2, Clements 2, Edelston.
Wales: Francis, Griffiths.

Ireland 0 England 1, Cliftonville, 18 February 1939.
Scorer: England: Bell.

England 8 Scotland 3, Dulwich, 11 March 1939.
Scorers: England: Edelston 3, Parr 2, Finch 2, Gibbons.
Scotland: Kyle 2, Cross.

Scotland 1 Ireland 1, Firhill Park, 19 April 1939.
Scorers: Scotland: McLean. Ireland: Kelleher.

GREAT BRITAIN XI IN THE 1936 OLYMPICS

Great Britain 2 China 0, 6 August 1936. Att, 9,000
Hill (Yorkshire Amateurs), Holmes (Ilford), Fulton
(Belfast Celtic), Gardiner (Queen's Park), Joy (Casuals),
Pettit (Corinthian), Crawford (Queen's Park), Kyle
(Queen's Park), Dodd (Queen's Park), Edelston
(Wimbledon), Finch (Barnet).
Scorers: Dodds, Finch

Poland 5 Great Britain 4, 8 August 1936. Att. 11,000
Hill (Yorkshire Amateurs), Holmes (Ilford), Fulton
(Belfast Celtic), Gardiner (Queen's Park), Joy (Casuals),
Sutcliffe (Corinthian), Crawford (Queen's Park),
Shearer (Corinthian), Clements (Casuals), Riley
(Casuals), Finch (Barnet).
Scorers: England: Joy 2, Shearer, Clements.
Poland: Wodarz 3, Gad, Piec.

AMATEUR INTERNATIONAL PLAYERS IN THE 1930s.

ENGLAND

Ainsworth,E .(Hull City), 1933 W,I.
Anderson,J.C. (Enfield), 1930 I.
Anderson,P. (Crittalls Athletic), 1931 I.
Anderson,R.S. (Dulwich Hamlet) 1938 W,I 1939 S.
Ashton,C.T. (Corinthians), 1930 I 1932 S,I,W.
Ball,H.J. (Dulwich Hamlet) 1938 S 1939 I.
Banks,R. (Birmingham Univ) 1934 W.
Barnes,H.E.R. (Wimbledon) 1935 S.
Beswarwick,R.C. (Enfield) 1931 I.
Beswick,S.M. (Bournemouth & Boscombe Athletic) 1930 W.
Bradbury,L. (Manchester Univ) 1936 I.
Burschell,G.S. (Romford) 1936-7-8-9 S,W,I.
Burns, J.C. (Queens Park Rangers, Brentford) 1930 W 1931-2-3-4-5 S,W,I.
Chadder,A.H. (Corinthians) 1933 S.
Charlton,W. (Wimbledon, Queens Park Rangers) 1936 S,I,W 1937 S.
Clements,B.A. (Casuals) 1939 W.
Clements,H. (Ipswich Town) 1937 I.
Coates, Rigger H.L. (Royal Navy, Southampton) 1930 S,W,I 1931 S 1932 I 1933 W,I.
Collins,E.C. (Leyton, Walthamstow Avenue) 1934 S,I 1937 S 1939 I.
Cornelius, Lieut D.G. (Royal Navy) 1933 W,I.
Creek,F.N.S. (Corinthians) 1932 S,W.
Davis,F.W. (Cheltenham Town) 1934 W.
Dudley,R.A. (Apsley) 1935 I.
Eastham, L/Cpl S. (KORR) 1936 S,I,W.
Edelston,M. (London Univ, Brentford) 1937 S 1938 S 1939 S,I,W.
Ellis,R. (Wealdstone) 1939 W
Evans,F.P. (Golders Green) 1934 W.
Ewer,F.H. (Corinthians) 1930 S,W,I.
Fabian,A.H. (Cambridge Univ, Casuals, Derby County) 1932 S,I 1933 S,W,I 1934 W.
Finch,L.C. (Barnet) 1933 S,I,W 1934 S,I 1935 S,W,I 1936 S,I 1937 S 1938 W 1939 S,W.
Firth,J.W. (Yorkshire Amateurs) 1939 S,I.
Fitzsimmons,P. (Preston North End) 1935 W.
Foreman,G.A. (Walthamstow Avenue) 1939 I.
Garland-Wells,H.M. (Oxford Univ) 1930 I.
Gates,E.H. (London Caledonians) 1930-1 S,W,I.
Gibbins,W.V.T. (West Ham United, Brentford) 1930 S 1931 S,W,I 1932 S,W.
Gibbons,A.H. (RAF, Tottenham Hotspur) 1938-9 S,W,I.
Gilderson,E.I. (Ilford) 1930 S,W.
Grant,R.S. (Cambridge Univ) 1933 S.
Gregory,F.J. (Leyton) 1930 I 1931 S,W,I 1933 S,W,I 1934 S,I.
Hammond,S.J. (Northern Nomads) 1932 I.
Hegan, Capt K.E. (Army, Corinthians) 1931 S,W 1932 S,I,W.
Hill,H.C.H. (Yorkshire Amateurs, Sheffield Wednesday, Dulwich Hamlet) 1935 S,W,I 1936 S,I 1937 S 1938 S,I.
Hobson,G.D. (Yorkshire Amateurs) 1931 S,W.
Hockaday,L.N. (Enfield) 1938-9 S,I.
Holmes,G.G. (Ilford), 1934 I,S,W 1936 I,W.

James, Sgt G.T. (RAF) 1935 W.
Jenkins,R.G. (Casuals) 1932 I.
Joy,B. (Casuals, Arsenal) 1934-5-6 I,S,W 1937 S.
Kail,E.L. (Dulwich Hamlet) 1930 S,I 1932 S,W 1933 S,I,W.
Kilkenny,J.C. (Yorkshire Amateurs) 1937 S 1938 I.
Knight,J.G. (Casuals) 1930 S.
Leek,T.H. (Moor Green) 1936-8 S,W 1939 S,I,W.
Lewis,J.W. (Queens Park Rangers, Walthamstow Avenue) 1931 S 1932 I 1934 S,I,W 1937 S,W 1938-9 S,W,I.
Lister,W.H.L. (Cambridge Univ, Corinthians) 1933 W,I 1934 S,I.
Lodge,H.S. (Stockton) 1934 I,S 1937 W.
Loveday,A.W. (Leyton, Wealdstone) 1936 S 1937 I.
McIntosh,R.J. (Barrow) 1936 W.
Mathews,R.J. (Walthamstow Avenue) 1937 W,I.
Millington,A.E. (Liverpool Police) 1930 W.
Mitton,H. (Bishop Auckland) 1937 W.
Morrish,L.B. (Dulwich Hamlet) 1930 S 1935 I,W.
Mulley,E.J. (Nunhead) 1936 W.
Mulrenan,B.W. (Sheffield Univ) 1935 S.
Murray,C.F.(Dulwich Hamlet) 1931 I 1933 S 1935 I.
Parr,W.W. (Blackpool) 1936 S,I,W 1937 W,I 1938 S,W,I 1939 S.
Partridge,G.B. (Corinthians) 1932 S,W.
Peploe,G. (Ilford) 1931 I.
Perkins,G.S. (Cheltenham Town) 1939 W.
Pettit,D.E.A. (Cambridge Univ) 1938 W.
Preston,J.W. (Leyton) 1930 S,W.
Riley,F. (Casuals) 1939 W.
Rimmer,J. (Southport) 1930 I.
Robbins,H.S. (Dulwich Hamlet) 1934 W 1935 S 1938 S,W,I.
Roberts,J. (Southport) 1933 S.
Robinson,J.R.C. (RAF) 1930 I.
Roylance,G. (Yorkshire Amateurs) 1935 S,I,W.
Russell,A.M. (Casuals) 1930 S.
Russell,J.F.C. (Clapton) 1932 S,W.
Sanders,E.M. (Chester) 1935 W.
Shearer,E.D.R. (Casuals) 1934 S,I 1935 W,S,I 1936 S,W.
Shield,J.G. (Bishop Auckland) 1937 W.
Simms,H.A. (Northern Nomads) 1935 S,I,W.
Smithies,G.H. (Preston North End, Northern Nomads) 1930 S,W 1932 I.
Sowerby,J.W. (Ipswich Town) 1937,S,W,I.
Sutcliffe,l.J. (Corinthians, Casuals) 1937 S,I.
Tewkesbury,K.C. (Birmingham Univ) 1931-2 S,W,I.
Thornton,L.C. (Kingstonian, Derbyshire Amateurs) 1936 S,W 1937 W,I 1938 S,W,I.
Tunnington,E. (Lloyds Bank) 1935 S 1937 W,I.
Warnes,W.H. (Woking) 1931 S,I,W.
Watkinson,A. (Congleton) 1936 I.
Watson,G.S. (Charlton Athletic) 1930 I,W.
Webster,W.H. (Cambridge Univ, Corinthians) 1931 W 1933 S 1934 S,I,W 1935-6 I.
Welsh,V.F. (Ilford) 1931 W.
Whewell,W.T. (Corinthians) 1930 W 1931-2-3 S,I,W.
White,R. (Royal Navy) 1934 W.
Whitehead,G.K. (Bury Amateurs) 1939 S,I,W.
Whittaker,W. (Kingstonian) 1939 W.
Wood,J. (Leytonstone) 1938 I.

Woodcock,J. (Yorkshire Amateurs) 1932 I 1933 W,I.
Woolcock,A.H. (Cambridge Univ) 1937 I 1938 W.
Wright,R.E. (Walthamstow Avenue) 1937 I.

SCOTLAND

Anderson,A. (Murrayfield Amateurs, Queen's Par) 1931 E,W 1932-3-4 E,W,I.
Arnott,J. (Weir;s XI) 1932 W.
Blackwood,D. (Goirock High School FP) 1934 W,I.
Bonomy,J. (Queen's Park) 1938-9 E,I.
Bootland,L. (Seaforth Highlanders) 1938 E.
Bremner,T.H. (Queen's Park) 1931 E,W 1932 E 1934 E,I 1935 W.
Brown,C. (RAF) 1936 W.
Browning,W. (Queen's Park) 1934 E 1939 E,I.
Buchanan,W. (Clydebank) 1930 W.
Buchanan,W.D. (Queen's Park) 1936 E,W 1938 E,I 1939 I.
Campbell,T.K. (Queen's Park) 1930 E,W 1931 I 1932 W,E 1933-4 E,W,I 1935 E,W 1937 E.
Christie,D. (Edinburgh Univ, Queen's Park) 1936 I 1937 E,I,W 1938-9 E,I.
Christie,M.J. (Queen's Park) 1932 W,I.
Clark,W. (Falkirk Amateurs) 1935 I.
Clyne,J. (Queen's Park) 1938 E,i.
Cooper,J.C. (Queen's Park) 1933 E 1935 I.
Cordiner,W.L. (Queen's Park) 1931 W.
Crawford,J. (Queen's Park) 1931 E,I 1932 E,W 1933 E,I,W 1935 E,W
Cross,R.M. (Queen's Park) 1936 I 1938-9 E,I.
Cumming,J.M. (Edinburgh City) 1932 W 1933 W.
Curvill,A. (Falkirk Amateurs) 1938 I.
Dodds,J,M,. (Queen's Park) 1931 I 1932 E 1933 E,I 1935 E,I,W 1936 I.
Donnelly,J. (Linfield) 1936 I.
Duncan,S. (Edinburgh City) 1939 I.
Fitzgerald,L. (Queen's Park) 1931 I.
Garden,J. (London Caledonians) 1935 E,W 1936 E W.
Gardiner,J. (Queen's Park) 1932 W 1933-4-5 E,I,W 1936 E 1937 E,W.
Gardiner,P.E. (Edinburgh City) 1933 E,W.
Gilbert,J. (Murrayfield Amateurs) 1930 I 1931 E,W,I.
Gillespie,R. (Queen's Park) 1930 E,W,I 1931 E,I 1932 E 1933 E W.
Gordon,R,D.G. (Edinburgh Univ) 1937 E,I,W.
Grant,R. (Queen's Park) 1930 E,W 1931-2 E 1934 I,W 1935 I.
Hall,G. (Edinburgh City) 1939 E.
Hall,J. (Queen's Park) 1937 I.
Hamilton,W. (Falkirk Amateurs, Edinburgh City) 1933 I,W 1935 E,I,W 1936,E,W.
Harvie, Lieut T,M. (Highland Light Infantry) 1932 W 1933 E,I,W.
Hosie,A. (Queen's Park) 1931 E 1934 E,I 1936 I 1937 E,I,W 1938 E,I 1939 I.
Hunter,H.G. (Queen's Park) 1939 E.
Johnstone,T. (Queen's Park) 1939 E.
Kerr,A. (Third Lanark) 1933 I.
King,W.S. (Queen's Park) 1930,E,W,I 1931 I.
Kinghorn,W.J.D. (Queen's Park) 1937 E,I,W 1938 I.
Knowles,J. (Murrayfield Amateurs) 1939 I.

Kyle,J.R. (Queen's Park) 1935 E,W 1936 E,I 1937 E,I,W 1938-9 E,I.
Lennie,S.G. (Dumbarton) 1931 W.
McCartney,A. (Queen's Park) 1931 W 1932 W,I 1933 I.
McCree,J. (London Caledonians) 1930 E.
McDonald,I. (Murrayfield Amateurs) 1930 E,W,I.
McDonald,J. (Queen's Park) 1931 W.
McDonald,W.S. (Queen's Park) 1937 E,I,W 1939 E.
MacFarlane,T. (Barnet) 1938 E.
McIlroy,W. (London Caledonians) 1939 E.
McIntosh,F. (Coats Amateurs) 1938 I.
McKay, Piper R. (Army) 1934, E,W,I.
McKell,J. (Edinburgh City) 1934, E,W,I.
McKenzie,G.D. (Queen's Park) 1930 E 1931 E,W,I 1932 E I 1933 E,W.
McKenzie,W. (Clydebank) 1930 W.
McLean,A. (Dundee Anchorage) 1939 I.
McLelland,D. (Queen's Park) 1930 E,W 1931 I.
McPherson,W. (Clydebank) 1934 W.
McShane,J,J. (Edinburgh City) 1936 W.
Martin,W. (Queen's Park) 1935 E,I 1936 E,W 1937 E,I,W.
Moncrieff,R. (Glasgow Transport) 1930 I.
Mooney,J. (Edinburgh City) 1939 E.
Munro,R.S. (Murrayfield Amateurs) 1932 E,W.
Murray,R. (Stenhousemuir) 1936 W.
Parlane,J.A. (Dumbarton, Raith Rovers) 1932 I 1933 I,E,W.
Parlane,W. (Dumbarton) 1931 E 1932 I.
Patterson,G.W. (Queen's Park, Romford) 1932 I 1935 E,I,W 1936 E,W.
Paul,E.P.J. (Queen's Park) 1934 W.
Peattie,R.W. (St Monance Swifts) 1936 E,I,W.
Peden,R.G.C. (Queen's Park) 1930 W,E,I 1931 W,E,I.
Ross,A (Calmeron Highlanders) 1930 I.
Russell,F. (Edinburgh City) 1931 I.
Russell,J. (Queen's Park) 1932 I.
Scott,J. (Queen's Park) 1936 I.
Shepherd,K. (St Bernard's) 1939 I.
Sibbald,T. (Edinburgh Univ) 1930 I.
Simpson,G.H. (Kennoway) 1938 I.
Sloan,E. (St Mirren) 1932 I.
Smith,T.G. (Queen's Park, Ayr United, St Bernard's) 1932 E,I 1933 I 1934 W,E,I 1935 E 1936 W,I 1937 I,W.
Souter,T.H. (Queen's Park) 1935 I.
Stewart.A. (St Mirren) 1930 I.
Stewart,J. (Queen's Park) 1934 E,W 1935 E,I,W.
Taylor,F.P. (Queen's Park) 1930 E 1932 I.
Thomson,S. (Queen's Park) 1937 I.
Turner,A.D. (Partick Thistle) 1931 W.
Walker, Lt-Col (Black Watch) 1936 W.
Walker,W.O. (Queen's Park) 1931 E,W 1932 E.
Wann,R. (Edinburgh City) 1932 W.
Watt,R. (Gourock High School FP) 1930 W.
White,D. (Edinburgh City, Queen's Park) 1935 W,I 1936-7-8 E.
Whitehead,D. (Kingstonian) 1934 E,I 1936 E 1937 E,W 1938 E.
Wiseman,W. (Queen's Park) 1930 E,W.I.
Wright,W. (Queen's Park) 1936 E,I.
Young,T. (Queen's Park) 1936 I 1937 I,W.
Yuill,G.C. (Falkirk Amateurs) 1930 I.

WALES

Anthony,R.F. (Treharris) 1936 E 1937 S.
Arnold,M. (Swansea Town) 1933 S.
Beavan,J.G. (Llanerch Celtic) 1937 S.
Bennett,G. (Barry) 1935 E,S.
Bevan,E.J. (Aberystwyth) 1938 E.
Clarke,A. (Lovells Athletic) 1935 S 1938 E.
Davies,Glyn. (Swansea Town, Casuals, Norwich City, Wrexham) 1930-1-2 E,S 1933 E 1935 E,S.
Davies, Rev Hywel (Wrexham) 1931 E,S.
Davies,J. (Blaenau Festiniog) 1930 E.
Davies,J. (Ebbw Vale) 1932 S.
Davies,O.T. (Llanidloes) 1938 E.
Davies-Owen,R. (Northern Nomads, Liverpool Univ, Aberystwyth) 1930 E 1932-3 E,S.
Deakin,A. (Caergwrie) 1938 E.
Dearson,D. (Barry) 1934 E.
Dewey,F.T. (Cardiff Corinthians) 1930-1-2-3 E 1930-1-2-3 S.
Dugdale,T.C. (Blaenau Festiniog) 1938 E.
Dunne,T. (Epsom) 1935 E.
Edwards,G. (Swansea Town) 1939 E.
Ellis,E. (Nunhead, Oswestry) 1930-1-2 E 1931 S.
Evans,D.B. (Wimbledon) 1931 E,S 1932 S.
Evans,G. (Oxford Univ) 1937 E.
Evans,L. (Cardiff City) 1930-1-2 E,S.
Evans,N. (Northfleet) 1939 E.
Evans,W.J. (Troedyrhiw) 1932 E,S 1933 E.
Fielding,I. (Royal Navy) 1935 E,S 1937 E.
Fisher,K. (Lovells Athletic) 1938 E.
Ford,J. (Arsenal) 1937 E.
Forse,T.R. (Cardiff City) 1937 E,S 1939 E.
Foulkes,R. (Flint) 1934-5 S.
Francis,E. (Hounslow) 1939 E.
Friend,H, (Cardiff Corinthians) 1933-4 S.
Gear,D. (Cardiff City) 1939 E.
George,C.V. (Leyland Motors) 1934 S,E.
Gilbert,D.G. (Troedyrhiw, Treharris) 1932 S 1933-4 E.
Griffiths,M. (Blackburn Rovers) 1932 E.
Griffiths,M. (Llandudno, Ilford) 1935 S 1937 S 1938-9 E.
Hamer,A.H, (Dulwich Hamlet) 1932 S 1933 E,S 1934-5 E.
Hassall,J.K. (Manchester United) 1939 E.
Heal,W.C. (Enfield) 1934 S,E.
Hitchcock,B. (Nunhead) 1933-5-6 E,S.
Hughes,J. (Llanerch Celtic, Blackburn Rovers) 1933 E.
Jenkins,E. (Lovells Athletic) 1930-1 E,S.
John,R. (Cardiff Corinthians) 1931 E,S.
Jones,Bryn (Notts County) 1935 S.
Jones,E. (Rhyl) 1932 E.
Jones,F. (Llanidloes) 1933 S.
Jones,G.H. (Cariff City) 1936 E,S 1937 S.
Jones,H. (Mold) 1930 S.
Jones,M. (Rhyl) 1933 S.
Jones,R.T. (Bangor Univ)1932 E.
Jones,S. (Lovells Athletic) 1934 E.
Jones,Trevor (Uxbridge) 1936 E,S.
Leahy,D. (Southall) 1937 E.
Lewis, A/C S. (RAF) 1939 E.
Lewis,C. (Tranmere Rovers) 1933 S.
Lewis,P. (Shrewsbury Town) 1939 E.

Lewis,R,O. (Aberdovey) 1938 E.
Lewis,W.F. (Southall) 1934 E.
Lloyd,J. (Llanerch Celtic) 1938 E.
Love,R.W. (Llanerch Celtic) 1935 E.
McCarthy,D. (Cardiff City, Crittalls Athletic) 1936 E,S 1939 E.
Miller,P.G. (Trent College) 1932 S 1933 E 1934 S.
Mills,H.B. (Llanidloes) 1934 E,S 1935-6-7 S.
Moore,W.A. (Cardiff City) 1935 E.
Mudford, Sgt R.R. (Army) 1936 E,S 1938 E.
Nicholls,J. (Cardiff Corinthians) 1930 E,S.
Norris,T.A. (Carshalton Athletic) 1937 E.
Pearce, Pte (Army) 1932 E.
Peart,W.C. (Royal Navy, Gloucester City) 1936 E,S. 1937 S.
Piper,F. (Tredomen) 1939 E.
Piper-Cole,W. (Marlborough) 1930 S.
Pitt,H.V. (Northern Nomads) 1930 S.
Pryce,H. (Machynlleth) 1934 S.
Pugh,A.R. (Newport County) 1930 E,S.
Pugh,T. (Talgarth) 1931,E,S.
Randall, Gdsm H.S. (Welsh Guards) 1935 E.
Roberts, Bombardier (Royal Engineers) 1932 E.
Roberts,M. (Colwyn Bay) 1935 S.
Roblings,G. (Llanelly) 1931 E,S.
Rogers,E. (Chirk) 1934 S.
Sidlow,C. (Llandudno) 1937 S.
Smallwood,F. (Wrexham) 1934 S.
Thomas,E. (Llanerch Celtic, Oswestry) 1934 E,S.
Thomas,E. (Lovells Athletic) 1930 E,S.
Thomas,W.G. (Wimbledon) 1937 E.
Vale,R. (Leavesden Mental Hospital) 1934 E.
Vereker,W. (Llanidloes) 1938 E.
Waite, Pte S. (RASC) 1937 E.
Ward,T. (Cardiff City) 1936,E,S.
Webb,J.G. (Flint, Liverpool Marine) 1934 E 1936-7 S.
Wheeler,G.H. (Newport County) 1931 E,S.
Williams,A. (Brymbo Green) 1934 S.
Williams,D.H (Llanerch Celtic, Oxford Univ, Liverpool Marine) 1935 S 1937 E,S.
Williams,F.C. (Lovells Athletic) 1933 S.
Williams,F.H. (Northern Nomads, Shrewsbury Town, Buxton) 1930 E,S 1932 S 1933 E.
Williams,H. (Druids) 1936 E,S.
Williams,J. (Bangor) 1936 E.
Williams,J.H. (Epping) 1935 E.
Williams, Pte R. (KSLI) 1935 E.
Williams,S. (Jurgen's Purfleet) 1933 E,S.
Williams,T. (Cardiff City) 1937 E.
Williams,T.S. (Aberaman) 1936-7 E,S.

NORTHERN IRELAND

Agnew,J. (Larne) 1931 S.
Alexander,M. (Glenavon) 1934 S.
Allen,C. (Cliftonville) 1935 E.
Allen,S. (Ards) 1938 E.
Banks,S.J. (Cliftonville) 1936 S 1937-8 E.
Bell,H. (Linfield) 1939 S.
Bermingham,J. (Bohemians) 1931 E.
Billingsley,J. (Cliftonville) 1934 S 1935 E.
Bingham,J. (Glenavon) 1931 S.
Bruce,W. (Bangor) 1935 E,S.

Buckley,A. (Ballymena United) 1935 E.

Burns,H. (Glenavon, Linfield) 1935 S,E 1937 S 1938 E,S.

Clarke,B. (Portadown) 1934 E,S.

Connell,A.S. (Glenavon, Ballymena United) 1934 S 1935-6 E,S.

Crawford.C. (Cliftonville) 1938 S.

Crymble,J. (Linfield Swifts) 1930 E.

Doherty,J. (Portadown, Ards) 1930-1-2 E 1930-1 S.

Dornan,J. (Glenavon) 1936 E.

Duffy,P. (Newry Town) 1937 S.

Falloon,R. (Cliftonville) 1930 E.

Foye,R. (Linfield) 1936 E,S.

Fulton,R.P. (Belfast Celtic) 1931-2-3-4-6-7-8-9 E 1930-1-2-3-4-5-6-8 S.

Galway, Fusilier. (Royal Inniskilling Fusiliers) 1932 E.

Gardinier,A. (Cliftonville) 1930-1-2-3 E1930 1-2 S

Gibb,J. (Cliftonville) 1935-6-7 E,S 1938 E.

Gordon,J.C. (Portadown) 1939 E.

Graham,J. (Bangor) 1938 S,E.

Hare,W. (Cliftonville) 1934 E,S.

Hewitt,H.C. (Linfield, Cliftonville) 1932 E,S 1934 E,S.

Hood,W.J. (Cliftonville) 1937 E.

Horlacher,F.N. (Bohemians) 1931 E.

Horner,R. (Ballymena United) 1939 E.

Irvine,R.G. (Glentoran) 1939 E.

Jennings,J. (Newry Town) 1930 S.

Johnstone,R. (Cliftonville) 1938-9 S.

Jones, L/Cpl J. (King's Own Scottish Borderers, Linfield) 1930-1 E,S.

Kelleher,D. (Barnet) 1938 S 1939 E,S.

Kelly,A. (RAF) 1930 E,S.

Kernaghan,N. (Cliftonville) 1935 E,S.

Kerr,W.C. (Glenavon) 1930 E.

Kilpatrick,A. (Coleraine) 1937,E,S.

Leckey,E. (Cliftonville) 1934,E,S.

Lillie,J. (Cliftonville) 1936,E,S.

Lyness, Cpl A. (Army) 1936 S 1937 E,S.

Lynn,T. (Ards) 1930 S.

McCappin,E. (Cliftonville) 1937 E.

McCarthy,J. (Barnet) 1937 E,S 1938 E 1939 E,S.

McCaw,S.N. (Cliftonville) 1931-2-3 E,S 1934-5 E 1936 S.

McConkey,W.J. (Cliftonville) 1930 S.

McCurry,F. (Cliftonville) 1935 S 1937-8-9 E,S.

McDowell,E.W.J. (Crusaders, Ballymena) 1934 E,S 1935 E.

McIlroy,C.R. (Ballymena) 1934 E.

McIlveen,S. (Larne) 1930 S.

McKay,N. (Glentoran) 1937 S.

McFarlane,J. (Cliftonville) 1930 S.

McGuire,R. (Cliftonville) 1930 E.

McKnight,E. (Bangor) 1933 E.

McLelland,J. (Cliftonville) 1932 S.

McMahon,J. (Derry City, Bohemians) 1930 E 1931-2-3 E,S.

McMillen,W.S. (Cliftonville) 1933 E,S.

McNeill,J. (Cliftonville) 1932 S 1935-6 E,S.

Martin,D. (Royal Ulster Rifles, Belfast Celtic) 1932-3 E,S.

Maynes,A. (Linfield) 1935 S.

Miller,J. (Cliftonville) 1930 E 1931 E,S 1932 E 1933 S 1934 S.

Mitchell,E.J. (Cliftonville) 1933 E,S 1935 S.

Mitchell,G, (Cliftonville)1932-3-6 E,S 1934 E.

Moore,S.S. (Cliftonville) 1933 S.

Moore,W. (Ballymena United) 1938-9 E,S.

Morton,V. (Bohemians) 1931 E.

Murray,G. (Belfast Celtic) 1934 E,S.

Olphert,R.E. (Ballymena United) 1939 E,S.

Preston,J. (Cliftonville) 1936 E,S.

Priestley,T. (Coleraine) 1932 S 1933 E,S.

Quinn,J. (Cliftonville) 1930 E.

Rainey,J. (Larne) 1930 S.

Roche,I.E. (St Albans City, Uxbridge) 1930-1 S.

Roden,G. (Clapton) 1939 S.

Ronnell,A. (Ballymena) 1938 S.

Rosbotham,J. (Glenavon) 1936 S 1937 S.

Shannon,A. (Cliftonville) 1937 E,S.

Skelton,R.M. (Cliftonville) 1931-2-3 E,S.

Tarrant,R. (Sutton United) 1935 S 1936 S 1937 S.

Todd,A. (Linfield) 1938 E,S.

Vincent,W. (Ballymena United) 1939 S.

Wallace,J. (Ballymena United) 1938-9 E,S.

Weir,F.E. (Glenavon) 1939 E.

Wilkin,T. (Newry Town) 1936 E.

Wishart,W. (Cliftonville) 1934 E.

England international Lester Finch, of Barnet

ENGLISH LEAGUE CHAMPIONS

1929-30 Manchester City
Allen JDA 41, Beeson GW 2, Blenkinsop E 39, Brown JH 41, Burgess H 39, Burridge BJH 2, Gregg RE 5, Hooper M 42, Jones TJ 1, Leach TJ 40, Mackey TS 1, Marsden W 37, Mellors RD 1, Millership W 6, Rimmer EJ 40, Seed JM 32, Smith WS 4, Strange AH 41, Walker T 34, Whitehouse JC 4, Wilkinson J 1, Wilson C 9
Goals: Allen JDA 33, Burgess H 19, Hooper M 18, Rimmer EJ 15, Seed JM 9, Strange AH 3, Marsden W 3, Leach TJ 2, Millership W 1, own goals 2

1930-31 Arsenal
Baker A 1, Bastin CS 42, Brain J 16, Cope HW 1, Hapgood EA 38, Harper W 19, Haynes AE 2, Hulme JHA 32, Jack DBN 35, James AW 40, John RF 40, Johnstone W 2, Keizer GP 12, Lambert J 34, Male CG 3, Parker TR 41, Preedy CJF 11, Roberts H 40, Seddon WC 18, Thompson L 2, Williams JJ 9
Goals: Lambert J 38, Jack DBN 31, Bastin CS 28, Hulme JHA 14, James AW 5, Brain J 4, John RF 2, Williams JJ 2, Johnstone W 1, Jones C 1, Roberts H 1

1931-32 Everton
Bocking W 10, Clark A 39, Coggins WH 1, Cresswell W 40, Critchley E 37, Dean WR 38, Dunn J 22, Gee GW 38, Griffiths PH 7, Johnson TCF 41, Lowe H 1, Martin GS 2, McClure JH 7, McPherson L 3, Rigby A 3, Sagar E 41, Stein J 37, Thompson JR 39, White TA 23, Williams BD 33
Goals: Dean WR 45, Johnson TCF 22, White TA 18, Dunn J 10, Stein J 9, Critchley E 8, Griffiths PH 3, Clark A 1

1932-33 Arsenal
Bastin CS 42, Bowden ER 7, Coleman E 27, Compton LH 4, Cope HW 4, Hapgood EA 38, Haynes AE 6, Hill FR 26, Hulme JHA 40, Jack DBN 34, James AW 40, John RF 37, Jones C 16, Lambert J 12, Male CG 35, Moss F 41, Parker TR 5, Parkin R 5, Preedy CJF 1, Roberts H 36, Sidey NW 2, Stockill RR 4
Goals: Bastin CS 33, Coleman E 24, Hulme JHA 20, Jack DBN 18, Lambert J 14, James AW 3, Stockill RR 3, Bowden ER 2, Hill FR 1

1933-34 Arsenal
Bastin CS 38, Beasley AE 23, Birkett RJE 15, Bowden ER 32, Coleman E 12, Cox G 2, Dougal PG 5, Drake EJ 10, Dunne J 21, Hapgood EA 40, Haynes AE 1, Hill FR 25, Hulme JHA 8, Jack DBN 14, James AW 22, John RF 31, Jones C 29, Lambert J 3, Male CG 42, Moss F 37, Parkin R 5, Roberts H 30, Sidey NW 12, Wilson AA 5
Goals: Bastin CS 13, Bowden ER 13, Beasley AE 10, Dunne J 9, Drake EJ 7, Birkett RJE 5, Hulme JHA 5, Jack DBN 5, James AW 3, Coleman E 1, John RF 1, Lambert J 1, Roberts H 1, own goal 1,

1934-35 Arsenal
Bastin CS 36, Beasley AE 20, Birkett RJE 4, Bowden ER 24, Compton LH 5, Copping W 31, Crayston WJ 37, Davidson RT 11, Dougal PG 8, Drake EJ 41, Dunne J 1, Hapgood EA 34, Hill FR 15, Hulme JHA 16, James AW 30, John RF 9, Kirchen AJ 7, Male CG 39, Marshall J 4, Moss F 33, Roberts H 36, Rogers E 5, Sidey NW 6, Trim RF 1, Wilson AA 9
Goals: Drake EJ 42, Bastin CS 20, Bowden ER 14, Hulme JHA 8, Beasley AE 6, James AW 4, Crayston WJ 3, Hill FR 3, Birkett RJE 2, Davidson RT 2, Kirchen AJ 2, Rogers E 2, Compton LH 1, Dougal PG 1, Hapgood EA 1, Moss F 1, own goals 3

1935-36 Sunderland
Carter HS 39, Clarke MMcNC 28, Connor J 42, Davis H 25, Duns L 17, Gallacher P 37, Goddard G 3, Gurney R 39, Hall AW 38, Hastings AC 31, Hornby CF 8, Johnston R 10, Mapson JD 7, McDowell LJ 1, McNab A 13, Middleton MY 9, Morrison TK 21, Murray W 21, Rodgerson R 3, Russell JW 1, Shaw HV 1, Thomson CM 42, Thorpe JH 26
Goals: Carter HS 31, Gurney R 31, Gallacher P 19, Davis H 10, Connor J 7, Duns L 5, Hornby CF 2, Goddard G 1, McNab A 1, Thomson CM 1, own goal 1

1936-37 Manchester City
Barkas S 30, Bray J 40, Brook EF 42, Cassidy JA 1, Clark GV 13, Dale W 36, Doherty PD 41, Donnelly R 7, Freeman RH 1, Heale JA 10, Herd A 32, Marshall RS 38, McCullough K 2, McLeod JS 3, Neilson R 2, Percival J 42, Regan RH 4, Rodger C 9, Rogers JH 2, Swift FV 42, Tilson SF 23, Toseland E 42
Goals: Doherty PD 30, Brook EF 20, Herd A 15, Tilson SF 15, Rodger C 7, Toseland E 7, Heale JA 6, Bray J 2, McLeod JS 2, Donnelly R 1, Neilson R 1, Percival J 1

1937-38 Arsenal
Bastin CS 38, Biggs AG 2, Boulton FP 15, Bowden ER 10, Bremner GH 2, Carr EM 11, Cartwright S 6, Collett E 5, Compton DCS 7, Compton LH 9, Copping W 38, Crayston WJ 31, Davidson RT 5, Drake EJ 27, Drury GB 11, Griffiths WM 9, Hapgood EA 41, Hulme JHA 7, Hunt GS 18, Jones LJ 28, Joy B 26, Kirchen AJ 19, Lewis RJ 4, Male CG 34, Milne JV 16, Roberts H 13, Sidey NW 3, Swindin GH 17, Wilson AA 10
Goals: Drake EJ 17, Bastin CS 15, Carr EM 7, Kirchen AJ 6, Griffiths WM 5, Crayston WJ 4, Milne JV 4, Hunt GS 3, Jones LJ 3, Cartwright S 2, Davidson RT 2, Hulme JHA 2, Lewis RJ 2, Bowden ER 1, Bremner GH 1, Compton DCS 1, Compton LH 1, own goal 1

1938-39 Everton
Barber AW 2, Bell RC 4, Bentham SJ 41, Boyes WE 36, Britton CS 1, Caskie J 5, Cook W 40, Cunliffe JN 7 , Gee CW 2, Gillick T 40, Greenhalgh N 42, Jackson G 2, Jones TG 39, Lawton T 38, Mercer J 41, Milligan GH 1, Morton H 1, Sagar E 41, Stevenson AE 36, Thomson JR 26, Trentham DH 1, Watson TG 16,
Goals: Lawton T 34, Gillick T 14, Stevenson AE 11, Bentham SJ 9, Cook W 5, Boyes WE 4, Bell RC 3, Cunliffe JN 3, Caskie J 1, Greenhalgh N 1, Trentham DH 1, own goals 2

FA CUP FINALS:

All finals played at Wembley Stadium

1929-30, 26 April 1930, Arsenal 2 Huddersfield Tn 0, att. 92,486
Arsenal: Preedy, Parker, Hapgood, Baker, Seddon, John, Hulme, Jack, Lambert, James, Bastin
Huddersfield: Turner, Goodall, Spence, Naylor, Wilson, Campbell, Jackson, Kelly, Davies, Raw, Smith
Scorers: Arsenal; James 16, Lambert 88
Referee: T.Crew (Leicester)

1930-31, 25 April 1931, West Bromwich Alb. 2 Birmingham 1, att. 92,406
West Bromwich Albion: Pearson, Shaw, Trentham, Magee, W Richardson, Edwards, Glidden, Carter, WG Richardson, Sandford, Wood
Birmingham: Hibbs, Liddell, Barkas, Cringan, Morrall, Leslie, Briggs, Crosbie, Bradford, Gregg, Curtis
Scorers: West Bromwich; WG Richardson 26 and 58. Birmingham; Bradford 57
Referee: A.H.Kingscott (Derby)

1931-32, 23 April 1932, Newcastle United 2 Arsenal 1, att. 92,298
Newcastle United: McInroy, Nelson, Fairhurst, McKenzie, Davidson, Weaver, Boyd, JR Richardson, Allen, McMenemy, Lang
Arsenal: Moss, Parker, Hapgood, Jones, Roberts, Male, Hulme, Jack, Lambert, Bastin, John
Scorers: Newcastle United; Allen 38 and 72 Arsenal; John 15
Referee: W.P.Harper (Worcs.)

1932-33, 29 April 1933, Everton 3 Manchester City 0, att. 92,900
Everton: Sagar, Cook, Cresswell, Britton, White, Thomson, Geldard, Dunn, Dean, Johnson, Stein
Manchester City: Langford, Cann, Dale, Busby, Cowan, Bray, Toseland, Marshall, Herd, McMullan, Brook
Scorers: Everton; Stein 41, Dean 52, Dunn 80
Referee: E.J. Wood (Sheffield)

1933-34, 28 April 1934, Manchester City 2 Portsmouth 1, att. 93,258
Manchester City: Swift, Barnett, Dale, Busby, Cowan, Bray, Toseland, Marshall, Tilson, Herd, Brook
Portsmouth: Gilfillan, Mackie, W Smith, Nichol, Allen, Thackeray, Worrall, J Smith, Weddle, Easson, Rutherford
Scorers: Manchester City; Tilson 74, 86 Portsmouth; Rutherford 27
Referee: S.F.Rous (Herts)

1934-35, 27 April 1935, Sheffield Wednesday 4 West Bromwich Albion 2, att. 93,204
Sheffield Wednesday: Brown, Nibloe, Catlin, Sharp, Millership, Burrows, Hooper, Surtees, Palethorpe, Starling, Rimmer

West Bromwich Albion: Pearson, Shaw, Trentham, Murphy, W Richardson, Edwards, Glidden, Carter, WG Richardson , Sandford, Boyes
Scorers: Sheffield Wednesday; Palethorpe 2, Hooper 67, Rimmer 88, 89.
West Bromwich Albion; Boyes 21, Sandford 72
Referee: A.E.Fogg (Bolton)

1935-36, 25 April 1936, Arsenal 1 Sheffield United 0, att.93,384
Arsenal: Wilson, Male, Hapgood, Crayston, Roberts, Copping, Hulme, Bowden, Drake, James, Bastin
Sheffield United: Smith, Hooper, Wilkinson, Jackson, Johnson, McPherson, Barton, Barclay, Dodds, Pickering, Williams
Scorer: Arsenal; Drake 74
Referee: H.Nattrass (Durham)

1936-37, 1 May 1937, Sunderland 3 Preston North End 1, att. 93,495
Sunderland: Mapson, Gorman, Hall, Thomson, Johnston, McNab, Duns, Carter, Gurney, Gallacher, Burbanks
Preston North End: Burns, Gallimore, A Beattie, Shankly, Tremelling, Milne, Dougal, Beresford, F O'Donnell, Fagan, H O'Donnell
Scorers: Sunderland; Gurney 52, Carter 73, Burbanks 78.
Preston North End; F. O'Donnell 38
Referee: R.G. Rudd (London)

1937-38, 30 April 1938, Preston North End 1 Huddersfield Town 0, a.e.t., att. 93,357
Preston North End: Holdcroft, Gallimore, A Beattie, Shankly, Smith, Batey, Watmough, Mutch, Maxwell, R Beattie, H O'Donnell
Huddersfield Town: Hesford, Craig, Mountford, Willingham, Young, Boot, Hulme, Isaac, MacFadyen, Barclay, Beasley
Scorer: Preston North End; Mutch 119 (pen)
Referee: A.J.Jewell (London)

1938-39, 29 April 1939, Portsmouth 4 Wolverhampton Wanderers. 1, att. 99,370
Portsmouth: Walker, Morgan, Rochford, Guthrie, Rowe, Wharton, Worrall, McAlinden, Anderson, Barlow, Parker
Wolverhampton W: Scott, Morris, Taylor, Galley, Cullis, Gardiner, Burton, McIntosh, Westcott, Dorsett, Maguire
Scorer: Portsmouth; Barlow 30, 46, Anderson 43, Parker 73.
Wolverhampton W; Dorsett 65
Referee: T.J. Thompson (Northumberland)

FA AMATEUR CUP FINALS

1929-30 Apr 12 1930 Ilford 5 Bournemouth Gasworks Ath. 1,Upton Park, London, att. 21,800
Ilford: G.Watson, W.B.Triesman, H.W.Winterburn, H.Sheppard, L. Craymer, W.Webb, V.C.Potter, V.F. Welsh, R.C.Dellow, F.A.Drane, G.Peploe
Bournemouth Gasworks Ath. G.Joyce, R.Saunders, H.G. Cobb, S.Turner, H.W.Phillips, T.W.Gillingham, B.Smith, T.Petty, P.Lavell, H.J. Cornbeer, C.J.Tapper
Scorers: Peploe 2, Dellow, Welsh, Potter. Bournemouth Gasworks; Petty
Referee: L.E.Gibbs (Reading)

1930-31 Apr 11 1931 , Wycombe Wanderers 1 Hayes 0, Highbury Stadium, London, att. 32,000
Wycombe Wanderers: J.E.Kipping, S.Crump, R.S.Cox, F.Rance, L.R.Badrick, A.Greenwell, C.Simmons, W.Brown, D.S.Vernon, F.C.Braisher, A.J.Britnell
Hayes: T.Holding, J.Maskell, H.H.Gower, E.J.Caesar, A.Wainwright, W.Caesar, C.Knight, R.G.Rowe, J.Morgan, T.D.Welsh, E.Lloyd
Scorer: Wycombe W; Britnell
Referee: P.Graham (Coventry)

1931-32 Apr 16 1932 Dulwich Hamlet 7 Marine (Liverpool) 1, Upton Park, London, att. 22,000
Dulwich Hamlet: R.F.Miles, A.J.Hugo, B.Osmond, C.Murray, A.H.Hamer, A.Aitken, L.Morrish, E.Kail, W.G.Goodliffe, H.Moseley, H.S.Robbins
Marine: H.Drury, G.Jackson, S.Rankin, J.Crilley, A Kelly, W.Halsall, N.Keir, J.Garvey, G.O'Donnell, L.King, A.Bamford
Scorers: Dulwich Hamlet; Moseley 4, Kail 2, Goodlifffe. Marine; O'Donnell
Referee: A.H.Adams (Nottingham)

1932-33 Apr 8 1933 Kingstonian 1 Stockton 1, Champion Hill, Dulwich, att. 20,744
Kingstonian: E.G.Brodrick, F.G.Rassell, I.W.Urpeth, G.S.C.Lee, J.V.Daley, G.Keene, E.McCarthy, H.Gibson, D.Whitehead, F.Macey, F.Okin
Stockton: R.Newton, J.Thompson, J.C.Little, G.L.Foster, J.Butler, R.P.Edwards, W.J.Stephenson, R.A.Smith, J.M.Coulthard, J. Stirling, S.Henderson
Scorers: Kingstonian; Whitehead. Stockton; Henderson
Referee: J. Milward (Derby)

Replay Apr 22 1933 Kingstonian 4 Stockton 1, Feethams, Darlington, att.16,492
Kingstonian: E.G. Brodrick, F.G. Rassell, I.W. Urpeth, G.S.C. Lee, J.V. Daley, G. Keene, E. McCarthy, H. Gibson, D. Whitehead, F. Macey, F. Okin
Stockton: R. Newton, J. Thompson, J.C. Little, G.L. Foster, D. Pass, R.P. Edwards, W.J. Stephenson, R.A. Smith, J.M. Coulthard, A.J. Prest, S. Henderson
Scorers: Kingstonian; Whitehead 2, Gibson, Urpeth (pen). Stockton; Coulthard
Referee: J. Milward (Derby)

1933-34 Apr 21 1934 Dulwich Hamlet 2 Leyton 1, Upton Park, London, att. 33,000
Dulwich Hamlet: N.Cummings, A.J.Hugo, H.S.Robbins, C.Murray, A.H.Hamer, E.W.Toser, L.Morrish, W.Miller,W.G. Goodliffe, H.F.Benka, D.S.Court
Leyton: T.Holding,A.W. Loveday,F.J. Gregory,E. Caesar, R.Richardson, C.Mercer, E.C.Collins, W.V.T.Gibbins, W.Skeels, H.L.Coates, F.Davis
Scorers: Dulwich Hamlet; Robbins, Court Leyton; Davis
Referee: J.M.Wiltshire (Sherborne)

1934-35 Apr 13 1935 Bishop Auckland 0 Wimbledon 0, Ayresome Park, Middlesbrough, att. 23,335
Bishop Auckland: T.W.Hopps, H.Minton,S. Scott, J.B.Birbeck, G.A.Straughton, J.G.Shield, N.R.Dodds, R.Bryan, A.Wilson, F.Stephenson, W.Hogg
Wimbledon: W.D.Irish, R.A.Goodchild, E.H.Balkwill, J.K.Wright, H.H.Bridge, A.G.Reeves, M.W.Batchelor, E.R.Barnes, W.W.C.Dowden, E.C.Turner, L.Smith
Referee: Dr A.W.Barton (Repton School)

Replay Apr 20 1935 Bishop Auckland 2 Wimbledon 1, Stamford Bridge, London, att. 32,744
Bishop Auckland: T.W.Hopps, H.Minton,S. Scott, J.B.Birbeck, G.A.Straughton, J.G.Shield, N.R.Dodds, R.Bryan, A.Wilson, F.Stephenson, W.Hogg
Wimbledon: W.D.Irish, R.A.Goodchild, E.H.Balkwill, J.K.Wright, H.H.Bridge, A.G.Reeves, L.Smith, E.R.Barnes, W.W.C.Dowden, E.C.Turner, E.Zenthon
Scorers: Bishop Auckland; Wilson, Bryan Wimbledon: Dowden
Referee: Dr A.W.Barton (Repton School)

1935-36 Apr 18 Casuals 1 Ilford 1, Selhurst Park, London, att. 25,064
Casuals: L.T.Huddle, W.T.Whewell, F.de L.Evans, G.Allen, B.Joy, L.T.Couchman, E.D.R.Shearer, A.H.Fabian, B.A.Clements, W.H.Webster, F.Riley
Ilford: M.F.Tietjon, G.C.Holmes, A.C.Hayes, L.V.Male, A.E.Myers,F.L. Craymer, E.C.Gilderson, T.G.Manley, J.Watts, S.R.Halcrow, E.H.Braund
Scorers: Casuals; Riley. Ilford; Braund
Referee: C.E.Argent (St. Albans)

Replay May 2 1936 Casuals 2 Ilford 0, Upton Park, London, att. 27,000
Casuals: L.T.Huddle, W.T.Whewell, F.de L.Evans, G.Allen, B.Joy, L.T.Couchman, E.D.R.Shearer, A.H.Fabian, B.A.Clements, W.H.Webster, F.Riley
Ilford: M.F.Tietjon, G.C.Holmes, A.C.Hayes, L.V.Male, A.E.Myers,F.L. Craymer, E.C.Gilderson, T.G.Manley, J.Watts, S.R.Halcrow, E.H.Braund
Scorers: Casuals; Riley. Ilford; Braund
Referee: C.E.Argent (St. Albans)

1936-37 Apr 7 1937 Dulwich Hamlet 2 Leyton 0, Upton Park, London, att. 33,516
Dulwich Hamlet: H.H.C.Hill, D.S.Weymouth, H.S.Robbins, C.Murray, A.J.Hugo, E.W.Toser, L.B.Morrish, R.S.Anderson, J.K.Wright, A.L.Ingleton, H.S.Ball
Leyton: W.Self, S.Gentry, P.B.Clark, L.Hunt, S.Preston, J.C.Burns, F.Smith, J.Leek, A.Avery, F.Boatwright, L.C.Camerson
Scorers: Dulwich Hamlet; Morrish 2
Referee: F/Sgt F.Warner (R.A.F.)

1937-38 Apr 23 1938 Bromley 1 Erith & Belvedere 0, The Den, Millwall, att. 33,000
Bromley:P.T.Bartaby, L.G.Gray, G.H.Clark, F.P.Wade, V.J.Weeks, E.W.Barnes, W.G.Thomas, A.G.Stroud, G.R.Brown, W.T.Holbrook, S.A.Reece
Erith & Belvedere: A.Gibbs, J.C.Little, P.O'Hara, C.Smee, C.Fuller, A.E.Bennett, G.H.Young, L.Scott, W.J.Southcombe, R.Beal, C. Saunders
Scorers: Bromley; Stroud
Referee: J.H. Lockton (South Norwood)

1938-39 Apr 22 1939 Bishop Auckland 3 Willington 0, a.e.t., Roker Park, Sunderland, att. 20,200
Bishop Auckland: J.Washington, J. Kirtley, K.Humble, E. Wanless, G.A.Straughan, R. Paisley, K. Twigg, L. Wensley, M. Slee, W. Evans, H. Young
Willington: J. Coe, F. Cooper, R. Etheridge, G. Hardy, J. Lumby, J.W.Hindmarsh, M. Mitchell, L. Pratt, M. McLean, W. Davidson, J. Elliott
Scorers: Bishop Auckland; Wensley 3
Referee: G.Hewitt (St Helens)

FOOTBALL ASSOCIATION CHARITY SHIELD

Arsenal 2 Sheffield Wednesday 1, Stamford Bridge, London, 8 October 1930, 25,000.
Arsenal: Keizer; Parker, Hapgood, Seddon, Roberts, John, Hulme, Brain, Lambert, Jack, Bastin.
Sheffield Wednesday: Brown; Walker, Blenkinsop, Strange, Leach, Wilson, Hooper, Seed, Ball, Burgess, Rimmer.
Scorers: Arsenal: Hulme, Jack. Sheffield Wednesday: Burgess (pen).

Arsenal 1 West Bromwich Albion 0, Villa Park, Birmingham, 7 October 1931, 21,276.
Arsenal: Preedy; Parker, Hapgood, Jones C, Roberts, Haynes, Hulme, Jack, Lambert, James, Bastin.
West Bromwich Albion: Pearson; Shaw, Trentham, Magee, Richardson W, Edwards, Glidden, Raw, Richardson W G, Sandford, Wood.
Scorer: Arsenal: Bastin.

Everton 5 Newcastle United 3, St James's Park, Newcastle. 12 October 1932, 15,000.
Everton: Sagar; Williams, Cresswell, Britton, White, Thomson, Critchley, McGourty, Dean, Johnson, Stein.

Newcastle United: Burns; Nelson, Fairhurst, Bell, Davidson, Weaver, Boyd, Richardson, Allen, McMenemy, Lang.
Scorers: Everton: Dean 4, Johnson. Newcastle United: McMenemy 2, Boyd.

Arsenal 3 Everton 0, Goodison Park, Liverpool, 18 October 1933, 30,000.
Arsenal: Moss; Male, Hapgood, Jones C, Sidey, John, Birkett, Coleman, Bowden, James, Hill.
Everton: Sagar; Cook, Bocking, Britton, Gee, Thomson, Geldard, Dunn, White, Johnson, Stein.
Scorers: Arsenal: Birkett 2, Bowden.

Arsenal 4 Manchester City 0, Highbury, London, 28 November 1934, 10,888.
Arsenal: Moss; Male, Hapgood, Hill, Sidey, Copping, Birkett, Marshall, Drake, James, Bastin.
Manchester City: Swift; Dale, Barnett, Busby, Cowan, Bray, Toseland, McLuckie, Tilson, Heale, Brook.
Scorers: Arsenal: Birkett, Marshall, Drake, Bastin.

Sheffield Wednesday 1 Arsenal 0, Highbury, London, 23 October 1935, 30,000.
Sheffield Wednesday: Brown; Nibloe, Catlin, Rhodes, Millership, Burrows, Hooper, Starling, Dewar, Bruce, Rimmer.
Arsenal: Wilson; Male, Hapgood, Hill, B Joy, Copping, Milne, Crayston, Dunne, Davidson, Bastin.
Scorer: Sheffield Wednesday: Dewar.

Sunderland 2 Arsenal 1, Roker Park, Sunderland, 28 October 1936, 11,500.
Sunderland: Mapson; Hall, Collin, Thomson, Johnston, McNab, Duns, Carter, Gurney, Gallacher, Burbanks.
Arsenal: Swindin; Compton L, Hapgood, Crayston, B Joy, Copping, Milne, Bowden, Kirchen, Davidson, Compton D.
Scorers: Sunderland: Carter, Burbanks. Arsenal: Kirchen.

Manchester City 2 Sunderland 0, Maine Road, Manchester, 3 November 1937, 30,000.
Manchester City: Swift; Dale, Barkas, Percival, Marshall, Bray, Toseland, Herd, Tilson, Doherty, Brook.
Sunderland: Mapson; Gorman, Hall, Thomson, Johnston, Hastings, Spuhler, Carter, Gurney, Gallacher, Rowell.
Scorers: Manchester City: Herd, Doherty.

Arsenal 2 Preston North End 1, Highbury, London, 26 September 1938, 35,000.
Arsenal: Swindin; Male, Compton L, Crayston, B Joy, Copping, Kirchen, Jones L, Drake, Jones B, Cumner.
Preston North End: Holdcroft; Gallimore, Beattie A, Shankly, Batey, Milne, McGibbon, Mutch, Dougal, Beattie R, Maxwell.
Scorers: Arsenal: Drake 2.
Preston North End: Beattie R.

THIRD DIVISION NORTH AND SOUTH CUP FINALS.

SOUTHERN SECTION.

Winners
1933-34: Exeter City.
1934-35: Bristol Rovers.
1935-36: Coventry City.
1936-37: Watford & Millwall.
1937-38: Reading.
1938-39: Not decided.

Exeter City 1 Torquay United 0,
Home Park, Plymouth, 2 May 1934, 6,198.
Exeter City: Chesters; Gray, Miller, Clarke, Webb,
Angus, Scott, Poulter, Hurst, Wrightson, Barnes.
Torquay United: Maggs; Rees, Tapp, Lievesley, Welsh,
Pickersgill, Steele, Orr, Flavell, Hutchinson, Bird.
Scorers: Exeter City: Hurst.

Bristol Rovers 3 Watford 2,
The Den, Millwall, 15 April 1935, 5,294.
Bristol Rovers: Ellis; Pickering, Donald, Wallington,
McLean, McArthur, McNestry, McKay, Taylor,
Harwood, Wipfler.
Watford: McLaren; Brown, Moran, Davies T,
Armstrong, Woodward, Davies W, Lowe, Lane W,
O'Brien, McPherson.
Scorers: Bristol Rovers: McKay, Wipfler, Harwood.
Watford: Lane W, O'Brien.

First Leg: Swindon Town 0, Coventry City 2,
25 March 1936, 3,610.
Swindon Town: Rutherford; Duckworth, Smith,
Cousins, Shanks, Wilcockson, Peters, Storey, Fowler,
Lowry, McPhail.
Coventry City: Morgan; Astley, Smith, McCaughey,
Elliott, Frith, Pritchard, Lauderdale, Crawley, Jones,
Liddle.
Scorers: Coventry City: Frith, Lauderdale.

Second Leg: Coventry City 3 Swindon Town 2,
2 April 1936, 2,077.
Coventry City: Morgan; Brook, Smith, McCaughey,
Elliott, Boileau, McNestry, Jones, Crawley, Lake,
Liddle.
Swindon Town: Rutherford; Duckworth, Smith,
Cousins, Shanks, Wilcockson, Peters, Storey, Fowler,
Parmley, McPhail.
Scorers: Coventry City: Jones, Liddle, Lake. Swindon
Town: Peters, McPhail.

NB: 1936-37 Final held over:
First Leg: Watford 2 Millwall 2,
29 September 1937, 2,714.
Watford: McLaren; O'Brien, Lewis DJ, Morgan,
Armstrong, Reed, Jones TJ, Black, Lewis TG, Evans,
Ovenstone.
Millwall: Pearson; Smith E, Inns, Lea, Wallbanks,

Sykes, Steele, Mangnall, Burditt, McCartney, Smith
JCR.
Scorers: Watford: Evans 2. Millwall: Burditt, Mangnall.

Second Leg: Millwall 1 Watford 1,
18 October 1937, 3,368.
Millwall: Pearson; Smith E, Inns, Lea, Chiverton,
Forsyth, Steele, Burditt, Walsh, McCartney, Smith JCR.
Watford: McLaren; O'Brien, Gallimore, Morgan,
Armstrong, Reed, Walters, Barnett, Black, Hawkins,
Evans.
Scorers: Millwall: McCartney. Watford: Walters.
Aggregate 3-3; both teams held trophy for six months.

NB: 1937-38 Final held over:
First Leg: Reading 6 Bristol City 1,
28 September 1938, 1,097.
Reading: Whittaker; Hayhurst, Fullwood, Dougall,
Holmes, Young, Doran, Tait, MacPhee, Glidden,
Smallwood.
Bristol City: Dawson; Bridge, Hick, Caldwell, Roberts,
Armstrong, Morgan, Bourton, Clayton, Gallacher,
Willshaw.
Scorers: Reading: MacPhee 4, Tait, Smallwood. Bristol
City: Willshaw.

Second Leg: Bristol City 1 Reading 0,
12 October 1938, 718.
Bristol City: Pearson; Brook, Turner, Caldwell, Pearce,
Armstrong, Willshaw, Brain, Clayton, Laidman,
Thorley.
Reading: Whittaker; Hayhurst, Fullwood, Wilks,
Young, Glidden, Watkin, Tait, MacPhee, Layton,
Deverall.
Scorer: Bristol City: Brain.

*NB: 1938-39 Semi-final replay between Queens Park
Rangers and Port Vale not played; Torquay United
had qualified for final. Both matches held over to 1939-
40 season.*

NORTHERN SECTION.

Winners:
1933-34: Darlington.
1934-35: Stockport County.
1935-36: Chester.
1936-37: Chester.
1937-38: Southport.
1938-39: Bradford City.

Darlington 4 Stockport County 3,
Old Trafford, Manchester, 1 May 1934, 4,640.
Darlington: Beby; Whelan, Scott, Cassidy, Strang,
Hodgson, Eden, Middleton, Best, Alderson, Edgar.
Stockport County: Finnegan; Vincent, Jenkinson,
Robinson, Stevens, Jones L, Foulkes, Humpish,
Lythgoe, Stevenson, Downes.
Scorers: Darlington: Cassidy, Middleton, Best,
Alderson. Stockport County: Lythgoe, Vincent (pen),
Stevenson.

Stockport County 2 Walsall 0,
Maine Road, Manchester, 1 May 1935, 4,035.
Stockport County: McDonough; Bocking, Jenkinson, Robinson, Jones L, Still, Foulkes, Hill, McNaughton, Green, Scott.
Walsall: McSevich; Bennett, Wiles G, Reed, Morgan, Bradford, Haddleton, Ball, Alsop, Bate, Woolhouse.
Scorers: Stockport County: McNaughton, Foulkes.

Darlington 1 Chester 2,
Feethams, Darlington, 27 April 1936, 7,820.
Darlington: Walker; Coulthard, Allan, Logan, Strang, Hodgson, Smith, McFarlane, Best, Alderson, Atkiin.
Chester: Burke; Common, Hall, Pitcairn, Wilson, Howarth, Horsman, Wharton, Wrightson, Sanders, Sargeant.
Scorers: Darlington: Alderson. Chester: Horsman, Wrightson.

Southport 1 Chester 3,
Haig Avenue, Southport, 27 April 1937, 7,820.
Southport: Rutherford; Purdon, Grainger J, Royston, Frame, Crawford, Kitchen, Newcomb, Patrick, McKay, Wardle.
Chester: Gray; Common, Hall, Howarth, Wilson, Davies, Horsman, Chambers, Wrightson, Alderson, Sargeant.
Scorers: Southport: Purdon (pen). Chester: Frame og, Davies, Horsman.

Southport 4 Bradford City 1,
Haig Avenue, Southport, 4 May 1938, 4,642.
Southport: Rutherford; Royston, Grainger J, Newcomb, Hill, Scott, Stapleton, Hampson, Patrick, Miller, Atkinson.
Bradford City: Parker; McDermott, Pallister, Murphy, Mackie, Moore, Gore, Robertson, Whittingham, Scrimshaw, Bartholomew.
Scorers: Southport: Hampson 2, Robertson 2. Bradford City: Whittingham.

Bradford City 3 Accrington Stanley 0,
Valley Parade, Bradford, 1 May 1939, 3,117.
Bradford City: McCloy; Murphy, McDermott, Molloy, Beardshaw, Moore, Whittingham, Hinsley, Deakin, Hastie, Smailes.
Accrington Stanley: Daniels; Hamilton, Randle, Calvert, Johnson, Dooley, Storey, Waring, Moir, Hann, Mee.
Scorers: Bradford City: Hastie, Hinsley, Smailes.

ENGLISH LEAGUE: FINAL PLACINGS

Columns are final year of season, division, played, won, drawn, lost, goals for and against, points, position in table, and a symbol to indicate promoted (P), relegated (R), final season in League (X), former club returning to League (F), and transferred between divisions three north and south(T)

Accrington Stanley

1930	3N	42	14	9	19	84	81	37	16	
1931	3N	42	15	9	18	84	108	39	13	
1932	3N	40	15	6	19	75	80	36	14	
1933	3N	42	15	10	17	78	76	40	13	
1934	3N	42	13	7	22	65	101	33	20	
1935	3N	42	12	10	20	63	89	34	18	
1936	3N	42	17	8	17	63	72	42	9	
1937	3N	42	16	9	17	76	69	41	13	
1938	3N	42	11	7	24	45	75	29	22	
1939	3N	42	7	6	29	49	103	20	22	

Aldershot

1933	3S	42	13	10	19	61	72	36	17	
1934	3S	42	13	12	17	52	71	38	14	
1935	3S	42	13	10	19	50	75	36	18	
1936	3S	42	14	12	16	53	61	40	11	
1937	3S	42	7	9	26	50	89	23	22	
1938	3S	42	15	5	22	39	59	35	18	
1939	3S	42	16	12	14	53	66	44	10	

Arsenal

1930	1	42	14	11	17	78	66	39	14	
1931	1	42	28	10	4	127	59	66	1	
1932	1	42	22	10	10	90	48	54	2	
1933	1	42	25	8	9	118	61	58	1	
1934	1	42	25	9	8	75	47	59	1	
1935	1	42	23	12	7	115	46	58	1	
1936	1	42	15	15	12	78	48	45	6	
1937	1	42	18	16	8	80	49	52	3	
1938	1	42	21	10	11	77	44	52	1	
1939	1	42	19	9	14	55	41	47	5	

Aston Villa

1930	1	42	21	5	16	92	83	47	4	
1931	1	42	25	9	8	128	78	59	2	
1932	1	42	19	8	15	104	72	46	5	
1933	1	42	23	8	11	92	67	54	2	
1934	1	42	14	12	16	78	75	40	13	
1935	1	42	14	13	15	74	88	41	13	
1936	1	42	13	9	20	81	110	35	21	R
1937	2	42	16	12	14	82	70	44	9	
1938	2	42	25	7	10	73	35	57	1	P
1939	1	42	16	9	17	71	60	41	12	

Barnsley

1930	2	42	14	8	20	56	71	36	17	
1931	2	42	13	9	20	59	79	35	19	
1932	2	42	12	9	21	55	91	33	21	R
1933	3N	42	19	8	15	92	80	46	8	
1934	3N	42	27	8	7	118	61	62	1	P
1935	2	42	13	12	17	60	83	38	16	
1936	2	42	12	9	21	54	80	33	20	
1937	2	42	16	9	17	50	64	41	14	
1938	2	42	11	14	17	50	64	36	21	R
1939	3N	42	30	7	5	94	34	67	1	P

Barrow

Year	Div	P	W	D	L	F	A	Pts	Pos	
1930	3N	42	11	5	26	41	98	27	22	
1931	3N	42	15	7	20	68	89	37	16	
1932	3N	40	24	1	15	86	59	49	5	
1933	3N	42	18	7	17	60	60	43	9	
1934	3N	42	19	9	14	116	94	47	8	
1935	3N	42	13	9	20	58	87	35	17	
1936	3N	42	13	12	17	58	65	38	15	
1937	3N	42	13	10	19	70	86	36	16	
1938	3N	42	11	10	21	41	71	32	21	
1939	3N	42	16	9	17	66	65	41	13	

Birmingham

Year	Div	P	W	D	L	F	A	Pts	Pos	
1930	1	42	16	9	17	67	62	41	11	
1931	1	42	13	10	19	55	70	36	19	
1932	1	42	18	8	16	78	67	44	9	
1933	1	42	14	11	17	57	57	39	13	
1934	1	42	12	12	18	54	56	36	20	
1935	1	42	13	10	19	63	81	36	19	
1936	1	42	15	11	16	61	63	41	12	
1937	1	42	13	15	14	64	60	41	11	
1938	1	42	10	18	14	58	62	38	18	
1939	1	42	12	8	22	62	84	32	21	R

Blackburn Rovers

Year	Div	P	W	D	L	F	A	Pts	Pos	
1930	1	42	19	7	16	99	93	45	6	
1931	1	42	17	8	17	83	84	42	10	
1932	1	42	16	6	20	89	95	38	16	
1933	1	42	14	10	18	76	102	38	15	
1934	1	42	18	7	17	74	81	43	8	
1935	1	42	14	11	17	66	78	39	15	
1936	1	42	12	9	21	55	96	33	22	R
1937	2	42	16	10	16	70	62	42	12	
1938	2	42	14	10	18	71	80	38	16	
1939	2	42	25	5	12	94	60	55	1	P

Blackpool

Year	Div	P	W	D	L	F	A	Pts	Pos	
1930	1	42	27	4	11	98	67	58	1	P
1931	1	42	11	10	21	71	125	32	20	
1932	1	42	12	9	21	65	102	33	20	
1933	1	42	14	5	23	69	85	33	22	R
1934	2	42	15	13	14	62	64	43	11	
1935	2	42	21	11	10	79	57	53	4	
1936	2	42	18	7	17	93	72	43	10	
1937	2	42	24	7	11	88	53	55	2	P
1938	1	42	16	8	18	61	66	40	12	
1939	1	42	12	14	16	56	68	38	15	

Bolton Wanderers

Year	Div	P	W	D	L	F	A	Pts	Pos	
1930	1	42	15	9	18	74	74	39	15	
1931	1	42	15	9	18	68	81	39	14	
1932	1	42	17	4	21	72	80	38	17	
1933	1	42	12	9	21	78	92	33	21	R
1934	2	42	21	9	12	79	55	51	3	
1935	2	40	26	4	12	96	48	56	2	P
1936	1	42	14	13	15	67	76	41	13	
1937	1	42	10	14	18	43	66	34	20	
1938	1	42	15	15	12	64	60	45	7	
1939	1	42	15	15	12	67	58	45	8	

Bournemouth

Year	Div	P	W	D	L	F	A	Pts	Pos	
1930	3S	42	15	13	14	72	61	43	10	
1931	3S	42	15	13	14	72	73	43	10	
1932	3S	42	13	12	17	70	78	38	15	
1933	3S	42	12	12	18	60	81	36	18	
1934	3S	42	9	9	24	60	102	27	21	
1935	3S	42	15	7	20	54	71	37	17	
1936	3S	42	16	11	15	60	56	43	8	
1937	3S	42	20	9	13	65	59	49	6	
1938	3S	42	14	12	16	56	57	40	13	
1939	3S	42	13	13	16	52	58	39	15	

Bradford City

Year	Div	P	W	D	L	F	A	Pts	Pos	
1930	2	42	12	12	18	60	77	36	18	
1931	2	42	17	10	15	61	63	44	10	
1932	2	42	16	13	13	80	61	45	7	
1933	2	42	14	13	15	65	61	41	11	
1934	2	42	20	6	16	73	67	46	6	
1935	2	42	12	8	22	50	68	32	20	
1936	2	42	15	13	14	55	65	43	12	
1937	2	42	9	12	21	54	94	30	21	R
1938	3N	42	14	10	18	66	69	38	14	
1939	3N	42	22	8	12	89	56	52	3	

Bradford Park Avenue

Year	Div	P	W	D	L	F	A	Pts	Pos	
1930	2	42	19	12	11	91	70	50	4	
1931	2	42	18	10	14	97	66	46	6	
1932	2	42	21	7	14	72	63	49	6	
1933	2	42	17	8	17	77	71	42	8	
1934	2	42	23	3	16	86	67	49	5	
1935	2	42	11	16	15	55	63	38	15	
1936	2	42	14	9	19	62	84	37	16	
1937	2	42	12	9	21	52	88	33	20	
1938	2	42	17	9	16	69	56	43	7	
1939	2	42	12	11	19	61	82	35	17	

Brentford

Year	Div	P	W	D	L	F	A	Pts	Pos	
1930	3S	42	28	5	9	94	44	61	2	
1931	3S	42	22	6	14	90	64	50	3	
1932	3S	42	19	10	13	68	52	48	5	
1933	3S	42	26	10	6	90	49	62	1	P
1934	2	42	22	7	13	85	60	51	4	
1935	2	42	26	9	7	93	48	61	1	P
1936	1	42	17	12	13	81	60	46	5	
1937	1	42	18	10	14	82	78	46	6	
1938	1	42	18	9	15	69	59	45	6	
1939	1	42	14	8	20	53	74	36	18	

Brighton & Hove Albion

Year	Div	P	W	D	L	F	A	Pts	Pos	
1930	3S	42	21	8	13	87	63	50	5	
1931	3S	42	17	15	10	68	53	49	4	
1932	3S	42	17	12	13	73	58	46	8	
1933	3S	42	17	8	17	66	65	42	12	
1934	3S	42	15	13	14	68	60	43	10	
1935	3S	42	17	9	16	69	62	43	9	
1936	3S	42	18	8	16	70	63	44	7	
1937	3S	42	24	5	13	74	43	53	3	
1938	3S	42	21	9	12	64	44	51	5	
1939	3S	42	19	11	12	68	49	49	3	

Bristol City

Year	Div	P	W	D	L	F	A	Pts	Pos	
1930	2	42	13	9	20	61	83	35	20	
1931	2	42	15	8	19	54	82	38	16	
1932	2	42	6	11	25	39	78	23	22	R
1933	3S	42	12	13	17	83	90	37	15	
1934	3S	42	10	13	19	58	85	33	19	
1935	3S	42	15	9	18	52	68	39	15	
1936	3S	42	15	10	17	48	59	40	13	
1937	3S	42	15	6	21	58	70	36	16	
1938	3S	42	21	13	8	68	40	55	2	
1939	3S	42	16	12	14	61	63	44	8	

Bristol Rovers

Year	Div	P	W	D	L	F	A	Pts	Pos	
1930	3S	42	11	8	23	67	93	30	20	
1931	3S	42	16	8	18	75	92	40	15	
1932	3S	42	13	8	21	65	92	34	18	
1933	3S	42	15	14	13	61	56	44	9	
1934	3S	42	20	11	11	77	47	51	7	
1935	3S	42	17	10	15	73	77	44	8	
1936	3S	42	14	9	19	69	95	37	17	
1937	3S	42	16	4	22	71	80	36	15	
1938	3S	42	13	13	16	46	61	39	15	
1939	3S	42	10	13	19	55	61	33	22	

Burnley

Year	Div	P	W	D	L	F	A	Pts	Pos	
1930	1	42	14	8	20	79	97	36	21	R
1931	2	42	17	11	14	81	77	45	8	
1932	2	42	13	9	20	59	87	35	19	
1933	2	42	11	14	17	67	79	36	19	
1934	2	42	18	6	18	60	72	42	13	
1935	2	42	16	9	17	63	73	41	12	
1936	2	42	12	13	17	50	59	37	15	
1937	2	42	16	10	16	57	61	42	13	
1938	2	42	17	10	15	54	54	44	6	
1939	2	42	15	9	18	50	56	39	14	

Bury

Year	Div	P	W	D	L	F	A	Pts	Pos	
1930	2	42	22	5	15	78	67	49	5	
1931	2	42	19	3	20	75	82	41	13	
1932	2	42	21	7	14	70	58	49	5	
1933	2	42	20	9	13	84	59	49	4	
1934	2	42	17	9	16	70	73	43	12	
1935	2	42	19	4	19	62	73	42	10	
1936	2	42	13	12	17	66	84	38	14	
1937	2	42	22	8	12	74	55	52	3	
1938	2	42	18	5	19	63	60	41	10	
1939	2	42	12	13	17	65	74	37	16	

Cardiff City

Year	Div	P	W	D	L	F	A	Pts	Pos	
1930	2	42	18	8	16	61	59	44	8	
1931	2	42	8	9	25	47	87	25	22	R
1932	3S	42	19	8	15	87	73	46	9	
1933	3S	42	12	7	23	69	99	31	19	
1934	3S	42	9	6	27	57	105	24	22	
1935	3S	42	13	9	20	62	82	35	19	
1936	3S	42	13	10	19	60	73	36	20	
1937	3S	42	14	7	21	54	87	35	18	
1938	3S	42	15	12	15	67	54	42	10	
1939	3S	42	15	11	16	61	65	41	13	

Carlisle United

Year	Div	P	W	D	L	F	A	Pts	Pos	
1930	3N	42	16	7	19	90	101	39	15	
1931	3N	42	20	5	17	98	81	45	8	
1932	3N	40	11	11	18	64	79	33	18	
1933	3N	42	13	7	22	51	75	33	19	
1934	3N	42	15	8	19	66	81	38	13	
1935	3N	42	8	7	27	51	102	23	22	
1936	3N	42	14	12	16	56	62	40	13	
1937	3N	42	18	8	16	65	68	44	10	
1938	3N	42	15	9	18	57	67	39	12	
1939	3N	42	13	7	22	66	111	33	19	

Charlton Athletic

Year	Div	P	W	D	L	F	A	Pts	Pos	
1930	2	42	14	11	17	59	63	39	13	
1931	2	42	15	9	18	59	86	39	15	
1932	2	42	17	9	16	61	66	43	10	
1933	2	42	12	7	23	60	91	31	22	R
1934	3S	42	22	8	12	83	56	52	5	
1935	3S	42	27	7	8	103	52	61	1	P
1936	2	42	22	11	9	85	58	55	2	P
1937	1	42	21	12	9	58	49	54	2	
1938	1	42	16	14	12	65	51	46	4	
1939	1	42	22	6	14	75	59	50	3	

Chelsea

Year	Div	P	W	D	L	F	A	Pts	Pos	
1930	2	42	22	11	9	74	46	55	2	P
1931	1	42	15	10	17	64	67	40	12	
1932	1	42	16	8	18	69	73	40	12	
1933	1	42	14	7	21	63	73	35	18	
1934	1	42	14	8	20	67	69	36	19	
1935	1	42	16	9	17	73	82	41	12	
1936	1	42	15	13	14	65	72	43	8	
1937	1	42	14	13	15	52	55	41	13	
1938	1	42	14	13	15	65	65	41	10	
1939	1	42	12	9	21	64	80	33	20	

Chester

Year	Div	P	W	D	L	F	A	Pts	Pos	
1932	3N	40	21	8	11	78	60	50	3	
1933	3N	42	22	8	12	94	66	52	4	
1934	3N	42	17	6	19	89	86	40	10	
1935	3N	42	20	14	8	91	58	54	3	
1936	3N	42	22	11	9	100	45	55	2	
1937	3N	42	22	9	11	87	57	53	3	
1938	3N	42	16	12	14	77	72	44	9	
1939	3N	42	20	9	13	88	70	49	6	

Chesterfield

Year	Div	P	W	D	L	F	A	Pts	Pos	
1930	3N	42	22	6	14	76	56	50	4	
1931	3N	42	26	6	10	102	57	58	1	P
1932	2	42	13	11	18	64	86	37	17	
1933	2	42	12	10	20	61	84	34	21	R
1934	3N	42	27	7	8	86	43	61	2	
1935	3N	42	17	10	15	71	52	44	10	
1936	3N	42	24	12	6	92	39	60	1	P
1937	2	42	16	8	18	84	89	40	15	
1938	2	42	16	9	17	63	63	41	11	
1939	2	42	20	9	13	69	52	49	6	

Clapton Orient

Year	Div	P	W	D	L	F	A	Pts	Pos	
1930	3S	42	14	13	15	55	62	41	12	
1931	3S	42	14	7	21	63	91	35	19	
1932	3S	42	12	11	19	77	90	35	16	
1933	3S	42	8	13	21	59	93	29	20	
1934	3S	42	16	10	16	75	69	42	11	
1935	3S	42	15	10	17	65	65	40	14	
1936	3S	42	16	6	20	55	61	38	14	
1937	3S	42	14	15	13	52	52	43	12	
1938	3S	42	13	7	22	42	61	33	19	
1939	3S	42	11	13	18	53	55	35	20	

Coventry City

Year	Div	P	W	D	L	F	A	Pts	Pos	
1930	3S	42	19	9	14	88	73	47	6	
1931	3S	42	16	9	17	75	65	41	14	
1932	3S	42	18	8	16	108	97	44	12	
1933	3S	42	19	6	17	106	77	44	6	
1934	3S	42	21	12	9	100	54	54	2	
1935	3S	42	21	9	12	86	50	51	3	
1936	3S	42	24	9	9	102	45	57	1	P
1937	2	42	17	11	14	66	54	45	8	
1938	2	42	20	12	10	66	45	52	4	
1939	2	42	21	8	13	62	45	50	4	

Crewe Alexandra

Year	Div	P	W	D	L	F	A	Pts	Pos	
1930	3N	42	17	8	17	82	71	42	11	
1931	3N	42	14	6	22	66	93	34	18	
1932	3N	40	21	6	13	95	66	48	6	
1933	3N	42	20	3	19	80	84	43	10	
1934	3N	42	15	6	21	81	97	36	14	
1935	3N	42	14	11	17	66	86	39	13	
1936	3N	42	19	9	14	80	76	47	6	
1937	3N	42	10	12	20	55	83	32	20	
1938	3N	42	18	9	15	71	53	45	8	
1939	3N	42	19	6	17	82	70	44	8	

Crystal Palace

Year	Div	P	W	D	L	F	A	Pts	Pos	
1930	3S	42	17	12	13	81	74	46	9	
1931	3S	42	22	7	13	107	71	51	2	
1932	3S	42	20	11	11	74	63	51	4	
1933	3S	42	19	8	15	78	64	46	5	
1934	3S	42	16	9	17	71	67	41	12	
1935	3S	42	19	10	13	86	64	48	5	
1936	3S	42	22	5	15	96	74	49	6	
1937	3S	42	13	12	17	62	61	38	14	
1938	3S	42	18	12	12	67	47	48	7	
1939	3S	42	20	12	10	71	52	52	2	

Darlington

Year	Div	P	W	D	L	F	A	Pts	Pos	
1930	3N	42	22	6	14	108	73	50	3	
1931	3N	42	16	10	16	71	59	42	11	
1932	3N	40	17	4	19	66	69	38	11	
1933	3N	42	10	8	24	66	109	28	22	
1934	3N	42	13	9	20	70	101	35	16	
1935	3N	42	21	9	12	80	59	51	5	
1936	3N	42	17	6	19	74	79	40	12	
1937	3N	42	8	14	20	66	96	30	22	
1938	3N	42	11	10	21	54	79	32	19	
1939	3N	42	13	7	22	62	92	33	18	

Derby County

Year	Div	P	W	D	L	F	A	Pts	Pos	
1930	1	42	21	8	13	90	82	50	2	
1931	1	42	18	10	14	94	79	46	6	
1932	1	42	14	10	18	71	75	38	15	
1933	1	42	15	14	13	76	69	44	7	
1934	1	42	17	11	14	68	54	45	4	
1935	1	42	18	9	15	81	66	45	6	
1936	1	42	18	12	12	61	52	48	2	
1937	1	42	21	7	14	96	90	49	4	
1938	1	42	15	10	17	66	87	40	13	
1939	1	42	19	8	15	66	55	46	6	

Doncaster Rovers

Year	Div	P	W	D	L	F	A	Pts	Pos	
1930	3N	42	15	9	18	62	69	39	14	
1931	3N	42	13	11	18	65	65	37	15	
1932	3N	40	16	4	20	59	80	36	15	
1933	3N	42	17	14	11	77	79	48	6	
1934	3N	42	22	9	11	83	61	53	5	
1935	3N	42	26	5	11	87	44	57	1	P
1936	2	42	14	9	19	51	71	37	18	
1937	2	42	7	10	25	30	84	24	22	R
1938	3N	42	21	12	9	74	49	54	2	
1939	3N	42	21	14	7	87	47	56	2	

Everton

Year	Div	P	W	D	L	F	A	Pts	Pos	
1930	1	42	12	11	19	80	92	35	22	R
1931	2	42	28	5	9	121	66	61	1	P
1932	1	42	26	4	12	116	64	56	1	
1933	1	42	16	9	17	81	74	41	11	
1934	1	42	12	16	14	62	63	40	14	
1935	1	42	16	12	14	89	88	44	8	
1936	1	42	13	13	16	89	89	39	16	
1937	1	42	14	9	19	81	78	37	17	
1938	1	42	16	7	19	79	75	39	14	
1939	1	42	27	5	10	88	52	59	1	

Exeter City

Year	Div	P	W	D	L	F	A	Pts	Pos	
1930	3S	42	12	11	19	67	73	35	16	
1931	3S	42	17	8	17	84	90	42	13	
1932	3S	42	20	7	15	77	62	47	7	
1933	3S	42	24	10	8	88	48	58	2	
1934	3S	42	16	11	15	68	57	43	9	
1935	3S	42	16	9	17	70	75	41	11	
1936	3S	42	8	11	23	59	93	27	22	
1937	3S	42	10	12	20	59	88	32	21	
1938	3S	42	13	12	17	57	70	38	17	
1939	3S	42	13	14	15	65	82	40	14	

Fulham

Year	Div	P	W	D	L	F	A	Pts	Pos	
1930	3S	42	18	11	13	87	83	47	7	
1931	3S	42	18	7	17	77	75	43	9	
1932	3S	42	24	9	9	111	62	57	1	P
1933	2	42	20	10	12	78	65	50	3	
1934	2	42	15	7	20	48	67	37	16	
1935	2	42	17	12	13	76	56	46	7	
1936	2	42	15	14	13	76	52	44	9	
1937	2	42	15	13	14	71	61	43	11	
1938	2	42	16	11	15	61	57	43	8	
1939	2	42	17	10	15	61	55	44	12	

Gateshead

Year	Div	P	W	D	L	F	A	Pts	Pos	
1931	3N	42	16	13	13	71	73	45	9	
1932	3N	40	25	7	8	94	48	57	2	
1933	3N	42	19	9	14	78	67	47	7	
1934	3N	42	12	9	21	76	110	33	19	
1935	3N	42	13	8	21	58	96	34	19	
1936	3N	42	13	14	15	56	76	40	14	
1937	3N	42	11	10	21	63	98	32	21	
1938	3N	42	20	11	11	84	59	51	5	
1939	3N	42	14	14	14	74	67	42	10	

Gillingham

Year	Div	P	W	D	L	F	A	Pts	Pos	
1930	3S	42	11	8	23	51	80	30	21	
1931	3S	42	14	10	18	61	76	38	16	
1932	3S	42	10	8	24	40	82	28	21	
1933	3S	42	18	8	16	72	61	44	7	
1934	3S	42	11	11	20	75	96	33	17	
1935	3S	42	11	13	18	55	75	35	20	
1936	3S	42	14	9	19	66	77	37	16	
1937	3S	42	18	8	16	52	66	44	11	
1938	3S	42	10	6	26	36	77	26	22	X

Grimsby Town

Year	Div	P	W	D	L	F	A	Pts	Pos	
1930	1	42	15	7	20	73	89	37	18	
1931	1	42	17	5	20	82	87	39	13	
1932	1	42	13	6	23	67	98	32	21	R
1933	2	42	14	13	15	79	84	41	13	
1934	2	42	27	5	10	103	59	59	1	P
1935	1	42	17	11	14	78	60	45	5	
1936	1	42	17	5	20	65	73	39	17	
1937	1	42	17	7	18	86	81	41	12	
1938	1	42	13	12	17	51	68	38	20	
1939	1	42	16	11	15	61	69	43	10	

Halifax Town

Year	Div	P	W	D	L	F	A	Pts	Pos	
1930	3N	42	10	8	24	44	79	28	21	
1931	3N	42	13	9	20	55	89	35	17	
1932	3N	40	13	8	19	61	87	34	17	
1933	3N	42	15	8	19	71	90	38	15	
1934	3N	42	20	4	18	80	91	44	9	
1935	3N	42	25	5	12	76	67	55	2	
1936	3N	42	15	7	20	57	61	37	17	
1937	3N	42	18	9	15	68	63	45	7	
1938	3N	42	12	12	18	44	66	36	18	
1939	3N	42	13	16	13	52	54	42	12	

Hartlepools United

Year	Div	P	W	D	L	F	A	Pts	Pos	
1930	3N	42	17	11	14	81	74	45	8	
1931	3N	42	12	6	24	67	86	30	20	
1932	3N	40	16	5	19	78	100	37	13	
1933	3N	42	16	7	19	87	116	39	14	
1934	3N	42	16	7	19	89	93	39	11	
1935	3N	42	17	7	18	80	78	41	12	
1936	3N	42	15	12	15	57	61	42	8	
1937	3N	42	19	7	16	75	69	45	6	
1938	3N	42	10	12	20	53	80	32	20	
1939	3N	42	12	7	23	55	94	31	21	

Huddersfield Town

Year	Div	P	W	D	L	F	A	Pts	Pos	
1930	1	42	17	9	16	63	69	43	10	
1931	1	42	18	12	12	81	65	48	5	
1932	1	42	19	10	13	80	63	48	4	
1933	1	42	18	11	13	66	53	47	6	
1934	1	42	23	10	9	90	61	56	2	
1935	1	42	14	10	18	76	71	38	16	
1936	1	42	18	12	12	59	56	48	3	
1937	1	42	12	15	15	62	64	39	15	
1938	1	42	17	5	20	55	68	39	15	
1939	1	42	12	11	19	58	64	35	19	

Hull City

Year	Div	P	W	D	L	F	A	Pts	Pos	
1930	2	42	14	7	21	51	78	35	21	R
1931	3N	42	20	10	12	99	55	50	6	
1932	3N	40	20	5	15	82	53	45	8	
1933	3N	42	26	7	9	100	45	59	1	P
1934	2	42	13	12	17	52	68	38	15	
1935	2	42	16	8	18	63	74	40	13	
1936	2	42	5	10	27	47	111	20	22	R
1937	3N	42	17	12	13	68	69	46	5	
1938	3N	42	20	13	9	80	43	53	3	
1939	3N	42	18	10	14	83	74	46	7	

Ipswich Town

Year	Div	P	W	D	L	F	A	Pts	Pos
1939	3S	42	16	12	14	62	52	44	7

Leeds United

Year	Div	P	W	D	L	F	A	Pts	Pos	
1930	1	42	20	6	16	79	63	46	5	
1931	1	42	12	7	23	68	81	31	21	R
1932	2	42	22	10	10	78	54	54	2	P
1933	1	42	15	14	13	59	62	44	8	
1934	1	42	17	8	17	75	66	42	9	
1935	1	42	13	12	17	75	92	38	18	
1936	1	42	15	11	16	66	64	41	11	
1937	1	42	15	4	23	60	80	34	19	
1938	1	42	14	15	13	64	69	43	9	
1939	1	42	16	9	17	59	67	41	13	

Leicester City

Year	Div	P	W	D	L	F	A	Pts	Pos	
1930	1	42	17	9	16	86	90	43	8	
1931	1	42	16	6	20	80	95	38	16	
1932	1	42	15	7	20	74	94	37	19	
1933	1	42	11	13	18	75	89	35	19	
1934	1	42	14	11	17	59	74	39	17	
1935	1	42	12	9	21	61	86	33	21	R
1936	2	42	19	10	13	79	57	48	6	
1937	2	42	24	8	10	89	57	56	1	P
1938	1	42	14	11	17	54	75	39	16	
1939	1	42	9	11	22	48	82	29	22	R

Lincoln City

Year	Div	P	W	D	L	F	A	Pts	Pos	
1930	3N	42	17	14	11	83	61	48	5	
1931	3N	42	25	7	10	102	59	57	2	
1932	3N	40	26	5	9	106	47	57	1	P
1933	2	42	12	13	17	72	87	37	18	
1934	2	42	9	8	25	44	75	26	22	R
1935	3N	42	22	7	13	87	58	51	4	
1936	3N	42	22	9	11	91	51	53	4	
1937	3N	42	25	7	10	103	57	57	2	
1938	3N	42	19	8	15	66	50	46	7	
1939	3N	42	12	9	21	66	92	33	17	

Liverpool

Year	Div	P	W	D	L	F	A	Pts	Pos
1930	1	42	16	9	17	63	79	41	12
1931	1	42	15	12	15	86	85	42	9
1932	1	42	19	6	17	81	93	44	10
1933	1	42	14	11	17	79	84	39	14
1934	1	42	14	10	18	79	87	38	18
1935	1	42	19	7	16	85	88	45	7
1936	1	42	13	12	17	60	64	38	19
1937	1	42	12	11	19	62	84	35	18
1938	1	42	15	11	16	65	71	41	11
1939	1	42	14	14	14	62	63	42	11

Luton Town

Year	Div	P	W	D	L	F	A	Pts	Pos	
1930	3S	42	14	12	16	64	78	40	13	
1931	3S	42	19	8	15	76	51	46	7	
1932	3S	42	20	7	15	95	70	47	6	
1933	3S	42	13	13	16	78	78	39	14	
1934	3S	42	21	10	11	83	61	52	6	
1935	3S	42	19	12	11	92	60	50	4	
1936	3S	42	22	12	8	81	45	56	2	
1937	3S	42	27	4	11	103	53	58	1	P
1938	2	42	15	10	17	89	86	40	12	
1939	2	42	22	5	15	82	66	49	7	

Manchester City

Year	Div	P	W	D	L	F	A	Pts	Pos	
1930	1	42	19	9	14	91	81	47	3	
1931	1	42	18	10	14	75	70	46	8	
1932	1	42	13	12	17	83	73	38	14	
1933	1	42	16	5	21	68	71	37	16	
1934	1	42	17	11	14	65	72	45	5	
1935	1	42	20	8	14	82	67	48	4	
1936	1	42	17	8	17	68	60	42	9	
1937	1	42	22	13	7	107	61	57	1	
1938	1	42	14	8	20	80	77	36	21	R
1939	2	42	21	7	14	96	72	49	5	

Manchester United

Year	Div	P	W	D	L	F	A	Pts	Pos	
1930	1	42	15	8	19	67	88	38	17	
1931	1	42	7	8	27	53	115	22	22	R
1932	2	42	17	8	17	71	72	42	12	
1933	2	42	15	13	14	71	68	43	6	
1934	2	42	14	6	22	59	85	34	20	
1935	2	42	23	4	15	76	55	50	5	
1936	2	42	22	12	8	85	43	56	1	P
1937	1	42	10	12	20	55	78	32	21	R
1938	2	42	22	9	11	82	50	53	2	P
1939	1	42	11	16	15	57	65	38	14	

Mansfield Town

Year	Div	P	W	D	L	F	A	Pts	Pos	
1932	3S	42	11	10	21	75	108	32	20	T
1933	3N	42	14	7	21	84	100	35	16	
1934	3N	42	11	12	19	81	88	34	17	
1935	3N	42	19	9	14	75	62	47	8	
1936	3N	42	14	9	19	80	91	37	19	
1937	3N	42	18	8	16	91	76	44	9	T
1938	3S	42	15	9	18	62	67	39	14	
1939	3S	42	12	15	15	44	62	39	16	

Merthyr Town

Year	Div	P	W	D	L	F	A	Pts	Pos	
1930	3S	42	6	9	27	60	135	21	22	X

Middlesbrough

Year	Div	P	W	D	L	F	A	Pts	Pos
1930	1	42	16	6	20	82	84	38	16
1931	1	42	19	8	15	98	90	46	7
1932	1	42	15	8	19	64	89	38	18
1933	1	42	14	9	19	63	73	37	17
1934	1	42	16	7	19	68	80	39	16
1935	1	42	10	14	18	70	90	34	20
1936	1	42	15	10	17	84	70	40	14
1937	1	42	19	8	15	74	71	46	7
1938	1	42	19	8	15	72	65	46	5
1939	1	42	20	9	13	93	74	49	4

Millwall

Year	Div	P	W	D	L	F	A	Pts	Pos	
1930	2	42	12	15	15	57	73	39	14	
1931	2	42	16	7	19	71	80	39	14	
1932	2	42	17	9	16	61	61	43	9	
1933	2	42	16	11	15	59	57	43	7	
1934	2	42	11	11	20	39	68	33	21	R
1935	3S	42	17	7	18	57	62	41	12	
1936	3S	42	14	12	16	58	71	40	12	
1937	3S	42	18	10	14	64	54	46	8	
1938	3S	42	23	10	9	83	37	56	1	P
1939	2	42	14	14	14	64	53	42	13	

Nelson

Year	Div	P	W	D	L	F	A	Pts	Pos	
1930	3N	42	13	7	22	51	80	33	19	
1931	3N	42	6	7	29	43	113	19	22	X

New Brighton

Year	Div	P	W	D	L	F	A	Pts	Pos	
1930	3N	42	16	8	18	69	79	40	13	
1931	3N	42	13	7	22	49	76	33	19	
1932	3N	40	8	8	24	38	76	24	20	
1933	3N	42	11	10	21	63	88	32	21	
1934	3N	42	14	8	20	62	87	36	15	
1935	3N	42	14	8	20	59	76	36	16	
1936	3N	42	9	6	27	43	102	24	22	
1937	3N	42	13	11	18	55	70	37	15	
1938	3N	42	15	8	19	60	61	38	13	
1939	3N	42	15	9	18	68	73	39	16	

Newcastle United

Year	Div	P	W	D	L	F	A	Pts	Pos	
1930	1	42	15	7	20	71	92	37	19	
1931	1	42	15	6	21	78	87	36	17	
1932	1	42	18	6	18	80	87	42	11	
1933	1	42	22	5	15	71	63	49	5	
1934	1	42	10	14	18	68	77	34	21	R
1935	2	42	22	4	16	89	68	48	6	
1936	2	42	20	6	16	88	79	46	8	
1937	2	42	22	5	15	80	56	49	4	
1938	2	42	14	8	20	51	58	36	19	
1939	2	42	18	10	14	61	48	46	9	

Newport County

Year	Div	P	W	D	L	F	A	Pts	Pos	
1930	3S	42	12	10	20	74	85	34	18	
1931	3S	42	11	6	25	69	111	28	21	X
1933	3S	42	11	7	24	61	105	29	21	F
1934	3S	42	8	17	17	49	70	33	18	
1935	3S	42	10	5	27	54	112	25	22	
1936	3S	42	11	9	22	60	111	31	21	
1937	3S	42	12	10	20	67	98	34	19	
1938	3S	42	11	16	15	43	52	38	16	
1939	3S	42	22	11	9	58	45	55	1	P

Northampton Town

Year	Div	P	W	D	L	F	A	Pts	Pos	
1930	3S	42	21	8	13	82	58	50	4	
1931	3S	42	18	12	12	77	59	48	6	
1932	3S	42	16	7	19	69	69	39	14	
1933	3S	42	18	8	16	76	66	44	8	
1934	3S	42	14	12	16	71	78	40	13	
1935	3S	42	19	8	15	65	67	46	7	
1936	3S	42	15	8	19	62	90	38	15	
1937	3S	42	20	6	16	85	68	46	7	
1938	3S	42	17	9	16	51	57	43	9	
1939	3S	42	15	8	19	51	58	38	17	

Norwich City

Year	Div	P	W	D	L	F	A	Pts	Pos	
1930	3S	42	18	10	14	88	77	46	8	
1931	3S	42	10	8	24	47	76	28	22	
1932	3S	42	17	12	13	76	67	46	10	
1933	3S	42	22	13	7	88	55	57	3	
1934	3S	42	25	11	6	88	49	61	1	P
1935	2	42	14	11	17	71	61	39	14	
1936	2	42	17	9	16	72	65	43	11	
1937	2	42	14	8	20	63	71	36	17	
1938	2	42	14	11	17	56	75	39	14	
1939	2	42	13	5	24	50	91	31	21	R

Nottingham Forest

Year	Div	P	W	D	L	F	A	Pts	Pos	
1930	2	42	13	15	14	55	69	41	10	
1931	2	42	14	9	19	80	85	37	17	
1932	2	42	16	10	16	77	72	42	11	
1933	2	42	17	15	10	67	59	49	5	
1934	2	42	13	9	20	73	74	35	17	
1935	2	42	17	8	17	76	70	42	9	
1936	2	42	12	11	19	69	76	35	19	
1937	2	42	12	10	20	68	90	34	18	
1938	2	42	14	8	20	47	60	36	20	
1939	2	42	10	11	21	49	82	31	20	

Notts County

Year	Div	P	W	D	L	F	A	Pts	Pos	
1930	2	42	9	15	18	54	70	33	22	R
1931	3S	42	24	11	7	97	46	59	1	P
1932	2	42	13	12	17	75	75	38	16	
1933	2	42	15	10	17	67	78	40	15	
1934	2	42	12	11	19	53	62	35	18	
1935	2	42	9	7	26	46	97	25	22	R
1936	3S	42	15	12	15	60	57	42	9	
1937	3S	42	23	10	9	74	52	56	2	
1938	3S	42	16	9	17	50	50	41	11	
1939	3S	42	17	9	16	59	54	43	11	

Oldham Athletic

Year	Div	P	W	D	L	F	A	Pts	Pos	
1930	2	42	21	11	10	90	51	53	3	
1931	2	42	16	10	16	61	72	42	12	
1932	2	42	13	10	19	62	84	36	18	
1933	2	42	15	8	19	67	80	38	16	
1934	2	42	17	10	15	72	60	44	9	
1935	2	42	10	6	26	56	95	26	21	R
1936	3N	42	18	9	15	86	73	45	7	
1937	3N	42	20	11	11	77	59	51	4	
1938	3N	42	19	13	10	67	46	51	4	
1939	3N	42	22	5	15	76	59	49	5	

Plymouth Argyle

Year	Div	P	W	D	L	F	A	Pts	Pos	
1930	3S	42	30	8	4	98	38	68	1	P
1931	2	42	14	8	20	76	84	36	18	
1932	2	42	20	9	13	100	66	49	4	
1933	2	42	16	9	17	63	67	41	14	
1934	2	42	15	13	14	69	70	43	10	
1935	2	42	19	8	15	75	64	46	8	
1936	2	42	20	8	14	71	57	48	7	
1937	2	42	18	13	11	71	53	49	5	
1938	2	42	14	12	16	57	65	40	13	
1939	2	42	15	8	19	49	55	38	15	

Port Vale

Year	Div	P	W	D	L	F	A	Pts	Pos	
1930	3N	42	30	7	5	103	37	67	1	P
1931	2	42	21	5	16	67	61	47	5	
1932	2	42	13	7	22	58	89	33	20	
1933	2	42	14	10	18	66	79	38	17	
1934	2	42	19	7	16	60	55	45	8	
1935	2	42	11	12	19	55	74	34	18	
1936	2	42	12	8	22	56	106	32	21	R
1937	3N	42	17	10	15	58	64	44	11	
1938	3N	42	12	14	16	65	73	38	15	T
1939	3S	42	14	9	19	52	58	37	18	

Portsmouth

1930	1	42	15	10	17	66	62	40	13	
1931	1	42	18	13	11	84	67	49	4	
1932	1	42	19	7	16	62	62	45	8	
1933	1	42	18	7	17	74	76	43	9	
1934	1	42	15	12	15	52	55	42	10	
1935	1	42	15	10	17	71	72	40	14	
1936	1	42	17	8	17	54	67	42	10	
1937	1	42	17	10	15	62	66	44	9	
1938	1	42	13	12	17	62	68	38	19	
1939	1	42	12	13	17	47	70	37	17	

Preston North End

1930	2	42	13	11	18	65	80	37	16	
1931	2	42	17	11	14	83	64	45	7	
1932	2	42	16	10	16	75	77	42	13	
1933	2	42	16	10	16	74	70	42	9	
1934	2	42	23	6	13	71	52	52	2	P
1935	1	42	15	12	15	62	67	42	11	
1936	1	42	18	8	16	67	64	44	7	
1937	1	42	14	13	15	56	67	41	14	
1938	1	42	16	17	9	64	44	49	3	
1939	1	42	16	12	14	63	59	44	9	

Queen's Park Rangers

1930	3S	42	21	9	12	80	68	51	3
1931	3S	42	20	3	19	82	75	43	8
1932	3S	42	15	12	15	79	73	42	13
1933	3S	42	13	11	18	72	87	37	16
1934	3S	42	24	6	12	70	51	54	4
1935	3S	42	16	9	17	63	72	41	13
1936	3S	42	22	9	11	84	53	53	4
1937	3S	42	18	9	15	73	52	45	9
1938	3S	42	22	9	11	80	47	53	3
1939	3S	42	15	14	13	68	49	44	6

Reading

1930	2	42	12	11	19	54	67	35	19	
1931	2	42	12	6	24	72	96	30	21	R
1932	3S	42	23	9	10	97	67	55	2	
1933	3S	42	19	13	10	103	71	51	4	
1934	3S	42	21	12	9	82	50	54	3	
1935	3S	42	21	11	10	89	65	53	2	
1936	3S	42	26	2	14	87	62	54	3	
1937	3S	42	19	11	12	76	60	49	5	
1938	3S	42	20	11	11	71	63	51	6	
1939	3S	42	16	14	12	69	59	46	5	

Rochdale

1930	3N	42	18	7	17	89	91	43	10
1931	3N	42	12	6	24	62	107	30	21
1932	3N	40	4	3	33	48	135	11	21
1933	3N	42	13	7	22	58	80	33	18
1934	3N	42	9	6	27	53	103	24	22
1935	3N	42	11	11	20	53	71	33	20
1936	3N	42	10	13	19	58	88	33	20
1937	3N	42	13	9	20	69	86	35	18
1938	3N	42	13	11	18	67	78	37	17
1939	3N	42	15	9	18	92	82	39	15

Rotherham United

1930	3N	42	11	8	23	67	113	30	20
1931	3N	42	13	12	17	81	83	38	14
1932	3N	40	14	4	22	63	72	32	19
1933	3N	42	14	6	22	60	84	34	17
1934	3N	42	10	8	24	53	91	28	21
1935	3N	42	19	7	16	86	73	45	9
1936	3N	42	16	9	17	69	66	41	11
1937	3N	42	14	7	21	78	91	35	17
1938	3N	42	20	10	12	68	56	50	6
1939	3N	42	17	8	17	64	64	42	11

Sheffield United

1930	1	42	15	6	21	91	96	36	20	
1931	1	42	14	10	18	78	84	38	15	
1932	1	42	20	6	16	80	75	46	7	
1933	1	42	17	9	16	74	80	43	10	
1934	1	42	12	7	23	58	101	31	22	R
1935	2	42	16	9	17	79	70	41	11	
1936	2	42	20	12	10	79	50	52	3	
1937	2	42	18	10	14	66	54	46	7	
1938	2	42	22	9	11	73	56	53	3	
1939	2	42	20	14	8	69	41	54	2	P

Sheffield Wednesday

1930	1	42	26	8	8	105	57	60	1	
1931	1	42	22	8	12	102	75	52	3	
1932	1	42	22	6	14	96	82	50	3	
1933	1	42	21	9	12	80	68	51	3	
1934	1	42	16	9	17	62	67	41	11	
1935	1	42	18	13	11	70	64	49	3	
1936	1	42	13	12	17	63	77	38	20	
1937	1	42	9	12	21	53	69	30	22	R
1938	2	42	14	10	18	49	56	38	17	
1939	2	42	21	11	10	88	59	53	3	

South Shields

1930	3N	42	18	10	14	77	74	46	7

Southampton

1930	2	42	17	11	14	77	76	45	7
1931	2	42	19	6	17	74	62	44	9
1932	2	42	17	7	18	66	77	41	14
1933	2	42	18	5	19	66	66	41	12
1934	2	42	15	8	19	54	58	38	14
1935	2	42	11	12	19	46	75	34	19
1936	2	42	14	9	19	47	65	37	17
1937	2	42	11	12	19	53	77	34	19
1938	2	42	15	9	18	55	77	39	15
1939	2	42	13	9	20	56	82	35	18

Southend United

1930	3S	42	15	13	14	69	59	43	11
1931	3S	42	22	5	15	76	60	49	5
1932	3S	42	21	11	10	77	53	53	3
1933	3S	42	15	11	16	65	82	41	13
1934	3S	42	12	10	20	51	74	34	16
1935	3S	42	11	9	22	65	78	31	21
1936	3S	42	13	10	19	61	62	36	18
1937	3S	42	17	11	14	78	67	45	10
1938	3S	42	15	10	17	70	68	40	12
1939	3S	42	16	9	17	61	64	41	12

Southport

1930	3N	42	15	13	14	81	74	43	9
1931	3N	42	22	9	11	88	56	53	5
1932	3N	40	18	10	12	58	53	46	7
1933	3N	42	17	7	18	70	67	41	12
1934	3N	42	8	17	17	63	90	33	18
1935	3N	42	10	12	20	55	85	32	21
1936	3N	42	11	9	22	48	90	31	21
1937	3N	42	12	13	17	73	87	37	14
1938	3N	42	12	14	16	53	82	38	16
1939	3N	42	20	10	12	75	54	50	4

Stockport County

1930	3N	42	28	7	7	106	44	63	2	
1931	3N	42	20	9	13	77	61	49	7	
1932	3N	40	13	11	16	55	53	37	12	
1933	3N	42	21	12	9	99	58	54	3	
1934	3N	42	24	11	7	115	52	59	3	
1935	3N	42	22	3	17	90	72	47	7	
1936	3N	42	20	8	14	65	49	48	5	
1937	3N	42	23	14	5	84	39	60	1	P
1938	2	42	11	9	22	43	70	31	22	R
1939	3N	42	17	9	16	91	77	43	9	

Stoke City

1930	2	42	16	8	18	74	72	40	11	
1931	2	42	17	10	15	64	71	44	11	
1932	2	42	19	14	9	69	48	52	3	
1933	2	42	25	6	11	78	39	56	1	P
1934	1	42	15	11	16	58	71	41	12	
1935	1	42	18	6	18	71	70	42	10	
1936	1	42	20	7	15	57	57	47	4	
1937	1	42	15	12	15	72	57	42	10	
1938	1	42	13	12	17	58	59	38	17	
1939	1	42	17	12	13	71	68	46	7	

Sunderland

1930	1	42	18	7	17	76	80	43	9	
1931	1	42	16	9	17	89	85	41	11	
1932	1	42	15	10	17	67	73	40	13	
1933	1	42	15	10	17	63	80	40	12	
1934	1	42	16	12	14	81	56	44	6	
1935	1	42	19	16	7	90	51	54	2	
1936	1	42	25	6	11	109	74	56	1	
1937	1	42	19	6	17	89	87	44	8	
1938	1	42	14	16	12	55	57	44	8	
1939	1	42	13	12	17	54	67	38	16	

Swansea Town

1930	2	42	14	9	19	57	61	37	15	
1931	2	42	12	10	20	51	74	34	20	
1932	2	42	16	7	19	73	75	39	15	
1933	2	42	19	4	19	50	54	42	10	
1934	2	42	10	15	17	51	60	35	19	
1935	2	42	14	8	20	56	67	36	17	
1936	2	42	15	9	18	67	76	39	13	
1937	2	42	15	7	20	50	65	37	16	
1938	2	42	13	12	17	45	73	38	18	
1939	2	42	11	12	19	50	83	34	19	

Swindon Town

1930	3S	42	13	12	17	73	83	38	14	
1931	3S	42	18	6	18	89	94	42	12	
1932	3S	42	14	6	22	70	84	34	17	
1933	3S	42	9	11	22	60	105	29	22	
1934	3S	42	17	11	14	64	68	45	8	
1935	3S	42	13	12	17	67	78	38	16	
1936	3S	42	14	8	20	64	73	36	19	
1937	3S	42	14	11	17	75	73	39	13	
1938	3S	42	17	10	15	49	49	44	8	
1939	3S	42	18	8	16	72	77	44	9	

Thames

1931	3S	42	13	8	21	54	93	34	20	
1932	3S	42	7	9	26	53	109	23	22	X

Torquay United

1930	3S	42	10	11	21	64	94	31	19	
1931	3S	42	17	9	16	80	84	43	11	
1932	3S	42	12	9	21	72	106	33	19	
1933	3S	42	16	12	14	72	67	44	10	
1934	3S	42	13	7	22	53	93	33	20	
1935	3S	42	18	6	18	81	75	42	10	
1936	3S	42	16	9	17	62	62	41	10	
1937	3S	42	11	10	21	57	80	32	20	
1938	3S	42	9	12	21	38	73	30	20	
1939	3S	42	14	9	19	54	70	37	19	

Tottenham Hotspur

1930	2	42	15	9	18	59	61	39	12	
1931	2	42	22	7	13	88	55	51	3	
1932	2	42	16	11	15	87	78	43	8	
1933	2	42	20	15	7	96	51	55	2	P
1934	1	42	21	7	14	79	56	49	3	
1935	1	42	10	10	22	54	93	30	22	R
1936	2	42	18	13	11	91	55	49	5	
1937	2	42	17	9	16	88	66	43	10	
1938	2	42	19	6	17	76	54	44	5	
1939	2	42	19	9	14	67	62	47	8	

Tranmere Rovers

1930	3N	42	16	9	17	83	86	41	12	
1931	3N	42	24	6	12	111	74	54	4	
1932	3N	40	19	11	10	107	58	49	4	
1933	3N	42	17	8	17	70	66	42	11	
1934	3N	42	20	7	15	84	63	47	7	
1935	3N	42	20	11	11	74	55	51	6	
1936	3N	42	22	11	9	93	58	55	3	
1937	3N	42	12	9	21	71	88	33	19	
1938	3N	42	23	10	9	81	41	56	1	P
1939	2	42	6	5	31	39	99	17	22	R

Walsall

1930	3S	42	13	8	21	71	78	34	17	
1931	3S	42	14	9	19	78	95	37	17	T
1932	3N	40	16	3	21	57	85	35	16	
1933	3N	42	19	10	13	75	58	48	5	
1934	3N	42	23	7	12	97	60	53	4	
1935	3N	42	13	10	19	81	72	36	14	
1936	3N	42	16	9	17	79	59	41	10	T
1937	3S	42	13	10	19	63	85	36	17	
1938	3S	42	11	7	24	52	88	29	21	
1939	3S	42	11	11	20	68	69	33	21	

Watford

1930	3S	42	15	8	19	60	73	38	15	
1931	3S	42	14	7	21	72	75	35	18	
1932	3S	42	19	8	15	81	79	46	11	
1933	3S	42	16	12	14	66	63	44	11	
1934	3S	42	15	7	20	71	63	37	15	
1935	3S	42	19	9	14	76	49	47	6	
1936	3S	42	20	9	13	80	54	49	5	
1937	3S	42	19	11	12	85	60	49	4	
1938	3S	42	21	11	10	73	43	53	4	
1939	3S	42	17	12	13	62	51	46	4	

West Bromwich Albion

1930	2	42	21	5	16	105	73	47	6	
1931	2	42	22	10	10	83	49	54	2	P
1932	1	42	20	6	16	77	55	46	6	
1933	1	42	20	9	13	83	70	49	4	
1934	1	42	17	10	15	78	70	44	7	
1935	1	42	17	10	15	83	83	44	9	
1936	1	42	16	6	20	89	88	38	18	
1937	1	42	16	6	20	77	98	38	16	
1938	1	42	14	8	20	74	91	36	22	R
1939	2	42	18	9	15	89	72	45	10	

West Ham United

1930	1	42	19	5	18	86	79	43	7	
1931	1	42	14	8	20	79	94	36	18	
1932	1	42	12	7	23	62	107	31	22	R
1933	2	42	13	9	20	75	93	35	20	
1934	2	42	17	11	14	78	70	45	7	
1935	2	42	26	4	12	80	63	56	3	
1936	2	42	22	8	12	90	68	52	4	
1937	2	42	19	11	12	73	55	49	6	
1938	2	42	14	14	14	53	52	42	9	
1939	2	42	17	10	15	70	52	44	11	

Wigan Borough

1930	3N	42	13	7	22	60	88	33	18	
1931	3N	42	19	5	18	76	86	43	10	X

Wolverhampton Wanderers

1930	2	42	16	9	17	77	79	41	9	
1931	2	42	21	5	16	84	67	47	4	
1932	2	42	24	8	10	115	49	56	1	P
1933	1	42	13	9	20	80	96	35	20	
1934	1	42	14	12	16	74	86	40	15	
1935	1	42	15	8	19	88	94	38	17	
1936	1	42	15	10	17	77	76	40	15	
1937	1	42	21	5	16	84	67	47	5	
1938	1	42	20	11	11	72	49	51	2	
1939	1	42	22	11	9	88	39	55	2	

Wrexham

1930	3N	42	13	8	21	67	88	34	17
1931	3N	42	21	12	9	94	62	54	3
1932	3N	40	18	7	15	64	69	43	10
1933	3N	42	24	9	9	106	51	57	2
1934	3N	42	23	5	14	102	73	51	6
1935	3N	42	16	11	15	76	69	43	11
1936	3N	42	15	7	20	66	75	37	18
1937	3N	42	16	12	14	71	57	44	8
1938	3N	42	16	11	15	58	63	43	10
1939	3N	42	17	7	18	66	79	41	14

York City

1930	3N	42	15	16	11	77	64	46	6
1931	3N	42	18	6	18	85	82	42	12
1932	3N	40	18	7	15	76	81	43	9
1933	3N	42	13	6	23	72	92	32	20
1934	3N	42	15	8	19	71	74	38	12
1935	3N	42	15	6	21	76	82	36	15
1936	3N	42	13	12	17	62	95	38	16
1937	3N	42	16	11	15	79	70	43	12
1938	3N	42	16	10	16	70	68	42	11
1939	3N	42	12	8	22	64	92	32	20

Charles Sutcliffe, President of the Football League, presents medals and the Third (South) Championship shield to Notts County, April 1931

SCOTTISH LEAGUE CHAMPIONS

Appearances and goals

1929-30 Rangers.
Archibald A 34; Brown G 17; Buchanan J 25; Craig T 27; Fleming J W 34; Gray D 34; Hamilton R 29; Hamilton T 38; Ireland R 1; Lockie T 2; McCandless W 2; McDonald R 13; McMillan G 5; McPhail R 23; McPherson A 6; Main R 1; Marshall J 26; Morton A 24; Meiklejohn D 31; Muirhead T 20; Nicholwon W 12; Osborne J l; Purdon J 4; Simpson J 8; Smith J 1.
Goals: 94: Fleming 27, McPhail 17, Marshall 14, Archibald 12, Brown 11, Morton 5, Craig 2, McPherson 2, Nicholson 2, Muirhead 1, Smith 1.

1930-31 Rangers.
Archibald A 28; Brown G 29; Buchanan J 26; Conlin G 2; Craig T 14; Dawson J 1; Fleming J W 13; Gray D 38; Hamilton R 27; Hamilton T 37; McAulay R 3; McDonald R 13, McGowan R 12; McMillan G 1; McPhail 34, Main R 2; Marshall J 32; Meiklejohn D 31; Morton A 32; Murray J 4; Nicholson W 6; Simpson J 12; Smith J 21.
Goals: 96: Smith 21, McPhail 20, Marshall 20, McGowan 10, Morton 7, Archibald 6, Fleming 5, Brown 3, Gray 2, Craig 1, Meiklejohn 1.

1931-32 Motherwell.
Blair J 4; Craig A 37; Douglas T 7; Dowall W 32; Ellis B 38; Ferrier R 36; Hunter A 1; Johnston J W 7; McClory A 38; McFadyen, W 34; McKenzie T 1; Mackrell J 2; McMenemy J 31; Moffat W 11; Murdoch J L 26; Stevenson G 35; Telfer W 37; Wales W 36; Wyllie T 5.
Goals: 119: McFadyen 53, Ferrier 13, Stevenson 12, Murdoch 10, Moffat 8, Douglas 6, McMenemy 6, Dowall 4, Wyllie 4, Craig 1, Wales 1, own goal 1.

1932-33 Rangers.
Archibald A 28; Brown G 38; Campbell H 2; Craig T 4; Dawson J 20; Deans W R 1; English S 25; Fleming J W 21; Gray D 37, Hamilton R 18; Kennedy J 10; McDonald R 29; McPhail R 31; Main R 3; Marshall J 34; Mason C 2; Meiklejohn 31; Morton A 6; Nicholson W 2, Russell T 5; Simpson J 32; Stevenson A 1; Smith J 34.
Goals: 113: Smith 33, McPhail 29, Marshall 16, Fleming 12, English 10, Archibald 4, Morton 3, Meiklejohn 2, Campbell 1, McDonald 1, Nicholson 1, own goal 1.

1933-34 Rangers.
Archibald 15; Brown G 35; Cheyne W 3; Craig T 8; Dawson J 30; Fleming J W 13; Gillick T 2; Gray D 37; Hamilton T 1; Jenkins G 7; Kennedy J 7; Macaulay A 5; McDonald R 38; McPhail R 25; Marshall J 21; Main R 25; Mason C 1; Meiklejohn D 29; Nicholson W 26; Russell T 3; Simpson J 29; Smith J 32; Stevenson A 11; Venters A 15.
Goals: 118: Smith 41, McPhail 22, Fleming 16, Nicholson 8, Marshall 7, Stevenson 7, Venters 5, Main 4, Archibald 2, Meiklejohn 2, Brown 1, Macaulay 1, Simpson 1, own goal 1.

1934-35 Rangers.
Brown G 34; Cheyne W 6; Craig T 6; Dawson J 37;
Fiddes J 3; Fleming J W 4; Gillick T 27; Gray D 36; Hay
W 1; Jenkins G 1; Kennedy J 13; Kinnear D 4; Macaulay
A 16; McDonald R 35; McPhail R 30; Main R 27;
Meiklejohn D 22; Nicholson W 13; Roberts S 5;
Simpson J 37; Smkith J 32; Venters A 28; Winning A 1.
Goals: 96: Smith 36, Gillick 17, McPhail 14, Venters 10,
Main 5, Macaulay 4, Meiklejohn 3, Brown 1, Craig 1,
Fleming 1, Nicholson 1, Roberts 1, Simpson 1, own goal
1.

1935-36 Celtic.
Buchan W 38; Crum J 38; Delaney J 30; Divers J 2;
Fagan W 5; Fitzsimmons 2; Foley J 5; Geatons C 34;
Hogg R 38; Hughes W 4; Kennaway J 33; Lyon W 38;
MacDonald M 10; McGonagle T 14; McGrory J 32;
McInally J 1; Millar A 1; Mills H 1; Morrison J 27;
Murphy F 29; Paterson G 36.
Goals: 115: McGrory 50; Delaney 18, Murphy 14,
Buchan 11, Crum 9, Lyon 6, Fagan 3, Hughes 2,
Geatons 1, McInally 1.

1936-37 Rangers.
Brown G 35; Cheyne W 17; Dawson J 38; Drysdale 7;
Fiddes J 4; Gray D 36; Kennedy J 21; Kinnear D 37;
Macaulay A 9; McDonald R 22; McKillop T 17; McPhail
R 33; Main R 23; Reid J 1; Simpson J 31; Smith J 37;
Soutar T 10; Thornton W 5; Venters A 33; Winning A 2.
Goals: 88: Smith 31, McPhail 25, Venters 10, Kinnear 8,
Main 6, Simpson 2, Brown 1, Cheyne 1, Fiddes 1,
Macaulay 1, McKillop 1, Thornton 1.

1937-38 Celtic.
Boyle J 1; Buchan W 16; Carruth J G 19; Crum J 38;
Delaney J 26; Davitt M 1; Divers J 20; Doyle T 2; Duffy
R 1; Fitzsimmons J 1; Geatons C 22; Hogg R 38;
Kennaway J 36; Lynch M 14; Lyon W 36; MacDonald M
27; McGrory J 10; Millar A 5; Morrison J 31; Murphy F
37; Paterson G 37.
Goals: 114: Crum 24, Divers 19, Carruth 15, Buchan 13,
MacDonald 12, Murphy 10, Delaney 7, McGrory 5, Lyon
3, Geatons 2, Lynch 1, own goals 3.

1938-39 Rangers.
Brown G 19; Cheyne W 2; Dawson J 33; Fiddes J 19;
Galloway J 2; Gilmour T 2; Gray D 35, Harirson R G 4;
Jenkins G 5; Kinnear D 26; Little A 4; Lyness A 4;
McKillop T 25; McPhail R 23; Main R 8; Reid J 2; Ross
R 1; Shaw J 36; Simpson J 25; Symon S 22; Smith J 7;
Thornton W 36; Turnbull J 6; Venters A 33; Waddell W
27; Woodburn W 12.
Goals: 112: Venters 35, Thornton 23, McPhail 13,
Kinnear 9, Waddell 7, Fiddes 6, Smith 4, Harrison 3,
Main 3, Symon 3, Brown 2, Lyness 2, Turnbull 1, own
goal 1.

SCOTTISH FA CUP FINALS

All finals played at Hampden Park

1929-30 12 April 1930, Rangers 0 Partick Thistle 0,
att. 107,475
Rangers: Hamilton T, Gray, Hamilton R, Buchanan,
Meiklejohn, Craig, Archibald, Marshall, Fleming,
McPhail, Nicholson.
Partick: Jackson, Calderwood, Rae, Elliot, Lambie,
McLeod, Ness, Grove, Boardman, Ballantyne, Torbet.
Referee; W.Bell (Motherwell).

1929-30 Replay 16 April 1930, Rangers 2
Partick Thistle 1, att. 103,686
Rangers: Hamilton T, Gray, Hamilton R, McDonald,
Meiklejohn, Craig, Archibald, Marshall, Fleming,
McPhail, Morton.
Partick: Jackson, Calderwood, Rae, Elliot, Lambie,
McLeod, Ness, Grove, Boardman, Ballantyne, Torbet.
Scorers: Rangers: Marshall, Craig.
Partick: Torbet.
Referee: W.Bell (Motherwell).

1930-31 11 April 1931, Celtic 2 Motherwell 2,
att. 104,803
Celtic: Thomson J, Cook, McGonagle, Wilson, McStay
J, Geatons, Thomson R, Thomson A, McGrory, Scarff,
Napier.
Motherwell: McCloy; Johnman, Hunter, Wales, Craig,
Telfer, Murdoch, McMenemy, McFadyen, Stevenson,
Ferrier.
Scorers: Celtic: McGrory, Craig (og).
Motherwell: Stevenson, McMenemy.
Referee: P.Craigmyle (Aberdeen).

1930-31 Replay 15 April 1931, Celtic 4 Motherwell 2,
att. 98,579
Celtic: Thomson J, Cook, McGonagle, Wilson, McStay
J, Geatons, Thomson R, Thomson A, McGrory, Scarff,
Napier.
Motherwell: McClory, Johnman, Hunter, Wales, Craig,
Telfer, Murdoch, McMenemy, McFadyen, Stevenson,
Ferrier.
Scorers: Celtic: Thomson R 2, McGrory 2.
Motherwell: Murdoch, Stevenson.
Referee: P.Craigmyle (Aberdeen).

1931-32 16 April 1932, Rangers 1 Kilmarnock 1,
att. 111,982
Rangers: Hamilton T, Gray, McAulay, Meiklejohn,
Simpson, Brown, Archibald, Marshall, English,
McPhail, Morton.
Kilmarnock: Bell, Leslie, Nibloe, Morton, Smith,
McEwan, Connell, Muir, Maxwell, Duncan, Aitken.
Scorers: Rangers: McPhail.
Kilmarnock: Maxwell.
Referee: P.Craigmyle (Aberdeen)

1931-32 Replay 20 April 1932, Rangers 3 Kilmarnock 0, att. 104,695
Rangers: Hamilton T, Gray, McAulay, Meiklejohn, Simpson, Brown, Archibald, Marshall, English, McPhail, Fleming.
Kilmarnock: Bell, Leslie, Nibloe, Morton, Smith, McEwan, Connell, Muir, Maxwell, Duncan, Aitken.
Scorers: Rangers: Fleming, McPhail, English.
Referee: P.Craigmyle (Aberdeen).

1932-33 15 April 1933, Celtic 1 Motherwell 0, att. 102,339
Celtic: Kennaway; Hogg, McGonagle, Wilson, McStay J, Geatons, Thomson R, Thomson A, McGrory, Napier, O'Donnell H.
Motherwell: McClory; Crapnell, Ellis, Wales, Blair, Mackenzie, Murdoch, McMenemy, McFadyen, Stevenson, Ferrier.
Scorer: Celtic: McGrory.
Referee: T.Dougray (Glasgow).

1933-34 21 April 1934, Rangers 5 St Mirren 0, att.113,403
Rangers: Hamilton T, Gray, McDonald, Meiklejohn, Simpson, Brown, Main, Marshall, Smith, McPhail, Nicholson.
St Mirren: McCloy, Hay, Ancell, Gebbie, Wilson, Miller, Knox, Latimer, McGregor, McCabe, Phillips.
Scorers: Rangers: Nicholson 2, McPhail, Main, Smith.
Referee: M.Hutton (Glasgow).

1934-35 20 April 1935, Rangers 2 Hamilton Academicals 1, att. 87,286
Rangers: Dawson, Gray, McDonald, Kennedy, Simpson, Brown, Main, Venters, Smith, McPhail, Gillick.
Hamilton: Morgan, Wallace, Bulloch, Cox, McStay, Murray, King, McLaren, Wilson, Harrison, Reid.
Scorers: Rangers: Smith 2.
Hamilton: Harrison.
Referee: H.Watson (Glasgow).

1935-36 18 April 1936, Rangers 1 Third Lanark 0, att. 88,859
Rangers: Dawson, Gray, Cheyne, Meiklejohn, Simpson, Brown, Fiddes, Venters, Smith, McPhail, Turnbull.
Third Lanark: Muir; Carabine, Hamilton, Blair, Denmark, McInnes, Howe, Gallacher, Hay, Kennedy, Kinnaird.
Scorer: Rangers: McPhail.
Referee: J.Martin (Glasgow).

1936-37 24 April 1937, Celtic 2 Aberdeen 1, att. 147,365
Celtic: Kennaway, Hogg, Morrison, Geatons, Lyon, Paterson, Delaney, Buchan, McGrory, Crum, Murphy.
Aberdeen: Johnstone, Cooper, Temple, Dunlop, Falloon, Thomson, Benyon, McKenzie, Armstrong, Mills, Laing.
Scorers: Celtic: Crum, Buchan.
Aberdeen: Armstrong.
Referee: M.Hutton (Glasgow).

1937-38 23 April 1938, East Fife 1 Kilmarnock 1, att. 80,091
East Fife: Milton, Laird, Tait, Rujssell, Sneddon, Herd, Adams, McLeod, McCartney, Miller, McKerrell.
Kilmarnock: Hunter, Fyfe, Milloy, Robertson, Stewart, Ross, Thomson, Reid, Collins, McAvoy, McGrogan.
Scorers: East Fife: McLeod.
Kilmarnock: McAvoy.
Referee: H.Watson (Glasgow).

1937-38 Replay 27 April 1938, East Fife 4 Kilmarnock 2 (aet), att. 92,716
East Fife: Milton, Laird, Tait, Russell, Sneddon, Harvey, Adams, McLeod, McCartney, Miller, McKerrell.
Kilmarnock: Hunter, Fyfe, Milloy, Robertson, Stewart, Ross, Thomson, Reid, Collins, McAvoy, McGrogan.
Scorers: East Fife: McKerrell 2, McLeod, Miller.
Kilmarnock: Thomson (pen), McGrogan.
Referee: H.Watson (Glasgow).

1938-39 22 April 1939, Clyde 4 Motherwell 0, att. 94,799
Clyde: Brown, Kirk, Hickie, Beaton, Falloon, Weir, Robertson, Noble, Martin, Wallace, Gillies.
Motherwell: Murray, Wales, Ellkis, Mackenzie, Blair, Telfer, Ogilvie, Bremner, Mathie, Stevenson, McCulloch.
Scorers: Clyde: Wallace, Martin 2, Noble.
Referee: W.Webb (Glasgow).

East Fife, Scottish FA Cup winners in 1938. Back; Russell, Laird, Tait, Milton, Harvey, Herd. Front; Adams, Miller, McCartney, Sneddon, McLeod, McKerrell

SCOTTISH LEAGUE: FINAL PLACINGS

Columns are final year of season, division, played, won, drawn, lost, goals for and against, points, position in table, and a symbol to indicate promoted (P), relegated (R), final season in League (X), former club returning to League (F), new club (N)

Aberdeen

1930	1	38	23	7	8	85	61	53	3
1931	1	38	17	7	14	79	63	41	6
1932	1	38	16	9	13	57	49	41	7
1933	1	38	18	6	14	85	58	42	6
1934	1	38	18	8	12	90	57	44	5
1935	1	38	17	10	11	68	54	44	6
1936	1	38	26	9	3	96	50	61	3
1937	1	38	23	8	7	89	44	54	2
1938	1	38	15	9	14	74	59	39	6
1939	1	38	20	6	12	91	61	46	3

Airdrieonians

1930	1	38	16	4	18	60	66	36	12	
1931	1	38	17	5	16	59	66	39	9	
1932	1	38	13	6	19	74	81	32	14	
1933	1	38	10	3	25	55	102	23	18	
1934	1	38	10	6	22	59	103	26	18	
1935	1	38	13	7	18	64	72	33	14	
1936	1	38	9	9	20	68	91	27	19	R
1937	2	34	18	8	8	85	60	44	4	
1938	2	34	21	5	8	100	53	47	3	
1939	2	34	21	5	8	85	57	47	4	

Albion Rovers

1930	2	38	24	6	8	101	60	54	3	
1931	2	38	14	11	13	83	84	39	9	
1932	2	38	13	2	23	81	104	28	16	
1933	2	34	19	2	13	82	57	40	5	
1934	2	34	20	5	9	74	47	45	1	P
1935	1	38	10	9	19	62	77	29	16	
1936	1	38	13	4	21	69	92	30	16	
1937	1	38	5	6	27	53	116	16	20	R
1938	2	34	20	8	6	97	50	48	2	P
1939	1	38	12	6	20	65	90	30	16	

Alloa Athletic

1930	2	38	9	6	23	55	104	24	19	
1931	2	38	15	5	18	65	87	35	13	
1932	2	38	14	7	17	73	74	35	13	
1933	2	34	14	5	15	60	58	33	11	
1934	2	34	11	9	14	55	68	31	15	
1935	2	34	12	10	12	67	60	34	10	
1936	2	34	19	6	9	65	51	44	4	
1937	2	34	13	7	14	64	65	33	9	
1938	2	34	11	4	19	78	106	26	11	
1939	2	34	22	4	8	91	46	48	2	P

Arbroath

1930	2	38	16	7	15	83	87	39	9
1931	2	38	15	4	19	83	94	34	15
1932	2	38	17	5	16	82	78	39	11
1933	2	34	14	5	15	65	62	33	10
1934	2	34	20	4	10	83	53	44	3
1935	2	34	23	4	7	78	42	50	2
1936	1	38	11	11	16	46	69	33	11
1937	1	38	13	5	20	57	84	31	14
1938	1	38	11	13	14	58	79	35	11
1939	1	38	11	8	19	54	75	30	17

Armadale

1930	2	38	13	5	20	56	91	31	15	
1931	2	38	13	2	23	74	99	28	18	
1932	2	38	10	5	23	68	102	25	18	X

Ayr United

1930	1	38	16	6	16	70	92	38	9	
1931	1	38	8	11	19	53	92	27	18	
1932	1	38	11	7	20	70	90	29	17	
1933	1	38	13	4	21	62	95	30	16	
1934	1	38	16	10	12	87	92	42	8	
1935	1	38	12	5	21	61	112	29	18	
1936	1	38	11	3	24	53	98	25	20	R
1937	2	34	25	4	5	122	49	54	1	P
1938	1	38	9	15	14	66	85	33	17	
1939	1	38	13	9	16	76	83	35	14	

Bo'ness

1930	2	38	15	4	19	67	95	34	13
1931	2	38	9	4	25	54	100	22	20
1932	2	38	15	4	19	70	103	34	14

Brechin City

1930	2	38	7	4	27	57	125	18	20	F
1931	2	38	13	7	18	52	84	33	16	
1932	2	38	9	7	22	52	97	25	19	
1933	2	34	11	4	19	65	95	26	15	
1934	2	34	13	5	16	60	70	31	14	
1935	2	34	10	6	18	51	98	26	15	
1936	2	34	8	6	20	57	96	22	16	
1937	2	34	8	9	17	64	98	25	16	
1938	2	34	5	2	27	53	139	12	18	
1939	2	34	11	9	14	82	106	31	10	

Celtic

1930	1	38	22	5	11	88	46	49	4
1931	1	38	24	10	4	101	34	58	2
1932	1	38	20	8	10	94	50	48	3
1933	1	38	20	8	10	75	44	48	4
1934	1	38	18	11	9	78	53	47	3
1935	1	38	24	4	10	92	45	52	2
1936	1	38	32	2	4	115	33	66	1
1937	1	38	22	8	8	89	58	52	3
1938	1	38	27	7	4	114	42	61	1
1939	1	38	20	8	10	99	53	48	2

Clyde

1930	1	38	13	11	14	64	69	37	11
1931	1	38	15	4	19	60	87	34	12
1932	1	38	13	9	16	58	70	35	13
1933	1	38	15	5	18	69	75	35	12
1934	1	38	10	11	17	56	70	31	14
1935	1	38	14	10	14	71	69	38	10
1936	1	38	10	8	20	63	84	28	18
1937	1	38	16	6	16	59	70	38	10
1938	1	38	10	13	15	68	78	33	15
1939	1	38	17	5	16	78	70	39	9

Clydebank

1930	2	38	7	10	21	66	92	24	18	
1931	2	38	10	2	26	61	108	22	19	X

Cowdenbeath

Season	Div	P	W	D	L	F	A	Pts	Pos	
1930	1	38	13	7	18	64	74	33	16	
1931	1	38	17	7	14	58	65	41	7	
1932	1	38	15	8	15	66	78	38	12	
1933	1	38	10	5	23	65	111	25	17	
1934	1	38	5	5	28	58	118	15	20	R
1935	2	34	13	6	15	84	75	32	12	
1936	2	34	13	5	16	76	77	31	10	
1937	2	34	14	10	10	75	59	38	6	
1938	2	34	17	9	8	115	71	43	6	
1939	2	34	28	4	2	120	45	60	1	P

Dumbarton

Season	Div	P	W	D	L	F	A	Pts	Pos	
1930	2	38	14	2	22	77	95	30	16	
1931	2	38	15	8	15	73	72	38	10	
1932	2	38	14	10	14	70	68	38	12	
1933	2	34	14	6	14	69	67	34	9	
1934	2	34	17	3	14	67	68	37	6	
1935	2	34	9	4	21	60	105	22	16	
1936	2	34	5	6	23	52	121	16	18	
1937	2	34	11	5	18	57	83	27	15	
1938	2	34	17	5	12	85	66	39	7	
1939	2	34	9	12	13	68	76	30	11	

Dundee

Season	Div	P	W	D	L	F	A	Pts	Pos	
1930	1	38	14	6	18	51	58	34	14	
1931	1	38	17	5	16	65	63	39	8	
1932	1	38	14	10	14	61	72	38	11	
1933	1	38	12	9	17	60	77	33	15	
1934	1	38	15	6	17	68	64	36	12	
1935	1	38	16	8	14	63	63	40	8	
1936	1	38	11	10	17	67	80	32	12	
1937	1	38	12	15	11	58	69	39	9	
1938	1	38	13	6	19	70	74	32	19	R
1939	2	34	15	7	12	99	63	37	6	

Dundee United

Season	Div	P	W	D	L	F	A	Pts	Pos	
1930	1	38	7	8	23	56	109	22	19	R
1931	2	38	21	8	9	93	54	50	2	P
1932	1	38	6	7	25	40	118	19	19	R
1933	2	34	14	4	16	65	67	32	13	
1934	2	34	10	4	20	81	88	24	17	
1935	2	34	18	6	10	105	65	42	4	
1936	2	34	16	5	13	108	81	37	7	
1937	2	34	9	9	16	72	97	27	14	
1938	2	34	9	5	20	69	104	23	14	
1939	2	34	15	3	16	78	69	33	9	

Dunfermline

Season	Div	P	W	D	L	F	A	Pts	Pos	
1930	2	38	16	6	16	99	85	38	10	
1931	2	38	20	7	11	83	50	47	3	
1932	2	38	17	6	15	78	73	40	10	
1933	2	34	20	7	7	89	44	47	3	
1934	2	34	20	4	10	90	52	44	2	P
1935	1	38	13	5	20	56	96	31	15	
1936	1	38	12	8	18	67	92	32	14	
1937	1	38	5	11	22	65	98	21	19	R
1938	2	34	17	5	12	82	76	39	9	
1939	2	34	18	5	11	99	78	41	5	

East Stirlingshire

Season	Div	P	W	D	L	F	A	Pts	Pos	
1930	2	38	16	4	18	83	75	36	12	
1931	2	38	17	7	14	85	74	41	7	
1932	2	38	26	3	9	111	55	55	1	P
1933	1	38	7	3	28	55	115	17	20	R
1934	2	34	14	7	13	65	74	35	9	
1935	2	34	11	7	16	57	76	29	14	
1936	2	34	13	8	13	70	75	34	8	
1937	2	34	18	2	14	81	78	38	7	
1938	2	34	9	7	18	55	95	25	13	
1939	2	34	9	4	21	89	130	22	17	

East Fife

Season	Div	P	W	D	L	F	A	Pts	Pos	
1930	2	38	26	5	7	114	58	57	2	P
1931	1	38	8	4	26	45	113	20	20	R
1932	2	38	18	5	15	107	77	41	8	
1933	2	34	15	4	15	85	71	34	7	
1934	2	34	12	8	14	71	76	32	13	
1935	2	34	16	3	15	79	73	35	9	
1936	2	34	16	6	12	86	79	38	6	
1937	2	34	15	8	11	76	51	38	5	
1938	2	34	19	5	10	104	61	43	5	
1939	2	34	21	6	7	99	61	48	3	

Edinburgh City

Season	Div	P	W	D	L	F	A	Pts	Pos	
1932	2	38	5	7	26	78	146	17	20	N
1933	2	34	4	4	26	39	133	12	18	
1934	2	34	4	6	24	37	111	14	18	
1935	2	34	3	2	29	44	133	8	18	
1936	2	34	8	9	17	57	83	25	15	
1937	2	34	2	3	29	42	120	7	18	
1938	2	34	7	3	24	77	135	17	17	
1939	2	34	6	4	24	58	119	16	18	

Falkirk

Season	Div	P	W	D	L	F	A	Pts	Pos	
1930	1	38	16	9	13	62	64	41	7	
1931	1	38	14	4	20	77	87	32	14	
1932	1	38	11	5	22	70	76	27	18	
1933	1	38	15	6	17	70	70	36	11	
1934	1	38	16	6	16	73	68	38	10	
1935	1	38	9	6	23	58	82	24	20	P
1936	2	34	28	3	3	132	34	59	1	P
1937	1	38	6	13	98	66	44	7		
1938	1	38	19	9	10	82	52	47	4	
1939	1	38	19	7	12	73	63	45	5	

Forfar Athletic

Season	Div	P	W	D	L	F	A	Pts	Pos	
1930	2	38	18	5	15	98	95	41	8	
1931	2	38	15	6	17	80	84	36	12	
1932	2	38	19	7	12	90	79	45	6	
1933	2	34	12	4	18	68	87	28	14	
1934	2	34	13	7	14	77	71	33	11	
1935	2	34	13	8	13	77	73	34	11	
1936	2	34	10	7	17	60	81	27	13	
1937	2	34	11	8	15	73	89	30	12	
1938	2	34	8	6	20	67	100	22	15	
1939	2	34	11	3	20	74	138	25	15	

Hamilton Academical

Season	Div	P	W	D	L	F	A	Pts	Pos	
1930	1	38	14	7	17	76	81	35	13	
1931	1	38	16	5	17	59	57	37	10	
1932	1	38	16	6	16	84	65	38	10	
1933	1	38	16	6	14	90	78	42	8	
1934	1	38	15	8	15	65	79	38	11	
1935	1	38	19	10	9	87	67	48	4	
1936	1	38	15	7	16	77	74	37	6	
1937	1	38	18	5	15	91	96	41	8	
1938	1	38	13	7	18	81	76	33	13	
1939	1	38	18	5	15	67	71	41	7	

Heart of Midlothian

Season	Div	P	W	D	L	F	A	Pts	Pos	
1930	1	38	14	9	15	69	69	37	10	
1931	1	38	19	6	13	90	63	44	5	
1932	1	38	17	5	16	63	61	39	8	
1933	1	38	21	8	9	84	51	50	3	
1934	1	38	17	10	11	86	59	44	6	
1935	1	38	20	10	8	87	51	50	3	
1936	1	38	20	7	11	88	55	47	5	
1937	1	38	24	3	11	99	60	51	5	
1938	1	38	26	6	6	90	50	58	2	
1939	1	38	20	5	13	98	70	45	4	

Hibernian

Year	Div	P	W	D	L	F	A	Pts	Pos	
1930	1	38	9	11	18	45	62	29	17	
1931	1	38	9	7	22	49	81	25	19	R
1932	2	38	18	8	12	73	52	44	7	
1933	2	34	25	4	5	80	29	54	1	P
1934	1	38	12	3	23	51	69	27	16	
1935	1	38	14	8	16	59	70	36	11	
1936	1	38	11	7	20	56	82	29	17	
1937	1	38	6	13	19	54	83	25	17	
1938	1	38	11	13	14	57	65	35	10	
1939	1	38	14	7	17	68	69	35	13	

Kilmarnock

Year	Div	P	W	D	L	F	A	Pts	Pos	
1930	1	38	15	9	14	77	73	39	8	
1931	1	38	15	5	18	59	60	35	11	
1932	1	38	16	7	15	68	70	39	9	
1933	1	38	13	9	16	72	86	35	14	
1934	1	38	17	9	12	73	64	43	7	
1935	1	38	16	6	16	76	68	38	9	
1936	1	38	14	7	17	69	64	35	8	
1937	1	38	14	9	15	60	70	37	11	
1938	1	38	12	9	17	65	91	33	18	
1939	1	38	15	9	14	73	86	39	10	

King's Park

Year	Div	P	W	D	L	F	A	Pts	Pos	
1930	2	38	17	8	13	109	80	42	6	
1931	2	38	14	6	18	78	70	34	14	
1932	2	38	14	5	19	97	93	33	15	
1933	2	34	13	8	13	85	80	34	8	
1934	2	34	14	8	12	78	70	36	7	
1935	2	34	18	2	14	86	71	38	7	
1936	2	34	11	5	18	55	109	27	14	
1937	2	34	11	3	20	61	106	25	17	
1938	2	34	11	4	19	64	96	26	12	
1939	2	34	12	2	20	87	92	26	13	

Leith Athletic

Year	Div	P	W	D	L	F	A	Pts	Pos	
1930	2	38	23	11	4	92	42	57	1	P
1931	1	38	8	11	19	51	85	27	17	
1932	1	38	6	4	28	46	137	16	20	R
1933	2	34	10	5	19	43	81	25	16	
1934	2	34	12	8	14	63	60	32	12	
1935	2	34	16	5	13	69	71	37	8	
1936	2	34	15	3	16	67	77	33	9	
1937	2	34	13	5	16	62	65	31	11	
1938	2	34	16	5	13	71	56	37	10	
1939	2	34	10	4	20	57	83	24	16	

Montrose

Year	Div	P	W	D	L	F	A	Pts	Pos	
1930	2	38	14	10	14	79	87	38	11	F
1931	2	38	19	3	16	75	90	41	8	
1932	2	38	11	6	21	60	96	28	17	
1933	2	34	8	5	21	63	89	21	17	
1934	2	34	11	4	19	53	81	26	16	
1935	2	34	7	6	21	58	105	20	17	
1936	2	34	13	3	18	58	82	29	12	
1937	2	34	11	6	17	65	98	28	13	
1938	2	34	7	8	19	56	88	22	16	
1939	2	34	10	5	19	82	96	25	14	

Morton

Year	Div	P	W	D	L	F	A	Pts	Pos	
1930	1	38	10	7	21	67	95	27	18	
1931	1	38	11	7	20	58	83	29	16	
1932	1	38	12	7	19	78	87	31	15	
1933	1	38	6	9	23	49	97	21	19	R
1934	2	34	17	5	12	67	64	39	5	
1935	2	34	17	4	13	88	64	38	6	
1936	2	34	21	6	7	117	60	48	3	
1937	2	34	23	5	6	110	42	51	2	P
1938	1	38	6	3	29	64	127	15	20	R
1939	2	34	11	6	17	74	88	28	12	

Motherwell

Year	Div	P	W	D	L	F	A	Pts	Pos	
1930	1	38	25	5	8	104	48	55	2	
1931	1	38	24	8	6	102	42	56	3	
1932	1	38	30	6	2	119	31	66	1	
1933	1	38	27	5	6	114	53	59	2	
1934	1	38	29	4	5	97	45	62	2	
1935	1	38	15	10	13	83	64	40	7	
1936	1	38	18	12	8	77	58	48	4	
1937	1	38	22	7	9	96	54	51	4	
1938	1	38	17	10	11	78	69	44	5	
1939	1	38	16	5	17	82	86	37	12	

Partick Thistle

Year	Div	P	W	D	L	F	A	Pts	Pos	
1930	1	38	16	9	13	72	61	41	6	
1931	1	38	24	5	9	76	43	53	4	
1932	1	38	19	4	15	58	59	42	6	
1933	1	38	17	6	15	75	55	40	10	
1934	1	38	14	5	19	73	78	33	13	
1935	1	38	15	5	18	61	68	35	13	
1936	1	38	12	10	16	64	72	34	10	
1937	1	38	11	12	15	73	68	34	13	
1938	1	38	15	9	14	68	70	39	7	
1939	1	38	17	4	17	74	87	38	11	

Queen of the South

Year	Div	P	W	D	L	F	A	Pts	Pos	
1930	2	38	18	6	14	65	63	42	7	
1931	2	38	18	6	14	83	66	42	6	
1932	2	38	18	5	15	99	91	41	9	
1933	2	34	20	9	5	93	59	49	2	P
1934	1	38	21	3	14	75	78	45	4	
1935	1	38	11	7	20	52	72	29	17	
1936	1	38	11	9	18	54	72	31	15	
1937	1	38	8	8	22	49	95	24	18	
1938	1	38	11	11	16	58	71	33	16	
1939	1	38	17	9	12	69	64	43	6	

Queen's Park

Year	Div	P	W	D	L	F	A	Pts	Pos	
1930	1	38	15	4	19	67	80	34	15	
1931	1	38	13	7	18	71	72	33	13	
1932	1	38	13	5	20	59	79	31	16	
1933	1	38	17	7	14	78	79	41	9	
1934	1	38	13	5	20	65	85	31	15	
1935	1	38	13	10	15	61	80	36	12	
1936	1	38	11	10	17	58	75	32	13	
1937	1	38	9	12	17	51	77	30	15	
1938	1	38	11	12	15	59	74	34	12	
1939	1	38	11	5	22	57	83	27	19	R

Raith Rovers

Year	Div	P	W	D	L	F	A	Pts	Pos	
1930	2	38	18	8	12	94	67	44	5	
1931	2	38	20	6	12	93	72	46	4	
1932	2	38	20	6	12	83	65	46	3	
1933	2	34	16	4	14	83	67	36	6	
1934	2	34	15	5	14	71	55	35	8	
1935	2	34	13	3	18	68	73	29	13	
1936	2	34	9	3	22	60	96	21	17	
1937	2	34	16	4	14	72	66	36	8	
1938	2	34	27	5	2	142	54	59	1	P
1939	1	38	10	2	26	65	99	22	20	R

Rangers

Year	Div	P	W	D	L	F	A	Pts	Pos	
1930	1	38	28	4	6	94	32	60	1	
1931	1	38	27	6	5	96	29	60	1	
1932	1	38	28	5	5	118	42	61	2	
1933	1	38	26	10	2	113	43	62	1	
1934	1	38	30	6	2	118	41	66	1	
1935	1	38	25	5	8	96	46	55	1	
1936	1	38	27	7	4	110	43	61	2	
1937	1	38	26	9	3	88	32	61	1	
1938	1	38	18	13	7	75	49	49	3	
1939	1	38	25	9	4	112	55	59	1	

St Bernards

1930	2	38	13	6	19	65	65	32	14	
1931	2	38	14	9	15	85	66	37	11	
1932	2	38	19	7	12	81	62	45	5	
1933	2	34	13	6	15	67	64	32	12	
1934	2	34	15	4	15	75	56	34	10	
1935	2	34	20	7	7	103	47	47	3	
1936	2	34	18	4	12	106	78	40	5	
1937	2	34	22	4	8	100	51	48	3	
1938	2	34	20	5	9	75	49	45	4	
1939	2	34	15	6	13	79	79	36	7	

St Mirren

1930	1	38	18	5	15	73	56	41	5	
1931	1	38	11	8	19	49	72	30	15	
1932	1	38	20	4	14	77	56	44	5	
1933	1	38	18	6	14	73	60	42	7	
1934	1	38	9	9	20	46	75	27	17	
1935	1	38	11	5	22	49	70	27	19	R
1936	2	34	25	2	7	114	41	52	2	P
1937	1	38	11	7	20	68	81	29	16	
1938	1	38	14	5	19	58	66	33	14	
1939	1	38	11	7	20	57	80	29	18	

St Johnstone

1930	1	38	6	7	25	48	96	19	20	R
1931	2	38	19	6	13	76	61	44	5	
1932	2	38	24	7	7	102	52	55	2	P
1933	1	38	17	10	11	70	55	44	5	
1934	1	38	17	6	15	74	53	40	9	
1935	1	38	18	10	10	66	46	46	5	
1936	1	38	15	7	16	70	81	37	7	
1937	1	38	14	8	16	74	68	36	12	
1938	1	38	16	7	15	78	81	39	8	
1939	1	38	17	6	15	85	82	40	8	

Stenhousemuir

1930	2	38	11	5	22	75	108	27	17	
1931	2	38	12	6	20	75	101	30	17	
1932	2	38	19	8	11	88	76	46	4	
1933	2	34	18	6	10	67	58	42	4	
1934	2	34	18	4	12	70	73	40	4	
1935	2	34	17	5	12	86	80	39	5	
1936	2	34	13	3	18	59	78	29	11	
1937	2	34	14	4	16	82	86	32	10	
1938	2	34	17	5	12	87	78	39	8	
1939	2	34	15	5	14	74	69	35	8	

Third Lanark

1930	2	38	23	6	9	92	53	52	4	
1931	2	38	27	7	4	107	42	61	1	P
1932	1	38	21	4	13	92	81	46	4	
1933	1	38	14	7	17	70	80	35	13	
1934	1	38	8	9	21	62	103	25	19	R
1935	2	34	23	6	5	94	43	52	1	P
1936	1	38	15	5	18	63	65	35	9	
1937	1	38	20	6	12	79	61	46	6	
1938	1	38	11	13	14	68	73	35	9	
1939	1	38	12	8	18	80	96	32	15	

Eddie Falloon, Aberdeen

Robert Harrison, Hamilton

*Neil Dewar,
Third Lanark*

Matt Armstrong, Aberdeen

BIBLIOGRAPHY

A CD Record of Pre-War Scottish Players 1890-91 to 1945-46, John Litster & "Scottish Football Historian" magazine 2012.

A Century of English International Football 1872-1972, Morley Farror & Douglas Lamming, Robert Hale & Co 1972.

All in the Day's Sport, Roland Allen, W H Allen & Co.Ltd 1946.

All the FA Cup Finals, Roland Allen, Mark Goulden Ltd 1947.

Allison Calling, George F Allison, Staples Press 1948.

Association Football, F N S Creek, J M Dent & Sons Ltd 1937.

Bass Sports Book of Irish Soccer, Noel Dunne & Sean Ryan, Mercier Press 1975.

Behind the Scenes in Big Football, Leslie Knighton, Stanley Paul & Co Ltd 1947.

British & Irish Special and Intermediate Internationals, Keith Warsop, Soccerdata 2002.

Cliff Bastin Remembers (with Brian Glanville), The Ettrick Press Ltd 1950.

Dunfermline Athletic Centenary History, John Hunter 1985.

England v Scotland, Brian James, Pelham Books 1969.

English League Football, Reginald C Churchill, Nicholas Kaye 1958.

Everton – the Official Centenary History, John Roberts, Mayflower Granada Publishing 1978.

FIFA Handbook 1937.

Fifty Years of Football, Sir Frederick Wall, Cassell & Co. Ltd, 1935.

Football All Round the World, R B Alaway, Newservice Ltd 1948.

Football League Players' Records 1888-1939, Michael Joyce, Soccerdata 2012.

Forward, Arsenal! Bernard Joy, The Sportsmans Book Club 1954.

Herbert Chapman on Football, John Graves, Garrick Publishing Co, 1933.

Het Nederlands Elftal (History of Dutch national team) 1905-89, Voetbal International 1989.

History of Aldershot Football Club, Jack Rollin, F K S Pubishers Lrd 1975.

L'Integrale de L-Equipe de France 1904-98, First Editions 1998.

Milestones 1911-37, History and Records of Halifax Town AFC, T T Dickinson, Halifax Branch of the National Union of Journalists, 1937.

North American National Teams 1885-2007, Gabriel Mantz & Romeo Ionescu, Ploiesti Printeuro 2007.

One Hundred Years of Scottish Football, John Rafferty, Pan Books Ltd 1973.

Pompey, The History of Portsmouth Football Club, Mike Neasom, Mick Cooper & Doug Robinson, Milestone Publications 1984.

Rags to Riches, The Official History of Dundee United, Mike Watson, David Winter & Son Ltd 1985

Raith Rovers FC, A Centenary History, John Litster, Tullis Russell & Co Ltd 1983.

Rothmans Book of Football Records, Jack Rollin, Headline Book Publishing 1998.

Scottish League Players' Records Division One 1890-91 to 1938-39, Steve Emms & Richard Wells, Soccerdata 2007.

Servowarm History of the FA Amateur Cup, Bob Barton, Tyneside Free Press.

Soccer, David Jack, Putnam & Co. 1934.

Soccer Nemesis, Brian Glanville, Secker & Warburg 1955.

Soccer Revolution, Willy Meisl, Phoenix Sports Books 1955.

Soccer Round the Globe, Brian Glanville, Abelard-Schuman 1959.

The AB-Z of World Football, Maurice Golesworthy & Roger Macdonald, Pelham Books 1966.

The Army Game, Red & Khaki, Jack Rollin, Soccerdata 2013.

The Encyclopaedia of Association Football, Maurice Golesworthy, Robert Hale Ltd 1956.

The FA Amateur Cup Results, Fred Hawthorn, Soccerdata 2009.

The FA Challenge Cup Complete Results, Tony Brown, Soccerdata 2006.

The Football Fact Book, Jack Rollin, Guinness Publishing 1990, 1993.

The Football League Match by Match books for 1929-30 to 1938-39, Tony Brown, Soccerdata 2005.

The Guinness Book of Facts & Feats, Jack Rollin, Guinness Superlatives Ltd 1978, 1979, 1980, 1981, 1983.

The Guinness Record of the FA Cup, Mike Collett, Guinness Publications 1993.

The Inside Story of Football, George F Allison, Quaker Oats Ltd 1938.

The Macadam Road, John Macadam, The Sportsmans Book Club 1954.

The Story of the Football Leagu 1888-1938, Charles E Sutcliffe, J A Brierley, F Howarth, Football League Ltd 1938.

The World Cup, Sixty Glorious Years 1930-1990, Jack Rollin, Guinness Publishing Ltd 1990.

Topical Times, Weekly magazine, various issues 1929-39. D C Thomson & Co.

Up Wl' The Bonnets! The Centenary History of Dundee FC, Norrie Price, N Price 1993.

We Are The Champions 1888-1972, Maurice Golesworthy, Pelham Books 1972.

Who's Who of Welsh International Soccer Players, Gareth M Davies & Ian Garland, Bridge Books, Wrexham, Clwyd 1991.

World Soccer from A to Z, Edited by Norman Barrett, Pan Books Ltd 1973.

40 Years in Football, Ivan Sharpe, The Sportsmans Book Club 1954.

50 Years of Sport, Edited by Ernest A Bland, Daily Mail Publications 1946.

100 Years of Irish Football, Malcolm Brodie, Blackstaff Press 1980.

Various Football Club histories by Breedon Books, Yore Publications, Polar Publishing, Amateur Football Yearbooks and Soccer History Ltd. Athletic News Football Annuals, Athletic News weekly magazine and News Chronicle Football Annuals. Other acknowledgements appear in the text.

BY THE SAME AUTHOR

The Men who Never Were tells the story of the football season of 1939-40. The outbreak of war in September 1939 led to the immediate cancellation of the Football League programme after just three games had been played. The match results and players' appearances were deleted from the official records. Consequently, many players who turned out for a new club in 1939 do not appear in the records.

The book includes line-ups and scorers for the Football League and Football League War Cup matches, tables and results grids for the English regional leagues that were formed later in 1939, Scottish results and tables; and details of summer tours in 1939.

THE ENGLISH NATIONAL FOOTBALL ARCHIVE

www.enfa.co.uk

The database of the English National Football Archive contains every games line-ups and scorers from 1888-89 to date, including the period covered by *Soccer in the 1930s* of course. You can search for matches by date, or by club, and from the line-ups follow any player's complete career game by game. You can also search on players' names, then follow through to look at every game they played. Planned enhancements include match reports, copies of programmes, and videos or film reports when available.